Theoretical-Practical Theology

Volume 2: Faith in the Triune God

PET. VAN MASTRICT.

PHILOSOPH. ET·THEOL. DOCT. ET PROFESSOR,

in Academiis: Francofurt: ad Oderam, Duisburg, et Ultrliectinâ.

SYMBOL

Ὅταν ἀ϶ϵνῶς ῥόϵι devalós

ἔιαι.

Theoretical-Practical Theology

Volume 2: Faith in the Triune God

by

Petrus van Mastricht

Todd M. Rester, Translator
Joel R. Beeke, Editor
Michael T. Spangler, Assistant Editor and Translator

REFORMATION HERITAGE BOOKS
Grand Rapids, Michigan

Reformation Heritage Books
3070 29th St. SE
Grand Rapids, MI 49512
616-977-0889
orders@heritagebooks.org
www.heritagebooks.org

Printed in the United States of America
23 24 25 26 27 28/10 9 8 7 6 5 4 3

Library of Congress Cataloging-in-Publication Data

Names: Mastricht, Peter van, 1630–1706, author.
Title: Theoretical-practical theology / by Petrus van Mastricht ; translated by Todd M.
    Rester ; edited by Joel R. Beeke.
Other titles: Theologia theoretico-practica. English
Description: Grand Rapids, Michigan : Reformation Heritage Books, 2018–
Identifiers: LCCN 2018014361 (print) | LCCN 2018028430 (ebook) ISBN
    9781601785602 (epub) | ISBN 9781601785596 (v. 1 : hardcover : alk. paper)
Subjects: LCSH: Reformed Church—Doctrines—Early works to 1800.
Classification: LCC BX9422.3 (ebook) | LCC BX9422.3 .M2813 2018 (print) |
    DDC 230/.42—dc23
LC record available at https://lccn.loc.gov/2018014361

For additional Reformed literature, request a free book list from Reformation Heritage Books at the above regular or e-mail address.

Contents

Part One, Continued
PROLEGOMENA AND FAITH

Book Two: **Faith in the Triune God**

Chapter 1: *Saving Faith*

The Exegetical Part

The Dogmatic Part

Chapter 2: *The Existence and Knowledge of God*

The Exegetical Part

The Dogmatic Part

The Elenctic Part

The Practical Part

Chapter 3: *The Essence and Independence of God*

The Exegetical Part

First Theorem—*The Imperceptibility of the Divine Essence*
The Dogmatic Part

The Elenctic Part

The Practical Part

Second Theorem—*The Very Essence or Independence of God*
The Didactic Part

The Elenctic Part

---

1. The original skips §XIII; its numbering is retained for ease of reference.

---

2. The Latin repeats the paragraph number XXI; as in the Dutch translation it is corrected here through the end of the chapter, §§XXII–XXVII.

Preface

As editors and translators we are thankful to the Lord for the enormous privilege we have to bring this major work of Latin theology by Petrus van Mastricht to the English-speaking world. To help our readers profit, we offer a few prefatory notes of explanation.

This volume reveals three reasons why the *Theoretical-Practical Theology* stands out in comparison to other systematic theologies. First is its division. This second volume is comprised of book 2, the subject of which is God himself: his existence, his essence (revealed in his names and attributes), and his subsistence (in the three persons), a fairly standard outline for treating the doctrine of God. What makes Mastricht's treatment noteworthy, however, is that this consideration of theology proper is preceded by a substantial chapter on saving faith. Said more accurately, saving faith is the heading under which falls not only book 2 on God, but also all of books 3–8 on the works of God. This reflects Mastricht's division, presented in 1.1.3, of theology into faith (pt. 1, English vols. 2–6) and observance (pts. 2 and 3, vol. 7), and shows the practical goal for which he wrote the whole work: that readers may believe with true faith for the salvation of their souls, and bear faith's good fruit in a life of humble obedience to God. In this division of theology into faith and observance, Mastricht is following a path well trodden by, among others, Reformed theologians such as William Ames, Amandus Polanus von Polansdorf, and Pierre Ramus, to name a few.

Mastricht's contribution at this point is a lengthy consideration of the nature and necessity of saving faith, which joins together his related emphases on effective preaching, doctrinal content, and faithful practice. By comparison, Mastricht's former pastor and professor, Johannes Hoornbeeck, in his *Practical Theology* emphasized seeking first the kingdom of God through care for eternal salvation, the practice of religion, and zeal for the divine Word, in three chapters between his prolegomena and theology proper. He reserved the topic of faith for later, well after his discussion of God, the law and conscience, sin, grace, calling, conversion, and repentance: it was not until book 7, after over seven hundred pages, that Hoornbeeck introduced the topic of faith. And this is perhaps why Mastricht was so insistent on maintaining that from the very beginning of the study of theology saving faith must be distinguished from presumption while at the same time even weak faith must be sheltered and nurtured. Pastors must tear down the former and build up the latter both in themselves and in others.

Second, Mastricht recognizes that he is somewhat unusual in his ordering of the divine attributes. In 1.2.5 §VIII he affirms standard divisions of the attributes, such as into positive and negative, or communicable and incommunicable, but in §IX explains his preference to arrange them "as though according to their functions," that is, by the questions they help to answer: first *quid sit*, what God is, then *quantus sit*, how great God is, then *qualis sit*, what qualities God has—a line of inquiry which has a long pedigree in scholastic disputations, and which provides Mastricht a useful and orderly method of proceeding in chapters 6–23.

Third, by his own testimony (1.2.24 §XI) Mastricht differs from his contemporaries in his more thorough treatment of the Trinitarian economy, which is woven into his broader consideration of God's personal subsistence in chapters 24–27. It is particularly striking how he describes the three persons as members of a *familia*, a "household" (broader than the English "family"), all having within the household economy, according to their distinct modes of subsisting, distinct economic offices, periods, attributes, and worship. He uses this teaching to answer questions in Trinitarian theology found vexing even today, and also to encourage believers to serve the divine persons with distinct devotion according to their distinct economy.

Those who have read volume 1 will find the basic outline of each chapter familiar. After a paragraph of contextual introduction, Mastricht begins with a word-by-word exegesis of a carefully chosen Scripture text. Note here that he often translates the same verse in different ways, even within the same paragraph, departing not infrequently from the rendering he gives in the chapter's heading text. Whatever the reason for this, it should not make readers doubt the translation, which intentionally reflects Mastricht's own variations. In the Exegetical Part and elsewhere, we translated the Latin and original language Scripture citations literally, but where possible we also sought conformity to familiar literal English versions. Greek and Hebrew were preserved in the text body where helpful for understanding Mastricht's discussions of interpretation and etymology, and Hebrew quotations reflect his habit of rarely using vowel points.

Following the Exegetical Part is the Dogmatic Part, where Mastricht usually begins with a proof from other Scripture passages, proceeds to a confirmation from reason or nature, and then makes further explanation, often anticipating objections that will be answered more fully later. Attention should be paid here and elsewhere to Mastricht's in-text citations of Scripture, which are always chosen with good reason, though the reason is not always immediately obvious. Sometimes his intent will become clear by comparing with other cited passages, or by using the Scripture index to find a fuller treatment of the same passage. We encourage you to look up the citations, for they reveal among other things that Mastricht's words, and even his theological terms, are closely bound to the language of Scripture itself. His New Testament citations usually follow the *textus receptus*, so sometimes they point to portions missing in modern Bibles. At other times, he grapples with textual variants, and translation differences found in, for example, the Septuagint, various editions of the Vulgate, and various translations and annotations of early modern Protestants, such as Tremellius and Junius, Beza, and Grotius. And though we have tried to use quotation marks to distinguish between quotation and paraphrase, for Mastricht that distinction was not strict, even when he wrote in Greek and Hebrew. Furthermore, all Old Testament citations are given in standard English versification, though Mastricht almost always cited according to the Hebrew, which differs mostly in the Psalms. Where textual variances from modern convention are significant, we have mentioned in a footnote what versions he might have used.

In each section of the succeeding Elenctic Part, Mastricht typically gives a short statement of the question, then outlines the response of those in error, giving their name, then the ideological motivation for their error, followed by the specific error itself, before he goes on to present the orthodox, Reformed opinion and to answer objections. Many of the elenctic sections, as Mastricht explained in his 1699 preface,[1] present orthodoxy as the golden mean between two extremes. This part features the most abundant use of technical terms, sometimes presented with a marker (e.g. "as they say"), and occasionally joined with a brief explanation. Mastricht is quick to indicate when the use of a helpful term compels him, reluctantly, to speak in "barbarous" Latin. In this volume we have footnoted fewer Greek terms, both to conserve space and to reduce distraction in reading, recognizing that for Mastricht, Greek was often simply an extension of Latin. In most places, whether a term was in Latin or Greek, we simply used an accepted English equivalent without comment, but where necessary for clarity or scholarship, we indicated the original term in a footnote, in most cases only at its first occurrence in the volume. Where helpful, comparison has also been made to the eighteenth-century Dutch translation.

In the final Practical Part, most notable is the shift in Mastricht's rhetoric. Careful analysis, didactic instruction, and reasoned defense yield to heartfelt

---

1. Vol. 1, pp. 43–44.

persuasion, full of questions, exclamations, biblical phrases, rhythmic repetition, figures of speech, and sometimes plays on words. Readers will enjoy and profit from these experiential and practical sections, and will observe how intimately and inextricably bound together are theory and practice in Christian theology. Thus they should be careful not to set Mastricht's rhetorical persuasion against his precise teaching: for example, when in the practical parts he movingly "communicates" the incommunicable attributes of God to believers, calling them to be, in their own way, simple (1.2.6 §§XXVI–XXIX), infinite (1.2.9 §XIV), and omnipotent (1.2.20 §XXXIII), he is not denying the division of the attributes into communicable and incommunicable, which he carefully defended in 1.2.5 §§VIII and XII, but rather, powerfully driving home his oft-repeated teaching that our chief perfection consists in the imitation of God. Similarly, for explanatory clarity and rhetorical power, Mastricht makes frequent use of etymological connections in Latin that do not always carry over into English (e.g. *sanctus*, "holy," but *sanctificatio*, "sanctification"). We have done our best to convey these connections, but some are inevitably lost in translation.

An important help in understanding the four parts is to read them always in parallel. Mastricht is a careful teacher, but he is also eager to save space, so he leaves many explanations for later, or assumes them from before. Often he points readers to appropriate places for clarification, and where he does we replicated his original cross-references, expanding incomplete or obscure citations with a footnote.[2] But even where there is no such cross-reference, patient readers who encounter challenges will in almost every instance have their questions answered by the end of the chapter. This is especially so in the Elenctic Part, which in meeting the objections of opponents greatly expands the teaching of the Dogmatic Part. Furthermore, the four-part structure occasionally becomes more complicated, when Mastricht subdivides larger topics into various theorems, each having their own Dogmatic, Elenctic, and Practical Part. In this volume this occurs in chapters 3, 6, and 12.

In addition to observing these things in the various parts, readers should note a few features of the translation as a whole. Nearly all the paragraph headings are Mastricht's, but they were originally marginal notes, and did not divide a section (to Mastricht, a *paragraphus*) into multiple paragraphs, as we have done for ease of reading. Mastricht wrote with brevity, and sometimes used *etc.* in

---

2. Our editorial citations of the *TPT* follow this form: part.book.chapter §section, e.g. 1.2.7 §VI. The part, book, and chapter numbers are indicated at the top of the odd pages of each chapter. When Mastricht gives citations with only book and chapter, he is speaking of part 1. See vol. 1, p. 47 for his outline of the whole work.

place of logical conclusions considered obvious. We have usually filled these in without comment. Moreover, his original printing occasionally used capitalization for emphasis. We have used italics instead. Note also that to preserve the unity of the text and to help our English readers, in most cases we have translated the titles of books Mastricht cites by their Latin or Greek name, a good number of which have no English translation. We follow each of these citations with our own footnote reference, pointing to an edition of the original work and, if available, an English version or at least a critical edition.

Our translation policy has been to adhere closely to the original text. Besides the few things mentioned above, we have done very little to clarify, expand, or update Mastricht's original. Indeed, it hardly needed any such work: as we hope this translation conveys, Mastricht's own prose is accessible, engaging, and at times quite beautiful. We hope that it will not only powerfully teach and exhort our English readers, but also encourage some of them to return to the Latin original, in order to drink more deeply from the fountains of classic Reformed orthodoxy. Our prayer is that through the reading of authors like Mastricht, and the wise application of their teaching to the needs of today's church, we will see in our day a renaissance of true theology, and especially of theology's great goal, that of living for God through Christ.

—Joel R. Beeke
Todd M. Rester
Michael T. Spangler

Abbreviations

ANF	*Ante-Nicene Fathers*
BWDN	*Biographisch Woordenboek der Nederlanden*
BDBI	*Dizionario Biografico degli Italiani*
LCL	*Loeb Classical Library*
NNBW	*Nieuw Nederlandsch Biografisch Woordenboek*
NPNF1	*Nicene and Post-Nicene Fathers,* Series I
NPNF2	*Nicene and Post-Nicene Fathers,* Series II
PG	*Patrologia Graeca*
PL	*Patrologia Latina*
PRRD	*Post-Reformation Reformed Dogmatics*
ST	*Summa Theologiae*
TPT	*Theoretico-Practica Theologia*

Book Two

Faith in the Triune God

CHAPTER ONE

Saving Faith

He came to his own, and his own did not receive him. But as many as received him, to them he gave authority to become sons of God, that is, to those who believe in his name.

—John 1:11–12

The first part of theology and spiritual life is faith.

I. The life lived for God, whose norm is Scripture, contains two acts, just as natural life does: the first act, by which we can operate spiritually, which is the faith by which the righteous live (Rom. 1:17; Gal. 2:20), and the second acts, which faith produces, namely acts of observance, inasmuch as through them faith is at work (Gal. 5:6). Consequently, first in the spiritual life comes faith. And in this faith is contained two things: first, the habit by which we believe, that is, the faith *by which* we believe; and second, the object which, or in which, we believe, that is, the faith *that* we believe. In this chapter we will explain the former, with the text of John 1:11–12 lighting the way; the exegesis of the text will demonstrate most of its essential parts.

The Exegetical Part

The text is opened and explained.

II. The text presents to us the matter of faith in two parts:

    A. Unbelief. The text presents to us the unbelief of the Jewish nation in the rejection of Christ who offered himself to it. Here there are:

        1. The unbelievers: οἱ ἴδιοι, "his own." That is, they are his own first by right of creation and governance (John 1:3, 11), and then by right of redemption and covenant, at least as offered, though not received, by which right the elect alone are ἴδιοι τοῦ θεοῦ, "God's own" (Gal. 5:24).

2. The offering, which they rejected in unbelief: ἦλθεν, "He came." That is, he came to them in the incarnation, whereby he offered himself to them as the Mediator who must be received by faith.

3. The unbelief: καὶ οἱ ἴδιοι αὐτὸν οὐ παρέλαβον, "and his own did not receive him." That is, either they simply did not desire to admit him as their Savior or Lord, or they did so only in a certain respect: if they did in fact receive him as their Savior, from whom they would receive remission and salvation (which sometimes happens in the case of hypocrites), they did not receive him as their King and Lord, to whom they should subject themselves (Luke 19:27).

B. Faith: ὅσοι δὲ ἔλαβον αὐτόν, ἔδωκεν αὐτοῖς ἐξουσίαν τέκνα θεοῦ γενέσθαι, τοῖς πιστεύουσιν εἰς τὸ ὄνομα αὐτοῦ, "But as many as received him, to them he gave authority to become sons of God, that is, to those who believe in his name." Here there is denoted:

1. In the first place, faith: "as many as received him." Here are designated:

a. Believers: "as many as," ὅσοι, namely each and every one of this class, and indeed, these only.

b. Faith, or the act of believing: παρέλαβον, they "received" him. That is, they desired to have him as their one and only Mediator as well as their Priest, who would redeem them by the offering of his blood; their King, who would govern them by his Word and Spirit; and their Prophet, who would teach them.

c. The object of faith: αὐτόν, "him." That is, not only his words, the gospel promises; nor only his benefits, the remission of sins and eternal life; but him, that is, first his person, that they may be united to him, and then his benefits, that they may obtain with him a communion of goods, from the tenor of the divine gift and offering (Rom. 8:32).

2. In the second place, the fruit of faith: "to them he gave authority to become sons of God," by which is shown:

a. The source of this fruit: ἔδωκεν, "he gave"; and the efficacy of faith in relation to spiritual benefits, namely that faith procures them for us not by its own intrinsic dignity or merit, but by the pure, unadulterated gift and kindness of God, without which saving faith itself could accomplish absolutely nothing at all for salvation.

b. The fruit itself of faith, that is, ἐξουσία τῆς υἱοθεσίας, the authority of adoption. In this is included, first, union with Christ, as with a brother, by which we together with him obtain one God and Father (John 20:17); second, communion with all his benefits by way of inheritance. Just as the natural Son himself by title of inheritance possesses all things from his Father (Ps. 2:8), so by right of inheritance we possess all things from him (Rom. 8:17). And since this sonship involves the enjoyment of God as the highest end, it follows that faith brings one not only to Christ as the Mediator but also to God as the highest end (John 14:1).

c. The prerequisite condition for conferring the fruit: τοῖς πιστεύουσιν εἰς τὸ ὄνομα αὐτοῦ, "to those who believe in his name," that is, the name of him in whom the previously designated reception provided a paraphrase for faith. In this the following stand out:

i. The act of faith: πιστεύουσιν, "who believe." For the habit of faith is not sufficient, but the act is also required, namely, wherever it can and ought to exist.

ii. The object of faith: εἰς τὸ ὄνομα αὐτοῦ, "in his name." That is, either in the name of God, who had been most recently named, and hence in God, for הוא שמו ושמו הוא, "he is his name and his name is he," according to the common saying of the Hebrews; or in the name of Christ, that is, in Christ, who bears the name of God in himself (בקרבו, Ex. 23:21); or in the name of God and Christ, and thus it is indicated that the object of saving faith is God as the end and Christ as the Mediator.

iii. The relation or relationship of the act to its object, signified in the preposition εἰς, "*into* his name." By this word is indicated that faith is brought to its object, not only by knowledge, or even by some kind of assent, but also by a consent of the will by which you desire to have Christ, as the coming bridegroom who offers himself and all that he has, to be before all others your Mediator.

The Dogmatic Part

The definition of saving faith is constructed from the text.

III. If not all, then at least most of the ingredients of saving faith are made known to us from the text, and especially this, that saving faith is nothing other than the act of the whole rational soul by which it receives God as the highest end and

Christ as the one and only Mediator, for this purpose, that we may be united with him, and being thus united obtain communion with all his benefits. Most, I say, of the ingredients of this definition are expressed in the text. There is the *definitum* of saving faith: "those who believe in him." And here saving faith is understood as revealed by its fruit: adoption. Its saving act is called receiving. The object of the act, God himself as its highest end, is not expressed, unless perhaps you refer the phrase "in his name" to God, who was recently named. But it is more than certainly presupposed in the secondary object, "as many as received *him*." For no one can receive Christ as his Mediator who has not previously received God as his highest end (John 14:6). Finally, the end or fruit of this faith or reception, namely, union and communion with Christ, is contained in that one word "adoption," since by the reception of Christ we who have been made his brothers are rendered heirs of God and joint heirs with Christ. And in this consists every bit of our blessedness. Meanwhile, we will demonstrate each of these parts individually and explain them in order.

The etymology of the word fides

IV. Then next, *fides*, "faith" is said to be from *fio*, "I am made," just as πίστις from πέπεισται, "he has been persuaded," and אֱמוּנָה from נאמן, "to be firm." In Latin it denotes some sort of persuasion of mind concerning the truth of something (Mark 15:32; Rom. 14:2). Improperly speaking, it is employed for that which produces faith, whether it be an argument that teaches something (Acts 17:31), or the trustworthiness[1] of the one speaking (Rom. 3:3), or the thing spoken and believed (Gal. 1:23; 3:23). More strictly it denotes that persuasion of mind which results from the faithfulness of the one speaking.

The distributions of faith

V. Therefore persuasion, just as it can depend on a twofold faithfulness, so produces a twofold faith: divine and human.[2] Divine faith, which belongs to this passage, designates these four things: either (1) bare assent given to anything that has been said; and this is called historical faith (on which see James 2:17–20); or specifically, (2) assent given to the divine promise of working or receiving miracles, which is called the faith of miracles, both active (Matt. 17:20–21; 1 Cor. 13:2) and passive (Matt. 13:58; Mark 5:34–36); or (3) assent that in addition

---

1. ἀξιοπιστία

2. Simply put, human faith rests on human authority and credibility whereas divine faith rests on divine authority and credibility. For a helpful overview of the historical and theological issues in play, see Herman Bavinck, *Reformed Dogmatics* (Grand Rapids: Baker Academic, 2008), 1:510–17.

stirs up motions in the will that are in some way good, but transient (Matt. 13:21; Heb. 6:4–6), which is called temporary faith;[3] or (4) assent that also stirs up such motions in the will by which we take hold of God as our highest end and Christ as our one and only Mediator, which is called saving faith (on which see John 1:12; 3:16; Rom. 10:10). It has been called saving faith not because it effects salvation or merits it, but because it is the condition, according to the pure good pleasure of God, that is prerequisite to conferring salvation. This saving faith is sometimes taken more strictly, in a more philosophical sense, insofar as it denotes one particular and simple act (John 3:16); and sometimes more broadly, in a more theological sense, insofar as it speaks of many acts of faith that are prerequisite for salvation, insofar as in saving faith coincide knowledge, assent, reception, and particular application. We will speak about it in this latter sense in the following sections.

Saving faith is an act.
VI. We call this faith an act—an act of the rational soul that consists in receiving God as the end and Christ as the Mediator. Its mode is in that preeminence[4] wherein we receive God as the highest end and Christ as the one and only Mediator, and its ends and fruits are first union with Christ and then communion with him. We will briefly present each of these again one by one. So then, the faith that is stipulated for salvation is an act. And there is on the one hand (1) seminal faith, which belongs through regeneration even to infants, and which is otherwise called the spirit of faith, or the seed and root of faith. There is also (2) the disposition or state of faith, a διάθεσις, produced from effectual calling or conversion. There is (3) habitual faith, if not produced, at least confirmed by repeated acts of believing. It is called the power of faith, which, even when believers are asleep, and when they lay buried under the most weighty trials, immovably clings to them. Finally, there is (4) actual faith, or the believing itself. The first three types of faith are useful and necessary for salvation, but ordinarily insufficient in adults, because the continual tenor of Scripture presents believing, receiving, and willing as prerequisites for salvation (John 1:12; 3:16; Acts 10:43).

It is an act of the entire rational soul.
VII. Faith is therefore an act, but of what? Certainly not of the body, although faith is attributed to it in its own way (Rom. 10:10; 1:8), but of the soul, for with the heart one believes (Rom. 10:10), and indeed, of the whole soul: "If you believe

---

3. *fides* πρόσκαιρος; cf. Matt. 13:21
4. ὑπεροχῇ

with your whole heart..." (Acts 8:37). For it is the first act of life, by which the whole person lives spiritually (Rom. 1:17; Gal. 2:20). Moreover, it is an act of each of the soul's faculties—the intellect, the will, the affections, and so forth.

The act of faith in the intellect

VIII. Indeed in the intellect faith requires: (1) knowledge of the promises of the gospel, of God and Christ (John 17:3; Isa. 53:11; 2 Tim. 1:12); (2) assent, given not only implicitly to the whole Word of God (Acts 24:14; Luke 16:29), but also explicitly to the fundamental dogmas, and in particular to the promises of the gospel, without which there cannot be any reception of God or Christ (Phil. 3:8, 10). In particular, (3) assent to this great proposition: Christ is that once-promised Messiah without whom there is no hope of salvation at all (John 11:25–27; 1 John 2:22, 4:2–3; Acts 4:12). But finally, (4) a theoretical knowledge and assent is not sufficient, but a practical knowledge, by which you have been convicted and the will is moved to take hold of what has been offered, namely, God and the Mediator (Rom. 7:18, "I know..."; v. 21, "I find..."; v. 24, "O wretched man that I am! Who will deliver me?").

The act of faith in the will

IX. In a word, in the will saving faith requires consent, in which we earnestly will to have God and the Mediator as they offer themselves to us in the gospel, and in willing, receive them (John 1:12), which we will soon address expressly.[5]

The act of faith in the affections

X. In the affections (although they are really nothing but acts of the will) faith will stir up: (1) love toward God and the Mediator (Matt. 10:37); (2) a desire for both, together with their promised benefits (Ps. 42:1–2); (3) joy and acquiescence (Ps. 16:5; 73:25–26); (4) hatred and detestation of anything contrary to them (Ps. 139:22). Finally, from all of these, faith in all its operations thrives and is at work through love (Gal. 5:6).

The act of faith is receiving.

XI. But, because several acts coincide in saving faith—knowledge, assent, consent, trust, and so forth—we must observe that one particular act is predominant among them—the act that when present, salvation is present, and when absent, salvation is absent; thus the act that is called saving. What act is it then? The text answers, "Receiving," and the apostle gives this his support (Col. 2:5–7; Phil.

---

5. §XI

3:8–9, 12; Gal. 4:14; cf. Matt. 26:26). To this end, (1) our God and Mediator offers himself to us so that we may receive him (Isa. 55:1–2; John 7:37–39; Rev. 22:17), and that certainly by faith (John 1:12). (2) He acts as a suitor, standing at the door, knocking and speaking sweetly so that he may be received (Rev. 3:20; Song 5:2; Hos. 2:14). (3) He seeks spiritual matrimony (Hos. 2:19), surely so that he may be received by consent, which makes a marriage (Song 2:16). For this reason, (4) we do not become partakers of any of the gospel's benefits unless by faith we receive the covenant of grace and the conditions of the covenant, together with its Mediator (2 Cor. 1:20; Rev. 22:17). For this reason, (5) not receiving Christ, rejecting him, despising him, and not believing in him are synonyms in the gospel (John 1:11–12).

What it is to receive Christ

XII. Moreover, this reception of Christ consists in consent, namely when the will assents to Christ as he offers himself in the gospel, and does so by this law, that he be received as the one and only Mediator, in the way that a bride receives a bridegroom, that is, by assenting to him as he offers himself. For this reason, receiving, consenting, and desiring earnestly seem to be of equivalent force in the gospel (John 1:12; cf. Rev. 22:17; Matt. 23:37; 22:3). I say desiring earnestly, that is, (1) desiring absolutely, without any condition or restriction (Ps. 73:25–26; Matt. 19:16–17, 20–21); (2) desiring Christ himself, not only his benefits (John 1:12), just as God gives us first the Son, then those things that belong to the Son (Rom. 8:32); (3) desiring Christ entirely, not only as Priest or Redeemer, but also as King, as Lord, in the way he is given to us by God (1 Cor. 1:30). And (4) not only him entirely but also him exclusively (Ps. 73:25–26), that is, conjugally; (5) not only as a king but also as a servant—not only his glory but also his misery (Luke 9:23). Finally, (6) desiring him on those terms and conditions by which he offers himself, that is, under the condition of the denial of one's very self, and so forth (Gal. 5:24; Luke 9:23).

The names given for this receiving

XIII. Indeed this receiving is represented in Scripture in various ways and terms. For it is named (1) reception, more strictly so-called (Col. 2:6–7; Rev. 22:17), which speaks of a desiring of Christ as he has been offered. (2) Consenting with Christ as the one and only Mediator (Matt. 23:37; Ps. 81:11; John 5:40), which speaks of the same desiring, but according to a previous invitation and persuasive arguments (Matt. 11:28; Isa. 55:1–2). (3) Choosing Christ (Song 5:9), which denotes desiring and reception with delight, and disregard for others (John 6:68; Ps. 73:26–27). (4) Covenanting, which speaks of a receiving conjoined with the surrendering of ourselves, as happens in marriage (Hos. 2:18–19; Jer. 31:33). Therefore, there is no saving act of faith except receiving our God and Mediator; no receiving him without consenting and earnestly desiring him, that is, desiring him in the same way as he desires to give himself—in a word, to receive Christ conjugally, that is, in such a way that by the same act you surrender yourself to him.

What the object of saving faith is not

XIV. From this the object of faith is evident. In its breadth, it takes various objects according to the various faculties of the soul in which it is found. As it is in the intellect, its general object is the whole Word of God (Acts 24:14), its partial object[6] is the gospel promises (Acts 10:43), and its foundational object, on which all assent rests, is God's trustworthiness in regard to the true, but the particular thing in regard to the good (Rom. 4:21; Heb. 11:3).[7] Accordingly, the object is not (1) the promises, except figuratively, insofar as they contain and offer goods and impel us to receive them. Nor (2) the benefits of God and the Mediator, which supply the end of our receiving (1 Peter 1:9), and its fruit (John 1:12).

What then is the object of saving faith?

XV. What then is the object of saving faith? God and the Mediator themselves: "As many as received him" (John 1:12). Accordingly, the object is twofold (John 12:44; 14:1; Ps. 78:22), for no one comes to the Father except through Christ (John 14:6). The highest and primary object is God, for which reason both Testaments so frequently speak of believing in God. The subordinate and secondary

---

6. Latin: *objectum…inadaequatum*; Dutch: *het ondergeschikte voorwerpen*. Cf. "Object Adäquates" and "Object Inadäquates" in Johann Heinrich Zedler, *Grosses vollständiges Universal-Lexicon aller wissenschaften und Künste* (1731–1754), 25:199. In short, an *objectum adaequatum* is the unified object necessary to understand the operation and maintenance of its purpose (*Würckung und Erhaltung eines zweckes*) in its totality. But when the object is understood by a portion of its subordinate or component parts, operations, or dispositions, it is an *objectum inadaequatum*. Zedler also provides the synonymous terms *objectum totale* and *objectum partiale*.

7. *sub ratione veri…sub ratione boni*. Cf. Bernard of Clairvaux, *De consideratione ad Eugenium V*, 5.14.31 in *S. Bernardi Opera*, ed. J. LeClercq and H. M. Rochais (Rome, 1963), 493.20–23. Mastricht's language here is similar to Bernard of Clairvaux. According to Bernard, for the contemplative life there are four kinds of contemplative considerations (meditation on God's promises, memory of his benefits, contemplation of his majesty, and consideration of his judgments). These contemplative considerations rouse a combination of proper religious affections ranging from love to fear, which move the soul toward the truth and also to the good. Thus, religious considerations *sub ratione veri* and *sub ratione boni* accord with faith and lead to their respective proper religious affections and actions.

object is Christ, but only as the Mediator, insofar as through him we believe in God (1 Peter 1:21; Rom. 6:11) and have confidence through Christ before God (2 Cor. 3:4). God indeed is the object as the end, and Christ is the object as the means, or the Mediator.

Christ is the object of faith as the Mediator, according to his threefold office.
XVI. Yet, the proper object of faith, as it is the faith of a sinner, is Christ the Mediator (Acts 10:43; John 1:11–12; 2:23; Acts 4:12; 1 Tim. 2:5; etc.), neither as God only, nor as man only, but as the God-man, distinguished by his mediatorial work (1 Tim. 2:5); and not according to this or that function of his office separately—either as Prophet, Priest, or King only—but as it embraces the threefold office in its entirety. For this reason we are commanded to believe without qualification "in him" (John 1:12; 3:16), in "Jesus Christ," which designates his person together with his office (Acts 8:37), and in "the Mediator" (1 Tim. 2:5; Heb. 9:15), which unites the three functions. Accordingly, we receive Christ as Prophet by hearing him (Matt. 17:5), by learning from him as from a teacher (Matt. 23:8, 10), and by not resisting him (2 Cor. 10:5). We receive him as Priest by resting on him as our one and only Redeemer (Isa. 10:20), by seeking remission, salvation, and all things from him alone (Gen. 49:18; John 8:56), and moreover, by promptly devoting to him whatever we have (Phil. 3:7–9). Finally, we receive him as King by acknowledging his lordship (Rom. 14:8), by subjecting ourselves to him and to his pleasure (Ps. 2:11–12), and by devoting our whole life to his glory and interest (Rom. 14:7; 2 Cor. 5:15).

Specifically, not only as our Redeemer but also as our Lord
XVII. Therefore, specifically, he must be received by faith not only as the Redeemer through whom we are freed from the punishments of our sins and eternal destruction, but also as the Lord to whom we offer ourselves obedient in all things. Thus he is in many places called "Lord" and "Savior" (1 Tim. 1:1; Titus 1:4). Likewise, he is called "the Lord Jesus Christ," and believers are also expressly said to receive him as such: "Therefore, just as you have received Christ Jesus the Lord…" (Col. 2:6). For this reason he comes to us and offers himself to us as King and Lord (Zech. 9:9). Nor does anyone receive him as the complete Mediator who does otherwise, because he is both Savior and Lord; indeed, nor even as the complete Redeemer, since he redeems not only from the guilt of sins but also from their stain, and he is for us not only righteousness, but also sanctification (1 Cor. 1:30). Although, the believer in receiving him first seeks his justification, as from the Redeemer (Phil. 3:8–9), just as in the exploration of his faith he first

senses and experiences the power of sanctification and obedience, as the power of the Lord (Ps. 2:10–12).

The saving way of receiving is this, that it be done with respect to his prerogative.
XVIII. Moreover, the way of this reception by which saving faith is most safely distinguished from common faith is this: that we receive God not only as an end, but as the highest end, and that we receive Christ not only as a mediator, but as the one and only Mediator, that is, that we receive both, God as well as the Mediator, before all others, and that we esteem them above all things (Matt. 10:37; Luke 14:26, 33), that we seek them first (Matt. 6:33) and consider all else with indifference (Phil. 3:7–8), that for their sake we readily accept the loss of our goods, any disgrace, imprisonment, and even death itself (Acts 20:23–24; Heb. 10:32–34; cf. v. 23). Thus in this way we overcome the world by our faith (1 John 5:4–5; 4:4; Rev. 2:7, 11, 17, 26), whereas hypocrites are overcome and conquered by the world (2 Peter 2:19).

The ends or fruits of faith: Union
XIX. Furthermore, the end or fruit of faith and saving reception is twofold: union with Christ and communion in his goods, as indicated by the apostle in Philippians 3:8–9. First, we receive Christ so that we may have him (Ps. 73:25–26), or so that we may be united with him, that he may be in us (Eph. 3:17) and we in him (Eph. 1:13).

Communion with Christ
Second, we receive Christ so that in and with him we may obtain every kind of saving goods (Rom. 8:32), so that from his fullness we may receive grace upon grace (John 1:12; cf. v. 16), to such a degree that we may be perfect in him (Col. 2:9–10), no different than the way that from the conjugal union flows communion of goods. For this reason it is also said that he who has the Son has life (1 John 5:12).

Justification, Adoption, Sanctification, Glorification
Moreover, the goods of this communion are the following: (1) justification (Phil. 3:9; Acts 10:43). (2) Adoption (John 1:12; Gal. 3:26), for having been united to Christ by faith, having been made his brothers, with him we gain one God and Father (John 20:17). (3) Sanctification (Acts 15:9), since established by faith in him we experience the power of his resurrection and gain "the fellowship of his sufferings, being conformed to his death" (Phil. 3:9–10); likewise, since having gained Christ we gain his sanctifying blood (Heb. 9:13–14); and finally, since we

receive by faith all the arguments that rouse us to a zeal for holiness (Titus 2:14; 2 Cor. 5:15). (4) Glorification (1 Peter 1:3–5, 9), first inchoate glorification, which indicates the certainty of future salvation (Gal. 5:5; 2 Cor. 5:1), a confident rest in God (Isa. 10:20; Jer. 17:7), a taste of the firstfruits (Rom. 8:23), spiritual peace (Rom. 5:1), ineffable joy (1 Peter 1:8; Rom. 5:2), comfort and tranquility of soul in adversity (Col. 2:2), and the experience of the divine benevolence (Rom. 5:1; cf. v. 3; 1 Peter 2:2–3); then consummated glorification (John 3:16; 1 Peter 1:9).

The degrees of faith
XX. It remains to discuss the degrees of faith, by which faith is sometimes called great (Matt. 15:28), and from it some are called full of faith (Acts 6:5–8); sometimes very small, and thus some are those of little faith (Matt. 6:30; 8:26; 14:31) or weak in faith (Rom. 14:1); sometimes most small, like a mustard seed (Matt. 17:20; Luke 17:6), so small that it is almost nothing: "Where is your faith?" (Mark 4:40; Luke 8:25). According to these degrees, faith is said to increase (2 Cor. 10:15), to be established (Col. 2:7), to grow exceedingly (2 Thess. 1:3), all the way to full assurance of faith (Heb. 10:22).

Concerning these degrees, three things must be observed.
Meanwhile, three things must be observed here. First, from one perspective faith can be robust when from another perspective it is weak. This is evident in Christ's disciples (Matt. 8:26) compared with the Syrophoenician woman (Matt. 15:28) and with the centurion (Matt. 8:10). In the former there was no doubt a more distinct knowledge of Christ and of Christianity than in the latter; whereas at the same time the former are called "you of little faith," while Christ marvels at the faith of the latter.

Second, this disparity is visible not only in different subjects but also in the same subjects at different times, as is evident in David (Ps. 30:6–7; and throughout the Psalms, compared with each other, e.g. 3:6; 18:1–2; 13:5 with 42:5–7, 11; 43:5), and likewise in Peter (Matt. 16:17 with 26:70–72).

Third, faith is not called strong or weak only as there belongs to it a more clear and distinct knowledge of divine things, or a more solid assent, or a more unmoved confidence, or a more confirmed certainty of salvation, but also, and this especially, due to its appetite, to the more intense or more lax reception and submission of itself, because the act of faith, at least the act that is properly called saving faith, does not consist so much in knowledge or assent as in reception.

The principal cause and origin of faith

XXI. The principal cause of the faith that we have delineated thus far is God, the Father of lights, from whom comes every saving good (James 1:17); and the Spirit of faith (2 Cor. 4:13), among whose fruits is numbered faith (Gal. 5:22). Nor can that faith come to us from any other place, because we are blind in mind (Eph. 4:18), stony in heart (Ezek. 11:19), and dead in sins (Eph. 2:1–2). Moreover, God works faith, first, in regeneration, whereby he confers the seed of faith, that by it we may be able to believe at the proper time, once all things needed are supplied. Before this regeneration, as we said, a person is dead to every spiritual good. Second, God works faith in conversion, whereby the seed of faith sends forth shoots, such that we actually believe, take hold of Christ as our one and only Mediator, and having been drawn to him, come (John 6:44), run (Song 1:4), and lean on Christ (Song 8:5). Third, God works faith in sanctification, whereby faith puts out flower and fruit, and is at work through love (Gal. 5:6).

The instrumental cause

In all these things, God uses as his instrument the Word (Rom. 10:17), both the law, that he may instill in us a sense of our misery and the necessity of receiving a deliverer, for which reason it is called our tutor to Christ (Gal. 3:24); and the gospel, that by it he may show us the Mediator who must be taken hold of, and add motives for taking hold of him (1 Cor. 1:23–24). Nevertheless, the efficacy of this Word is nothing other than a moral and instrumental efficacy (1 Cor. 3:6–8).

The Elenctic Part

It is asked: 1. Does saving faith consist only in the assent of the intellect?

XXII. It is asked whether saving faith consists only in the assent of the intellect. Here on one side the papists, so that they are not compelled to grant the received Protestant way of thinking, wherein saving faith is a trust of the heart through which each person applies Christ to himself and is persuaded that Christ is his Redeemer, state that saving faith consists in the general assent of the intellect, although they do not deny that a certain inclination in the will toward God is presupposed, by help of which the believer accepts the divine trustworthiness. And they also make this assent separable from all pious motions in the will. With these points a fair number of Protestants agree, at least insofar as they place saving faith in the assent of the intellect alone; but they do not place it in such an assent that is general, toward anything revealed, nor in such an assent that is detached from all pious affections in the will, but rather in such an assent that is alive and effective, by which a believer is persuaded that Christ is his

Redeemer. On the other side, most of the practical writers among the British place saving faith in the will alone, whereby we rest in God through Christ. They do this because they judge that no assent of the intellect is itself sufficient for receiving Christ. There are those who choose the middle way of thinking, in which saving faith consists neither in the intellect alone nor in the will alone, but in the whole spiritual life of a person—indeed radically in the intellect, but formally in the will and operatively in the remaining faculties of the soul. This seems, at least to me, the most careful way of thinking, principally for this reason, that faith is the first act of spiritual life that informs all human faculties, as we have already taught.

It is proved by the Scriptures

In all events, it can be proved that saving faith does not exist only in the assent of the intellect, first by testimonies of Scripture: (1) those in which we are not only called to believe God or Christ but to believe *in* God (2 Kings 17:14; Rom. 10:11; John 14:1; 3:16; 1 Peter 2:6). (2) Those in which faith is either called, or to it is attributed, trust (2 Cor. 3:4), courage (Matt. 9:2; 2 Cor. 5:6), boldness (Eph. 3:12), full assurance (Rom. 4:21; Col. 2:2; Heb. 10:22), substance (Heb. 11:1), and access (Rom. 5:2; Eph. 2:18; 3:12). (3) Those in which faith is designated by the terms *trust* or *to trust* (Ps. 78:22; 25:2; Isa. 50:10). (4) Those in which we are said to lean on Jehovah in faith (Isa. 10:20; 50:10; 2 Chron. 16:8); (5) through faith to cast ourselves upon God (Ps. 37:5; Prov. 22:9); and likewise (6) to keep ourselves for God and embrace God (Deut. 4:4; 2 Kings 18:6; Ps. 119:31). Pointing to this are all those Old Testament passages that speak of a resting and trust of the heart in God and are referred to in the New Testament by the term *faith*. For example, Psalm 33:21 is referred to in the parallel of John 1:12; again, Proverbs 3:5 is referred to in Acts 8:37, and likewise, Psalm 31:1 and 25:2 are brought forward in Romans 10:11. By all of these testimonies it shines forth more clearly than the sun that saving faith is not in the intellect alone, nor is its act a mere assenting, nor is it brought indifferently to anything that has been said by God.

And by reasons

Second, it is confirmed with these reasons: (1) The object of saving faith as such we have demonstrated to be not some sort of axiom, but rather God and the Mediator. (2) For this purpose God and the Mediator are offered to us in the gospel: that they may be received by faith. (3) We come to God in faith (Isa. 55:1; Matt. 11:28; 1 Peter 2:4; Rev. 22:17). (4) Union and communion with Christ, which without doubt is by faith, also does not belong to mere assent of any sort.

(5) Not desiring Christ (Matt. 23:37; John 5:40), rejecting and despising him (Matt. 22:5; Acts 13:46), and not receiving him (John 1:11; 5:43–44) constitute unbelief, from which by the law of contraries it remains that faith is earnestly desiring Christ (Rev. 22:17), as we demonstrated in its own place.[8] Add to these reasons that (6) though saving faith is particular to the justified (2 Thess. 3:2), this faith of the papists may be observed in anyone (John 12:42). (7) Although to saving faith belongs the promise of salvation (John 3:16; Acts 10:43), to this faith of the papists belongs no such promise (James 2:1; 1 Cor. 13:2). (8) Although the fruit of saving faith is union and communion with Christ (Phil. 3:9), justification, adoption, sanctification, and glorification, as we have shown in their own place,[9] none of these is connected with the papist faith.

Objections

If our opponents should allege for their position (1) that Scripture constantly locates faith in the assent of the mind to the truth presented to it (John 1:50), I respond: (a) We have already recognized that the assent of the intellect is in more than one way a part of saving faith, and we have also demonstrated it in the dogmatic part.[10] But whether assent exhausts the term *faith*, this only is the question; and we deny that it does. Then (b) it is also certain that the trust of the heart, or the will, in the Messiah without qualification is applied to our Jesus by the kind of words that speak of an act of assent of the intellect in such a way that the trust of the heart is not excluded, but rather presupposed. If they allege (2) that philosophers are in agreement in locating all faith in the assent of the mind (except those who with Descartes, in order to support their hypotheses, refer judgment to the will), I will say that faith can be considered either philosophically, as denoting one certain act of the rational soul, and thus without any doubt it denotes the assent of the intellect alone; or it can be considered theologically, as denoting several acts, namely, knowledge, assent, trust, and particular application. In this latter way we say that included in faith is, besides the assent of the intellect, also trust, or the consent of the will.

2. Is knowledge also included in saving faith?

XXIII. It is asked, second, whether knowledge is also included in saving faith. Those who follow Descartes, philosophers as well as theologians, do recognize that there is knowledge in faith, but a knowledge that should be presupposed

---

8. §XII, above
9. §XIX, above
10. §VIII, above

by faith rather than included in its nature. On the other hand, the papists completely deny that there is knowledge in faith; in fact, more accurately they want to describe it as ignorance (Bellarmine, *On Justifying Faith*, bk. 1, ch. 7).[11] Of course, they hold to this so that they may maintain their implicit faith, or coal miner's faith,[12] in which someone believes whatever the church believes while at the same time remaining ignorant of what the church believes, and thus is made more compliant to the dictates of the pope.

Arguments

The Reformed distinguish between the knowledge called *scientia* and the knowledge called *notitia*, insofar as *scire*, "to know," is to know a thing from its causes or effects. In this way, they do not believe that *scientia* is necessarily required in faith, yet they do teach that *notitia*, which does not involve causes or effects, is necessary in faith. This is because Scripture: (1) expressly requires in faith knowledge[13] (Deut. 4:6; Ps. 32:9; Dan. 9:22; Col. 1:6; 2:2; 2 Tim. 3:7); (2) attributes salvation to knowledge as well as to faith (Isa. 53:11; John 17:3); and (3) commands a confession of our faith, which presupposes knowledge (Rom. 10:10; 1 Peter 3:15). Moreover, (4) we cannot desire God and the Mediator, or by desiring receive them, without knowledge.

Objections

Nor is it valid to argue to the contrary: (1) that faith is a way, and also a means, to knowledge (from Isa. 7:9, poorly translated), because implicit faith could be for us the reason that we come to know distinctly the things that must be believed, and that we assent to them with explicit faith. (2) That knowledge is distinguished

---

11. Robert Bellarmine (1542–1621) argues against Calvin that "faith is not so much knowledge (*notitia*) as assent (*assensus*)," in *De fide justificante*, bk. 1, ch. 7, in *Disputationes Roberti Bellarmini…de controversiis Christianae fidei* (Lyon: Jean Pillehotte, 1610), 4:948–51. Volume 4 has three general controversies: the grace conferred on the first parents, the grace lost, and the grace restored. The last controversy has three parts: grace and free choice, justification of the ungodly, and good works and the fruits of the justified. *De fide justificante* is a five book subsection in the third part of the third controversy.

12. *fides carbonaria*, a common Protestant turn of phrase for the Roman Catholic doctrine of implicit faith. Among the Reformed, see Thomas Cartwright, *Thomae Cartwrighti…harmonia evangelica commentario analytico, metaphrastico, practico* (Amsterdam: Ludovicus Elsevier, 1647), 188; among Lutherans, Johannes Eisenhart, *De fide historica commentarius* (Helmstadt: J. M. Sustermann, 1702), 14; among Remonstrants, Étienne de Courcelles, *Opera theologica* (Amsterdam: Daniel Elsevier, 1675), 458, "For this reason, those of the papists are mistaken who think that a collier's faith, as they say, is true faith and sufficient for salvation, wherein that which the Roman Church believes is implicitly believed even if one is ignorant of what that is."

13. *notitia*. So throughout this paragraph and next.

from faith in 1 Corinthians 13:2. For aside from the fact that the discussion at that particular place is not about saving faith but only about the faith of miracles, knowledge can and ought to be distinguished as a part from the whole, and therefore not excluded from the whole. (3) That we are commanded to take our reasonings captive and to bring our intellect under obedience to Christ (2 Cor. 10:5). For it is not reason simply speaking that must be taken captive, but reason inasmuch as it is corrupt. And moreover, much less is it commanded that all knowledge must be eliminated from faith, since knowledge and reasoning differ.

3. Does saving faith consist in observing the commands of Christ?

XXIV. It is asked, third, whether saving faith consists in obedience to the commands of Christ. The papists, so that they might more easily hold to the idea that a person is justified by works, state not only that faith is a good work, but also that it must be considered as a work in this matter of justification.[14] The Remonstrants in the same spirit say that faith is indeed not perfect obedience, but is nevertheless considered and admitted by God through acceptilation in the place of perfect obedience in the matter of justification.[15] The Socinians, that they might more effectively remove the satisfaction and merits of Christ from saving faith as well as from the Christian religion, and maintain that we are justified not by faith alone in Christ, but by observance of the commands of Christ, and thus by "evangelical works," as they love to say, state that saving faith does not consist of anything but observance of the commands of Christ. The Reformed, although they do not deny that faith in itself and materially considered is a sort of work (John 6:29), and a work or act of obedience, even so do deny that in the matter of justification it is considered as a work or an act of obedience, as we will

---

14. Cf. Bellarmine, *De fide justificante*, 1.13.

15. Latin: *per acceptilationem a Deo*; Dutch: *door ene aannemende schatting van Godt*. In Roman Law, an *acceptilatio* is an *imaginaria solutio*, i.e. an imaginary payment, when a creditor chooses to accept either nothing or something less from the debtor in lieu of full payment, Justinian, *Institutes*, 3.29.1. Hugo Grotius (1583–1645) builds his understanding of Christ's satisfaction, not as a *solutio* or full payment, but as an *acceptilatio* or partial payment, in *Defensio fidei catholicae de satisfactione Christi adversus Faustum Socinum* (Leiden: Joannes Patius, 1617), 80; see also "Acceptilatio. Hugo Grotius on Satisfaction" in *Grotiana*, 38, no. 1 (2017):1–27. Philip van Limborch (1633–1712), while commenting on Romans 4:3, argued that God received Abraham's faith and imperfect obedience by graciously accepting it as "full and perfect in every way" for his righteousness. Furthermore, Limborch asserts that Christ's righteousness is never imputed to us and argues, "righteousness is imputed to us due to Christ, or rather, our faith is imputed to us as righteousness" in his *Commentarius in Acta Apostolorum et in epistolas ad Romanos et ad Hebraeos* (Basel: Johann Rudolph, 1740), 293. Cf. Charles Hodge, *Systematic Theology* (New York: Charles Scribner's Sons, 1898), 3:188–89.

see expressly in its own place.[16] In addition, they deny that faith is observance of the commands of Christ and affirm that it chiefly consists in the reception of God as the supreme end and Christ as the one and only Mediator.

Arguments

In any case, Scripture teaches that faith does not consist in the observance of the commands of Christ. It does so in more than one way, when: (1) in its definitions it distinguishes faith and works, saying that the former is receiving Christ (John 1:12) and "the substance of things hoped for and the evidence of things not seen" (Heb. 11:1), and that the latter on the contrary is the "fulfillment of the law" (Rom. 13:10). (2) It distinguishes faith and obedience as cause and effect (Gal. 5:6; 1 Tim. 1:5). (3) It assigns different effects to each: it assigns to faith justification (Rom. 3–4; Gal. 2–3; Eph. 2:8), adoption (John 1:12), and union with Christ (Eph. 3:17), and takes these things away from obedience or good works (Gal. 3:2, 5). (4) It also asserts a different norm for each: for faith, the gospel (Mark 1:15); for obedience, the law (Matt. 22:37; Rom. 13:8–10). In fact, (5) at least in the matter of justification, it opposes faith and obedience or good works (Rom. 3:20; Gal. 2:16). I will not mention (6) the absurdities of the Socinian opinion, which are quite intolerable to Christians. For it excludes (a) the satisfaction of Christ from faith; (b) a person from participation in Christ (Rom. 10:3; Gal. 5:4–6); (c) Christ from the perfect glory of redemption, for if any works whatsoever are our righteousness,[17] then Christ alone is not; (d) all hope of salvation from anyone, since there is no salvation apart from Christ received by faith (Acts 4:12; John 14:6; 3:16); (e) all Christian godliness, inasmuch as godliness results from Christ alone received by faith (John 15:4–5). In addition, (f) it leads us right back to popery, which seeks justification in works.

Objections

Neither does it follow that faith consists in obedience because of the fact: (1) that it is said that Christ promised salvation to those who obey him, and that no one is saved who is not obedient to Christ's words (Heb. 12:14). For this indicates nothing else than that obedience is inseparable from faith, not however that it is faith itself (Gal. 5:6). (2) That James states that faith without works is dead (James 2:26). For faith without any operation is called dead only in the sense that works flow forth from faith just as operations do from life. (3)

---

16. 1.6.6 §§XIV, XXII, XXVI, XXVIII
17. δικαίωμα

That the godly and obedient are called believers (Heb. 11). For this happens only because faith and obedience are inseparable, not because they are the same.

4. Is particular application the very essence of saving faith?

XXV. It is asked, fourth, whether particular application or persuasion, by which someone is certain that Christ is his own Mediator, is the very essence of saving faith. Here the Pelagians, papists, and as many as deny that infallible certainty of salvation can be obtained by ordinary means, in order that they may not injure the independent indifference of free choice; these, I say, respond to the question in the negative. Protestants speak in more than one way. Among the majority it is agreed that knowledge, assent, and trust[18] coincide in saving faith, but some locate trust in a person's particular persuasion and application of the benefits of Christ to himself, while others do not understand trust as anything other than choosing Christ and resting in him. The former refer trust to the intellect, the latter to the will. There are also those who locate that trust in a certain conjugal reception, by which we receive the Mediator as he offers himself to be possessed by certain laws, namely that we reciprocate and return ourselves to him (Song 2:16), and afterward this trust is taken up by particular application and the indubitable persuasion that Christ is our bridegroom, that his goods, however many there are, are ours. Thus this persuasion is not formally the saving act itself of faith, but rather a consequence of reception. This, at least in my judgment, is the safest way of thinking. So then, concerning this particular application, it seems to me that sin is committed at both extremes: first in defect, by the papists and others, when they entirely separate this application both from faith and from religion, contrary to the express testimonies of Scripture (Gal. 2:20; Rom. 8:38; 2 Cor. 5:1; 2 Tim. 4:8; Ps. 103:1–3; 2 Sam. 12:13). We will see a specific consideration of this in its own place, in the matter of the certainty of salvation.[19] Second, sin is committed in excess by very many Protestants, who place faith's saving act properly and formally in this application, such that when it is present, salvation is present, and when it is absent, salvation is absent. We prove this generally by these reasons: (1) this particular persuasion has no promise of justification or salvation in the Scriptures. For nowhere, either in words or in substance, is it said that whoever has been persuaded that Christ is his own Savior, that his own sins have been forgiven, and so forth, has been justified or

---

18. *fiducia*: cf. Question 21, "What is true faith?" in German Reformed Church in the USA, *The Heidelberg Catechism in German, Latin, and English, with an historical introduction* (New York: Charles Scribner, 1863), 152–53; *certa fiducia*, "a hearty trust," *hertzliche vertrawen*.

19. 1.6.1 §XXII; cf. §§LV–LVI, below

will be justified. (2) There can be no peculiar persuasion of this sort unless there is presupposed a saving act of faith from which you may infer and gather that Christ is your Savior and that your sins have been forgiven. (3) That applicative assent, if only it wishes to be divine faith, requires for its object the Word of God that speaks, for where God does not speak, there I also cannot believe. Now, however, God nowhere says: "Peter or Paul, Christ is your Savior, he died for you; your sins have been forgiven you." (4) By this reasoning, either Christ will have died for the reprobate also, or many of them will believe by divine faith what is false. The reasoning is that each and every one to whom Christ is announced, among whom there are very many reprobate, is obligated to believe in Christ (Mark 16:14; John 6:28–29, 64–65; 12:36). (5) That particular persuasion, at least with respect to the essence of the act, can be present in the unregenerate and hypocrites (Luke 18:11–12), and even more evidently (Ps. 78:34–36). Conversely, on this view (6) there would exist a believer destitute of saving faith, since it is evident that neither is this particular persuasion present in all believers, nor is it present all the time (Ps. 77:7–9; Ps. 88; Rom. 7:24).

Objections
Those Scripture passages that could be and customarily are urged in favor of the contrary (Gal. 2:20; Rom. 8:38; 2 Cor. 5:1; 2 Tim. 4:8; Ps. 103:1–3; 2 Sam. 12:13; etc.) do not extend further than to say that the persuasion of special grace was not uncommon in believers, and that in addition believers can acquire, and ought with utmost zeal to acquire, this persuasion with the help of ordinary means, especially the means of saving faith. But in no way do these passages assert that saving faith is nothing other than this very persuasion of special grace.

Nor does faith consist in trust alone.
XXVI. Nor also, as some think on the other hand, does trust, or any other act of the will, exhaust the whole nature of saving faith, because it also manifestly includes the operations of the intellect, knowledge and assent, as per §VIII. The arguments customarily produced to the contrary, if carefully weighed, prove nothing but that trust is included in the nature of faith, not that it exhausts it. Or if they seem to prove even more, and they ascribe salvation to those who trust (Ps. 2:12; Jer. 17:7–8), this must be taken figuratively, with the part understood in place of the whole, because without the knowledge of God and the Savior (2 Tim. 1:12; Job 19:25), and without assent to the divine promises, this trust cannot exist at all (Rom. 4:20–21).

5. Can divine faith be based on something false?

XXVII. It is asked, fifth, whether divine faith can be based on something false. The sense of the question could be twofold: first, whether the faith that is in God (Rom. 3:3), or the divine trustworthiness, can be based on something false, that is, whether God can say something false; and second, whether the divine faith that is in us can be based on something false. With reference to the former sense, there are some Scholastics who suppose that God by his absolute power can lie or say something false, although he cannot do so by his ordinary power,[20] a view promoted by Franciscus Sylvius (on Aquinas's *Summa theologiae*, IIa IIae, q. 1, art. 3).[21] Among our theologians one or two follow this view, estimating that God can deceive if he should will, but he does not will to do so. We have examined these in our *Gangrene of the Cartesian Innovations* (sect. 2, ch. 12).[22] But this sense of the question does not exactly fit this locus. With reference to the second sense, there is one man that I know of among the Reformed, in other respects a most learned theologian, whom I suspect was carried away in the heat of a disputation occasioned by this Pelagian argument for universal grace: whatever everyone is bound to believe for himself by divine faith is true of each and every person; but everyone is bound to believe by divine faith that Christ died for him; therefore this is true of each and every person. Now he upheld that the major premise must be denied, and thus stated that divine faith could be based on something false. And for this his colleague, a man just as famous, opposed him in his particular disputation *On the Truth of Divine Faith*, in which he examines as carefully as possible the thought of his colleague on both points.[23] Regarding this argument there is hardly anything to add, and since this theologian has no one who follows him, it will not be worthwhile to cast any further aspersions on his opinion here.

---

20. *potentia ordinaria*, a synonym for *potentia ordinata*, "ordained power." Cf. 1.2.20 §XIII.

21. Thomas Aquinas, *Summa theologiae (ST)*, IIa IIae, q. 1, art. 3.

22. Mastricht, *Novitatum Cartesianarum gangraena* (Amsterdam: Jansson-Waesburg, 1677), 257–73.

23. This is a discreet reference to a controversy at Franeker University between an anonymous *antagonista* and William Ames (1576–1633). Ames's disputation, *De fidei divinae veritate*, was appended to his *Medulla theologiae* in the London Cotes editions of 1627, 1629, and 1630, pp. 423–69, and the 1641 Amsterdam Jansson edition, pp. 369–408. The disputation in these editions also includes the phrase "repeated and vindicated" (*repetita et vindicata*). Subsequent editions of the *Medulla*, however, do not contain it.

The Practical Part

The first practice concerns unbelief.

Its nature in general

XXVIII. The first practice of faith concerns unbelief, which is pointed out in our text: "His own did not receive him." We will refer this matter to these four heads, the (1) nature, (2) origin, (3) evils, and (4) remedies of unbelief. Concerning the nature of unbelief we will be more brief, since from the faith that is opposed to it, which we have delineated in its parts, the innate character of unbelief can be perceived adequately. Therefore, first in general, whether in the mouth, the heart, or both, unbelief is to not receive God as its highest end, nor Christ as its only Mediator. Thus, in unbelief: (1) its act is not receiving (John 1:11), not desiring (John 5:40; Matt. 23:37), despising (Matt. 22:5), and casting away or rejecting (John 12:48). (2) Its object is first God as the end (Ps. 78:22), and next Christ as the Mediator (John 5:46–47). (3) Its instrument is either the mouth (Matt. 26:72) or the heart (Heb. 3:12; Mark 6:52), or the heart and mouth together, as is gathered from Romans 10:10 and expressed in Job 21:14.

Its nature in specific: 1. Ignorance

XXIX. Individually, the following things are ingredients of unbelief. First, crass ignorance of God and the Mediator, and of divine things (Jer. 10:25; 2 Thess. 1:8; Ps. 95:10), whether this ignorance is negative only, the sort that prevails among the pagans, or positive and privative, the sort that is observed in those who are blind under the very light of the gospel.

2. Disbelief

Second, disbelief, or lack of assent in the intellect (John 5:46–47; Acts 28:24; 19:9; John 20:25, 27), whether it bears either upon the whole Word of God, the sort that occurs among the pagans; or upon some essential part, the sort that happens among the Jews, who reject the New Testament, and likewise among the Muslims and many others who reject most books of both Testaments; or only upon this or that proposition of both Testaments, as an integral part of the Word, the sort that happens not only among heretics but also among true believers, albeit in a different way. For this reason we observe that there are degrees of unbelief as regards assent: first, doubt (Rom. 4:20); next, denial of assent (John 10:25–26); and finally, resistance added to denial (Acts 19:9).

3. Non-reception

Third, non-reception or non-willing, which has already been noted from the Scriptures. This is either total, when we wholly and entirely reject and do not desire God and the Mediator (Job 21:14; Ex. 5:2; John 1:11), or partial, when we indeed would desire, but do not desire them, that is, we desire under a condition, with a limitation, or with mental reservation, which is called willingness[24] (the sort we find in Matt. 19:21–22 and John 12:42). Moreover, it regards, as we have already observed, either God or the Mediator, which in each case involves distinct sins. Insofar as unbelief does not receive God it connotes one of three sins: (1) atheism, which does not receive any God (Ps. 14:1); (2) idolatry, which either rejects the true God and substitutes another for him, or at least joins with him a false god (Rom. 1:25); or (3) profanity, which certainly receives God in profession, but in reality denies him by withholding worship (Titus 1:16; Ps. 10:4; Rom. 1:21). Moreover, insofar as unbelief does not receive the Mediator, it likewise involves one of three sins: either (1) it simply does not acknowledge Christ as the Mediator (John 1:11; 5:40); or (2) it does not receive the whole Mediator, when it indeed admits him as Redeemer, but rejects him as King (Luke 19:27; Ps. 2:1–3)—and this sin is also most common among those who are Christians as far as their profession; or (3) if to some extent it does also receive him, yet it scorns the conditions stipulated by Christ when he offers himself (Matt. 7:22), such as self-denial (Luke 9:23), mortification of the flesh (Gal. 5:24; 1 John 3:3), contempt for the world and for worldly things (Luke 14:26–27), and constant and serious zeal for holiness (2 Cor. 7:1).

4. Lack of trust

Fourth, lack of trust, either (1) toward God, that he either is not able (Gen. 4:13), or does not desire, to fulfill his own promises, even if we ourselves do not fail in our duty (Zeph. 3:2; Ps. 78:22, 32; 106:24), which is unbelief and despair most properly so-called, and is especially detestable and damnable; or (2) toward Christ, that he is either no Savior, or not the only and sufficient Savior (Jer. 2:13; Rom. 10:3–4), or at least that he neither desires nor is able to save, even though we received him by believing (John 5:40). From this result such great fear, anxiety, and faintheartedness, which are most frequently noted in the Scriptures by the black mark of unbelief (Mark 4:40; 9:23). Yet meanwhile it is observed that this lack of trust easily besets believers themselves, which is evident at least in part from the passages just cited.

5. Disobedience

Fifth, disobedience, in which we accept God and the Mediator with a certain kind of trust as Savior, but obstinately refuse to give ourselves to them, that is,

---

24. *velleitas*

to return and submit ourselves and our belongings, however many there are, to them as our Lord. For this reason unbelievers are called "sons of disobedience" (Eph. 2:2; 5:6; Col. 3:6), that is, insofar as this disobedience is opposed to the "obedience of faith" (Rom. 1:5; 16:26), and thus by this disobedience we refuse to receive the yoke and lordship of Christ (Matt. 11:29), and we kick against him (Ps. 2:1–3), more prompt to heed our own lusts than God and the Mediator (Rom. 6:12).

6. Carnality
And finally, sixth, carnality, or the mind of the flesh, by which we indeed receive God and the Mediator to some degree, but the better portions of our heart, care, and labors we reserve for ourselves, the world, and sin, being "lovers of pleasure rather than lovers of God" (2 Tim. 3:4). A clear example of this is seen in the young Pharisee (Matt. 19:21–22) and the leaders of the Jews (John 12:42–43).

The degrees of unbelief
XXX. Nevertheless, we have not reviewed these ingredients so much because we suppose that each and every one of them come together in any sort of unbelief, whereas in faith each and every requirement is required, but rather that when one or another of the ingredients is present, unbelief is present. For this reason there are degrees in unbelief, just as there are in faith. And thus there is: (1) the greatest and universal form of unbelief, which either rejects the true God as paganism does, or rejects Christ as Judaism does, or his mediatorial office as Islam does. (2) The lesser form of unbelief, the kind that heresy displays, denying the fundamental articles of the faith with obstinacy. (3) The least form of unbelief, which is shown by all who deny, not as much in profession as in substance and in fact, the prerogative of God and the Mediator, and thus in practice set them behind others. This form is found (sadly, all too often) to be frequent among the very confessors of the true faith.

Nine causes of unbelief
XXXI. Next follows the origin of unbelief. It is (1) Satan (2 Cor. 4:4), who is "at work in the sons of disobedience" (Eph. 2:2): (a) by removing their sense of sin and by raising their opinion of their own righteousness (Luke 18:11); (b) by making light of their sins (1 Sam. 15:15); (c) by abusing the divine mercy (Rom. 6:1); or on the contrary, (d) by making their sins excessively great (Gen. 4:13). (2) The perversity of the human heart, an evil heart of unbelief, falling away from the living God (Heb. 3:12), for which reason they are called the "sons of disobedience" (Eph. 2:2), namely a heart blinded, burning with love of self and thus

neglecting God and the Mediator (Luke 18:11). (3) Foolishness and insensibility, by which they do not experience in themselves any need to receive God or the Mediator (Rev. 3:17–18; Luke 18:11–12). (4) Ignorance of God, of Christ, and of his promises and benefits (John 1:10–11; 4:10). (5) Love and desire for sin (John 5:44), for while they give their attention to those, they do not seek Christ, nor receive him (2 Cor. 6:14–15). (6) Fear of persecution (Matt. 16:24–25; Acts 14:22; 2 Tim. 3:12). (7) Self-love or selfishness,[25] for since most inordinately pursue themselves, they cannot sincerely love God and the Mediator (Luke 16:13). For this reason, in order to receive Christ you must deny yourself (Luke 9:23), crucify yourself (Gal. 5:24), and abandon everything (Luke 14:26), which is incompatible with self-love. (8) Excessive faintheartedness, in which by the sense of his own unworthiness one is afraid to come to Christ (Matt. 9:20). And often (9) contempt for the grace offered so long and abundantly by God (John 12:38–41; cf. Prov. 1:23–26; Ezek. 22:18–23; Heb. 6:7–8).

The evils of unbelief

XXXII. The worst evils of unbelief follow next, that they may drive us away from it. For (1) it is injurious (a) to God and his glory (cf. Rom. 4:20), and to each of the persons: the Father and his counsel of peace (Luke 7:30; Matt. 22:5), the Son and his redemption and merits (Heb. 10:29; 6:6), and the Holy Spirit (Heb. 10:29; 1 Thess. 5:19; Act. 7:51; Eph. 4:30; Heb. 3:17, 19). (b) To his attributes: his truth (John 3:33; 1 John 5:10; Rom. 3:3); his goodness and love toward man (Titus 3:4); his grace and love (Rom. 2:4); his wisdom, conspicuous in the Mediator and in redemption (Rom. 11:33; 1 Cor. 1:24); and his power (1 Cor. 1:24), when we limit God (Ps. 78:41). (c) To God's works, that is, to his decrees and counsels (Luke 7:30); his promises, which in Christ through faith are yes and amen (2 Cor. 1:20); the wishes and expectations of God (Ps. 81:13; Matt. 21:34, 36, 37; Isa. 5:2, 4); his redemption and the Redeemer (Matt. 22:5; Acts 13:46); and the sufferings of Christ (Heb. 10:29). (2) It is harmful to the unbeliever, insofar as it renders him unfit for all works of piety (John 15:4), indeed unfit that such works might please God (Heb. 11:6; Rom. 14:23).

---

25. αὐτότης, Dutch: *eigen-zelfsheit*, literally "one's own self-ness." Contrary to classical Greek usage, that this word does not mean "identity" here can be evidenced from other Dutch theological writing and translation in the period. Cf. George Hutcheson (1615–1674) on Job 10:18–19, "Selfishness is an ill root with much distemper," translated into Dutch (1751) as "De eigenzelfsheit is een kwade wortel van veele ongestalten." George Hutcheson, *An Exposition of the Book of Job being the sum of CCCXVI lectures, preached in the city of Edenburgh* (London: printed for Ralph Smith, 1669), 143; idem, *Sakelyke en prackticale verklaringe van het boek Jobs*, trans. Jan Ross (Leiden: Abraham Kallewier, 1751), 379.

Conversely, it is (3) the mother and nurse of all kinds of vices (Heb. 3:12): ignorance (2 Cor. 4:4), carnal security (Matt. 24:38–39), apostasy (Heb. 3:12), and atheism (Eph. 2:12). In addition, it is (4) the cause of every kind of death, as is evident in our first parents (Gen. 3): namely, bodily death (2 Kings 7:2 with v. 20; Ps. 106:26 with Num. 20:8, 10–12), spiritual death (Eph. 2:1–2), and eternal death (John 3:18, 36).

The remedies for unbelief

XXXIII. Now it remains for us to add the remedies of unbelief that must be applied by the spiritual physician and received by the patient. These are, namely, (1) the recognition and sense of unbelief (Lam. 3:40), to which end self-examination aims (2 Cor. 13:5), in which on the one hand we hold clearly before us the nature of unbelief, and on the other hand compare ourselves with it. (2) The consideration of the evils of unbelief that were discussed in the preceding section. (3) The investigation of the cause, not so much of unbelief in general (as discussed in §XXXI), but indeed of our own personal unbelief: does it arise (a) from ignorance, (b) from foolishness and insensibility, (c) from love of this age, or (d) from fear of the cross and of persecutions? This investigation is needed so that the remedies may be suitably applied to whichever of these we may be personally striving against. (4) Waiting on God to remove an unbelieving and stony heart and create a new heart, and this happens in the constant and faithful use of the means by which God customarily works faith, which include the hearing of the Word (John 5:25; Ezek. 37:4), prayers (Ps. 51:10), living among believers, and so forth. At the least, (5) let us not obstinately struggle against God as he builds faith in us by the proclamation of the Word and other things, by which we would provoke his wrath, and thus he would depart from us (Isa. 63:10; Gen. 6:3), or even harden us (Isa. 63:17); and let us not harden our hearts (Heb. 3:7–8), or extinguish the Spirit of faith (1 Thess. 5:19), or shut the door to Christ as he knocks (Rev. 3:20; Song 5:2–3). And finally is (6) the use of the means by which faith customarily is generated, which we will show in their own place.[26]

The second practice, of exploration

XXXIV. The second practice concerns the exploration of faith (2 Cor. 13:5; 1:12; Gal. 6:4), which faith the apostle calls more precious than gold that perishes (1 Peter 1:7). But since this work is exceedingly hard and tiresome, both because of the deceitfulness of our own heart (Jer. 17:9) and because of the similarity and affinity that common faith has with saving faith, it is entirely necessary that

---

26. §§XLV, XLVII, XLIX, below

we be roused and urged to this work by several motivating reasons. Therefore, here it helps to consider: (1) how easy it is to be deceived in the matter of faith, as is evident in so many and such great examples (Matt. 7:26–27; Luke 18:9, 11; Rev. 3:17; Luke 13:25–26). At the same time (2) how dangerous, harmful, and indeed deadly it is to be deceived in a matter of such great importance (1 Cor. 3:18; Eph. 4:22; James 1:16). Conversely, (3) how sweet and pleasant it is to be persuaded of the truth and the sincerity of our faith (2 Tim. 1:12), on which depends all good conscience (1 Tim. 1:19), all comfort, and all certainty of salvation (2 Tim. 4:7–8). What is more, (4) how useful it is (a) for godliness (2 Peter 1:8–10), so that we may fight to the finish the illustrious fight of the faith (2 Tim. 4:7); (b) for patience (Heb. 12:2; 10:34–35); and (c) for eternal life (John 3:18, 36). (5) How shameful it is to know other things, but to be ignorant of ourself and our own faith, on which all things depend (Gal. 6:3). Finally, (6) how necessary it is not only from the divine command (2 Cor. 13:5), but also because God will one day examine us, whether we are willing or not, in righteousness and vengeance, though this will not occur if we have first examined ourselves (1 Cor. 11:31–32); and because our conscience itself will examine us, and torment us as well, after the example of Cain (Gen. 4:13–14). For one or the other is unavoidable: either we examine ourselves, or God, the searcher of hearts and the just judge, will examine us.

The things that must be distinguished concerning faith
XXXV. So that this work of exploration may better turn out as we wish, we must on the one hand have before us the things that must be distinguished, and on the other the marks of the distinction. The things that must be distinguished are: (1) true and real faith from counterfeit and oral faith, the form from the power (2 Tim. 3:5), faith that only *says* from faith that also *does*, faith that clings to the lips from faith that springs forth from the heart (Matt. 7:21; 15:8). These things are easily distinguished, first by sense, whereby the one who truly believes also senses in reality that he believes, and then by reasoning, from the fruits (Matt. 7:16; James 2:17, 26). (2) Great faith, small faith, and the smallest faith must each be distinguished from its rivals. That is, (a) truly great faith must be distinguished first from carnal security and then from temerity; (b) small faith and the smallest faith must be distinguished from unbelief on the one hand and from common faith on the other.

Great faith is distinguished from presumption.
XXXVI. William Ames vigorously distinguishes truly great faith from carnal security and presumption in his *Cases of Conscience* (bk. 2, ch. 6, §16). He says,

"A lively and strong faith is easily manifest and known to them in whom it is present, because (1) they have the testimony of it in themselves (1 John 5:10), that is, the Spirit of God bearing witness with their spirit that they are children of God (Rom. 8:16), which Spirit they have as the earnest of their inheritance (Eph. 1:13–14), and by it they are sealed for the day of redemption (Eph. 4:30). (2) They have the love of God poured out in their hearts (Rom. 5:5), for which reason they have peace and joy unspeakable, and full of glory (Rom. 5:1; 1 Peter 1:6–8). (3) They have and bring forth those fruits by which true faith is customarily manifested and brought to completion (James 2:18; Gal. 5:6)."[27] To these add (4) an insatiable desire for God and the Mediator joined to a resolution of profound submission of the self, and of universal obedience, which in no way belongs to presumption.

Great faith is distinguished from temerity.

XXXVII. Great faith is distinguished from temerity and audacity in undertaking and bearing with dangers and evils, by the following: (1) it not so much undertakes and seeks these dangers as it accepts them as offered and imposed on it by God and on account of God (Luke 9:23). Conversely, temerity loves these dangers and dives into them head first (Matt. 26:33, 35). Or if (2) faith also undertakes danger, it does not do so except by divine command (Gen. 12:1; Acts 20:23); temerity does this of its own accord, or for the sake of a little glory (Matt. 4:6–7; 1 Sam. 15:32). Next (3) faith, when it undertakes dangers or bears with evils, leans on the strength God gives (Phil. 4:11–13; Rom. 8:37–39; Ps. 23:4), whereas temerity relies on its own strength alone (2 Cor. 1:9–10; Matt. 26:33–35).

Lesser faith is distinguished: First, from lack of trust

XXXVIII. Lesser faith struggles, whether in confidence, or in joy and full assurance, and it approaches a lack of trust. Therefore Ames carefully distinguishes the one from the other by the marks gathered in *Cases of Conscience*, book 2, chapter 6, §17 to the end of the chapter, which has not been copied here for the sake of brevity.[28]

---

27. William Ames, *De conscientia et eius jure, vel casibus, libri quinque* (Amsterdam: Joannes Janssonius, 1631), 2.6 §16, pp. 58–59; idem, *Conscience, with the Power and Cases thereof* ([Leiden, London]: [W. Christaens, E. Griffin, J. Dawson], 1639), 2.6 §16, 2:14.

28. In §17–22 Ames gives six marks to discern that a faint and weak faith is true and genuine. In summary, it (1) has a sincere desire for union and communion with Christ; (2) depends on an effective ministry of the Word; (3) embraces the whole Word of God; (4) seeks to purify the heart from all sin; (5) stirs up sincere love for God and desire to glorify him; and (6) stirs up sincere

Next, from common faith

We add here this one thing: that in weaker trust, provided it is sincere, there must be observed more vehement zeal for submission and obedience, and indeed more vehement ardor and desire to receive Christ, or else by reason of its more tepid reception, submission, and giving of the self, it verges on common faith. At this point the desire for accepting Christ and giving of the self to Christ is so frail that it scarcely can be acknowledged and distinguished from common faith. In this case, I would recommend to the one struggling that he pay attention not so much to distinguishing his faith as rather to increasing it, that by its size it might become visible and evident to him. We will describe the means for this in their own place.[29]

The smallest faith is distinguished: 1. From unbelief

XXXIX. Likewise, the smallest faith is lacking, first, in trust, joy, and particular application, as is apparent in spiritual desertions, and it seems to verge on despair (Job 7:14–16; 10:1–3; Ps. 43:2, 5; 77:7–9; 88). It is distinguished from it by these marks: (1) the smallest trust desires God, Christ, and salvation (Ps. 6:1–3; 77:1–3); unbelief by no means does this (Job 21:14). (2) The smallest faith, although it does not yet receive Christ as its Redeemer in whom it rejoices with Mary (Luke 1:47), nevertheless receives him as its Lord (John 20:28). Although it is destitute of the comfort of faith, it is even so not destitute of the obedience of faith (Rev. 3:8); otherwise, it would be unbelief (Eph. 2:1–3). (3) The smallest faith acknowledges its own infirmity, experiences it, and laments it (Mark 9:24), whereas unbelief is free from care (Rev. 3:17; Luke 18:11–12). (4) The smallest faith pants after remedies (Mark 9:24; 1 Peter 2:2); conversely, unbelief, as it is dead, is therefore without sense and without desire (John 5:40; Matt. 23:37).

2. From common faith

The weakest faith may also be lacking, second, in the vigor of its reception, when love for God and the Mediator is as it were in equilibrium with love for anything else, so that the prominence of saving faith, whereby it can be most safely distinguished (as we have said above), cannot be recognized. In this case and even more so I would recommend what I did in the preceding section concerning

---

love for the brethren. Ames, *De conscientia*, 2.16.17–22, pp. 57–58; idem, *Conscience*, 2.16.17–22, 2:14–16.

29. §XLVII, below

lesser faith, namely that a person who is struggling should devote his effort not so much to distinguishing his faith as to increasing it.

3. From any sort of common faith

XL. Finally, saving faith must be distinguished from any sort of common faith (concerning which, see John 2:23–24; 12:42), whether it be historical faith, or the faith of miracles, or temporary faith. We have made this distinction above in §V and it will also be clearly evident in the subsequent paragraph.

The marks of saving faith

XLI. Concerning saving faith of whatever kind, we will not advance marks for distinguishing it from common faith so much as we will advance a single mark, namely, the definition of saving faith explained in the dogmatic part and here to be applied a little more distinctly. Therefore, faith that is indubitably saving is that in which all those essentials concur which we have expressed piece by piece in the previously given definition, that is, its parts, its objects, and the relation or proportion of the act to its object.

1. From its parts

Therefore, saving faith consists in (1) knowledge sufficient for accepting God and the Mediator, and also the promises and conditions under which they are offered. For this reason *faith* and *knowledge* are used indiscriminately in the Holy Scriptures, as we have taught above from Isaiah 53:11 and John 17:3. Meanwhile any other kind of faith is mostly ignorant of the one in whom it believes (John 4:21). (2) Firm and unmoved assent given to the law and the gospel, not only generally and implicitly to all those things that Scripture sets forth as necessary to believe concerning God and Christ (Acts 24:14–15; 2 Tim. 1:12; Rom. 4:20), but specifically and explicitly. Meanwhile on the contrary, any other kind of faith often either does not believe at all what it knows concerning God and Christ (Titus 1:16), or if it does believe, it does so with great hesitation, and at least never so solidly that it dares, having abandoned all other things, to commit itself without fear to the promises of God and of the Mediator (John 12:42–43). (3) Consent of the will, by which, once they have been known through assent to the divine Word, we truly accept God and the Mediator (John 1:12; Col. 2:6). Meanwhile, any other kind of faith either stops with bare assent (James 2:19) and does not at all accept God and the Mediator (John 1:11), or if it should accept them, it does so not as much with the heart as with the mouth (Matt. 15:8). These are the essential parts of faith.

2. From its object

XLII. Furthermore, those parts have for their object (1) not only Christ as the Mediator but also God as the highest end (John 14:1; Ps. 78:22); thus they truly have God as their own God, and they fear him according to the first table of the law, and they also truly have Christ as the Way and Mediator by whose aid they come to God (John 14:6–7). This is the character of saving faith, while any other kind of faith is generally brought only to Christ that he might redeem it from imminent evils, and does not seek to be led through Christ to the Father, to be united with him, and to rest in him as its highest end. Furthermore, (2) the parts of saving faith are brought to Christ not only as Redeemer, in the trust and repose of the heart, but also as Lord, as King, in most absolute submission (Col. 2:6). Whereas meanwhile, any other kind of faith desires Christ only as its Redeemer, that he might take away from it the punishments for sins, and thus it seeks the benefits of Christ rather than Christ himself (John 4:26). And the parts of true faith do not only receive Christ, but also (3) the conditions under which Christ offers himself to them to be received: the denial of the self (Luke 9:23) and the mortification of the flesh (Gal. 5:24). Meanwhile, any other kind of faith indeed would desire Christ in some way, and his benefits, but rejects the offered conditions of which we have spoken (Matt. 19:21; Luke 19:27).

3. By its way of receiving

XLIII. Finally, the parts of saving faith are brought to God and the Mediator in such a way that they constantly yield to them before all other worldly things (Ps. 73:25–26; Matt. 19:27). Conversely, any other kind of faith, if it sometimes seems to receive God and the Mediator, nevertheless does so in such a way that it prefers the world and worldly things to them (Matt. 19:21; John 12:42–43). All these things, although they coincide in saving faith not with equal necessity, yet coincide to such a degree that if one of them is entirely absent, faith is not saving. Also, each of these—namely, knowledge, assent, reception, trust, and submission—have their own rivals that imitate their character, from which they deserve to be distinguished carefully, if only the concise method of this book of common places would bear it. In the meantime, whoever desires to pursue this topic further can go to our *Syntagma on Saving Faith* (ch. 13).[30]

---

30. Mastricht, *De fide salvifica syntagma theoretico-practicum…cum praefatione de membris Ecclesiae visibilis* (Duisburg: Sas, 1671), 320–55.

The third practice, concerning zeal for faith, motivated by its: 1. Excellence
XLIV. Therefore, we advance to the third practice of faith, which concerns zeal
for faith in general. Recommending this practice is first, its excellence (2 Peter
1:1; 1 Peter 1:7). For this reason the Savior counted faith among the "weightier
matters of the law" (Matt. 23:23). On account of it, whatever was gain for him,
the apostle considers as excrement, indeed as loss (Phil. 3:7–9). Faith obtains this
excellence: (1) from its source, that is, the eternal love of election (Titus 1:1; Acts
13:48); (2) from its rarity (2 Thess. 3:2; Luke 18:8); (3) from its objects, not only
so many precious promises (2 Peter 1:4), but God himself and the Mediator,
who are most all-sufficient (Gen. 17:1); and (4) from its effects, for it ennobles
the believer's person (Rev. 1:6; 1 Peter 2:5, 9); nature (2 Peter 1:1, 3, 4); prayers
(Heb. 11:4); works (Heb. 11:6); state, since it renders us servants, friends, and
children of God, and likewise brides, members, brothers, and children of Christ;
and his inheritance (Ps. 16:6; Rom. 8:17; 2 Tim. 4:8; 1 Peter 1:4–5).

2. Pleasantness
Second, faith's pleasantness (Matt. 11:28–30; Isa. 55:1–2; Song 5:1): it calms the
soul in many ways (John 14:1), comforts it in adversities (Ps. 42:5), fills it with
ineffable joy (1 Peter 1:8; Rom. 5:2; 15:13), and brings it the experience of divine
benevolence (Rom. 5:1, 3; Ps. 34:7–9) and the indubitable hope and certainty of
eternal rest (Gal. 5:5; Heb. 11:1).

3. Utility
Third, faith's utility. For it is conducive in general for the whole life, insofar as
we live by faith (Rom. 1:17; Gal. 2:20). In particular, faith is the bond of union
with Christ, the foundation of communion with him, the productive cause of
justification, adoption, and glorification both inchoate and consummated, as we
have specifically shown above.[31] Namely, faith supplies to the believer an unconquerable strength by which we may conquer the world (1 John 5:4), Satan (Eph.
6:16), ourselves and our own passions (2 Cor. 10:5; Heb. 11:17), persecutions
and any sort of the harshest evils (Heb. 11:33), death itself (Phil. 1:23), and what
is more, God (Gen. 32:28) and Christ (Matt. 15:28).

4. Equity
Fourth, faith's equity. For if God with such great preparation designated the Son
as the Redeemer from all eternity (Isa. 42:1; 1 Peter 1:20) and sent and gave
him in time (John 3:17; Rom. 5:8), if he so readily offers the Son and all that is

---

31. §XIX

his (Matt. 22:2–4), if Christ offers himself and all that is his (Isa. 55:1; Matt. 11:28; Isa. 65:1–2), is it not most equitable that we should also readily receive them by faith? Indeed, if we deservedly receive the gifts of God and the Mediator (1 Tim. 6:17), and their ministers and ambassadors (2 Cor. 7:2; Gal. 4:14, 16), then should we not all the more receive those who give and send them? I need not add that the God and Mediator who are to be received by faith are equally and infinitely more "worthy of all acceptance" than the word that offers them (1 Tim. 1:15), such that it is most inequitable not to receive them (John 1:11).

5. Necessity
Fifth, its most absolute necessity. For without faith we are still enemies of God (Eph. 2:1), nor is there open any access to him (Rom. 5:1–3; Eph. 2:14–15, 17), nor can we please him (Heb. 11:6). Without faith we have no business with Christ, in whom all the promises of God are yes and amen (2 Cor. 1:20). We are still in our sins, under the wrath of God, the curse of the law, eternal condemnation (Acts 26:18); without faith we are shut out of every hope of salvation (John 3:16, 18, 36).

The supports of zeal for faith
XLV. Moreover, the general supports that promote zeal for faith are: (1) the use of a living and effective ministry (Rom. 10:14, 17), since by the most effective impulses it inclines the intellect both to a knowledge of the God and Mediator who are to be received, and to an assent to the promises, and the will to a promptness in consenting and receiving. (2) The contemplation of God and the Mediator (Heb. 12:2), and of that sufficiency that is in them (Gen. 17:1; John 1:16): of their all-sufficiency, that we may be complete in them (Col. 2:10; 3:2); of their sole-sufficiency (Ps. 73:25–26; Acts 4:12; John 14:6); and, still more, of the abundance of their fullness (Eph. 3:8; Col. 1:19). (3) The use of whatever means by which God customarily generates and fosters faith (2 Peter 1:6, 10, 11), which are: the reading, hearing, meditation, and application of the divine Word (Rom. 10:14, 17); participation in the sacraments (Rom. 4:11); and living among believers (Prov. 13:20; Luke 24:32; Acts 18:27). (4) Prayers (Mark 9:24; Luke 17:5), namely, that God would: illumine the mind (Eph. 1:18), that we may know by faith (John 17:3); open the heart, that we may receive the things offered (Acts 16:14; Ps. 81:10); and confer the Spirit of faith (2 Cor. 4:13), whose fruit is faith (Gal. 5:22); that he would make every use of any of the means fruitful by his grace (1 Cor. 3:6–7). Moreover, since this zeal for faith in general flows forth particularly into zeal for acquiring, preserving, and increasing faith, for living by

faith, and for rising by the power of faith to particular application and persuasion, we will treat each of these individually.

The fourth practice, concerning the acquiring of faith
XLVI. Let then the fourth practice be in zeal for acquiring faith: not indeed seminal faith, or the power of believing, which God, without our zeal, confers immediately by virtue of regeneration, by making us alive, taking away our stony heart, and so forth, as we have demonstrated above;[32] but rather actual faith, by which once made alive in regeneration and having obtained the ability to believe, we strive that in actuality we may take hold of God as our highest end and Christ as the one and only Mediator. The general arguments that we produced in §XLIV will encourage and persuade to this end. Moreover, the way to acquire this actual faith is chiefly in these two things: first, we must have clearly before us the nature, causes, and remedies of actual unbelief, not only in common, but also in particular, the character, causes, and remedies of our own unbelief, according to the things we taught in their own places in §§XXVIII–XXXIV (cf. our *Syntagma on Saving Faith*, ch. 17, §2).[33]

The way of creating faith, on God's part
Then second, we must consider the steps and turns by which God customarily generates actual faith in the heart. Namely, after he has, as we have said, conferred the power of believing immediately through regeneration: (1) he convicts the mind (John 16:8), such that it acknowledges the universal truth and divine authority of Scripture, and in particular the infallible certitude of the threats that are directed against sins and sinners. Thus from this (2) it intimately senses its own misery (2 Sam. 24:10; Acts 2:37; Rom. 7:24; Ps. 38:3–4; Job 31:4), confesses and deplores it (Luke 15:18), is displeased with itself and flooded by shame (Luke 18:13), and is worn out and laboring (Matt. 11:28). Next, (3) he drives us to pious desperation and perplexity (Acts 2:37) about ourselves (Rom. 7:18–19) and about all things other than God, because they cannot free us from our misery (Rom. 7:24). This sense is designated as a "contrite heart," a "crushed spirit" (Ps. 34:18; 51:17), a "spirit of slavery to fear" (Rom. 8:15), and also a "spirit of timidity" (2 Tim. 1:7), without which we will never pant for a physician and medicine, and never stoop to the conditions under which Christ offers himself

---

32. §VI

33. *Cap. XVIII §2.* Chapter 18 is the method of preserving faith, whereas chapter 17 is the method of acquiring it. Chapter 17 §§1–5 addresses the removal of the obstacle of natural inability. Cf. Mastricht, *De fide salvifica syntagma*, 449–56.

as the Redeemer (Luke 9:23; Acts 9:6). And after that (4) he opens the heart: to it he shows and offers himself and the Son, the Mediator and most all-sufficient Redeemer; he entices it so that it may receive the conditions of liberation (Matt. 11:28). Moreover, (5) he allures and excites the will: he draws it so that it may come in actuality and take hold of God as the highest end and Christ as its one and only Mediator (Acts 26:18). Following after this are all the acts of conversion, trust, tranquility, consolation, joy, and so forth.

The way of receiving faith, on our part
XLVII. From those things it is easy to see what it is necessary to do in order to acquire actual faith, namely: (1) we must eagerly observe these acts of God that as it were give birth to faith. If, for example, such things occur that could convince us of our sin and misery, immediately we should think that God is now building faith in us. (2) We must prudently prepare ourselves for these acts, as it were direct ourselves and our faculties toward God as he gives birth to faith in us, cooperate with him, and having been drawn, run with him. (3) We must diligently take heed that we do not strive against God, quench the Spirit (1 Thess. 5:19) or grieve him (Eph. 4:30), or resist him (Isa. 63:10), much less insult him (Heb. 10:29). (4) We must personally seek out all those supports by which we can be stirred up and moved to the acknowledgment and sense of our sins and misery, to the knowledge of how to receive God and the Mediator, and to receiving them. (5) To these may be added the general things that we have already pointed out in §XLV.

The fifth practice, concerning the preserving of faith
XLVIII. The fifth practice concerns zeal for the preserving of faith: certainly not seminal faith, which is born in regeneration and which can never be altogether lost (1 John 3:9), because the solid foundation of God stands, and God knows those who are his (2 Tim. 2:19), because the gifts of God are irrevocable (Rom. 11:29); but rather, actual faith, and also the sense and fruits of faith— consolation, joy, and so forth—which through sluggishness and carelessness can be lost, or at least can become inactive, and which faith, together with the things that accompany it, God does not will to preserve apart from our zeal (Rom. 11:20–21).

The impelling reasons
The things that urge this zeal are: (1) the repeated exhortations of the Holy Spirit (Acts 14:22; 1 Cor. 16:13; Col. 1:23; 2:7). The fact that (2) preserved faith preserves us (Rev. 2:10). And (3) God does not preserve us by his own power

from Satan, the world, and the flesh except through faith (1 Peter 1:5). Nor (4) does Christ preserve us for salvation except through faith (John 3:16, 18, 36; Rom. 1:16). Nor (5) does faith itself preserve us unless it is preserved (Heb. 10:38). And (6) there are so many and such great enemies that attack our faith: Satan (Luke 22:31–32; Eph. 6:12); the world, by its people, or its enticements (1 Thess. 3:4–5), or its persecutions (Acts 14:22); the corrupted flesh (Heb. 3:12).

The means
XLIX. The means of preserving faith will be (1) to make much of faith, as a thing most precious (2 Peter 1:1). (2) For the preservation of faith, to depend not on one's own strength (2 Cor. 3:5–6), but on the Father of lights (James 1:17), on Christ, the author and finisher of our faith (Heb. 12:2), on the Spirit of faith (2 Cor. 4:13); and to weary God with prayers that he not remove his Spirit from us (Ps. 51:10–11). (3) Not to grieve the Spirit of faith (Eph. 4:30). (4) The obstructions to faith, chief among which are insensibility (Rev. 3:17–18; Luke 18:11–12), ignorance (John 1:10–11), love for the world and desire for sin (John 5:44; 12:42), faintheartedness (Matt. 9:20), and contempt for the means (John 12:37–41; Heb. 6:7–8)—these obstructions, I say, should be cautiously avoided. (5) To undertake the most tender care of faith, in regard to its nourishment (1 Peter 2:2); its exercise, that it may not perish from neglect (Luke 24:25); its health (Titus 1:13; 2 Tim. 1:13; 1 Tim. 6:3); and its defense against enemies (Eph. 6:16; 1 Peter 2:11). (6) To frequently inspect or examine our faith, that it may be vigorous (2 Cor. 13:5). (7) By prayers to entrust our faith to God, that it may not fail (Luke 22:31–32), that by his power he may keep us in faith (1 Peter 1:5; Heb. 12:2). Joined to these should be the general means furnished in §XLV.

The sixth practice, concerning the increasing of faith
L. The sixth practice is aimed at a zeal for increasing our faith. It presupposes the theory of the degrees and imperfection of faith that was taught above in §XX, which the apostle confirms in Philippians 3:12, 13, 15. Accordingly, it is right to take care that our faith increase (2 Cor. 10:15), be established (Col. 2:7), increase greatly (2 Thess. 1:3), that we may be full of faith (Acts 6:5) and reach the full assurance of faith (Heb. 10:22).

The impelling motives
In this zeal is: (1) a mark of true and living faith, inasmuch as it is a faith that grows (1 Peter 2:2; Matt. 13:31–32). (2) The increase of our whole life and

spiritual perfection (2 Peter 1:3, 5–8), insofar as in receiving by faith the Christ who is our life (Col. 3:4), he himself lives in us (Gal. 2:20), that is, his holiness, humility, longsuffering, and so forth. And at the same time (3) the increase of joy, peace, comfort, certainty of salvation, and so forth, inasmuch as they lean with all their weight upon robust faith, as we have taught above in §XIX. (4) A great protection (Eph. 6:10, 12) for our infirmity against so many and such great enemies, whom we already mentioned in the preceding section, and also against so many and such powerful attacks and fiery darts from those enemies. (5) That God offers to our faith the most fruitful means of growth, and accordingly expects from us its more fruitful increase (Isa. 5:1–7).

Its supports

LI. Moreover, to this end the following are profitable: (1) constant and religious zeal for the divine Word (1 Thess. 3:10). (2) Frequent and worthy use of the sacraments, inasmuch as they are seals by which faith is confirmed (Rom. 4:11), and which are given in remembrance of the death of Christ (1 Cor. 11:25). (3) Ardent prayers (Mark 9:24; Luke 17:5). For just as Paul plants faith and Apollos waters, so God gives the increase (1 Cor. 3:6–7), for which reason he is called the finisher of our faith (Heb. 12:2)—and this increase is not obtained without our prayers (Matt. 7:7–8). (4) Daily exploration of our faith, so that it may be apparent whether it has increased or decreased, together with a careful concern that no day go by without a line,[34] and that something is always added to it little by little. (5) Assiduous exercise of our faith (2 Tim. 1:6), so that it may not contract dirt, rust, and lethargy, but on the contrary that it may gain strength through exercise. For practice makes the artist, even here, and by repeated actions even faith, if not generated, is at least augmented (cf. 1 Tim. 4:7, 12, 14–15). (6) An intimate sense of our weak faith (Mark 9:24), by which "You should always be dissatisfied with yourself for what you are, if you wish to arrive at what you are not yet; for where you are satisfied, there you remain," as Augustine says.[35] Paul speaks in a similar way (Phil. 3:13–14), as does Christ against the Laodiceans (Rev. 3:17).

The signs of increasing or decreasing faith

LII. Meanwhile, in order that our progress may become more evident, it will

---

34. That is, after the example of the ancient painter Apelles, who never spent a day without some practice of his art. Pliny the Elder, *Natural History*, 35:36.

35. From *Sermo* CLXX, cap. 15 on Phil. 3:3–16, Augustine in *Patrologia Latina (PL)*, ed. Jacques Paul Migne (Paris, 1841–1855), 38:926.

help to have the marks of increasing and of decreasing faith clearly before us. It is discerned from: (1) doubts, fear, and similar things, as they increase (Luke 8:25) or decrease (Rom. 4:20). (2) Trust or lack of trust with respect to God and his goodness and providence (Matt. 14:29–31). (3) The cares and concerns of this life, as they increase or decrease (Matt. 6:30–31). (4) Progress or regress in the duties of holiness. For faith is at work through love (Gal. 5:6), and therefore it ought to be shown by those duties (James 2:18). (5) The struggle to resist all the attacks of enemies. For the one who yields easily is a weak soldier, while the one who resists to bloodshed is reckoned strong (Heb. 12:4).

The seventh practice, concerning the life of faith
LIII. The seventh practice concerns the use of faith, for which reason it is said that faith is at work (Gal. 5:6), and that we walk by faith (2 Cor. 5:7), and also live by faith (Hab. 2:4; Rom. 1:17; Gal. 3:11; Heb. 10:38): "The life I live, I live by faith in the Son of God" (Gal. 2:20). In general, this means to us nothing else than this: having received God and the Mediator, committing our whole self to them, depending on them in all necessities, and in return giving to them our whole self, with all that is ours. In specific, it involves three acts, one essential act—receiving God and the Mediator, on which we spoke expressly above—and then two subsequent acts, namely, first confident dependence, and next obedient submission. (1) In dependence, in any misfortune or difficulty, whether spiritual or temporal, and especially either in an uncertain circumstance, when we lack all the supports of our trust, we walk not by sight but by faith (2 Cor. 5:7). That is, we perceive clearly our own need and impotence (Luke 15:16–17), we go out of ourselves, as it were (Heb. 13:13), being persuaded of the all-sufficiency, goodness, and faithfulness of God and the Savior (Phil. 4:12–13; Rom. 8:36–37). We await his help (Rom. 7:24–25) with patience, resting on (a) his all-sufficiency (Gen. 17:1), by which he is a buckler and a shield (Ps. 84:11); (b) his goodness (Ex. 34:6–7), by which he who did not spare his own Son will with him graciously give us all things (Rom. 8:32); and (c) his truthfulness and faithfulness in his promises (Rom. 4:19–20; 2 Tim. 2:13). On the other hand, (2) in obedient submission, faith lives by (a) obedience (Rom. 1:5), by which we show our faith in works (James 2:18), we walk by faith (2 Cor. 5:7), not by our own impulse but by the divine command (Deut. 12:32), nor by our own strength, but in the power of God (1 Cor. 15:10; Gal. 2:20), urged on not by worldly desire, but by the divine promises (2 Cor. 7:1). And (b) the merit of Christ, in which all faith's works are dyed, so to speak, that they may please God (Heb. 11:6; Rom. 14:23; Heb. 10:22), and thus by a more certain faith they speed toward God.

Incitements

LIV. Urging this usage and life of faith is the fact that: (1) without it, faith is dead (James 2:17) and is being buried as it were (Matt. 25:18–25). Indeed, (2) it languishes, wilts, and perishes, for which reason the apostle commands it to be rekindled by the exercise of good works (2 Tim. 1:6). (3) The more industrious it is, the more perfect it is (for the perfection of a habit is in operation) and also the more glorifying to God (Rom. 4:20; Matt. 5:16). (4) The more industrious it is, the sweeter it is in life as well as in death (2 Tim. 4:6–8; Isa. 38:2–3; Rev. 14:13). Indeed also, (5) the more glorious it is for us, both here (Heb. 11:2), and hereafter, in the judgment (Matt. 25:34). Let us add that (6) to this end Christ died, that we might live for God through faith (2 Cor. 5:15; Rom. 14:7–9); and thus (7) by his grace we ourselves live (Acts 17:25, 28), undoubtedly so that we may live for him by faith. I need not say that in this way our life is rendered (8) truly Christian, namely, when we walk not by our senses, which belongs to brute beasts, not by sight, which belongs also to unbelievers, but by faith (2 Cor. 5:7); yet it is not only rendered Christian, but also (9) tranquil and secure, insofar as in every circumstance through faith we rest in God and in his providence (Ps. 37:3–5); and indeed also (10) blessed (Ps. 2:12).

The eighth practice, concerning particular persuasion

LV. The eighth and last practice of faith concerns application or particular persuasion, that by which you endeavor by faith to hold without doubt that God is your God, that Christ is your Mediator, your Bridegroom, that he has loved you, devoted himself to you, procured for you the remission of sins, the right to eternal life, and all things, following the example of Paul in Galatians 2:20, "I live by faith in the Son of God, who loved me and gave himself for me," and in 2 Timothy 1:12, "I know whom I have believed and am persuaded that he is able to keep that which I have committed until that day." This persuasion is born of faith or the saving act of faith, that is, reception, just as the bride knows without doubt that her bridegroom is hers from the consent by which she receives him as he offers himself (Song 2:16). It is born, I say, by virtue of this practical syllogism: All who believe in God and the Mediator, and by believing receive them, then God and the Mediator are undoubtedly theirs (John 3:16; 1:12); but I believe, and by believing I receive them, so then they are mine. Thus it is evident that this persuasion includes three things—faith, sense, and reasoning: (1) faith, with regard to the proposition, whereby you know the Scriptures, you are convinced that they are undoubtedly true and divine, and that they supply this mark of identification that is found in the major proposition (2 Tim. 1:12); (2) sense (Phil. 1:9), whereby you perceive faith as truly present, and you say, "I believe" (Mark 9:24); (3) reasoning (2 Cor. 4:13), whereby you infer from the effects the presence of the cause, that is, faith; the faith which you have gathered you distinguish from any sort of common faith; and from the premises you infer the conclusion. Therefore the conclusion, or the particular persuasion, is not saving faith itself, but its effect, and not an effect of faith alone, but also of sense and reasoning. This must be carefully noted lest we ourselves obstruct our pathway to particular persuasion: this is what the spiritually deserted do, when they judge that saving faith is this particular persuasion itself, and for this reason, because they do not sense it, they infer that they are devoid of faith, and from this at last infer that Christ is not their Savior.

The benefits of this persuasion
LVI. In this particular persuasion is the apex and choicest fruit of saving faith. And in particular: (1) it is the sharpest spur for all promptness and alacrity in piety, inciting a person to repentance (2 Cor. 7:1), divine love (Ps. 18:1–2), trust (Ps. 23:1), fortitude (Ps. 27:1), patience (Job 19:25), gratitude (Ps. 103:1–4; Gen. 32:10), and spiritual battle (2 Tim. 4:7–8). (2) It is the perpetual spring of all spiritual tranquility (Rom. 5:1), consolation (Col. 2:2), and joy (Ps. 16:5, 6, 9, 11). (3) In favorable circumstances, in good health, wealth, and honors, it is a sweetness, when we possess all these things as pledges of paternal love (Ps. 23:1–3), and in them as it were we see and taste how good the Lord is (Ps. 34:8). (4) In adverse circumstances it is a solace, such that we are even able to glory that the love of God has been poured out in our hearts, persuaded that all these things have been sent by our Father (Matt. 10:29–31), and that none of them will separate us from his love in Christ Jesus (Rom. 8:39), but in fact that all these things will be directed to our salvation (Rom. 8:28). It is a solace: (5) in death, such that we mock it with the apostle (1 Cor. 15:55, 57), and desire it (Phil. 1:23; Luke 2:29–30); (6) against the horrors of the last judgment, such that we look up and lift up our head because our redemption draws near (Luke 21:28; Rom. 8:23); (7) against hell (1 Cor. 15:55). Indeed, (8) by this persuasion, it will be as if heaven is on earth, making known what eye has not seen nor ear heard (1 Cor. 2:9); it is as if to hear that sweetest phrase, "Well done, good and faithful servant..." (Matt. 25:21).

The means
LVII. The following things promote that particular persuasion: (1) zeal for augmenting faith (concerning which see §§L–LII), since this persuasion does not belong to just any kind of faith, however much it may be true and saving, but only to a more robust faith (Rom. 4:21). (2) Exploration of our faith, whether

it is saving, that is, so that in place of persuasion we do not allow presumption
(1 Peter 1:5, 7). (3) Let us beware of any sort of obstructions there are to our
faith, such as: (a) errors, by which we take common faith for saving faith; or a
common act of faith for a saving act; or we constitute the nature of saving faith in
special persuasion; or we take the fruit of faith—tranquility, consolation, joy—
for faith itself; or we do not believe that persuasion is true if it is not perfect
and if it is conflicted with various hesitations; (b) that meagerness or idleness
of faith by which it occurs that faith cannot be recognized and distinguished;
(c) the disturbance of conscience through more heinous sins (Ps. 51:11–12).
(d) Momentary spiritual desertions should be cautiously distinguished from
total and perpetual ones (Isa. 54:7–10). Finally, (e) zeal for this persuasion
should be distinctly devoted to acquiring, preserving, augmenting, and using it,
regarding which an express treatment can be seen in our *Syntagma on Saving
Faith*, a kind of summary of which we have offered in this whole chapter.[36]

---

36. What here Mastricht terms a zeal for this persuasion, *studium hujus persuasionis*, in his
1671 *De fide salvifica syntagma* he seems to call a zeal for faith, *studium fidei*, which he distinguishes into a general, special, and most special zeal for faith. The most special zeal is "so that we
aspire through faith to a personal certainty of salvation." Cf. Mastricht, *De fide salvifica syntagma*,
416–668.

CHAPTER TWO

The Existence and Knowledge of God

*For the one who comes to God must believe that he exists and that he will be
a rewarder of those who seek him.*
                                                    —Hebrews 11:6

*The connection with the preceding things, and an outline of the things
to be treated concerning God*
I. In saving faith, so that we may seek after God and receive him as our highest
end, it is entirely necessary that we are persuaded that: (1) God exists; (2) he is
such a God who is perfectly sufficient for himself and for us; and (3) he is such
a God who is able and willing to share this sufficiency of his with us through
his efficiency or operations. And, because the all-sufficiency of God results from
two things—partly from his essence and essential perfections and partly from
his subsistence and persons, insofar as every good thing redounds to us from
the love of the Father, the grace of the Son, and the fellowship of the Holy Spirit
(2 Cor. 13:14)—the entire topic concerning God divides into these four heads:
(1) the existence and knowledge of God; (2) his essence, names, and essential
attributes; (3) his subsistence and persons; and (4) the efficiency and operations
of God. We will treat the first three matters in this book, and the fourth in the
next. In Hebrews 11:6 the apostle expressly teaches the necessity of the divine
existence and knowledge.

The Exegetical Part
The text is resolved and explained.
II. In it, in order to confirm the necessity of habitual faith (πίστις), he brings
forth the necessity of the act of believing (πιστεύειν) and of its use in the persuasion of the twofold *principium* on which all religion rests, namely, that God
exists and that he will be a rewarder of those who seek him. With respect to this
necessity of faith, three things occur:

A. Those who believe, for whom it is necessary to believe (πιστεύειν): προσερχόμενοι τῷ θεῷ, "those who come to God." For this coming to God, with the Savior standing between, is what faith intends (John 14:6; Matt. 11:28; Isa. 55:1). Moreover, the Greek phrase προσέρχεσθαι τῷ θεῷ may denote any of the following: (1) walking along with God, either in the same paths, in equal step with God (Gen. 6:9; Job 31:7; Mal. 2:6, 8), or in the ways of God, through the pursuit of holiness; or (2) walking before God, in the sight of God (Gen. 17:1; 24:40; 2 Cor. 2:17), through sincerity; or (3) walking after God (Deut. 12:4), by following him and imitating his virtues; or (4) walking in the name of God (Mic. 4:5); or (5) coming to God, namely, so that you may find him—for which reason the verb ἐκζητεῖν, "to seek," is in the text—so that you may be united with him, have communion with him, enjoy him, glorify him, and in him have every kind of blessedness. The last of these meanings seems to be the most suitable to the text.

B. Believing and its necessity: δεῖ πιστεύειν, "he must believe." Here the verb "to believe" could, on the one hand, be spoken of more broadly as any sort of knowledge, drawn either from sense or from reasoning, since God's existence is known to us not only by faith, at least not faith alone, but by reasoning as well. Or it could, on the other hand, be spoken of more strictly, denoting a knowledge that is born from assent. For God has not left himself, nor has the world and every person's conscience left God, "without witness" (Acts 14:17). And so this believing is called necessary (δεῖ)—not merely fitting in whatever way, but unavoidably necessary for this purpose: that we may come to God. For without an acknowledgment of the deity, no love, worship, and obedience of him can subsist—no impetus to find him, no finding him, and finally no salvation.

C. What must be believed, namely, the two supports of all faith and religion. Of these the first regards the existence of God: ὅτι ἔστι, "that he exists," which is the common *principium* of religion and presupposition of faith. The second regards the grace whereby he is a μισθαποδότης, "rewarder," and he communicates his own self, the exceedingly great reward (Gen. 15:1), not to just anyone, but τοῖς ἐκζητοῦσιν αὐτόν, "to those who seek him," those who not only seek him by faith and religion, but who diligently seek him, that is, who seek in such a way that they find him, and having found him, receive him as their highest end, and enjoy that end eternally.

The Dogmatic Part

It is proved that God exists.

III. Therefore at the least this is evident to us: that the knowledge of the divine existence is the first *principium* and foundation of all religion. For, according to the meaning of the text, we cannot "come to God" by faith or "seek him" unless we have been persuaded that he exists. For this reason, the psalmist locates the source of all falsehood and iniquity in the denial of God's existence (Ps. 10:4; 14:1).

By eight reasons

IV. Therefore we must argue the case for his existence before we explain the reason for the knowledge of him. In order to argue the case firmly, it must be presupposed that we do not want by the term *God* to be understood anything but "the absolutely first being," and that we will demonstrate the existence of this being first by reasons, because atheists ridicule testimonies, and then by testimonies, because once atheists are convinced by reasons, they can be remarkably confirmed by testimonies of every kind.

1. From the subordination of causes

Therefore, the first and foremost among this class of reasons proceeds from effects, for we cannot without contradiction construct from causes a demonstration of the first cause. At this point therefore, I know well enough that an atheist—provided he is not senseless, a masked scoffer, or a jester—will acknowledge the existence of those things that occur daily before his eyes, and likewise will acknowledge that they do not have their existence from themselves, nor also do those things from which they derive their existence. So then it must be stated that in these things there is either (1) an infinite regress; or (2) the same thing produced itself; or (3) in causations there is circularity, by which, for example, A is the cause of B, B is the cause of C, C is the cause of D, and D in turn is the cause of A; or (4) there is some first being that derives its existence from nothing or no one. There is no fifth option. Now however, the first three cannot be admitted in any way, because they imply more than one contradiction. And indeed, an infinite subordination of causes results in the following. (1) If it should stand, absolutely nothing can exist, which is contrary to what was acknowledged at the outset. This is the case because nothing can exist except by its own proximate cause that produces the effect. But now if an infinite number of causes should have to precede a proximate cause, then a proximate cause will never be able to exist, and thus also nothing will be able exist. Then (2) in this way an infinite thing would be made greater, since we daily observe causes being added to infinite causes, and numbers would be added to an infinite number. And thus there will be an infinite that is not actually infinite. Furthermore, (3) the order of prior and posterior which occurs in a sequence will be left without a first thing, from which by its nature all flow arises. For when there is no first thing, then there is also neither second nor third, and in turn there is not second and third when there is no first, and accordingly there will be a subordination that is not a subordination. Therefore an infinite subordination cannot be admitted in any way. Nor can it any more be admitted that the same thing can produce itself. For in this way the same thing would simultaneously exist and not exist. For insofar as it produced it would certainly exist, and insofar as it was produced it would not exist. If the atheist should insist, "Yet God, in your opinion, is from himself," then we would reply, "True, but he did not produce himself." He is from himself negatively, insofar as he was not produced by anyone, but he is not from himself positively, such that he produced himself, as we will demonstrate in its proper place.[1] But what if, finally, in causes the circularity that we mentioned should be admitted—then would a first thing not be required? I will say that then the same thing, although in a roundabout way, would produce itself, since A will be the cause of itself through B, C, and D. Now, I do not see anything that the atheist could allege against these reasons except perhaps that we do not observe that the sun, moon, and the rest of the stars have been produced from other things, and this perhaps is why, by the first idolaters, the sun under the name Molech, the moon under the name Melecheth, and the stars under the phrase "the army of heaven" were considered as gods. But here also a response is easy: Although we do not observe by our senses that those things were produced, yet by our mind or reasoning we gather it more certainly than certain because we observe that all these things are finite, and, since nothing determines and limits itself and its own perfection, they acquired their limits from another who is greater and who produced them. Now, I do not see even one crack through which an atheist could escape the force of this reasoning.

2. From the creation of the world

V. From here we will descend to the particulars in which this world stands before us, and from this we are supplied with a second demonstration: The world is created; therefore God exists. We presuppose, in agreement with any atheist, that the world exists. This world either produced itself, or from eternity it was not produced, or it was produced by another. In the third case it was produced either from another preexisting thing or from nothing, and if from nothing, then

---

1. 1.2.3 §XXII

it was created, seeing that creation is to us nothing but production from nothing, and the one who produces the world is, by necessity, more excellent than the world that has been produced. And nothing is more excellent than the whole world than that one who produces it, whom we call God. We demonstrate these things in a summary; now let us briefly develop it. That this world did not produce itself, and that it could not produce itself, is evident from the preceding section. That the same world did not exist from eternity is taught by more than one thing. For (1) eternity is infinity, which a finite world cannot contain. If the atheist should affirm that the world is infinite, then this will be easily refuted from the parts of the world. Either these parts will be infinite, and thus there will be several infinites, and in consequence none. For a part would have all the perfection of its co-part, or not. If it had all the perfection of it, then it would not be distinct but one and the same, which an inspection of the parts of the world refutes. If it did not have it, then it would not be infinite. But from many finite parts cannot result one infinite world, unless an effect should be infinitely better than its cause, and finite causes should have produced infinity in their effect. Then (2) if the world had existed from eternity, thus an infinite number of years, which eternity would imply, ought necessarily to have preceded today, and because that number is never complete, even today could not have followed it—but without doubt the mind of the atheist will cry out against this. Finally, (3) from this eternity of the world it will follow that something can be added to an infinite thing and thus, there is an infinite that is not infinite. For eternity is an infinite duration, and yet to it (as our sense and experience cry out) there are continually added years, months, days, hours, and so forth. Furthermore, from this it follows that there can be an infinite greater than infinite, insofar as the world, which one hundred years before by its eternity was infinite in duration, is now greater through those hundred years. Let it remain therefore that the world by no means existed from eternity and, in consequence, it was produced by another. Furthermore, if it was produced by another, then either it was produced from another thing existing prior to it, or from nothing. If it be claimed that it was produced from another thing existing prior to it, then the difficulties that were set forth in this and the preceding section will reappear. If the production is from nothing, then the world exists by creation, because by "creation" we understand nothing else than production from nothing. And because the essence of creation is to remove that infinite distance of difficulty that exists between nonbeing and being, it remains that it demands an infinite power to remove it, and because that power does not occur in any but the first being, whose power alone is not and cannot be determined and limited by another, it remains that if the world should be created, then there exists a first and infinite being, which we call God.

3. From the preservation of the world

VI. The third demonstration comes to us from the preservation of the world: If the world has been continuously preserved up to the present day, then God exists. For to very many learned men, preservation is nothing but continued creation, different from creation in this alone, that the former includes newness of existing, which the latter excludes. If the atheist should deny that the world is preserved, saying that it only endures, in nearly the same way in which our God endures, even though he is not preserved, then we will respond that the world does indeed endure, but by preservation, because it is produced by another, per the preceding section. Thus emerges a dissimilar reckoning between the duration of God and the preservation of the world: God is simply from himself, and thus the first and independent being, who accordingly cannot be preserved by anything, while the world exists by another (as has been proved), can be preserved by another, and must be. Now if the world is preserved it is either preserved by itself or by another. It is not preserved by itself, for that which could not give itself existence also cannot preserve the existence given to it by another; so then, it is preserved by another. And finally, what is this other if not the one that gave it its existence? Indeed, if it were something else it would without doubt be a part of the world, and accordingly a part of the world would preserve the whole world. For whatever preserves the whole also preserves the part. Furthermore, given that there are in this world different parts which among themselves are not only heterogeneous but also opposed, to their mutual destruction, parts in which one strives with all its strength for the destruction of another, for example, fire and water, water and earth, then the fact that the world has been so far thus preserved, that water has not extinguished fire or inundated the dry land, or that one kind of the parts of the world has not been taken away—from where does this come, if not from the first and omnipotent being?

4. From the governance of the world

VII. Let the fourth demonstration follow, from the governance of the world. We presuppose on the basis of simple inspection—which I know well enough that an atheist will not deny—that the world consists of various parts, not only heterogeneous but also opposed to each other, and those for the most part irrational, parts which at the same time hold together in a way so well-ordered and agreeable to reason, parts among which all pursue their own perfection, yet not only their own but also that of the whole universe, such that despite and contrary to the innate character of their own nature they are conveyed toward the conservation of the whole universe, as is evident in heavy things that, contrary to their nature, strive upwards, so that the universe does not suffer from emptiness, and likewise that the changes of the year recur so accurately and put forth fruits suitable to themselves. We likewise presuppose that all these things are governed. Now let the atheist tell me by whom they are governed—by themselves or by another? He will not say by themselves, because most of them are devoid of reason and the vast majority of them strive against one another; hence it is by another. And who at last is that? Is there any other that can be thought of besides some omnipresent, omnipotent, most wise, and most good being? And who is such a being besides that first being, whom we call God? Let us make the matter clear by a simile: let there be several gears in one clock that cooperate with one another for its ticking or tolling precisely at this or that time, while none recognize either their own goal or each other. Do they not powerfully argue that there had been before them a craftsman who prudently joined them together, who as exactly as possible conceived their shape and distances? And will you then assert that this most pleasant and constant unity and harmony of the parts of this world, though they are very often irrational and lifeless, exist without a certain most wise, omnipotent, and omnipresent builder and maker (Heb. 11:10)? If the atheist should insist that all these things result from the peculiar nature and innate character of the individual parts, then there recur to him the many great difficulties already set forth: From where does this nature come? This arrangement so wise, constant, and ordered? So then, I do not see through what crack an atheist can escape the force of this demonstration.

5. From the heavens
VIII. The fifth demonstration specifically arises for us from the heavens: Their vastness and their constant and regular motion, what do they declare but the glory of God (Ps. 19:1)? Thus you can perhaps denominate this theory "astrology," because it is the ἄστρων λόγος, "the word of the stars," that is, whereby they declare God (Ps. 19:2), just as "astronomy" is so called because a νόμος, a "law," was established for the motion of the stars undoubtedly by a supreme lawgiver. For surely the sun and the stars are moved by another, by whose might their motions are so strictly fixed by laws that all their eclipses through tens of thousands of years can be certainly predicted by astronomers, down to the minute. From where does this order, this law, come, if not from a certain most wise lawgiver?

6. From man
IX. Likewise, each person in many ways shows the sixth demonstration to himself. For (1) the so skillful formation of us in our mother's womb, even while we and our parents were ignorant of it—does this not argue for a certain most

wise one who formed us (Ps. 139:5, 15–16)? (2) Our soul, designated by the pagans themselves (and not entirely inappropriately) as a "particle of the divine Spirit,"[2] by its spiritual essence a whole class nobler than the body—does this not argue for a certain supreme Father of spirits (Heb. 12:9) who formed the spirit of man within him (Zech. 12:1)? In fact, (3) the existence of each person supplies him with an argument for the divine existence. For since each knows that he is from his parents, just as his parents are from his grandparents, by necessity each must acknowledge that either there is an infinite concatenation in this series, given which his own parents could not have existed, and thus neither could he himself, or that he must stop at some first parent, who did not exist except by the Father of spirits, by analogy with §V.

7. From commonwealths and laws

X. We would add a seventh reason, namely, from the preservation, constancy, order, and changes[3] of commonwealths, against the many machinations of such great men intended for their destruction. Indeed even civil laws argue for a divine mind that first reveals them to men and then preserves them, so that they do not fall to ruin, dissolved by the hatred and machinations of the devil and the ungodly. For who would not conclude from this that there exists some God of order, who desires all things to be done decently and in order (1 Cor. 14:40)?

8. From miracles and predictions

XI. Furthermore, we would add an eighth reason, from miracles accomplished throughout both sacred and secular history. Because they exceed nature, they cannot but lay the foundation for accepting a force superior to nature, for it involves a contradiction for something to act beyond its own forces. And what is there that exceeds nature if not God? And thus we would add also a ninth reason, from certain predictions of future contingencies, which because in themselves they do not have a determined truth cannot but argue for a mind predetermining

---

2. *divinae particula aurae*. Horace, *Satires*, 2.2.79.

3. *revolutio*: Current historical scholarship on this term in the early modern period indicates a range of meanings from a substantial change, alteration, or turnover in an order of government or a regime. In some primary sources it could involve a cyclical change, in others more of an oscillating spiral, in others a rebellion. The latter meaning of *revolutio* as an upheaval or rebellion, and especially a violent one, in the process of political progress is a much broader usage in the eighteenth century political climate of the French Revolution and in the nineteenth century political thought of dialectical historical materialism of Marx and Engels. For an excellent, brief overview of the early modern period usage, see Tim Harris, "Did the English have a script for Revolution in the Seventeenth Century?" in K. M. Baker and D. Edelstein, eds., *Scripting Revolution: A Historical Approach to the Comparative Study of Revolutions* (Stanford: Stanford University Press, 2015), 25–40.

all events by a certain decree. I say that we would add these things, if our pursuit of brevity would endure it, or if the preceding things were not sufficient.

By three kinds of testimony
So then, we should proceed to testimonies, if perhaps the mind of the atheist, softened by the proofs, may be confirmed by them, or at the least so that they who admit a deity may from this *principium*, which is first of all, be strengthened in their faith and observance. Therefore let us proceed.

1. Conscience
XII. First is the testimony that each person's conscience gives to God. For this reason "what may be known of God" is said to be "manifest in them" (Rom. 1:19), namely insofar as it either excuses or accuses, delights or terrifies them (Rom. 2:15; Isa. 33:14; 57:20; Mark 6:14, 16). Examples of this are not only offered in the sacred writings (Gen. 42:21) but also in secular writings, as in the case of Nero, who because he had killed Agrippina was more frequently (by his own admission) terrified in his spirit; or Caligula, who was accustomed during thunder and lightning to hide himself because of the wicked deeds on his conscience; or King Richard III of England, who after his villainies was harassed by frenzies of nightmares, as if by the torments of Satan, such that Polydore Vergil said of him, "I believe that it was not a dream, but the conscience of his wicked deeds."[4] And thus comes the line of Statius, "Fear it was that made the world's first gods."[5] See Grotius, *On the Truth of the Christian Religion*, book 1.[6] Meanwhile on the contrary, the faithful, because of their conscience toward God, can sing sweetly in their very chains (Acts 16:25), sleep securely, and triumph in the gravest dangers (Ps. 3:5–6; 1 Sam. 30:6; Ps. 46:1–2). "If the globe should break and fall, it shall strike him down still fearless" (Horace).[7] And from what does all this come, except the fact that they bear the law of God inscribed on their hearts, that they hear the voice of the Judge, as if before the tribunal, either condemning or absolving them?

---

4. Polydore Vergil of Urbino (1470–1555), was commissioned by Henry VII to compose a pro-Tudor history, which was published in five editions as *Historia Anglia* (Basel, 1534, 1546, 1555, 1556, 1570). Polydorus Vergilius, *Three books of Polydore Vergil's English History comprising the reigns of Henry VI, Edward IV, and Richard III*, ed. H. Ellis (London: John Bowyer Nichols and Son, 1844), 178–79.

5. Statius, *Thebaid*, 3:661.

6. There is a similar but much lengthier list of extra-biblical sources in Hugo Grotius, *De veritate religionis Christianae, editio nova* (Paris: Sebastian Cramoisy, 1640), 16–22.

7. *Odes*, 3.3.7–8.

2. The world

XIII. The world presents the second testimony to God for his existence, by the universal and constant approval of all nations, which Paul considers in Romans 1:20 and 2:15. This approval is so great that, as evidenced by the cosmographers, Abraham Ortelius,[8] Sebastian Münster,[9] and others, there is no nation so barbarous that it does not acknowledge a deity, as Cicero states in *On the Nature of the Gods*.[10] And Epicurus himself, who was not ashamed of anything shameful, was nevertheless ashamed to deny God.[11] In fact, our own Phillipe du Plessis Mornay says in chapter 1 of *On the Truth of the Christian Religion*, "Although there are found those who live without a king or without a law, who wander naked in the woods like wild beasts, seeking trackless places and feeding off whatever they find; yet nevertheless there have not been found, nor are there found, those who entirely lack some kind of religion, who lack holy things, who lack a sense of a divinity."[12] And even their idolatry itself gives testimony to God. For such senseless idolatry would never have prevailed so broadly throughout the nations, even those not entirely barbarous, that they would even prefer to have a leek and onion as their god than to have none at all—just as Juvenal says in his *Satires*, 15, "It is a sin to violate or break the leek and onion with a bite: oh how holy are the nations in whose gardens such gods are born!"—unless they had presupposed a god or some deity. See also these authors on idolatry: Vossius, Juan Luis Vives, and John Owen, among others.[13]

---

8. Abraham Ortelius (1527–1598), *Theatrum Orbis Terrarum* (Antwerp: Gilles Coppes de Diest, 1570). Idem, *Theatrum Orbis Terrarum. Gedruckt zu Nuremberg durch Johann Koler Anno MDLXXII. Mit einer Einführung und Erläuterungen von Ute Schneider* (Darmstadt: Wissenschaftliche Buchgesellschaft, 2007).

9. The most well known of his editions are, Sebastian Münster (1466–1552), *Cosmographia, B[e]schreibung aller Lender durch Sebastianum Munsterum in welcher begriffen* (Basel: Heinrich Petri, 1544). Idem, *Cosmographia, das ist, Beschreibung der gantzen Welt, darinnen aller Monarchien, Keyserthumben, Königreichen, Fürstenthumben, Graff- und Herrschaften, Länderen, Stätten vnd Gemeinden, wie auch aller Geistlichen Stifften…Beschaffenheit* (Basel: Petri, 1622).

10. Cicero, *De natura deorum*, 1.16.43–1.17.45, cf. 1.43; idem, *De legibus*, 1.8.

11. Epicurus, *Letter to Menoeceus* (*Ep. Men.*), 123.

12. Philippe du Plessis Mornay (1549–1623), *De la verité de la religion chrestienne : contre les athées, epicuriens, payens, Juifs, Mahumedistes, et autres infideles* (Antwerp: Christophe Plantin, 1581), 13–14; idem, *De veritate religionis Christianae liber adversus atheos, epicureos, ethnicos, Judaeos, Mahumedistas et caeteros infideles* (Antwerp: Christopher Plantin, 1583), 14; idem, *A woorke concerning the trewnesse of the Christian religion* (London: for Thomas Cadman, 1587), 10.

13. Cf. Gerardus Joannes Vossius (1577–1649), *De theologia gentili et physiologia Christiana, sive de origine ac progressu idolatriae deque naturae mirandis quibus homo adducitur Deum*, 2 vols. (Amsterdam: Joannes Blaeu, 1668); Juan Luis Vives (1492–1540), *De veritate fidei Christianae libri quinque* (Lyon: Joannes Frellonius, 1551); John Owen (1616–1683), Θεολογούμενα Παντοδαπά, *seu de natura, ortu, progressu, et studio verae theologiae* (Oxford, 1661), bk. 3,

3. God

XIV. Finally, God personally presents the third testimony to himself for his existence, not only by acting in nature—the sort of testimony that the Savior presented for himself (John 5:20, 36)—but also by speaking in Scripture, whose every line, or at least whose every page, shouts that God exists: its head, "In the beginning God" (Gen. 1:1); its tail, "If anyone should take away from the words of this prophecy, God will take away his part from the book of life" (Rev. 22:19); and its middle, in most of its prophecies, "thus says the Lord," "the word of the Lord," "Hear, O heavens, and perceive, O earth, for the Lord speaks" (Isa. 1:2). And indeed this testimony, although the atheist is indifferent to it, and the Pharisees (John 8:13), is still of the highest authority, according to the Savior (John 8:14).

Several objections to the contrary are resolved.

XV. The sorts of things that atheists could object to the existence of God are so thin, indeed so futile, that they scarcely deserve to be recounted, much less refuted. Nevertheless, with one or two words we will point them out for the sake of the system.

First, those who allege that God does not exist object most crassly that people do not see him, and he does not live among them. I respond: (1) This is plainly irrational and brutish. For if what is not seen does not exist, then to such persons there will be no rational souls, as they surely do not see them, and thus they will be brute beasts themselves. Then (2) God daily makes himself conspicuous in his own way, by his works.

Second, with not much more subtlety they allege, If God exists, then he would not tolerate the prosperity of the wicked and the misery of the good; he would not tolerate himself to be blasphemed; he would not tolerate such great disorder in these earthly affairs. We oppose this objection with this: These affairs that appear to us each on their own to be so confused, so unjust, so perverse, would show themselves to us to be by far most just and most well-ordered if we were granted, like God, to view all of them at the same time, at a single glance, in their construction with other things, and in the harmony of the whole.

Finally, third, the atheists want religion to be nothing but a human invention or political stratagem devised for the sake of magistrates, in order to restrain

---

chs. 3–14, pp. 184–286; idem, *The Works of John Owen*, 20 vols. (Edinburgh: T & T Clark, 1862), 20:179–260.

subordinates in their duty. I respond: But they only want this to be so, or rather they would want it, as fools (Ps. 14:1). For religion has existed from the cradle of the world, it exists throughout the whole world, and without a doubt it will continue to exist to the end of this universe. From these things it is most readily concluded that religion is not a human invention, and it does not come from anything but God.

It is proved that the knowledge of God is necessary.
XVI. It is not, however, sufficient that God exists, but it is necessary in addition that we know him who exists: "For he must believe" (Heb. 11:6). It is necessary, I say, not only by a necessity of command (Jer. 31:34), but also by necessity of means, for just as on the one hand God assigns life to the knowledge of himself (John 17:3), so in turn he assigns to the ignorance opposed to it eternal flames (2 Thess. 1:8).

By reasons
XVII. Thus in fact, even as our text says, the knowledge of God is necessary in many ways. It is necessary (1) for faith. For how will we believe in him of whom we have not heard, or whom we have not come to know by someone speaking (Rom. 10:14)? And thus it is necessary (2) for pleasing him, as also without faith it is impossible to please God, and consequently without knowledge no one can be pleasing to God or do what is pleasing to him. From which it is necessary (3) for the worship of God, since just as without faith, thus also without knowledge, no one can seek out God. And furthermore, because of that, it is necessary (4) for union and communion with God, since without knowledge, just as a person cannot seek him, so he cannot find him, or "come to God." Finally, it is necessary (5) for experiencing the kindness of God. For since without knowledge a person cannot believe, cannot by believing, seek, and cannot by seeking, come, likewise he cannot ever experience God as a "rewarder." To these reasons I will add that (6) apart from the knowledge of God, not only would the intellect have been given to man in vain, and likewise man would have been created in vain, but even this whole world, at least the terrestrial one, would have been created in vain. For to what end did God make all things, if not for the sake of man (Ps. 8:6)? And to what end did God make man, if not so that as God's treasurer he might gather the goodness of all the irrational creatures and bring it back to the Creator? And this does not happen except by the knowledge and glorification of God.

The nature and character of the knowledge of God

XVIII. Thus we must carefully and thoroughly investigate the character as well as the supports of this knowledge. As regards its character, it is either comprehensive, a knowledge which perceives God as he is in himself and indeed according to everything that is knowable in him, and thus a knowledge perfect in every respect; or, it is apprehensive, a knowledge which knows him to a certain extent, knowing *that* he is rather than *what* he is, what he is *not* rather than what he *is*. First and foremost, that prior comprehensive knowledge regarding himself must be left to him alone (1 Tim. 6:16). The latter knowledge, however, is either the knowledge of the homeland,[14] and the more perfect knowledge hereafter, when we will see God as if face to face (1 Cor. 13:12; Job 19:26–27), or the more imperfect knowledge of the journey[15] here, when we see God as it were from his back and not his face (Ex. 33:23), as if through a mirror, as if in an enigma (1 Cor. 13:12). God in his Word conveys this knowledge to us as if by lisping to us, as infants. For this reason in Scripture occur so many anthropopathies[16] concerning God, and in addition very many things concerning God are explained according to our capacity, following the method of our conception, rather than from the nature of God himself. Furthermore, this more imperfect knowledge is either natural, a knowledge that we hold by nature, or that we are able by the help of nature to obtain for ourselves, and this knowledge is distributed by theologians into (1) inborn or innate knowledge, which freely comes into existence without reasoning, about which the apostle speaks in Romans 1:19, and (2) acquired knowledge, which we obtain by discursive reasoning, by ascending from the subordination of motions to the prime mover, from the concatenation of inferior causes to the supreme cause, in the modes and ways already demonstrated. Paul likewise speaks about this in Romans 1:20 (cf. Ps. 19:1–2; Acts 17:27–28). Or, this more imperfect knowledge is revealed, a knowledge not different from the prior natural knowledge in kind, but only in degree and in perfection; indeed it absorbs, as it were, the prior knowledge as a larger number absorbs a smaller one. For whatever natural knowledge has, revealed knowledge provides the same in its entirety, and that much more perfectly. And this revealed knowledge is in turn either (1) common and theoretical only, a knowledge that only wanders about in the mind, the kind made known in our text by the phrase "to believe that God exists" (cf. Rom. 1:21; Titus 1:16), or (2) proper to the elect, an experiential,

---

14. *cognitio patriae*

15. *cognitio viae*

16. *anthropopathiae*. In Mastricht's usage this term includes both anthropopathism and anthropomorphism, as does the adverb ἀνθρωποπαθῶς, "in a human way," which he uses in other chapters.

practical, and saving knowledge, penetrating from the mind to the heart by efficaciously affecting it and stirring up pious affections in it. With this knowledge seems to agree, in our text, the knowledge of God "as a rewarder," which impels us to approach him, to please him, a knowledge about which Scripture speaks throughout (John 17:3; Isa. 53:11; Phil. 1:9–11; 3:8–10; Col. 1:9–10).

The means for the knowledge of God: The more general means
XIX. Now, concerning the supports by which we arrive at the knowledge of God, they are observed to be of two kinds. In the first more general kind are enumerated three ways to arrive at the knowledge of God, namely: (1) the way of causality, whereby having moved through various second causes as if by Jacob's ladder, we finally arrive at the highest step, where God is, according to the mode which we described above in §VI. And this knowledge is what the apostle seems to indicate in Romans 1:19. (2) The way of eminence, by which whatever there is of absolute perfection in creatures we attribute with the highest eminence to the Creator, because of the fact that no one can confer on another what he does not have either formally or eminently, nor can an effect be conceived such that it is on the whole more excellent than its own cause. The psalmist seems to use this way in Psalm 94:9. Indeed, it is fitting by this support to interpret all anthropopathic and metaphorical expressions. (3) The way of negation, by which we entirely remove from him any imperfection that occurs in the creatures, for example, corporality, mortality, finitude, and the like. Scripture seems to follow this way in Numbers 23:19 and Psalm 90:2–3. And indeed in this manner, we arrive by this threefold way at the knowledge of God, such that (1) the first way chiefly leads to his relative attributes, through which he is called Creator, preserver, governor, and mover; (2) the second way leads to his communicable and affirmative attributes, for example, wisdom, righteousness, and so forth, which we will discuss in their own place; and (3) the third leads to his incommunicable and negative attributes, such as infinity, immutability, and so forth.

Four more specific means
XX. In the second kind of supports, which is more specific, there are: (1) the divine names, of which some present to us what must be known about the essence of God, names such as אהיה, יה, יהוה, to which κύριος, "Lord," corresponds in the New Testament; some his power, such as אל and אלהים, "God"; some his self-sufficiency,[17] such as שדי; and some his excellence, such as עליון, and so forth. (2) The divine attributes, which by inadequate concepts relate that

---

17. αὐτάρκειαν

single, infinite perfection of God as if by parts, so that by their assistance we may know first how great God is and next what sort of God he is, as will become distinctly evident, each in its own place.[18] (3) The works of God, from which, as is customary, the nature of a cause is made known. Finally, (4) the Word of God, which presents God to us in all the preceding things as perfectly as can possibly be done.

The Elenctic Part

It is asked: 1. Is it permitted to doubt the existence of God in any way or for any cause?

XXI. We have already elaborated on questions concerning the existence of God, natural theology innate and acquired, and the insufficiency of natural theology for salvation in previous sections: the first question in this chapter, and the remainder in bk. 1, ch.1, §§XXIII–XXIV. Furthermore, it is asked whether it is permitted to doubt the existence of God in any way or for any cause. Long ago the Academic and Skeptical philosophers, whom you might call the "deliberators,"[19] otherwise known as seekers,[20] doubters,[21] and Pyrrhonians (from Pyrrho, the head as it were of the Skeptics, who following in the footsteps of the ancient philosophers—Socrates, Arcesilaus, Carneades, Anaxarchus, and others— gave preeminence to the dogma of acatalepsy[22]), stated that all things must be doubted, even the existence of God. (See Aulus Gellius, bk. 11, ch. 5,[23] and Sextus Empiricus in his *Against the Mathematicians* and *Outlines of Pyrrhonism*.)[24] Drawing on their defects in our own age, that most acute Frenchman René Descartes, seeking to construct a new foundation for a new philosophy, stated that the one who would philosophize legitimately must at least once doubt all things, and that earnestly and for some time, until he has perceived a matter clearly

---

18. The question of God's quantity, *quantus sit*, will be addressed in 1.2.8–11, and of his quality, *qualis sit*, in 1.2.12–20.

19. *quasi considerantios dicas*

20. Ζητητικοί

21. ἀπορητικοί

22. ἀκαταληψίας *dogma*, the Academic contention that nothing can be known with full certainty. Cf. Cicero, *Epistulae ad Atticum*, 13.19.3.

23. Aulus Gellius, *Attic Nights* (*Noctes Atticae*), 11.5.1–8.

24. E.g. Sextus Empiricus, *M* 9.55–56, 191–94, in which he speaks first, with Protagoras, "I am not able to say either whether [the gods] exist or of what sort they are," and second, of suspension of judgment with respect to the gods; in *Outlines of Pyrrhonism* (*Pyrrhoniae hypotyposes*), *PH* 1.10, 1.12. Sextus Empiricus articulates a doctrine of ἐποχή in which the skeptic's goal is to suspend judgment on all matters by posing equally weighty but opposing arguments in order to achieve ἀταραξία (*PH* 1.12), that is, mental tranquility.

and distinctly. Indeed it is true that he seems occasionally to make exception for matters of faith and common life or conversation, though he does so without any reason at all; but his disciples nevertheless go further and extend this doubt to matters of faith, a notable specimen of which is expressly supplied by the *Paradoxical Exercise Concerning Philosophy, the Infallible Interpreter of Scripture*,[25] and the famous Christoph Wittich in his *Peaceable Theology*,[26] and also with particular reference to this matter of doubting, as we have demonstrated elsewhere in our *Gangrene of the Cartesian Innovations*.[27] Specifically it is asked whether the existence of God is not among the things that we are permitted to doubt. Descartes, when asked, responded that we must distinguish between that which pertains to the intellect—and in this way it ought not to be asked whether it is permitted to be doubted, but whether it is able to be, and here he determines and grants that this ability belongs to all who are not convinced of it by solid reason—and that which has to do with the will. And here he proceeds, "We ought to distinguish between that doubt which considers the end and that doubt which considers the means: whoever lays before himself doubt about God as an end sins gravely, because he desires to remain uncertain concerning a matter of such great moment; yet however, if someone proposes to himself doubt as a means to arrive at a clearer knowledge of the truth, he does what is *especially pious and upright*, because no one can desire an end unless he desires the means."[28]

---

25. Lodewijk Meijer (1638–1671), *Philosophia Scripturae interpres, in qua veram philosophiam infallibilem S. Literas normam interpretandi esse apodictice demonstratur* (Amsterdam, 1666); idem, *De philosophie d'uytleghster der h. Schrifture* (Amsterdam, 1667); idem, *Philosophy as the Interpreter of Holy Scripture (1666)*, trans. S. Shirley (Milwaukee: Marquette University Press, 2005).

26. Christoph Wittich (1625–1687), *Theologia pacifica…simul usus philosophiae Cartesianae in diversis theologiae partibus demonstratur* (Leiden: Arnoldus Doude, 1671). Cf. *Biographisch Woordenboek der Nederlanden (BWDN)* (Haarlem: van Hardewijk & Schotel, 1852–1878), 20:399–400; *Nieuw Nederlandsch Biografisch Woordenboek (NNBW)* (Leiden: Sijthoff's Uitgevers-Maatschappij N. V., 1911–1937) 10:1233–34.

27. Cf. Mastricht, *Gangraena*, 1.2.

28. See René Descartes, "Epistola X ad Dominum à Buitendijk" in *Epistolae, partim auctore Latino sermone conscriptae, partim ex Gallico translatae…pars secunda* (Amsterdam: Daniel Elzevier, 1668), 2:34; cf. Latin citation in Mastricht, *Gangraena*, 16. This letter from Descartes to a Leiden student of theology, surnamed Van Buitendijck, was published in part and in Latin by Tobias Andreae in 1653 in order to defend Cartesianism, and cited in response by Jacob Revius. See Tobias Andreae (1604–1676), *Methodi Cartesianae assertio opposita Jacobi Revii…Methodi Cartesianae considerationi theologicae* (Groningen: Cöllen, 1653), 1:947–48; Jacobus Revius (1586–1658), *Kartesiomania…succincte et solide confutatum* (Leiden: Lopez de Haro, 1654), 364–67; cf. Jacob Revius, *A Theological Examination of Cartesian Philosophy*, ed. A. Goudriaan (Leiden: Brill, 2002), 48–49. For a critical translation of this letter, see Letter 66, Descartes to Van Buitendijck (1642–1649), in *The Correspondence of René Descartes 1643*, ed. T. Verbeek, E. J. Bos, J. van de Ven (Utrecht, 2003), 174–76; translation in French, "A Monsieur de Bvitendiich, lettre X" in *Lettres de M. Descartes*, 3 vols. (Paris: C. Angot, 1657–67), 2:53–55.

Here he acknowledges that there exists a kind of doubt that is especially pious and upright. But his followers, without these evasions, roundly profess that all things must be doubted, even the existence of God. This is what we have demonstrated in our *Gangrene of the Cartesian Innovations* (sect. 1, ch. 2, §§1–3).[29]

What do the Reformed say?
The Reformed (1) confess that sometimes things should be doubted, but (2) they deny that all things should be doubted, because this most inflexibly obstructs the way to arrive at any firm knowledge of anything, insofar as we are led to the knowledge of what is uncertain only by what is certain. Furthermore, (3) by no means and at no time should matters of faith, and particularly that God exists, be doubted. At the same time (4) they do not deny that while we are already persuaded by the divine testimonies concerning what must be believed, and especially concerning the existence of God, we should investigate the reasons by which we may be strengthened in this faith more and more. Given these things, they deny that it is ever lawful to doubt concerning matters of faith, and especially concerning the existence of God.

The arguments of the Reformed
They do so because: (1) God in Scripture constantly demands faith in the matters that must be believed (Heb. 11:6), and expressly excludes any sort of doubt whatsoever (Rom. 4:20–21; James 1:6), that in this way we might certify that God is truthful (John 3:33), whereas by doubting we make him a liar (1 John 5:10). (2) It destroys all faith in God, for if you doubt that someone exists, how will you believe that he speaks? How will you place your confidence in him? (3) It destroys all divine worship. For how will you worship, revere, and love a God whom you doubt exists in the nature of things? Hence doubt produces an atheist. (4) According to the determination of the Cartesians, ignorance of the deity and unbelief will sometimes not be regarded as sinful, but will be viewed as a pious and upright thing! (5) If universal doubt be presupposed, you will not have anything to help you ever emerge from doubt, for that which is uncertain to you cannot free you from doubt.

Objections
Meanwhile, in favor of their doubt, the opponents allege (1) that it is an extraordinary support for a certain knowledge of things, indeed that it is also such a support that without it we can know nothing at all for certain. To this we

---

29. Mastricht, *Gangraena*, 13–20.

answer: (a) We acknowledge in doubtful and uncertain matters that doubt can offer some sort of use, but in matters that are certain by the certain revelation of God, such as are all matters of faith, especially the existence of the deity, doubt conveys entirely nothing, in fact it is rather a hindrance. And at the least, (b) universal doubt is so far from being conducive to certitude that it actually obstructs every way to certitude in everything. They allege (2) that by this doubt of theirs they intend nothing other than the suspension of judgment. I respond, Neither do we intend anything else to be understood by doubt, and thus we also declare that it is impious and atheistic to suspend judgment as to whether God exists and whether matters of faith are true or not. They allege (3) that they do not desire a permanent doubt, but a doubt that only subsists for a brief period of time. I respond, They demand a doubt that endures until you have perceived a matter clearly and distinctly—a doubt that in Descartes's case lasted nine years! But what if a duller nature takes more years? What if it never happens? What will happen to simple folk and other uneducated people who do not have the ability to examine the philosophical reasons by which you arrive at certainty? Will they not cling perpetually to atheism, and die in the same frame of mind? Anyone who desires to see these things and more like them considered on both sides can consult my *Gangrene of the Cartesian Innovations* (sect. 1, ch. 2).[30]

2. Are we supplied from the idea of God solid support for acknowledging
and demonstrating the existence of God?

XXII. It is asked, second, whether we are supplied from the idea of God in our mind a solid support for arriving at a knowledge of the divine existence, and also an argument for convincing atheists of the same. The term *idea*, from ἰδεῖν, "to see," for the most part denotes that exemplar that a craftsman carries around in his mind, so that as he prepares to work he sees and considers it beforehand, and directs his work according to it. And this is the practical idea which we will show in considering the divine intellect (bk. 2, ch. 13).[31] Nevertheless, it is not uncommon to employ the term *idea* in reference to any concept of any thing, and in this way an idea is theoretical. By this signification, Plato and his Academics once thought that the ideas of all things were innate to human beings, and that all our effort ought to be expended in digging up these hidden ideas, rousing them, and contemplating them. Descartes and his followers, intent on a new philosophy and seeking new arguments for demonstrating the divine existence, found a twofold idea in man: one innate, the other acquired from the

---

30. Mastricht, *Gangraena*, 13–33.
31. 1.2.13 §§VIII–IX

former by reasoning. First, by *idea* he understands either some sort of concept or thought concerning an infinite being; or a representation or certain similitude of a perfect, infinite being, which representation, with respect to its representative essence, is of the same perfection as God himself. Second, he determines that by the help of this idea alone we should both attain for ourselves the knowledge of the divine existence and demonstrate the same to others. The Reformed gladly acknowledge some concept of God, but such an idea in us that according to its representative essence is of the same perfection with God himself they reject, because they acknowledge only one that is infinitely perfect. In addition, they do not admit that an atheist can be solidly convinced of the existence of God from the idea of God, whatever kind it may be. For (1) if the Cartesians understand by *idea* a simple concept of an infinite being, then the argument will proceed in this way: Whatever I personally have a concept or thought of exists in reality; but I have a concept of an infinitely perfect being; therefore, there is an infinitely perfect being in reality. The atheist will ridicule this by insisting that an Anthropomorphite holds the concept of a corporeal God; does such a God therefore exist? And any atheist has a concept of a God who does not exist; therefore, God does not exist. And (2) if the Cartesians should argue from *idea* as a representation, likeness, or image of an infinite being, infinite in regard to its representative essence, such that from it you conclude the following: If I have a representation of an infinite being, then an infinite being exists; but I have such a representation; therefore, such a being exists—then the atheist will respond (a) to the major premise, that it is incoherent. For I may have an idea of a corporeal God; does such a God therefore exist? (b) To the minor premise, that if he should deny that you have such a representation, how will you demonstrate that you do? If he should say that he does not have it, how will you convince him? If he should add that it is impossible that it exists, since no more than one infinite can exist, and additionally since the finite cannot contain the infinite, how will you solidly oppose him? If you should strive to convince him by piling up the following reasons: (1) You yourself cannot form this idea in your mind, nor can you do so from the instructions of others, or from mere sounds vanishing into the air; he will deny all these things by his experience in receiving instructions, which speaks constantly against this. If you should insist, (2) Say your arguments are true; even so, no finite creature can fashion such an idea, as it is in some sense infinite; he will retort that an infinite idea of this sort, by the reasons already mentioned, is nothing except a chimera. If finally you should press him (3) that every representation requires a certain exemplar from which it has been represented; he will escape by saying that this indeed can be admitted in true ideas, which this is not, but by no means can it be admitted in false ideas, such as that of a corporeal God, a chimera, or wood made of iron. How difficult will it be for you to solidly convince him! Accordingly, the argument from ideas is futile in more than one way. You may consider many similar arguments of this sort in our *Gangrene of the Cartesian Innovations* (sect. 2, ch. 4).[32]

The Practical Part

The first practice, concerning atheism

XXIII. The first practice, then, concerns atheism, that we may beware of it more than a dangerous dog or snake. For since (1) this is the first point known by any theology and religion, that God exists, then whoever denies or doubts that God exists is surely far from all religion. Since (2) "The one who comes to God must believe that he exists," then whoever does not believe, who denies, or who doubts that he exists is certainly far from God, from the highest good, and from salvation. Since (3) the "seeking" of God presupposes his existence, then certainly the negation or doubt of it thoroughly excludes all seeking, all worship of God, and all piety. And if (4) whoever will experience God as a "rewarder" must believe that he exists, and seek the God he knows to exist; then the one who does not even believe that he exists, still less that he should seek him, will certainly experience God as a most fearful avenger.

Three things that are undertaken concerning atheism

Therefore, there are all kinds of reasons why we should beware of atheism, and that we may more successfully do so, we must remember: (1) what atheism is, and how many kinds there are; (2) the reasons why it ought to be avoided; and finally, (3) by what helps it ought to be avoided.[33]

First, what atheism is and how many kinds there are

XXIV. Therefore, atheism, which the Dutch quite appropriately call *god-deloosheit*, "godlessness," is either when we have no God (Eph. 2:12), that is, no God covenanted with us, or when we do not acknowledge God, or rather we do not have him since we do not acknowledge him. And this occurs either in the

---

32. Mastricht, *Gangraena*, 198–217.

33. For the citations in this section on atheism, Mastricht seems to depend heavily on Gisbertus Voetius (1589–1676), *Selectae disputationes theologicae*, 5 vols. (Utrecht: Joannes à Waesberg, 1648–1669), 1:114–226; the original set of disputations over which Voetius presided was held at Utrecht, June 22–July 13, 1639; idem, *Disputationum theologicarum…de atheismo*, 4 parts (Utrecht: Aegidius Roman, 1639). Mastricht also references Gottlieb Spitzel (1639–1691), a Lutheran theologian also known as Theophilus Spizelius, *Scrutinium Atheismi historico-aetiologicum* (Augsburg, 1683), which cross-references Voetius as well.

mind (Ps. 10:4), or in words (Ps. 14:1), or in deeds (Titus 1:16). Thus atheists are either theoretical or practical ones.

Three types of theoretical atheism are observed.

Theoretical atheists, that is, atheists in the most proper and strict sense, those who have denied that God exists not only with their mouth but also fully in their heart, without fear of the contrary, and who constantly have sensed that God does not exist, are (according to Cicero) named in vain, because no such thing has ever existed in reality. For in all the nations, God has not left himself without witness (Acts 14:16–17) and has inscribed his law in their hearts (Rom. 2:14–15). So I marvel that there are even among the Reformed those who, albeit in a way hardly consistent with their principles, have maintained that speculative atheists exist. Moreover, you might perhaps not find more than two or three of those who in a broader sense are speculative atheists, who, although not constantly, nevertheless have openly denied God. But you will have perhaps counted a few more who are such atheists in the broadest sense, those who by public profession have denied the providence, righteousness, or goodness of God. Those who secretly think to themselves that they are so, and who as occasion requires pretend to be so to their followers, are by far in every place the greatest number. Among these are without doubt Lucilio "Julius Caesar" Vanini,[34] Spinoza, and those in France who call themselves deists, or "brave spirits," because they have hardened themselves against all sense and fear of divine providence, punishments, or rewards. Even if paganism had some who were atheists by profession, such as Diagoras of Melos, Protagoras, Theodorus, and others, these were rather those who denied the pagan gods or plural deity rather than God or deity itself, as attested by our own Du Plessis Mornay in *On the Truth of the Christian Religion*, chapter 1.[35] In fact, the aforementioned Theodorus, on account of his profanity called "the Atheist" preeminently, according to Diogenes Laertius fell from atheism into self-theism,[36] and thus he was not fixed in his atheism. Others doubted rather

---

34. Lucilio "Julius Caesar" Vanini (1585–1619) was an early modern free thinker and pantheist executed by the parliament of Toulouse, France for the crimes of atheism and blasphemy on February 9, 1619. See "Vanini, Giulio Cesare Lucio" in *Dizionario di filosofia* (2009). His primary works were: idem, *Amphitheatrum aeternae providentiae divino-magicum, christiano-physicum, nec non astrologo-catholicum* (Lyon: Antoine de Harsy, 1615); idem, *De admirandis naturae reginae deaeque mortalium arcanis libri quatuor* (Paris: Adrian Perier, 1616). Cf. Emile Namer, *La vie et l'œuvre de J.C. Vanini : prince des libertins, mort à Toulouse sur le bûcher en 1619* (Paris, J. Vrin, 1980). Cf. Voetius, *Disputationes selectae*, 1:147–48.

35. Du Plessis Mornay, *De la verité de la religion chrestienne*, 1–20.

36. *authotheismus*. Diogenes Laertius, *Lives of Eminent Philosophers*, 2.85, *Loeb Classical Library* (*LCL*) (Cambridge, Mass.: Harvard University Press, 1972), 184:217.

than denied that God exists, among whom should be numbered Protagoras, who was sent into exile because he made the following introduction to his treatise: "Indeed concerning the gods I cannot decide whether they exist or not."[37] And with him you could number Pope Clement VII, who, being in agony, professed that he was mostly still undetermined on these three things that were doubtful to him throughout his whole life, namely, (1) whether God exists, (2) whether the immortal soul exists, and (3) whether heaven and hell exist. Thus Bellarmine himself, and not without reason, pronounced concerning him, "As far as I know, as far as I understand, he descended into hell."[38]

Practical atheism

But on the other hand are practical atheists, who doubt that God exists, who would prefer that he did not exist, who do this so that they may shake off all sense and fear of deity, who set their belly as their god and live as if they perfectly perceived that God does not exist. Day by day in every place they are observed in large numbers before our eyes, among Christians themselves, in all parts of Europe, as Gottlieb Spitzel shows at length in his *Scrutiny of Atheism*, §§5–13.[39] The sacred page deals chiefly with this sort (Ps. 10:4; 14:1; Eph. 2:12; Phil. 3:19; 2 Tim. 3:4; Titus 1:16).

Second, six motives against atheism

XXV. We understand now what atheism is and how many kinds there are. Now, why it should be carefully avoided, Psalm 14 could teach even nearly on its own, being as it were the seat of this matter. It teaches, namely, that (1) it renders people stupid and irrational; (2) it corrupts a person in his soul, body, and whole life and conversation; (3) it renders him abominable to God as well as to men; (4) it renders him unfit for doing anything good, that is, for any duty either of piety or humanity, and on the contrary casts him headlong into all the crimes that are reviewed in Psalm 10; and (5) it exposes a person to the most dreadful

---

37. Protagoras, *De deis* is no longer extant. Cf. Cicero, *De natura deorum*, 1.63.

38. The pope in the anecdote that Bellarmine is alleged to have remarked upon was Sixtus V, not Clement VII. Cf. William Watson, *A decacordon of ten quodlibetical questions concerning religion and state wherein the author…decides an hundred interrogatorie doubts…betwixt the seminarie priests and the Iesuits at this present* ([London]: Richard Field, 1602), 57. Watson cites an anecdote that Bellarmine said this of Pope Sixtus V (d. 1590): *Qui sine penitentia vivit et sine penitentia moritur, procul dubio ad infernum descendit*, "Whoever lives without penitence and dies without penitence, without a doubt descends to hell." And also, *Conceptis verbis, quantum capio, quantum sapio, quantum intelligo descendit ad infernum*, "With these words uttered, as far as I can grasp, as far as I can perceive, as far as I understand, he descended to hell."

39. Spitzel, *Scrutinium Atheismi*, §§5–13, pp. 13–53.

threats of God. For this reason, Paul connects destruction with atheism (Phil. 3:19), and the psalmist calls on God to break the arm of the wicked and evil man, to pursue his wickedness until he no longer finds any (Ps. 10:15). In fact, (6) it subjects an atheist to the terrible judgments of God, so much so that Guillaume d'Assonleville de Bouchault does not hesitate to pronounce, in his *Atheomastix* (bk. 1, ch. 15), that hardly an atheist can be named, whether in the Holy Scriptures, or in church history, or in the writings of the heathen, who did not meet horrible destruction.[40] Calvin has an especially memorable example in his *Commentary* on Psalm 115:16. "It once happened," he says, "that while we were dining in a certain inn a profane despiser of God, deriding our conversation concerning the hope of heavenly life, was repeatedly vomiting out this mockery: 'The heaven, even the heavens, are the Lord's, but the earth he has given to the children of men.' At that moment, suddenly convulsed in torments, he began to cry out, 'O God! O God!', and as he had a large throat, so he filled the whole dining room with his bellowing. I, who had begun to burn with indignation against him, proceeded in my own way, angrily denouncing him so that then at least he would perceive that God was not mocked with impunity; but one from our party, a good and religious man, yet witty, said, 'You invoke God: have you forgotten your philosophy? Why do you not allow God to rest in his own heaven?'"[41] Spitzel brings forth similar examples in sufficiently great abundance in his *Scrutiny of Atheism*, §29.[42]

Third, the remedies of atheism: Preventative remedies

XXVI. The remedies of atheism remain: remedies of both kinds, namely, preventative and restorative ones. Among the preventative remedies are those

---

40. Guillaume d'Assonleville de Bouchault (1565–1597), a Roman Catholic minor nobleman from the environs of Brussels and Antwerp, *Atheomastix, sive, adversus religionis hostes universos (politicos maxime) dissertatio* (Antwerp: Joannes Moret Plantin, 1598). This work, however, being a *dissertatio*, is too short to have books and chapters, and is ill-suited to Mastricht's detailed citation and general point; namely, the argument of d'Assonleville de Bouchault's work is that enemies of the Roman Catholic faith should be suppressed politically. Thus it seems Mastricht is probably citing the *Atheomastix* indirectly. There is another work entitled *Atheomastix* in English that is not authored by d'Assonleville de Bouchault. It is a substantial volume, and perfectly fits Mastricht's citation. Cf. bk. 1, c. 15, "That God hath at all times powred downe his iust iudgments, vpon the heads of atheists,… (2) examples out of Scriptures, (3) examples out of ecclesiastical histories, (4) examples out of heathen writers…" in Martin Fotherby (1559–1619), *Atheomastix clearing foure truthes against atheists and infidels* (London: Nicholas Oakes, 1622), 158–62.

41. On Psalm 115:16, John Calvin, *Calvin's Commentaries* (Grand Rapids: Baker Books, 1999), 6:356; cf. G. Spitzel, *Scrutinium Atheismi*, 132–33.

42. Spitzel, *Scrutinium Atheismi*, 130–35.

things that must be shunned. First, we must shun the opinions that directly seduce us to atheism. Included in this kind are, among many others, (1) that anyone can be saved in his own religion, which, as the apostle warns, must be cautiously avoided (Eph. 4:14–15; Mic. 4:5). (2) That divine providence does not keep watch over every minute individual thing particularly, and not over the individual operations of men (Ps. 94:7–12), whether by punishing evil deeds or by rewarding good ones (Ps. 75:7). (3) That the immortality of souls is a fiction (Eccl. 3:19). Second, we must shun the practice of impiety, by which someone inordinately loving himself, and for the sake of himself loving his sins, acts in hatred toward first the law of God, since it is hostile to his sins, and from there the Lawgiver himself. From this at last he begins to turn over in his mind and to persuade himself of the nonexistence of God, which he greatly prefers.

The causes of atheism: First, the more general causes

Third, we must shun the causes of atheism, both general and specific ones. Appearing in the first category are: (1) nefarious teachers of atheism, such as once was Lucilio Vanini with his thirteen worthless associates in Naples who were sent out to spread that venom throughout all Europe (as reported by Marin Mersenne in *Renowned Questions on Genesis*),[43] and recently among the Dutch, Benedict Spinoza, a man greatly celebrated in atheistic societies. (2) Books of the same sort, among which is the infamous *Treatise of the Three Impostors*, which they attribute to Pietro Aretino;[44] Geoffroy Vallée's book *The Art of Believing Nothing*;[45] especially

---

43. Cf. Marin Mersenne, O.M. (also Marin Mersennus, 1588–1648), *Quaestiones celeberrimae in Genesim...in hoc volumine athei, deistae impugnantur et expugnantur, et Vulgata editio ab haereticorum calumniis vindicatur* (Paris: Sebastian Cramoisy, 1623), 477–78; on the spread of atheism across Europe, see 671, cf. Voetius, *Selectae disputationes*, 1:131.

44. Pietro Aretino (1492–1556) was infamous for his ribald sonnets, satirical pasquinades, and sexually explicit prose and plays. *De tribus impostoribus* was a work rumored to exist from the medieval period onward, in which Moses, Christ, and Muhammad are shown to be frauds. There were works that were penned in the early modern period claiming to be the lost manuscript. "But whether or not [*De tribus impostoribus*] (which ought not to have been written), exists, was extant, or ever existed, it touches upon a true issue: there once were not lacking and even now there are not lacking those who claim that Moses, the prophets and apostles were frauds," Christian Kortholt (1633–1694), *De tribus impostoribus magnus liber* (Kiel: Joachim Reumann, 1680), 2. Kortholt's work is a Protestant response that the three impostors and "founders of the new wisdom" are in fact Edward Herbert of Cherbury (1583–1648), Thomas Hobbes (1588–1679), and Benedict Spinoza (1632–1677), 3. On Aretino as a possible author of *De tribus impostoribus*, see idem, *De tribus impostoribus magnus liber*, 1; Spitzel, *Scrutinium Atheismi*, 18–19.

45. Geoffroy Vallée II (c. 1535–1574), author of *La béatitude des Chrétiens ou le Fléau de la foy*, (Paris, ca. 1572), published recently under the title *L'Art de ne croire en rien: suivi de livre des trois imposteurs* (Paris, 2002), was condemned by the Parliament of Paris, hanged, and burned for "having held and maintained blasphemies and errors...against the honor of God and our holy mother

Spinoza's *Theological-Political Treatise*;[46] and Lucilio Vanini's *Amphitheatre of Eternal Providence*.[47] (3) Slippery conversations concerning God, his providence, and the immortality of our soul, among which is the well-known quodlibetal disputation held before Leo X, where between two men one proved with all reasons that God exists and the other denied it, and the pope at last pronounced to the former, "Indeed, your opinion is the truer one," and to the latter, "but yours makes for a merrier face."[48]

Next, four more specific causes

XXVII. In the category of specific causes of atheism, (1) the first place is occupied by the sacrilegious disparaging, reviling, and distorting of the Holy Book for any reason, such as that of Pietro Bembo, who said to Sadoleto about the Scriptures, "Give up this nonsense! Such follies are not fitting for a serious man!";[49] of Lazzaro Bonamico, "I prefer the odes of Pindar to the Psalms of David";[50] or of Angelo Ambrogini, "I once read through that book," that is, Scripture, "and I have never made a poorer use of time."[51] Next is (2) the profane religion of the Machiavellians, the Hobbesians, the pseudo-political theorists, and all of those who brazenly hold that all religion is only an instrument for preserving the civil state. To this end also we see Dietrich Reinking (*On Government*, bk. 2, ch. 1, no. 48) referencing this same so-called "Reason of State."[52] Then there is

---

Church," Frédéric Lachèvre, *Geoffroy Vallée (brûlé le 9 février 1574) et La béatitude des Chrestiens: l'ancêtre des libertins du XVIIe siècle* (Paris, 1920). Cf. Gisbertus Voetius, who refers to *La béatitude* as *De arte nihil credendi*, and dates it to 1572: idem, *Selectae disputationes*, 1:136.

46. Benedict Spinoza, *Tractatus theologico-politicus* (Hamburg [Amsterdam]: Henricus Künrath, 1670); idem, *Spinoza: Theological-Political Treatise*, ed. J. Israel (Cambridge: Cambridge University Press, 2007).

47. Vanini, *Amphitheatrum aeternae providentiae* (1615).

48. Cf. Voetius, *Selectae disputationes*, 1:131.

49. On Cardinal Pietro Bembo (1470–1547) see C. Dionisotti, "Pietro Bembo," in *Dizionario biografico degli Italiani (DBI)*, 88 vols. (Rome: Istituto dell'Enciclopedia Italiana, 1960–present), 8 (1966):133–51. For this anecdote, "Omitte has nugas, non enim decent gravem virum tales ineptiae," see Spitzel, *Scrutinium Atheismi*, 21; Gregory Michael, *Notae in Jacobi Gaffarelli curiositates* (Hamburg, Gothofredus Schultz, 1676), 111; "Bembus (Pierre)" in Pierre Bayle, *Dictionnaire Historique et Critique*, 5th ed. (Amsterdam, 1740), 1:516, note F; idem, *The Dictionary historical and critical of Mr. Peter Bayle*, trans. Des Maizeaux, 2nd ed. (London: 1734), 1:743, note F.

50. On Lazzaro Bonamico (1479–1552), or often Lazarus Buonamicus, see R. Avesani, "Bonamico, Lazzaro," *DBI* 11 (1969), 533–40.

51. *Angelus Politianus*: On the humanist poet, Angelo Ambrogini (1454–1494), also known as "il Poliziano" or Politian from his birthplace of Montepulciano (Lat. *Mons Politianus*), see *DBI* 2 (1960), 691–702.

52. See the excursus "Appendix de ratione status" in Dietrich Reinking (Theodorus Reinking, 1590–1664), *Tractatus de regimine seculari et ecclesiastico* (Frankfurt: J. M. Porss, 1659), 810–12; for bk. 2. ch. 1, no. 48, p. 811.

(3) repeated change of religion or crossing over from sect to sect, which finally unburdens itself in atheism, no different from polytheism, whether simultaneous or successive, which finally ends up in atheism. Lastly, (4) that perverse treatment of natural wisdom, by which a great many, with reckless (or should I say, insane) effort, so confine all things within the bounds of nature, not fearing, with the primary cause subordinated, to observe second causes alone, that they persuade themselves that all things, without the most high Director, follow this or that course according to their own natural disposition. Peter seems to allude to these in 2 Peter 3:3–5. And they search in such a way into the natural causes of things that in so doing they well enough take away supernatural and miraculous causes. For this reason, the elite assembly of cardinals in Rome branded doctors and philosophers in Italy who were otherwise preeminent priests of nature with the mark of atheism.

Five restorative remedies of atheism

XXVIII. Now comes what pertains to restorative remedies, those designed for routing atheism when it already exists. You will act most effectively if: (1) you use invincible arguments to convince the mind of an atheist of God's existence and God's providence. (2) You solidly refute his petty reasons to the contrary. (3) You prudently explain to him the book of nature and its three pages, as it were: heaven, earth, and the seas, with all that they contain. (4) You set the book of Scripture everywhere before his mind and eyes, by which strategy alone the father of Franciscus Junius, who was first an atheist and then a most renowned theologian, called him back from atheism to religion, by setting a volume of the Bible before his eyes in every room of his house.[53] Finally, (5) you tire out God by your prayers, that he might breathe his benediction on your efforts in the conversion of the atheist.

The second practice, concerning ignorance of God

XXIX. The second practice regards ignorance of God, which also must be avoided in all ways. For as the knowledge of deity is necessary in so many ways (according to §XVII), it is certain that in just as many ways the ignorance of it will be dangerous. By *ignorance* I mean: (1) simple ignorance, whether negative or privative, that is, ignorance of the true God (Gal. 4:8; Isa. 45:4–5). (2) Feigned or studied ignorance (Job 21:14; 2 Peter 3:5; Ex. 5:2). (3) Practical

---

53. Cf. Franciscus Junius (1545–1602), *A Treatise on True Theology with the Life of Franciscus Junius*, trans. David C. Noe (Grand Rapids: Reformation Heritage Books, 2014), 26–34.

ignorance, by which many people indeed know God with their brain or tongue, with a knowledge that is frigid and idle, but are ignorant as to their affection and its effective operation (Titus 1:16; Matt. 7:21).

Why must it be avoided?
All such ignorance must be sedulously avoided because (1) as God laments, it casts man lower than the beasts (Isa. 1:3). It renders people inept (2) for believing (Heb. 11:6; Rom. 10:14; Eph. 4:18); (3) for "seeking" God, for there is no desire for a thing unknown (John 4:10); (4) for finding or "coming to" God; (5) for "pleasing" God; and (6) for experiencing God as a "rewarder." (7) It exposes us to the danger of idolatry (Gal. 4:8). (8) It locates us outside the communion of the covenant of grace (Jer. 31:34). (9) It makes us liable to every kind of curse and plague in this life (Hos. 4:1–3; Jer. 10:25; Ps. 79:6); and (10) to eternal flames in the next (2 Thess. 1:8). For this reason, so that we may come to the aid of this ignorance, its causes and sources come forth for consideration: (1) the mind of the flesh (1 Cor. 2:14; 2 Cor. 10:5), (2) impiety (Isa. 28:9), (3) a lack of faithful instruction (Acts 8:30–31; 2 Tim. 2:25), and (4) a lack of assiduous study (2 Tim. 3:7).

The third practice, concerning the exploration of knowledge
XXX. The third practice is occupied with the examination of the true knowledge of God. For since not just any knowledge suffices, since not common knowledge but saving knowledge is required, an exploration is needed that we may know whether we are endowed with any knowledge of God, and whether with knowledge of the saving kind. Our text supplies the criteria of this knowledge: if (1) it generates faith in the "rewarder" (Prov. 3:6); (2) it rouses the appetite to "seek" him once recognized; (3) it leads toward God, toward "coming to him," that is, that we may by faith receive him once found (John 1:11–12); (4) it excites zeal in all circumstances "to please God" (Jer. 9:7; 1 John 2:3–4); (5) by a true confidence of the soul, it longs to experience, in him once known, that God is a "rewarder"; and furthermore, (6) it rejoices in the requirements and qualities of saving knowledge, such as (a) that it is experiential, not derived by hearing alone, or the reading of books, or the revelation of another, intruding into things which it has not seen (Col. 2:18), but by the very sense of experience, and as it were, by sight (Ps. 34:8; 1 Peter 2:3), that is, in knowledge and all discernment (Phil. 1:9). (b) That it is living and practical, bearing not only light but also heat, and is a burning lamp (John 5:35), by which the heart burns (Luke 24:32) and becomes prompt to love, to seek, and to worship the God that is known; and accordingly, not a knowledge which is only theoretical, frigid, sterile, and disengaged,

consisting rather in form than in power (2 Tim. 3:5), which is without love (1 Cor. 13:2). (c) That it is deep, resting upon the foundation of the prophets and apostles (Eph. 2:20), rooted in the depths of the heart (Col. 2:6–7), received from heaven, namely, the wisdom from above (James 3:17), a knowledge in which, by revealing himself, God shines, as it were, in the heart (2 Cor. 4:6), not a superficial and perfunctory knowledge.

The fourth practice, concerning zeal for the knowledge of God, in five particular things: 1. The persons whose responsibility it is to care for this knowledge
XXXI. At this point remains the fourth practice, concerning care for the knowledge of God (Hos. 6:3). And this care, if first you consider persons, applies to the following: (1) magistrates, that they may not be content to have provided a knowledge of God for themselves, but that they may in every way take care, by their example, by their calling of qualified teachers, and even as circumstances arise, by their own instruction, to confer and augment the knowledge of God in their subjects, according to the example of Moses, Joshua, David, Solomon, and others. (2) Ministers, upon whom it is preeminently incumbent by their office to instill in their hearers the knowledge of God, and namely that knowledge which is the basis of all faith, religion, and godliness, according to the judgment of the text, that God exists (John 14:8; 2 Peter 1:1–2; Phil. 1:9). (3) Every believer (see the same passages).

2. The character of this care for the knowledge of God
Second, if you consider the knowledge of God that must be cared for, it does not rest in some sort of common knowledge, by which it knows "that God exists," or it knows only theoretically, superficially, frigidly, and lazily, but it strives toward a knowledge that is experiential, living, and deep, a knowledge that impels it to "seek God," to "come to God," to "please him," that he might be experienced as a "rewarder," just as we taught in the preceding sections.

3. The parts of this care
Third, if you consider the care itself and its parts, not only should we equip ourselves with the knowledge of God, but we should daily strive to make progress in it more and more (2 Peter 3:18; 1 Peter 2:2; Col. 1:9–10; Rom. 15:14; 1 Cor. 2:4–5).

4. Motives
Fourth, if you consider the reasons recommending this zeal for the knowledge of God, then they will be supplied: (1) from its excellency, since it supplies to

us the chief argument for our worthiness and glorying (Jer. 9:23–24), and on account of it, Paul held everything in indifference (Phil. 3:8), just as if he had the privilege of eternal glory, where we will see (that is, we will know) God face to face (1 Cor. 13:12), indeed the privilege of angels (Matt. 18:10; Isa. 6:1–2), which accordingly Moses sought with such great zeal (Ex. 33:13–14). (2) From its pleasantness, for just as the chief felicity and sweetness of the chief part of our soul, namely the intellect, is in knowledge and wisdom, so the more excellent the object of knowledge is, the sweeter it is to come to know it. Thus in the knowledge of the one who is most excellent, there cannot but be the most excellent sweetness, such that not undeservedly, in the most perfect foreknowledge or vision of God is constituted the chief part of blessedness (1 Cor. 13:12; John 17:3; cf. 2 Peter 1:19). (3) From its utility, whereby the knowledge of God is conducive (a) to conversion (1 Tim. 2:4; 2 Tim. 2:25; 2 Peter 1:20); (b) to justification (Isa. 53:11); (c) to sanctification, so that we may believe (according to the text), we may seek God, come to God, and study to please God, so that we may not be lazy and sterile but abound in every duty and all piety (2 Peter 1:2–3, 6, 8); (d) to glorification (John 17:3); (e) to obtaining every kind of blessing, grace, and peace (2 Peter 1:2–3), that is, that we may always and everywhere experience God as a "rewarder"; and (f) to keep us from the perniciousness of ignorance, concerning which see §XXIX.

5. Means

Finally, fifth, if you consider the means, the following will assist: (1) a constant and assiduous use of the supports, both general and special, which we mentioned in §§XXVI–XXVIII.[54] In particular, I would recommend (2) that you ponder the book of nature, and each of its pages—heaven, earth, and the seas, and the things contained in all of them, as Augustine advises: "Ask the universe, the adornment of the heavens, the brilliance and arrangement of the stars, the sun, the sufficiency of the day, the moon, the solace of the night. Ask the earth, bearing fruit in herbs and trees, filled with animals, adorned with men. Ask the sea, full of such great and varied aquatic creatures! Ask the air, flourishing with such great flying creatures! Ask all things if they do not, in their own sense, as it were respond to you, 'God made us!'"[55] (3) That we especially ponder, constantly and devotedly, the book of Scripture, where God reveals himself to us as perfectly as can be done, such that on every page, it proclaims and points to

---

54. See also §§XIX–XX.
55. Augustine, Sermon 141 on John 14:6, cap. 2, PL 38:778.

God. (4) That we tire out God with our most eager prayers that he would reveal himself to us and inscribe the knowledge of himself on our hearts, according to the promise of the covenant of grace (Jer. 31:33–34), after the example of Moses (Ex. 33:13–14; cf. 2 Cor. 4:6).

CHAPTER THREE

The Essence and Independence of God

And Moses said to God, "Behold, I will go to the children of Israel, and I will say to them, 'The God of your fathers has sent me to you.' And they will say to me, 'What is his name?' What will I answer them?" And God said to Moses, "I WILL BE WHO I WILL BE." In addition he said, "Thus you will say to the children of Israel, 'I WILL BE has sent me to you.'"
—Exodus 3:13–14

What must be said about God is distinguished
I. We have demonstrated the existence of God and the way of knowing of him; now we will elaborate on his essence, which is made known to us partly by his names and partly by his attributes. We will treat each separately. Yet before all these things, as if on the threshold, we will set forth the imperceptibility of the divine essence. Thus in this chapter it is incumbent upon us to explain two points: the *imperceptibility* of the essence and the imperceptible *essence*. And who would teach both of these more successfully than God himself, and there especially in the place where he expressly intended to teach Moses about himself? That is, in the words prefixed above, Exodus 3:13–14.

The Exegetical Part
The text is resolved and explained.
II. In this text, it is as if an instrument promoting faith (commonly called "credentials") is placed by God into the hands of Moses as he is about to be sent to lead the Israelites out of Egyptian slavery. Regarding it we observe three things:
   A. The undertaking of the mission God offered to Moses in the preceding words. It consists in a twofold duty:
      1. Going to the children of Israel, which God had committed to him and he had declined (Ex. 3:10–11): "Behold, I will go to the children of Israel."

    2. Giving a message to the children of Israel, or delivering his creden-
tials: "I will say, 'The God of your fathers has sent me to you.'" By
this the Lord of this mission is described, first by his proper name
אלהים, *Elohim*, which we will treat in its own place,[1] and next by the
particular relation to the ancestors of the Israelites that arises from
his covenanting with them: "The God of your fathers."

B. The hindrance or difficulty that will be raised in objection to the mission: "They will say to me, 'What is his name?' What will I answer?"
This indicates:

    1. On the one hand, the difficulty that he would undoubtedly encounter
in the future: "They will say to me, 'What is his name?'" They will say
it, that is, either in disbelief, whereby they suspect that he should not
be trusted, unless by a prior investigation of the name and of other
circumstances they had examined his truthfulness, and so before anything else they will question him about the name of the one who sent
him (cf. Matt. 16:1; 21:23–24). Or, they will say it in fleshly curiosity,
whereby when they hear someone making noise about extraordinary
revelations of God, they will inquire about the divine essence and the
name by which it might be made known. This seems to be gathered
from the divine response, wherein seeking to curb their curiosity he
provides to Moses his name that represents his essence. With a similar
curiosity Jacob once asked about the name of the angel (Gen. 32:29),
and later so did Manoah (Judg. 13:17). See also Proverbs 30:4.

    2. On the other hand, his own concern over this difficulty: "What will
I answer them?" This is as if he said, "I myself do not perceive your
essence, I do not know it, and for this reason, I also cannot represent
it by a name. What am I to do?"

C. The removal of this hindrance: "And God said to Moses, 'I will be who
I will be,'" as if he intended to reprehend, first, the curiosity of the Israelites inquiring about his essence and essential name, and next, the
concern of Moses, who was so anxious about this name. For his essence,
as it is spiritual and infinite, is imperceptible to finite creatures, and
thus to require a name to supply such perception is entirely vain. So
then, he rejects the request as if to spurn it: "I am who I am," as if he
is saying, "This has nothing to do with the Israelites and nothing to do
with you," in nearly the same way in which he usually rejects the same

---

1. 1.2.4 §IX

request of others (Gen. 32:29; Judg. 13:17; Prov. 30:4). Unless you prefer to understand that by these words God is assenting to Moses's request, as if he is saying, "You want my name, that it might somehow represent my essence? It is 'Being'": אהיה אשר אהיה, "I am who I am," or "I will be who I will be," or "I will be who I am," or "I am who I will be." On this name, see the next chapter.[2]

FIRST THEOREM—The Imperceptibility of the Divine Essence

The Dogmatic Part

That the essence of God is imperceptible

III. Therefore, the first theorem of this chapter, the preliminary theorem as it were, should be that the very essence of God, what it is in itself, is inaccessible to our intellect. For when the Israelites question Moses, and Moses questions God about the name that would represent the essence of God, what do they imply but that it is unknown to them? And when God answers, "I am who I am," rebuking as it were the obtuseness of the question, what does he mean except that his essence is incomprehensible, and thus ineffable? This is what Zophar, even a bit more clearly, teaches his friend Job, "Will you by searching find out God? Will you reach all the way to the perfection of the all-sufficient one?" (Job 11:7). For this reason, it is said that he dwells in inaccessible light, that no man has seen him, or can see him (1 Tim. 6:16), that is, not only not with the eyes of the body, but also of the mind, for he is absolutely invisible (1 Tim. 1:17). For this reason, when God shows Moses only his back, he denies that his face, by which the essence of persons is as much as possible most properly discerned, can be seen (Ex. 33:20, 23). And so far this point has been beyond doubt among all Christians, against the Anthropomorphites, since all have acknowledged that regarding God's essence we know what he is *not* rather than what he *is*. Neither by his attributes do we consider the very essence of God as much as something about his essence. For they are called *attributes*, as we will show in its own place,[3] and they concern God as if in a certain secondary being, which presupposes his essence, as if a certain primary being.

It is proved.

IV. The reasons for this point are provided: (1) from his simplicity, by which he is one most simple and pure act, free from all composition, which simplicity

---

2. 1.2.4 §VIII

3. 1.2.5 §V

accordingly cannot be conceived of positively. The apostle seems to aim at this in
1 Timothy 6:16, when from the fact that he is light, in the abstract, not a light-
giving substance, in the concrete, the apostle concludes that God is not seen and
cannot be seen. (2) From his infinity, through which he cannot be comprehended
or perceived by a finite intellect. And this infinity, in a paraphrastic distribution,
seems to be pressed to this same end by the passage cited, Job 11:7–9: "Will
you reach all the way to the perfection of the all-sufficient one? It is higher than
the heavens; what will you do? Deeper than hell; what will you know? It is longer than the earth and broader than the sea." (3) From his most simple unity,
through which he is so different from all the creatures that he corresponds with
them in nothing and stands apart from them in everything, such that from no
thing can we borrow an idea of the divine essence, and thus neither can we form
a representation of essence,[4] or a definition properly so-called (which is nothing
other than a description of essence). We will say more about this a little later.[5]

An objection
V. The things that could be objected to this are: that in the Holy Scriptures,
God is frequently said to have been seen by the saints, for example, Abraham
(Gen. 18:1), Isaac (Gen. 26:2), Jacob (Gen. 32:29), Moses (Ex. 33:11), Job (Job
42:5), Isaiah (Isa. 6:1), Micaiah (1 Kings 22:19); and that it is believed that he
will one day be seen by the saints (Job 19:27), and indeed, "face to face" (1 Cor.
13:12), and so forth. Such passages must be understood to concern either a sym-
bolic vision, which perceives not his essence but his operation, under certain
signs; or the human nature of Christ, and in it, the nature of God himself (John
14:9), through emperichoresis;[6] or some sort of more perfect knowledge of God
in blessedness which in its perfection will be similar to vision or ocular knowledge, and in fact will surpass it. But by no means do these passages import a
vision or perception of the essence itself.

The sense of the theorem is explained.
VI. Yet at the same time, in order more fittingly to understand the intention of
our theorem, let us observe the following: (1) the discussion is not about God,
but precisely about the essence of God, insofar as in the formal sense it is conceived of as different from his attributes, subsistence, and actions, though it is a
received truth that all these things coincide in the identical sense; or, insofar as

---

4. λόγον οὐσίας
5. §IX
6. Here, the coinherence of Christ's two natures in his one person.

his essence is conceived of as some substratum or primary being, which his attributes, as it were, make complete. Next (2) regarding the essence, the discussion is not *that* it is, for our intellect in many ways most clearly perceives that, but rather, *what* it is, and that indeed in itself and not in its attributes, insofar as they are conceived of as distinct from his essence. Finally, concerning this quiddity of the divine essence, we declare that (3) it is inaccessible to our intellect (according to the preceding reasons), that is, we cannot touch it with our knowledge, whether comprehensive or apprehensive, since in this way we are not even able to grasp the essence of angels or of our own soul.

The Elenctic Part

It is asked: 1. Do we have a positive concept of the divine essence?

VII. It is asked, first, whether we have a positive concept of the divine essence. A positive concept is opposed to a negative concept in this way: in the former we ponder what a thing is on its own part; in the latter, what it is not. Since Descartes and his followers suppose that (1) the divine essence consists in nothing except mere, infinite thought; (2) man carries in his mind the idea of infinite being; and (3) absolutely nothing must be admitted except what we clearly and distinctly perceive; they state that we do have a positive concept of the very essence of God. The Reformed, although they admit positive concepts of several attributes of God, even so concerning the very essence of God commonly do not acknowledge any but negative concepts, by which we hold concerning the essence what it is not, rather than what it is in itself. We have already set forth the bases for this view in §IV. We do not add anything here except this one point, that we do not even have such a concept of our own soul, though it is finite; in fact, formally speaking, we do not even have such a concept of the essence of a dog or pig, indeed I say of any thing at all, except from its attributes, properties, and operations. For example, we have a concept of a dog from its barking. But what do we have regarding the divine essence, which is infinitely different from our soul and from all other things? If the Cartesians should say for themselves (1) that the essence of God consists in infinite thought, of which we have a positive concept, we respond: (a) It is false that the essence of God consists in mere thought, which we will expressly demonstrate in the following theorem.[7] And (b) even if it did entirely consist in mere thought, nevertheless there remains an infinite separation between the divine thought and any creature's thought, such that from the thought of the creatures you cannot form

---

7. §XIX

a concept of the thought of God, according to Isaiah 55:8. If they should say, (2) At the same time, we do have some concept of God and the divine essence, or, what is the same thing, some kind of idea of the divine essence, I respond, Yes, but we have a concept *that* it is; not, however, *what* it is in itself. We have a concept that he exists, for the reasons presented and vindicated in the preceding chapter, and thus that he has a certain essence. We have a concept of what that essence is not: for example, it is not material, not dependent, not mutable, not composite, not finite. We likewise have a concept, and indeed a positive one, of its properties: for example, intellect, will, goodness, love, grace, mercy, righteousness, holiness, omnipotence, and so forth. By joining these things together we do have some kind of concept of what sort of essence it is, but of that very essence, what it is in itself, we have entirely no concept. In the same way we also have a concept of the sun, that it is—namely, from our vision and from the effects that it produces in terrestrial things—but of the essence itself, what it is in itself— whether it is a solid or fluid, whether it is fire properly so called—we are deeply ignorant. If they should say, (3) To us, nothing should be admitted of which we do not have a clear and distinct perception, for such perception is the norm of all truth, and for this reason, if we do not have a positive conception of the divine essence, we will all be atheists, I respond: (a) We deny that we should properly admit nothing unless we have clearly and distinctly perceived it, until those who claim the opposite have solidly proven it. And (b) we likewise deny that a clear and distinct perception is the norm for acknowledging all truth. We can admit, for example, that the sun has an essence, although we may be ignorant what and of what sort that essence is. And thus by no means will we be atheists when we do know that God exists and that he has an essence, although what that essence is on its own part is hidden from us.

2. Do we have an idea representatively equal to God?

VIII. Here could recur the question whether there is in us an idea of the divine essence which, according to its representative or ideal being, is of the same infinite perfection as the divine essence itself? Descartes and his followers affirm this; the Reformed generally deny it. But because we already aired this question in both its parts in the preceding chapter, it is sufficient at present to refer the reader back to it.[8]

---

8. 1.2.2 §XXII

3. Can God be defined?

IX. It is asked, third, whether God can be properly defined. For since a definition properly speaking is a λόγος οὐσίας, a representation of essence, and since the divine essence is inscrutable, it is not inappropriate to examine this controversy here. John Duns Scotus and his Scotists, since he supposes that we can have a concept of an infinitely perfect infinite being, and also that we can represent it in words, affirm that God can be defined.[9] Likewise Conrad Vorstius and his Socinians, because he stated that God is finite in essence and exists in heaven alone, and is in addition a composite being, affirms the same. Descartes and his followers, since he located the essence of God in infinite thought, thus considered "infinite thought" as a definition properly speaking. The Reformed distinguish between a description and a definition in this way: a description is a representation of a thing from its attributes or properties, as when, for example, you say that man is a featherless biped. They willingly acknowledge that descriptions of God are of the same sort, as when, for example, you say that God is the absolutely first being, or Spirit from himself. But they by no means allow a definition of him, properly speaking, whereby his essence is represented as it exists in itself, because: (1) the essence of God is imperceptible, as we demonstrated in §IV, and accordingly it cannot be represented by a definition. (2) There is not a univocal genus that is appropriate for God and creatures, because he stands infinitely far apart from them all. And there is not a specific difference by which he differs from them, since he stands apart from all of them not in this or that respect, but in all respects. However, according to all logicians, those two parts are essential to any definition. (3) A definition properly speaking argues for composition, namely that of genus and difference, which composition, because it presupposes one who composes as prior, cannot be consistent with the absolutely first being. (4) By the same stroke it imports finitude and limitation, not only in our understanding of the *definitum*,[10] but also in the *definitum* itself. And so also (5) it argues for act and potency in God, because a genus is constituted as a potency that is actuated through difference. Finally, (6) it also argues for imperfection, because first is conceived the genus which, as if in potency, is to be actuated and perfected through the difference, and then second, although the difference is conceived of as more perfect than the genus, still both parts are presupposed to be more imperfect than the whole *definitum*.

---

9. Cf. John Duns Scotus, *Ord.* I, d. 2, qq. 1–2, n. 26, Vat. III:18, "I assert that God is not only conceived in a concept analogous to the concept of a creature (namely, a concept which is entirely different from a concept of said creature), but also in some concept that is univocal to God and creatures."

10. That is, the thing defined. See 1.1.1 §I, nn. 1, 2.

Three objections

X. It is not true what they object: (1) that we can have an idea of the divine essence actually present to us, and that we can also express it in words, which is what it means to define. Besides the fact that this objection presupposes what is in question, namely, that we have an idea properly speaking of the divine essence, also, a definition properly speaking is not immediately constructed from any sort of idea, because an idea can come from the accidents of a thing, whereas this sort of definition is a λόγος οὐσίας, a representation of essence. (2) That "the being perfect in the highest degree" is the definition of God. For not only is "being" not a univocal genus, but also, it does not so much explain the essence of God as it only proposes it. And in addition, we see that "perfect in the highest degree" expresses only the relation of God whereby he exceeds all creatures in perfection. Hence, from this emerges a definition no more accurate than if I should assert that man is the most perfect terrestrial being. (3) That at the least, "infinite thought" is such a definition of God. For neither does the essence of God consist more in thought than, for example, in reprobation, nor are finite and infinite so much properties of an action as rather properties of an agent, which things perpetually differ according to our ideas, that is, according to our clear and distinct perceptions. Our *Gangrene of the Cartesian Innovations* explains more things of this kind (sect. 2, ch. 5).[11]

The Practical Part

The first practice constrains fleshly curiosity.

XI. The first practice of the preliminary theorem restrains the vain curiosity of those who, either in order to satisfy an idle desire to know things higher than themselves, or so that they may seem wiser than the common lot, (1) examine in a prying way the divine essence and other similar things (Ex. 3:3; 33:18; John 14:8), as if by examining they might find out God and attain to the perfection of the all-sufficient one (Job 11:7). Such people accordingly (2) more audaciously make pronouncements about it, for example, that the divine essence is nothing but thought. Thus they are thinking beyond what is written (1 Cor. 4:6) and intruding into things which they have not seen (Col. 2:18). Then, (3) they boast of ideas of the infinite divine essence that according to their representative essence are entirely adequate to God. Is this not striving for the perfection of the all-sufficient one and aspiring to the secret things of God (Deut. 29:29)?

---

11. Mastricht, *Gangraena*, 217–25.

Why vain curiosity must be avoided

This curiosity is (1) rebuked by God himself (Ex. 3:4–5) and by our Savior (John 14:8–10), and (2) thus thoroughly forbidden (Ex. 19:21). Such curiosity is (3) not only desiring to know beyond what is written (1 Cor. 4:6) and beyond what is proper (Rom. 12:3), but also (4) desiring with a foolish arrogance to comprehend what is infinite (Job 11:7), (5) striving for nothing other than puffing people up with a vain swelling of knowledge (1 Cor. 8:1). It is (6) the first source of all idolatry, as indicated by God himself (Deut. 4:15–16) and by the example of the Gentiles (Rom. 1:22–23), namely, when men tried to represent before their eyes a fabricated appearance of God through likenesses and images, on which they afterward judged that divine honors ought to be conferred. Accordingly, (7) God declares that such curiosity must be restrained by the penalty of death (Ex. 19:21). And (8) sometimes he inflicted this penalty (1 Sam. 6:19).

The second practice encourages modesty.

XII. The second practice encourages us to pay attention to modesty when we are engaged with God's essence and essentials. This modesty is cultivated in these particulars: (1) we should not prepare ourselves for meditation on these things without first having sought divine direction and illumination (Eccl. 5:1; 2 Cor. 4:6), according to David's example (Ps. 119:18). (2) We should not be occupied in this meditation without a pious fear and apprehensiveness, because it is perilous to speak even true things about God. In this way Abraham conducted himself concerning God (Gen. 18:31). (3) We should not declare anything in this matter unless divine utterances have been consulted: "If they should say, 'What is his name?,' what will I answer?" (Ex. 3:13–14). And we should do these things (4) recognizing the blindness and ignorance of the mind (Prov. 30:3–4), and thus, (5) as it were, remove our shoes (Ex. 3:5–6) and cover our face, according to the example of the angels (Isa. 6:2–3).

The impelling reasons

(1) God requires this modesty of those who draw near to him (Lev. 10:3). (2) The nature of the thing requires it, namely, that a puny human being occupied with God and divine things must be zealous for modesty. For if Moses reverently took off his shoes on account of the place on which he was standing because it was holy, why not all the more on account of the very God with whom we deal (Ex. 3:5; 19:10–11)? (3) The judgments of God, which fall on those who treat divine matters with too little reverence, require modesty (Ex. 19:12); for example, the judgments on Korah, Dathan, and Abiram (Num. 16, esp. v. 35),

Uzzah (2 Sam. 6:6–7), the inhabitants of Beth-shemesh (1 Sam. 6:19), and Uzziah (2 Chron. 26:16–20).

The supports

Finally, so that we may be rendered more prompt toward this modesty, it will help to use these means, among others: (1) we must religiously compare the majesty of the divine essence and the divine essentials with our worthlessness, according to the example of Abraham (Gen. 18:27). Then (2) we must earnestly turn over in our mind the infinite distance of God and divine things from our intellect, namely, "It is higher than the heavens, what will you do? It is deeper than hell, what will you know? It is longer than the earth and broader than the sea" (Job 11:8–9). Thus here one may use the well-known adage, "God is infinite; we are finite" (cf. 1 Cor. 1:23; Rom. 8:7). So then (3) we must think about how disposed we are to be deceived in matters so removed from our natural capacity (1 Cor. 2:14), and also how perilous and harmful it is to stumble and err in matters of such great importance (Job 42:7). The things we have said here by way of preliminary introduction should be sufficient.

SECOND THEOREM—The Very Essence or Independence of God

The Didactic Part

God's essence is that by which he is the absolutely first being.

XIII. Moreover, although according to the preceding theorem the essence of God, as it is in itself, is imperceptible, yet notwithstanding, so that God might accommodate himself as best as can be done to the weakness of our mind, that is, so that we might not perceive absolutely nothing about his essence, he willed to designate it by such a name that he might most suitably convey it. Namely, he is ὁ ὤν, "the one who is," or τὸ ὄν, "the thing that is," which is to say that he does not exist from any other, or that he is the absolutely first being, or the one utterly independent of any other prior cause: of an efficient cause from which he would exist, of a material cause from which he would have been formed, of a formal cause through which he would be what he is, and of a final cause to which he would have been directed. This is what he wanted to signify to Moses as he asked him what his name was, that is, his essential name, when he responded, אהיה אשר אהיה ("I will be who I will be," or "I am who I am," or "I will be who I am," or "I am who I will be"). This is to signify that he is that being, or he has such an essence, that coexists with all types of time, as he is in eternity. For this reason, as a name to bring to the Israelites, he attributed to himself אהיה, "I

will be," namely, "I will always be the same." Psalm 102:26–27 says ואתה הוא,
"you are that הָוָא," where וא, separate from ה, means "he was," which is numbered
among the names of God by the kabbalists.[12] So then afterwards, speaking to
Moses he names himself יהוה, the LORD, and adds that this is *his own* name
and *his own* memorial, so proper to him that he wants it to be shared with no
one (Isa. 42:8). Regarding this name we will say more things expressly in its own
place.[13] The summary of what God said amounts to this: he intended to have signified to Moses that he exists, that is, preeminently so, that he possesses essence,
indeed that he alone is essence, that is, universal essence, and essence from himself, whereas all creatures have only a small part of essence, they lack the essence
of the other creatures, and thus by that reckoning it is more true to say that they
do not have essence than that they have it. God intended to say that he has such
an essence from which is derived, and upon which depends, all the essence of
all things, that he has such an essence that comes from no one and nothing, and
accordingly that he is the first being, not in this or that species only, in the way
that Adam was the first among men, but absolutely first.

It is proved by the Scriptures.
XIV. John indicates the same thing paraphrastically in Revelation 1:8, "'I am the
Alpha and the Omega,' says the Lord (Jehovah) God, 'who is and who was and
who is to come,'" and in 16:5, with added words in 21:6, "the beginning and the
end," and also in 22:13, "the first and the last." Isaiah had already said the same
thing in Isaiah 44:6: "Thus says Jehovah…'I am the first and the last, and besides
me there is no god,'" and in 41:4 (cf. Prov. 8:22–30; Ps. 90:2).

And by two reasons: 1. The subordination of causes argues for a first being.
XV. Neither do reasons prove otherwise. For first, wholesome philosophy
presupposes rather than demonstrates that God is being from himself, being
through essence,[14] and the absolutely first being. For if what is apparent to all
is granted, that there is a certain subordination of things, and, with respect to
essences, that they depend upon each other; and additionally, if it is conceded
what, supposing that there exists some being, cannot be reasonably denied, that

---

12. For Christian receptions of Kabbalah in the early modern period, see Johann Reuchlin
(1455–1522), *De arte cabalistica libri tres* (Hannover, 1530); Francesco Giorgi (1467–1540), *De
harmonia mundi totius cantica tria* (Venice, 1525); Christian Knorr von Rosenroth (1636–1689),
Kabbala denudata, 2 vols. (1677–1678).
13. 1.2.4 §VIII
14. *ens per essentiam*, that is, being that exists by virtue of its own essence, not, as creatures do,
by participation in another being. Cf. §XVII, below.

this dependence cannot be extended into infinity, because otherwise nothing could exist, since that infinite number of preceding causes, never being complete, would exclude the existence of the proximate cause upon which the existence of its effect depends; furthermore, if it stands to reason that nothing can be its own cause because that openly involves a contradiction, since it says that the same thing simultaneously exists (insofar as it produces) and does not exist (insofar as it is produced); and finally, if it is admitted that creatures could not have been circularly the causes of each other's existence, on account of the fact that this circle also connotes the contradiction we just mentioned—then it cannot but remain that there exists some being from himself, being through essence, the absolutely first being, one that produced all things and by no means produced itself. And furthermore, we presuppose from common usage that this being is God.

2. Because all the attributes of God are established in this primacy.

XVI. Then, second, that this is the very thing we can best think about as the essence of God could be made plain from the following. On the one hand, it is accepted that the thing best called the essence of something is that on which all its attributes are grounded, and from which they take their origin, as it were. On the other hand, it is accepted that all the attributes of God are grounded on this aseity, independence, and primacy, which could be made plain through induction, in the following ways. (1) Unity: for that which is the absolutely first being cannot be but one. But if several such beings should be conceived, none will be absolutely first, since one does not precede another. (2) Immutability: for if this being were changed, it would be changed by another, and to that extent that other would undoubtedly be prior to the absolutely first being, which is contradictory. (3) Infinity: for that which is limited, is limited by another, for nothing limits itself and restricts its own perfection, and that other would certainly be prior to the absolutely first being. (4) Simplicity: for that which is composed is, by the same measure, composed by another that is prior to it. (5) Life: for since there is no imperfection involved in the concept of life, it cannot but belong to the one who is simply from himself, and thus it applies to the one to whom this perfection cannot be denied by another. By the same consequence, (6) intellect: for by common consent it is more perfect to understand than not to understand. And also (7) will: for as all confess, to operate from free choice[15] is more perfect than to act by nature. Equally, (8) omnipotence: for he who does not admit a being prior to himself also cannot be restricted and limited in his power. (9) You could easily demonstrate similar things concerning the virtues of the intellect

---

15. ἐκ προαιρέσει

and the will—wisdom, goodness, grace, holiness, and others—which, since they without any doubt imply absolute perfection, cannot be removed from the absolutely first being, because if they were removed, they would be removed by another, who would then become prior to the absolutely first being.

XVII. Now, in order to properly understand the intention of the theorem, we must observe the following: (1) by the word *essence* we intend nothing other than what Scripture designates by θεότης, "deity" (Col. 2:9), θειότης, "divinity" (Rom. 1:20), φύσις, "nature" (Gal. 4:8), and μορφὴ θεοῦ, the "form of God" (Phil. 2:6). Thus we do not use the word *essence* profanely with regard to God, as not a few adversaries of the Trinity, out of hatred for the doctrine, misrepresent us. (2) God exists through essence, not simply a being, but *the* being par excellence—that is, not only nominally, in the way that something that does not exist is also called a being, but also participatively, such that he is understood as a being existing in actuality, though nevertheless by this law, that "being" not be taken in the concrete as something composed of essence and existence, but in the abstract, such that existence is the same thing as essence. And accordingly, we say that God is "being through essence," or, what is the same thing, that existence is of his essence, because we cannot think of a most perfect essence that does not exist. And (3) by such a being, we mean nothing but that he is a being from himself, certainly not in the positive sense, as if God were the producing cause of himself or his essence—for this would involve a most open contradiction, as we have said and will say again—but only in the negative sense, insofar as he was not produced by another. And from this we add that (4) he is the first being through his essence: certainly not first in his own genus only, in which sense in all species there is some first being, as, for example, Adam is in the human species, but also absolutely first, in every genus. And indeed he is so in such a way that he excludes not only such a being that would have been prior to himself, but also one that would exist simultaneous to himself. He is the first being, but without a beginning, just as he is the last being without an end, that is, he is a being that is eternal in every way; he is first indeed comparatively, or rather superlatively, in rank to any creatures. And he is first not only by a priority of nature, in which sense things that exist simultaneously in time can be prior and posterior with reference to each other, as for example the sun and the sun's rays; but by a priority of time, yet in his own way, such that nothing has coexisted with God from eternity. In a word, he is first by a primacy that excludes not only a preexisting being but also a coexisting being, because not only infinity in general, but also eternity, is among the incommunicable attributes of God. And finally, in this sense (5) he is said to be simply from himself, as he is uncaused, in every way free from entirely every cause: an efficient cause that would have produced him, a material cause by which he would consist, a formal cause through which he would be what he is, and a final cause on account of which he would be and exist, just as we already taught.[16] Accordingly, through his essence, God is independent in every way, both with respect to his existence and with respect to his operations. And if you would prefer to say besides these things something more distinct about the essence of God, you could say (6) that he is a "Spirit living from himself." For, that I might speak with Ames, "The formally quidditative concept of God ought to be as it were the ultimate reckoning, one that fulfills his nature, as it were in the most perfect species of being; but we have no more perfect concept than that of a Spirit living from himself" (*Marrow of Theology*, bk. 1, ch. 4, §33).[17] But we will consider these topics again more distinctly in their own place.[18]

The Elenctic Part

It is asked: 1. In reference to God, do we use the word essence *accurately enough?*
XVIII. It is asked, first, whether in reference to God we use the word *essence* accurately enough. The Remonstrant Apologists, who are secretly Socinianizers, in order to undermine through devices the mystery of the Trinity, in which is stated that there is one essence in God and three persons, think that the word *essence* is not attributed to God accurately enough. The Reformed teach that it applies to God most properly, indeed par excellence, before all others. This is because: (1) תושיה is expressly attributed to God, and it denotes *essence*, from יש, "it is" (Prov. 8:14). (2) Synonyms of the word are used in the Scriptures concerning God: θειότης, "divinity" (Rom. 1:20), θεότης, "deity" (Col. 2:9), and θεῖα φύσις, "divine nature" (Gal. 4:8). (3) Scripture calls him אהיה and likewise יהוה, as well as ὁ ὤν (Rev. 1:4, 8), all which cannot but imply *essence*. Finally, (4) if *essence* does not properly and rightly apply to God, then neither does the verb *est*, "he is," which inclines toward atheism. Let me add (5) if *essence* does not properly apply to God, it also cannot rightly be said that God is one in essence and three in persons. Given these things, the Remonstrant Apologists will not now sustain their allegation to the contrary, that the word does not appear in Scripture. And even if the word did not appear there, but at the same time the idea did, what then? If they should say that God is "above essence,"[19] we

---

16. §XIII, above
17. William Ames, *Medulla theologica* (Amsterdam: Joannes Janssonius, 1656), I.4 §33, p. 22. The 1639 English translation revises and omits most of this section of Ames; see *The Marrow of Theology*, trans. J. D. Eusden (Grand Rapids: Baker Books, 1997), I.4 §33.
18. §XXII, below
19. ὑπερούσιον

will indeed grant that in rank to creatures, his essence exceeds theirs infinitely, but this does not deprive him of his essence; indeed, it rather confirms it for him. For this reason, and not inappropriately, very many call him the "essence above essence."[20]

2. Does the essence of God consist in thought alone?

XIX. Second, it is asked whether the divine essence consists in mere thought. Descartes, along with his followers, since he enumerated only two kinds of substance on which he built the whole of his philosophy—thought and extension—and since he could not refer the divine essence to extension, asserted that it was thought. The Reformed, although they willingly admit thought, indeed thoughts, in God, and also grant that they entirely coincide with the divine essence, since through the omnimodal simplicity of God they recognize nothing in God different from the divine essence, notwithstanding deny that the divine essence is mere thought. And for this reason they say that the thought of God ought to be considered in a twofold sense, namely, identical and formal, as the Scholastics meaningfully speak. Under the identical sense, they state that all divine things are the very divine essence itself, in such a way that, for example, even reprobation is the very essence of God. But on the other hand, in the formal sense, in which that essence is constructed with our concepts, thought is something different from the essence of God, just as reprobation also is. And for this reason just as it cannot be said that reprobation is the essence of God or that the essence of God is reprobation, in the same way it ought not to be said that the essence of God is thought, but rather that thought is a certain action of the divine essence. The reasons of the Reformed are: (1) God, who best knows his own essence, neither in our text, where he expressly intends to represent himself to Moses and the Israelites by his essential names, nor in any place in the entirety of the Holy Scriptures, calls himself "thought" or declares that his essence consists in thought. In fact, (2) throughout Scripture he attributes many thoughts to himself, and thus more than adequately distinguishes his thoughts

---

20. οὐσίαν ὑπερούσιον: cf. John of Damascus, Ἔκδοσις ἀκριβὴς τῆς ὀρθοδόξου πίστεως, *De Fide Orthodoxa, Patrologia Graeca (PG)*, ed. Jacques-Paul Migne (Paris, 1857–1866), 94:799–800, καὶ τὸ ἀνάπαλιν τὸ ὑπὲρ οὐσίαν, καὶ γνῶσιν ἔσται, *quod est supra essentiam, cognitionem superabit*; idem, *An Exact Exposition of the Orthodox Faith*, 1.4, *Nicene and Post-Nicene Fathers*, Series II (*NPNF2*), ed. Philip Schaff and Henry Wace (New York: Christian Literature Co., 1885–1896; reprint Peabody, Mass.: Hendrickson, 1994), 9:4; cf. Richard Muller, *Post-Reformation Reformed Dogmatics (PRRD)* (Grand Rapids: Baker Academic, 2003), 3:237n47.

from his essence (Isa. 55:8; Ps. 92:5; 139:17; Jer. 51:11, 12, 29; Mic. 4:12; etc.), distinguishing, that is, himself the agent from his action in order that we may understand that although on his part the agent and action, the thinker and the thought, are entirely one and the same, yet, that he and his essence are by no means what we understand when we conceive of thinking only. And also (3) by this reckoning we could have a concept of the divine essence that is absolutely positive, since thought furnishes such a concept for us; but this is what we expressly rejected in the previous theorem.[21] I may add (4) that in this manner the essence of God and of creatures would be the same, since the essence of God and of angels and rational souls would coincide in this point, that the former as much as the latter would be nothing but thought, which hitherto was exceedingly crude to Reformed ears.

The first objection

XX. The first falsehood[22] of Descartes's previously unheard of novelty is that Descartes, in his hyperbolic doubt, either while still clinging to it or while emerging from it, discovered (1) that he was thinking and had extension; and from there (2) next concluded that his soul consisted in thought, and indeed in thought alone, but his body in extension alone; and not only this, but also (3) that all substances consisted in either thought or extension, and so (4) since God was not extension, he could not be anything other than thought. These, then, are the supports of such a great mass, but they are in fact quite full of sand. For as to the first hypothesis, namely, that man thinks and has extension, we receive it with open arms, but in no way is it concluded from this that the soul consists in thought, and indeed in thought alone, but that the body consists in extension alone, just as it in no way follows that because man is able to laugh or laughs that therefore he consists in laughter or the ability to laugh. And even if such a thing did follow, by no devices would you wrench from this that all substance is either thought or extension. And from there follows least of all that grand postulate that God, because he is not extension, is precisely thought, indeed that his entire essence consists in thought alone.

The second objection

XXI. The chief point that one could object to these things is that since God is a most simple act, then for this reason his thought cannot but be the same thing as his essence. But from this it is no more demonstrated that the essence of God

---

21. §VII, above
22. πρῶτον ψεῦδος

consists in thought alone than that it consists in reprobation alone, since reprobation is equally identical with the essence as thought is with the same essence. Therefore, granted that thought is the same thing in the identical sense, through which all things in God are one and the same, yet all things are not one in the formal sense, through which we conceive of the divine attributes as different, as much from the essence as among themselves. Therefore in the sense, for example, that reprobation differs from the divine essence, in that sense thought also differs from the same essence. If you, reader, should desire more arguments of this sort, you will be able to compare our *Gangrene of the Cartesian Innovations* (sect. 2, ch. 6).[23]

3. Is God from himself positively?

XXII. It is asked, third, whether God is from himself positively. Descartes, together with his followers, because he does not support negative concepts about God and divine things, is not content to declare that God is from himself negatively, that is, insofar as he is not from any other, and stated in addition that God is from himself as positively as possible, insofar as through his immense and incomprehensible power, by a certain and most perfect causation, from eternity he is the cause of his very self, because he willed to be, and to be that which he is, and in this very fact consists his singular perfection. But indeed by this kind of aseity (1) the omnimodal aseity of God is thus quite weakened. For by this method (a) the following will have to be conceived of in God as different things: his immense power and all-sufficiency, as the cause; his eternal willing, as the most perfect causation; and his essence, existence, and properties, as the thing caused. Furthermore (b) concerning that immense power which would, by the most perfect causation, be the cause of God and of all his perfections, one of two things must be stated: either it is not from itself positively, and thus it is deprived of this eminent perfection, which they will not say; or it is from itself positively. Then, pray tell, what is the cause through which this immense power, the origin of God and of all the divine perfections, is from itself positively? Or, by the help of what perfection is this power from itself? If they should not be able to answer, just as they have not been able, then it will have to be stated conclusively that that immense power is from itself only negatively, and hence it is deprived of positive aseity, and thus the omnimodal aseity of God is weakened. I need not add to these things that (2) for something to be the cause of its own self involves a most open contradiction, as we taught above in §XV. Nor that (3) if the immense power of God should be conceived as the cause of God, that is, of his essence and

---

23. Mastricht, *Gangraena*, 225–36.

divine perfections, by this method the power of God will have to be conceived of as prior (if not in time, at least in nature) to his essence, since every cause is by nature prior to its effect. Nor need I add that (4) if aseity is the highest and chief perfection of God (which our opponents recognize), and therefore must be located in the first place, because from it the rest of his perfections flow, then how can it be claimed that it has some sort of cause? Nor finally that (5) if God therefore is from himself positively, or is the cause of himself, since from eternity he willed to be, and to be such as he is, then will not the will of God be the cause of God's essence, existence, and divine perfections? Could we not therefore use in reference to the Creator what John has in reference to the creatures, "By your will they exist" (Rev. 4:11)? But then, finally, what will be the cause of that very will through which he is positively from himself?

Three objections

XXIII. If they should say (1) that nevertheless aseity is a certain perfection of God, indeed the primary perfection, which accordingly cannot consist in something purely negative, I will respond that (a) the negative attributes of God also involve in their material concept, besides a negation of imperfection, an affirmation of the highest perfection. Thus, for example, just as immutability and infinity do, in entirely the same way, aseity involves sufficiency, all-sufficiency, and self-sufficiency[24] as a most positive perfection, although God is not by it positively from himself. In fact, (b) for something to contain the cause of itself by no means speaks of perfection, but rather of imperfection. If they should say (2) that it is attributed to the Father to have life in himself (John 5:26), the response is easy: (a) It does not say that he has life *from himself*, which is our question, but *in himself*, which is a difference as wide as heaven. (b) Nor does it say that God has life from himself positively, but simply. And (c) it does not say that God has his own being from himself, which is the point in question, but life, insofar as it is in the formal sense distinct from his essence. If they should say (3) that God nevertheless from eternity has willed to be, and to be what he is, I will say on the contrary that it by no means follows from this that the willing of God is the *principium* or cause of his own essence, existence, and attributes, since he is God, and he is such a God, through his nature, and not through his will, insofar as in the formal sense his nature is conceived of as distinct from his will, although concomitantly, insofar as he does not exist by coercion, he could be said to exist voluntarily.

---

24. ἄρκειαν, πανάρκειαν, *et* αὐτάρκειαν

The Practical Part

The first use is for comfort. 1. The evils it remedies; 2. The arguments for comfort XXIV. Now, the use of the observation concerning the essence of God can be, first, for comfort in all sorts of adverse circumstances. For since, if not all, at least most of our sorrow and anguish of soul arises from the fact that what we would want to be *is not*, according to that phrase of Jeremiah, "Rachel is weeping for her children, because they are no more" (Matt. 2:18), where at last could a more effective source of comfort and remedy come from than from him who *is* by his essence, and *is* preeminently? If therefore, (1) there are not for us goods of fortune: (a) our dearest relatives are no more, or have perished, as for Job (Job 1:19), Rachel (Matt. 2:18), and Naomi (Ruth 1:3, 5); (b) there are not resources necessary for preserving life, as for Lazarus (Luke 16:20–21); (c) there are not honors to make life honorable, if we are "the scum of the world" (1 Cor. 4:13). If (2) there are not for us goods of the body: if (a) there is not good health, if there is nothing sound from head to toe (Isa. 1:6; 53:3), if the body and the soul should waste away (Ps. 73:26), as in the example of Job, Lazarus, and others; if (b) there is not peace or rest (2 Cor. 6:4–5), if enemies, persecutors, and taskmasters should threaten, as they did the Israelites (Ex. 1:14; 3:7); if (3) there are not for us goods of the soul: if (a) there is not for us, for example, faith, hope, or charity (Mark 9:24); if (b) there is not necessary wisdom (James 1:5); if (c) there is not for us spiritual light, such that we walk in the darkness of spiritual desertions (Isa. 50:10; Ps. 77:2, 7–9); if (d) there is not for us whatever sort of thing we would want to be, and about which we are vexed because it is not there for us—then what could encourage us more effectively than to think, (1) that God *is* by his essence, by which argument God encourages the Israelites in our text, and Asaph encourages himself in Psalm 73:25–26, "If my body and soul should waste away, *you are....*" (2) That God is eminently all being: he is (a) all-knowing, he who most perfectly knows what for his own is not, or is lacking (Rev. 2:2); he is (b) all-powerful, in whose hand are power and might (2 Chron. 20:6), so that he is able to help if he wills (Matt. 8:2); he is (c) most highly good, gracious, and merciful (Ex. 34:6), the one who also wills (Matt. 8:3), indeed who does not will to forsake his own (Heb. 13:5); in fact, he is (d) most all-sufficient (Gen. 17:1), a sun and shield (Ps. 84:11). (3) God *is* not only for himself, but also for us; he is not only preeminently essence, but also the Essencer (to speak barbarously),[25] for in him we live, move, and *are* (Acts 17:25, 28), and by him we are whatever we are (1 Cor. 15:10) and can be whatever we ought or desire to be. For he *is* for

---

25. *Essentiator*, "Essencer," is not classical Latin (thus he is speaking "barbarously"); cf. John Calvin, *Institutes*, 1.13.23.

us all in all (1 Cor. 15:28) and in him we can be complete (Col. 2:10). (4) He is by essence being from himself, utterly independent, whose help does not depend on any creatures, even if they are unwilling, or upon any instruments (1 Sam. 14:6). Finally, (5) he is by essence the absolutely first being, who accordingly, if heretofore he has not been something for us, he can be it hereafter, which he promises to the Israelites: "I will be" to you "what I am." From these arguments there cannot but be supplied to us all comfort in all miseries, if only we do this one thing: enter with him into covenant (Gen. 17:1–2), that through it he may become our God (Jer. 31:33). And thus Moses could declare to us also what he declares to the Israelites in our text: "The God of your fathers...," indeed, also *your* God.

The second use is for rebuking. Here are noted: 1. Those who must be rebuked
XXV. The second use can be for restraining all of the following: (1) those who would openly want essence and existence to be abolished from God (Ps. 14:1; 10:4). (2) Those who, at least interpretatively,[26] so to speak, infringe upon the aseity and independence of the divine essence, when in the matter of predestination they make the grace of God dependent on the free choice of man, on faith and unbelief, or also on foreseen good works, and thus on the one hand strip God of his omnimodal independence, and on the other hand bestow independence on man and his choice, mixing up heaven and earth. Indeed, (3) those who, at least practically, nip at the independence of God, when they make his help depend on means, either through total desperation (2 Kings 7:2) or through some sort of distrust (Num. 11:21, 23; John 11:21; 4:49). (4) Those who limit God (Ps. 78:41), prescribing to him as it were the time, mode, order, and means of his helping (Ps. 78:18–19; John 4:49). (5) Those who through disobedience dispute with God, as it were, for the independence of his lordship, and thus strive themselves for independence, according to the example of Pharaoh (Ex. 5:1–2), and of the wicked (Job 21:14). (6) Those who do not rest in God's counsels, decrees, and works (Rom. 9:20; Matt. 20:12–16; cf. Jer. 18:6).

2. Arguments for rebuking
Now, all those (1) though in different ways and degrees, overthrow the very essence of God, inasmuch as it consists in his aseity and omnimodal independence. And thus they are atheists, or at least they participate in atheism. Then (2) that God whom they do not want to be, or to be that kind of God,

---

26. That is, when the logical consequences of their thought are "interpreted" or explained.

nevertheless will be no matter how they snarl, and will be the kind of God they do not want. He will be to them a severe judge; he will be a consuming fire; he will be a lion, a bear whose cubs have been snatched away. And (3) he will be entirely the kind of God to them that he is threatened to be throughout the prophets (Jer. 16:21; cf. 2:19); indeed (4) the kind of God that Pharaoh the atheist once experienced (Ex. 5:2; cf. 14:28), and that all like him will without a doubt experience—either here, or hereafter, or both.

The third use is for exhortation, and it is fivefold: 1. That we would glorify God
XXVI. The third use can be for exhortation, toward the study of the divine essence and independence. That is, (1) it must be known, for to this end God reveals himself to Moses, that he may be described also to the Israelites; and he does this also elsewhere, in the passages designated above in §XIV. (2) It must be used: first, for the glorification of God, according to his commandment (Isa. 42:8) and God's example, since to this end he describes himself throughout the Scriptures, that he is not only "Jehovah, I am," but also "he who is, who was, and who is to come," "the Alpha and the Omega," "the first and the last" (we gave these passages in §XIV). He does this namely so that we would acknowledge and celebrate his glory as the one who *is*, who *is* above all persons and all things, who is, namely, *being* preeminently—in fact, who is such alone.

2. That we would be humbled
Second, it must be used for the humbling of ourselves, because the divine essence, by all means proper to God, consists in this, that he *is*. So then, it is as if we are not, and thus are nothing: "Surely every man is entirely emptiness" (Ps. 39:5, 11); and likewise, "All the nations are as nothing before him (or in comparison with him); they are accounted as less than nothing and empty in comparison with him," that is, "a drop from a bucket and fine dust on the scales" (Isa. 40:17, 15); "dust and ashes" (Gen. 18:27). So then, in a way analogous to these texts, before him we should as it were annihilate ourselves, ἐξουθενοῦντες, as the Greeks meaningfully say, counting ourselves as nothing. We should be nothing in the world (1 Cor. 1:28; cf. 3:7). Thus at last God will be all in all, and thus by the grace of God we will be what we are (1 Cor. 15:28, 10).

3. That we would deny ourselves
From this, third, it must be used for the denial of ourselves, our will, our strength, and our actions, according to the example of our Savior—"Not my will, but yours be done" (Matt. 26:39)—and the warning of James (James 4:13, 15), and

moreover, in the offering of daily prayer (Matt. 6:10), always mindful that he alone is independent, and also the prime mover of all things.

4. That we would have confidence in God

Fourth, it must be used for placing our confidence in him alone (Jer. 17:5, 7), namely because he, since he is "the one who is" and "being through essence," can at his own pleasure call into existence those things that do not exist (Rom. 4:17), cailing light out of the very darkness (2 Cor. 4:6). And in this matter it is extremely helpful to add that he *is*: (1) a living and life-giving being in whom we live (Acts 17:28); (2) an intelligent being who understands our needs (Rev. 2:2); (3) a willing being who wills not to forsake us (Heb. 13:5); (4) a merciful, gracious being who by nature is inclined to help those in misery (Ex. 34:6); (5) an omnipotent being who can in addition do far more than all that we think and desire (Eph. 3:20); (6) an immutable being in his love and in his promises, always the same, who will be what he is; and (7) a being from himself, independent, free from every hindrance.

5. That we would receive the emissaries of God

Finally, it must be used for the receiving of the Word of God and his ministers. To this end Moses in our text is equipped with these credentials: "Go to the Israelites. Say, 'I AM has sent me to you.'" To this same end points the received prophetic phrase, "Thus says the LORD" and likewise "The word of the LORD."

Motives

Finally, if we do not by this method or one similar eagerly seek to know God in his essence, (1) whatever we have professed with our mouth, we have denied in reality (Titus 1:16), in a manner quite like that of atheists (Ps. 14:1). In fact (2) all our knowledge of the divine essence, however great and however effective it may appear to be, will be hollow and useless to us, for it will never be answered by the loving knowledge of God (Matt. 7:23). In fact, (3) it will be not only hollow, but in addition harmful, when God by inflicting punishments will make us more certainly than certain experience that he truly *is*, not as a rewarder, but as an exactor, as is evident in the case of Pharaoh and others. These five duties, which for the sake of brevity we have joined into one exhortatory use, can be individually, as circumstances require, explained in detail as so many uses and fitted with their own motives and means.

CHAPTER FOUR

The Names of God

"The Lord God of your fathers, the God of Abraham, the God of Isaac, the God of Jacob, has sent me to you." This is my name forever, and this is my memorial from generation to generation.

—Exodus 3:15

The transition from God's essence to his names

I. Of the two helps, that is, the names and attributes of God, by which the essence of God outlined in some sense in the previous chapter is made known to us, we take up first, in this chapter, his names. God himself precedes us in this, when intending to reveal himself to the Israelites through his commissioned ambassador, he uses the names אלהים, יהוה, אהיה ("I AM," "Lord," "God") and appends to them, "This is my name forever, this is my memorial," namely, "that by them I may be made known."

The Exegetical Part

The text is resolved and explained.

II. By the words of the text, God, intending to procure authority for himself the commissioner, for the one commissioned, and for the commission, places as it were into Moses's hands, like an instrument of the commission (what they elsewhere call "credentials") a word in praise of his names and titles, to be set before the Israelites. In it two things occur:

A. The instruction, by which, in order that the trustworthiness and authority, first of the commissioner, then of the one commissioned, and finally of the commission, would be more effective among the Israelites, the God who commissions portrays himself. He does so:

1. By three names:

   a. The essential name: יהוה, "Lord," that is, the one who, as he is from himself, is thus most perfect, who is faithful, not knowing how to be deceived or to deceive, who is steadfast and omnipotent, the one who is able both to make promises and to provide what has been promised. On this name more is soon to come.

b. The personal name: אלֹהִים, "God," subsisting in three persons, each of which is God, and thus steadfast and faithful by the testimony of three witnesses, such that the Israelites do not have anything at all for which to question the trustworthiness of the commission. Likewise on this name there is a fuller treatment to come.

c. The covenantal name: "the God of your fathers," and thus also your God, that is, due to the covenant of grace, by which he has devoted himself in all he is both to them and to you—"I will be a God to you and to your seed." Namely, he is:

   i. "The God of Abraham," the most famous of the patriarchs. Concerning this covenant, see Genesis 17:7–8.

   ii. "The God of Isaac." See Genesis 46:1 and 32:9.

   iii. "The God of Jacob." See Exodus 3:6. So then this God, as he has never failed his covenant, so also he never will.

2. By the commission: "…has sent me to you." Here stands out:

a. The commission: "He has sent," that is, he has instructed me by his own authority.

b. The one commissioned: "me," whom you know to be an Israelite, and thus your brother, educated in the court of your king. And for your sake, because as a sign of your future deliverance I struck down the Egyptian in your midst, I was sent into exile.

c. The object of the commission: "to you," who are oppressed so strenuously in the present circumstance by your king, Pharaoh, and who have cried out in anguish, sighing to your God from the distress of your slavery.

B. A commendation of the name, especially the essential name. This includes:

1. The ownership of the name: "This is *my* name forever," that is, that essential name by which I will be named, I will be known, I will be distinguished from all others—my name, that is, my very own, peculiar to me and incommunicable to anyone else (Isa. 42:8). And so it will be forever, through all generations to the end of the world, indeed to all eternity. The word לְעוֹלָם, "forever," is by the rabbis translated based

on the verb עלם, "to conceal," to mean "for concealing," because they determine that the pronunciation of his name has been prohibited and therefore must be concealed.

2. Its use: "This is my memorial" (Ps. 135:13; 102:12; Hos. 12:5). That is, by this means I will preserve the memory of myself and of my independence, eternity, steadfastness, and faithfulness through all ages, so that I will be known, loved, and worshiped, and so forth.

The Dogmatic Part

The nature of God is made known to us by his names.

III. So then, it is therefore evident that the nature of God is made known to us by his names. For in the text, God attributed to himself the names Jehovah, Elohim, and "the God of your fathers," and he adds, "This is my name, this is my memorial," namely, this is how I may be known, distinguished, and come to be remembered by men. Several passages make this point: Exodus 6:3, "By my name Jehovah I was not made known to them"; likewise Acts 9:15, "He will bear my name," that is, he will reveal my name, "among the Gentiles"; and Isaiah 42:8, "This is my name; my glory," that is, the glory of this name, "I will not give to another." Particularly since this is the innate character of names, and the reason why the Latin word *nomen*, "name," is spoken of as a sort of *novimen*, a distinguishing characteristic, or a *notamen*, a mark of designation,[1] because it leads to a knowledge of the thing named. But it is not of great importance to confirm this laboriously with reasons. For since we are led to a knowledge of things, first by those things that indicate their essence, second by those things that distinguish them from similar things, and third by those things that reveal their properties, it cannot happen that the names of God would not lead us to a knowledge of him. For (1) they reveal his essence, as do אהיה, "I am," ὁ ὤν, "he who is," and so forth; (2) they distinguish him, not only from the false gods, but also from all creatures whatsoever, for which reason the Greeks derive the word ὄνομα, "name," from νέμω, "I divide"; and (3) they make known his properties

---

1. Latin: *unde nomen, quasi notamen aut notamen, dicitur*; Dutch: *waarvandaan het Latynsche woordt Nomen, een Naam, als zeide men novimen of notamen, dat is een onderscheident kenmerk, of merktekens*. Cf. Sextus Pompeius Festus, *De significatione verborum*, book 12: *nomen dictum quasi novimen, quod notitiam facit*, "the word *nomen* is like a distinguishing characteristic because it results in knowledge." Cf. Cledonius in *Grammatici Latini* (Leipzig: Teubner, 1855–1880; Hildesheim: Olms, 1961 [1981]), 5.10.8–9, *nomen dictum quasi notamen, quod res nobis notas efficiat*, "the word *nomen* is like a distinguishing characteristic that makes things known to us."

and qualities.[2] And this is said more precisely of God's names than of any others, because they were assigned not by ignorant men but by the one who is most wise, who alone knows himself perfectly, and not rashly, but as by the most deliberate counsel.

Does a name properly belong to God?

IV. Therefore, let us proceed directly to the theory of the divine names, first the more general theory and then the more specific. In the former the first thing that occurs is the question whether a name properly belongs to God. In the past this was denied by Philo in *On the Life of Moses*, Justin Martyr in *Exhortation to the Greeks*, and Rabbi Haccados (according to Pietro Colonna Galatino's *On the Hidden Mysteries of Catholic Truth*, bk. 2, ch. 10),[3] as well as others. They denied it especially for this reason: the essence of God is incomprehensible to us, and thus it cannot be represented by a name. It seems that Scripture also denies this (Prov. 30:4; Gen. 32:29; Judg. 13:18), and with Scripture it should be denied entirely, if a name is understood to be a perfect representation of a thing. Particularly since God, because he is a most singular being, and is most distinct from anything else in his own nature and infinity, does not need a distinguishing name (whether it be understood as an appellative name, which distinguishes a species within the same genus, or as a proper name, by which individuals are discerned within the same species). Nevertheless, not only so that he may be distinguished both from the creatures and from the false gods, but also so that he may become more fully known to us, God throughout Scripture attributes a name—indeed, names—to himself.

What does a name mean with respect to God?

V. Then, in the second place, here occurs the question, What do names mean about God? Specifically, in the Scriptures the name of God frequently designates: (1) God himself (Ps. 5:11; 7:17; 1 Kings 5:5; Isa. 12:4; Joel 2:32); and sometimes (2) all that is divine or that concerns God, for example, (a) his attributes (Ex. 15:3; 34:14), (b) his will and commandments (Deut. 18:19; 1 Sam. 17:45; Matt. 28:19), (c) his worship and the confession of him (Mic. 4:5; Acts 21:13), and why not (d) Christ himself, who not only has the name of God in himself (Ex. 23:21), but also leads us to the knowledge of God the Father (John

---

2. Latin: *proprietates et affectiones*; Dutch: *eigenschappen en hoedanigheden*

3. For Pietro Colonna Galatino (1460–1540), see *DBI* 27 (1982), 399–402; idem, *De arcanis catholicae veritatis libri XII, quibus pleraque religionis Christianae capita contra Judaeos, tam ex Scripturis veteris testamenti authenticis, quam ex Talmudicorum commentariis* (Frankfurt: Jacob Gottfried Seyler, 1672), 80–84.

5:24; 14:9; Heb. 1:1, 3). But more properly (3) it denotes the words by which
the essence of God, or something similar, is represented.

How many kinds of names of God are there?
VI. Furthermore, in the third place, how many kinds of names of God are there?
This question is answered in various distributions, when the divine names are
said to be either essential, such as *Jehovah* and θεός, *God*; or personal, such as
Elohim, Father, Son, and *Holy Spirit.* The former (God's essential names) are
either proper or figurative, and the figurative names (as secondary) apply to God
either metonymically, when, for example, he is called our strength, help, light,
and salvation (Ps. 18:1; 27:1), or metaphorically, as when he is called a shield
or sun (Ps. 84:11; Isa. 10:17), or when these metaphorical names are obtained
from man or any other creatures. Regarding names that are proper but that
nevertheless in a certain way, by analogy, are communicable to creatures (for
there are certain names such as יהוה that are incommunicable in every respect),
theologians observe that in a primary sense they apply to God, and in a secondary
sense to creatures, that is, if you consider the thing signified. Although, with
reference to the mode of signifying, inasmuch as it is borrowed from creatures,
in a primary sense they regard creatures. Then also, though by a more tenuous
conjecture, several observe that names attributed to God in most languages quite
often consist of four letters, for designating the Trinity of persons in the unity of
essence. On the other hand, the personal names either include the three persons,
such as אלהים, or designate the individual persons individually, such as *Father,
Son,* ὁ λόγος (the *Word*), and *Holy Spirit.*

A specific consideration of the divine names
VII. That was the more general theory of the divine names; now the more
specific theory follows, according to which the names of God either represent
his essence, such as יהוה, *Jehovah,* or אהוה, *Ehyeh;* or his power, such as אל, *El,*
or אלהים, *Elohim;* or his excellence and preeminence, such as עליון, *Elyon;* or his
lordship, such as אדני, *Adonai.*

What does the name Jehovah include?
VIII. Among these, the first place goes to the great name of the first kind, יהוה,
Jehovah, and in some places *Jehovi* (Deut. 3:24; 9:26).[4] It comes from the היה

---

4. *Jehovi* is Mastricht's Latin representation of the unusual Masoretic pointing, יְהֹוִה. The
vowels reflect those of *Elohim,* the alternate Jewish pronunciation of the name when the usual
Adonai is already present. Cf. §XII, below.

customarily employed more in Aramaic, or from the היה that is more in use
in Hebrew, which means *to be*, because God is from himself and for himself,
because he always is, always lives, and is always the same, because he is immutable, as Drusius says in his *Tetragrammaton*, chapter 24,[5] and likewise because
he alone exists, as it were: he alone has all essence, while all other things have
only some small part of essence, and consequently they rather do not exist than
do exist, and they also exist only for a moment or a flow of moments, in which
past things are no more, future things are not yet, and what remains is nothing
but a moment, whereas God, or the eternity of God, is the possession, at once
whole and perfect, of boundless life, as Boethius says.[6] For this reason, in the
three syllables of this name several authors observe all the periods of time—the
past, present, and the future, in such a way that ' *Je* designates the future, ה *ho*
the present, and וה *vah* the past. Or, as others have it, ה designates the past, ו the
present, and ' the future (so Girolamo Zanchi, *On the Divine Attributes*, bk. 1,
ch. 13; and Nicholas Fuller, *Miscellanea theologica*, bk. 2, ch. 6).[7] That seems also
to be what the Savior intended to say in Revelation 1:8: "who is, who was, and
who is to come." The translators of the Septuagint render it in most instances by
the word κύριος, which is the same as אדוני, the very *Lord* of all, inasmuch as
he is from himself, and all things depend upon him, and in very rare instances
by the word θεός, God. The French in their Bibles continuously translate יהוה
as *l'Éternel*, "the Eternal One." It seems that something of this word flowed down
to the Gentiles when they called the supreme god among their gods *Jove*. Many
want this name to be ineffable, inexpressible, and unutterable,[8] a name that *de
facto* cannot be pronounced, or *de jure* ought not to be. For this reason, while
reading they always substitute for it either *Adonai* or *Elohim*; or they do so
because it cannot be portrayed by the Greek alphabet, since Greek lacks marks of
aspiration for the middle of a word. It is employed sometimes substantially, for
the whole essence insofar as it includes the individual persons jointly (Ex. 20:2,
5, 7), and at times hypostatically, for the Father (Ps. 110:1; Gen. 19:24), the Son
(Num. 6:25), and the Holy Spirit (Ex. 4:12; Num. 12:6), which, according to the
circumstances and by a comparison of passages of the Old and New Testament,

---

5. Johannes Drusius (1550–1616), *Tetragrammaton, sive de nomine Dei proprio, quod tetragrammaton vocant* (Franeker: Aegidius Radaeus, 1610), 64–65.
6. Cf. Boethius, *The Consolation of Philosophy*, LCL 74:422–23; idem, *De consolatione philosophiae*, lib. 5, prosa 6, PL 63:858–59.
7. Girolamo Zanchi (1516–1590), *De natura Dei, seu de divinis attributis* (Heidelberg, 1577),
35–47; (Neustadt, 1598), 26–36; Nicholas Fuller (c. 1557–1623), *Miscellanea theologica* (Strassburg: Lazarus Zetzner, 1650), 187–97.
8. ἄρρητον, ἀνεκφώνητον, ἄφραστον

must be carefully distinguished. Also, they observe that all the component letters of this name are quiescent, and from this—perhaps more subtly than solidly—they infer that this very name intends to signify not only the profound rest of God, but also that we as human beings must seek all solid rest in Jehovah alone. With respect to the efficacy of signifying, it denotes: (1) God's self-existence,[9] by which he subsists through himself in such a way that he exists for all things as the cause of their existing and subsisting. (2) His preeminence, because although by every other name is designated some mode of being, this name *Jehovah*, ὁ ὢν, "he who is," determines no mode of being, and thus it signifies that God preeminently *is*. (3) His aseity, by which he alone is independent and uncaused, in such a way that for all creatures he is the source of being and existing. As Bernard of Clairvaux says, "God is what he is, that is, the being of himself and of all other things: he exists for himself, he exists for all things, and through this, in a certain way he alone exists" (*On Consideration, to Eugenius*, bk. 5).[10] (4) His immutability, by which he always *is*, and properly speaking never was and never will be, or, he is the one who is what he was, who will be what he is, always the same and like to himself, not only with respect to his existence and essence, but also with respect to his will, Word, and promises (cf. Ps. 102:26; Heb. 1:12). Hence (5) his eternity, because that alone *is* which is eternal. For in time, past things are no more, future things are not yet, and present things are transient and cease in a moment, as it were. Therefore God alone, since he is eternal and thus beyond succession, properly speaking, *is*. Finally, (6) his truthfulness and faithfulness in his promises, since also in these it is more certain than certain that he will be who he is, such that on this foundation the things promised that *will be*, in their own way *are*, indeed so truly that for this reason our faith is deservedly called "the substance of things hoped for, and the conviction of things not seen" (Heb. 11:1). Furthermore, these things that are signified, since they are applicable to God alone, establish in addition that the name *Jehovah* is in every way proper to God alone, as our text witnesses, for in it, in an exceedingly emphatic way, God calls this *his own* name and also *his own* memorial, and so for that reason expressly appropriates it for himself (Isa. 42:8). I say "in every way," for while all other names of God are univocally incommunicable, yet analogically they are common to creatures. But this name is not read to have been communicated, either univocally or analogically, except in composition or in an oblique case. Plato, since he was in Egypt and might have heard something of this name, seems to

---

9. αὐτύπαρξιν; Dutch: *Godts van zich zelfs zyn*

10. Bernard of Clairvaux (1090–1153), *De consideratione ad Eugenium papam tertium* in *PL* 137:796.

have recognized this in his own way, when he teaches in the *Timaeus*, "God alone properly exists, but the other things that arise, change, and perish, more truly do not exist than exist."[11] And so also in the *Sophist* and *Parmenides*, he calls God τὸ ὄν, "the one that is" and in the *Theaetetus* he says that every created thing has more non-being than being,[12] just as is apparent, for example, in man, who has only human being, but by no means angelic, heavenly, or divine being, while God has all being, eminently at least, of all things, such that in this sense he alone is rightfully said *to be*. If you should want more on this name (besides the controverted points that will occur in their own place in the elenctic part below), go to Drusius in his *Tetragrammaton*; Buxtorf in his *Dissertation on Hebrew Names*; Gataker in his *Dissertation on the Tetragrammatic Name*; Fuller, *Miscellanea theologica* (bk. 2, ch. 6); Sixtinus Amama, *Dissertation on the Name Jehovah*; Jean Mercier on Genesis 2:4 and 15; and Louis Cappel in his *Dissertation* (after "The Secret of Punctuation"); and others.[13]

The name Elohim. *Where does it come from and what is it?*
IX. Therefore, with the remaining matters concerning the name *Jehovah*, whether problematic or elenctic, reserved for their own place, next comes אלהים, *Elohim*. According to some it derives from אל, whose plural form אלים is interspersed with the וה of the Tetragrammaton, because Jehovah is Elohim. Thus the force of the expression is: they, namely, Father, Son, and Holy Spirit, are God or Jehovah—perhaps more subtly than truly. According to others it is as it were a composite from אל, "strong," and אלה, "he swore," because through his strength he binds created men to worship as if by an oath. To others it is simply from אלה, either because one ought to swear only by the name of God, or because he confirmed the covenant of grace with an oath (Ps. 110:4; Heb. 7:20–21; cf. Deut. 29:12–13). Rav Nachman bar Yitzchak thinks that it is a saying, as it were אל הם, "their strength," that is, the strength of the things that have been created.[14]

---

11. Plato, *Timaeus* 28a.

12. E.g. Plato, *Sophist* 236–64b; idem, *Parmenides* 137c–59b; idem, *Thaetetus*, 170e–71c.

13. Jean Mercier (1510–1570), *In Genesim…commentarius* (Geneva: Matthieu Berjon, 1598), 39–42, 55–56. The other works may be found in Adriaan Reland (1676–1718), *Decas exercitationum philologicarum de vera pronunciatione nominis Jehova* (Utrecht: Coster, 1707): Drusius, *Tetragrammaton*, 1–120; Johannes Buxtorf, Sr. (1564–1629), *Dissertatio de nomine* יהוה, 385–412; Fuller, *Miscellanea theologica*, 187–97; Sixtinus Amama (1593–1626), *De nomine tetragrammato dissertatio cum responsio ad argumentum…D. Nicolai Fulleri*, 173–286; Louis Cappel (1585–1658), *Oratio de SS. Dei nomine tetragrammato*, 267–312.

14. Rav Nachman bar Yitzchak (d. 356) is one of the Talmudic commentators. One possible vector of Nachman's opinions was Paul Fagius (1504–1549): see "אֱלֹהִים Deus" in *Exegesis sive explicatio dictionum Hebraicum literalis et simplex* (Isne, 1542), 3–5.

But others believe that none of these agree exactly with Hebrew etymology, and thus they think that seeking an etymology is questionable and even futile. So then it is more rightly derived from אלוה, "God," which occurs repeatedly (Job 4:9; 12:4; etc.). By enallage of number it is in the majority of cases constructed with singular adjectives, and it is used in various ways: first substantially (Gen. 1:1), then hypostatically (Gen. 1:2), with respect to a certain person of the Holy Trinity (Ps. 45:6–7; Hos. 1:7), that is, on account of emperichoresis. Why it usually occurs in the plural in the Holy Scriptures will be evident in its own place in the elenctic part.[15] The Jews—Maimonides, Rabbi Salomon Rashi, Rabbi David Kimchi, and the talmudists—observe that it is the name of judgment, just as *Jehovah* is the name of grace and mercy, but the rationale for this is not apparent. It applies to the Creator properly, to the creatures analogically: to some indeed in truth, though secondarily; to others only in appearance or mimetically, as in the case of idols. The rabbis write אלקים or אלודים for אלוהים, just as the Chaldeans also write אלקא for אלה, which is among the names of God, and the Hebrews, in the names יהוה and אהיה, put ד in place of ה. In this they were undoubtedly led by superstition, namely, that if a book ever were desecrated, the name of God would not be desecrated as a result.

The name God. *Where does it come from and what is it?*

X. Θεός, God, which stands for *Elohim* in the New Testament, is either from די, "all-sufficient," according to Genesis 17:1, or from θέειν, "to run," because the sun and the stars, which were generally the first gods of the pagans, seemed to run continuously; or from θεᾶσθαι, "to observe," according to Basil in his *Epistles*, 141, because God is the observer and commander of all things;[16] or jointly from θέειν and θεᾶσθαι, as Dionysius thinks (*The Divine Names*, ch. 12), because God observes all things and as it were runs around all things by his marvelous providence; or from αἴθειν ("to burn"), because he as it were burns up the wicked by his wrath;[17] unless you prefer with John of Damascus (*On the Orthodox Faith*, bk. 1, ch. 2) to combine these three Greek derivations.[18] It matters little, provided it is not thought of, in the way the Socinians do, as a name of office, or an appellative name only, concerning which see the elenctic part below.[19]

---

15. §XVI
16. Basil, *Ep.* 141 in *LCL* 215.
17. Pseudo-Dionysius the Areopagite, *Works*, trans. J. Parker (London, 1897), 119–22.
18. Basil, *Ep.* 141 in *LCL* 215; John of Damascus, PG 39:797; idem, *The Orthodox Faith* in *NPNF2* 8:1b–2b.
19. §XV

Certain other names of God

XI. The name אל, *El*, is so called from איל, from "might." Accordingly, Franciscus Junius everywhere renders it "the mighty God." On account of a pun with אלים, the idols of the Gentiles are frequently called אלילים, which comes either from אלל, from which is derived אליל, "vain," "useless," "nothing," to which Paul alludes in 1 Corinthians 8:4; or, by composition from אל אלים, "not gods," though they bear the name *god* in front of themselves, or rather they counterfeit it; or, from אלה, "to curse," because they are things that should be cursed. The name שדי, *Shaddai*, is either from שדד, "to lay waste," because as he is the Creator, he therefore also can lay waste to all things; or, from שד, "breast," because he nourishes and cherishes all things as though by his own breasts (for which reason the Greeks called Diana "the breasted goddess"); or, from the pronominal prefix ש and די, "sufficient," as if to say, "the one who is preeminently sufficient for himself and for all things." The names אהיה, *Ehyeh* and יה, *Yah*, are with יהוה of the same origin and also of the same power, except that certain people prefer to derive the last one from יאה, which denotes "beauty" and "decency." More rightly, in my judgment, it is thought to be an abbreviation of the Tetragrammaton, arisen from very rapid pronunciation in at least the common pronunciation, although in the priestly benediction they pronounced it most distinctly. The name אדני, *Adonai*, in plural form (whose singular occurs in Deuteronomy 10:17 and in other places), perhaps with the suffix of the first person plural, unless you prefer to recognize it as an irregular termination, but at least with a *qamets*, is among the proper names for God,[20] and is regularly substituted for *Jehovah* in reading, unless this *qamets* is, for a grammatical reason (for example in a *sof pasuq* at the end of a verse), put in place of a *patakh*, for then it remains in the common meaning. This name expresses the most absolute lordship of God. The name צבאות, *Sabaoth*, is usually joined with the words *Jehovah* and *Elohim* and denotes that God uses all things according to his own pleasure, as his armies. The term עליון, *Elyon*, "Most High," should be called an adjective expressing his majesty, rather than a name of God.

The Elenctic Part

It is asked: 1. Can the name Jehovah be pronounced, or is it permissible to do so?

XII. In elenctic matters, first, the name *Jehovah* comes up again, and regarding it, first its problematics and then its elenctics. Among its problematics is the reading or pronunciation of it, in which respect, not only to the rabbis but also to

---

20. I.e. אֲדֹנָי

certain Christians it is inexpressible and unutterable (see Eusebius, *Preparation for the Gospel*, bk. 1, ch. 8).[21] For this reason, when reading they always substitute *Adonai*, or if that name is immediately joined to *Jehovah*, they substitute *Elohim*.

2. Is the name Jehovah *miraculous?*

XIII. It is asked, second, whether the name *Jehovah* is miraculous. Just as the papists, not content through superstition to have attributed too much to the name *Jesus*, also assert for *Jehovah* the power to perform miracles, drive out demons, heal diseases, and so forth, so also the Jews, no doubt to the end that from the miracles of Christ, from which we assert his divine power and deity, they might more ably take away his divinity, state that he did not perform them by some divine virtue, but that by virtue of this name, which through deception he had stolen from the holy of holies, he hatched all his miracles. That is, Jesus did his miracles by the *Shem ha-Mephorash*, "the excellent name," which we presuppose, according to the opinion of Maimonides (*The Guide of the Perplexed* pt. 1, ch. 62), to have been the very name *Jehovah*, although others think differently.[22] Luther wittily, and indeed deservedly, mocks this fable in his book entitled *Vom Schem Hamphoras und vom Geschlecht Christi*.[23] The Reformed, although they embrace with open arms the fact that the one named Jehovah is miraculous, nevertheless deny that this should be referred to the name itself (1) because nowhere does the sacred page maintain this, and the Jews cannot prove this very thing with sufficient reason; (2) because in the formation of any sound there is no other power than a moral power, that is, a power of signifying the interior things of the soul; and (3) because to undertake this kind of thing tends toward magic or practical kabbalah, which Scripture everywhere condemns (Nah. 3:4; Deut. 18:10; Mic. 5:12; etc.). Meanwhile the Jews allege on the contrary that: (1) by virtue of this name which he carried inscribed on his staff, Moses performed all his miracles; (2) by this name, he slew the Egyptian (Ex. 2:14); and (3) by this name, Elisha destroyed by means of bears those boys who were cursing him (2 Kings 2:23–24). They add (4) from Scripture, Psalm 44:5, "Through your *name* we will trample our adversaries." This is, they say, through the *Shem ha-Mephorash*. To these things we respond: (1) As for the first three allegations, the Jews deeply presuppose that these miracles of Moses, Elisha, and Christ were done through the *Shem ha-Mephorash*, the

---

21. *lib. 1…c. viii.* Cf. Eusebius, *De praeparatione evangelica* 11.6 in PG 21:857; idem, *Preparation for the Gospel*, trans. E. H. Gifford (Oxford, 1903), 517

22. See Moses Maimonides, *Liber Moreh Nevukhim Doctor Perplexorum* (Basilae: Ludwig I. Konig & Johann Jakob Genath [the older], 1629); idem, *The Guide of the Perplexed*, trans. Michael Friedlander (London: George Routledge & Sons, 1956).

23. Martin Luther, *Vom Schem Hamphoras: und vom Geschlecht Christi* (Frankfurt, 1543).

very thing that was to be proved, especially since Scripture knows absolutely
nothing of this name. (2) As for the text in Psalm 44, its immediately preceding
words refer those victories to Jehovah himself: "Through you we will strike our
enemies." Nor is there hidden to the Jews their own well-known maxim, הוא שמו
ושמו הוא, "He is his name, and his name is he."

3. Is the name Jehovah proper to God alone?

XIV. It is asked, third, whether the name *Jehovah* is proper to God alone. There
are some who do not even admit it as a name of God, but as a fiction, but the
continuous citation of this name throughout the entirety of the Holy Scriptures
most powerfully refutes them. The Socinians, due to their hatred of the Holy
Trinity and the eternal deity of Christ and the Holy Spirit (which deity, presupposing the name belongs to them, has a most strong defense in it), deny that the
name is proper to God and rather affirm that it is common to creatures, and even
to idols. The Reformed do in fact grant that in an oblique case, in composition,
and thus in a diminished sense, it can happen that it is attributed to creatures,
but on the contrary, in the nominative case, in the simple and full sense, they
deny that it applies to any other throughout the Scriptures than to the God
who is, as they say, the highest. This is so because: (1) in the text God affirms
that this is his own name forever and his own memorial from generation to generation (likewise in Ps. 83:18; Ex. 15:3; Hos. 12:5). (2) It is expressly denied to
others (Isa. 42:8; 48:2). (3) The force and efficacy of this name, as explained in
§VIII, cannot belong to any other than the highest God. (4) The very rationale
of Hebrew grammar does not allow another explanation, for according to it,
this name is never read with the demonstrative ה, never with an affix, and never
in the plural—all of which belong to proper names. (5) With these things the
universal consent of all Jews agrees. Nevertheless, the Socinians cry out against
it: (1) that it is attributed to angels (Ex. 3:2; 19:11 with Acts 7:53; Gal. 3:19). I
respond, Not to angels but to an angel, that is, the one who is called the angel
of his presence (Isa. 63:9), the angel of the covenant (Mal. 3:1), who bears the
name of God, that is, God himself, "within him" (Ex. 23:21), and thus is God
himself. (2) That it is attributed to judges (Deut. 19:17), but this is denied; it
is said that litigators will stand "before Jehovah," that is, before the priests, inasmuch as Jehovah judges through them. (3) That it is attributed to the ark: "Rise
up, O Jehovah, and let your enemies be scattered" (Num. 10:35). I respond, It
is not attributed to the ark, but to Jehovah who is present with the ark in a
singular way. For it is an invocation that, as our adversaries acknowledge, does
not belong the ark, but to Jehovah alone; nor were the enemies to be scattered
properly enemies of the ark, but of Jehovah. (4) That it is likewise attributed

to the altar: "He built an altar and named it *Jehovah Nissi*, 'Jehovah Is My Banner'" (Ex. 17:15). I respond, He did not name the altar *Jehovah*, but *Jehovah Nissi*, in composition, just as occurs in the names יהונתן, *Jonathan*, יוצדק, *Jozadak*, and others, in which the force of the name *Jehovah* is not full, but diminished. The Reformed do not deny that the name can be spoken in this way about creatures, in the same way as also the altar is called יהוה שלום, "Jehovah is Peace" in Judges 6:24. (5) That it is also attributed to Jerusalem: "This is the one who will call her, 'Jehovah our Righteousness'" (Jer. 33:16). I respond, It is not said that Jerusalem will be so called, because as our adversaries confess, not Jerusalem but rather Jehovah was their righteousness, but rather the Messiah who was the righteousness of Israel: "This will be the name that they will call *him*: *'Jehovah our Righteousness'*" (Jer. 23:6); for Jerusalem was not the righteousness of Israel. (6) That finally it is attributed to idols in Exodus 32:5 and Judges 17:3ff. I respond: (a) Aaron does not call the idol Jehovah, but proclaims a feast for Jehovah. And (b) in Judges 17:3, Micah's idol is not called Jehovah, but his mother says only that she consecrated the silver to Jehovah, so that by it there might be a sacrifice made to Jehovah, that is, through the image. For this reason, the rabbis, in order to signify the fictitious gods of the Gentiles, through contempt call them, instead of *Elohim*, אלוהות, *Elohoth*, in the feminine form.

4. Is the name Elohim *a name designating only an office and not the divine essence?*
XV. It is asked, fourth, whether the name *Elohim*, to which θεός of the Greeks and *Deus* of the Latins corresponds, is a name designating only an office and not the deity or divine essence. The Jews commonly think—although without any firm reason—that this is the name of righteousness and judgment, and thus it is communicated to magistrates by analogy, but that this is no different than how *Jehovah* is the name of grace and mercy, though it still in its own special character and emphasis designates God alone. The Socinians,[24] since they observe that the name *Elohim* or θεός is often attributed to Christ and the Holy Spirit, so that they will not be compelled to admit that the divine essence or eternal deity belong to them, state that the words *Elohim*, θεός, and *Deus* do not signify the divine essence but only an office. The Reformed do not deny that there are among the names, if not each and every one, those that connote, together with the divine essence, some perfection of God, just as for example, the name *Adonai*, which without a doubt is proper to God, connotes his most absolute lordship over all created things. Nevertheless, they state that there is no name that excludes the divine essence. Thus it is also possible that *Elohim*, as in the opinion of the Jews,

---

24. *Judaei*: cf. §X, above, where this view is specifically ascribed to the Socinians.

connotes, together with the divine essence, his righteousness and judgment, and even more, from אֵל, his might. You will observe the same thing, for example, in *Shaddai, Elyon*, and others. Meanwhile, they also deny that *Elohim* connotes, together with the essence, any office of God, for (1) what would the office be that *Elohim*, θεός, and *Deus* denote? Next, (2) all the names of office are derived from something else that expresses its formal reason, just as *Rex*, "King," from *regendum*, "governing," and *Dominus*, "Lord" from *dominandum*, "ruling over," but neither *Elohim* nor θεός are derived from some other such thing. If they allege in support of their case that *Elohim* is attributed to magistrates (Ps. 82:6; John 10:34), we respond that from this it does not follow that it is a name of office, for many things are attributed to the magistrate that are not names of office.

5. Does the name Elohim *signify a plurality of persons in God?*
XVI. It is asked, fifth, whether the name *Elohim* signifies a plurality of persons in God. The Jews, with whom the Socinians are in complete agreement on this point, because, as they admit only one divine essence, so they also admit only one person, state (1) that *Elohim* is indeed plural in form but singular in force. (2) That if it should be also plural in force, then it connotes, together with the essence, the properties and virtues of God. (3) That in this plurality is the courtly manner of speaking, by which a plural word denotes one certain monarch. Among Protestants there are some who state that the name *Elohim* so cogently argues for plurality in God that even by itself, that is, conjoined with a word in the singular number, it can in a disputation sustain the doctrine of the Holy Trinity. The majority of the Lutherans, and in addition several of the Reformed—for example, Zanchi, Martyr, and Junius, and others—think in this way.[25] Others on the contrary deny that that argument should be advanced in conflict with anti-Trinitarians because it seems exposed to objections and exceptions that have too much appearance of truth, while other more evident arguments are available for this cause. Thus thought Calvin, Mercier, Daneau, Drusius, and others who otherwise frankly professed the Trinity of persons. I would think that in this matter the middle way is walked most safely, if we say that neither should the argument be placed at the beginning of the dispute, as Calvin prudently warned, nor ought it to be entirely neglected, but rather, that when the Trinity has been demonstrated by other more evident arguments, it can be subjoined, and that

---

25. E.g. Girolamo Zanchi, *De tribus Elohim*, 2 parts (Frankfurt, 1572), 1:1; on Gen. 1:1, Peter Martyr Vermigli (1499–1562), *In primum librum Mosis, qui vulgo Genesis dicitur* (Zurich: Christopher Froschuer, 1569), 2v; on Gen. 1:1, Franciscus Junius, *Libri Geneseos analysis* ([Geneva]: Sanctandreana, 1594), 5.

this was without a doubt the rationale of the Holy Spirit, that though there was available to him the singular אל and אלוה, he wished nevertheless nearly always to use אלהים in the plural.

Arguments

Meanwhile there is not, as far as I can tell, anyone among the Protestants who denies that it is a personal name. For why (1) when in fact there are several persons in God (just as in its own place, we will show, God willing, proved by unconquerable arguments),[26] would he not want this fact signified in the plural name? Why (2) to signify one person would he use the plural number, when the singular number of the same word is readily available and is not rarely used elsewhere (Deut. 32:17; Job 3:4, 23; 12:4; 36:2; Ps. 50:22; Hab. 3:3; etc.)? Why (3) to designate one person would he with the plural *Elohim* construct plural verbs and nouns: נעשה אדם, "Let *us* make man," and indeed בצלמנו, "according to *our* image" (Gen. 1:26; cf. 20:13; Deut. 5:26; Josh. 24:19; Jer. 10:10; Isa. 6:8)? Why these things?

Objections

If they should say on the contrary: (1) that in Hebrew there are nouns plural in number that are singular in force, we gladly admit this, but then only when their singulars are not prominent. If (2) they should say that this occurs in the style of the court, they themselves must demonstrate that such a style was in use at that time, and that it existed among the Hebrews, and even if it did, that such a vain way of speaking was used by God. If (3) they should say that nevertheless it is observed from our hypothesis that the word in the plural is used for some single divine person, then we will answer that in Psalm 45:7 this occurs by emperichoresis, on account of the one divine essence that is common to the individual persons. If they should say (4) that this is also observed to have occurred in the case of singular idols, we will respond that this is done improperly, or catachrestically, and mimetically, since to do so is customary among the Hebrews (Judg. 11:24; Amos 5:26 with Jer. 16:20; Hos. 8:6; Ps. 96:5; 1 Cor. 8:5; 2 Thess. 2:4; cf. John 17:3; 1 John 5:20). For the Hebrews usually designate "god" by *Elohim*. If (5) they should say that this occurs in order to indicate angels in Genesis 1:26, "And Elohim said, 'Let us make man…,'" will they not be attributing the name of God and his glory to another, when God cries out against this (Isa. 42:8)? Will they not be making the angels also into Elohim who are creators, which God abominates in Jeremiah 10:11? Will they not be saying

---

26. 1.2.24 §§III, IV, XVIII, XIX

that man was created in the image of angels, which is against the whole tenor of Scripture? Finally, if (6) they should say that God by this very thing wants to add to himself his own properties and virtues, then they will be saying what has neither an example in the Scriptures, nor reason, nor sense. For what, for example, does this mean: "And God along with his properties said, 'Let us make man in our image'"?

The Practical Part

The first practice, concerning the knowledge of God

XVII. With respect to practice, the theory of the divine names assists first in the knowledge of God. For it is among the first supports by whose help we arrive at the knowledge of God. Likewise, it is the first support by which we distinguish creatures and false gods from the true God, in which is founded all religion, faith, and divine worship (Heb. 11:6), and to which Scripture attributes justification (Isa. 53:11) and eternal life (John 17:3). For this is, from its root, the function of a *nomen* (for it is nothing other than a *novimen* or *notamen*, a characteristic trait or mark), that it may make the one named known (Ex. 6:3).[27] For this whole crowd of so many divine names, each of which represents the very same God but in a different way, what is its purpose if not to generate a more distinct knowledge of the one named? Hence there are names set forth that represent his essence, *Jehovah, Yah, Ehyeh*; that represent his subsistence in three persons, for example, *Elohim, Father, Word, Son,* and *Holy Spirit*; that convey his all-sufficiency, such as *El-Shaddai*; his dominion, *Adonai*; his strength or omnipotence, such as *El*; his majesty and excellence, such as *Elyon*—certainly so that in all these names and several others we may distinctly acknowledge him as God. See also chapter 2 on the existence and knowledge of God.

The second practice, concerning the glorification of God

XVIII. Then, second, it inculcates the glorification of God. For such an accumulation of so many names, of which each singular name sets before us something singular about the majesty of God, and the knowledge born from there—to what end do they serve except that we would acknowledge in our heart and declare with our mouth the majesty that is in these names sketched out, as it were, bit by bit? And what then is this, if not to glorify God? That is, when (1) "name" throughout the Holy Scriptures expresses fame, glory, and great esteem and renown (Gen. 11:4; 12:2; Prov. 22:1; Mark 6:14); when (2) "men

---

27. See §III, above.

of name" are those renowned for whatever special privilege (1 Chron. 5:24; Gen. 6:4); when (3) to "have a name" is to be commended by all (Rev. 3:1), and he whose name is said to be commended is most celebrated (2 Sam. 12:28); when (4) "children without a name" are considered disgraceful children of the earth (Job 30:8); indeed, when (5) in particular the "name of God" designates his fame and renown (1 Kings 8:42; Neh. 9:10; Dan. 9:15), and also his glory (Josh. 7:9; Ps. 23:3; etc.); and moreover, when (6) the "name of God" not rarely in the Holy Scriptures means nothing other than the recognition of his attributes and perfections (Ps. 76:1; Heb. 2:12; 13:15)—then what else would be the purpose of so many and such a variety of names of God? Do they not intend to raise a person up, so that (1) in his own heart, he may acknowledge and extol the virtues of God signified in his names; and (2) he may publicly declare and magnify them before others (1 Peter 2:9)? These are the two parts of divine glorification, about which we will speak expressly in the chapter on the glory of God.[28]

The third practice, concerning the profanation of the divine name
XIX. Furthermore, third, it condemns the violation and profanation of the divine names, which are intended for such precious uses, namely, for the increase of the knowledge of God and his glorification. Such profanation (1) God expressly prohibits by one certain, specific commandment out of the Ten, and with such great emphasis (Ex. 20:7). Upon it (2) he pronounces unavoidable punishment: "The Lord will not let him go unpunished." And (3) he also punished it by death (Lev. 24:11, 16). Moreover, this profanation occurs: (1) in the heart, through ignorance, by which the name that was given in order that God would be known is neglected; and through forgetfulness, by which the name is neglected as a memorial. (2) With the mouth, by using it rashly or without just cause, profanely without reverence and devotion, or impiously through blasphemy. (3) In one's work, for anyone who names the name of the Lord must depart from every kind of unrighteousness (2 Tim. 2:19). More things of this kind will be treated under the third commandment.[29]

The fourth practice, concerning the sanctification of the divine name
XX. Finally, fourth, it rouses us to the sanctification of the divine name, in which we generally embrace whatever could pertain to the genuine use of the divine names: for example, (1) the announcement and preaching of the divine

---

28. 1.2.22 §XVI
29. 1.6.8 §XVI; 2.2.14

name (Acts 9:15); (2) the invocation of the same (Joel 2:32); (3) a trust-filled resting in the same (Prov. 18:10); (4) the fear and reverence of the divine name (Ps. 143:11); (5) the profession of the name of God, or of Christ (2 Tim. 2:19; Acts 9:15); and (6) the glorifying of the same (Joel 2:26; etc.). About these things the sacred Book speaks throughout its pages, as do theologians when they treat the first petition of the Lord's Prayer. Furthermore, to develop the use and practice of each of the divine names one by one would require more space than the compendious plan of this Theology would allow.

CHAPTER FIVE

The Attributes of God in General

And he added, "Please show me your glory." And he responded, "I will make all my goodness pass before your face, and I will call out the name Jehovah before you...."

—Exodus 33:18–23[1]

The second help for knowing the divine essence is in the attributes of God.

I. Up to this point, we have presented the first help for knowing the divine essence, namely that which is found in the names of God. We now progress to the second help, which is found in the divine attributes, and we will speak of them in general, and then individually regarding each attribute. The text of Exodus 33:18–23 will lay the foundation of the prior theory.

The Exegetical Part

The text is resolved and explained.

II. In it is displayed Moses's request joined with God's certainly gracious but limited answer. Thus these two parts emerge:

A. Moses's petition, in verse 18: "Please show me your glory," or in verse 13, את דרכך, "your way." But what does this "glory" mean? Philo of Alexandria, in the section *On Monarchy*, understands this as the ideas and powers that are in God;[2] Tertullian, as the glory of the humanity of Christ that he would display later on Mount Tabor (Matt. 17); Jerome, Augustine, and others, as the glorious essence of God itself, which

---

1. Mastricht quotes only 33:18–19 but explains through v. 23 below.

2. *Philo Judaeus*, Philo of Alexandria (c. 20 B.C.–c. A.D. 50); also *de Monarchia*: "the section *On Monarchy*." This reference is known variously as Περὶ Μοναρχίας λόγος πρῶτος 1.6, *De Monarchia* 1.6, or as a subheading within *De legibus specialibus*; see idem, *Philonis Alexandrinis opera quae supersunt*, ed. L. Cohn and P. Wendland, 7 vols. (Berlin, 1896–1930), 5:10–12; idem, *The Works of Philo Judaeus*, trans. J. D. Yonge, 3 vols. (London: H. G. Bohn, 1855), 3:184–86; idem, *Philo volume VII*, LCL 320:122–27.

Moses desired to see with his eyes, either the eyes of his body, under some bodily appearance, or the eyes of his mind. God himself seems to refute this in denying that his face can be seen by the living. What if we should understand it as the glorious attributes of God, by which his very essence may in some way be made known to us? In the same way, the rabbis understand "the ways of God" to mean his properties, as Johannes Drusius attests in his *Observations*,[3] which elsewhere they call מדות, and which are reviewed quite copiously in Exodus 34:5–8.[4] This seems to be confirmed from the text when God substitutes for "glory" "goodness" (v. 19) and avenging justice: "But I will have compassion on whom I will have compassion," adding also, "Jehovah." By all these things, God's "posterior parts," as it were, or rather, God's essence *a posteriori*, are in the glorious name in some way made known to us.

B. God's answer, in which:

1. He assents to Moses's petition, promising him twin kindnesses, of which:

    a. One was visible: "I will make all my goodness to pass by before your face," קל תובי, "all my goodness," that is, "which is contained in all my attributes." Moses had asked for the glory of God, and God answers regarding his goodness, either because in the glory of God, Moses especially desired to perceive the goodness of God, or because the glory of God perhaps especially appears in the independent goodness of God (Matt. 19:17), or (what is most likely) because "face," glory, goodness, righteousness, mercy, and all things are one and the same on the part of God.

    b. The other was audible: "And I will call out the name *Jehovah* before you," or, "I will also proclaim that great name of mine, *Jehovah*, before you, so that in this way, both from my attributes and from this name, you may in some way see both my glory and my essence."

2. He restricts and limits, as it were, the same petition by two clauses, of which:

---

3. Johannes Drusius, *Observationes sacrae…lib. XII* (Antwerp: Aegidius Radaeus, 1584).

4. The שָׁלוֹשׁ עֶשְׂרֵה מִידוֹת הרחֲמִים or the thirteen attributes or "rules" of mercy in rabbinic Judaism are the divine attributes of God, whereby he governs the world, revealed to Moses. In Maimonides, מרה נבוחים, that is, *The Guide for the Perplexed*, trans. M. Friedländer, bk 1 ch. 54, pp. 75–78, these are not God's inherent qualities, but his principles of action from the perspective of the human observer.

a. The first regards his goodness: "But I will have compassion on whom I will have compassion, and I will be merciful to whom I will be merciful," just as if he should say, "You will truly see my goodness, but not such a goodness that is in itself different from or contrary to my avenging justice." For the attributes are not in reality different in God, much less contrary.

b. The second regards his essence: "You cannot see my face, for man shall not see me and live." Here the "face of God" seems to mean that essence which no one has seen or can see, because he dwells in inaccessible light (1 Tim. 6:16). Although, at the same time it is said that after this life we will see God "face to face," namely, in contradistinction to the vision that is "in an enigma" (1 Cor. 13:12).

3. Finally, he grants what was petitioned:

a. In assigning to Moses a place where he might receive it: "Behold, a place by me, and you shall stand upon a rock," regarding which there is nothing to teach under this topic.

b. In determining the mode of both conferring and receiving the petitioned benefit, "And when my glory passes by, I will place you in the cleft of the rock, and I will cover you with my hand until I have passed by."

c. In conferring the petitioned thing itself: "I will remove my hand," that is, from your eyes, "and you will see my posterior parts, but my face will not be seen."

Regarding these matters, many things could be asked and said, but those things are not for this chapter, for which reason out of zeal for brevity we will set them aside, being for the purpose of this topic content to have noted from the above matters the two following things.

The Dogmatic Part

The essence of God is invisible.

III. First, the essence of God as it is in itself is entirely invisible and imperceptible, inasmuch as it is said that the face of God cannot be seen. Since we expressly considered this observation in chapter 3 of this second book,[5] we set it aside for the present.

---

5. 1.2.3 §III

The essence of God is made known to us through his attributes.

IV. Yet meanwhile, that same essence is in some way made known from its attributes and properties, insofar as by them God shows Moses as it were his posterior parts, in his glory, goodness, mercy, and righteousness. To this end the divine attributes are amassed throughout the sacred Scriptures (Ex. 34:5–6; Neh. 9:5, 17; Ps. 103:8; Jer. 32:17–19; 1 Tim. 1:17; 6:15–16, etc.). And also from this, in the calling of God by names, his attributes come forth, as much in Scripture as in the fathers, as we taught above, namely because together with the names that are properly so-called, the attributes are a sort of *novimen* or distinguishing characteristic of the divine essence.[6] This fact, if it is obvious in the knowledge of any creature, will be much more so in the knowledge of the divine essence. For if (1) any substance, down to the smallest, and even a corporeal substance exposed to the senses, is not made known to our mind except by the help of its attributes, then (2) will we not all the more say this about spiritual substances, which are entirely inaccessible to the senses, that they are not made known to us except through their attributes? For clear witnesses to this reality are displayed in the angels, indeed in our very own soul. In fact, (3) will this not especially have to be asserted regarding an infinite substance? How could it come into our mind unless as if by parts, under various attributes, in various inadequate concepts? From these things there arises a threefold argument for the necessity of attributes as an aid in knowing this substance, namely, that it is a substance, and spiritual, and infinite.

How do attributes belong to God?

V. Therefore, they are called *attributes*, if you should attend to the term, not because they are in God, or because they are present and inhere in him as accidents and qualities, but rather because they are attributed by us to God, that is, they are predicated of him, they belong to him and are of his essence, or more rightly said, they are his essence itself. They are otherwise designated as *properties*, not insofar as they express the fourth of the predicables,[7] but as they denote the essential reckoning of a subject; and also as *names*, as we just taught.[8] If you want the thing they express, they are nothing but the one infinite perfection of God insofar as it is apprehended by us in various inadequate concepts. For to our formal concepts, as they say, which are in reality distinct among themselves,

---

6. 1.2.4 §§III, V

7. In scholastic logic based on Porphyry's *Isagoge* (chs. 2–11), there are five things that can be predicated about a subject: genus, species, difference, property, and accident.

8. §IV, above

on God's part respond various objective concepts which indicate in God nothing but his one infinite perfection, unknowable to our intellect through its native finitude and infirmity except in various acts, as if by parts. It is just as, when we would contemplate the entire horizon, although it is one and only one, yet we employ various actions of seeing, now turned toward the east, now toward the west, next toward the south, and finally toward the north, until we have exhausted the whole. Thus this hodge-podge of attributes arises not so much from God's perfection as from our imperfection. Namely, when from these things which we see belong to creatures, we attribute certain ones to God, we remove others from him; then, from the things attributed we remove all imperfection which in creatures customarily adheres to them, because in the most perfect one imperfection does not occur; and finally, in the remaining things attributed, we add the infinite preeminence that belongs to him by reason of the infinity of his essence. And this at last is the way to investigate the divine attributes.

All the attributes in God denote one most simple act.
VI. Therefore, so that we may more exactly understand their nature and character, above all this must be laid as a foundation: all the attributes together in God are nothing but one certain most simple and most pure act, his very essence, and his infinite perfection. For (1) in the absolutely first being, there cannot occur one thing and another, through composition, because that would require one who composed those things, who was prior to the absolutely first being. Also, (2) it cannot occur in an infinite being. For if one thing and another did occur, both things would be either infinite or finite: not infinite, because plural infinites involve an infinite contradiction; nor finite, because one infinite thing cannot coalesce from plural finite things. In addition, (3) it cannot occur in an immutable and incorruptible being. For when a thing is composed with another, then the one thing can also be separated from the other, and thus the thing can be changed and corrupted.

Ten inferences about attributes
VII. Thus with this laid as a foundation, we will best think about the nature of divine attributes by aid of the following inferences.

1. First, the attributes of God certainly differ among themselves, but not so much on God's part as on the part of our conception. Accordingly, they do not differ really, as one thing from another, but by our reason or thought, and yet not only by a reasoning reason which lacks reasons for distinguishing, but by a reasoned reason which receives the reasons for distinguishing from God himself, insofar

as it observes that God through his infinite perfection differs as it were in infinite ways, in his operations, when, for example, he builds up this one and destroys that one. And since it is persuaded that in the creatures, the former comes from love and the latter from hatred, it attributes both, from the likeness and identity of the effect, to God, and also distinguishes them in God, at least virtually and eminently. Moreover, it expresses them by different definitions, just as of one and the same thing there are different notions, or as they say, formalities, which belong to things not on their own part but on the part of our intellect.

2. Meanwhile, second, all the attributes truly belong to God. For he is good, wise, just, and so forth, not only through our thought, but from the condition of his own nature. And they belong to him not only in the concrete, as properties belong to the creatures; but in addition in the abstract, which is proper to God (compare these passages: 1 John 5:20 with 1 John 1:2; 1 Tim. 6:16 and Dan. 2:22 with 1 John 1:5; Ex. 34:5–6 with 1 John 4:8).

3. Indeed, third, all the attributes, if you should consider the thing that they signify, not only belong to God truly, but also first of all, or, more properly and perfectly than they belong to the creatures, namely insofar as the perfection of any divine attribute infinitely exceeds any analogous perfections in the creatures. Although at the same time, the names by which those perfections are designated belong first of all to the creatures, inasmuch as they are transferred from them to God.

4. Because all the attributes speak of one most simple act in God, it should be held, fourth, that in them there must not be admitted any degrees of increase, loss, dissimilarity, or inequality; that is, intrinsically and on God's part, each and every attribute indicates infinite perfection, in which any idea of more or less is not admitted. Although at the same time, it can happen that extrinsically one attribute extends itself to more objects than another, in which sense the intellect can be called greater than the will, or it acts more intensively upon one object than another, in which sense God loves the elect more than the reprobate.

5. On the same basis, fifth, much less ought there to be admitted any conflict or enmity among the attributes of God. And if there does appear some such thing, for example, between mercy and avenging justice, it is entirely in the object according to which the uniform perfection of God, since it is infinite, is occupied in different ways. Or, as you might say more accurately, it is this perfection of God which the creatures undergo in different ways.

6. Furthermore, sixth, we must conceive the divine attributes as divine perfections, and yet in such a way that every imperfection that usually attends such properties in creatures is carefully removed from the analogous attributes of God, and the remaining perfection is conceived with the greatest eminence, that is, according to the ways of causality, negation, and eminence, which we already demonstrated as the ways for investigating the divine attributes.[9]

7. In addition, seventh, it must be noted that the attributes belong to God, not only virtually, as heat belongs to the sun because it heats, nor also only eminently, just as the perfection of a thing caused belongs to its cause (Ps. 94:9), but formally, insofar as every perfection which is designated through analogous attributes, with every attached imperfection removed, belongs to God truly and properly, and indeed to a preeminent degree, although they do not belong to him as accidents or qualities, which pertains to the imperfections of those attributes in the creatures.

8. Moreover, eighth, the attributes belong to God as if in a certain secondary being, insofar as we conceive first of the essence of God, as the root from which the attributes arise. For we conceive that God exists before we can conceive that he is, for example, merciful, wise, and just. In this sense, essence, substance, and spirit must be removed from the category of divine attributes, since they concern primary being, and they do not have anything to which they may be attributed in the way of a perfection that arrives and qualifies, such as wisdom, and so forth. And this is also the case because there are incommunicable and communicable attributes, which we presuppose here, and which will be explained and confirmed in its own place.[10]

9. It should be observed, ninth, that those attributes which are incommunicable include in their formal concept something so peculiar to the divine essence that not even a trace of it may be discovered in any creature. In this place are especially those attributes called negative—for example, infinity, immutability, independence—and from the affirmative attributes also several, such as omniscience, omnipotence, eternity, and any others of the same character.

10. In the same way vice versa, tenth, those attributes that are called communicable do not correspond to God and the creatures univocally, because there is no

9. 1.2.2 §XIX
10. §§VII, XII

proportion at all between the infinite and the finite; nor also equivocally, such that they concur in name only, since from the knowledge of the one we can be led back to the knowledge of the other; but only analogically, such that the thing signified by the attributes belongs principally and originally to God, but to the creatures only participatively, and with a degree of diminution, just as health properly and in itself belongs to an animal, although on account of the animal it belongs to food, air, and medicine.

The distribution of the divine attributes
VIII. Therefore, from these theorems the common nature of the divine attributes will be made quite well known to us, and even more so if we should add their distribution. It is customarily arrayed in different ways by different theologians. The more received distributions are those in which the attributes of God are: (1) proper and metaphorical, the latter such as a lion, fire, and a rock. (2) Negative and positive, such that those which are called negative, while in their formal signification they remove imperfections from God, yet in their material concept involve positive perfections. The positive are (3) either relative, such as Creator, which are hardly admitted about him other than in the concrete; or absolute. They are (4) either personal, such as the generation of the Son, or natural. Finally, the natural attributes are (5) either communicable or incommunicable,[11] which distribution, the most received among theologians, we have vindicated in another place from injury.[12] We only add that those attributes which are called communicable belong to God (a) not only negatively, such that when, for example, he is called living, it is signified that he is not like lifeless beings. And (b) not only virtually or causally, as if he were only the cause of the signified perfections in creatures. And not (c) univocally, such that the thing signified by the attributes is equally present on both sides, in God and in creatures, because the attributes are infinite in God, from whom the finite is infinitely distant. Rather, they belong to God truly and substantially, eminently, and analogically, to such a degree that although a perfection signified by the attributes, which belongs to the creatures, belongs as such to God, nevertheless the perfection of this attribute is not, vice versa, to the extent that it is present in God, also present in the creatures, except perhaps by some sort of vestige of it.

---

11. κοινωνητὰ *vel* ἀκοινώνητα
12. §XII, below

The most preeminent distribution of the attributes

IX. Our preference is to arrange the divine attributes as though according to their functions. For they teach partly (1) what God is, namely those attributes which coincide as suitably as possible with God's description, by which he is "Spirit from himself," in which description these coincide, his spirituality (under which is his simplicity, invisibility, and so forth) and independence. Partly (2) how great God is, by which attributes he is called one, infinite, and eternal. Partly (3) what qualities God has. Attributes of this third kind return to us the divine perfection under the notion either of faculties, in which place are the intellect, will, and affections; or of virtues, whether in the intellect, such as omniscience, or in the will, where there is goodness (under which are grace and mercy), holiness, and righteousness; or under the notion of operations, the chief of which is omnipotence.[13] From all these coalesce (4) perfection and omnisufficiency, majesty and glory, and finally, blessedness. And this then is the order by which we will be engaged in the individual contemplation of the divine attributes.

The Elenctic Part

It is asked: 1. Are the divine attributes something different from his essence?

The variety of opinions

X. It is asked, first, whether the divine attributes are something different from his essence. The heretic Valentinus (c. AD 130), with his Gnostic followers, numbered thirty gods, whom he called aeons, partly male and partly female (without doubt different from the divine essence), from whose congress (συζυγία) or intercourse he stated that the Savior arose. He did this, namely, so that he would not be forced to admit that Christ is of the same essence with his Father. Concerning these things see Tertullian, *Against the Valentinians*; Irenaeus, book 2, chapter 4; and Epiphanius, *Panarion*, 31.[14] The kabbalist Jews had their own ספירות and אצילות, "numerations" and "emanations," which from the book יצירה, *Yetzirah*, which they claim is by Abraham, they enumerate ten as "lights," or properties of the divine essence, which are neither God nor creatures, but flow forth and emanate from God as rays from the sun, concerning which see Reuchlin's *On the Kabbalistic Art*.[15] Buxtorf philosophizes in this way in his

---

13. The three questions are (1) *quid sit Deus*, (2) *quantus sit*, and (3) *qualis sit*.

14. Tertullian, *Adversus Valentinianos* in *PL* 1:545–46, 552–54; idem, *Against the Valentinians* in *Ante-Nicene Fathers* (*ANF*) ed. Alexander Roberts and James Donaldson (New York: Christian Literature Co., 1885–1896; reprint Peabody, Mass.: Hendrickson, 1994), 3:504–5, 508; Irenaeus, *Adversus Haereses* in *PG* 7:718–22; idem, *Against Heresies* in *ANF* 1:362–64; Epiphanius of Salamis (d. 403), *Panarion* (or *Adversus Haereses*), Heresy 31 in *PG* 41:473.

15. Reuchlin, *De arte cabbalistica*, LXI v–LXII r.

Lexicon of the Talmud: "Behold, they," these ten *Sephiroth*, "are the ten divine names which we mortals conceive about God, names that are either essential, or personal, or notional, or communal. And they are named in this way: כתר, 'Crown'; חכמה, 'Wisdom'; בינה, 'Prudence' or 'Intelligence'; חסד, 'Clemency' or 'Goodness'; גבורה, 'Gravity' or 'Severity,' or 'Power'; תפארת, 'Adornment'; נצח, 'Triumph'; הוד, 'Confession of Praise'; יסוד, 'Foundation'; מלכות, 'Kingdom' (though it is placed above 'Crown'); and אין סוף, 'Infinity' (and this is 'Abyss')."[16] Conrad Vorstius, the Socinianizer, really distinguished between God's power and the divine essence, and he did so for this reason, so that the essence of God would be present only in heaven, while the power of God would be present also on earth, and thus the essence of God could not have been personally united with the human nature of Christ as long as it existed on the earth only, and in this way Vorstius powerfully lies in ambush for Christ the God-man. The Socinians, so that the Holy Spirit may not be God consubstantial with the Father, state that he is the power of God, different from the divine essence, and thus that the divine attributes really differ from the essence. In addition, so that we would not solidly gather from the divine attributes, which are asserted throughout the Scriptures for both the Son and the Spirit, that the divine essence belongs to them—and thus that God is three in persons and one in essence— they say that the divine attributes really differ from the essence. Furthermore, in the business of the decrees, predestination, and so on, so that when the divine will has changed the divine essence is not changed, they state that the attributes really differ from the divine essence.

The thought of the Reformed

The Reformed, although they admit that the essence does differ from the attributes, nevertheless do not admit that they differ really, in God himself, but by reason, in our conception, insofar as sometimes it conceives of the essence simply and abstractly from the attributes, and sometimes conceives of the same essence with various relations and operations in creatures, and from that arise the attributes, which do not differ really either from the essence or among themselves. For if, (1) they should differ, they would be different things in God, and thus there would not be pure deity in God, nor for that reason would God be the light in whom there is no darkness (1 John 1:5). Next, (2) if there were one thing and another in God, then in him there would exist composition, which would have as a prerequisite one who composes, and thus God would not be the absolutely

---

16. Johannes Buxtorf, Jr. (1599–1664), *Lexicon Chaldaicum, Talmudicum et Rabbinicum* (Basel: Ludovicus König, 1639).

first being. Furthermore, if composite, then also dissoluble and thus not incorruptible—and why not also annihilable? For neither the essence without the attributes nor the attributes without the essence are God. Thus, (3) God would be in part God and in part not, for if the attributes are not the divine essence, they are not God.

An objection ·
Adversaries in this business do not so much dispute with reasons as serve their own hypotheses. Nor is there anything that they could more speciously allege for their case than that there are contrary attributes in God, such as mercy and avenging justice. But this is not in God himself, but rather in the work of God, and in us who observe this contrariety in the divine effects and from it form such attributes. In this is the chief perfection of the most simple divine essence, that in things that are different it can produce things that are contrary.

2. Are only a few attributes necessary to know and believe?
XI. It is asked, second, whether only a very few attributes are necessary to believe for salvation. The Socinians, not only so that they might more comfortably bring into the Christian faith a Samaritanism under which someone lacking the fundamentals could more comfortably hide, but also so that they can more effectively eliminate from the bounds of Christianity those attributes of God by which the eternal and consubstantial deity of the Son and the Holy Spirit are customarily demonstrated, and furthermore, so that they may more securely hold to the dependence of God upon our free choice, the mutability of the divine decrees according to the pleasure of human choice, the real diversity of the divine essence, the incommunicability of the essence to the three persons, and other things, state, since independence, immutability, simplicity, and infinity have been excluded, that only these six attributes are necessary to know and believe: (1) that God exists, and that he is (2) one only, (3) eternal, (4) perfectly just, (5) perfectly wise, (6) and perfectly powerful (*Racovian Catechism*, ch. 1).[17] The Remonstrant Apologists, so that the Socinians might not be judged to be in error on the fundamentals, and so that they can have communion with them in their assemblies, are not far from the Socinians in stating that only a very few things are necessary for Christians to know and believe about God. The Cartesianizing theologians, in favor of their own philosophy, for which the divine essence is nothing but mere thought, enumerate none but two attributes of God: intellect and will,

---

17. Cf. Valentinus Smalcius, *Catechismus der Gemeine derer Leute* (Raków: Sternacius Sebastianus, 1608), 1–16; *The Racovian Catechism* (London, 1818), 1–13.

because these two alone are included in the nature of thought. The orthodox number more attributes of God than the six of the Socinians and the two of the Cartesians, and indeed account them as necessary to believe. This is because (1) Scripture numbers more, and also frequently amasses divine attributes, as we noted above in §IV. (2) Without the omitted attributes—independence, immutability, simplicity, infinity, grace and mercy, and likewise who God is—a person cannot have a thought about the true God, and thus also cannot have faith, love, and so forth, and for this reason, is by necessity an atheist. (3) Neither faith nor divine worship can subsist in any way unless we know who the true God is, namely, the God who is Father, Son, and Holy Spirit (John 17:3), unless we want to believe in and serve an unknown God, which is contrary to John 4:22, Acts 17:21, and 2 Kings 17:29. (4) The spirituality and simplicity of God (John 4:24), his invisible nature (Deut. 4:15ff.), immensity (Ps. 139:1–3ff.), and immutability (Ps. 102:26–28) are necessary for us to know. (5) The six Socinian attributes, if the rest are set aside, do not confer salvation, but concern only inexcusability (Rom. 1:19–21; 2:14–15), as the apostle declares (1 Cor. 1:21; Rom. 1:19). The Socinians do not have anything to allege for themselves, except that those six are required for salvation; but on the contrary they do not prove that they are sufficient for salvation when the others are removed. In regard to the Cartesians, their foundation is in the idea that the essence of God consists in thought alone, which we already expressly routed in a preceding section.[18]

3. Should the distribution of the divine attributes into incommunicable and communicable be accepted?

XII. It is asked, third, whether the distribution of the divine attributes into incommunicable and communicable, or rather, into proper and common, is accurate and useful, and whether it should be accepted, or rather eliminated. The Lutherans, so that they may hold secure the omnipresence of the flesh of Christ and in particular its presence in the Lord's Supper, state that by the hypostatic union of the two natures in Christ the attributes of the divine nature have been communicated to the human nature, and thus they well enough destroy the distribution into communicable and incommunicable attributes. We will refute them below in book 5, chapter 4 concerning the person of Christ and in book 7, chapter 5 concerning the Lord's Supper.[19] The Cartesian theologians, so that they may substitute for it a distribution more suitable to their philosophy, a distribution into intellect and will, judge that it should be removed from its place. The

---

18. 1.2.3 §XIX
19. 1.5.4 §XXIII; 1.7.5 §§XXI, XXV

Reformed think that although properly and univocally speaking, no attribute of God is communicable or common, because they are all an infinite distance apart from the creatures, nevertheless there are attributes of which some vestiges are observed by analogy in the creatures, and thus this distribution should be altogether accepted, since there are others in which no such vestige is observed: for example, independence, aseity, immutability, and so forth. They think this way because: (1) together with the Scriptures, experience itself teaches that life, intellect, will, goodness, love, grace, righteousness, and holiness, in that mode which we have said, are common to creatures and God. (2) This distribution is useful and also necessary in the demonstration of the consubstantial deity of the Son and of the Holy Spirit, inasmuch as it is not from the communicable attributes but from the incommunicable attributes alone that we can and customarily do demonstrate it. (3) Scripture teaches that God created man in his own image (Gen. 1:26), בצלמנו כדמותנו, that is, according to interpreters, in the most similar image possible; likewise that we are made partakers of the divine nature (2 Peter 1:4); and likewise that we will be transformed into the same image of God (2 Cor. 3:18). From these things it cannot but be concluded that there is some sort of communion of attributes.

Objections

The foundations of the thought of our adversaries are observed to be these two things: (1) If you take the word *communicable* more strictly, then the attributes of God are properties, and thus they are all incommunicable. I respond: (a) As true as this is in itself, it thus agrees little with the hypotheses of the Cartesians. For they desire the same essence to be actually and univocally common to God, angels, and our souls. For every mind, whether it is human, angelic, or divine, is a thinking thing, which the celebrated Wittich says (*Peaceable Theology*, §122).[20] They also want essence to be the first attribute of anything (e.g. Wittich, §120).[21] For this reason, if (i) the essence of the mind, that is, thought, is common to God, angels, and our souls; if (ii) essence is the first and foremost attribute of a thing; and if (iii) an attribute is a property of God—then how will all the attributes of God be incommunicable? But (b) communion is threefold, according to the philosophers: there is equivocal communion, in which only the name is common, as the word *cancer*, "crab," belongs to a disease, to a constellation, and to an animal. There is a univocal communion, when the word's referent is common according to the same rationale, equally common, to several things, just

---

20. Wittich, *Theologia pacifica*, §122.
21. Wittich, *Theologia pacifica*, §120.

as *substance* belongs to man and beast. Then there is analogous communion, when the word, with respect to what it signifies, belongs to one thing first and foremost, and to other things only on account of that first thing. In this way *health* belongs first and foremost to an animal, and then on account of the animal to food, air, and medicine. In this way the divine attributes belong first and foremost, indeed incommunicably, to God, but to creatures they belong not only equivocally, but also analogically. (2) Their second foundation is that if you understand communicability most broadly, as concerning some similarity that is greatly obscure, even certain attributes which are commonly called incommunicable could be called communicable (Wittich, *Peaceable Theology*, §194, resp. 1).[22] I respond: (1) That certain incommunicable attributes can be called communicable on account of such a greatly obscure similarity existing in the creatures, or even that such a greatly obscure similarity of the incommunicable attributes, for example, aseity, immutability, infinity, and so forth, exists, is false until it has been proved. (2) Even if it should be entirely proved that certain incommunicable attributes have such a greatly obscure similarity in the creatures, the distinction will not labor under this, as long as it has not been demonstrated that all the attributes are either communicable or incommunicable. If the reader wishes more on this matter, see our *Gangrene of the Cartesian Innovations*, the latter section, chapter 16.[23]

The Practical Part

The practice of the divine attributes

XIII. Regarding the practice of this topic, we will be briefer for two reasons: (1) because the whole practice that we assigned to the names in the preceding chapter could recur here with very little changes, since attributes agree with the names in this, that on both sides they are a means of knowing the divine essence. (2) The practice of the attributes generally results individually from the individual divine attributes, for which reason it will be subjoined individually to the individual attributes.

They assist: 1. The knowledge, glorification, and reverence of God

Therefore, first, no one can doubt that it excellently provides for the knowledge of God to perceive through the attributes what God is, as well as how great he is and what qualities he has. For in whatever knowledge, the more attributes are perceived regarding a subject, the more perfect the knowledge of it is called. And

---

22. Wittich, *Theologia pacifica*, §194.
23. Mastricht, *Gangraena*, 304–10.

no less, second, it provides for the glory and glorification of God to reflect on so many attributes in God, each of which represents the infinite perfection of the divine essence. For this reason they are amassed by the saints throughout the Scriptures (Ex. 34:5–6; Neh. 9:5; Ps. 103:8; 1 Tim. 1:17; 1 Peter 2:9). Moreover, third, it instills reverence for God and zeal for pleasing and obeying him (Neh. 9:17; etc.), namely, the God who is known by so many infinite attributes. See also §§III–V.

The strengthening of: 2. Other articles of faith
XIV. Specifically, second, the general theory of the divine attributes excellently provides for the reinforcement of the most fundamental articles of our faith—of the most holy Trinity, the eternal consubstantiality of the Son and the Holy Spirit with the Father—because even the incommunicable attributes, which entirely coincide with the divine essence, are in the holy Scriptures attributed not only to the Father, but also to the Son and the Holy Spirit. For this reason also the Socinians, who would undermine those articles, considered it necessary to pervert the majority of the attributes of God.

3. Our faith and confidence
XV. In addition, third, it offers an excellent foundation for our faith and confidence that so many perfections coincide in God—wisdom, power, goodness, and so forth—of which each are infinite, eternal, immutable, and also the very essence of God. And not only in God, but also in the Mediator, who, because he is God, and blessed with all the divine attributes, is able to save perfectly (Heb. 7:25), and so forth.

4. Our prayers
XVI. It also offers, fourth, an immovable foundation for our prayers, so that with boldness we may approach the throne of grace of him who by so many perfections both can and will supply all our defects (Jer. 32:17–19).

5. Certain other virtues
XVII. Furthermore, fifth, the general theory of the attributes supplies the material for our thanksgivings and celebrations, and it also adds spurs to obedience, divine worship, and all the Christian virtues. It will suffice in this place to have pointed out all these things as if with a finger (for with no trouble they will be amplified with added testimonies, and also elsewhere will be more broadly explained in the individual theory of each of the attributes).

6. The blessedness which is in communion with God

XVIII. Finally, sixth, the coming together of so many and such great attributes in the one God instructs us concerning the blessedness of those who have this God covenanted to themselves: "Blessed is the nation whose God is Jehovah, the people whom he chooses as his own inheritance" (Ps. 33:12; 2 Cor. 6:18). For when this God is our God, and for us (Rom. 8:31), will not all these attributes be for us, and ours? Individually, for example, (1) will not his immutability render us certain that he will remain our God to all eternity (Mal. 3:6; 2 Tim. 2:19)? (2) Will not his truthfulness make it so that we can rest unmoved upon his promises (Josh. 21:45; Isa. 34:16)? (3) Will not his goodness and love make it so that we may be secure, in adversities of whatever sort and however great, that all these things will serve to our advantage (Heb. 12:6; Rom. 8:28, 38–39)? (4) Will not his mercy give us hope that he will graciously remit our sins (Ps. 103:8–10; Ex. 34:6)? (5) Will not his wisdom persuade us that his governance of us will be most beneficial (2 Peter 2:9; 2 Sam. 15:25–26)? (6) Will not his omnipotence persuade us that he can furnish all the things that he has promised, and that will benefit us (Eph. 3:20; 2 Thess. 1:11)? And so forth.

CHAPTER SIX

The Spirituality and Simplicity of God

God is Spirit, and those who worship him must worship in spirit and truth.
—John 4:24

The first attribute of God is his spirituality.

I. Now the divine attributes should each follow individually. First come those that represent what God is, or that make up his description, such as spirituality and aseity, with the analogous and consequent attributes of simplicity and immutability. For in our view, God is Spirit from himself. Now, because we just treated his aseity and independence in chapter 3 of this book, in this chapter we will add spirituality and simplicity. The Savior will lay this chapter's foundation in John 4:24.

The Exegetical Part

The text is opened and explained.

II. The Savior's words contain a response regarding the nature of God and its efficacy[1] for the practice of piety. Accordingly, in this response we find:

A. A certain description of God, in which is contained:

1. The thing described, or the subject of the axiom (with its designating article): ὁ θεός, God, whom we have treated up to this point, and will treat in what follows.

2. The description, in the word πνεῦμα, "Spirit." (The copulative "is," left out by Hebraic ellipsis, is implied.) God is called Spirit, but improperly so, if you consider the word itself. Indeed this word, derived as it is from the word for respiration in Hebrew, Greek, and Latin, properly applies in corporeal things to a breath. It applies to God, though improperly, because people commonly consider a spirit to be the subtlest among

---

1. ἐνεργείᾳ; Dutch: *krachtdadigheit*

visible things. But if you consider what the word is meant to signify, then God is most properly called Spirit, because he is eminently subtle, immaterial, and simple, as we will show in what follows.

B. A practical consequence, from the utility of this description, for worshipers and for divine worship: "and those who worship him must worship in spirit and truth," and so forth, which words describe three things:

1. The worshipers whom the description serves: προσκυνοῦντας, those who prostrate themselves before God, adoring and worshiping him externally in their profession and ceremonies. The Greek denotes the same thing as the Hebrew השתחוה. Both mean worship: sometimes civil (Gen. 23:7; Matt. 18:26), more often religious (John 4:23; Ps. 96:9; Matt. 4:10), but external, or at least conjoined with external bodily actions. Thus προσκυνοῦντας means those who profess the worship of God and perform it.

2. The worship and its two qualities that follow from the nature of God. Worship must be done:

   a. In spirit, that is, proceeding from the worshiper's spirit or inward parts (Ps. 51:6; Matt. 22:37; Rom. 1:9), not by profession only or in external actions. Worship must be spiritual, even when it is external (John 4:22–23).

   b. In truth, that is: (1) not falsely through hypocrisy, but in sincerity of heart (1 Cor. 5:8); (2) not typically, through shadows, through ceremonies, confined to times and places, but by spiritual grace (John 1:17).

3. The relative obligation of the worshipers to this kind of worship, in the word δεῖ: "they must," or "it is necessary." This necessity is certain because, on the one hand, God is Spirit and therefore delights in spirit and in spiritual things, and on the other, because he has rejected the ceremonial shadows and requires, especially now under the New Testament, the spiritual worship that the ceremonies prefigured.

FIRST THEOREM—The Spirituality of God

The Dogmatic Part

That God is Spirit: Proved by testimonies

III. Thus according to this text, God is Spirit. Both testaments present him as such: the Old (Num. 24:2; Judg. 3:10; Ezek. 11:24) as well as the New (2 Cor.

3:17; Acts 5:9), although the Acts passage could also be understood to be speaking of the Holy Spirit hypostatically. Therefore Origen says in his first homily on Genesis, "Thinking that God is corporeal and of human form is manifestly impious,"[2] and Augustine in *The City of God* (bk. 8, ch. 5), "If our soul is not a body, how is God, the Creator of the soul, a body?"[3]

And by reasons

IV. Nor can God be anything but Spirit because: (1) he is the absolutely first being, who spurns the idea of corporeal parts, whether they preexisted his fullness or now coexist with him. (2) He is independent (Rom. 11:36), whereas a body depends upon its members. (3) He is simple, and most simple, as we will soon prove openly, and thus he does not allow us to think that he is a conglomerate of body parts. (4) He is infinite, which could not be true of a being made of finite parts. (5) He is immutable and incorruptible (James 1:17), which cannot be admitted regarding bodies and composites which can be dissolved. Finally, (6) he is most perfect (Matt. 5:48), and by the confession of all, a spirit is in many ways more perfect than a body.

In what sense God is Spirit

V. But God is not Spirit in a metaphorical sense, in which even corporeal realities—wind, animal spirits, gases—come under this term, because they approximate immaterial substances. Nor is he Spirit in an analogical sense, wherein angels and our own souls are called by the name "spirit," because of all things they most closely approximate the immateriality and the simplicity of God. Rather, God is Spirit in an especially proper and univocal sense, because he is far removed from all composition. Thus God is called Spirit: not the third Person only, speaking hypostatically by appropriation, because he subsists through a certain ineffable spiration of the Father and the Son; but rather, each Person is called Spirit essentially,[4] because all have the same immaterial essence.

---

2. Origen, *PL* 12:156 and *Origen: Homilies on Genesis and Exodus*, trans. Ronald E. Heine, *Fathers of the Church: A New Translation*, vol. 71 (Washington, D. C.: Catholic University of America Press, 1982), 63.

3. Augustine, *PL* 41:230; *Nicene and Post-Nicene Fathers*, series I (*NPNF1*), ed. Philip Schaff (New York: Christian Literature Co., 1887–1900; reprint Peabody, Mass.: Hendrickson, 1994), 2:148. Augustine has similar remarks against the Manichean claim that Christians held an anthropomorphite view of God, cf. *Aurelii Augustini…De Genesis contra Manichaeos libri duo* 1.17.27 in *PL* 34:186.

4. οὐσιωδῶς

What spirits require

VI. Moreover, the spirits of any being, and especially of the uncreated God, require that the spiritual nature be: (1) substance, not accident; (2) incorporeal and immaterial (Luke 24:39); (3) living, something that operates by itself, and thus we read of the Spirit of life (Rom. 8:2) and the life-giving Spirit (1 Cor. 15:45); (4) intelligent (1 Cor. 2:11); and (5) volitional, ordering all things just as it wills (1 Cor. 12:11). We will treat each one of these individually in the series of divine attributes.

What qualities follow

VII. Following logically from the nature of spirits are their qualities: (1) insensibility, through which the spiritual essence is entirely inaccessible to our senses, which of course require a corporeal object. Specifically, insensibility implies (a) invisibility (Ex. 33:20; 1 Tim. 1:17; 6:16; John 1:18; Heb. 11:27), because a spirit (since whatever is immaterial lacks spatial extension) neither has a shape, nor can it show off its features in a way that would touch our eyes. Moreover, that God is infinite also proves that he is invisible. Although we read in many places that from time to time he appeared in a vision[5] (Gen. 18:2; Judg. 13:22; 1 Kings 22:19), where, by a certain extraordinary symbol displayed to human eyes, God manifested his presence, nonetheless, he always was seen in this way: his invisible attributes were, as we read, perceived in created things (Rom. 1:20), the same way in which we see the Father in the Son (John 14:9; Ex. 3:2; cf. Heb. 11:27). Likewise, God appears to the mind (Matt. 18:10), and thus also in our minds will we see God, as it says, face to face (1 Cor. 13:12), surely no longer through a mirror and through an enigma (that is, obscurely), but clearly, like what we see right before our eyes. This sort of seeing is hinted at in Matthew 5:8, Hebrews 12:14, and Job 19:27. (b) Impalpability (Luke 24:39; cf. John 4:24). Although God is said to be able to be touched (Acts 17:27), the description is metaphorical, just as when he is said to be able to be tasted and seen (Ps. 34:8). This tasting and seeing is done, of course, by our mind and not by our body. (c) Indepictibility (Isa. 40:18), since a spirit does not present a figure, outlines, boundaries, or colors which a painter's art could portray (Deut. 4:15; Acts 17:29). Following also from God's spiritual nature are (2) his omnimodal simplicity and (3) his immutability, about which we will speak openly, each in its own theorem.

---

5. ἐν ὁράματι

The Elenctic Part

It is asked: 1. Is God, properly speaking, a spirit? The divergence of opinions
VIII. It is asked, first, whether God is, properly and exactly speaking, a spirit?
The Anthropomorphites, so that they might more conveniently explain the creation of man in the image of God, asserted that he was not a spirit, but a crass
body, like the human body. (Concerning these things, see the following section.)
Several of the Fathers, including Tertullian in *Against Praxeas*, indeed attribute
a body to God, but a subtle body, although others excuse him, saying he did not
want to signify anything except that God is not an accident but a substance.[6]
Vorstius and the Socinians together attribute a body to God, but in this sense,
that they acknowledge the body itself to be Spirit. (We will soon speak rather
copiously of these matters.) The Cartesian theologians, because the word "spirit"
cannot be sufficiently Cartesianized and because they prefer a word which agrees
in meaning more closely with "thought," say that God is Spirit improperly; more
properly, he is mind.

The orthodox opinion and its arguments

The Reformed certainly acknowledge that the word "spirit" is derived in Latin
from respiration, just as רוח, in Hebrew, is derived from רָוַח, and the corresponding Greek word from πνεύειν, which means, "to respire," and that therefore
the word "spirit" applies in the first place to creatures. Nevertheless, they teach
that the thing signified by the received use of the word means "immaterial substance" or "simplex," and applies to God not improperly but most properly, and
indeed in the first place, because (1) he is clearly called Spirit in the text, nor
does any necessity compel us to stray from the proper sense to an improper one.
(2) The thing expressed by the use of the word "spirit," namely, immateriality
and simplicity, applies (as even our adversaries admit) most properly to him, as
we have said. (3) If he is not properly a spirit then he is properly a body. Yet this
is so only if that body is substance, not accident, since the distinction of substance into spirit and body is immediate, insomuch as every substance is either
immaterial or material. (4) If God is not properly a spirit, then the argument of
the orthodox for divine simplicity derived from his spirituality will prove empty.
Moreover, (5) the Holy Spirit will be either something corporeal, or he will no
longer be a spirit, properly speaking, for a spirit, in the opinion of our opponents,
is properly something corporeal.

---

6. Cf. Tertullian, *Adversus Praxeas* in *PL* 2:161–62; *Against Praxeas* in *ANF* 3:601–2.

Objections

And the objections they bring have no weight. They say, (1) "Spirit" comes from respiration, but it is not proper to speak of God as being exhaled. I respond: (a) There must be a distinction between the word itself, which comes from respiration, and the thing it signifies, which does not come from respiration. (b) Not every spirit comes from respiration; for example, animal spirits and natural spirits. Nor did our souls or the angels come from respiration; therefore, neither should these properly be called spirits. What then should we properly call a spirit? Nothing, except perhaps the wind and the breath we breathe? But (as everyone knows) we would call these things "spirits" only very improperly. What then is a spirit, properly speaking? If (2) they should say that all spirits properly speaking are something material, such as wind, breath, animal spirits, or gases, I respond: (a) What would you say about our souls, and likewise about the angels? Are they not properly called spirits? (b) All those material things are not spirits except by some sort of analogical participation, and then only improperly speaking, insofar as by their own subtleness they most closely approximate our souls and the angels, and our souls and the angels most closely approximate God, while he alone remains Spirit properly speaking. If they should say that (3) God is thought, for which the word "mind" is more appropriate than "spirit," then I respond: (a) The Cartesians go even further, claiming that every spirit, whether human, angelic, or divine, is thought, as the renowned Wittich says.[7] (b) We deny that God is thought, because in the Scriptures, nowhere is he called either thought or mind. If they should say that (4) the word "spirit" in the Scriptures is attributed to both wind and breath, I respond, (a) Does it therefore not apply properly to God? Even the word "gods" is applied to others: for example, to angels (Ps. 8:5; cf. Heb. 2:7), to magistrates (Ps. 82:6), and to false gods (1 Cor. 8:5). On this account is God not properly called God? (b) Why not rather turn their argument on its head: God is spirit properly speaking (John 4:24); therefore wind, blowing, animal spirits, gases, are not spirits unless we are speaking improperly by analogy. What argument then could they bring to refute me? If the reader is hungry for more rebuttals like these, he can consult my *Gangrene of the Cartesian Innovations* (sect. 2, ch. 7).[8]

2. Is God a body, complete with human parts? The divergence of opinions
IX. It is asked, second, whether God is a body, complete with human parts. Long ago the pagans, because they considered their great men to be gods, believed that

---

7. Wittich, *Theologia pacifica*, §195, pp. 156–57.
8. "The Spirituality of God," *Gangraena*, 236–42.

their gods were corporeal, endowed with human parts, as we will mention in the following controversy. The Anthropomorphites (also called Audians, from a certain Audius), who disturbed the church in the fourth century, around the year 370, and also in the tenth century, whose opinion Tertullian at one point approached when he claimed our soul had a fixed shape,[9] these Anthropomorphites, in order more conveniently (or so they thought) to explain what the image of God in man was, believed that God was endowed with human parts, according to which he fashioned the human form.

The orthodox opinion with its arguments
The Reformed do indeed acknowledge that the Scriptures frequently attribute to God human members—eyes, ears, hands, feet, heart—but that this does not occur except by a human way of speaking,[10] and that it must be understood in a way worthy of God,[11] insofar as it is not these fleshly members, with their imperfections, that truly belong to God, but instead the perfections of these members, with every imperfection removed. Thus "eyes" does not denote anything in God except his knowledge, "hands" his power, "feet" his presence, "heart" his love. This is so without a doubt because (1) Scripture denies that God has a body (Rom. 1:23). (2) It presents God to us as invisible (Rom. 1:20), as Spirit (John 4:24) to whom belong no flesh and bones (Luke 24:39). (3) If God were made up of parts, he would be a composite thing, and thus would require someone to compose him who existed before him. For this reason, (4) he would be divisible and corruptible, which contradicts the apostle (Rom. 1:23). Moreover, (5) neither would God be infinite, because an infinite whole cannot come together from many finite members. Nor in addition (6) would he be most simple. Thus, (7) God would be, by all accounts, imperfect.

Objections
If they should allege for their case: (1) that in the Scriptures God is described with body parts, we respond that this is said in a human way[12] and must be understood in a way worthy of God. (2) If they allege that we read often in

---

9. Audius in fourth century Syria read Genesis 1:26–27 to mean that God's form was the basis for human creation. E.g. Heresy 70, "On the schism of the Audians" in Epiphanius, *The Panarion of Epiphanius of Salamis, Books II and III. De Fide*, trans. F. Williams (Leiden: Brill, 2013), 412; cf. Tertullian, *Against Praxeas* in PL 2:161–62; ANF 3:601–2; idem, *Adversus Marcionem*, 2.16 in PL 3:302–4; *Against Marcion*, 2.16 in ANF 3:309–10.

10. ἀνθρωποπάθειαν

11. θεοπρεπῶς

12. *hoc fieri* ἀνθρωποπαθῶς

the Old Testament that God appeared to men, I respond, He appeared either without any human form, manifesting his extraordinary presence only by some extraordinary sign, or, if he was present in some form, it was not his own but one that he had assumed. He appeared not in his own form but in a vision, the way Jesus appeared to Stephen, standing at the right hand of God (Acts 7:56), and to Paul (Acts 9:10, 12), the same way that Peter saw a vessel descending from heaven filled with animals (Acts 10:11–12; 11:5–6).

3. Does a subtle body belong to God? The divergence of opinions
X. It is asked, third, if body parts do not belong to God, whether a body does, or at least a subtle one. Just recently, we heard the opinion of certain Fathers, represented by Tertullian. Vorstius, so that he might covertly undermine the personal union of the two natures in Christ (which he did not dare deny openly), taught that God was a subtle body, whose power was indeed everywhere, but whose essence was in heaven only, from which it very closely follows that the Christ who lived on earth was not united with the divine nature. The Reformed affirm with our Savior that God is Spirit, that is, immaterial substance, and thus utterly removed from having any body or matter, for the reasons which we gave in §§III–IV, and in the preceding section, reasons which, if you change a few details, with equal force foil the Socinians and the Anthropomorphites. Nor, moreover, are any other arguments available to the Socinians than the ones available to the Anthropomorphites.

4. Can and ought God to be represented by images? The diversity of opinions
XI. It is asked, fourth, whether God, who is Spirit, can and ought to be represented by statues and images. The pagans, since they considered their gods to be corporeal, as we have said, answer in the affirmative. The papists and Lutherans acknowledge that God is Spirit, and yet, from a love of images, teach that God can and ought to be portrayed, yet with this difference, that the papists teach not only that we should have images of God, but also that we should adore them with *latria*, which the Lutherans do not tolerate.

The arguments of the Reformed
The Reformed, because God is Spirit, admit neither opinion. For (1) a spirit, since it is immaterial and thus lacks a shape, cannot be portrayed, and also ought not to be (Isa. 40:18; Deut. 4:15), unless you wish to think God would require a task that no one can do. Accordingly, (2) God throughout the Bible resists with great zeal imaginations of this sort, for example, in the second commandment, in Acts 17:29, and elsewhere, since, that is, (3) "they change the glory of

the incorruptible God into the likeness of the image of corruptible man" (Rom. 1:23). Since (4) such images generate concepts that are vain, crass, and unworthy of God. Therefore, heathen philosophers are said to have become vain in such thoughts of theirs, having become fools (Rom. 1:21–22).

Objections

The papists and Lutherans do not have anything to argue for their images, except what we recently rejected in §IX, namely, that God quite often appeared in the Old Testament under certain forms, even human ones. The reply is easy: He never appeared for the purpose that he might be portrayed; indeed, that is what, throughout Scripture, he has forbidden as strictly as possible, just as we have said. But because this controversy concerns the second commandment, for now we will put other arguments to the side.

5. *Is it permitted, while praying, to put God before us under the form of a man?*
What the Lutherans think
XII. It is asked, fifth, whether it is permitted, while praying in divine worship, to put God before us under the form of an old man. Because the Lutherans, as we mentioned recently, have allowed the use of images in public worship, which cannot but breed such crass concepts in onlookers' minds, they cannot criticize these concepts with any appearance of fairness. They believe that these sorts of concepts about God under the appearance of an old man occasion them no sin, provided that they do not believe that God's essence actually has such a shape. (See Friedrich Balduin, bk. 2, ch. 2, case 1 in his *Cases of Conscience*,[13] Andreas Prückner in his *Thousand Cases of Conscience*, and others.)[14]

What the Reformed say, and by what arguments
The Reformed, however openly they embrace the fact that it is lawful to have a concept of God, and even more, that it is most necessary—unless we want to be atheists!—nevertheless say that a concept of God under the form of a man, or of any corporeal entity at all, is altogether unlawful, because: (1) the Savior in John 4:24 commands us to have a concept of God that agrees with the nature of God, that defines God as Spirit, and that therefore leads to the result that God

---

13. Friedrich Balduin, *Tractatus… de casibus conscientiae* (Frankfurt: Caspar Wachtler, 1654), bk. 2, ch. 2, casus 1, pp. 75–77.

14. *Mille casibus consc.*: Prückner's work is entitled *Manuale mille quaestionum illustrium theologicarum, praecipue practicarum* (Nürnberg: Wolfgang Maurits Endter, 1679). This is probaby a reference to Philipp Müller's abridgment, *Notae ad B. Dn. M. Andreae Prückneri mille quaestiones de casibus conscientiae* (Nürnberg: Wolfgang Maurits Endter, 1696).

is worshiped and adored in spirit, that is, spiritually, without any such forms, and in truth, meaning in thoughts that are true and that agree with the concept. (2) Such kinds of concepts about God are false. Since they do not agree with the God who is conceived, they are therefore unlawful. (3) These concepts of theirs are vain: "They became futile in their thinking" (Rom. 1:21). (4) They obscure the glory of the incorruptible God and, as it were, change it "into the likeness of the image of corruptible man" (Rom. 1:23). (5) Through these concepts, the heart is darkened and the mind rendered senseless: "Their foolish heart was darkened" (Rom. 1:21). This darkening happens to the extent that they carry around in their mind concepts that are crass and unworthy of God. (6) Whoever worships God under such forms does not worship God, but an idol.

The objections of the Lutherans

Yet Balduin objects: (1) that since whenever we have a concept of God, and we therefore conceive a certain image of God, it is better to conceive of God under the image of a man rather than an image of anything else. I respond, Balduin presupposes that having a concept and conceiving an image are synonymous, when in fact they are worlds apart. For under what likeness or image will you conceive of a spirit as it exists in itself? But (2) God appeared in human form. I respond, We already answered this. God appeared (Gen. 18:2, Josh. 5:13, Dan. 7:9, and Isa. 6:1) so that those who saw might conceive of his extraordinary presence, and that whatever glory appeared they might ascribe to God. By no means did God appear so that they might thus conceive of an image inside themselves or might form one outside themselves, since he frequently prohibited this as strictly as possible.

The Practical Part

The first practice teaches us how, while praying and otherwise, we must think about God.

XIII. For the first practice, let us consider a rather important case of conscience that arises from what has been discussed: what sort of concept of God ought we to have in our prayers or in divine worship? It is presupposed that it is necessary that we should have some concept of God (Ps. 16:8), otherwise we would call upon nothing. Likewise, from the preceding paragraph, we presuppose that the concept of an old man, or of some sort of corporeal essence, here is invalid, because by this rationale we would invoke an idol instead of the true God. What kind of concept, then, is fitting here? And how must we think about God? I respond: (1) almost in the same way that we think about our own soul, which we cannot think about under a corporeal form endowed with human members. (2) In the way that we think about a spirit (John 4:24) or about an immaterial substance which does not have flesh and bones (Luke 24:39). He must be thought of just as we would think of: (3) an omnipresent being that fills heaven and earth (Jer. 23:23–24), in whom we live, move, and have our being, and who is not far from us (Acts. 17:27–28); (4) an invisible being whom no one has seen and no one can see (1 Tim. 6:16); (5) an omnipotent being, superlatively good and kind, who therefore is most perfectly sufficient for infinite blessedness for himself, and for his own, and for all (Gen. 17:1), because he can abundantly satisfy all your desires (Ps. 37:4–5). And finally, (6) one must think about his most glorious attributes rather than his imperceptible essence, which is the way God presents himself to us for thinking about him (Ex. 34:6). And in this way we will see his posterior parts, so to speak, while his face, or his essence, cannot be seen or thought (Ex. 33:19–20).

The second practice rebukes hypocrites.
XIV. Then second, the spirituality of God marks out all those who worship God, who is Spirit, without their spirit, who draw near to God with their lips, though they are as far as possible from him in their spirit (Matt. 15:8; Isa. 29:13), who approach holy things with their feet but without their spirit, who pray to God with their tongues but not in spirit and in understanding (1 Cor. 14:14–15), who distribute alms and other good things with their hands but without their spirit, who are content to offer to God their exterior things, having preserved their interior things for themselves, for the world, and for pleasures, though God examines the heart or the spirit (Prov. 26:23), and indeed the whole heart (Deut. 6:5; 10:12; 30:6; Luke 10:27). Their worship stops short at mere bodily exercises, which are almost useless (1 Tim. 4:8). The Savior calls such persons hypocrites (Matt. 15:7), and their worship, however attractive it may be, is devoid of spirit and soul, and thus dead (which is said of faith in James 2:20, 26): it reeks before God just like a putrid cadaver. And for this reason he also drives these sorts of hypocrites away from his eyes, together with this worship of theirs (Isa. 1:13), and pronounces woes on them (Matt. 23:25–26)—indeed, he counts them as dung, which he shows by flinging it back into their face (Mal. 2:3; Amos 3:13–14).

The third practice commands us to examine our worship.
XV. So then, the third practice persuades us that we should carefully examine our worship, whether it, consistent with the divine nature, is in spirit and in truth. We will conduct such examination according to these criteria: (1) if in our

external worship, the spirit always joins the body, such that we glorify God in our spirit and in our body (1 Cor. 6:20), and not with the body only, or the lips, while the heart is absent, as we have warned. (2) If the spirit that joins the body in external worship is spiritual and not carnal, for that which is from the flesh is flesh, and that which is from the Spirit is spirit (John 3:6). And those who live according to the flesh set their minds on the things of the flesh, and those who live according to the spirit, the things of the Spirit (Rom. 8:5). (3) If the end of our external worship is not carnal—the preservation or increase of our reputation (Matt. 6:1), the provisions of this life (John 6:26), or the merit (as they say) of the work performed (1 Tim. 4:7–8)—but spiritual: to glorify God, to edify our soul, to promote our salvation; that is, to serve God in spirit (Rom. 1:9), and to work out our own salvation (Phil. 2:12). (4) If in worship, all the faculties of the soul exert themselves: the intellect, in focus and understanding, for this, according to the apostle, is what it means to pray in the spirit (1 Cor. 14:15); the will, in love (2 Cor. 5:14; Ps. 27:4), in desire (Ps. 84:1–2), in delight and in joy (Ps. 84:1–2; 43:4), in sadness on account of its torpor and weariness (Ps. 43:5). (5) If we are Christians and religious not only in public but also in secret, that is, in the spirit and not in the letter (Rom. 2:28–29). (6) If in simplicity of heart we have done whatever we do sincerely, as to the Lord, and not to men (Col. 3:22–23). Finally, (7) if we are intent on spiritual exercises, the denial of ourselves, the mortification of our passions, the imitation of Christ, on faith, hope, and love, more frequently and more fervently than on the external and corporeal things, indeed, if we are intent on external things for no other reason than to augment those internal things (1 Tim. 4:7–8).

The fourth practice commands that we devote our spirit to God. Why?
XVI. Fourth, the fact that God is Spirit teaches us that we should devote our spirit to God, since he is the one: (1) who rejoices and delights in spirit, "for the Father seeks such persons" (John 4:23), just as like seeks like (Rom. 8:5); (2) who is the Father of spirits (Heb. 12:9) because he creates the spirit of man within him (Zech. 12:1); (3) who stamped and sealed our spirit as his own property so that, because it bears the image of God as a stamp of his ownership, we might offer it back to God, its possessor (Matt. 22:20–21); (4) who bears many unique relations to our spirit, since he is not only the Creator of our spirit, as we have seen, but also its Redeemer (Ps. 31:6); its governor and Lord (Prov. 21:1); and its examiner (Jer. 17:10).

How?

But in what manner, then, will we devote our spirit to God? I respond: (1) By denying it, by disowning it, whereby we strip ourselves, so to speak, of that which belongs to our spirit (1 Cor. 6:19), which we do when we so refuse to follow its faculties—the intellect with its thought and wisdom, the will with its inclination and appetite (Matt. 26:39), and all the affections with their passions—as if they were not our spirit or our right. (2) By handing it over, by surrendering it, by consecrating it, when we deny our spirit to ourselves and devote it instead to God—"you do not have a right to yourself," and therefore, "glorify God with your body and spirit, which are his" (1 Cor. 6:19–20); when we hand over our spirit to him (Prov. 23:16; 2 Cor. 8:5) so that it may live, not for itself (Rom. 14:7–8; Gal. 2:19–20), but for his glory (1 Cor. 10:31), according to his will (1 Peter 4:2, 6), and with him working in us (Phil. 2:13). (3) By purging the spirit from all impurity (2 Cor. 7:1; Jer. 4:14), that is, that it may be fit to be received by God (Isa. 1:15–16), regarding which we just recently said many things expressly. (4) By adorning our spirit with every virtue (1 Peter 3:3–5), namely, that it might be more readily received and possessed by God (cf. Matt. 12:44). (5) By entrusting it into the hands of God, who redeems it (Ps. 31:5), who washes and cleanses it in the blood of the Son (Ps. 51:9–10), who renews it by the work of his own Spirit (Ezek. 36:26–27), and who at last receives it in the hour of our death (Luke 23:46).

The fifth practice concerns the cleansing of our spirit.

From what kind of uncleanness?

XVII. Specifically, fifth, because God is Spirit, we should more and more cleanse our spirit, which has been stamped in his image and consecrated to him, from all impurity (2 Cor. 7:1; 1 Thess. 5:23; Jer. 4:14). From what sort of impurity? I respond, That which (1) the Savior notes in Matthew 15:19–20, which (2) the apostle notes when he surveys the works of the flesh, that is, of the carnal spirit (Gal. 5:19–20): not only adulteries and impurities, but also idolatries, wrath, contentions, and so forth. The chief of them are (3) spiritual ignorance and blindness, pride, unbelief, and hypocrisy. They are, moreover, (4) all lusts, which James calls "lusts of the spirit" (James 4:5), which war against the soul (1 Peter 2:11).

On account of what reasons?

But for what reasons, then, will we do this? I respond: (1) Because God is a spirit who, just as he delights in spiritual duties, is in the same way most of all offended by spiritual impurities. (2) Because those impurities are diametrically opposed to the perfection of the law, which is spiritual (Rom. 7:14). (3) Because sin is strongest in the spirit, inasmuch as the spirit is its source (Matt. 15:19). (4) Because by spiritual filthiness we are made just like devils, who are nearly nothing but spiritual wickedness.

By what means?

Finally, by what helps will we cleanse our spirit? I respond: (1) We should daily circumcise our hearts (Jer. 4:4). (2) We should wash and sprinkle ourselves, through faith, in the blood of Christ (Jer. 4:14; Heb. 9:14; Acts 15:9). (3) We should carefully guard each motion, thought, desire, and delight of our heart, so that they may not be contaminated from without by its objects, and these contaminate our spirit (Prov. 4:23). To this end, (4) we should have the Word of God as our norm within our heart (Prov. 4:20–21). (5) We should continually weary God with our prayers, that he create in us a clean heart and renew a right spirit in our inner parts (Ps. 51:10), that according to the covenant of grace, he put his law within us, that he write it on our heart (Jer. 31:33), and likewise that he put a new spirit within us (Ezek. 36:26–27).

The sixth practice, spiritual worship. What is it?

XVIII. Given these things, the fact that God is Spirit demands, sixth, that we worship him in spirit and in truth, as the text also concludes. That is, we are to worship (1) not only in body, but also in spirit; not corporeally only, but also even more, spiritually. This is proven by analogy in §§XIV–XV. (2) Not only in public worship with others but also in private worship with God and our soul alone (Matt. 6:6), in pious conversations with ourselves, meditations by which we pour out, as it were, our spirit onto God's bosom (Ps. 42:4), particularly (3) in matters of the gospel, of godliness, charity, petitions, and intercessions, after the example of Paul: "God is my witness, whom I serve with my spirit in the gospel, that ceaselessly I make mention of you in my prayers" (Rom. 1:9). And we should do this frequently, indeed incessantly, and with an attention so careful that it is as if we approached all our holy tasks bound in the spirit (Acts 20:22). Finally, we should also approach them sincerely, so that we can call forth God as our witness.

For what reasons must this be observed?

Spiritual worship of this sort (1) agrees with the spiritual nature of God (John 4:24); (2) is sought and desired, in fact even demanded by God (John 4:23; Prov. 11:20; 1 Chron. 29:17), to such a degree that (3) the spiritual is the whole of all our worship (1 Sam. 12:24; 1 Kings 2:4; Matt. 22:37), and without the spirit there is no worship whatsoever (Matt. 15:8), or rather, there is evil, hypocritical worship (Matt. 15:7), worship that is abominable, like a corpse without a spirit (James 2:17, 26), however it be otherwise attractive, as is evident in Ahab (1 Kings 21:27) and in Jehu (2 Kings 10:29–31). Moreover, (4) the greatest defects and failures in external worship are redeemed and offset by the presence and truth of the spirit (2 Chron. 30:18–19). Finally, (5) so great in God's eyes is the presence of the spirit, and truth and sincerity, that he defines evangelical perfection by it, and declares those who have it perfect (Job 2:3) and righteous (Ps. 32:11; 97:11; 2 Kings 20:3).

The seventh practice, spiritual prayers
XIX. We would add, seventh, that particularly in prayer, we should be occupied in spirit and truth, which is clearly demanded in the text. That is, we should pray not only with the voice or lips, nor only in the external actions (Isa. 1:15), not restricted to customary formulas of praying, but with a present mind, with understanding and attention (1 Cor. 14:15), and thus also with faith, hope, and love, with suitable preparation of the mind before praying, and finally, with vigorous desire and expectation, after prayer, of obtaining what we sought. We would add this, as I said, if fear of prolixity did not restrain us, and it did not already belong to its own chapter, on prayer.[15]

SECOND THEOREM—The Simplicity of God

The Dogmatic Part
Following the spirituality of God is his simplicity. Scripture teaches it.
XX. The consequent of spirituality is simplicity: not a shared and restricted simplicity, which applies to created spirits because they are spirits only analogically, but rather, an original and omnimodal simplicity, because God is Spirit from himself, and is called Spirit univocally. Scripture teaches this simplicity whenever it represents God, not only in composite and concrete terms, but in simple and abstract terms, when it calls him love (1 John 4:8, 16), life (1 John 5:20), light, in which there is no darkness (1 John 1:5), that is, a deity in which there is nothing heterogeneous, a deity that is nothing but pure deity.

15. 2.2.7

Reason confirms it.

XXI. And this is true because he is: (1) the absolutely first being. Accordingly, if he were, by composition, one thing and another thing, there would be more than one first being, and of these beings, none would be absolutely first, because it would not be prior to all the other parts that coexist with it. In addition, if he were composite, he would require someone to compose him who was prior to the first being. (2) Independent, which would not be so, if his whole depended upon component parts, if the union of his parts depended upon someone to unite them and to preserve their union. (3) Immutable, for when there is a unification of parts by composition, then there can also occur a dissolution of those parts, and thus an alteration. (4) Infinite, for composing parts, since they cannot but be finite, cannot come together to produce something infinite. (5) Eternal, for that which has been composed has, from the one who composes it, a beginning through its construction, and can have an end through the dissolution of its parts. (6) Most perfect, not only because it is, in the consensus of all, more perfect to be goodness itself (for example) than merely good, wisdom itself than merely wise, but also because a part contains various imperfections, since it does not possess the perfection of the whole, and because a part requires someone to have made it a part of the whole. Finally, (7) if there is composition in God, then he is not the light in which there is no darkness, not pure deity: for parts, as they are doubtless diverse, could not constitute such pure deity. Therefore Justin rightly says in *Questions and Answers to the Orthodox*, question 144, "God does not exist in the likeness of the creature, such that what he is and has should be understood in terms of composition, as with created nature. And even in regard to the fact that God does possess a nature, he should still be understood in the same way: what he is and what he has, he possesses beyond all composition."[16]

The simplicity of God excludes composition of five types.

XXII. By his simplicity, God is entirely free from all composition, in which one thing and another thing come together. Specifically, he is free from composition: (1) of quantitative, corporeal parts, for he is a spirit (from the preceding theorem), whereas parts belong to a body; (2) of essential parts, matter and form, which likewise do not occur except in a body; (3) of substance and accident, because all accidents are considered more imperfect than their substance, which is not fitting for the most perfect being, and because accidents are thought to perfect their substances, and that would thus make his substance liable to change

---

16. Pseudo-Justin Martyr, *Quaestiones et responsiones ad Orthodoxos* in *Corpus apologetarum Christianorum saeculi secundi*, ed. J. C. T. Otto, 3 vols. (Jena: 1876–1881), vol. 3.

and corruption; (4) of essence and existence, because his existence is nothing but the act of his essence, and not something different, which would imply composition; (5) of genus and difference, for the being who is above being[17] fits into no category with anything else, but stands apart in all respects from all things, and arranges all things into classes of genus and species, and accordingly there is also nothing in him that can be restricted by difference. In addition, because of his simplicity, not only is God free from all composition within himself, but also, he enters into no ordinary composition outside himself, for in such composition it is presupposed that each composing part is more imperfect than the whole. At the same time, we do not deny the fact of extraordinary composition in Christ's hypostatic union, because such does not connote an imperfection of this sort, since in this type of composition, the assuming nature possesses by way of eminence whatever there is of perfection in the nature assumed. For which reason, God with the creature does not speak of a greater perfection than do the two separately.

The Elenctic Part

It is asked: 1. Is God a most simple being?

XXIII. It is asked, first, whether is God a most simple being. The heathen, since they held their gods to be human, that is, illustrious men; the Anthropomorphites, because they taught that man was formed according to the image of the divine members; certain Fathers, among whom is Tertullian, perhaps because they considered substance and body as synonyms, so that God would not become an accident; the Socinians, so that they might have a finite God, existing only in the heavens, who accordingly could not be united with the human nature of Christ, since it existed only on the earth, and in addition so that they might hold that God is set against his own essence by those things which, in the business of predestination, suit the fancy of the human will, which changes every hour, though God's essence is not changed—all these deny that God is a most simple being. The Reformed, on the contrary, teach that God is in all ways most simple, from the Scriptures and reasons which we indicated in §§XX–XXI.

The chief points which our adversaries give are: (1) that human members are attributed to God, to which we have already given a satisfactory answer.[18] (2) That external actions differ from the agent himself. I respond, Indeed the thing produced extrinsically by an action does differ, though not the power and producing action. Nor does the relation with what is produced, which from

---

17. οὐσία ὑπερούσιος
18. §IX

the production belongs to the producer, make that producer a composite. For
that relation is not a being of any sort, nor does it imply composition in God
(for things are related to something, not in something).[19] (3) That even internal
actions (e.g. the decrees) undoubtedly differ from the agent, the one who decrees.
I respond, Indeed they do differ from the thing decreed, but not from the act
of decreeing, and that the relation that exists between these two things is not,
in regard to either, a relation that can make him composite. (4) That his attributes differ from his essence, for example, his mercy from his avenging justice.
I respond, They do not differ except in their objects and effects, and through
the relation which exists between the attribute and its object. (5) That there are
three persons in his one essence. I respond: (a) His essence does not differ from
his personality except in our reason or conception, which can think of one thing
only while it is not thinking of another thing. For God's personality is nothing
other than the subsistence of his essence, and his subsistence is nothing other
than the actual existence of his substance, which without doubt does not differ
from the God who himself exists. And (b) the persons in the abstract differ
among themselves, not as three subsistences, but as three modes of one subsistence, which, because they are not beings, do not compose, but only distinguish
and limit, as we will teach more distinctly in its own place.[20] (6) That two natures
are united in one person. I respond, From this there arises no composition in
God, although there does arise an extraordinary composition in the God-man,
of which we have spoken.[21]

2. Is the omnimodal simplicity of God taught in the Scripture?
XXIV. It is asked, second, whether Scripture teaches the omnimodal simplicity
of God. The Anthropomorphites or Audians, Vorstius in his *Theological Treatise
on God* and his *Notes on Disputation 3, on the Nature of God*,[22] and Socinus in
his *Defense of the Criticisms against the Assertions of the College of Poznań* and
his *Racovian Catechism* (ch. 1),[23] entirely expunge the simplicity of God from
the number of the divine attributes, by their hypotheses which we noted while
attending to the preceding controversy. The Remonstrant Apologists, in their

---

19. *relata enim sunt* πρὸς τί, *non ἐν* τινί
20. 1.2.24 §IX
21. §XXII, above
22. Conrad Vorstius (1569–1622), *Tractatus theologicus de Deo sive de natura et attributis Dei* (Steinfurt: Theophilus Caesar, 1610), 194–210.
23. Faustus Socinus (1539–1604), *Defensio animadversionum Fausti Socini Senensis in assertiones theologicas collegii Posnaniensis de trino et uno Deo* in idem, *Assertiones theologicae de trino et uno Deo, adversus novos samosatenicos* (Raków: Sebastian Sternacius, 1618), 94–462.

Apology, do not indeed deny the simplicity of God, for in that way they would cross into the camp of the Socinians, who have been banned from our shores by our civil laws.[24] But lest they be forced to ban the Socinians from their own communion, they sum up the issue of the simplicity of God with these three axioms: (1) there is not one iota concerning the simplicity of God in Scripture; (2) the whole doctrine of it is metaphysical, whether you consider the term or its content; (3) it is not necessary to believe the simplicity of God. Among the Reformed, there was always, all the way to the time of Socinus, a great consensus concerning divine simplicity. At this point, our only task is to demonstrate that Scripture teaches the simplicity of God, and thus, that it is no mere philosophical dogma, but one necessary to believe.

The orthodox arguments

The Reformed endeavor to maintain this by these arguments: (1) Scripture teaches that God is Spirit (John 4:24), and to all people, "spirit" speaks of a being that is immaterial, and accordingly, simple. If they insist that both angels and our souls are called spirits in the Scriptures, but they are not therefore omnimodally simple, an easy response comes to mind: The angels and our souls are spirits only by analogy, in a diminished sense, because they, of all creatures, most closely approximate the spirituality of God, since God is properly and most perfectly Spirit. (2) Scripture teaches that God is the absolutely first being (Rev. 1:8; 22:13; Isa. 41:4; 44:6; Rom. 11:35–36), who accordingly does not admit a prior being who would have composed God's various parts. (3) Scripture teaches that he is immutable (Mal. 3:6; James 1:17; Ps. 102:26–27; Heb. 1:11–12). But what has been composed also can be broken up, and thus changed. (4) Scripture teaches that God is incorruptible (Rom. 1:23; 1 Tim. 1:17). If, however, God were composite, he could be corrupted. Since he cannot be changed into something better, because nothing exists better than God, nor into something equally good, because this cannot exist either, then nothing remains except that he must be changed into something worse, and thus be corrupted. (5) Scripture teaches that God is infinite, as the one who fills heaven and earth (Jer. 23:23–24), who is higher than the heavens (Job 11:8), whom the heaven of heavens does not contain (1 Kings 8:27). But what is composite is finite, since the parts that compose it are always finite, being of course less than the whole, and since, then, from finite parts, an infinite whole cannot come together. (6) Scripture teaches that God is most perfect (Job 11:8; Matt. 5:48). But a being that is simple as well

---

24. Simon Episcopius (1583–1643), *Apologia pro confessione sive declaratione sententia eorum* (1629).

as most simple, is more perfect than a composite, and what has been composed consists in imperfect parts. These things should be sufficient, especially if they be considered together with §§XX–XXI.

Objections

Yet they allege in vain to the contrary: (1) that not even one iota about simplicity exists in the Scriptures. I respond: (a) We have already proven the contrary; (b) the term does not exist expressly, yet it does exist in its force and meaning.[25] Moreover, it is hardly solid to conclude, because the term does not exist expressly in this way, that it absolutely and entirely does not exist. For in this way, (c) neither the Trinity, nor the personal union, nor satisfaction, nor other mysteries, are taught in the Scriptures, since they happen not to appear there in as many syllables. (2) That the omnimodal simplicity of God denies that the free actions and volitions of God are truly distinct from his essence, which is not consistent with Scripture (Ezek. 18:24; 33:11). I respond, This fundamental assumption is false.[26] The freedom of the divine volitions stands no less safe and sound because, with no interference from God's simplicity, he acts according to counsel, from choice,[27] in which freedom consists. (3) That the attributes in God's essence imply composition. I respond, They do not imply composition because they do not differ from his essence, except in our manner of conceiving them. Nor do they differ among themselves except in our reason, which finds the foundation of distinguishing them in the variety of their operations and in the relations that arise from them. (4) That the three persons in one essence argues for composition in God. I respond, They do not argue for composition, because persons do not differ from essence in God, but rather in us and in our conception. Nor also do the persons differ between themselves except through their modes of subsisting, which, because they are not things or beings, but only modes of beings, do not compose, but only distinguish.

The Practical Part

1. *The omnimodal simplicity of God discloses to us the foundation of every perfection in God and of every imperfection in the creatures.*

XXV. Thus now for practice. Because the spirituality of God generally coincides with his simplicity, and the Savior deduces some sort of simplicity from spirituality (Luke 24:39), so also theologians, by God's omnimodal spirituality,

---

25. διανοίᾳ
26. hoc πρῶτον ψεῦδος
27. ἐκ προαιρέσει

want his simplicity to be understood. It remains that there are several practical uses, which we just recently dealt with under divine spirituality, that can be taken up, with the necessary changes made, in regard to divine simplicity. But to those, we will briefly add the following. First, then, the omnimodal simplicity of God reveals the foundation of both the perfection of God and the imperfection of creatures; indeed, of the divine perfection, because, by his omnimodal simplicity, he is pure and sheer deity, in which nothing is or can be that is less perfect than infinite deity itself. Each and every one of his attributes—wisdom, goodness, grace, truth, holiness, righteousness, power, and so forth—are the very deity itself. For which reason, not only in the concrete, as they say, but also in the abstract, are these attributes declared of God, such that he may be called not only wise, good, gracious, and so forth, but rather, wisdom, goodness, holiness, and life itself. And this is so not according to amplification, as in human rhetoric, nor in the manner of courtiers or dinner guests, when, for example, we salute a wise man as wisdom itself, for we can never declare too much good about the highest and infinite good. Because of all these things, he is called the light in which there is no darkness at all (1 John 1:5), that is, there is such an identity in his essence and attributes that in him there is found no darkness, no heterogeneity, no imperfections. The foundation and root of all these things is in the omnimodal simplicity of God. And it is taught to us in the Scriptures for this purpose, that (1) we may glorify God because of it, as it is the root of his every perfection. It is known that in the Scriptures the majesty and glory of God is designated by light, and thus he is said to dwell in light inaccessible (1 Tim. 6:16) and to clothe himself in light (Ps. 104:2). So then the Philosophers are condemned because, though they knew his deity, they did not therefore glorify him as God (Rom. 1:20–21). That (2) from his simplicity, we may depend wholly on God in whatever circumstance, however adverse, because he is (a) our light (Ps. 27:1); (b) love itself (1 John 4:8, 16), by which he cannot but love his own and confer all saving blessings upon them (Rom. 8:32). In addition, he is (c) our salvation, for he is able and willing to free his own from every evil (Ps. 27:1). Indeed, he is (d) eternal life (1 John 5:20), for he is able to be the fount and source of all life (Ps. 36:10). That (3) from all those things, we may glorify God as most simple goodness, by which he is called the only one who is good (Matt. 19:17), and that we would do so by faith, repentance, a zeal for pleasing him, and especially by covenanting with him, for how blessed is the nation whose God is Jehovah (Ps. 33:12)! So far we have seen that the omnimodal simplicity of God has revealed the foundation of every perfection in God. It likewise reveals the foundation of every imperfection in the creatures, because all, to the last one, are composite, and in them, or at least in most all of them, we see a perpetual mixture of good and evil, by which, if perhaps they can offer some profit as good creatures, they can likewise injure as evil creatures; if they can gladden, they can likewise embitter, and if they were entirely good, they are nevertheless, on account of composition, only mutably good. And this is what should direct us never to attribute too much to any sort of creatures, or at least not to depend upon them as upon God, who is most simple, most pure perfection and goodness.

2. It teaches us to lean in simple rest upon God alone.
XXVI. And even more, second, because God is most simple, and he thus gives simply (ἁπλῶς, James 1:5), that is, he gives himself, all that he is, and all his attributes, which, by simplicity, are inseparable—his wisdom, power, goodness, and grace—devoting them to us, let us also then with a simple and whole heart, rest in God alone, and because of his integrity and uprightness (which coincides with his simplicity), let us promise him all that is ours (Ps. 25:21). For this confidence, the divine simplicity supplies to us various grounds, since it is: (1) a pure goodness that profits us, in which there is no malice to harm us; (2) a universal goodness, which allows no exception (Ps. 34:9–10); (3) an unlimited and illimitable goodness, which cannot be restrained or impeded by any creature, no matter how powerful, which thus can be all things for us, and can supply all things to us, indeed, beyond what we ask or think in our mind (Eph. 3:20). Thus there is no reason that we should not say with David, "He is my portion" (Ps. 16:5), and with Asaph, "Whom have I in heaven? With you, I do not desire anything on earth. My flesh and my heart may fail, but God is the strength of my heart and my portion forever" (Ps. 73:25–26). To neglect this duty, what is that except by that very action to deny the simplicity by which God is the light in which there is no darkness? What is it except to set ourselves far from God (Ps. 73:27)?

3. It reminds us that we should attend to divine worship with a simple heart.
XXVII. Again, third, since God is simple, we should, in all our worship, devote ourselves with a simple heart (Matt. 10:16; Eph. 6:5), with simplicity of heart, as to Christ, with the simplicity and sincerity of God (2 Cor. 1:12), not with a double heart, which is attributed to hypocrites (Ps. 12:2), a heart which looks to itself, the world, temporal things, at the same time as it looks to God, but instead, with one simple heart, which is carried in one straight line to the one God.

What is this?
And indeed in this, three distinct things are included: (1) that the inward heart should be pure, that is, free from every admixture of corruption (Ps. 12:2–3), and likewise of every sinister intention, on account of which the Savior speaks of the simple eye (Matt. 6:22–23). Next, (2) that the heart, being pure and simple, should aim at one goal, the glory of God (Phil. 1:20–21), and subordinate to that, the salvation of its own soul, as well as the edification of its neighbor. (3) That the pure and simple heart should strive for its simple goal with a constant and (as much as possible) uniform endeavor. By lacking this, a person is called double-minded, unstable in all his ways (James 1:8).

Why must it be sought?
That we may more intently strive for a simple heart like this, we must consider the following: (1) we ourselves, in this effort, are striving to the imitation and likeness of the primary perfection of God, of that perfection which is the foundation of every perfection, the likeness of which is the chief perfection of the rational creature. This is what we call sincerity, which in Greek is ἁπλότης, and in Hebrew is םת, "perfection." (2) Those who are pure in heart are called blessed by our Savior (Matt. 5:8; Ps. 73:1), just as on the contrary, (3) those who are double in heart are called monstrous, abominable, and cursed (Ps. 12:2–3; cf. 1 Kings 18:21; Hos. 10:2). Furthermore, (4) the foundation of all constancy is in simplicity, just as in duplicity is the foundation of all instability (James 1:8). And finally, that our heart may become simple: (1) it must be cleansed from every mixture of that which is foreign, of depraved desires (2 Cor. 7:1; 1 John 3:3), cleansed by the blood of Christ (1 John 1:7) in sincere repentance (Jer. 4:14, 4). (2) We must fight against carnal desires, so that they do not contaminate our hearts (Gal. 5:17). (3) We must pray to God that he, according to the formula of the covenant of grace, would give us one heart (Ezek. 11:19) and create in us a clean heart (Ps. 51:10).

4. It urges sincerity in our manner of life.
XXVIII. And not in divine worship only must we work to achieve simplicity of heart, but also, fourth, in human life, according to the example of the apostle (2 Cor. 1:12), who lived with his Corinthian brothers in simplicity and godly sincerity, not in carnal wisdom, and who likewise also requires the same: "with simplicity of heart, fearing God" (Col. 3:22). What then does this mean? "To work heartily, as to the Lord, and not to men" (Col. 3:23). For in this simplicity is our security (Ps. 25:21), both our tranquility and our boasting, whereas a deceitful life is an abomination to God (Ps. 5:6; Prov. 11:20).

5. It moves us to the study of contentment.

XXIX. Fifth, the divine simplicity teaches us to acquiesce to our lot, however simple it may be. For the more simple anything is, the more constant it is, and durable, whereas the more composite, likewise the more dissoluble and corruptible. Thus, God is most immutable because he is most simple, while on the contrary the angels, because they exist with qualities that are distinct from their essence, were able to be corrupted by sin, and material things are the more corruptible the more composite they are, just as we see if we compare stable chemical elements with substances that are mixed. When it comes to our lot, the exact same is true: the more simple, the more solid, and the more variegated from composition by wealth, honors, friends, the more mutable, and the more you are distracted by so many objects, the more you are liable to cares and anxieties (Luke 10:41), for the more you possess, the more you can lose. It is thus on this account that we should, in godly self-sufficiency,[28] accustom our soul to simplicity, and should substitute, for the variety of things, the one God who is most sufficient in every way for all things (Gen. 17:1), who is accordingly for us the one thing necessary (Luke 10:42). So then let us possess him as our lot, with a simple acquiescence, and other things as corollaries (Matt. 6:33), looking to the apostle, who urges this contentment (1 Tim. 6:6) and lights our way in it with his own example (Phil. 4:11–12).

---

28. αὐταρκείᾳ

CHAPTER SEVEN
The Immutability of God

With whom there is no changing or shadow of turning.
—James 1:17

From God's independence and simplicity results his immutability.
I. From God's independence and simplicity, in which God is Spirit from himself, there cannot but arise omnimodal immutability. For he who is, by his independence, absolutely first, does not admit someone prior who would change him, and he who is most simple does not have anything that would, through change, be taken away or remain. Thus according to James, in the Father of lights, who is not only the light in which there is no darkness (1 John 1:5), but also the fount of life in whose light we enjoy light (Ps. 36:9), the very sun of righteousness, there is no intrinsic alternation between light and darkness.

The Exegetical Part
This is constructed upon the exegesis of the text.
II. Here the text offers, with respect to God as the Father of lights, an eminent testimony of his omnimodal immutability, in terms borrowed mostly from astronomy. In that testimony, two things appear:

A. The one to whom it renders testimony: παρ' ᾧ, "with whom," or "in whom." Without a doubt, God is the one understood, inasmuch as the expression in the preceding words was about him, calling him the Father of lights: not only the Light in whom, or in whose essence, there is no darkness (that is, nothing heterogeneous), as we taught in the preceding chapter, but also he who is the Father, that is, the fount and source, not of light, but of lights, namely, all of them, however many there are, whether natural—the sun, moon, and stars—or supernatural—those lights in the mind of rational creatures through the illumination of regeneration, conversion, and sanctification.

B. What it testifies: οὐκ ἔνι παραλλαγή, and so forth, denying, namely, that there is any change in him. Here there is:

1. The denial: οὐκ ἔνι, "there is not in," which means, "there is none." ἔνι comes from ἔνειμι, "to be in," and stands by syncope for ἔνεστι, except that one codex, whose source is Beza, reads ἐστί for ἔνι.[1]

2. The thing denied, which concerns the immutability of God, since it removes from him:

   a. παραλλαγήν, "changing over" from ἀλλάσσω, "to change," which seems to come entirely from ἄλλο, since in every change, there is ἄλλο καὶ ἄλλο, "one thing and another," and a succession between them, which παρά denotes. Here we see a persistent metaphor found among the astronomers, according to whom the sun (the created father of lights) and the moon have their own παραλλαγὰς or παραλλάξεις, "various appearances," for they look one way at dawn, another way at noon, and another way at dusk. Likewise, they have their various changes: now they shine, now they do not, as is evident in eclipses of both the sun and the moon, and also in their motions, for example, in the case of the sun, which changes its place when it moves from the east to the west, and from the Tropic of Cancer to the Tropic of Capricorn, and thus there is now day or light, and now night or shade, which is greater or lesser depending on a greater or lesser rising or setting of the sun. So then again, the sun now appears, now shines, now is hidden by vapors, clouds, and eclipses. The created father of lights, therefore, is subject to so many changes, but the text removes all of them, and all others, from the uncreated Father of lights.

   b. τροπῆς ἀποσκίασμα, "shadow of vicissitude," or "of turning." Both words, again, are from astronomy. Indeed, τροπή, according to the astronomers, refers to the sun, which has its annual excursions from us, which we call solstices and the Greeks, τροπάς. And because of these excursions, the sun casts shadows upon us differently, and thus we read ἀποσκίασμα, "shadow," from ἀποσκιάζειν, "to cast a shadow." Therefore, the whole context signifies not only that there is absolutely no change in God, but also that there is no appearance or shadow of change.

---

1. Cf. James 1:17 in *Jesu Christi D. N. Novum Testamentum Gr. et Lat. Theodoro Beza interprete* ([Geneva:] Henricus Stephanus, 1580).

The Dogmatic Part

God alone is immutable. It is proved from the Scriptures.

III. Therefore, God, and indeed only God, is entirely and in all ways immutable. This is taught by the sacred page in many ways, when (1) it removes from him all change, even so much as a shadow (James 1:17; Mal. 3:6; 1 Tim. 1:17; Rom. 1:23), and (2) whatever implies change, for example, repentance (Num. 23:19; 1 Sam. 15:29). Indeed, (3) it explicitly asserts his immutability (Ps. 102:26–27; Heb. 1:11–12). For which reason Proclus says in his *Sermon on Faith to the Armenians,*[2] "Deity remains higher than all mutability. Change is a passion of a nature that passes away, but immutability properly belongs to that nature that is everlasting and that lives forever in the same way."[3]

It is confirmed by reasons.

IV. For God is, by his independence: (1) the absolutely first being, for whatever is changed is changed by another which is prior to itself. And he is also (2) a most simple being, for in a change, what remains lasts forever, but what is added or taken away, is likewise an alternating vicissitude. He is in addition (3) a most perfect being, indeed an infinitely perfect being, and for this reason, there can be no perfection either added to him, for thus he would not be most perfect, or taken away from him, for thus he would not remain most perfect. So then, he cannot be changed either for the better, which is not possible, or for the worse, for this would corrupt him, or into something equally good, for thus there would be more infinitely perfect beings than one, and therefore, there would be none. For these reasons Hilary wrote in book 3 of *On the Trinity*, "God, I say, is not mutable, nor to his eternal being belong either vice, or cleansing, or improvement, or loss, but what he is, he always is: he cannot ever have it in his nature not to be."[4] He is (4) infinite, to whom nothing can be added or taken away by change without his ceasing to be infinite. He is (5) incorruptible, whereas a change in a most perfect being is nothing other than a corruption. Moreover,

---

2. *Serm. de fide ad Armenos*: Cf. Proclus of Constantinople, *Epistola de fide ad Armenos* in PG 65:855–74.

3. *Passio*, "passion," in the philosophical usage of the patristic and medieval period frequently means the state or fact of being acted upon. In this context its opposite is *actio*, "action." The quotation is from Proclus, *Epistola de fide* in PG 65:861–62, V: μένει γὰρ ἡ θεότης ἀλλοιώσεως ἀνώτερα· ἐπείπερ τὸ τρεπτὸν, παραρρεούσης φύσεως πάθος· τῆς δὲ ἀϊδίου καὶ ἀεὶ ὡσαύτως ἐχούσης τὸ ἄτρεπτον ἴδιον. *Manet namque divinitatis omni mutabilitate superior: mutatio enim, naturae fluentis est passio: sed perennis illius ac semper eodem se habentis modo naturae, incommutabilitas est propria.*

4. See bk. 3, ch. 13 in Hilary of Poitiers, *De Trinitate* in PL 10:83; idem, *On the Trinity* in NPNF2 9:65.

(6) he would be annihilated, for a change in a most simple being can be nothing but an annihilation, inasmuch as when a most simple being has been changed, nothing remains of that which existed previously. Thus, a change in God would lead to flagrant atheism.

It is explained in regard to different types of change.

V. Moreover, change differs from annihilation, because in change, something always remains of what existed previously; in annihilation, nothing. Thus, if the deity changed, none of it would remain. If you say that it could, by a change, become something else, then you are saying that there could be more deities than one, and that one of them could become another, that the one, having passed through the change, could be born as another. But thus it would also not be eternal, and thus not the deity. Therefore, not only change itself, but even the different types of change, cannot apply to him. For this reason, Augustine says in the prologue of book four of *On the Trinity*, "The divine essence has nothing mutable, either in its eternity, or in its truth, or in its will."[5] Therefore God is immutable: (1) with respect to his essence and existence (1 Tim. 1:17; Ps. 102:27; Rom. 1:23), because he is eternal, immortal, a most pure act, existing necessarily and by his essence. (2) With respect to accidents, which do not belong to him, because he is good, true, just, wise, by his essence. For this reason, he can neither deny himself (2 Tim. 2:13) nor lie (Titus 1:2). (3) With respect to his knowledge, because he is omniscient (1 Cor. 2:16; Job 11:7–9), knowing all things in himself, in eternity, intuitively,[6] however much the objects of his knowledge change. (4) With respect to his will and decree (Isa. 46:10; Rom. 9:11; Job 42:2). For although his will is free, yet it is constant and eternal, and what has once pleased him can never displease him. Nor in addition does his immutability stand in his way such that he would any less do his works according to his eternal counsel. (5) With respect to his words, his promises and threats (Num. 23:19; Heb. 6:18). For he who changes his words also changes his will, but God's will is his very essence. (6) With respect to place, "because he cannot be comprehended, either in a place, or in the whole world," according to Justin in his *Dialogue with Trypho*.[7] Thus, even in regard to place, he cannot change.

---

5. Augustine, *De Trinitate*, bk. 4, proem. in *PL* 42:87; idem, *On the Trinity* in NPNF1 3:70.

6. *uno intuitu*, "at one glance." The distinction is between God knowing something intuitively from himself, i.e. through his most simple, eternal essence, and knowing something discursively, i.e. by learning it. Thus, Mastricht is arguing that God does not learn, and God's knowledge cannot be increased or decreased. Cf. 1.2.13 §§VI, XVIII.

7. Cf. Justin Martyr, *Dialogue with Trypho* in ANF 1:263; idem, *Dialogus cum Tryphone Judaeo* in PL 6:769–72.

The Elenctic Part

It is asked: 1. Is God immutable in every way? The divergence of opinions

VI. It is asked, first, whether God is immutable in every way. All who pro-fess Christ (even if only with their mouths), and indeed, all who profess God, including even the pagans, acknowledge that he is immutable with respect to his essence, since they profess that he is incorruptible and immortal (Rom. 1:23). For there is nothing more frequently on the lips of the pagans than the phrase "the immortal gods." The semi-Pelagians, Jesuits, Remonstrants, Anabaptists, and indeed even the Lutherans, acknowledge a sort of divine will that depends on a condition to be supplied by man, that depends upon man's free choice, which choice consists in independent indifference. Thus, they indeed acknowledge that man is dependent in all things, but they make an exception for that divine will, inasmuch as, according to the changes of human choice, the divine will changes hour by hour. The full Pelagians (with whom today's Socinians agree in every way) conclude from these same hypotheses that not only the divine will, but also God's intellect, that is, his omniscience, is mutable, since day by day he also procures from the decisions of the human will (that is, human choice) a knowledge of new truths. For they state that because God does not have any certain knowledge of future contingencies, especially those contingencies that depend upon the determination of our choice (which choice consists in inde-pendent indifference), that therefore, from that determination, God's knowledge is increased hour by hour, and as a result, it is changed, and that in addition, God experiences in himself affections of the true and proper sort, affections that by their own nature imply change, for example, repentance, longings, wishes, pain, pleasure, joys, and anger. The Reformed, on the contrary, deny that there is change of any kind in God, by means of the Scriptures and the reasons which we presented in §§III–IV.

Objections

Meanwhile, consider what our adversaries allege for themselves and for God's immutability, or what could be alleged: (1) that this immutability of God destroys the liberty of our choice. I respond, By no means, since the liberty of our choice does not consist in indifference, and certainly not in independent indiffer-ence, but in the faculty of acting from counsel, from free choice,[8] from rational complacency,[9] and this faculty is not destroyed or injured by the immutability of God. (2) That in this way, free choice does not belong even to God, since

---

8. ἐκ προαιρέσει
9. *ex complacentia rationali*

he could not, by his omnimodal immutability, change his purpose once it has been conceived. I respond, This is not true either, because by the indifference of God's nature, he can, when given two options, will either one, and thus he wills whatever he wills from his rational complacency, and therefore, he wills freely. (3) That God wills and makes mutable things. I respond, Yes, but he does so immutably, just as from his own eternity, which lacks all succession, he directs successive and mutable things. (4) That God created the world in time, though he did not create it from eternity. I respond, God created by that power which has existed immutable from eternity, the power that, by the divine will, the world underwent in time. And from creation, nothing has been added to him, except a mere relation, which does not imply any change in him. (5) That God predicted future things that he did not fulfill. I respond, He predicted, or rather promised and threatened, under a future condition, and if this condition was not fulfilled, he did not predict the future. (6) That God sometimes repented. I respond, Yes, speaking in a human way,[10] according to the change in his works, not in him who worked them. (7) That what God wills does not always happen. I respond, On the contrary, what he wills always happens, but in the way that he wills it. If he wills only by commanding, with the intent that the thing commanded be our duty, then that happens. If he wills something by decreeing, with the intent that it exist, then it exists, or it will exist. (8) That the Word, the second person of the Trinity, became flesh (John 1:14). I respond, The Word became flesh by assuming or by acting, not by being acted upon, but every passive change occurs by being acted upon. (9) That God suffered death (Acts 20:28). I respond, He suffered death not in himself, but in the assumed human nature.

*2. If God was incarnated and the divine nature of Christ suffered,
is it not rightly inferred that God is mutable?*

VII. Some ask whether, second, if God was incarnated and the divine nature of Christ suffered, it is not rightly inferred that God is mutable and has changed. At one time the Patripassians, arising from Praxeas, threw the church into confusion in the beginning of the third century. Marcellinus Comes (in his *Chronicle*, under Emperor Anastasius)[11] calls them the "Deopassians" because they acknowledged not only one and the same nature in God and in the Son, but also one and the same person, which Noetus later imitated, and his disciple Sabellius. These

---

10. ἀνθρωποπαθῶς
11. Cf. Marcellinus Comes, *Chronicon Minora II* in *PL* 51:937; idem, *The Chronicle of Marcellinus: A Translation with Commentary* (Leiden: Brill, 2017), 17.

Patripassians stated that the Father also suffered and thus God was changed (see Augustine, *On Heresies*, §41;[12] Eusebius, *Ecclesiastical History*, bk. 7, ch. 6;[13] Epiphanius, *Panarion*, §§57, 62;[14] John Forbes, *Historical-Theological Instruction*, bk. 1, ch. 2, §5).[15] The Lutherans state that through the hypostatic union of the two natures in Christ, the divine essence, together with the subsistence of the second person, was communicated to the human nature, that in this way they might obtain the omnipresence of Christ's flesh, and thus its presence in the elements of the holy Supper. Therefore, they state that this divine nature both was incarnate and suffered, and thus, was changed. Yet they still deny that God is mutable. The Reformed, on the contrary, also acknowledge that the Son of God, the second person of the Trinity, can be called incarnate, but in this sense: not by being acted upon but only by acting, that is, by assuming a human nature. They also acknowledge that God suffered, though not in himself, but in the assumed human nature. In this way the Reformed affirm that if we say properly speaking that the divine nature became incarnate or suffered, then we call God mutable, because to be passively incarnated or to suffer in himself imports, without any doubt, a change. For to become what you were not, as in a passive incarnation, and to be no longer what you were—who would say that this does not import a change?

Yet there is no lack of excuses that the adversaries plead. (1) The Patripassians, on the one hand, allege that without any doubt the same nature is in the Father that is in the Son, and since therefore the divine nature suffered in the Son, it could not be but that it also suffered in the Father, and thus, the divine nature suffered in both. I respond, The divine nature suffered in neither, but rather, the person of the Son suffered. The Son indeed had a divine nature, the same as the Father's, but, acting by his characteristic or personal properties, he assumed a human nature that was bound, as it were, to the second person. It was, finally, in this nature that the Son of God suffered. (2) The Lutherans allege that through the personal union the subsistence of the Son of God has been communicated

---

12. Augustine, *PL* 42:32–33; idem, *De Haeresibus: A Translation with an Introduction and Commentary*, trans. and ed. L. G. Müller, vols. 90–91, *Catholic University of America Patristic Studies* (Washington, D.C.: Catholic University of America Press, 1956).

13. *Lib. v. cap. xi*: Eusebius of Caesarea, *PG* 20:420–57; *Eusebius Pamphili Ecclesiastical History: Books 1–5*, trans. R. J. Deferrari (Washington, D.C.: Catholic University of America Press, 2005), 304–6.

14. Epiphanius, *Panarion* in *PG* 41:903–1010, 1051–62.

15. John Forbes (1593–1648), *Instructiones historico-theologicae de doctrina Christiana et vario rerum statu* (Geneva: Jean Pictet, 1680), 2–3.

to the human nature of Christ, and because subsistence in God coincides with his essence, that therefore the divine essence, together with its properties, was communicated to that nature. Thus, when the human nature suffered, the divine nature also suffered, since it had been communicated to the human nature. We, however, deny that through the personal union the subsistence of the second person was communicated to the human nature, because by this rationale, the human nature would not only have become a person—for every rational substance which has some sort of subsistence, whether proper or communicated, is a person—but would also have become a divine person, since everything that has divine subsistence is a divine person. Likewise we deny that the divine nature of the Son of God has been communicated to the human nature, for in that way the human nature would have become a divine nature (since, undoubtedly, a nature is divine which has a divine nature), and thus, there would be, not a union of the natures in Christ, but an identity, which is plain Eutychianism. Therefore it remains that if the divine nature had been communicated to the human nature, it would have suffered in that human nature, and God would have changed, and thus, he would be mutable. These things, with God's help, will come up again more expressly in the chapter on the person of the Mediator.[16]

3. Is God mutable at least with respect to place?

VIII. Some ask, third, whether God is mutable at least with respect to place. Conrad Vorstius, not yet daring to deny openly the personal union of the two natures in Christ, lies in ambush to undermine it secretly, saying that the essence of God is finite and exists only in heaven, from which it follows that it could not have been united with a human nature, which exists only on earth, for which reason he acknowledges only a finite deity that could move from place to place. The Socinians, openly denying the personal union in Christ, openly teach that God is composite and finite, and that it is not contrary to his nature for him to move from place to place. The Reformed, just as they teach that God is in all ways immutable, such that there is not even a shadow of change in him, thus also teach that he is immutable in respect to place. Because his essence is infinite, omnipresent, immense, filling heaven and earth (Jer. 23:24; Josh. 2:11; Ps. 139:7–10; Acts 7:49; 17:24–28), he cannot change place. Concerning these things we will speak expressly in the following chapters. If they should say, (1) It is said throughout Scripture that he is in heaven, I will respond, Nowhere does it say that he is in heaven only; rather, it says the contrary, as is evident from the passages adduced just above. (2) It is said that he ascends and descends, he arrives and departs.

---

16. 1.5.4 §XXIII

I will respond, He does so in his own way, that is, the way an infinite, omnipresent being that fills heaven and earth can ascend and descend. It is, namely, whenever he reveals his extraordinary presence, for an extraordinary end and work, in an extraordinary way, that he is said to ascend and descend, unless you prefer to say that he ascends and descends, not in his own essence, but under some assumed form. These things spoken of in passing here will be treated more fully in the following chapters.[17]

The Practical Part

It is profitable: First, for his glorification

IX. With respect to practice, the immutability of God is profitable, first, for the glory and glorification of God. Thus we read of the glory of the incorruptible (that is, immutable) God (Rom. 1:23). By this glory, (1) God glorifies himself (Mal. 3:6), and his saints glorify him: (2) the church (Ps. 102:25–26), (3) Paul (1 Tim. 1:17), and others. And this is so not only because (1) he enjoys this excellent and weighty perfection on his own (Mal. 3:6; Ps. 102:25–26; 1 Tim. 1:17), but because (2) this perfection pours itself out into all his other perfections, since in his wisdom, in his goodness, in his love, grace, mercy, patience, righteousness, power, and so forth, he is wholly and utterly unchanging. Also because (3) amidst all the changes and vicissitudes, so many and so great, of the whole universe, he stands unmoved, and wholly unmovable. Indeed, the author of all change in all things exists himself unmoved (Ps. 102:25–26). So then, because of this incorruptible glory, let us join in glorifying him, following the example of God and of the saints, lest we also, with the pagan philosophers, be rebuked because we have changed the glory of the incorruptible God (Rom. 1:23).

2. For the despising of the creatures

X. Second, it directs us to despise all creatures, however stable and brilliant they seem, when we consider that God alone is immutable, and thus that anything under the sun that is different from him is fragile, fleeting, and passing away, including (1) republics, kingdoms, cities, kings, princes (Hag. 2:22; Jer. 13:18; Dan. 2:1–46); (2) riches, honors, pleasures, health (Prov. 30:8); (3) good fortune (Job 8:2ff.; 20:15; 24:24; Ps. 73:18–19). We should consider these things in this way so that: (1) we do not set our heart on any of them (Ps. 62:10; Prov. 23:5); and (2) we do not rest our confidence upon them, for they are unstable (1 Tim. 6:17). In fact, (3) we should condemn them (1 John 2:15–16), or at least,

---

17. 1.2.9 §VI; 1.2.10 §IX

(4) we should use present things with moderation (1 Cor. 7:29–31). And (5) we should rest in our immovable God alone, for he is the rock of our heart forever (Ps. 73:25), and his promises are immutable (Heb. 6:13–19).

3. For the detestation of sin

XI. Third, it frightens us away from sin, and from carelessness in sinning, that God is immutable in all ways (2 Tim. 2:19), that is, (1) with respect to his essence and existence, for he exists as the avenger of sins, even to all eternity (Isa. 66:24); (2) with respect to his attributes: his justice, his wrath, his hatred for sins and sinners, attributes that will not only never cease, but also never diminish; (3) with respect to his threats (Gen. 2:17); (4) with respect to the exercise of vengeance through his judgments, in which he always is and always will be who he has been from all eternity (Ex. 20:5; 34:7).

4. For confidence and comfort in any circumstances

XII. Fourth, it encourages confidence and comfort in the godly, in whatever fortune, no matter how adverse, that God is immutable (Heb. 6:17–18). For this reason he is called the rock (Deut. 32:31; Ps. 73:26) upon which the church has been built (Matt. 16:18). For if the godly are vexed, perhaps in regard to their eternal salvation, because of the inconstancy of their own heart, together with the immutable treacheries of their spiritual enemies, what will sustain them more effectively than the fact that their immutable God (Mal. 3:6) is a rock and unmoved boulder, whose firm foundation stands, by which the Lord knows those who are his (2 Tim. 2:19), whose saving gifts are without repentance (Rom. 11:29)? Or if they are vexed about the vicissitudes of temporal things, whether the stirrings of war, diseases, or whatever other calamities, what will more effectively comfort them than to consider that (1) the immutability of the one God is a law fixed in their favor, and that all other things are only immutable in their motion and flux (1 Cor. 7:29). At the same time that (2) God, through all these motions and vicissitudes, will be present, unmoved, for the sake of his own (Ps. 46:1–7), present in his perfection and strength, that they may not be shaken (Ps. 90:1). That (3) he is immutable in goodness, love, grace, and mercy (Isa. 54:10; Ps. 117:2; 118:1, 2, 5), and also (4) in his will and gracious decrees by which he knows his own (2 Tim. 2:19; Heb. 6:17–18), and in addition, (5) in his promises, so many and so great (Num. 23:19), all of which will be yes and amen in Christ (2 Cor. 1:20; Heb. 13:5), and especially in his faithfulness and covenant (Isa. 55:3; 54:10; Hos. 2:19). What could be more effective for our consolation than all these things? Especially when we have the examples of so many saints to prove them: David (Ps. 18:2; 37:33, 37) and others. Only let us devote ourselves,

(1) that the immutable God be *our* God through the covenant of grace, and (2) that we in turn be immovable in our keeping of that covenant, as well as (3) in our love, faith, confidence, holiness, worship, and so forth.

5. For fleeing inconstancy and fickleness

XIII. Fifth, the immutability of God draws us away from all mutability, inconstancy, and fickleness, (1) in our holy intentions (1 Cor. 15:58); (2) in the promises we offer to God (Rom. 1:13); (3) in the covenant we entered through baptism, that we have renewed often through the Lord's Supper, in sicknesses, in fasts, and so forth (Ps. 25:10; 103:18); (4) in our profession of Christ and of the Christian faith (Matt. 10:32–33); and (5) in love, trust, and good works (1 Cor. 15:58; Heb. 12:27–28). For surely (1) by all such fickleness we withdraw from the example of our immutable God, in whose imitation our every perfection consists (Matt. 5:48), for which reason also, (2) we incur those most disgraceful marks of this fickleness, which appear in Scripture (James 1:8; Matt. 11:6; Luke 7:24; 1 Kings 18:21; Eph. 4:14; Heb. 13:9; etc.).

6. For the study of constancy

XIV. On the contrary, sixth, the immutability of God invites us to a zeal for imitation, that in our duty toward God and neighbor we may be immovable, not in that Stoic insensibility[18] too eagerly endorsed by the Enthusiasts, but (1) by taking our affections, loves, desires, and joys, and binding them fast to the one God (Ps. 73:25); (2) by immutably fulfilling our promises and pacts made to God and men (Ps. 116:14); (3) regarding all duties of piety, (a) by undertaking them with fixed purpose (Acts 4:19), (b) by pursuing them with unmoved constancy (Rev. 2:26), (c) by vigorously removing and avoiding the difficulties in the way (Heb. 10:36); and to this end, (4) with our minds ever intent on the immutable goodness of God as our model, for in imitating him consists our perfection (Matt. 5:48; Lev. 11:44), (5) persuaded that nothing good, no virtue, faith, or righteousness, is true or perfect without constancy (Ezek. 18:24; Rev. 2:25–26); and to this end, (6) by wearying the immovable God with unmoved prayers that he renew a true spirit in our innermost parts (Ps. 51:10), that by his own immutability he support us in our unsteadiness, so that we may advance in constancy until finally we achieve that state of perfect immutability.

---

18. ἀπαθία

CHAPTER EIGHT

The Unity of God

Hear, O Israel, the Lord Our God, the Lord is one.
—Deuteronomy 6:4

In the second class of attributes, the first place is allocated to unity.

I. We have considered the first class of divine attributes, which represented *what* God is. After it comes the second class, that it might relate to us, under the idea of *quantity*, his unity, infinity, and eternity. Unity, the foundation of this class, appears in Deuteronomy 6:4, which was adduced by our Savior (Mark 12:29), and is, by the Jews, not only read daily, but also customarily inscribed on a clean parchment, on which, according to Fagius on Exodus 13:15,[1] they set down the chief points of their religion.

The Exegetical Part

It is built upon an analysis and explanation of the text.

II. The text commends to the church the hearing of the articles of faith that are most fundamental: the Trinity and the unity of God. Concerning these, it notes:

A. The hearing: שְׁמַע, "Hear." Of course, not only with the ears, but also with the mind, that is, know, believe, and hold fast to these things, as they are the deepest ground of all religion. The last letter in שְׁמַע is larger than usual, the ninth time this happens in the Hebrew Bible, and this feature is preserved not only by the Masoretes, but also by Christians, so that it may call us to careful attention. For this reason the Jews say these words daily, morning and evening, following a most ancient tradition,

---

1. Paul Fagius, *Thargum, hoc est, paraphrasis Onkeli Chaldaica in sacra biblia* (Strassburg: 1546), sigs. m4 recto–[m5] verso.

and in their book of prayers, they boast about it: "Blessed are we, who morning and evening say, 'Hear, O Israel....'"[2]

B. The hearers: "Israel." Not "Israelites" in the plural, but "Israel" in the singular. Thus it is signified that not only the Israelites as a whole, but every Israelite as an individual, has been entrusted with hearing it for himself. "Israel" is of course not only that carnal Israel which Moses led out of Egypt into the wilderness and Joshua led into the land of Canaan, in which signification this name occurs throughout the Scriptures, but also that spiritual Israel about which Romans 2:21, 29, and Galatians 6:16 speak. It signifies the church of both testaments, to whom what is to be heard ought to be most highly commended, since it is the most fundamental article of religion, and without it no other article can be safe, as is evident in the case of the anti-Trinitarians, who, because they neglected or corrupted it, violated the whole of religion. In a word, without hearing this, you cannot be that Israel of God, that is, the true church.

C. What must be heard, namely, two things about God:

1. His Trinity: יהוה אלוהנו, "Jehovah our God." Here note:

   a. "Jehovah," the especially proper name for God, and his memorial, which never occurs in the plural. We have already treated this name in detail in the discussion about the names of God (bk. 2, ch. 4).[3]

   b. "Our God," אלוהנו. Here אלוהים is his personal name, denoting a plurality in God, which by no means is a plurality of essences, but rather of persons. And the pronominal suffix for the first person, נו, "our," speaks of the covenant by which Jehovah was Israel's God, and Israel, vice versa, was Jehovah's people. The covenant can be understood either as the national covenant in which God chose that whole Israelite nation out of all other nations to be, as it were, his own property, which covenant concerned only the Israelite people and all its members, whether they were good or bad, or, as that especially gracious covenant which he enters into with each and every true believer, and with them alone, under both testaments, in any nation.

---

2. Mastricht is likely referring to the prayer books, the *siddurim*, and an element of the morning prayer service, the *shacharit*, שחרית, developed in the Talmudic period.

3. 1.2.4 §VIII

2. His unity: יהוה אחד, "Jehovah is one." Here again, the third letter
ד in אחד is larger than usual, the tenth time this happens, and it
is preserved by the Masoretes and others in order to commend to
Israel the necessity of this unity, so that they, on account of the plurality of persons, do not invent for themselves more than one god.
Thus אחד is one of the names of God (Isa. 66:17; Job 31:15), from
which in Syrian, "god" is *ahad*, and in Assyrian, *adad*, the name of the
greatest god of the Assyrians, as Macrobius testifies (*Saturnalia*, bk. 1,
ch. 23).[4]

The Dogmatic Part

The unity of God is proved: From divine testimonies

III. Therefore God is, according to the text, most perfectly one. That is, not only
one, but also one of a kind, indeed as Bernard says somewhere, "most one."[5] God
says this in his Word, and he would not be God if, whether through ignorance
or malice, he said what was not true. He says it in more than one way: (1) whenever he affirms it, saying, "I am one," as if in those exact syllables (Zech. 14:9;
Mal. 2:10; Matt. 19:17; Mark 10:18; Rom. 3:30; 1 Cor. 8:4–5; Gal. 3:20; Eph.
4:6; 1 Tim. 2:5). He says it (2) whenever he denies that all others, besides the
one, are gods (Deut. 4:35; 2 Kings 19:15; Ps. 83:18; 86:8; John 17:3). He says it
(3) whenever he denies to all others the rank of deity (Deut. 3:24; 1 Sam. 2:2;
2 Sam. 7:22; Ps. 18:31; Hos. 13:4; Mark 12:32; 1 Tim. 6:15; etc.).

From human testimonies

The Fathers agree, when by piles of arguments they wrench this unity from
the pagans. See Ignatius, *Epistles* (no. 9, to the Antiochans);[6] Justin Martyr in
Exhortation to the Greeks and in *On the Monarchy of God*;[7] Tertullian in *Against
Praxeas* and in his *Apology* (bk. 2, on idolatry);[8] in Cyprian, *On the Vanity of*

---

4. Macrobius, *Saturn.*, 1.23.10.

5. *unissimus*

6. The epistle of Ignatius to the Antiochians is considered among the spurious letters by later
scholarship; see Ignatius, *Ep.* 9 in PG 5:897–910; ANF 1:110–11.

7. Pseudo-Justin Martyr, Λόγος παραινετικὸς πρὸς Ἕλληνας, or *Cohortatio ad
Gentiles* in PG 6:279–99; idem, *Hortatory Address to the Greeks* in ANF 1:275–88; idem, Περὶ
Μοναρχίας or *De Monarchia* in PG 6:311–26.

8. Tertullian, *Adversus Praxeam*, ch. 4, in PL 2:159; idem, *Against Praxeas* in ANF 3:599–
600; idem, *Apologia* in PL 2:661–96; idem, *Apology* in ANF 3:61–76.

Idols;[9] Athanasius, *Against the Heathen;*[10] Gregory of Nazianzus, *Orations* (no. 2, on theology);[11] Basil, *Orations* (Against the Sabellians and Arius);[12] Ambrose, *On Faith* (bk. 1, ch. 1);[13] Lactantius, *Divine Institutes* (bk. 1, ch. 3);[14] Augustine, *On the Trinity* (bk. 1, ch. 4);[15] John of Damascus, *On the Orthodox Faith* (bk. 1, ch. 5).[16] Indeed, even the wiser among the pagans, at least whenever they speak in earnest, bear testimony to God's unity. Thus Plato says in his *Epistles* (no. 13, to Dionysius), "From this you will learn whether or not I am writing in earnest: when I write in earnest, I begin the epistle with the one God, when writing otherwise, I begin with the many."[17] And Lactantius, "How did men become persuaded that there were many gods? Without doubt, all those whom they worship as gods were men: they were the first and greatest kings. But who can deny that they either were afforded divine honors after their death on account of the virtue by which they benefited the human race, or, that they achieved an immortal memory on account of the benefits and discoveries by which they improved human life?" (Lactantius, *On the Wrath of God*; cf. John Selden, *On the Syrian Gods*, in the prolegomena).[18] Sophocles speaks in the same way: "In reality, there is one God who made heaven and earth…but we mortals, deceived by cunning," that is, of certain men, "set up…images of the gods…, and by dedicating sacrifices and vain assemblies to them, we thus repute ourselves to be pious."[19] Orpheus, after his *Theogony*, recites a recantation with these words, "There is one God, the immortal King of the world, who is from himself, from whom are all things."[20]

---

9. Cyprian, *De idolorum vanitate* in PG 4:563–82; idem, *On the Vanity of Idols* in ANF 5:465–69.

10. *Contra Idola*: see Athanasius, *Contra Gentes* in PG 25:75–78; *Against the Heathen* in NPNF2 4:24.

11. Gregory of Nazianzus, *Orations* 27 in PG 7:311–34; NPNF2 7:288–301.

12. Basil, *Contra Sabellianos, et Arium, et Anomoeos* in PG 31:600–17.

13. Ambrose, *De Fide* in PL 16:530–1; idem, *Exposition of the Christian Faith* in NPNF2 10:202–3.

14. Lactantius, *Divinae institutiones* in PL 6:122–27; idem, *Divine Institutes* in ANF 7:11–13.

15. Augustine, *De Trinitate* in PL 42:72–3; idem, *On the Trinity* in NPNF1 3:20.

16. John of Damascus, Ἔκδοσις ἀκριβὴς τῆς ὀρθοδόξου πίστεως (*Expositio accurata fidei orthodoxae*) in PG 94:801–2; idem, NPNF2 9:4.

17. Plato, *Ep.* 13, 363b, to Dionysius; idem, *LCL* 234:624–5.

18. Lactantius, *De ira Dei* in PL 7:79–148; idem, *A Treatise on the Anger of God* in ANF 7:259–80; John Selden (1584–1654), *De dis Syris syntagmata II* in *Opera omnia*, 3 vols. (1726), 2:225–53 (ch. 3 in the prolegomena).

19. Cf. the citation of pseudo–Sophocles, ch. 18, in pseudo-Justin Martyr, Λόγος παραινετικὸς πρὸς Ἕλληνας (*Cohortatio ad Graecos*) in PG 6:273–76; idem, *Hortatory Address to the Greeks* in ANF 1:280.

20. μοῦνον δὲ ἐσόρα κόσμοιο ἄνακτα ἀθάνατον…εἷς ἐστ᾽ αὐτογενής, ἑνὸς

From the testimony of nature

IV. Nor could they testify otherwise, since nature itself proclaims it. For it proclaims (1) that in the subordination of things, we must stop at one certain thing that is from itself and absolutely first, which nothing at all can preexist, or with whom nothing of the same nature can coexist. It proclaims (2) that this one thing is infinite, given that he is not bounded by a prior being, and accordingly, that he contains all being, either formally, as they say, or eminently. It proclaims (3) that this infinite being is, by the same logic, most perfect, one to whom no perfection of any other being can be lacking, while the contrary of this requires a plurality of gods. It proclaims (4) that this first, infinite, and most perfect being is, by the same logic, omnipotent, a being that some other god could not resist. It proclaims (5) that by this omnipotence, he formed one world, that every part unites in one harmony to preserve this one world, and that this preservation is administered, without doubt, by one most wise governor. It proclaims (6) that over this one world there stands one monarch, who, because he is supreme, cannot tolerate a superior, indeed, not even an equal (Isa. 46:5; Ps. 86:8). Thus Homer (*Iliad*, bk. 2) says, "Not good when many rule, let one be lord, // One king...."[21] Meanwhile, that no scruple against this most perfect unity of God may cling to us, we should understand that the divine unity does not contradict: (1) the plurality of his names, because they designate nothing but one God; (2) the plurality of his attributes, because they do not relate to us anything but the one infinite perfection of God, though in a way analogous to our inadequate concepts; (3) the Trinity of his persons, which our adversaries mock, but most speciously so, for in these three persons there is only one essence, one existence, one subsistence; we count three only in the modes of subsisting. These modes do not mean three gods, but rather, three who are one God.

The nature of the divine unity is explained.

V. And so God is one, and as we have said, most one, or most especially one, because he is the greatest and most perfect being. And he is so, not by a unity of species, which admits more than one individual of the same name and nature,

---

ἔγκονα πάντα τέτυκται. This exact quote appears in Clement of Alexandria, *Clementinì Alexandrini Protrepticus*, ed. M. Marcovich (Leiden: Brill, 1995), 112. The figure of Orpheus is used as a literary device in Clement's work. Also, a *theogony* is a description of the birth or origin of the gods. Translated from Mastricht's Latin rendering.

21. Mastricht: οὐκ ἀγαθὸν πολυκοιρανίη, εἷς βασιλεύς, εἷς κοίρανος ἔστω. The translation follows the order of the original, *Iliad* 2.204–5: οὐκ ἀγαθὸν πολυκοιρανίη εἷς κοίρανος ἔστω // εἷς βασιλεύς. In context, Homer is arguing for an absolute human monarch.

nor by a unity of composite parts, in the way that body and soul constitute one person, nor by a unity of subject and accident, which applies to all created spirits, the angels and our souls, but by a singular unity, a unity that also entirely excludes every composition, a unity through which he is one and only one, undivided in himself, and unable to be divided into more gods or more beings that have the same name and nature. Furthermore, this unity, when attributed to God, is not understood to be an arithmetic unity, which is a principle of number, but an essential unity, according to the sense of Basil, "We confess that God is one, not in number, but in nature,"[22] and a transcendental unity, according to the sense of Victorinus (*Against Arius*, bk. 3), "God is one in three persons more than he is one in number."[23]

The Elenctic Part

It is asked: 1. What and of what sort was the polytheism of unbelievers,
that is, of the pagans?

VI. It is asked, first, what and of what sort the polytheism of unbelievers, that is, of the pagans was. Polytheism was not accepted by all of the pagans, as we just previously taught (§III), and not by the wiser among them, but only by those of baser character. For this reason, the sect of the philosophers whom they often called Atheists, in which sect Theodorus, Protagoras, and Diagoras appear to have been, is thought by many to have been so called, not because they believed in no God, but because they resisted the mob of gods (as Gregory of Nazianzus says in his *Oration 38, On the Birth of Christ*),[24] that is, the polytheism of the Greeks. Indeed, Socrates, from his hatred of polytheism, did not hesitate to drink hemlock. These gods, for the common lot of the pagans, or for their common philosophers, arose from every kind of creatures. Thus Prudentius, not without wisdom, sang: "What earth, sea, sky bring forth that struck them strange // They called their gods: the hills, waves, streams, and flames."[25] Among these gods, Varro numbered three hundred Jupiters, and Hesiod, thirty thousand gods (see Augustine, *City of God*, bk. 6). Epiphanius, by reason of Colossians 3:11, separated these gods into barbarism, Scythianism, and Hellenism, in such

---

22. *Epist. 141*: cf. Basil, *Epistl.* 8 in PG 32:247–48.

23. Victorinus, *Adversus Arium* in PL 1098–113.

24. δήμῳ θεῶν. Gregory of Nazianzus, *In Theophania sive Natalia Salvatoria* in PG 36:312; idem, "Oration 38: On the Theophany, or Birthday of Christ" in NPNF2 7:347.

25. *Quicquid humus, pelagus, caelum mirabile signant // Id dixere Deos, colles, freta, flumina, flammas.* Prudentius, *The Reply to Symmachus* in LCL 387:372–73. Cf. the same citation of Prudentius (also paired with a citation of Gregory of Nazianzus, Oration 38) in Francis Turretin, *Institutio theologiae elencticae* (New York: R. Carter, 1847), loc. 3, q. 3, §11, 1:165.

a way that in his opinion barbarism prevailed from Adam to Noah, Scythianism from Noah to the age of Serug,[26] when Hellenism was introduced, just as Judaism takes its origin from the circumcision of Abraham.[27] By barbarism, he means that severity of morals and that violence that infested the antediluvian world. He places the distinction between Scythianism and Hellenism in this, that the making of statues,[28] which the former lacked, was introduced under the latter.

The Jesuit Petavius, in his *Animadversions*, warned that this chronology was not made carefully enough.[29] For this reason, some prefer to separate polytheism into Sabaism and Hellenism. Sabaism consisted in the worship of the heavens, sun, moon, and stars, to which Hellenism added the veneration of the images of departed people, although both held the adoration of the stars in common. Accordingly, Sabaism worshiped the sun (which Scripture labels Moloch) and the moon (which Scripture calls Melecheth), the sun as king and the moon as queen.[30] Because of this, they called the sun various names: God, the Most High, and so forth; Adrammelech, Kiyyun, Molech, Baal-zebub, Chemosh, Adoni, Bel, Baal,[31] and they added to these Saturn, Jupiter, Mithra, Mars, Apollo, Osiris, Pan, Bacchus, Janus, Belenus, and Helios, names which referred to nothing more than heavenly bodies. Job speaks of this sort of polytheism in Job 31:26–27, and so does Moses in Deuteronomy 4:19. They seem to have taken as the occasion for their polytheism or idolatry, that (1) perhaps word came to them, based on Genesis 1:16, that God established two great luminaries, one to rule the day, and the other, the night; (2) they observed the virtues, operations, and remarkable influences which celestial luminaries exert upon the earth and terrestrial things (Jer. 44:17–18); likewise, (3) they were astounded by the adornment of the heavens, the course of the stars, and the order of the celestial bodies, because of which the heavens are said to tell the glory of God (Ps. 19:1ff.). Both Lactantius (*Divine Institutes*, bk. 2, ch. 14)[32] and Diodorus Siculus (in his *Library of History*,

---

26. Gen. 11:21; 1 Chron. 1:26; Luke 3:35

27. Epiphanius, *Panarion* in PG 41:187–90.

28. ἀγαλματοποιία

29. Epiphanius, *Opera omnia*, ed. Dionysius Petavius (1583–1652), 2 vols. (Cologne: Jeremiah Schrey and Heinrich Johannes Meier, 1682), vol. 1, sigs. *aiij (recto)– *aviij (recto). It is Petavius's edition of Epiphanius that forms the basis for the text of PG 41:173–1199. See Petavius's warning in PG 41:151–54.

30. Moloch is related to the name Molech and the Hebrew *melech*, "king" (see Amos 5:26; Acts 7:43). Melecheth is Hebrew for "queen" (see Jer. 7:18).

31. האל, הליון, *etc.*, כיון, אדרמלך, מלך, בעלזבוב, כמוש, אדני, בל, בעל. Cf. 2 Kings 17:31, Amos 5:26, Lev. 18:21, 2 Kings 1:2, 1 Kings 11:7, Jer. 50:2, 1 Kings 18:21.

32. Lactantius, *Divinae institutiones* in PL 6:326–29; idem, *Divine Institutes* in ANF 7:63–64.

bk. 1),[33] regarded this to be the source of polytheism. This Sabaism gained strength during a long series of years, even among the ancient Greeks, though it had not yet come into the mind of men to project their own likenesses onto the throne of deity.

Now regarding Hellenism, it added two things to Sabaism: first, the apotheosis of illustrious men who generally lived in the East and were the leaders of tribes. Thus, for example, they made Noah into Saturn, Janus, and Bacchus, Ham into Jupiter Hammon, Japheth into Iapetus and Neptune, Shem into Pluto and Dis. And in the same way, after a while other illustrious men were adopted by the Greeks into the number of the gods. The motive for this apotheosis was either their admiration for their exceptional deeds, or their love for the benefits they amassed by them, or their hatred for tyrants who sought to persecute them, or their adulation, which is evident in the apotheosis of Herod in Acts 12:21–22. Then second, besides the apotheosis of men, Hellenism added to Sabaism the worship of images and statues, which are thought to have first been fabricated by Terah, the father of Abraham, whom they suppose was a statue-maker. These statues began in the succession of time to be placed in shrines, groves, and temples, and as a result, achieved the rank of deity.

The origin of all polytheism or idolatry is variously thought of by various people. Maimonides refers it to the time of Enosh, and for this argument twists the sentence in Genesis 4:26, אז הוחל לקרא בשם יהוה. While most all interpreters, and indeed the best ones, render these words, "Then men began to call upon the name of Jehovah," he translated it as, "Then men began to profane the name of the Lord," that is, because he adds with no warrant a tail to the verse, "through idolatry," although no mention at all of idolatry in antediluvian times occurs in the Scriptures. Some therefore refer the origin of idolatry to the construction of the tower of Babel. Others refer it to the times of Serug or Terah. But all these things are uncertain. The error that is fundamental[34] to all these resided in this one thing, that they were ignorant of the nature of deity, ignorant, namely that because of that nature, God is the absolutely first and infinitely perfect being, who cannot be anything but one. The entire system of polytheism is confounded by those most powerful arguments produced in §IV. The pagans do not dispute in favor of their polytheism with reasons, but rather, what they believe they deeply presuppose.

---

33. Diodorus Siculus, *Library of History* in *LCL* 279:1–342.
34. πρῶτον ψεύδους

2. What was the reason for the polytheism of the ancient heretics?

VII. It is asked, second, what the reason for the polytheism of the ancient heretics was. Marcion, the disciple of Cerdo, who lived in the second century around AD 145, perhaps because he regarded God as having acted more harshly with his own people under the Old Testament by imposing on them the yoke of the ceremonial law than he acted under the New Testament through the sweet gospel, talked of two gods: an evil god, the author of the world and the law, and a good god, the author of the gospel and redemption. Origen relates that Marcion set up three gods: one of the Jews, another of the Christians, and a third of the unbelievers (see Tertullian, *On the Prescription of Heretics* and *Against Marcion*; Irenaeus, *Against Heresies*, bk. 1, 3; Epiphanius, *Panarion*, 42; Augustine, *On Heresies*, 22; Origen, *The Dialogue of a Montanist and an Orthodox*).[35] Mani, from whom came the Manicheans, in the third century around AD 275, using the fanatical books of Scythianus and of his disciple Terebinthus, an adherent of the magical arts, supposed that there were two gods: the one god good, the author of good things, and especially of the good soul, the god whom he named Phos, "light," to whom also, together with Marcion, he attributed the gospel; the other god evil, equal in power with the good, whom he called Hyle, "matter," from whom the evil soul, the body, sexual intercourse, commands, and all evil things had their origin (see Epiphanius, bk. 2 of *Panarion*, 66; Augustine, *On Heresies*, 86, likewise his *On the Manichaean Way of Life*; Theodoret's book, *Compendium of Heretical Fables*, 10).[36] Valentinus the Egyptian, from whom came the Valentinians, under Emperor Antoninus Pius in the second century, circa AD 110, was excessively devoted to Platonic and Pythagorean philosophy, as well as to the theogonies of the ancients, of Orpheus and Hesiod, and building upon them and filling in their gaps, he asserts the existence of thirty aeons, that is, ages. Their

---

35. Tertullian, *De praescriptione haereticorum* in PL 2:9–74; idem, *The Prescription against Heretics* in ANF 3:243–65; idem, *Adversus Marcionem* in PL 2:239–524; idem, *Against Marcion* in ANF 3:271–474; Irenaeus, *Contra haereses* in PG 7:465–78; idem, *Against Heresies* in ANF 1:319–20; Epiphanius, *Panarion*, Heresy 42, in PG 41:695–848. For the spurious work Mastricht attributes to Origen, see in Latin *Dialexis montanistae et orthodoxi*, *Clavis Patrum Graecorum* (Turnhout: Brepols, 1974), 2572; in Greek, attributed to Didymus the Blind, *Widerlegung eines Montanisten*, ed. G. Ficker, *Zeitschrift für Kirchengeschichte* 26 (1905), 447–63; in English, *The Montanist Oracles and Testimonia*, ed. R. E. Heine (Macon, Ga.: Mercer University Press, 1989), 112–27.

36. Epiphanius, *Panarion*, Heresy 66, in PG 42:29–172. Augustine, *De haeresibus ad Quodvultdeum* in PL 42:46–47; idem, *De moribus Manichaeorum* in PL 32:1345–78; idem, *Morals of the Manichaeans* in NPNF1 4:65–89; idem, *The Catholic and Manichaean Ways of Life*, trans. D. A. Gallagher and I. J. Gallagher, *Fathers of the Church* series (Washington, D.C.: Catholic University of America Press, 1966), 56:65–118; Theodoret of Cyprus, *Compendium haereticarum fabularum* in PG 83:359–60; idem, "Compendium of heretical mythification" in *Theodoret of Cyprus*, trans. I. Pásztori-Kupán (New York: Routledge, 2006), 198–220.

first principle is Depth and Silence, or Bythus and Sige, and of these two, he also calls Depth the Father. He says that from these two, as from intercourse, proceeded Intellect and Truth, Nous and Aletheia, and they brought forth, in honor of the Father, eight aeons. Moreover, from Intellect and Truth proceeded the Word and Life, Logos and Zoe, and they brought forth ten aeons. Furthermore, from the Word and Life proceeded Man and the Church, and they brought forth twelve aeons. And so eight, ten, and twelve makes thirty aeons, which have, as we have said, their first principle from Depth and Silence. Moreover, Christ, who was sent by the Father, that is, from Depth, carried with him a spiritual or heavenly body and assumed nothing from the virgin Mary, but passed through her as if through a channel or pipe without having assumed flesh from her. Valentinus says that from the thirtieth age, the devil was begotten, and that from the devil others were born, who made this world. And thus he attributes evil not to choice, but to the nature of the world, that is, to its diabolical origin. It is in this way, following Augustine's *On Heresies*, that our Lambert Daneau delineates the aeons of Valentinus (in his commentary on Augustine's *On Heresies*).[37] Tertullian insightfully calls these aeons "infamies, not deities."[38] In sum, what we see is two first principles, Bythus and Sige, and thus two gods, as the primary gods from which the aeons, as secondary gods, took their origin. The refutation of all these things depends upon the right exposition of deity, which the reader may revisit in the chapter on the essence of God.[39]

3. What then was the reason for polytheism among the Tritheists and others?
VIII. It is asked, third, what then the reason for polytheism among the Tritheists and others was. In antiquity there used to be, as witnessed by Augustine in *On Heresies*, an anonymous sect which some called the Triformians. They asserted a triform God, in such a way that a certain part was the Father, a certain part the Son, and a certain part the Holy Spirit, that is, that the one God had parts that made up the Trinity, as if God were completed from these three parts, and that God was not perfect in himself, nor was the Father, or the Son, or the Holy Spirit. This sect disturbed the church in the fourth century, around AD 370, having taken its occasion from the Sabellians, who believed in only one divine person, or in three persons who differed in nothing but their names. Against them, the Triformians acknowledged divine persons that were different from

---

37. Lambert Daneau (1535–1590), *D. Aurelii Augustini Hipponensis episcopi liber de haeresibus, ad Quodvultdeum…commentariis illustratus* (Geneva: Eustace Vignon, 1576), 36–42, see chart on 40.
38. *crimina, non numina*: cited from Daneau, *Augustini de haeresibus…commentariis*, 40.
39. 1.2.3

the divine essence, and thus they actually asserted three gods, for whatever has divine essence is God. Likewise in antiquity there was Tritheism, begun by a certain grammarian, Philoponus by surname,[40] in the sixth century around AD 574, under Emperor Phocas.[41] These Tritheists, likewise in order more strongly to oppose the Sabellians, stated that there were three complete divine essences, belonging respectively to each divine person. They categorically professed that there were three gods. Finally, there were in antiquity the Tetratheists, prior to the time of Emperor Anastasius in the fifth century, around AD 485, afterwards known by different names—Theodosians, Damianists, Angelites—who taught that besides the three divine hypostases there existed a certain fourth essence which was common to the three and communicated itself to them, on account of which communication they became gods (concerning these, see Isidore of Seville).[42] Valentine Gentile, who lived last century in Switzerland, was nearly the same as the Tritheists: he numbered three different essences in God, essences that were indeed eternal, yet still subordinated to each other.[43] For this reason, speaking in barbarisms, he called the essence of the Father *essencing* and the essences of the Son and the Holy Spirit *essenced*. The fundamental error of all these men was in this, that they could not distinguish carefully enough between

40. That is, John Philoponus (c. 490–c. 570), also known as John the Grammarian or John of Alexandria. Near the time of the fifth Council of Constantinople (AD 553), he threw in his support for monophysite Christology. He argued in his work *Arbiter* that the term *hypostasis* is best understood in the Aristotelian sense of a primary substance, and *ousia* as a secondary substance or universal nature. Thus, for Philoponus the *ousia* of God was an essence in the abstract or functioned as a conception of divinity whereas in the concrete there were in reality three separate divinities. He was posthumously condemned at the Council of Constantinople (680–681) for tritheism. Among his works more accepted by Christian philosophers, Philoponus wrote, for example, two treaties against the pagan conception of the eternality of the universe, *Against Proclus* and *Against Aristotle*. Methodologically, he argues his case not on theological grounds but on philosophical grounds for creation *ex nihilo*, pointing to inconsistencies in Proclus's Platonist position, using Plato's *Timaeus* and offering a different interpretation of the processes of generation and corruption. In *Against Aristotle*, using the same strategy of demonstrating contradictions and inconsistencies, Philoponus argued against the eternity of the world on Aristotelian principles, citing the impossibility of an infinite regress of causes, the impossibility of an infinite number existing in actuality, and the impossibility of the eternal motion of the universe.

41. The Eastern Roman Emperor throughout the majority of AD 574 would have been Justin II, reigning 565–578, though due to his increasing insanity, the next emperor Tiberius II Constantine began to serve as regent in December of 574. The reign of Emperor Phocas was 602–610.

42. Isidore of Seville (560–636), *Chronica Maiora* in *Monumenta Germaniae Historica* 11, ed. G. H. Pertz (Hanover, 1854); *Corpus Christianorum Series Latina* 112, ed. J. C. Martin (Turnhout: Brepols, 2003).

43. E.g. Benedictus Aretius (d. 1574), *A short history of Valentinus Gentilis tryed, condemned, and put to death by the Protestant reformed city and church of Bern in Switzerland* (London: Robert South, 1696).

essence and person, which distinction we will supply, God willing, in the chapter on the Trinity, where the reader can revisit it.[44]

4. What then is the reason for polytheism among the papists?

IX. It is asked, fourth, what then the reason for polytheism among the papists is. The papists do indeed profess that there is one and only one God, yet meanwhile they have in heaven as well as on earth those to whom they offer divine or religious worship. In heaven, they have the angels, the blessed Virgin, and the departed saints. On earth, they have that which they call the host, they have images to be venerated with the same kind of worship that belongs to their prototypes, they have the relics of the saints. Now if a god is one to whom divine worship belongs and is attributed, then the papists will have many gods: they will have angelic gods, they will have human gods, they will have gods of stone, gold, and silver—they have a god of bread.[45] Let me not say anything about their pope, whom they hold as if he were a vice-God on earth. The fundamental error of all of these is the blind obedience they believe should be offered to the pope, upon which his universal absolute rule, his *monarchia*, is constructed, as well as their perverse exposition of the nature of religious worship. The reader may seek these topics in their own places, namely, the chapter on the absolute rule of the pope,[46] and likewise on the nature of religious worship, according to the first and second commandment of the Decalogue.[47] Moreover, it is vain for them to lean for assistance upon the distinction between *latria*, *dulia*, and *hyper-dulia*, which have no foundation in the Scriptures and in any event do convey religious worship.

5. What then is the reason for polytheism among the Socinians?

X. Finally it is asked, fifth, what then the reason for polytheism among the Socinians is. The Socinians, from their hatred of the Trinity, upon which the whole of our religion and worship rests, although they hold Christ to be a mere creature, nevertheless proclaim him to be true God, and also eternal (at least on the latter part), and in addition though they do not hold the Holy Spirit as God consubstantial[48] with the Father, they nevertheless hold him up in some way as God. Thus they distinguish between a created God and an uncreated God,

---

44. 1.2.24 §§VI, VIII

45. *habent Deum panaceum.* Referring to the bread of the Mass, thought to be transubstantiated into the body of Christ and therefore worshiped. Cf. 1.2.12 §XI.

46. 1.1.2 §§XXXVII–XXXVIII

47. 1.6.8 §XVII; 2.2.1–13

48. ὁμοουσίῳ

between the most high God and a subordinate God, between a God who has the divine essence, whom they believe to be only one, and a God who does not have the divine essence. We will overturn this distinction in its place, if God wills, in the chapters on the Trinity and the person of the Mediator.[49]

The Practical Part

Unity makes for: 1. Tranquility of mind

XI. Now as it regards practice, a godly consideration of the divine unity is extremely effective, first, for tranquility of mind. If at any time our mind is distracted (Luke 10:41) (1) by the variety of our cares, (2) by the clashes of civil wars, (3) by the variety of church quarrels, or (4) by private contentions with our neighbor, our mind wavers, what then could comfort us more effectively than taking note of (1) that fount of evil, namely, the baseness of our sins, by which the blessed unity was broken, first between us and God (Isa. 59:1–2), and then with all creatures, as they are God's servants, and at the same time, (2) the fact that for all these distractions and quarrels that come from our cares, there is no other remedy than to bind our soul to the one God (Ps. 73:25), and (3) to humbly beg him who is the fount of unity and concord, using the formula of the covenant of grace, that he give us in every circumstance one heart (Ezek. 11:19), that Jehovah may be one and his name one alone (Zech. 14:9).

2. The detesting of idolatry: First, the crasser type

XII. Then, second, it is effective for detesting every sort of idolatry, by which indeed the unity of God is invalidated; idolatry, I say, first the crasser type: (1) pagan idolatry, which worshiped as gods the sun and stars, men who excelled others (Hercules, Saturn, Jupiter, and so forth), their leaders, and others from whom they had acquired outstanding benefits (Asclepius, Bacchus, Ceres), all things that were stronger than themselves. By the same logic, they constructed temples for the Fevers, and similarly, for Fortune and others. Indeed they even worshiped virtues (Justice, Patience, etc.) as well as statues of their false gods. And also, (2) Romanist idolatry, which venerates the angels, the saints in heaven, and their relics and images, with religious worship, and hails them as divine, an idolatry from which we have, by divine clemency, been freed.

---

49. 1.2.24 §XVII; 1.5.4 §XIV; cf. 1.2.26 §XVIII

Second, idolatry of the subtler type

Then, second, God's unity makes us detest the subtler type of idolatry, where, by devoting our mind to, by serving, and by building our confidence upon riches, honors, pleasures, and so forth, we make our god our belly (Phil. 3:19), and thus commit idolatry (Col. 3:5). This is that great sin which God proscribes by the first commandment of them all (Ex. 20:3), and which both excels and includes the shame of all lesser sins.

3. The binding of our whole soul to the one God

XIII. Against such sin, third, it commands us to lead our soul back from multitude to unity and (1) to bind it to the one God (Ps. 73:25; 16:5), to rest in him alone, to desire him alone, to seek him alone, and to set all we have, ourselves and all that is ours, upon him alone, persuaded that he alone, because he is God, is sufficient for us in all things (Gen. 17:1), and that nothing at all can happen to us, either to benefit us or to harm us at all, apart from him (Rom. 8:28–30); and then, (2) to fix our faith, hope, and love on him alone, to acknowledge, revere, and worship him according to the tenor of the first commandment, which is like the frontispiece and summary of the whole Decalogue; and to this end, (3) when we intend to do our private holy tasks, to call back our souls from a multitude of thoughts to unity (Ps. 94:19), and our bodies from the noisy crowds to solitude (Matt. 6:6).

4. Zeal for ecclesiastical unity and concord

XIV. Finally, fourth, the unity of God offers to us an argument as well as an example for promoting ecclesiastical unity, both by our prayer and by our effort, as far as in us lies. Christ himself is the source of this practice: "I ask that they may all be one, just as you, Father, are in me and I in you, and they are one in us. The love that you have given to me I have given to them, that they may be one, even as we are one, I in them and you in me, that they may be made perfectly one" (John 17:21–22). On these words, Athanasius commented (*Orations against the Arians*, 4), "Just as the Father and the Son are one in essence, so are we, in a certain resemblance and rough likeness: while we gaze at him, we are made one, both in the one mutual harmony of mind and in the one unity of spirit among us."[50] So also Cyril (bk. 11, *Commentary on John*), "What manner

---

50. Athanasius, *Orationes adversus Arianos* in PG 26:467–526; idem, *NPNF2* 4:433–47. This exact quote was not located, but cf. Johann Gerhard, *Loci theologici* (Hamburg: Zacharias Hertelius, 1657), loc. 2, §103, p. 264. Gerhard utilizes precisely this citation from Athanasius as well as the following one from Cyril in the same order on the question of God's unity or oneness.

of petition is this, 'That they may be one, just as you, Father, are in me, and I in you, that they also may be one in us'? He is seeking the bond of charity, peace, and harmony, that it would lead spiritual believers to so great a union that we imitate the likeness of that natural and consubstantial union in the Father, Son and Holy Spirit."[51]

Motives

The apostle urges the same unity, and does so from the same principle, in Ephesians 4:4–6, where, to urge ecclesiastical unity, he heaps up various types of unity as so many motivating arguments, namely, that (1) we are all one mystical body and each of us are its individual parts—and to such parts, what is more suitable than harmony? And that there is (2) one Spirit, by whose power we have all been baptized into one body (1 Cor. 12:12–13). (3) One hope of our calling, the glory and communion of heaven (Eph. 4:4; Heb. 12:22–23). (4) One Lord, Jesus. (5) One faith in him. (6) One baptism. And finally (7) one God, the Father of all. Induced by reasons of this sort, the primitive church, it is written, was united in one accord (Acts 2:1, 44–46).

Supports

And so that we may pursue this blessed oneness more happily, it will help (1) to be often and greatly intent on the unity of God and the consubstantiality[52] of his persons, together with their unanimity,[53] which the Savior uses as an argument in prayer to his Father and at the same time gives to us to contemplate (John 17:21–22). (2) To beware, more than a dog or serpent, all schisms in the church, as well as schismatic contentions and arguments (1 Tim. 6:3; 2 Tim. 2:14; 1 Tim. 6:4–5; 20–21). (3) With the Savior, to procure this unity from God by our most fervent prayers, that he would so imprint in us a sense of his unity, that we might press toward a similar unity with all our strength. Finally, (4) to be intent on the benefits, so many and so great, which unity and harmony of spirit bring to the church and to each of her members in particular, benefits that are not only internal, but also external.

---

51. Cyril, *In D. Joannis Evangelium*, ed. P. E. Pusey, 3 vols. (Oxford: Clarendon Press, 1868–72), 2:731; idem, *Commentary on John*, trans. David R. Maxwell, ed. Thomas. C. Oden, 2 vols. (Downer's Grove, Ill.: IVP Academic, 2013–15), 2:302.

52. ὁμοουσίαν

53. ὁμονοίαν

CHAPTER NINE

The Infinity and Greatness of God

Great is Jehovah, and most greatly to be praised,
and his greatness is unsearchable.
—Psalm 145:3

The second attribute of quantity is the infinity of God.
I. Unity represented God to us under the idea of discrete quantity. Under the idea of a continuous quantity, *infinity*, called by another name, *greatness*, will convey the same God to us. That infinity is considered either absolutely, in the divine essence, or with a relation, partly to where he is, that is, to his presence, and thus called by the specific names *immensity*, *omnipresence*, and *ubiquity*, and partly to when he is, that is, his duration, and thus called *eternity*. Psalm 145:3 presents in paraphrase the infinity of his essence.

The Exegetical Part

This is constructed upon the explanation of the text.
II. The text contains an inscription of praise, or a certain celebration of God, and its argument is his infinite greatness. Two members of this celebration occur:

A. The object celebrated: יהוה, Jehovah, frequently with the description, אלהינו, "our God" (2 Chron. 2:4–6; Ps. 135:5). Thus the text indicates that not only the divine essence, but also all of its persons, are, in accord with that essence, infinite. Moreover, one should specifically observe in this passage that it is not the divine power or wisdom that are celebrated as infinite in their greatness (which, because of their identity with the essence of God, is not uncommon elsewhere in the Scriptures), but rather, Jehovah himself, named by his essence, that we may understand that God with respect to his essence is infinite.

B. The argument of this celebration, which provides a threefold description of God:

1. "Great," גדול. It refers either to quantity or to quality. If it refers to quantity, then either it refers to number, and thus Jehovah is one only, but in such a way that he eminently envelops all things, indeed, that he exceeds all things, because he is infinite. Or it refers to his greatness, strictly defined, and so it does in this passage, yet in such a way that he is conceived to be great beyond quantity, just as he is conceived to be just, good, and wise, for example, beyond quality.

2. "Greatly to be praised," מהלל מאד. Greatness in relation to quality denotes dignity, pre-eminence, excellence, of a thing or a person, and by it a thing is said to be praiseworthy, which means that it has a great amount of eminent good. Because Jehovah is great in every eminent good, he is thus called greatly or most greatly to be praised (מהלל מאד), in the superlative degree, above all creatures, that is, by his greatness which exceeds all things, or which is infinite, which is also more clearly stated when there is added:

3. "And his greatness is unsearchable," אין חקר. In other words, there is no end to it. For whatever is finite is also fully searchable, and in turn, whatever simply cannot be searched is also infinite (cf. in parallel Job 5:9; 9:10; Rom. 11:7–9, 33). And this is also intended with great emphasis when he is called, in comparative terms, great above the gods, and above all gods (2 Chron. 2:5; Ps. 135:5), not only to those who are named gods, magistrates, and kings, but also to those who are improperly named gods, that is, the false gods who in the opinion of their proponents are most great. Of these there were counted in the time of Hesiod more than thirty thousand, and to each was assigned his own greatness and particular perfection. Therefore, there should be no doubt that the one who is greater than all these gods ought to be celebrated as infinite.

The Dogmatic Part

That God alone is infinite: It is proved by testimonies.

III. It is without doubt then that God, by his essence, is infinite, and indeed God alone, in such a way that it would not even be possible for anyone besides him to be infinite. For although the holy Book does not have this concept expressly (perhaps because there is not one word in Hebrew that is sufficient to express infinity, and the New Testament follows the style of the Old), nevertheless it does have the concept in its intended force, that is, whenever (1) it simply calls him great (1 Chron. 16:25), that is to say, preeminently great, and "the Great One" (הגדול, Neh. 4:14),[1] and does so by describing him as so great that we do not know him, that is, so great that by thinking we cannot reach him: "Behold, God is great, and we know him not; great is the number of his years, and there is no searching them" (Job 36:26). (2) It denies that he has boundaries (Job 36:26; Ps. 145:3ff.). (3) It shows him to excel all of the greatest things in greatness: heaven and the abyss (Job 11:7–9), all nations, such that they are like nothing before him, indeed less than nothing (Isa. 40:12, 15, 17; Dan. 4:32), likewise, all the gods of the nations, as we have said, to which we will add Exodus 18:11 and Psalm 77:13. Also applicable here are all those passages by which he will be proven in particular to be immense, omnipresent, and everywhere, in the following chapter. For all these same reasons, Ambrose (*Commentary on Ephesians*, 3:18) says, "Just as in a sphere there is as much length as breath, and as much height as depth, so also in God are all things equal in the immensity of his infinity. Moreover, God does not only fill all things but also exceeds them, for he is not hemmed in, but he holds all things within himself, and thus he alone may be held to be ineffable and infinite."[2]

And also by reasons

IV. For he is (1) the absolutely first being, who for this reason does not admit a prior being which would bound and limit him. He is, accordingly, (2) independent, bounding and limiting all things, and thus, he is limited by no one. (3) He is simply the most perfect being, while when it comes to a finite being, we can think of something more perfect, since we recognize that a finite being by definition lacks some sort of perfection. (4) He is Jehovah, "being," that is, all being that there is, or that can be conceived, being that is by necessity infinite. Also (5) he created the world from nothing, which demands an infinite power that removes the infinite distance between nothing and something, and by that very fact, an infinite essence. Finally, (6) everything we can observe in the creatures that argues for limit and lack in them entirely disqualifies them from being God: for example, a lack in essence, in knowledge, in presence, in duration, in power, on account of which they are called finite. But right reason would not deduce that such a lack applies to God. Furthermore, reasons from

---

1. Hebrew, Neh. 4:8. Cited as Ezra 5:8, which speaks of "the great God," but does not use הגדול.

2. Ambrose, *Commentaria in epistola ad Ephesios* in *PL* 17:384.

the immensity, omnipresence, and ubiquity of God will be supplied by the following chapter.

What and how manifold is the infinity of God?

V. Moreover, we do not understand *infinite* here to describe that which is not yet finished or absolute, that which is still to be finished, in which sense a work that is not yet complete could be called infinite, though in itself finite and incomplete;[3] nor that which is so large and so great that we cannot grasp what its limits are, that which, in a wholesome sense, could be called indefinite, in which sense the world could be called indefinite; nor that which is ever so perfect that it could not be further perfected, which the philosophers call a syncategorematic infinite, in which sense all created things are infinite;[4] but rather, we call infinite that which has every perfection that anyone can conceive, or that can possibly exist. Indeed, this infinity of God regards, on the one hand, his attributes: his presence (Jer. 23:24), duration (Ps. 90:1–2), power (Ps. 115:3), wisdom (Rom. 11:33), righteousness (Job 37:23), goodness, grace, and mercy (Ps. 103:11–12), all which we will treat in their own places. Or it regards, on the other hand, his essence, since it cannot be bounded or limited, either extrinsically by a body that encompasses him, as with material things, or intrinsically by his own boundaries, as with created spirits. Therefore God is infinite, not (1) because he has yet to be finished, in which sense things that are nearly perfect are infinite, as long as they are not yet perfect. Nor (2) because he is infinite in potentiality, or as they say, syncategorematically, in the same way that a continuous quantity is considered infinitely divisible and a discrete quantity is considered infinitely multiplicable. Rather, he is called infinite positively, in actuality, and categorematically, in such a way that he possesses in actuality whatever he can possess, and in that which he possesses, there are no limits. Thus it is also true that he alone is infinite, and that there can be nothing infinite besides him, as argued in §§III–IV. This infinity can be thought about either in its general perfection or as it exists in each of his

---

3. In Latin, *infinitus* is the opposite of *finitus*, which can mean either "finite" or "finished."

4. Cf. "Categorematice-Syncategorematice" in Nunzio Signoriello, *Lexicon peripateticum philosophico-theologicum*, (Naples: Officina Bibliothecae Scriptorum, 1872), 56, "A thing is affirmed categorematically to be something when it is actually (*actu*) and absolutely such; for example, God is said to be categorematically infinite. A thing is affirmed syncategorematically to be something when it is such potentially (*in potentia*); for example, a mathematical quantity, since it can be understood as something without an end, is said to be syncategorematically infinite. Therefore, the description "syncategorematic infinite" or "potentially infinite" is given to that which is actually finite, but still is never divided into so many parts that others could not be added to it." See also G. Klima, "Syncategoremata" in *Concise Encyclopedia of Philosophy and Linguistics*, ed. A. Barber and R. J. Stainton (Elsevier, 2010), 714–17.

attributes: presence, duration, and so forth. In this place we are representing it in the former way; we will represent it in the latter way in the chapters to follow.

The Elenctic Part

It is asked: 1. Is God infinite in every way? The difference of opinions
VI. It is asked, first, whether God is infinite in every way. Some time ago, the Anthropomorphites or Audians, because they taught a composite God who was endowed with human and corporeal parts—hands, feet, heart, eyes, etc.—which, after his own image, God exhibited in man, they could not but deny that he was infinite in respect to his essence. Vorstius, aiming by devices to tear down the personal union of the two natures in Christ (which he did not dare contradict openly), likewise denied the infinity of the divine essence, for otherwise, of course, it might have been present with the human nature of Christ in the time when he lived only on earth.[5] The Socinians, so that they might not be compelled to admit that one and the same divine essence is common to the three persons, which we customarily prove from the infinity of the divine essence, and also, that they might underhandedly cancel the infinite value of the death and obedience of Christ in its application to the myriads of those who would be redeemed, and thus also cancel the satisfaction and merits of Christ, deny the omnimodal infinity of God. The Reformed on the contrary assert the omnimodal infinity of God by the testimonies of Scripture and the arguments which we produced in §§III–IV.

Objections
They do not have anything that they may oppose to this except: (1) that his infinity is not taught by Scripture. I respond, Perhaps it is not taught expressly, yet against this claim cries out the fact that in our text and elsewhere there is ascribed to him a greatness for which אֵין חֵקֶר, there is no end, no searching out. Indeed, God's infinity is taught by implication in many ways, as proven in §III. (2) That God is that certain something distinct from all other things, and is thus something finite. I respond, Yes, formally, he is that certain something, but such that he is, eminently, all things. And yet he is distinguished from all other things by his infinity itself. (3) That by the infinity of God, all creatures would be equally perfect, since they would be equally distant from the infinite God, that is, infinitely distant. I respond, It is wrongly presupposed that the measure of perfection consists in the distance, whether greater or smaller, from

---

5. Vorstius, *Tractatus theologicus de Deo*, 21.

the most perfect, when in fact it consists in the degrees of perfection, whether more or fewer, that are conferred by the most perfect. (4) That God has been seen by creatures and will be seen hereafter, and that he is thus finite. I respond, He is not visible with the eyes, but with the mind, not in his essence, but in his attributes, nor will he be comprehended by our vision, but only apprehended. (5) That he can be defined. I respond, We have in fact already denied this with many reasons in chapter 3.[6]

2. Is the world infinite, or could it be?
VII. It is asked, second, whether the world is infinite, or whether it could be. The Scholastics, so that they could more conveniently imagine for themselves and declare to others the infinity of the divine essence, stated that beyond the world there were imaginary spaces, infinite in their own way, in which God dwelt by the infinity of his essence, though they were not in fact beings. The Cartesians, because they consider these spaces true bodies, actually endowed with extension in three dimensions, state that because of these spaces, the world can be infinite, although we cannot solidly determine that it is infinite, and thus they state that it is indefinite. And so that they may anticipate the objection that infinity is an incommunicable attribute of God, they distinguish between the infinity of perfection, which they leave to God alone, and the infinity of quantity and of mass, stating that this latter could belong to the world, and that perhaps it actually does. The Reformed, although they do not disapprove of the imaginary spaces of the Scholastics (except insofar as they keep them imaginary, since they are truly spaces), nevertheless deny all positive, actual, and categorematic infinity to the world and assert it for God alone.[7]

Arguments
And they do so (1) by the Scriptures and reasons which we mentioned in §§III–IV. Next, (2) because for the world to be infinite implies more than one contradiction. For, to have parts and to be infinite is a most manifest inconsistency, for these parts will be either infinite in their greatness or not infinite, that is, finite: a mean is not allowed between contradictories. Now if you should say

---

6. 1.2.3 §IX

7. On post-Reformation Reformed approaches to God's attributes and controversies with the Cartesians on divine omnipresence and God's infinity, see Muller, *PRRD*, 2:338–45; Aza Goudriaan, *Philosophische Gotteserkenntnis bei Suárez und Descartes: Im zussamenhang mit der niederländischen Reformierte Theologie und Philosophie des 17. Jahrhunderts* (Leiden: Brill, 1999), 101–8; R. T. te Velde, *The Doctrine of God in Reformed Orthodoxy, Karl Barth, and the Utrecht School* (Leiden: Brill, 2013), 157–58.

these parts are infinite, you will say that from many infinite things one infinite thing comes together; if you should choose that they are finite, then you will say that from many finite things one infinite thing is put together. Which one of these is the more absurd, let them decide. (3) Because for a body to be a whole, such as the world without doubt is, and for it not to have parts, is a contradiction. But an infinite world would involve such a contradiction, because this world could have neither finite nor infinite parts and thus, it could not have any parts. In addition, (4) it implies that the world is created but that it cannot even in the least bit be increased by its own Creator; and this would hold true of the world if it were infinite. I will not press hard (5) that the psalmist declares that he sees a limit in every perfection (Ps. 119:96), that (6) heaven and earth, from which the world is knit together (Gen. 1:1; Ex. 20:11), are finite: indeed heaven is (Isa. 40:12; 48:13; Deut. 4:32) and so is earth (Job 38:5, 13). I will not add anything but (7) this one thing, that all consider it beyond doubt that it involves a contradiction for a finite subject to have an infinite property.

Objections

At the same time, they have no lack of arguments to oppose us, (1) indeed, from the Scriptures, that in Jeremiah 31:37, God himself declares that the heavens above cannot be measured. I respond: (a) Even so, in the meantime the Cartesians are still not sure whether there are other bodies beyond the heavens of heavens (see Wittich, *Peaceable Theology*, §86).[8] (b) By this rationale, the heavens will be immense, for whatever cannot be measured is immense. However, I think that the Cartesians will not say this. (c) They cannot be measured because of human inability, in the same way that the text says that the foundations of the earth cannot be searched out. (2) That all of us have such an idea of the world in our minds that we cannot conceive any boundaries for it. I respond, (a) An idea in a person is not an infallible rule of truth. (b) The prophets, apostles, fathers, and philosophers all the way up to Descartes did not have such an idea. In fact (c) it is evident from their concept of imaginary spaces that they had an idea of a finite world. (3) That those spaces which are beyond the highest heaven, in which God by his infinity dwells, are not imaginary but are true bodies. I respond, We deny this, because in that way a body would be in a body, since a body exists in space, and thus a penetration of dimensions would have to be admitted, which, by the consent of all, overturns the nature of a body. If (4) they should try to prove their case by explaining that these spaces are extended and have their own three dimensions, we will deny this also, because such extension

---

8. Wittich, *Theologia pacifica*, §86.

and threefold dimension is not properly said to be in the containing space but rather in the thing it contains, since a thing located in space is so long, so wide, so deep, or it could be if it were located in it. If the reader is eager for more arguments of this kind, he can consult our *Gangrene of the Cartesian Innovations* (sect. 2, ch. 20).[9]

3. *Does the infinity of God consist only in the idea that he thinks all things by one act?* The opinion of the Cartesians and of the Reformed, with their reasons

VIII. It is asked, third, whether the infinity of God consist in this, that God by a single and most simple act, thinks all things. The Cartesians, since they state that the whole essence of every spirit—angelic, human, and divine—consists in mere thought, and since they cannot distinguish spirits that differ from God from the Spirit that is God, except that God's Spirit is infinite, and since they do not find anything else in which the infinity of God consists than in this, that he thinks all things by a single and most simple act, therefore, in this idea alone they place the divine infinity. The Reformed grant that there is thought in God, and that it proceeds by a single and most simple act, because all things in God are a single and most simple act, that is, in the identical sense (as they say). Yet in the formal sense, the Reformed make the thought of God distinct and refer his infinity to his greatness, because: (1) the text does so, and all the passages of Scripture that speak of the infinity of God do the same. (2) There is no one, whether theologian or philosopher, until Descartes, who placed God's infinity in this idea that he thinks all things by a single act. (3) The Cartesians themselves attribute to created spirits no more than one thought, just as men have no more than one mind, which thinks of its objects in diverse ways according to their diversity, though it does not, of course, think of all objects. (4) Thought, in itself and in its own nature, has no relation to greatness, or to infinity. Our adversaries, in defense of this opinion of theirs, do not press any arguments except their own hypotheses, that a spirit is nothing but mere thought, and that in thought nothing is found by which the thought of God can be called infinite, other than the idea that he thinks all things by a single act. But we have routed these hypotheses already by proving that the essence of God does not by any means consist in thought alone, and that the infinity of God consists in his greatness, that is, his omnimodal perfection.[10]

---

9. Mastricht, *Gangraena*, 360–83.
10. 1.2.3 §VII; this chapter, §V

*4. Is the infinity of God so particular to God that it cannot be
communicated to any creature?*

IX. It is asked, fourth, whether infinity is so particular to God that it cannot be communicated to any creature. The Lutherans, so that they may have the flesh and blood of Christ essentially present in the holy Supper, state that through the personal union the subsistence of the Son of God has been communicated to the human nature of Christ, and that by the same action, so have the divine nature and its properties, and thus its infinity as well. The Reformed on the contrary state that God's infinity, according to the nature of any of God's properties, is entirely incommunicable.

The reasons of the Reformed

And they do so because (1) if infinity had been communicated, it would not be a property of God, which the Lutherans themselves acknowledge. (2) By this rationale, the human nature of Christ, though finite, would have also become infinite, which involves a blatant contradiction. (3) If infinity had been communicated to the human nature, it would have become the divine nature, since the divine nature and essence consists in infinity, which they themselves acknowledge. (4) If infinity had been communicated to the human nature, all its parts, all its members would have become infinite. (5) Christ's parts, his body and soul, could not have been torn apart, and accordingly, he could not have died, nor resurrected, nor ascended, nor could he return from there to judge, inasmuch as all these things presuppose the finitude of the human nature. I pass by the fact that (6) Scripture nowhere teaches that the infinity of the divine nature has been communicated to the human nature.

The hypotheses of the Lutherans

The Lutherans have nothing in their favor but their own hypotheses, which we have consigned to the chapter on the person of the Mediator that, by God's help, we might vanquish them there.[11]

The Practical Part

The infinity of God shapes us: 1. To be modest

X. This infinity of God, first, shapes us to be modest in our thought about the divine mysteries. Whenever in the articles of faith, such as the Trinity, the hypostatic union of the two natures in Christ, and others, whenever likewise in our

---

11. 1.5.4, esp. §§XXII–XXV

reading and meditation upon the Scriptures we run across things hard to understand, to which our little capacity is not equal, then what will more effectively
captivate our reasoning than for us humbly to call to mind that Jehovah is great,
and greatly to be marveled at, and that his greatness is unsearchable? Or why
not instead Zophar's remark in Job 11:7–9, "Would you find out the depth of
God? And would you reach to the perfection of the Almighty? It is higher than
the highest heavens—what would you do?" Or why not Paul's exclamation, "Oh,
the depth of the riches of the wisdom and knowledge of God! How inscrutable
are his judgments! And how unsearchable are his ways!" (Rom. 11:33). More
application like this can be found in the practical part of chapter 3 of this book.[12]

2. To glorify God

XI. Then, second, the infinite greatness of God supplies an argument for us
to make him great with infinite praises (Luke 1:46). For he is (1) great, and
therefore, greatly to be praised. Indeed, he is (2) most great, infinitely great: "and
his greatness is unsearchable." And also (3) he is the only one who is such (Isa.
40:12; 15, 17). Indeed, (4) great in so many ways; great, in fact, in all ways: in his
essence, his presence, his duration, his wisdom, his strength and power, his grace
and mercy (Ps. 147:5). And in this greatness he is (5) above the gods, whether
earthly, such as kings and magistrates, or heavenly (at least in the opinion of the
pagans), the false gods; and above all gods (2 Chron. 2:5; Ps. 135:5). For if, then,
we celebrate the sun for its great greatness, and the heavens for their greater
greatness, why would we not celebrate God for his greatest greatness, for his infinite greatness? Let us therefore make him great (1) in our heart (Ps. 103:1; Luke
1:46), by always thinking of him great things, indeed the greatest things, for he is
the one who is infinitely greater than all our thoughts (Eph. 3:20); by esteeming
as great, indeed, as most great, both him and all that is his—his presence, favor,
promises, worship—in such a way that we approach him and all these things
of his with an infinite (that is, an insatiable) appetite and desire (Ps. 84:1–2).
(2) In our mouth, that with a great voice, in the presence of others, we celebrate
him who is infinitely great (Ps. 103:8), indeed that we call others to celebrate him
with us (Ps. 103:20–22). Finally, (3) in our work, that we do it (a) with profound
reverence for the infinite deity, and with fear of offending him, even in the least
things, because he is the most great King (Mal. 1:14; Deut. 10:17; Neh. 1:5; Dan.
9:4). (b) By a careful zeal for obeying and pleasing him (2 Cor. 5:9). (3) By an
infinite desire or concern for possessing and enjoying him (Ps. 73:25).

---

12. 1.2.3 §XXVI

3. It wards off all despising of him.

XII. Furthermore, third, the thought of the infinity of the divine greatness drives away from us every sort of despising of him, by which we disparage: (1) God himself, putting him beneath us in our speaking or thinking, joining Pharaoh in asking, "Who is Jehovah…?" (Ex. 5:2). Or (2) his statutes and worship: "…that I should obey him?" (Ex. 5:2), "Depart from us!…Who is the Almighty, that we should serve him?" (Job 21:14–15). Or (3) his patience, longsuffering, and kindness (Rom. 2:4). Or (4) his ambassadors (Luke 10:16). Moreover, we despise him whenever (1) we do not think about him in a sufficiently great way, saying, "Who is Jehovah?" (Ex. 5:2; Ps. 10:4; 14:1); (2) we do not conduct his business with sufficient diligence and care (Jer. 48:10; Col. 3:22–23); (3) we place something we possess ahead of God (Phil. 2:21), such as riches, honors, and desires (2 Tim. 3:4).

4. It stirs us up to humility.

XIII. In addition, fourth, the devout comparison of infinite greatness with human nothingness batters down man's pride and shapes us to humility, as in the example of Abraham (Gen. 18:27) and of the angels (Isa. 6:2). For God is infinite in essence, wisdom, power, and even if we look great and splendid, what are we but locusts, a shadowy dream, alive for but a day, worms (Ps. 22:6), fine dust on the scales, little drops from a bucket (Isa. 40:6, 15), indeed, nothing (Ps. 39:5, 6, 12), and even less than nothing (Isa. 40:17)? For there is no proportion at all between the infinite and the finite. All these things surely compel us to cry out, "What is man," that momentary vessel of clay, "that you should think of him?" (Ps. 8:4).

5. It shapes our souls to be great.

XIV. Finally, fifth, the example of the infinite divine greatness should produce a greatness in our soul, by which: (1) in our service to God, we take up great labors, great difficulties, great dangers, all with a great spirit, persuaded that God will be our exceedingly great reward (Gen. 15:1). (2) In our thoughts, our loves, our desires, we become great, and, in our own way, infinite, that is to say, insatiable, unable to be satisfied except by an infinite object (Ps. 16:5; 73:25), as those to whom the infinite God conferred an infinite appetite, for this very reason, so that nothing would satisfy us except for that infinite God himself. (3) Our souls become great in their contempt for worldly things, for they are vain and worthless (Heb. 10:34). And on the other hand, (4) in our meditation and pursuit of divine, spiritual, heavenly matters, those matters that are truly great, we act with a great spirit (Heb. 11:24–26; Matt. 6:33; 2 Cor. 4:17–18). God encourages this greatness of soul in Abraham (Gen. 15:1; 17:1); Paul, in the Colossians (Col. 3:1); the Savior, in his hearers (Matt. 6:33–34); David, in himself (Ps. 27:1–2).

By what motives should this be urged?

And all of us should realize that our condition is great: we bear the image of the great King, we are subjects of the great King, we were made, redeemed, and destined for great things, so great, indeed, that we are set above all great things, and beneath only the greatest thing, that is, our infinitely great God. All these things, so many and so weighty, should they not make our spirits great (Phil. 3:8; James 1:9)?

By what helps should it be acquired?

And so that they might do so more effectively: (1) let us be intent on our most great God, who is ours by covenant, that we may not only imitate him (as far as that is possible and proper), but also rest in him, and rest so fully that we hold all things besides him to be vain and trifling (Ps. 73:25). (2) Let us put before us, in all great dangers, our great God as our great shield. Trusting in him, Moses before the great king of the Egyptians (Heb. 11:27), Daniel and his friends before the absolute ruler of the Chaldeans (Dan. 3:17–18), and the unarmed apostles before the great Sanhedrin (Acts 4:19), heard all their great threats, and with a great soul, paid them no heed.

CHAPTER TEN

The Immensity and Omnipresence of God

Where shall I go from your Spirit? And where shall I flee from your face?
If I ascend to the heavens, you are there. If I make my bed in hell, behold,
you are there. If I take the wings of the dawn, and dwell in the farthest sea,
behold, there your hand will lead me, and your right hand will hold me.
—Psalm 139:7–11

God's immensity and omnipresence
I. We have considered the infinity of God absolutely, as it is in itself. Now it follows for it to be considered as it is relative to space or location. Either that space is without a body, and thus is a vacuum, in which case we call infinity *immensity*, or that space is filled with a body, and thus is a place, in which case we call infinity *omnipresence*.[1]

The Exegetical Part
It is constructed upon the exegesis of the text.
II. The words of the above text picturesquely represent the immensity and omnipresence of God. By these words the psalmist, in offering an argument for the providence of God, sketches as it were the parts and terms of the immensity of God, in the following order:

    A. He propounds it more generally, in verse 7, with a double inquiry:

        1. "Where would I go from your Spirit," that is, so that I may avoid you and your presence? The answer: nowhere. By "your Spirit" some understand a certain person different from the Father, namely, the

---

1. Mastricht throughout this chapter uses three terms: *locus*, "place," *ubi*, "location," and *spatium*, "space." Place is where a body is located, location is where that place is without regard to what is in it, and space has the property of location, but it may or may not contain a body. See below, esp. §§VI, XII.

Holy Spirit, just as by "your face" in the following question, they understand the Son, as in Exodus 33:14–15 and Isaiah 63:9. In this way, immensity might be signified not only of God, but also of each person of God. But I do not know whether this is well enough established. Therefore, it is safer to say "Spirit" means God theologically considered, as in John 4:24.

2. "Where would I flee from your face?" The response: nowhere. Regarding both questions in this passage, here we only need to observe that they are asked, not only about God's knowledge, or only about his power and operation, but also about his very essence, which is stated emphatically, since the questions concern his Spirit and his face (by which the essence of God is often indicated, Ex. 33:20, 23, cf. v. 18).

B. The psalmist declares and proves it by a merism, that is, by a distribution of the omnipresence of God's immensity into his presence at the world's boundaries, according to the three types of distance. For the boundaries of this world are either the outermost, the heavens; or the innermost, hell; or the intermediary, the earth and the farthest parts of the seas. It is as if he intended to reason this way: if someone is present in the outermost boundary, the innermost boundary, and in the middle boundary of this universe, then he is undoubtedly immense and omnipresent, such that you would try in vain to flee from his Spirit and face; but God is present in all those places; therefore, he is immense and omnipresent. With the proof of the major premise presupposed, he confirms the minor premise by induction, with three inquiries:

1. The first teaches his presence in the outermost boundary, in the heavens, and it includes:

   a. A question: "Shall I ascend to heaven?" That is, to the outermost, empyrean, third heaven, to paradise.[2] The statement is plainly hyperbolic, the sort which also occurs in Obadiah 4, Proverbs 17:22, Deuteronomy 30:12, and Job 23:8–9.

   b. An answer: "You are there." That is, by your essence, by your knowledge, and by your power.

2. The second teaches his presence in the innermost boundary, in hell, again by:

---

2. Cf. 1.3.6 §XXVI. On early modern cosmology and the empyrean heaven, see E. M. W. Tillyard, *The Elizabethan World Picture*, 38; cf. 2 Cor. 12:2; John Milton, *Paradise Lost*, bk. 3, v. 57.

a. A question: "Shall I make my bed in hell?" שאול, *sheol*, here could speak of hell, the place of the damned, as in Job 11:8 and 26:6, inasmuch as it is set apart from heaven by the greatest distance. But in that hell, we do not make for ourselves a bed. It could be read more suitably here as the grave, as in Genesis 42:38, Acts 2:27, and Psalm 16:10, because graves are like beds for the dead. But here it is opposed to heaven as the deepest place, at the greatest distance from it. What, then, are we to think? You could understand it as the deepest lairs of the earth or the center of the earth. And to place a bed somewhere does not mean anything but to hide oneself or to dwell somewhere.

b. A response: "Behold, you are there," that is, you are certainly present.

3. The third gives us God's presence in the middle boundary, in the earth, and in the furthermost part of the seas, once more by:

a. A question: "Shall I take the wings of the dawn and dwell in the farthest parts of the seas?" Here "the wings of the dawn" denote the rays of the rising sun, projected as if by an instantaneous flight to the furthermost parts of our horizon. Moreover, wings are attributed to the dawn, just as elsewhere they are attributed to the wind (Ps. 18:10; 104:3), to wealth (Prov. 23:5), and to the sun (Mal. 4:2). In addition, "the furthermost parts of the seas" denotes the parts of this earthly circle most distant from Judea (Ps. 65:5; 72:8; Isa. 24:14–16). Thus the sense is, If I fly away like the rays of the sun do, in a single moment of time, to the remotest limits of the earth.

b. A response: "Even there your hand will guide me and your right hand will take hold of me." This means, Not only will you be there by your essence, not only will you find me or know me, but also, you will sustain and govern me by your providence.

The Dogmatic Part

God is immense and omnipresent.

III. From this text, therefore, nothing is more clearly evident than that God is immense and omnipresent by his essence, as well as by his knowledge, and also by his operation, coexisting with every space and with every creature in space. For he is said to coexist, by his Spirit and face, with all the boundaries of the world, and in every place to see David, to know him, and also to lead him and to sustain him.

It is proved by testimonies: of Scripture, of the Fathers

IV. And this is taught on the sacred page not once or twice, but often and in many ways (Eph. 4:6; Jer. 23:24; 1 Kings 8:27; 1 Cor. 12:6). It is likewise taught by the Fathers. For in this way Hilary spoke in *On the Trinity* (bk. 1, ch. 6): "In God there is no absence, nor any nowhere. He is in the heavens, he is in hell, he is beyond the seas, he is within as the God inside, and he is without as the God outside. Therefore when he thus holds and is held, neither is he in anything, nor is he not in everything."[3] And a little afterwards, "God himself in his entirety contains all things inside and outside of himself, such that neither is the infinite one absent from all things, nor are all things not present in him who is infinite."[4] Likewise Augustine in *City of God* (bk. 7, ch. 30) says, "The same God is everywhere in his entirety, hemmed in by no places, bound by no bonds, divided into no parts, mutable in no part, filling heaven and earth, and where his power is present, his nature is not absent."[5] And, according to Hermes Trismegistus, God is a sphere whose center is everywhere, whose surface is nowhere.[6]

It is confirmed by reasons.

V. And right reason does not differ from this. For he who is, with respect to his essence: (1) infinite, cannot be restricted to any finite place; (2) independent, cannot be bound to one place by anyone; (3) a most simple act, thus cannot be in the potency of arriving at any place in which he is not present; (4) immutable, cannot be transferred from one place to another; (5) omnipotent, thus can work everywhere, and thus exists everywhere; (6) most perfect, for this reason cannot be robbed of the perfection of his immensity and omnipresence. Persuaded by these reasons, even the pagans believed "all things" to be "full of Jove."[7]

---

3. Hilary of Poitiers, *De Trinitate* in *PL* 10:83; idem, *On the Trinity* in NPNF2 9:41.

4. Hilary of Poitiers, *De Trinitate* in *PL* 10:83; idem, *On the Trinity* in NPNF2 9:42.

5. Augustine, *De Civitate Dei* in *PL* 41:220; idem, *City of God* in NPNF1 2:140.

6. This is a common dictum in the medieval period, continuing through the early modern period, attributed to Hermes Trismegistus as well as others. Cf. dictum 2, *Deus est sphaera cuius centrum est ubique, circumferentia nusquam*, in the critical Latin text and a French translation of *Liber XXIV philosophorum*, see *Le livre des XXIV Philosophes* (Grenoble: Millon, 1989). Hermes Trismegistus was mentioned or engaged by some patristic era church fathers (e.g. Lactantius, *The Divine Institutes*, bk. 1, ch. 6; bk. 2., chs. 15–16, bk. 4, chs. 6, 9; and Augustine, *City of God*, bk. 7, chs. 23–26; bk. 17, ch. 39).

7. *Jovis esse omnia plena*. Virgil, *Eclogues*, 3.60.

Its nature is explained.

VI. God's immensity, incomprehensibility, ubiquity, and omnipresence all represent the same thing in a different way. For infinity, insofar as it cannot be delimited in any one place, is called immensity and incomprehensibility; insofar as it coexists with every location, ubiquity; insofar as it coexists with every creature, omnipresence. Thus, this concept could not be defined more fittingly than as the infinity of the divine essence insofar as it coexists with every space. Next, by a space we understand nothing other than where a creature exists or can exist. Accordingly, a space is of two kinds, either a vacuum where a creature can exist, or a place where a creature actually exists. And so a space, properly speaking, is not some sort of being, much less a body, for thus a body would be in a body while that body is in a place. Nor is it the same thing as the body that is contained in that place, for we understand that when the body that was contained has been taken away and moved elsewhere, the place that had contained it still remains. Nor also are a body's dimensions of length, breadth, and depth properly said to be in a space, but rather in the body that exists, or could exist, in a space.

And its modes

VII. God is not coextensive with a space of this sort, whether that space is empty or full, nor is he diffused throughout it, as several thinkers, both ancient and modern, conceive and speak, because all these properties belong only to bodies. Rather, God only coexists with space. And he coexists with all spaces not (1) by a multiplication of himself (as the papists pretend concerning the body of Christ in the Mass), for he is one. Nor (2) by division, as if by parts, partly in heaven and partly on earth, for God is a most simple being. Nor (3) circumscribed by space or encircled by place, for he is a spirit. Nor (4) delimited and restricted to a certain place by the finitude of his essence, like a created spirit, for he is infinite. Nor (5) as one who is in a space as an accident is in its subject, for he is most pure substance. Rather, he coexists by filling (Jer. 23:24), that is, by filling the whole world with his whole self, and every one of its parts with his whole self, not hemmed in by any space, not excluded from any space, indeed even the space beyond the world, because the essence of God is infinite, whereas the world is finite.

And in addition, the different species of the divine presence

VIII. But as this immensity and omnipresence of God, first and foremost, concerns the essence of God, it thus also, through his essence, considers his knowledge, since all things are bare and intimately open to his eyes (Heb. 4:13; Ps. 139:12–13; Jer. 23:24), and also his operation and providence (Heb. 1:3; John

5:17; 1 Cor. 12:6). And in this respect, when it comes to his operation, we speak of the different modes in which he is present to creatures. Specifically, he is present: (1) to the human nature of Christ, by the hypostatic union (Col. 2:9; John 1:14; 1 Tim. 3:16; Rom. 1:3–4; 9:5); (2) to believers, through the Spirit of faith, sanctification, adoption, consolation, and strengthening (John 14:16, 17, 23; 2 Cor. 13:14; Rom. 8:14–17, 26; Gal. 4:6; Ps. 145:18); (3) to the prophets, through wisdom and revelation (1 Peter 1:11; Heb. 1:1); (4) to the church, through the unifying Spirit who distributes gifts and savingly rules (1 Cor. 12:12–13; John 17:21; Matt. 28:20); (5) to the heavens, through his majesty and glory, now manifested to his angels and soon to be manifested to men (Isa. 66:1; Matt. 18:10; Heb. 12:22–23; Phil. 3:20–21; John 14:2–3); (6) to hell, through his avenging justice (Ps. 139:8; Matt. 10:28; 2 Thess. 1:9; Mark 9:44, 46, 48). Concerning these modes of presence, Bernard says perceptively in his *Meditations*, chapter 1, "God is present in himself as the incomprehensible one, because he is the beginning and the end, the beginning without a beginning and the end without an end; in the angels as the desirable one, because they desire to look upon him; in the saints as the delightful one, because they are perpetually blessed to delight in him; in the creatures as the admirable one, because he powerfully creates, wisely governs, and kindly disposes all things; in men as the loveable one, because he is their God and they are his people."[8] Or, as he says in another place, "God is present in himself as the alpha and omega, in the world as its author and director, in the angels as their savor and beauty, in the church as a father in his house, in the soul as a bridegroom in the marriage bed, in the righteous as an assistant and protector, in the reprobate as a fear and a horror."[9]

The Elenctic Part

It is asked: 1. Is God, even with reference to his essence, omnipresent?
The diversity of opinions
IX. We already occupied ourselves with most of the controversies of this chapter, at least those that respect its foundation, when in the preceding chapter we asserted against various opponents the infinity of the divine essence. And when that infinity has been taken away, the omnipresence built upon cannot but fall. Even so, it will be helpful to vindicate God's omnipresence more distinctly. It is therefore asked, first, whether God, with respect to his essence, is present in all things. We already heard and refuted Vorstius, who with the Socinians denied

---

8. Bernard of Clairvaux, *Meditationes* in *PL* 184:485.
9. Bernard of Clairvaux, *Sancti Bernardi Opera*, 9 vols. (Rome: Brepols, 1957–2017), 6–2:143.

the infinity of God's essence, together with their hypotheses.[10] As far as omnipresence is concerned, Vorstius (*On God*, pp. 41ff.) counts the omnipresence of the divine essence as something impossible, and indeed has even stated that it was unbecoming to the divine majesty, for it would make him coexist with unclean things, though at the same time he grants that God is present with all things by his power and activity,[11] and thus he makes a real distinction between God's essence and his power and efficacy.[12] Socinus does the same thing in his *Treatise against Franciscus David*.[13] The Remonstrant Apologists, to gain favor with the Socinians, though they do not deny the omnipresence of the divine essence, nevertheless still do not confirm it: in their *Confession*, they pass it by in silence and in their *Apology* they put the omnipresence of the divine essence up for debate.[14] A Cartesian rationalist, in his public disputation, said that it was a figment of the Scholastics.[15]

The thought of the Reformed with their foundations

The Reformed, although they do not deny that God is omnipresent by his power and activity, nevertheless, because both power and operation (if you exclude the works that it produces) are one and the same in God, also do not deny that the divine essence is omnipresent. In the preceding chapter we already laid the foundation for this idea in the omnimodal infinity of God, to which we attached, in §§IV–V, Scripture passages and reasons in favor of the divine omnipresence. And given those, we add that if with respect to his power and working God is omnipresent, he is also omnipresent with respect to his essence, unless we want to tear apart that which is altogether one and the same.

Objections

On the contrary, our adversaries allege: (1) that the omnipresence of his essence is not taught in the Scriptures. I respond, We demonstrated the contrary in §IV. On the contrary, (2) that it is taught by the Scriptures that God's essence is in heaven. I respond, Not in heaven exclusively, but in a unique and special way.

---

10. 1.2.9 §VI

11. ἐνεργείᾳ; so also below.

12. Vorstius, *Tractatus theologicus de Deo*, 41ff.

13. Faustus Socinus, *De Jesu Christi invocatione disputatio* (Valentinus Radekius, 1595).

14. Cf. Simon Episcopius, *Confessio sive declaratio sententiae pastorum qui in Foederato Belgio remonstrantes vocantur* (Harderwijk: Theodore Daniels, 1622); idem, *Apologia pro confessione sive declaratione sententiae eorum* (1629).

15. On the debate surrounding the views and work of Antonius Perizonius (1626–1672), see Dirk van Miert et al., eds., *Scriptural Authority and Biblical Criticism in the Dutch Golden Age* (Oxford: Oxford University Press, 2017), 325–50.

(3) That it is unbecoming for the divine essence to coexist with unclean things. I respond: (a) If it is not unbecoming for his power and activity to coexist with them, nor will it be unbecoming for his essence to coexist with them, because in God all these things are one and the same. (b) Neither is it unbecoming for the divine essence to create, sustain, and govern such unclean things. (c) Neither is God's spiritual essence touched or defiled by corporeal things. (4) That God approaches and recedes, descends and ascends. I respond: (a) His power and activity, since they are abstracted from his essence, properly speaking do not approach or recede. (b) He approaches and recedes, etc., not by a change in his place, but by a change in his works, such as when he makes an extraordinary declaration of his grace or justice. (c) At most, he approached and receded not in his essence but in some sort of assumed appearance (Gen. 18:1–2; etc.). Furthermore, (5) that he is not present with the wicked (Num. 14:42–43). I respond, He is not present with the wicked in his grace (Matt. 28:20; 2 Cor. 13:14), although he is in his essence (Acts 17:28). In addition, (6) that he fills heaven and earth. I respond: (a) This fact, if understood in regard to his essence, strongly implies that his essence is omnipresent. (b) Nor does it imply what our adversaries intend, that his essence does not exist outside of heaven, because Scripture plainly teaches the contrary (Job 11:7–8; 1 Kings 8:27). Finally, (7) that for the power of something to extend further than its essence is a mark of its perfection. I respond, However much this may be true with respect to corporeal beings, whose power is different from their essence, it is nonetheless not true with respect to spiritual beings, and even much less with respect to the spiritual being who is most perfect, and who is also infinite.

2. In what order ought the omnipresence of God's essence, virtue, and operation be conceived? The thought of the Cartesians

X. It is asked, second, in what order it is fitting to conceive of the omnipresence of the divine essence, power, and operation. The Cartesians want to help out their hypothesis that the essence of any spirit, even the divine Spirit, consists in nothing but mere thought, which hypothesis does not allow a spirit to have any relation to place or location, and they have not dared to deny the divine omnipresence openly, so on this issue, they contort themselves into all kinds of shapes by stating: (1) God, with respect to his essence, is not properly speaking in any place, space, or location, because that imparts to his essence some sort of extension. For this reason (2) he is not, properly speaking, everywhere in his essence. In fact (3) he is nowhere, in the sense that no location circumscribes him, delimits him, or is filled by him. Although (4) he is present to all things by his external operation, and therefore it is more rightly said that he is omnipresent, than that he exists everywhere. Meanwhile, (5) only to the extent that his power and operation coincide with his essence can he be called omnipresent in his essence. Nevertheless, (6) in so conceiving the divine omnipresence, we ought to think of his external operation, then of his power, and last of his essence, and that only to the extent that his omnipresence coincides with his essence. All these things come to this point, that the divine essence, considered properly and in itself, is not omnipresent, which their first hypothesis expressly intends, yet even so they do not say with Vorstius that it is altogether not omnipresent. A certain disputation held at Deventer by a certain rationalist cut the knot when he said as a corollary that the divine omnipresence is nothing but a figment of the Scholastics.[16]

And the thought of the Reformed

The Reformed, although they consider it useless to contend with someone about the manner and order of conceiving the divine omnipresence, provided that he does not intend to lay a trap for the truth and to eliminate entirely the omnipresence of God's essence, and although they likewise think that someone can, by ascending, first conceive of the divine operations, and from there move on to God's power, and finally from both arrive at the divine existence and essence, just as most customarily do in the demonstration of the deity, despite all this, commonly judge that once the existence and essence of God have been demonstrated and presupposed, in this matter of divine omnipresence it is best to begin our thought from God's essence, to which the concept of presence is most properly applicable, and from there to progress to the omnipresence of his power, insofar as in the formal sense (as they say) it differs from his operation, and finally, to finish at his operation itself.

The arguments of the Reformed

And they do so because: (1) in this manner the text of Psalm 139:7 lights the way: "Where shall I go from your *Spirit*?" And this Spirit is surely not a divine operation. "Where shall I flee from your *face*?" And the face of God constantly denotes the essence of God. Furthermore, verse 8, "If I would ascend to the heavens, *you* are there," not an operation, but *you*. Thus, the text begins its consideration of the omnipresence of God from his Spirit, from his face, and from God himself, and from there it proceeds to the omnipresence of the divine power, in verses 9 and 10: "If I would take the wings of the dawn...even there your *hand* would lead me." And in the Scriptures what else ultimately is God's hand than

---

16. See n15.

his power or ability? Lastly, the text finishes at God's operation, in verse 10: "and your right hand would *sustain* me." And from the other side, (2) there is not, as far as I know, a passage of Scripture that begins its consideration of God's omnipresence from his operations, proceeds to his power, and concludes with his essence. (3) Because the goal of this order that our adversaries promote openly colludes with, if it does not thoroughly coincide with, the opinion of Vorstius and the Socinians, insofar as with them it has removed God's presence from his essence and placed it in the presence of his power and operation, although on the nature of the divine essence (which does not belong to this chapter), the Cartesians and Socinians do differ on this point: the Cartesians want the divine essence to exist in pure thought, which Vorstius and the Socinians do not allow. (4) Because the Cartesian hypothesis, which locates God's omnipresence in his operation, terribly confuses divine omnipresence with divine providence, which two things the Scriptures carefully distinguish, namely, as an attribute from an operation. Of these, the prior is conceived of as existing in God, the latter as flowing forth from God. Finally, (5) this order in which our adversaries conceive God's omnipresence does not help their hypothesis. For if in thinking about the divine omnipresence you were to begin from his operations and proceed to his power, nevertheless, no one will conclude that his essence properly and in itself is not omnipresent. For whether you should conceive of his essence in the third place or in the first place, the result will be the same.

The basis of the Cartesian opinion
The basis of our adversaries' opinion rests on these three points: (1) that a thought does not admit a relation to place or space. (2) That just like the essence of an angelic and human spirit, so also the essence of the divine spirit consists in thought alone. (3) That place, space, and location imply extension, and thus are something corporeal, and consequently cannot apply to spirits. The first of these is most false, and it will not do much for the Cartesian cause unless the second assist it, namely, that the divine essence is nothing but mere thought, which we have already vanquished in chapter 3 of this second book.[17] If anyone would like more of these sorts of arguments, let them consult our *Gangrene of the Cartesian Innovations*, (sect. 2, ch. 15).[18] Their third argument, that place, space, and location is extension, will be examined in the controversy of §XII.

---

17. 1.2.3 §XIX
18. Mastricht, *Gangraena*, 285–304.

3. Presupposing the finitude of the world, can we conceive of the omnipresence of God without the concept of supra-celestial spaces?

XI. It is asked, third, whether, presupposing the finitude of this world,[19] we can have a concept of the divine immensity and omnipresence without a concept of supra-celestial spaces. Those who deny the immensity of the divine essence, as Vorstius and the Socinians do, do not need a concept of spaces, and the same for those who teach that this world is infinite in its quantity or mass. Among the Reformed, there is not one theologian who does not genuinely acknowledge both that the world is finite and that the divine omnipresence and divine essence are infinite, yet neither is there any who does not affirm the concept of imaginary spaces. The Cartesians, since they join Vorstius and the Socinians in denying the omnipresence of the divine essence, therefore also join them in not needing a concept of spaces. But at the same time, because they state that the world is indefinite, such that it could be infinite, just as much as it could be finite, they certainly allow in the latter case for there to be spaces beyond it, but these spaces would be true bodies, and thus would coalesce with the world.

The difference of opinions

The Scholastics taught these supra-celestial spaces for the purpose of conceiving of the divine immensity, but they taught that these spaces arise from our imagination, and for that reason they designated them imaginary spaces. The Reformed, at least those who think more carefully, because they presuppose two things, the finiteness of the world and the infinity of God's omnipresence, state that it is impossible to conceive of an infinite presence which subsists within the finite world unless you invoke the assistance of some sort of spaces beyond the world, so that God, who by his immensity is also beyond the world, might coexist there within those spaces, all the way to infinity. And besides this, given the finitude of this world, I do not think it would be denied by anyone that through the unexhausted power of God some body could exist beyond this world, and that not except by divine creation, because not only does this not involve a contradiction, but in addition, because denying it would deny the infinite power of God. But I cannot conceive that such a body would be created without also conceiving that it would exist in a location or a space, and that with that space, the infinite power of God, or his essence and operation, would likewise coexist. If it should be said on the contrary that (1) God, just as he did before the creation of the world, exists in himself, then I would say this is true everywhere, but that

---

19. Mastricht employs *mundus*, "world," to mean the entire created order or universe, not simply the earth.

this does not stand in the way of the fact that God coexisted with the space in which he later created the world to exist, for if that were not true, then he would have changed, and would be mutable. If (2) it should be said that this space will thus be infinite, and thus there will be two infinite things, I will then reply by denying this claim, for to be finite or infinite does not properly belong to a space, but to a true being, and that alone, for such a being is not a space, as the following arguments in the following section will prove. If they should say that (3) this space will be a true body, and thus the world will be infinite, then I will respond by denying that the world is infinite, as we have already demonstrated.[20]

4. Are those supra-celestial spaces, with which the divine omnipresence coexists, true bodies? The diversity of opinions

XII. It is asked, fourth, whether those supra-celestial spaces with which the divine immensity or omnipresence coexists are true beings, or indeed, true bodies. The Scholastics, because these spaces neither are nor could be true beings, judge that they depend upon our mere imagination, and therefore they commonly call them imaginary spaces. The Cartesians, so that they may more effectively rescue their idea of a swirling world,[21] a world which in their opinion is actually infinite, and also so that they may thus not leave a place for a possible body to exist beyond that world of theirs, and moreover (I need not add), since two immense or infinite things are mutually incompatible with themselves, so that they may take the infinity they removed from God and refer it to that world of theirs, state that those supra-celestial bodies are true bodies.

The opinion of the Reformed

The Reformed are compelled to acknowledge those supra-celestial spaces, first so that they may hold the divine infinity, immensity, and omnipresence safe and sound, and then so that they may avoid the idea of the infinity of the world, for if that were allowed, no infinity would remain for God. Nevertheless they do not understand those supra-celestial spaces to be real beings, much less real bodies, for they allow no entity at all in them; they allow in them rather the *location* of beings, and especially the location of bodies. For whatever exists, coexists with some location, and if it coexists with no location, it does not exist. A space or

---

20. 1.2.9 §VII

21. The Cartesians believed that the entire universe was a collection of connected swirling vortices. This theory is an attempt to explain planetary motion as well as to deny the existence of vacuum. Cf. René Descartes, *Principles of Philosophy*, trans. V. R. Miller and R.P. Miller (Dordrecht: Kluwer Academic Publishers, 1983), 2.10; idem, *The World*, trans. M. S. Mahoney (New York: Abaris Books, 1979).

location, if it should be filled by a body, is called a place; if it lacks a body, it is called a vacuum. Now we undergird this fact that those spaces are not bodies chiefly with the following supports.

Its supports

(1) Because if they were bodies, a body would be in a body, and therefore there would be a penetration of dimensions, which destroys the nature of a body. For according to the meaning common to men, which clear and distinct perception applauds, a body is in a space, a place, a location, and it is there in such a way that while the space remains, the body may move, or while the body remains, its place or space may be changed. Thus you cannot escape by saying that a space and the body contained in it are one and the same. (2) Because God, by his own absolute power, can annihilate whatever exists that partakes of real being. For example, if he did so within a room such that its walls remained and stood where they already stand, then there would certainly be nothing real within those walls, and yet the space would remain, the same space that could be filled with just as much air as God annihilated. If you should say that God cannot do this because it involves a manifest contradiction, since though we presuppose that these walls would stand apart from each other, they would at the same time not stand apart because there would be nothing set between them through which they stood apart, I would reply: (a) In Descartes' thinking, God can also do those things that are contradictory, or at least contradictory in regard to the things themselves. (b) I will instead deny that there is a contradiction, for I grant that those walls would not stand apart by some sort of thing. Yet even so, they would stand apart by some sort of space. (3) Because if these spaces were bodies, then the world would be infinite, so then there would be plural infinite things, and thus, none. Moreover, God could not, by his own infinite power, create other worlds, for he could not even add anything to the one he created.

An objection

There is one objection they make to the contrary that has some appearance of truth, namely, that these spaces nevertheless have their own extension and dimensions of length, breadth, and depth, which apply only to a body. The ready response is that these do not properly belong to spaces that contain bodies, but to the bodies which are contained in them, or that would be contained in them, if they were created in them. In the same way, for example, all the fathoms of length, breadth, and height that belong to the world in its own space, the space with which it coexists, are improperly attributed to that space. And here is the origin of their error, that they take properties that apply to things that are contained or will be contained and they refer them to the space that contains them.

5. Does omnipresence belong to the human nature of Christ?
The opinion of our adversaries
XIII. It is asked, fifth, whether immensity, omnipresence, and ubiquity belong to the human nature of Christ, having been communicated through the hypostatic union with the divine nature. The papists want the human nature to be present indeed in many places, namely, in all places where their Mass is celebrated, but not in all places, not in other places. The Lutherans at this point divide into factions. The Calixtians, named after Georg Calixt of Helmstedt, agree entirely with the papists. On the other side, the others whom they call the Ubiquitarians, that they might have the flesh and blood of Christ in the holy Supper, state that the omnipresence of the divine nature has been communicated to the human nature through the hypostatic union.[22]

The opinion of the Reformed, with its foundations
The Reformed, as with infinity in the preceding chapter, so also with immensity and ubiquity, judge these attributes are proper to God, such that they have not been and cannot be communicated, or else through that communication the human nature would have become divine. Likewise then one and the same nature would be omnipresent and not omnipresent, God and not God, and by the same logic, the human nature would also be divine, and in fact there would cease to be a hypostatic union. We gave the rest of our arguments in the preceding chapter, §IX.

The exception of the Ubiquitarians
If they take exception, saying that we should distinguish between immensity as proper to God and immensity as communicated to the human nature, they will accomplish nothing at all, for whether it is conceived of as proper or as communicated, it remains the same immensity, and if the human nature possesses it in any way, it will really be the divine nature. For if anything is immense in any way, that thing is God. I need not add that immensity cannot be communicated without ceasing to belong to God's incommunicable properties, nor besides this, that to be infinite is not possible for finite being, apart from the most evident

---

22. E.g. Johannes Brenz (1499–1570), *De personali unione duarum naturam Christi* (Tübingen: Morhard, 1561).

contradiction. We gave more arguments on this subject in the preceding chapter, concerning God's infinity.

The Practical Part

The practice of divine immensity serves: 1. For the consolation of the godly
XIV. The practical force of God's immensity and omnipresence is, first, in the consolation, in any dangers and troubles, whether impending or currently pressing, that God is present with his people, not only by his essence, but also by his grace. Therefore, even if they walk through the valley of the shadow of death, there is no evil that they fear, "For you," they say, "are with me, and your rod and your staff, they comfort me" (Ps. 23:4; Isa. 43:1–2; Rom. 8:31).

In what circumstances?
Namely (1) in loneliness, in the farthest part of the seas (Ps. 139:9–10); (2) in exile and on dangerous journeys (Gen. 39:2); (3) in prison (Gen. 39:21); (4) in the persecutions of enemies oppressing the godly (Ps. 46:5); (5) in diseases, in death itself, when all people and all things desert us (Ps. 23:4); and (6) in any arduous labors (Ex. 3:11–12).

By what arguments?
In these and all similar circumstances, what will more effectively sustain our soul than to think that (1) the immense God is at our right hand (Ps. 16:8), and (2) with God, our Savior, who is also God himself (Matt. 28:20), who as a fiery wall dwells among us (Zech. 2:5, 10). "Thus with Christ by our side, even cobwebs are bulwarks, // Yet with Christ far away, every wall is a cobweb."[23] Just as Julius Caesar said to his captain, "Confide in fortune, sailor, Julius is on the battleship,"[24] and Alexander to his soldier, "When I am present, fear not the arms of any foe, though you should be unarmed."[25] And Augustine, "What adversary do you fear, since God the King is in you as your portion?" And likewise, "What man do you fear, you who have been set in the bosom of God?"[26] (3) He is present to us through his immensity, not only in his essence, but also in his wisdom and counsel in doubtful situations, and in addition, in his power in arduous and

---

23. *Sic ubi Christus adest nobis, vel aranea murus, // Sic ubi Christus abest, vel murus aranea fiet.* These lines are adapted from Paulinus of Nola, cf. *Poema* XVI, *PL* 51:480.

24. Plutarch, *Caesar*, trans. C. Pelling (Oxford: Oxford University Press, 2011), 38.4–5, pp. 105–6.

25. Justinus, *Hist. phil. epit.* 12.16.

26. See Augustine on 1 Tim. 1:5, Sermo CXII, *PL* 39:1968. This sermon is located among sermons of doubted authenticity.

hopeless situations; in short, he is present in his grace and providence, that is, his rod and his staff (Ps. 23:4).

By observing what things?
This is the case provided that we make sure (1) that this immense and omnipresent God become our God through the covenant of grace and through the Mediator received by faith (Isa. 43:1–3; Ps. 23:1, 4; Gen. 17:1); (2) that he be reconciled to us and a friend toward us (2 Cor. 5:19), so that he might be at our right hand and not our left (Ps. 16:8), so that he might be for us, not against us (Rom. 8:31); and also (3) that he remain with us and not depart from us, driven away by the shamefulness of our sins (Isa. 59:2); indeed (4) that day by day he also be invited and summoned by our prayers, that he would come to us and remain with us (Ps. 91:15; Luke 24:29).

2. For the fear and reverence of God

XV. Second, in producing fear and reverence in our souls, that by it (1) we may dread the commission of any sin, even the least, because it would be done in the presence and indeed the sight of God. Indeed, that by it (2) we may be frightened away from thinking, saying, or doing anything except what is holy, honorable, and godly, because we have everywhere present to us our most holy God, the Judge himself, who stands close by and sees all things, even the most remote (Heb. 4:13; Amos 9:1–4). Because of this God commanded the Israelites to remove every uncleanness from their camp (Num. 5:2–3; Deut. 23:13–14), and he used this argument: "For the Lord your God walks in the midst of your camp." Indeed, (3) that by sincere repentance we may remove every shameful thing from the sight of God, so that no uncleanness at all would appear, lest he turn away from us (Deut. 23:14; Isa. 1:16). How, especially when you can hardly but withdraw from sins in the presence of some sober and upright man, and even less in the presence of a judge, will you not do the same at the thought of the presence of God, the judge as well as the avenger, and such a strict one at that (Gen. 18:20–21, 25; Dan. 5:26–28; Rev. 3:15–17)? Certainly it is the root of all carnal security and license to think inwardly that God is stuck in heaven and therefore has no business with us on the earth (Ps. 10:3–4; 14:1; 94:7). But for the godly, this root has been removed: because they have God present to them, right before their eyes, even though they be far removed from men, they shudder at the thought of sinning (Gen. 39:9; Job 31:1, 27).

3. *Against hypocrisy and for sincerity*

XVI. Third, in removing every mask and hypocrisy, and in summoning sincerity of heart through the whole of divine worship. That is, whenever we think that God, by his immensity, is present even in the innermost chambers of our heart, and that he sees our most secret thoughts, sees them even from afar (Ps. 139:5) with eyes in infinite ways more bright than the sun, whose sharp sight neither clouds, nor roofs and walls, nor subterranean caverns shut out. For he is "all an eye, and thus sees all our affairs; all an ear, and thus he hears them all…" (Augustine, *On the Psalms*, Ps. 36).[27] So then in the Scriptures to act sincerely and without a mask is to act as in the sight of God (Gen. 24:40; 2 Cor. 2:17) and to have God always and everywhere before us (Ps. 16:8).

4. *For zeal in walking with God*

XVII. Finally, fourth, in stirring up a sincere zeal for always and everywhere walking and living with God present, following the example of Enoch (Gen. 5:24) who התהלך, "walked" in the frequentative sense, that is, he went about unceasingly, just like Noah (Gen. 6:9), and Abraham (Gen. 17:1). We are to do so because the sacred page demands it of us in many ways, when it urges that we should walk, not only with God (Job 31:5; Mal. 2:6), but also before God, that is, in the sight of God (Gen. 24:40; 2 Cor. 2:17), after God (Deut. 11:1, 4), in the name of God (Mic. 4:5), by the Spirit of God (Gal. 5:16). This walking involves many things, for example: (1) that we know and sense that he is present with us (Ps. 16:8). (2) That we who have been separated from him by our sins strive to be reunited with him through reconciliation (cf. Amos 3:3; 1 Sam. 24:19). And indeed, (3) that we also seek his friendship, so that like Moses we may converse with him as a friend with a friend (Ex. 33:11). And because of this, (4) that we continuously desire his gracious presence (Ps. 23:4). Furthermore, (5) that we talk with him in prayers and soliloquies (Song 1:2–8; 7:4). In addition, (6) that in all our affairs we consult him in his Word (Ps. 42:6; 43:3–4). And (7) that we feast with him in holy fellowship (Matt. 22:4; Ps. 36:8). Especially (8) that always and everywhere we conduct ourselves as in the sight of God (2 Cor. 2:17), with reverence and fear (Prov. 23:17; Neh. 5:9), on the one hand by abstaining from all evil on account of the fact that God is present, "for a great part of sins goes away if a witness stands nearby those about to sin" (Seneca, *Epistles*, 11),[28]

---

27. This could be a close citation from Augustine, *Ep.* 148 in *NPNF* 1:449, but it more closely approximates Jerome on Psalm 94:9, Homily 22, see Jerome, *The Homilies of St. Jerome*, trans. M. L. Ewald, *Fathers of the Church* series (Washington, D. C.: Catholic University of America Press, 1963), 48:177.

28. Seneca, *Ep.* 11.

and on the other hand by attending to every good thing (Isa. 38:3), and that without any hypocrisy, with all sincerity (Col. 3:22). Our *Prodromus* has more on this subject, in proof 3, on life with God.[29]

---

29. Mastricht, *Theologiae didactico-elenchtico-practicae prodromus tribus speciminibus* (Amsterdam: Johannes van Someren, 1665), 173–201. See below, p. 456, n. 10.

CHAPTER ELEVEN

The Eternity of God

Lord, you have been our dwelling place from generation to generation. Before the mountains were brought forth and you formed the earth and the world, even from everlasting to everlasting, you are God.

—Psalm 90:1–2

The eternity of God

I. The infinity of God can be thought of either absolutely, with respect to his essence, as it is in itself, and this could be properly called and named the infinity of the divine essence. Or it can be thought of in relation or reference to his coexistence, either with other beings, whether they are spiritual or corporeal, or with the spaces in which beings exist or can exist, and thus God's infinity is called either *omnipresence* or *immensity*. Or it can be thought of in relation simply to his existence, that is, to his duration, which is eternity. We brought out the infinity of God's existence in chapter 9, and his coexistence in the preceding chapter. Therefore, there is nothing remaining under the notion of quantity except the infinity of his existence, that is, of his duration, which we have designated under its own name as *eternity*. And of this eternity, Moses furnishes us with a most elegant summary in Psalm 90:1–2.

The Exegetical Part

It is built upon the exegesis of the text.

II. In order to draw a picturesque outline of the flux and fragility of human life, Moses compares it with the eternal constancy and immutability of God by a certain address, or a word of praise and a celebration of God. In it we are to observe:

A. The thing celebrated: אֲדֹנָי, "Lord," with the vowel *qamets*, and thus used in place of the name *Jehovah*, which, as we taught expressly above in our theory of the divine names, comes from the perpetuity of his being and existing.[1]

B. The celebration, which under a double relation represents the eternity of God. Namely, it is considered:

1. In respect to his own people: "You have been our dwelling from generation to generation." That is to say, in all the time since human beings have been in the world, you have been the same thing for us that a house is for its residents, protecting them from whatever harm may come from the weather. Here, מעון denotes a dwelling place, a place to stay, that is, a perpetual one, not an inn, not a hut, under which the Israelites spent a season during their traveling in the desert (Ex. 33:10; Deut. 33:18). It also denotes a refuge, that is, from harm by the weather. And the text continues, you were such a dwelling place לנו, "for us," that is, for us Israelites, for your own people, not for all people, and especially for the true believers among that people. And for how long? בדר ודר, "from generation to generation," that is, as long as a generation exists, or as long as people exist on the earth. And this is the eternity of God as he coexists with time.

2. In respect to himself, in relation to the infinite duration of his own existence, which the text describes:

   a. Comparatively, in three steps:

      i. "Before the mountains were brought forth." Namely, those unmoved and immovable bodies, before they יולדו, "were brought forth," that is, by your eternal power.

      ii. "Before you formed the earth and the world." Here ארץ denotes the circle of the earth, whether it is habitable or not, insofar as it also includes the seas, and תבל speaks more strictly of the world insofar as it is habitable, which the Greeks designate as the οἰκουμένη. And the text says, before תחולל, "you labored to give birth" to them, that is, before you, as if by laboring to give birth, formed or created them (Deut. 32:18; Job 26:13). The verb תחולל can be taken either actively in the Piel (as in Prov. 25:23; Deut. 32:18), so that it means, "before you had given birth," or passively in the Pual (as in Ps. 51:5; Prov.

---

1. 1.2.4 §§VIII, XI

8:24–25), meaning, "before the earth had been brought forth by your power."

    iii. This is all to say, before the whole world existed. (Note that with several others you could, not without reason, understand the word תבל also to mean the whole world.) All this proves irrefutably that whatever existed before the world is eternal, for whatever existed before time existed in eternity.

  b. Absolutely: "from everlasting to everlasting, you are God." מעולם לעולם, "from eternity to eternity." Thus eternity, when absolute in every part, is designated in the Scriptures by its prior as well as its latter part. When eternity is partial, it is designated by only one use of the word עולם. Therefore by these words, the eternity of God is shown by its lack of three things:

    i. Of a beginning: "from everlasting," מעולם.

    ii. Of an end: "to everlasting," לעולם. And in this way it is signified that the existence of God has, in eternity, neither beginning nor end: he is the first and the last, the alpha and the omega.

    iii. Of succession: "You *are* God," where the substantive "you are" (which, as all agree, is included in the אתה, "you," according to Hebrew usage) denotes that God, by his eternity, coexists as present with all types of time, past, present, and future, just as in the Savior's words in John 8:58, "Before Abraham was, *I am*." The phrase in Exodus 3:14, אהיה אשר אהיה, "I am who I am," points in the same direction.

The Dogmatic Part

It is proven by the Scriptures.

III. From all this, it now naturally follows that God alone is eternal. The sacred page teaches this in many ways, when: (1) it expressly affirms, מעולם עד עולם אתה אל, "from eternity to eternity you are God." It does so likewise in Proverbs 8:25, Genesis 11:33, as well as in Psalm 55:19, ישב קדם, "sitting in time past," that is, dwelling in the beginning, in Isaiah 40:28, יהוה אלהי עולם, "The Lord is the God of eternity," and in Isaiah 57:15, שכן עד, "inhabiting forever." See also Daniel 6:26 and Romans 16:26. (2) It denies to him time and succession (Job 36:26, "Of the number of his years, there is no finding out"; Isa. 43:10; Ps. 90:5; 2 Peter 3:8). (3) It attributes to him eternal properties and operations, in Psalm 103:17 when eternal mercy, in Exodus 15:18 when eternal rule, in Daniel 6:26

when eternal dominion, and in 1 Peter 5:10 when eternal glory are attributed to him. (4) It describes him metaphorically by attributing to him days and years, though his differ from ours as much as heaven differs from earth (Dan. 7:9, 22, "the Ancient of Days"; Ps. 102:26, "your years are not consumed"; Job 10:5; Isa. 43:13). The Fathers assist on this point: Irenaeus (bk. 2, ch. 34, sec. 2) writes, "without beginning and without end, truly and always the same, keeping himself in the same mode, he alone is God, and he is Lord of all."[2] And Hilary in *On the Trinity* (bk. 2, ch. 6), says, "Run with your senses toward whatever seems ultimate to them—you will always be aimed at him, always moving in his direction. Again, cycle through the centuries—you will always find him, and though you will run out of numbers to count his days, God will never run out. Stir up your understanding and embrace his whole being with your mind—you have nothing, because he has everything left, and what he has left is always whole."[3] Especially consider Augustine on Psalm 102:24, commenting on "your years are in the generation of generations": "But what are 'your years'? What are they but years that will not come and go? What are they but years that do not come only to vanish? For in this world of time, each day comes only to pass away. Each hour, each month, each year, none stands firm. Before it comes, it will be, but after it comes, it will not be. Thus these your years, eternal years, your years that do not change, they will remain 'in the generation of generations.'... For God's years are not one thing, and God's self another, but God's years are God's eternity. Eternity is God's very substance, which has nothing changeable. There, nothing is past, as if it now were not; nothing is future, as if it were not yet. Rather, there is nothing there but *is*. What will be, is not yet, but there, whatever is, simply *is*."[4] Indeed, even the pagans affirm God's eternity: Thales, in Diogenes Laertius, when asked what God was, responded, "the one who has neither beginning nor end."[5] And Plato in the *Timaeus* says that there is nothing past, nothing future, that can be attributed to God without blasphemy.[6]

---

2. Irenaeus, *Contra Haereses* in PG 7:835; idem, *Against Heresies* in ANF 1:412.

3. Hilary of Poitiers, *De Trinitate* in PL 2:55; idem, *On the Trinity* in NPNF2 9:53–54.

4. Hebrew Ps. 102:25, Latin Ps. 101:25; Augustine, *Enarrationes in Psalmos* in PL 37:1310–11; idem, *Expositions on the Psalms* in NPNF1 8:501–2.

5. ὁ μήτ᾿ ἀρχὴν ἔχων, μήτε τέλος: For a Greek transcription and English translation, see Diogenes Laertius, *Lives* 1.1.36 in LCL 184:36–37.

6. This does not appear to be an exact quote but seems to summarize Plato, *Timaeus* 37e–38a. On blasphemy in applying time to God, compare 37e, "although we apply them wrongly, without noticing, to Eternal Being," LCL 234:76–77.

It is confirmed by reasons.

IV. Right reason applauds the Scriptures. For (1) if God had not existed from eternity, then at some point he would not have existed, and thus he would not exist even now, and thus, we would have atheism instead of religion. For either he would have produced himself before he existed, and thus he would have existed and not existed at the same time, for if he had been the producer, he would have existed, but if he had been yet to be produced, he would not have existed before he was produced; or, another being would have produced him, and that being would have existed before the first being. In either case, God would not exist, for by *God* we understand nothing other than the absolutely first being, that is, a being that excludes the idea, not only of a preexisting being, but also of a coexisting being. (2) If God were not from eternity, then nothing would exist, for if the first being does not exist, then neither does the second, and so on. We demonstrated this above when we considered the subordination of beings or of causes.[7] (3) If that which is God had not existed from eternity, then God would not exist: for that which is God is a most perfect being, that is, a being that has every perfection that there is, or that can be, or that can be conceived. But a being that lacks existence also lacks the perfection that is in existence. Indeed, it would also lack essence, since existence and essence denote one and the same thing in God. (4) God, when he is presupposed by us to be the Creator of all things and all times, is also presupposed to be before all things, before all times, and that which is before time is by that very fact eternal. We will not add more in a matter that is beyond controversy.

God alone is eternal.

V. Indeed, not only is God eternal, but also, God alone is eternal, for the text restricts eternity to God: "You, O Lord...from eternity to eternity, *you* are God." Also, Scripture throughout its pages distinguishes God from everything else by his eternity (Ps. 92:8; 102:24–27; Rom. 1:23; 1 Tim. 1:17; 6:16). He alone is called the first and the last, the alpha and the omega (Isa. 41:4; 44:6; Rev. 21:6; 22:13). Nor does reason fail to help us here, since: (1) from the subordination of causes, God alone remains the absolutely first being, that is, the being that excludes not only a pre-existing being, but also a coexisting being. (2) God's eternity is nothing but his duration, and his duration is nothing but his existence, and his existence is nothing but his essence. So then, if the essence of God cannot be held in common with another, neither can his eternity. (3) Everything different from God is created, which implies that at some point its existence was

---

7. 1.2.2 §IV

new. (4) Otherwise, there would be, besides God, something immutable, and consequently, something over which God has no power. The reason for this is that an eternal being without a beginning excludes the idea of the variety that comes through succession, inasmuch as succession progresses from a beginning. Thus if another being were eternal, it would have no succession, and therefore it would be, with God, immutable.

What the word eternity *means is explained.*

VI. Moreover, *eternity* signifies, sometimes a duration that has a beginning and an end, but one that is very long and that does not have a defined end (thus Gen. 17:13; 49:26; Lev. 17:7; Ex. 21:6); sometimes a duration that has a beginning but not an end, whether that duration is by nature, such as belongs to the angels and our souls, or by grace or justice, such as will one day, after this world, belong to our bodies also; sometimes a duration that lacks a beginning as well as an end, which is represented distinctively in the periphrasis, "from everlasting to everlasting," or by the joining of two synonymous expressions, עולם ועד "forever and ever" (Ex. 15:18; Ps. 9:5; 10:16; Dan. 12:3; Mic. 4:5). It is also customary to call eternity *sempiternity.* This eternity is variously described by various people. It could be described negatively as a duration that lacks beginning, end, and succession. Or, it could be described in another way, as the infinite duration of God, as long as by the word *duration* we do not mean the flow of some sort of existence, speaking successively, a duration like that of the creatures, through years, months, days, etc. But rather, we mean it abstractly and simply, in the sense that enduring is the opposite of ceasing to exist. In Boethius it is defined quite accurately as "the possession, at once whole and perfect, of boundless life" (*Consolation of Philosophy*, bk. 5, prose 6).[8] By "life," he does not understand here anything but the very essence of God, such that based on this definition, eternity could be not improperly described as the very essence of God insofar as it is conceived by us as lacking boundaries and succession. This life is called, in Boethius, "boundless," that is, not only unbounded in actuality, but also a life that cannot be bounded, either by a beginning or by an end, entirely different from the life of the creatures. For although there are creatures whose life is unbounded, either by their own nature, as is evident in spirits, or by unending divine preservation, which will be the case for our bodies after the resurrection, still, when it comes to creatures, there is no boundless life, nor can there be, no life to which God through his infinite power could not put an end, at least through annihilation.

---

8. *Aeternitas igitiur est interminabilis vitae tota simul et perfecta possessio:* Boethius, *Consolation of Philosophy*, bk. 5, prose 6, ln. 4; LCL 74:422–23.

Boethius adds that this eternity is the "possession, at once whole and perfect," of this boundless life, intending to signify that in eternity, every idea of before and after, every flow and succession of minutes, is altogether banished; he means an eternity that cannot be divided by our measures of time. We will find more on this subject in the elenctic part.[9]

It is explained with help from the concept of temporal spaces.
VII. And that we might have at least some idea of this eternity, it will be not unsuitable to represent for it the concept of certain temporal spaces, and by that concept to construct our concept of the divine duration. For just as in the preceding chapter we could not conceive of God's immensity and omnipresence without spaces, that is, local spaces, so likewise can we scarcely, and not even scarcely, conceive of his eternity without spaces, that is, temporal spaces. This, however, should be done according to these laws: (1) we may not conceive of them as true beings. Just as in the case of the local spaces we did not intend that they be true beings, neither also should we do so in the case of these temporal ones, so that we do not conceive of more than one eternal being. (2) As in the case of local spaces we did not allow true extension, true dimensions of length, breadth, etc., so also in these temporal spaces we may not allow any flow of moments or succession of duration in the God that coexists with these spaces, although such can be allowed in the creatures that coexist with them.

What the idea itself means is likewise explained.
VIII. Furthermore, the nature of this eternity will be made further known to us if we consider that there are, in total, three measures of duration. The first belongs to things that by their nature are mutable and that wear out. It possesses a beginning and an end, and it is called *time*. Its nature consists in a continuous succession of moments, such that properly speaking not but one moment exists at a time, and only when the preceding moments have ceased to exist and the following moments do not yet exist. In this measure of duration it is proper to observe periods: the past, the present, and the future. The second measure of duration belongs to things that by their essence are incorruptible or immaterial. It has a beginning but it is without end, and it is named *forever*.[10] The third measure is simply immutable, and thus it lacks beginning, end, and succession. And only this measure is that *eternity* which the Scholastics define as "interminable, indivisible, and independent duration": "interminable," meaning that it lacks

---

9. §XI, below
10. *aevum*

both outer boundaries; "indivisible," meaning that it also lacks succession; and finally, "independent," meaning that it lacks all imperfection and change. Thus in this eternity, three things come together: the absence of a beginning, the absence of an end (which all admit), and the absence of succession. This last absence Vorstius as well as the Socinians deny, and we will demonstrate and vindicate it in the elenctic part.[11]

God through his eternity coexists immutable with all types of time.
IX. Finally, through his eternity, God coexists, unchanged and immutable, with the types in which all times are included: with the past, the present, and the future. The ancients made for this concept a sketch of sorts using the explanatory picture of a circle, whose center coexists unmoved with all the moving points on its circumference. We also can make a sort of sketch of it with this similar image: for a person sitting on a river bank, only the water that is present is visible, but not the water that has gone or that is to come, though if he were meanwhile lifted on high, the whole river, both its source and its mouth, would be visible and present to him. In the same way, God with his eye, because he is by his eternity above time, coexists invariable with the past, the present, and the future, and with the whole flow of things, such that nothing either flows from him or to him. And this is so though those very things neither coexist with God (except when they do happen to exist and be present), nor even with themselves. For they do not coexist with God's eternity, because they would thus become eternal, unless you use the verb *coexist* only in an inadequate sense.

The Elenctic Part
It is asked: 1. Is eternity such a property of God that belongs to him truly, and to him alone? The difference of opinions
X. It is asked, first, whether eternity is such a property of God that belongs to him truly, and to him alone. The pagans, because they cherished gods that were human, liable to the common lot of being born and of dying, for which reason their most ancient theological writers were occupied with theogony, cannot hold to eternity as a property inseparable from God. At one time the Manicheans, that they might more conveniently hold to their two principles of good and evil, or their two gods, invented the idea that they were both eternal. The Arians, though they in some way accepted Christ as true God, and though they confessed that he existed before this world, nevertheless denied that he had existed

---

11. §XI, below

from eternity, and they did not tolerate the thought of deducing, from this fact that he had existed before the world, the conclusion that he had existed from eternity, contrary to the Scriptures, in which these two ideas are synonymous (Ps. 90:2; Eph. 1:4; Matt. 25:34; John 17:5; etc.), and contrary to reason, which understands that what is outside of time is in eternity. The Peratae (a name scarcely read in the catalogues of the ancient heretics), or the Tritheists, counted instead of three divine persons three divine essences, and they attributed eternity to each, and thus they set up three eternal beings.[12] Last century, Valentine Gentile agreed exactly with these Tritheists and was on that account burned in Switzerland. He counted that there were three essences, and that they were eternal essences. He called the first of them, the Father, the *essencing* essence, and the others, the Son and the Holy Spirit, *essenced* essences, that is, essences that were created by the Father. The Socinians deny that eternity is attributed to God expressly in the Scriptures, and they assert that it is therefore not necessary to believe in it. Furthermore, they accept two true gods, the Father and the Son, but between these they attribute eternity to the Father and deny it to the Son, and thus they hold to a true God who was not from eternity. Finally, lest Christians safely infer from the eternity that the Scriptures assert for Christ that Christ is God consubstantial with the Father, they state that eternity is not an attribute proper to God because there is nothing that opposes the idea that a creature may have existed from eternity. The Reformed state that eternity is the type of property of God which belongs to God truly, and to him alone, and they do so by the arguments, first from the Scriptures and then from reason, which we presented just above in §§III–IV. Our opponents do not have anything that they may object, except to say that we cannot prove it, but this topples to the ground by the arguments we have already brought forth.

2. Does succession belong to eternity as it belongs to time?

XI. It is asked, second, whether succession belongs to eternity, just as it belongs to time. Vorstius and the Socinians would like more powerfully to overthrow the omnimodal immutability of God, and also more easily to hold, in favor of the volatility of our free will, to the mutability of the divine decrees, by which they mean in the matter of predestination that God's opinion changes as often as it

---

12. Hippolytus of Rome (170–235) is the primary historical source for the Peratae ("those from beyond the Euphrates"), their origin, and their beliefs. The *Philosophumena* was originally attributed to Origen, but in the nineteenth century manuscripts were found that supported the authorship of Hippolytus. See Hippolytus of Rome, *Philosophumena*; idem, *Refutation of All Heresies*, bk. 5, chs. 7–12, bk. 10, ch. 6 in *ANF* 5:58–64, 142; bk. 5, chs. 7–12, bk. 10, ch. 10 in *PG* 10:3125–62, 3419–20.

seems good to the rational creature to redirect his course of life. Therefore, they state that in eternity there is the same succession and flow of moments as there is in time, and thus that God coexists with moments that are continually new, and therefore also that in that regard he changes. The Reformed state on the contrary that in eternity there neither is nor can be any succession of minutes. This is so because (1) Scripture testifies in this way. For when it says that a thousand years to God are nothing but one day (Ps. 90:4; cf. 2 Peter 3:8); when it says that God endures forever, that he endures in all generations, that he is the same, and that his years have no end (Ps. 102:11–12, 24, 26–27); when it says that today God has begotten his Son (Ps. 2:7), but that the Son's coming forth is from the beginning, from the days of eternity (Mic. 5:2)—what is it saying except that in eternity there is no past or future, but only present? (2) Such succession is opposed to God's immutability (Mal. 3:6; James 1:17), which without doubt excludes the flow of duration. (3) It is opposed to the essence of God, for since eternity is nothing but God's duration, and his duration nothing but his existence, and his existence nothing but his essence, then, if his eternity is liable to succession, it cannot be but that his essence is also. Accordingly Augustine says, commenting on Psalm 102, "Eternity is God's very substance, which has nothing changeable. There, nothing is past, as if it now were not; nothing is future, as if it were not yet. There is nothing there but *is*: there is no *was* or *will be* there, because what was, is not now, and what will be, is not yet, but there, whatever is, simply *is*."[13] Because (4) in many ways, including those above, it is repugnant to right reason. For right reason teaches: (a) that in all succession there is an order of before and after, and that such an order presupposes a beginning from which the flow of that order comes. But eternity rejects this idea, as it lacks a beginning and likewise an end. (b) In every succession there are parts that succeed each other, but in an infinite duration, such parts cannot have a place. For those flowing parts would be either finite—but in that way, an infinite would come together from finite parts, and an effect would be in every way more noble and perfect than its cause, though from its cause it has all its perfection—or, they would be infinite—but in that way, one infinite would come from many infinite parts, which is repugnant to reason. I will not add that to speak of an infinite part is to speak of a part which is not smaller than the whole, or what is the same thing, a part which is not a part, and likewise that it implies a number of parts to which not even a unity could be added, and furthermore, that there thus exists an infinite that is greater than infinite, and consequently, an infinite which is not infinite, for that infinite duration of eternity would imply infinite centuries,

---

13. Cf. §III above. Augustine, *PL* 37:1310–11; idem, *NPNF1* 8:501–2.

and these centuries more years, and those years more months, days, hours, and so forth. Also, nature teaches (c) that in every successive duration there is some nonbeing, for what is past is no longer, what is future is not yet, and what is present will very soon be past, and will not be. Likewise, (d) that duration, flowing as it does through points of time, is never infinitely perfect, and thus it is also not compatible with the infinity of God's existence and perfection, for that to which something is continuously added, as happens in successive duration, is never perfected. Furthermore, nature teaches that (e) what is continually being actuated cannot be independent, for however much potential there is in things, there is also that much dependence.

Five objections are resolved.
But they proffer: (1) Years, days, past and future, before and after, are all asserted of God throughout the Scriptures. I respond, This does not happen except by condescension,[14] on account of the infirmity of our intellect, that is, so that it might more fittingly portray for itself the eternity of God. And what is thus done in a way suitable to man is not to be received otherwise than in a way worthy of God, nor by these statements are we to think of anything other than his most simple and most perfect duration. (2) Eternity coexists with succession and the vicissitudes of time. I respond, Yes, but without succession, just as he coexists with changeable things without change (Mal. 3:6) and imperfect things without imperfection, and just as spirits coexist with bodies spiritually. (3) If he coexists with the types and successions of time without succession, then the types of time—past, present, and future—would also coexist with themselves: for when two things join a third thing, they also join each other. I respond, This does not follow, in the same way as the points on a circumference, although the center coexists with them, nevertheless do not mutually coexist with each other. Nor also do the types of time coexist with eternity, except speaking inadequately—indeed, properly speaking, no time coexists with him except the present, since the past and future do not exist, although eternity coexists with them all. (4) In this way, time would coexist with all of eternity and consequently, it would be eternal as well. I respond, Time does indeed coexist with all of eternity, but not adequately and totally, for it coexists only according to the present, not according to the past and future. (5) The order of before and after are observed in the eternal operations of God themselves. I respond, Indeed, that order is observed in his works, but not, however, in their working or in their worker. And this is so

---

14. *per* συγκατάβασιν

in this way: by his single and most simple operation, God decreed from eternity, then produces in time, all things that are liable to succession.

3. If there was not anything besides God from eternity, at least could there have been?

XII. It is asked, third, if there was not anything besides God from eternity, whether there at least could have been. It is related (by what right, I will not here determine) that Aristotle, because he lacked Scripture, could not extend his mind back to the first man, and because he thus judged that he should proceed backward into infinity, stated that the world had existed from eternity. The Tritheists and Valentine Gentile, because they could not distinguish in God anything apart from his singular essence, counted three divine essences, in which two were created, namely, the Son and the Holy Spirit; yet even so they still asserted eternity for them no less than for the Father. Several of the Jesuits, although they acknowledge that nothing besides God existed in actuality from eternity, nevertheless state (by pure insolence) that something besides God could have existed from eternity, and therefore deprive both themselves and us of the argument for the consubstantial deity of the Son and of the Holy Spirit that is supplied from the eternity of God's essence. Vorstius and the Socinians, that they might more ably dodge the force of our argument for the consubstantial deity of the Son and of the Holy Spirit, which we construct from the eternity asserted for both of them in the Scriptures, do not deny that God alone has existed from eternity in actuality, but nevertheless affirm that something besides God could have existed from eternity. On the contrary, the Reformed state that perfect eternity is proper to God, such that whatever is besides God neither has nor could have existed from eternity, and they do so on account of the Scriptures and reasons which we have already set forth in §§III–IV. We will add nothing to those, besides the following problems: (1) from this hypothesis, an infinite number of days would have to precede an existing day—this day, for example—but since this number would never have been completed, neither would this day have been able to follow it. Or (2) if we did believe it to have been completed, and we said that an infinite number of days had preceded the present day, then a much greater number of hours would have preceded it, and thus an infinite will be greater than an infinite. Indeed also (3) we will end up stating that something can be added to an infinite thing. I will not say (4) that the authors of this possible eternity, at least those who accept the holy Trinity, weaken the argument for the deity of the Son and the Holy Spirit which is made from their eternity. The Jesuits and Socinians do not even try to adduce anything from the Scriptures, nor from reason, except for one most specious argument, which is this: if God could have created the world from eternity, then the world also could have existed from eternity; but he could have created the world from eternity, and therefore the world could have so existed. But the terms of the proposition insufficiently cohere. For although that power which created the world in time, and by which it can be said that God could have created from eternity, was at his disposal, nevertheless it does not immediately follow from this that the world could have existed from eternity, since this involves, not on God's part but on the world's part, this problem: from finite moments, with which the time of the world coexists, would result an eternity, that is, an infinite duration. Or, if they prefer to call the moments infinite, then from many infinites would emerge a single infinite. But I say in sum (if I may resist the Scholastics scholastically), that an infinite world could have been created according to the potency of the cause, but it could not have been created according to the potency of the effect.

4. Has what existed before the world existed from eternity?
What do our adversaries say?
XIV.[15] It is asked, fourth, whether what existed before the world has existed from eternity. Conrad Vorstius, to gain favor with the Socinians, openly denies that existing before the world is the same thing as existing from eternity (*Sum of Apologetic Exegesis*, §14).[16] The Arians, or Homoiousians, since they acknowledge that Christ existed before this world but at the same time deny that he existed from eternity, are compelled to answer the question in the negative.[17] Among the Cartesians, the famous Wittich, in his *Peaceable Theology* (§§180–181), on this topic speaks in an exceedingly slippery fashion about whether angels could have existed before this world, and does so to promote the Cartesian hypotheses, in which an angel is nothing except pure thought, and a thought, so that it may exist, does not require any space with which to coexist, and for this reason it could have existed when as of yet no space existed, and thus, before the world. In this matter he acknowledges that angels did not exist before this world or before the first beginning of creation, but at the same time he refuses to state, on account of the reasons of the famous Maresius, his opponent, that they could not have existed before the world, and adds that instead he simply does not deny that they could not have existed before the world. Nevertheless, he nowhere asserts that they could not have existed before this world, and much less does

---

15. The original skips §XIII; its numbering is retained for ease of reference.
16. See §§ XIII–XIV in Vorstius, *Epitome exegeseos apologeticae* (Steinfurt: T. Caesar, 1611), sigs. B1 recto–B2 recto.
17. Wittich, *Theologia pacifica* (1671), 152–53.

he mention any arguments by which he might be brought to assert that they could not have existed before the world. Yet since he does not expressly declare that angels could have existed before the world, and since he does declare that they do not exist from eternity, we will not harass his opinion with more arguments, though you may also consider our *Gangrene of the Cartesian Innovations* (sect. 2, ch. 22).[18]

What do the Reformed say?

The Reformed state that whatever existed before the world has existed from eternity. For with the Reformed, (1) Scripture states the same thing, for to it, existing before the world is a perpetual periphrasis for eternity. This is so in our text (Ps. 90:2): what Moses says at first, "before the mountains were brought forth, before you had produced the earth and the world," he explains in terms of eternity, "from eternity to eternity, you are God," ומעולם עד עולם אתה אל. A second passage that applies here is Micah 5:2, where it is said about the Messiah that his coming forth (that is, the coming forth of the person of the Son through eternal generation from the Father, about which Psalm 2:7 also speaks) was מקדם, "from of old," that is, before the creation of the world. And how does it explain this? מימי עולם, "From the days of eternity." For this reason קדם, "of old," when it is used in reference to God, designates his eternity (Deut. 33:27), or at least in this passage, it signifies the eternity of the Messiah, as is evident by comparing other passages (Prov. 8:22–24, 30–31; John 1:1). One may advance a third passage, John 17:5. In it, what does the phrase "before the foundations of the world were laid" mean, or what could it mean, other than eternity (see also 1 Peter 1:20; Eph. 1:4ff.)? Also with the Reformed, (2) nature or right reason states the same thing, for to it, what exists before the world also exists before time, since time was created with the world, and what exists before the world cannot but exist in eternity or from eternity.

An objection

Vorstius together with the Arians do not have anything to allege to the contrary other than the fact that God can do that which does not imply a contradiction, and moreover, that for a creature to exist before the world does not imply a contradiction, and accordingly, that God can produce such a creature. To this I respond, It does indeed imply a contradiction for a creature to exist and yet not to exist in time, since a creature which does not exist in time, exists never, and what exists never, does not exist, just as what exists nowhere or no place, does not exist at all.

18. Mastricht, *Gangraena*, 396–403.

The Practical Part

The eternity of God: 1. Rouses us to the celebration of God.

XV. The eternity of God rouses us first, as the text teaches us, to the celebration of God, and to gratitude (Ps. 93:2; 102:12, 24, 26–27; 1 Chron. 16:36; 1 Tim. 1:17), that (1) in himself God is eternal, alone eternal, and eternal in all his perfections—wisdom, goodness, righteousness—and thus that he not only is so, but will be so eternally, according to his name in Exodus 3:14, "I will be who I will be." (2) He made us to be eternal in our own way, with respect to our soul (Matt. 10:28), and immortal, with respect to our whole person, unless we sinned (Gen. 2:17; Rom. 6:23). (3) He predestined us for eternal blessedness (1 Peter 1:4); and he did so (4) from all eternity past (Eph. 1:4), and thus immutably, since in eternity there is no variation or change; and he did so also (5) by an eternal covenant (2 Sam. 23:5; Ps. 111:9; Hos. 2:19). Let us acknowledge all this with a grateful mind, let us preach it with a willing mouth, and let us imitate it with a constant and eternal purpose (Ps. 119:106; 103:18; 139:24).

2. It shows us the vanity of all things.

XVI. Second, it shows to us the vanity and natural fragility of ourselves and of all things that are distinct from God, as in Psalm 90:2–12, with which the apostle's words in Hebrews 1:11, part of his quotation from Psalm 102:25–27, agree. Indeed, though such things lasted for a thousand years, even so, in respect to eternity they would not last but one day, indeed less than one day, because between a thousand years and one day there is at least some sort of proportion, whereas between a thousand years and eternity there is no proportion. Indeed, even speaking absolutely, without respect to eternity, however long such things might endure, because they endure by succession and flux, they last but for a moment, since what is past has ceased to exist and what is future has not yet begun to exist, and what remains present is not but a moment. Thus the apostle rightly speaks of "this light momentary affliction" (2 Cor. 4:17). From all this it is apparent how vain and foolish it is to promise ourselves anything constant and unchangeable from any created things—riches, honors, pleasures, indeed even our own life (1 Tim. 6:17)—or to fix our heart on them as if they were lasting, and on the other hand, how prudent it is to drag our affections away from transient things and to bind them to God alone, who through his eternity has neither end nor succession, and thus is always the same, that he alone may be for us as a habitation from generation to generation, after the example of the patriarchs (Heb. 11:9–10; Ps. 39:12).

3. It offers solace in the face of all evils.

XVII. Third, it offers sure solace to the soul (1) in the face of the terrors of sin, when it accuses us of being exiles from eternal life and liable to eternal death. When this happens, what will more effectively lift up our soul than to remind it, "But the mercy of God abides into eternity" (Ps. 103:17; 117:2)? (2) In the face of spiritual desertions, doubts about the love and mercy of God (Ps. 77:7–9), what will succor us more effectively than to think, "For a small moment I have forsaken you, but with great mercies I will gather you. In a moment of wrath, I hid my face from you for a moment, but in eternal mercy I have pitied you" (Isa. 54:7–8)? And also, what more than Isaiah 40:27–28? What more than to set our hope in the eternal God, whose mercy is eternal (Ps. 117:2), who keeps the truth given in his promises forever (Ps. 146:6)? For this reason, if the mountains be moved, if the hills give way, God's mercy will not depart from us, and his covenant of peace will not be moved (Isa. 54:10). (3) In the face of all calamities, what will be more powerful for us to think than that these afflictions are momentary and that they "are working for us an eternal weight of glory beyond all comparison" (2 Cor. 4:17), and that God presides over all these things as King to eternity (Ps. 10:16)? And indeed, (4) in the face of the terrors of death, what will be a sweeter subject for our meditation than the fact that God is eternal (Ps. 102:11–12; Hab. 1:12) and that he will substitute for our death eternal life, indeed that temporal death will open for us the way to eternal life (John 5:24)?

4. It draws us back from sins.

XVIII. Fourth, it most effectively draws us back from sin to think that (1) the offended God will be present to sinners as a most just, most strict judge and avenger, and that eternally (Ex. 20:5). And therefore also that (2) the sinner who offends him will exist eternally (Dan. 12:2). And that (3) the very offense that sinners give, together with their guilt, without a redeemer, will also exist eternally (Matt. 5:25–26). Furthermore, (4) their prison, Gehenna, will be eternal too (2 Peter 2:4; Jude 6), and in it (5) the fire will be eternal (Matt. 25:41; Jude 7), flowing from the breath of the Lord, the eternal judge, like a torrent of burning brimstone, and its smoke will not be extinguished (Isa. 30:27–28; 34:8–10; 66:24). In addition, (6) the punishment of loss, the privation of the highest and infinite good, will be eternal (2 Thess. 1:9; Matt. 25:41). Likewise (7) the punishment of sense will be an eternal torment (Matt. 25:46), the worm that gnaws eternally (Isa. 66:24). And all this on account of a temporary— indeed, a momentary—enjoyment of sin (Heb. 11:25; cf. 1 Sam. 14:43). Surely all these things should inflame us (1) to sorrow seriously over our past sins (Ps. 51:4); (2) to seek their remedy in him who has obtained eternal redemption

(Heb. 9:12); and (3) to send our future sins a bill of eternal divorce (Ps. 80:18). Consider also Drexel, *Reflections on Eternity* (reflection 2, §1).[19]

5. *It invites us to a zeal for eternal blessedness.*

XIX. Finally, fifth, the eternity of God most sweetly summons us to believe, to strive, and to live for eternity, as the apostle teaches in 2 Corinthians 4:18: "Looking not to the things that are seen, for the things that are seen are transient, but the things that are not seen are eternal." In saying *believe* I mean that we should believe both that God is eternal, together with all his attributes—his goodness, his mercy, his righteousness—and that we, whether we are good or evil, will be, in our body and soul, eternal, and that life, as well as death, will last eternally. If we believe these and similar things firmly and frankly, how much throughout our whole life will they move our affections to piety, to flight from evil, and to zeal for good! Furthermore, let us also be zealous for eternity, that is, daily let us spend even a quarter of one small hour contemplating it, not only that we may succeed, with help from so many explanatory pictures and similar things given to us, first by the Fathers, then even by the pagans themselves, in sketching its nature in our mind (a practice Drexel mentions in *On Eternity*), but also that we might feel its *moment*, whether for salvation or for destruction, in our heart (2 Cor. 4:17). Finally, let us also live for eternity, that is, let us think on eternity and on those things that are eternal, not momentary, not earthly (Phil. 3:19), let us speak about eternity and eternal things (1 Thess. 4:17–18), let us strive for eternal blessedness, "looking" to it (2 Cor. 4:18), let us work for eternity (John 6:27), let us suffer for eternity (2 Cor. 4:17; Rom. 8:18), let us pray for eternity (Matt. 6:13).

---

19. Jeremias Drexel, S. J. (1581–1683), *De aeternitate considerationes* (Munich: Raphael Sadeler, 1621), 40; idem, *The considerations of Drexelius upon eternitie*, trans. R. Winterton (Cambridge: Roger Daniel, 1666), 36–37.

CHAPTER TWELVE

The Life and Immortality of God

Just as the Father has life in himself, so he has
granted the Son to have life in himself.
—John 5:26

The contemplation of the life of God

I. We have considered, among the divine attributes, those that represent to us what God is, that is, the attributes that are included in his description, that he is Spirit from himself. We have likewise considered those that represent how great God is, that in number, he is one; in greatness, infinite; in presence, immense or omnipresent; in duration, eternal. It remains that we should pass to those attributes that represent what qualities God has, namely those attributes by which he is conceived by us to work. And we will see them under two types: first his life, his intellect, and so forth, then those that arise from these first attributes: his all-sufficiency, majesty, and blessedness. We will begin with the first attributes, and in these first attributes we will begin with God's life, the most general attribute of this order, which the Savior explains to us in John 5:26.

The Exegetical Part

It is constructed upon the exegesis of the text.

II. The text contains a comparison between the life of the Father and the life of the Son, and in this comparison, the former communicates and the latter has been communicated. Therefore since two things are being compared, we see two subjects for consideration:

    A. The Father's life, which communicates: "Just as the Father has life in himself." The most learned Lightfoot judges that in these words is a periphrasis of the name *Jehovah*, which signifies both that he has being in himself and that he gives being to every creature, so that the sense of the passage is this: just as the Father is Jehovah, he gives the same name to the Son. Perhaps this judgment has more wit than substance. On this point there are three things worth considering more distinctly:

1. He who lives, the Father: "Just as the Father." This indicates that, just as in earthly matters, a father communicates life to his son, a life that is the same in kind, so also in divine matters, the Father communicates to the Son a life that is the same in number. This act of communication belongs to the Father, and indeed to him alone. For although both the Son and the Holy Spirit, because they are God, have life, indeed both life from themselves and that same life together with the Father, even so, the Son does not communicate that same life to the Father, nor does the Holy Spirit communicate it to the Son or to the Father.

2. His life, that is, his essence as we conceive it to be active in itself. As we proceed, we will say more on this subject.

3. His life-giving, or his possession of life: "the Father has." It does not say he "receives" life that has been communicated from another person (the Son or the Holy Spirit), in the same way as the Son and the Holy Spirit have that life. The Father has it, not only as God, just as the other divine persons also have it, but also as the first person, and thus in a manner that the rest of the persons do not have it, that is, from himself.

4. He who gives life, or who is the origin of life: "in himself." This means either "in his own essence," inasmuch as God fully coincides with his essence, except that our intellect conceives of that essence by means of its activity and by this conception distinguishes for itself God's essence from God's life; or it means "from himself," that is, independently in all ways. This phrase certainly does not speak positively, as if God had produced this life for himself though it previously did not belong to him. For in this way, he would have lived and not lived at the same time. Rather, it speaks only negatively, insofar as God's life comes neither from any other essence, a fact common to all the divine persons, nor from another person, a fact proper to him as the first person, as we have said.

B. The Son's life, which has been communicated: "so he has granted the Son to have life in himself." Here four things stand out:

1. The giving: "he has granted." That is, certainly not by grace, in the way that God gives life by grace to all living creatures, but rather, by

eternal generation, about which Psalm 2:7 speaks. He has granted him life, that is, a life the same in number with his own. For he could not be the Son without this communication of essence and life, whatever the modern Rationalists may think to the contrary. Thus also for this reason, the Son is also rightly called *autotheos*, God from himself, that is, with respect to his essence, although not with respect to his subsistence or personality.

2. The one to whom it is given, the Son: "he has granted the Son." "Son" here means not one who before this giving was already the Son, but one who by this communication of essence and life became the Son, so to speak. For as by his essential aseity, he is God, so by this giving or communication, he is the Son.

3. The gift: "life." This is not so much the life he obtained by his death (John 10:11), which is spiritual life for his people (Col. 3:4), the life by which they live, that is, by faith in the Son of God, by which the Son of God lives in them (Gal. 2:20), a life that is also eternal (John 3:16), such that anyone who believes in him has eternal life. Yet, I do not deny that he did indeed receive omnimodal life, so that he might communicate it, together with all other things, to his own. Thus Psalm 68:18 says, "you received gifts for men,"[1] that is, in order to communicate those gifts to them. For this reason it is said that he became for us wisdom, righteousness, sanctification, and redemption (1 Cor. 1:30). Nevertheless, the word *life* in this passage is not intended in that way. Rather, it means the life which the Father has in himself, given that the Son might have it in himself, about which we will now speak.

4. The manner of giving: "to have it in himself." This either means "in himself," that is, not in another, as is the case with us believers, who have our life in Christ ("You are in Christ, who has been made for us righteousness…," 1 Cor. 1:30); or it means "from himself," just as God has life and all things from himself, though we understand also that insofar as Christ is a divine person, he has life communicated to him from the Father, as we have heard.

---

1. לקחתה מתנות באדם

FIRST THEOREM—The Life of God

The Dogmatic Part

God lives, and is the source of all life.

III. From these things, we have every right to say not only that God lives, but also that he lives preeminently, and in addition, that he is the source of all life, for he is the one who communicates life, not only to the Son through generation, but also to all living things through grace. For this reason, he is called "the living God" throughout the sacred page (Deut. 5:26; 32:40; Isa. 37:17; Dan. 4:34; Josh. 3:10; Ps. 42:2; 84:2; Jer. 2:13; 5:2; Matt. 16:16; Acts 14:15). Indeed, he is also called life (1 John 5:20; Col. 3:4), and the fountain of life (Ps. 36:9; Jer. 2:13), for he is the one in whom we live, move, and have our being (Acts 17:28). For this reason, he distinguishes himself from idols by his life (Jer. 10:10; Acts 14:14–15). Thus the Greeks call God Ζῆν, because he is "living" par excellence, just as ὄν, "being," is from the verb εἶναι "to be."[2] And this is also why God, in many passages, often swore by his life (Zeph. 2:9; Jer. 46:18; Isa. 49:18; Deut. 32:40; and fourteen times in Ezekiel[3]), and the saints also, following God's example (Jer. 5:2; 12:16).

Life is attributed to each divine person specifically.

IV. And not only is life attributed to God, but also hypostatically, to each person individually: to the Father (John 5:26); to the Son (John 5:26; Job 19:25; John 14:19), and that indeed through the Father (John 6:57), and thus he is called the Prince of life (Acts 3:15), for he is the one in whom is life (John 1:4), and who is also our life (Col. 3:4), and who rejoices in life that is indestructible, that is, eternal (Heb. 7:16), such that by it he lives forever and ever (Rev. 1:8); and also to the Holy Spirit (Rom. 8:2; 2 Cor. 3:3).

It is proven that life belongs to God.

V. Moreover, life cannot but belong to God: (1) because without doubt it is a perfection that does not involve any imperfection, which is why everything that lives is reckoned to be more perfect than that which does not. (2) Because by his own essence, he is most active: he knows, wills, works, decrees, and does all this entirely from himself. (3) Because he is the source and spring of life for all living things (Ps. 36:9). (4) Because if he did not live, all the rest of his attributes, and

---

2. Mastricht takes this alternate name for Zeus to be a participle of the verb ζῆν, "to live." See also below, §X.

3. The oath "as I live" in fact occurs sixteen times in Ezekiel: 5:11; 14:16, 18, 20; 16:48; 17:16, 19; 18:3; 20:3, 31, 33; 33:11, 27; 34:8; 35:6, 11.

even he himself, would be in vain, and thus he would not differ from an idol, since all God's remaining attributes are active by his life.

What is life, and how many types of it are there?
VI. Furthermore, those things are called living that act of themselves, not that are actuated by something else, and we consider this definition either in light of secondary causes only, which is the sense in which life belongs to the creatures, or in light of the prime mover of every cause, which is the way God lives. Among creatures, or at least material creatures such as human beings, all life comes from some sort of composition: natural life comes from the conjunction of the soul with the body, and when this is taken away, every operating faculty ceases to operate naturally; spiritual life comes from the conjunction of original righteousness with the soul, and when this ceases, it is unable to operate spiritually; and eternal life comes from the perfect union of the soul with God as our highest good, and when this is absent, it is unable to enjoy God, to exult in God. Furthermore, among the creatures, life is enumerated in four types. There is vegetative life, which looks to the acquiring and preserving of the full strength of nature as well as to the propagating of the species. There is sensitive life, in which living things distinguish what is profitable from what is harmful, that they might choose the one and reject the other. Both of these types of life involve much imperfection, and thus they cannot belong to God. There is rational life, in which a living being by free choice determines itself to act, and this life belongs to angels and rational souls. And there is life that is mixed, combining either the first two types, which is evident in animals, or all three, which exists in human beings.

What sort of life belongs to God?
VII. So then for God, inasmuch as he is the most perfect being, nothing can be fitting but the most perfect type of life, that is, rational life, in which his intellect and will are understood to be active. This life is in fact nothing but his essence insofar as it understands, wills, and performs works—first internal works, then external. That is to say, this life is the essence of God insofar as it is conceived by us as simply active from itself.

How do the life of God and the life of the creatures differ?
VIII. Although between God and rational creatures there is life that is held in common, and although this is so not just in name, for if it were, then we could not be led through the life of the creatures to the life of the Creator, even so, this does not mean that in reality these two do not stand as far apart as earth and heaven, indeed, as far apart as the finite and the infinite. This is true particularly in the

following points: whereas (1) creatures are only living beings, God is life itself
(1 John 5:20), or what is the same thing, whereas creatures have a life different
from their essence, and a life that is a faculty of their essence, God rejoices in a
life that entirely coincides with his essence. (2) Creatures live their life dependently, for it has been communicated to them by God, who is the source of life
(Ps. 36:9; Acts 17:28); God has life in himself. For this reason, whereas (3) creatures possess life that comes from another, God possesses his own life. (4) The
life of creatures is finite either from both directions, from head to toe, or from
head only, and thus at some point they did not have life, and at some point some
of them will not have it; God rejoices in a life that is infinite, immortal, and eternal, and thus when we say that he has life, we always speak in the present tense.
(5) The life of the creatures slips by in continual motion, succession, and flux; to
God belongs "the possession, at once whole and perfect, of boundless life."[4]

How does it agree with the life of creatures and differ
from the thought of God?

IX. Because of this, it is clear that the life of God differs not only from the life
of creatures but also from his own thought, intellect, and will. That is to say,
(1) life, according to its basic idea, is nothing but active force, or, if I may speak in
a barbarism, *actuative* force, and in this sense, life is common to God and to living creatures, though to each in its own way. But (2) because this actuative force
requires an object to be actuated, namely, a faculty, whether this faculty is vegetative, and thus we speak of vegetative life, or sensitive, and thus of sensitive life, or
rational, and thus of rational life, it remains true that although thought, intellect,
and will are, with respect to God, entirely one and the same thing as his life, in
the identical sense (as they say), yet in our reason, that is, in the formal sense,
we conceive that life stands apart from these faculties as that which actuates
from that which is actuated, since we conceive that it is through his life that God
thinks, knows, and wills in actuality. But (3) because of the fact that, according to
whether the faculty that is to be actuated by life is more or less noble, the life that
actuates it is itself required to be more or less noble, by which fact sensitive life is
said to be more noble than vegetative life, and rational life more noble than either
of those prior two, it remains true that, because the faculties of thinking, knowing, and willing in God, and the same faculties in his creatures, differ in infinite
ways, there is also an infinite distance between the life of God and the life of his

---

4. Quoted from Boethius, *Consolation of Philosophy*, bk. 5, prose §6, as above in 1.2.11 §VI,
and below in this chapter, §XX.

creatures. Accordingly, life is said to be common to them, neither equivocally (as they say) nor univocally, but rather, analogically.

The Elenctic Part

It is asked: 1. Is there a god, or ought anything be held to be a god, that does not live a rational life? The difference of opinions

X. Compared to his other attributes, God's life is not as exposed to the darts of enemies. Nevertheless, it is asked, first, whether there is a god, or whether anything ought to be held to be a god, that does not live a rational life. The pagans, at least those that were wiser—for example, Socrates, Plato, Cicero—whenever they spoke seriously (which they did not usually do in their conversation), allowed only one god to be God. That god was a god who lived rationally, and they designated him as Ζῆν, "living,"[5] that is, living preeminently. But the common people of the pagans, and all the philosophers who followed the wisdom of the common people, had gods who neither lived nor lived rationally. The first idolaters, those of the East, had gods that were lifeless and irrational,[6] the heavenly bodies—the sun, the moon, and so forth—which various regions designated by various names, for example, Bel, Moloch, and so forth. They had gods of stone, wood, gold, and so forth, in their statues and images. They had gods blessed with vegetative life alone, such as trees, garlic, onions. They also had gods who were in some measure nobler, gods bearing sensitive life, such as, among others, Apis.[7] They had their noblest gods, who for a brief period of time were endowed also with rational life, that is, men illustrious either for kindness or for brutality. Such were the gods of the West and of the Greeks. All these are compelled to affirm that what did not live rationally could be a god. The living God sharply ridicules these gods (Jer. 10:3; 16:23; 44:6–21; 46:5–7; Ps. 105:5–6) and so do the pagans themselves, at least those who were a bit more prudent, for example, Juvenal in his *Satires*, 15: "It is a sin to violate or break the leek and onion with a bite: oh how holy are the nations in whose gardens such gods are born!"[8]

The opinion of the Reformed

The Reformed, though they do not deny that magistrates, on account of a certain communication of divine power, are now and then called gods (e.g. Ps. 82:1, 6), nevertheless do not allow anything to be called God truly and properly if it does

---

5. See note above in §III.
6. ἀζώους καὶ ἀλόγους
7. An Egyptian God in the form of an ox.
8. Cf. 1.2.2 §XIII.

not live rationally. We have set forth their reasons in §V. The more ignorant pagans cannot make the case for their lifeless gods by arguments and reasons.

2. Do not those who with religious worship venerate creatures that are devoid of life have gods who are not living? The opinion of the papists is explained.

XI. It is asked, second, whether those who venerate lifeless things with religious worship do not have lifeless gods, or at least, whether we should not call them lifeless. The pagans, whom we just now considered, at least acknowledge and profess that those lifeless things that they religiously venerate are gods. The papists have various lifeless things that they honor with religious worship, and that in various degrees. They have their images and statues—of God, the holy Trinity, the blessed Virgin, and the departed saints—as well as their relics—little parts of the body of Christ, of the virgin mother of God, of the departed saints, or of garments or other things that in some way or another touched the body of Christ—all of them lifeless. They have above all, in the Mass, their god of bread, which is lifeless. And indeed they teach that images should be venerated with the same kind of religious worship with which they venerate the prototypes, and so likewise for relics. In the same way they also honor the images of God, Christ, and the Trinity with the same worship of *latria* with which they honor God and the Trinity himself. In the same way they also venerate the images of the departed saints and their relics with the same worship of *dulia* with which they venerate those holy saints themselves, and the host, as they call it, which is to them Christ the God-man himself, transformed from bread, with the same *latria* they render to Christ in heaven. Concerning these things, since they are all devoid of life, it is now asked whether indeed they have gods devoid of life, or at least whether we should say they do. The Romanists deny that they do; the Reformed affirm that they do, chiefly by the following reasons, and those like them.

The thought of the Reformed, with their reasons
(1) Scripture pronounces that every form of idolatry, that is, of perverse religious worship, is the making of other gods (Ex. 20:3–5), and consequently, that he who bows downs before lifeless things, who worships lifeless things, makes lifeless things his gods. (2) Religious worship, the sort that adoration offers, rests upon the preeminence of deity alone: "I am Jehovah...I will not give my glory to another, nor my praise to graven images" (Isa. 42:8). Here, the glory of God and his praise is built upon his deity, by which he is called *Jehovah*, and consequently, whoever refers the glory of God and his praise (which is without doubt part of religious worship) to lifeless things has lifeless things for gods. (3) The Savior in Matthew 4:10 binds the religious worship of adoration to God alone, and

consequently, if anyone extends the same thing to those things which lack life, he has lifeless things as gods. Finally, (4) all worship is divided into civil worship and religious worship in such a way that religious worship is given to an object as it is reckoned to be a god, and thus religious worship, if it is given to lifeless things, is given as to gods.

The evasions of the papists

The Romanists do not have any arguments that might help them evade this charge, except these two: (1) they allege that not all religious worship is given as to God: not *dulia* or *hyperdulia*, but only *latria*. I respond: (a) Laboriously demonstrating the vanity of this distinction is not our task in this place, but (b) even if we granted those distinctions that we do not concede, *latria* itself is extended by the papists to lifeless things, to images of God, of the Trinity, of Christ, as well as to bread in the Eucharist. (2) They allege that this religious worship of theirs does not terminate on the images, but passes through and stops at their prototypes, and thus, they are not so much adoring these lifeless things, but rather, the God who is signified by them. I respond: (a) The pagans could also allege the same thing in the adoration of their own images, for they were convinced that their gods dwelt in heaven and not among men (Dan. 2:11). Next, (b) that honor, passing through the representative to the one represented, at the least touches that representative, even if it does not stop there.

3. Does the life of God not differ from his intellect and will?

The opinions of various factions

XII. It is asked, third, whether the life of God does not differ from his intellect and will. Vorstius and the Socinians, that they might more conveniently have a God who is composite and finite, who does not exist except in heaven, who for that reason could not have been united to Christ because Christ existed only on the earth, and, at last, that they might have a Christ, or rather, that in Christ they might have a God, who is nothing but a mere man,[9] state that life, intellect, and will in God himself differ as so many separate things. On the contrary, the Cartesians conclude that God's life does not differ from his intellect and will because for them God is nothing but mere thought, in which there is nothing but intellect and will, which are so many attributes.

---

9. ψιλὸς ἄνθρωπος

The opinion of the Reformed
The Reformed pursue the middle course: they do not grant that in God life, intellect, and will differ as so many separate things. They do grant that God is a single most pure and most simple act, and thus that his life, intellect, and will, are, at least on God's part, entirely one and the same thing, that they are one and the same most simple essence, but that on the part of our mind, his life, intellect, and will differ, for while we are thinking about God's life, we are not thinking about his intellect or his will, and vice versa. And this distinguishing thought has its reason for distinguishing in the things to be distinguished,[10] for it conceives of intellect and will as faculties in God, and life as that actuative force by which those faculties are actuated, just as we briefly represented in §IX, and with greater abundance in our *Gangrene of the Cartesian Innovations* (sect. 2, ch. 8, §2).[11]

The reasons of the Reformed
Our reasons are: (1) in what we have already said. (2) That Scripture constantly distinguishes between God's life, intellect, and will, since in God's oaths, God says these words (or words like them): "As I live" (Isa. 49:18; Jer. 22:24; Ezek. 5:11; Hos. 4:15; etc.). He does not say, "as I understand" or "as I will" or "as I think," which would be the case if God's life, intellect, and will meant one and the same thing. (3) If God's life and his intellect and will, or his thought, are the same thing, such that God's living is nothing but his thinking, then one or the other of the following conclusions will have to be admitted: either the act by which God delights in himself according to his infinite blessedness, and likewise the act by which he can and does work all things, and even the act by which the Father begets the Son, and, with the Son by spiration sends the Holy Spirit, do not pertain to the life of God, or, if they do pertain to it, then all those acts are nothing else than thinking. Which of these two is more absurd, I surely do not know. At the least, (4) there is no obstacle at all to the idea that life is different from intellect and will, or thought, just as according to the Cartesian hypotheses, in thought itself, the intellect and will are different.

Objections
The foundation of the Cartesian opinion rests on these two things: (1) That God is nothing but thought. I respond: (a) We have already vanquished this idea more than once with the proofs we adduced, especially in this book, chapter 3, §XIX. (b) Just as in thought, the Cartesians distinguish the intellect

---

10. *distinguendi rationem habet in rebus distinguendis*
11. Mastricht, *Gangraena*, 243–44.

and the will, and thus from these two admit that there are two attributes of God, and two only, that are, properly speaking, divine, why then is it not permitted for us likewise to distinguish between life and intellect and will in God? (2) That God is a single most simple and most pure act, and from this fact, his life cannot be distinguished from his intellect and will. I respond: (a) Despite this fact, the Cartesians nevertheless distinguish between intellect and will in the one most simple divine thought, and indeed they distinguish them as two different attributes. (b) That same fact notwithstanding, the Cartesians themselves distinguish between, for example, the divine essence and divine reprobation, although these two from the perspective of God are one and the same thing. Therefore it must be said that (c) God's life and his intellect and will are one and the same, in the identical sense (as the Scholastics say—barbarously for sure, but meaningfully),[12] since all that is in God is God himself, and the essence of God. But this is not so, however, in the formal sense, the sense in which I conceive of one divine perfection when I think of God's life and another when I apprehend his intellect and will. If this were less than true, you would have to say with equal confidence that the life of God is the same as his righteousness, his decree, his creation, his providence, his reprobation, and so forth, since all these things together denote one and the same thing in God.

4. Does the life of God agree with the lives of his creatures in any other way than in name only? The opinions of each side are explained.

XIII. It is asked, fourth, whether the life of God agrees with the lives of his creatures—of plants, of animals, of man and angels—in any other way than in name only. The Cartesians, because they state that the life of God is entirely the same thing as his intellect and will, or as his thought, and that these are the same thing as his very essence, which is nothing but a single and most simple act of thinking, judge that there is nothing in which these two types of life agree, other than in their name alone. The Reformed enumerate three possible types of agreement between things. First is univocal agreement, in which the matter signified by one name applies truly and properly to two things. The Reformed by no means acknowledge this sort of agreement between the life of God and that of his creatures, because the life of God is infinite, whereas the life of all of his creatures is finite, and the infinite stands infinitely far apart from the finite, and thus agrees with it univocally in nothing. Next is equivocal agreement, when one thing agrees with another with respect to its name alone. Last is analogical

---

12. Mastricht is speaking "barbarously" because *identicus,* "identical," is not a classical Latin word.

agreement, when the matter signified by a name belongs first, or principally, and that in its own proper way, only to one thing, and yet it also is, through some sort of analogy, common to other things. In this way, to be an *animal* is common univocally, or in an equal sense, to a man and to a beast; to be called *cancer*, "crab," is common equivocally to a shoreline animal, to a constellation of stars, and to a feminine disease;[13] and the term *health* applies analogically to an animal, to air, to food, or to medicine, in such a way that what the term signifies applies principally and in a proper way to the animal alone, and to the other things only according to how they are related to the animal, insofar as they serve that animal in nourishing, preserving, and restoring its health.

The Reformed also acknowledge a manifold distinction between the life of God and the life of his creatures, for example, that (1) the force of actuating the faculties, in which life consists, in God is entirely one and the same with the faculties to be actuated, though in the creatures it is actually different from those faculties. (2) The faculties to be actuated, the intellect and the will, are in God one and the same thing, whereas in the creatures, they differ. (3) In living creatures, faculties are constituted in potency and are in fact actuated by their life, whereas in God, faculties are never in potency, but always in act through his life. (4) Through life, creatures do indeed act from themselves, but in respect to secondary causes only, whereas God through his life acts simply from himself. Furthermore, to the Reformed, life is nothing but that force through which a living being works from itself, or that force through which the faculties of a living being are actuated, and thus when this force is absent, the being is dead. When this force of life actuates the faculty of growing, it is called vegetative. When it actuates the locomotive and sensitive faculties, it is called sensitive. When it actuates the rational faculties, the intellect and the will, it is called rational.

Furthermore, from these truths, the Reformed conclude three things. (1) The force of actuating, which is called life, and the faculties to be actuated by it, are conceived of as different things. (2) Nevertheless, this force of actuating is, in the idea, common to all living things. But (3) the more perfect and noble the faculties to be actuated are, an accordingly more noble and perfect actuative force is required, because due proportion is always required between a work to be produced and the force that is to produce it. Thus sensitive life is more perfect than vegetative life, and rational life is more perfect than both, and the life of God is most perfect, indeed, infinitely perfect.

---

13. Mastricht may be referring to a discussion of a particular form of feminine cancer that Pliny asserts can be cured with the application of a paste made of a female crab, Pliny, *Nat. Hist.*, 32.46.

Given these things that are as it were clear in themselves, the following are easily perceived: (1) the fact that, and the manner in which, God's life, intellect, and will are conceived to differ. Namely, his life is understood to be the foundation,[14] both of these and of all the divine operations, all of which, though they are on God's part or in the identical sense (as they say), one most simple and most pure act, they are even so, in the formal sense, on our part, different, because we think one thing when we conceive of God's life, and another when we conceive of his intellect and will. (2) Because the intellect and will of God, faculties that are as it were to be actuated by his life, are of infinite perfection, and thus stand infinitely far apart from all the faculties of all living beings, so also the life of God is of infinite perfection. But at the same time, with respect to its actuation simply considered, God's life agrees with all living beings, certainly not univocally or equivocally, but rather, analogically. Finally, to these things, (3) this also must be added: because living is operating by oneself, unmoved by another, living cannot apply to creatures, except only in a secondary and dependent manner, insofar as they operate by themselves, unmoved by others, only in respect to second causes. Rather, living applies to God alone par excellence, because he operates by himself, simply and independently. On these matters we needed to spend more time than usual because they bear very greatly upon not only the determination of the question, but also upon our understanding of the divine life in a more lucid way. Therefore the Reformed commonly deny that the life of God and of the creatures agree in almost nothing but their name only.

The reasons of the Reformed

They deny this because (1) in this way, through the life of the creatures we could in no way be led to the knowledge of the divine life. And thus (2) the life of God would be nothing to us but an idle phrase, offering us in practice no profit at all. (3) We should allow the same agreement between the life of God and the life of his creatures as we allow between the intellect of God and of his creatures. (4) We observe that the force of actuating is common to God and to his creatures, each in their own way, as has been said. And this is so, finally, just as (5) to the Cartesians themselves, thought, in which by their own hypothesis God's very essence and even his life consists, is common to God and created spirits, according to the comment of the famous Wittich in his *Peaceable Theology*, §122: "Every mind, whether angelic or divine, is thought."[15]

---

14. *substratum*
15. Wittich, *Theologia pacifica* (1671), 90–91.

Objections

I do not see now what they could allege to the contrary, for if they should say:
(1) that God is pure thought; notwithstanding, that thought is common to God
and to created spirits—then why not also his life? Especially since the life of all
spirits consists in thought, at least according to them. Besides the fact that we
have demonstrated with solid reasons in another place that God, or any other
spirit, does not consist in thought alone.[16] If they should say (2) that God is a
most simple act; nevertheless this does not hinder us in any way from saying that
life is in its own way common to him, just as in the case of his thought, intellect,
and will. And (3) they cannot say that God is infinite spirit, for even so, this does
not hinder us in any way from saying that thought is common to him, and thus
also life. Besides the fact that to the Cartesians, the infinity of God consists in
nothing but this, that he thinks all things by a single act, which implies nothing
at all about life.

The Practical Part

From the life of God, we are furnished with: 1. An argument for glorification.

XIV. In practice, we are furnished from the life of God, first, with an argument
for the divine glory and glorification (Rev. 4:9; 1 Tim. 1:17; 6:16) because not
only is it true that (1) God has life, for life is the first and primary perfection,
and indeed the universal perfection of man (Job 2:4), since by its strength, all
his faculties, all his perfection, is actuated in such a way that without life, all his
perfection would be nothing (cf. Eccl. 9:4), indeed, it would also be an abomination, and in entirely the same way, the life of God also actuates all his other
perfections, such that all of them are nothing apart from his life. But it is also
true that (2) he is life itself (1 John 5:20), and thus he is nothing but the highest
possible degree of this perfection. Indeed, (3) this life is a life that is independent,
infinite, eternal, immutable, and so forth. Add also that (4) he is also the source
and spring of life for all things (Ps. 36:9), such that nothing has life without having it from his life. These are the reasons on account of which God himself so
often glories, so to speak, in his own life, as often as (1) he swears by his life (Jer.
46:18), (2) he distinguishes himself by his life and calls out all false gods as devoid
of life (Ps. 115:3–8). And not only God does this, but also (3) the saints as well
(Ps. 42:2), all the way to the inhabitants of heaven themselves (Rev. 4:9).

---

16. 1.2.3 §XIX

2. An argument for gratitude

XV. By the same token, second, we are therefore furnished with an argument for gratitude, since as God is the fountain of life, he shows himself to be the spring of all the life we have: natural life (Acts 17:28; Ps. 103:4), spiritual life (Eph. 2:4–6), and in the future, eternal life, and so to this end he gave his only begotten Son over to death (John 3:16). All this shapes us through gratitude that we might (1) acknowledge him with our mind (Ps. 103:1–4), (2) celebrate him with our mouth (Ps. 116:8, 12), and (3) render, by our work, our whole life to him from whom we receive it, rendering it for his glory by readily devoting to him, in particular, (a) our natural life (Phil. 1:20–21), (b) our spiritual life (Rom. 6:2; Gal. 2:19–20), and (c) our eternal life (Isa. 6:3).

3. An argument for rebuke

XVI. Third, we are furnished with an argument for rebuking all of the following: (1) those who not so much in their words as in their deeds, deal with God as if they considered him lifeless and senseless, a God who neither sees, nor hears, nor observes, nor understands, nor rewards or avenges whatever they do on the earth (Ps. 94:6–8; Ps. 10:4, 11). (2) Those who refuse to love, to seek, to fear, to revere, to call upon, to worship God, as if he were lifeless and could not bring to pass anything either good or evil (Lam. 3:38; Zeph. 1:12). (3) Those who, set amidst whatever difficulties, despair for their souls as if they did not believe that God in heaven is the one who lives, who sees and knows their lot, and who can bring them help. Such despair is contrary to the practice of Job (Job 19:25). Do not all these people in various ways pass over to the madness of the pagans, which was noted in the elenctic part, and also, much worse, do they not make for themselves, from the true God, an idol? And so then, what should they expect other than that the living God, in his vengeance, will prove to them that he is alive, according to the oft-repeated phrase of Ezekiel, "And they shall experience that I am Jehovah" (Ezek. 25:14; 35:9)?

4. An argument for consolation

XVII. Fourth, we are furnished with a foundation for solace, in whatever difficulties of all our life, that we have been persuaded that God our Redeemer lives (Job 19:25) and that he is the strength of all our life (Ps. 27:1). Namely in the difficulties (1) of natural life: if (a) disease threatens the end of life (Ps. 6:2, 5; John 11:25); if (b) poverty takes away the means of life, such that we say, "From where will bread be supplied?" (John 6:5; Matt. 6:25); if (c) an enemy lays traps for our life, seeking our soul (Ps. 7:2, 5; 35:4; 38:12; cf. 42:3); if (d) fear of death chokes us (Heb. 2:15), and (e) the horror of rotting (Ps. 16:10)—in these and

similar cases, what will be a more effective help than to think that even then our
God and Redeemer lives, indeed that he is life itself and the source of life, and as
he has given us our life, so also he can preserve it, whatever may strive against it,
even more, that when our life is lost he can restore it to us; to think that our Jesus
is the resurrection and the life (John 11:25), and he has become a life-giving
spirit (1 Cor. 15:45); to think that the Holy Spirit is the Spirit of life (Rom. 8:2)
and that if he is in us, he will also give life to our mortal bodies (Rom. 8:11)?
Again (2) in the difficulties of spiritual life, if we sense that we are dead in our
sins (Eph. 2:1), unfit for all operations of spiritual life, for our conversion, faith,
hope, and love, what then could more effectively raise us up than to think that
God has life in himself, that he has given that same life to the Son, that he gave
it to him that we might have life in him (1 John 4:9), indeed, that he is our life
(Col. 3:4), the way, the truth, and the life (John 14:6)? Finally, (3) in the difficulties of eternal life, when the fear of death (Heb. 2:15) presses upon this body of
death, such that we sigh, "Who will deliver me?" (Rom. 7:24), "What must I do
that I may have eternal life?" (Matt. 19:16), "What will we do, men and brothers?" (Acts 2:37), then what will more effectively raise us up than to think that:
(a) God is living (Ps. 42:2), and he is life and the source of life; and that (b) our
Redeemer lives, and he is our life, who was given by the Father for this reason,
that we may not perish, but have eternal life, indeed who died for this reason,
that we might live; and finally, that (c) the Holy Spirit is the Spirit of life, for he
gives us life (John 6:63)? What, I say, will more effectively raise us up in all such
difficulties? But it will only do so if we act in earnest (1) to know him, for this
eternal life (John 17:3), (2) to believe in him, for whoever believes will not perish
but will have eternal life (John 3:16), to receive him by believing (John 1:12), and
to do so for this purpose, (3) that we may be united with him as members with
the head, branches with the vine (John 15:4–6), that (4) planted together with
him we may become like him in his death and resurrection (Rom. 6:5), that (5)
we may follow the life-giving spirit (1 Cor. 15:45), and that (6) Jesus himself may
live in us (Gal. 2:20), and his life become manifested in us (2 Cor. 4:10), and in
this way, that (7) we ourselves may come to live for God (Rom. 6:11).

5. An argument for living for God

XVIII. Fifth, we are furnished by the life of God with a manifold argument for
living for God (Gal. 2:19), namely, (1) that our God lives, and in his life consists
the greatest perfection, and that our life consists in imitating him (Matt. 5:45).
(2) That he exists as the source and author of all our life, and therefore, it must
be rendered back to him (Rom. 11:36). (3) That our Redeemer has life in himself, that he is our life, indeed, that he died that we might live, not for ourselves,

but for him who died for us (2 Cor. 5:15; Rom. 14:7–9). (4) That the Holy Spirit is the Spirit of life, for his special work is to give life (John 6:63). But what, finally, is living for God? I respond, It is (1) living to the glory of God; (2) living according to the will of God (1 Peter 4:2, 6); (3) living by the strength of God, that is, that he might live in us (Gal. 2:19–20); (4) turning ourselves to the living God (Acts 14:15); (5) striving that you may be a living member of the body of Christ (1 Cor. 12:27); (6) a living stone (1 Peter 2:4–5); (7) equipped with living faith (James 2:17–18); (8) lively and active, not sluggish in the business of God (1 Thess. 1:9; Heb. 9:14). Compare what we considered on this matter above in book 1, chapter 1.[17]

SECOND THEOREM—The Immortality of God

The Dogmatic Part

It is proved that God is immortal: By the Scriptures

XIX. As in the case of creatures, the concomitant of life is death, so in the case of the Creator, it is immortality. And although God's immortality, in regard to the thing itself, coincides with his immutability and eternity, and thus is for the most part explained from those chapters, even so, in regard to the term, it denotes the immutability and eternity that are peculiar to his life. (1) The text asserts this immortality for him when it says not only that he "has life," in the present tense, that is, by always continuing to have life, but also that he has life "in himself," and thus, his life was not received from another, and it will not be taken away by another. Then (2) Scripture also asserts it elsewhere, when it calls him incorruptible and immortal, and indeed him alone (Rom. 1:23; 1 Tim. 1:17; 6:16). Likewise, (3) when in many places it attributes life to him, indeed, when it calls our Savior the true God and eternal life (1 John 5:20).

And by seven reasons

XX. Nor can he be anything but immortal: (1) who through his independence has life from himself, and consequently also preserves it from himself, and cannot be deprived of it by anything that is different from him. (2) Who through his simplicity is life itself, and consequently, if he were to die, he would be annihilated, for which purpose an infinite power, different from him who would be annihilated, would be required. (3) Who through his eternity obtains life without any succession at one and the same moment, that is, the one who, according

---

17. 1.1.1 §§LI–LVII

to Boethius, obtains "the possession, at once whole and perfect, of boundless life."[18] (4) Who through his immutability most greatly rejects the most great of all changes, death. For this reason he alone is said to have immortality (1 Tim. 6:16). Augustine most elegantly demonstrates this in book 2, chapter 12 of *Against Maximinus*: "In every changeable nature, the very fact of change means some measure of death, because it makes something in that nature not to be, something that beforehand was. And so the soul itself, which is called immortal on account of the fact that in some certain way, according to its mode, it never ceases living, has nonetheless, in that same mode of life, its certain kind of death, for if it lives in righteousness, then sins, it dies to righteousness, but if it is a sinner, then is made righteous, it dies to sin. Even the nature of heavenly creatures could have died, because it could have sinned. For even angels sinned, and those that did not sin, still could have sinned."[19] So then, the one who is entirely and altogether immutable is also immortal. (5) The one who through the highest perfection of his essence cannot be deprived of the perfection of life. (6) The one who through his omnipotence does not allow anyone to take away from him his life. Finally, (7) the one who through his blessedness cannot but enjoy himself, which is not so if he is without life. For this reason, in the Scriptures, to live and to be blessed are sometimes used as synonyms (Ezek. 37:14).

It is shown in what manner immortality belongs to God alone.
XXI. Indeed, because other things are also recognized either to have had immortality, as our first parents did, or to have it now, as angels and human souls do, or to have it in the future, as the blessed in heaven one day will, it could be asked, How is God alone said to have immortality (1 Tim. 6:16) and he alone to live (Deut. 32:40)? For a response, consider immortality to be of three kinds. The first kind of immortality is that which comes through the grace of another. It belongs to what in its own nature is mortal, and it is nothing more than a potential immortality, by which a living thing is able not to die. This kind belonged to our first parents, and it will be ours in glory. The second kind of immortality comes indeed through nature, a nature that is in its own simplicity indissoluble but that even so is able to be altered, corrupted, and annihilated through the Creator's absolute power, and thus is in some way mortal. This kind describes the mortality of the angels and of souls. The third kind of immortality comes through omnimodal independence and entirely lacks all change, corruption,

---

18. Quoted from Boethius, *Consolation of Philosophy*, bk. 5, prose §6, as above in 1.2.11 §VI, and above in this chapter, §IX.

19. Augustine, *Contra Maximinum Arianum* in PL 42:763.

annihilation, and death of any sort. And this at last is the immortality that belongs to God alone, on which account he is called incorruptible (Rom. 1:23; 1 Tim. 1:17).

The Elenctic Part

The Anthropomorphites, Vorstius, and the Socinians insult the immortality of God.
XXII. It seems that those who deny that God is immortal, have not, as far as I can tell, ever existed. For even the pagans themselves had nothing more frequently on their lips than the phrase, "the immortal gods." Yet there are those who state things that are terribly inconsistent with immortality: thus were the Anthropomorphites of old, who believed God had human parts, and thus are Vorstius and the Socinians, who believe that God is composed from parts, and likewise from subject and accidents. These men can never solidly defend the omnimodal immortality of God. For what is composed in any way is both dissoluble, and also to that extent mortal, or at least corruptible. Furthermore, those things that could apply to the defense of this theorem we dealt with just above under God's life, and they can be transferred here as needed.

The Practical Part

The immortality of God makes: 1. For God's glorification
XXIII. In practice, the immortality of God, makes first for the glory of God, as the apostle shows (Rom. 1:23; 1 Tim. 1:17; 6:16; Ps. 102:26–27), and as the heathen themselves prove, when on account of immortality they not only called God Ζῆν,[20] but also continuously boasted about their immortal gods. This practice coincides with the first practice of the preceding theorem.

2. For our humbling
XXIV. On the other hand, second, it makes for the humbling of ourselves, we who carry our breath in our nostrils (Isa. 2:22; Ps. 144:4), who are exposed to all kinds of death—natural, spiritual, and eternal—who can be deprived of life by the most trivial causes, by a fly or by a pinprick (as the histories teach us),[21]

---

20. See note above, §III.

21. Mastricht may be referring obliquely to the death of Pope Adrian IV. Upon his papal election, Nicholas Breakspear (c. 1100–1159) became Pope Adrian IV, or sometimes Pope Hadrian IV, and ruled from 1154–1159. Popular accounts of his death in the medieval and early modern periods report that he choked to death on a fly in his wine before he could excommunicate Emperor Frederick I Barbarossa. More recent scholarship concludes his death was due to a case of quinsy, that is, an inflammation of the tonsils also known as peritonsillar abscess.

who personally bring this mortality upon ourselves by our own recklessness. So then we all die, and like water, are poured out and spilled upon the ground (2 Sam. 14:14), and our days pass away like a shadow (Ps. 144:4). They run away, just like a rushing stream, just like a flower, which thrives in the morning, is plucked, and withers in the evening, according to Psalm 90:6, and Job 14:1: "Man who is born from a woman is short of days and full of wrath." Commenting on these words, Bernard of Clairvaux insightfully says, "Man is born for labor, not for honor. Man is born of woman, and on account of this, with guilt. He lives for a brief time, and thus, with angst. He lives filled up with many miseries, and therefore, with grief, and truly, many griefs, the griefs of body and of soul. For in these words of Job are sketched the brevity of our life, its fragility, its inconstancy, and its manifold misfortune" (*On Consideration*, bk. 2).[22] Indeed it helps us in this way to consider this mortality of ours, that by it (1) we may be humbled, for when by it we are compared with God we realize that we are but dust and ashes (Gen. 18:27); (2) we may never think upon a long-lived life (Ps. 39:4–5); (3) from the vanity of our life, we may deduce the vanity of all things, for they cannot be present for us more constantly than life itself (Ps. 39:4–5); (4) we may pant for eternity and immortality (2 Cor. 5:1, 4); and (5) we may seek it in the immortal God himself, so that if our flesh and our heart should fail, he may be the strength of our heart forever (Ps. 73:26).

3. For the consolation of the godly

XXV. Furthermore, third, it conveys to the godly, even in the horror of death, the sweetest solace, that they have God covenanted to them, the God who is immortal, who in his own image built us long ago for immortality, who by an eternal decree destined us to blessed immortality (Matt. 25:34), and though we had lost our inborn immortality by sin (Eph. 2:1), to restore us, delivered his Only Begotten over to death, that he might abolish death and bring life and immortality through the gospel (2 Tim. 1:10), the God who, in pledge of our future immortality, when we were dead in our offenses, made us alive together with Christ, and raised us up together, and set us together in the heavens in Christ Jesus (Eph. 2:5–6), who finally, when we have died naturally, will raise us up to blessed immortality, where what was sown in corruption will be raised in incorruption, and what was sown in weakness will be raised in power, and what was sown a natural body will be raised a spiritual body. For the corruptible must put on incorruption, and the mortal, immortality. And thus they may now triumph, "O death, where is your sting?" (1 Cor. 15:42–44, 53, 55). At the thought

---

22. Bernard of Clairvaux, *De consideratione ad Eugenium*, bk. 2, ch. 10, PL 182:753.

of this, David's heart greatly rejoiced and his tongue exulted (Ps. 16:9–11). And it is with such words that the apostle commands the Thessalonians to comfort one another (1 Thess. 4:18).

4. For zeal for blessed immortality

XXVI. Finally, fourth, the immortality of God entices us by its example to a zeal for immortality, and at the same time it shows us the source and means of pursuing it. The desire for immortality is inborn in all, the desire that they might not die (Gen. 42:2; Job 2:4), the desire that though dead they might yet live, either in seed and successors (Ps. 89:29, 36) or in name and fame (Gen. 12:2, 5; 2 Sam. 7:25), and the desire that they might be restored from death to life (Phil. 3:11). They strive for this immortality either by natural works, by the use of food, medicine, defenses, and the most studious avoidance of death, or by heroic works (2 Sam. 23:8–12), or by virtuous works such as wisdom, erudition, and so forth, or even by criminal and shameful works (Gen. 11:4), as when Herostratus burned the temple of Diana, or by religious works (Phil. 3:10–11). It was to this end that the immortal God conferred on us an immortal soul, and on the soul an appetite for immortality; indeed, in forming our first parents he made them immortal, and when we lost our immortality by apostasy, he restored it to us, even by the death of his only begotten Son, and now at last he has shown us the path of immortality in the gospel, an immortality that will be conferred at its proper time, at the last judgment.

The means of pursuing immortality

But finally, in what way will we acquire the immortality for which we long? I respond: (1) Its source and spring is God, who is alone immortal, and who is united to us by burning love and desire (Ps. 42:2; 73:25). (2) Its one and only means is the Savior Jesus, to whom the Father granted to have life in himself, that he would be the way, the truth, and the life (John 14:6), indeed life itself for his own (Col. 3:4). (3) The instruments for acquiring these things are (a) the knowledge of God and of the Mediator (John 17:3); (b) faith in both of them (John 14:1; 3:16); (c) a burning desire for blessed immortality (2 Cor. 5:2–4); (d) a good life,[23] and that in all things (Phil. 3:20–21); (e) a good death,[24] and that in faith (Rev. 14:13). And after all these things cannot but follow a blessed deathlessness[25] (Rev. 2:11; 3:5).

---

23. εὐζωΐα
24. εὐθανασία
25. ἀθανασία

CHAPTER THIRTEEN

The Intellect, Knowledge, and
Wisdom of God

*Oh, the depth of the riches both of the wisdom and knowledge of God! How
incomprehensible are his judgments, and his ways past finding out! For who
has known the mind of the Lord? Or who has been his counselor?*
                                                            —Romans 11:33–34

Through the life of God is made active, first, the intellect of God.
I. The life of which we have spoken, inasmuch as it is the active force of God,
makes active in God, first, his intellect, not because it moves it from potency into
act, for God and all that is in God is a most simple act, but because that act in
God has its existence from his life. And belonging to God's intellect is its act, as
it were, knowledge, and its perfection, wisdom. And all these are concerned with
their object as it is true. The apostle expresses most of these things in the text,
when he makes mention of intellect as the faculty, and of knowledge as the act,
and of wisdom as their power and perfection, all which are distinct, that is, due
to our mode of conceiving them.

The Exegetical Part
Its theory is constructed upon the exegesis of the text.
II. The text presents a certain exclamatory conclusion of praise, in which the
apostle both admires and extols the conspicuous preeminence of God's intellect,
knowledge, and wisdom in the matter of redemption, and especially of predestination. In it, two things occur:
  A. A certain exclamation of the admirer, and in it:
    1. The exclamatory marker, in the little word ὦ, "Oh," which here is a
       particle of the admirer, signifying that the thing commended is so
       great and so excellent that it can neither be perceived by the mind of
       any rational creature according to its proper dignity, nor be declared
       by the mouth.

2. The thing commended by the particle of the admirer, namely:

    a. "The depth," βάθος. This denotes height above and depth beneath, implying that the thing commended far exceeds all the boundaries of perfection, as much of height as of depth, and thus it is infinite, as explained in the paraphrase of Zophar in Job 11:8–9, "higher than the heavens…deeper than hell…longer than the earth, and broader than the sea." Nevertheless, the word most properly expresses depth, and thus it is applied to what is bottomless (Rev. 2:24; 1 Cor. 2:10).

    b. "Of the riches," πλούτου. And what are riches? They are an excess of wealth by which someone has more than he requires. Thus there is in the thing commended a certain abundance, not of poverty or of misery, but of the wealth that can make its possessor rich and happy. It is disputed whether βάθος, "depth," ought to be referred and restricted to πλούτος, "riches," so that the text reads, "Oh, how great the depth in his riches!" or whether it ought to be extended all the way to σοφία, "wisdom," so that it says, "Oh, the depth of the riches of wisdom!" and likewise to γνῶσις, knowledge, "Oh, the depth of the riches of the knowledge of God!" The following seem to argue for the latter: (1) the καί, "both," after πλούτου, "of the riches," (2) a comparison with verses 34 and 35, (3) a comparison with the preceding verses, where mention is made of the divine mercy toward Gentiles and Jews, the magnitude of which the apostle admires, using the word "riches" (Rom. 2:4; Eph. 2:7), which is a familiar habit of Paul's, as is evident in the passages adduced (as also in Eph. 1:18; 3:8; Col. 1:27).

    c. "Of the wisdom and knowledge of God," σοφίας καὶ γνώσεως. These two genitives are governed by the first, πλούτου, "of the riches," just as occurs in Colossians 2:3, "the treasures of wisdom and knowledge." Wisdom and knowledge here mean, according to some, the same thing, but to others, they differ such that wisdom is a species of knowledge. At least from the perspective of God they without doubt denote one and the same thing, although from our perspective, they are distinguished in various ways, including the following: (1) mind (νοῦς) represents to us the faculty of knowing, knowledge (γνῶσις), its act, and wisdom (σοφία), the perfection and power of both; (2) wisdom is something absolute, knowledge is something relative; (3) wisdom comprehends

all the intellectual habits, knowledge denotes only one of them;
(4) knowledge is a theoretical habit, wisdom is a practical habit,
and elsewhere it coincides with prudence, as Beza observes on
1 Corinthians 1:17.[1]

B. Four questions from the admirer, showing more distinctly the reason for
the preceding admiration. Of these questions:

1. The first is occupied with the judgments of God: ὡς ἀνεξερεύνητα
τα κρίματα αὐτοῦ, "How unsearchable are his judgments!" Here
we find:

a. The thing commended by the question, in the words, "his
judgments," κρίματα αὐτοῦ. Κρίματα names first the decrees of
God and then the execution of his decrees, especially in punishment,
according to the custom of the Hebrews, in which חקים also
denotes both. In particular, this word points to the judgments
God exercised in his rejection of the Jews and in his substitution of
the Gentiles.

b. The perfection on account of which it commends the thing, ὡς
ἀνεξερεύνητα, "How unsearchable!" This is the same as what is
said in Psalm 36:6, "Your judgments are a great deep." The verb
ἐρευνᾶν means to search deeply, and ἐξερευνᾶν, to find after
searching deeply. And the adjective ἀνεξερεύνητον implies not
finding, and not being able to find, that for which you deeply
searched. That is, it describes that which cannot, even by the
sharpest mind and the most careful searching, be inquired into.
And the particle of seeking, ὡς, "how," also increases this perfection of the utter unsearchability of his judgments: "How utterly
unsearchable!" That is, so much so that they cannot be searched
out by any creature of any kind, no matter how great.

2. The second is occupied with the ways of God: καὶ ἀνεξιχνίαστοι αἱ
ὁδοὶ αὐτοῦ, "and his ways past finding out." Here, there is:

a. The subject of the question: αἱ ὁδοὶ αὐτοῦ, "his ways" (in Hebrew,
דרכים). These are understood either generally, as the methods

---

1. While not directly mentioning theoretical habits, practical habits, and prudence in his
majores annotationes, Theodore Beza (1519–1605) does distinguish between σοφία and φρόνε-
σις so that the former tends toward contemplation whereas the latter toward action; but taken
more broadly σοφία means every kind of skilled action. For his Greek text, his Latin translation,
a comparison with the Vulgate, and his longer notes on 1 Cor. 1:17, see Theodore Beza, *Novum
testamentum…eiusdem Th. Bezae annotationes*, 4th ed. (Geneva: Henricus Stephanus, 1588), 100.

of his counsels and deeds of any kind, or specifically, as the arrangements of predestination, election, and reprobation, insofar as those ways are, for us, entirely and utterly past finding out.

b. The attribution: ἀνεξιχνίαστοι, "past finding out," which applies to that of which not even a trace can be found by any cleverness or by any arts, or to those things that cannot be sought by any trace of anything, or that of which no trace is furnished to our natural intellect apart from revelation, and indeed scarcely even by revelation.

3. The third is devoted to God's mind or intellect, which sustains his knowledge and wisdom, and from which his judgments and ways flow: Τίς γὰρ ἔγνω νοῦν κυρίου;, "For who has known the mind of the Lord?", from Isaiah 40:13, מי תכן רוח יהוה, "Who has measured the Spirit of Jehovah?" Here, there is:

a. The knower: Τίς, "Who?", indicated interrogatively: Who upon earth? Who in heaven? Who will point out anyone, anywhere? So then, the knower is no one.

b. The thing known: νοῦς κυρίου (Hebrew, רוח, "Spirit," יהוה, "of the Lord"), meaning the mind or the intellect of the Lord, of Jehovah. Νοῦς denotes the intellect to the extent that we understand it as the faculty from which comes knowledge, and in which is the power of wisdom. But in this passage it does not exclude the things God's intellect knows, namely, the decrees of predestination, election, the reprobation of the Jews, and their replacement by the Gentiles: Who has known the intellect of the Lord concerning these things?

c. The knowing: ἔγνω, in Hebrew תכן, "has weighed, measured, found out." Thus τίς ἔγνω, "Who has known?", that is, Who has known perfectly? We know several things about the mind or intellect of God: for example, that it truly belongs to God, what its properties are, and also many of its thoughts, that is, those that he has revealed to us in his own Word. But who has known them in such a way that he has weighed, measured, and found them out, that is, that he has come to know the intellect or Spirit of the Lord perfectly? No one. (1 Cor. 2:10–11).

4. The fourth is devoted to the counsels of God: σύμβολος αὐτοῦ ἐγένετο, "or has been his counselor," with the τίς, "Who?", understood to repeat from the previous phrase. These words also seem to

be taken, following the Septuagint version, from Isaiah 40:13–14: ואיש עצתו יודיענו את מי נועץ, "And a man made him to know his counsel" (with מי, "Who?" understood from the previous half-verse, resulting in, "Who is that man who…"). That is, Who is the man with whom he devised his counsels? Here we find:

a. The counselor, denied to exist: σύμβολος, "counselor." Such a man is understood to be one who shows the one seeking counsel what should be done, that by his choice he may either accept the counsel or reject it. The counselor is presupposed to be more skilled than the one he is counseling, or than the one who seeks counsel.

b. The one who seeks counsel, likewise not allowed, in the word αὐτοῦ, "his," that is, God's. Now, if from the preceding half-verse, you bring back the interrogative τίς, "Who?", this sense emerges: Who was present with God when he determined his counsels, that is, of providence, predestination, election, reprobation, the rejection of the Jews, and the substitution of the Gentiles? Who can show such a man to us? No one.

The Dogmatic Part

It is proved that intellect belongs to God: 1. From the Scriptures

III. And so according to the text, not only do intellect, knowledge, and wisdom belong to God, but also such that are most perfect, most full, infinite, and past finding out. Those three, intellect, knowledge, and wisdom[2]—different in the creatures though the same in God—we will, for our own sake, that we might reach an understanding of the one perfection of the divine intellect, consider separately. So then, intellect belongs to God, or, what is the same thing, he is the being that is intelligent in the highest degree. For the text attributes to him a mind, which in another place, Scripture designates as his eyes: "The eyes of the Lord traverse the whole earth" (2 Chron. 16:9; cf. 6:20). And thus it is said that to his eyes nothing is hidden (Heb. 4:13). Therefore he is called the God of knowledge[3] (1 Sam. 2:3; cf. Job 12:13; Ps. 136:5; 147:5; Prov. 3:19). And pointing in the same direction are all those passages where wisdom, omniscience, foreknowledge, and providence are asserted for God, passages that we will bring forth in their proper places.

---

2. νοῦν, γνῶσιν, σοφίαν

3. *Deus scientiarum*, lit. "God of knowledges," following the Hebrew, אל דעות in 1 Samuel 2:3.

2. From reasons

IV. It is not through Scripture alone that we know God to be intelligent, but also in many ways through nature. For (1) since being intelligent is numbered among God's perfections, perfections that involve no imperfection, then apart from a contradiction, it cannot be denied to the most perfect being. Next (2) God's intellect is the source and spring of the intellect of all intelligent beings, since only by his light do they enjoy light (Ps. 36:10). Accordingly we read, "Should he who implanted the eye not see? Should he who formed the ear not hear?" (Ps. 94:9). Furthermore (3) since God does his external works, not as one determined by his nature, as the sun in its shining, and also not randomly, nor under compulsion, but according to reason, counsel, and free choice,[4] he could not exist without an intellect. And (4) if he did exist without an intellect, what would he be but an idol, such as those about which Psalm 115:5–6 speaks: "They have eyes, but do not see; ears, but do not hear"? But since no one would be so barbarous, unless he were an atheist, to deny to God his intellect, there is no reason to exert ourselves any further to prove it for him.

What is it to understand in creatures?

V. Therefore, it will be more useful to investigate what the intellect is and what sort it is,[5] which will be made known by no other means more clearly than by a comparison of the human intellect with the divine. For intellect belongs to the class of communicable attributes, attributes that belong to creatures in their own way, by analogy. The verb meaning "to understand," *intellegere*, seems to come from *intus legere*, "to gather inwardly," that is, to gather intelligible species, or to contemplate sensory images,[6] according to the common proverb, "It is proper to an intelligent being to examine sensory images."[7] For this reason two things are required for understanding: intelligible species, which when they are to be represented in a work, are usually called ideas; and the examination of those ideas. The latter requires: (1) the reception of those ideas from the external senses, from common sense, and from the imagination,[8] for which reason we

---

4. προαιρέσει

5. *Quid sit?* explores the nature of something whereas the *qualis sit?* explores its qualities.

6. *phantasmata*

7. *oportet intelligentem phantasmata speculari.* As Mastricht explains below, when the senses sense an object, they provide an image of that object to the mind, that it may contemplate that image and deduce from it the intelligible species, or universal idea, of the object. Cf. *phantasma, intellectus agens,* and *species impressa* in Richard Muller, *Dictionary of Latin and Greek Theological Terms* (Grand Rapids: Baker Academic, 2017).

8. *phantasia,* the faculty of the soul that represents *phantasmata,* images from the senses, to the mind. Cf. 1.3.9 §VI.

speak of the receptive intellect; and (2) the contemplation of the ideas received, which consists, partly in collecting them—composing or dividing, affirming or denying—from which arises noetic judgment, and partly in discourse or reasoning, by which we move from things more known down to things less known, from which arises dianoetic judgment and the active intellect.[9] And this is the process of understanding in creatures.

What is it to understand in God?

VI. In the intellect of God, two things are also required, things that differ in our conception: the presence of ideas and the examination or perception of them. Because of this, the intellect of God can be defined in no way more accurately than as the most perfect intuition of himself or of his own ideas, and yet without any reception of them, that is, without a receptive intellect, and also without any composition and division, without any discourse, because all these things involve imperfection, which must be most scrupulously secluded from the most perfect being.

In what sense do ideas belong to God?

VII. Thus we have attributed ideas (so called from the verb ἰδεῖν, "to see") to God here in a broader sense, insofar as they denote not only a practical species to be represented in a work, but also an intelligible species of any sort, even one that will not be expressed. Concerning these matters Scripture speaks sparingly; concerning them it is common to take up the phrase from Hebrews 11:3, "The things which we see have been made from things that are not seen." In creatures the term properly denotes what exists in the mind of the artisan and will be expressed in his work. In God (as Ames says in his *Marrow of Theology*, bk. 1, ch. 7, §14), an idea is nothing other than "his very essence insofar as it is understood by him as imitable in the creature, or such that an image of its perfection, or some trace of it, can be expressed in some way in the creatures."[10] That is, the

---

9. On *intellectus patiens*, receptive intellect, as opposed to *intellectus agens*, active intellect, see Aristotle, *De Anima* III.5, 430 a. 11. On the distinction between axiomatic and dianoetic judgment, see Petrus Ramus (1515–1572), *Dialecticae libri duo scholiis Guilelmi Tempelli*, 2nd ed. (Frankfurt: Johann Wechelus and Petrus Fischer, 1591), 49. For Ramus, the dianoetic judgment, utilizing syllogism and method, is employed in conjunction with the axiomatic judgment, which formulates propositions that are self-evidently true, to determine the truth or falsity of a question that is not self-evidently true.

10. Ames, *Medulla* (1634), 26; idem, *Marrow* (1639), 24. The 1639 English edition translates *idea omnium rerum* as "the platforme of all things."

creatures themselves as they are conceived in the divine mind are the ideas of that nature which they have in themselves.

How does an idea differ in God and in the creatures?
VIII. An idea in man, who acquires his knowledge through analysis, is collected from things themselves, and thus, things first exist in themselves, then they come to one's sense, and from there to one's intellect, where they can constitute some idea for directing a subsequent operation. But since God understands all things through genesis and does not acquire knowledge through analysis, therefore all things exist in his mind before they exist in themselves. In man, things themselves are the pattern and our knowledge is the image, but in God, the idea is the pattern and the things themselves are the expressed image. In man an idea is first impressed and afterwards expressed in things, but in God, an idea only expresses, properly speaking, and is not impressed, since it does not come from any other source. These words of this section are from Ames, in the passage already cited, §15–17.[11]

In God, does the idea exist as one and as manifold?
IX. So then, the idea, as it is considered absolutely in God, is a single idea only, since it is his essence. But it is manifold insofar as it connotes various considerations of the creatures, and it does that insofar as it is true that the idea of one creature is not an idea of another. In addition, ideas exist in God of all the perfections that are in the creatures, namely because they come into being from the active power of God, but not of any of their imperfections, if the creatures are considered formally by reason of their imperfections. However, at the same time even the knowledge of evil belongs to God, though only such knowledge as depends upon the negation of good, since being evil consists in the privation of good. For only in this way are things truly known in the way they are. Also, insofar as there exist plural ideas in God, they are as it were connected among themselves and also mutually depend upon each other. For this reason there is that order of prior and posterior that we observe in predestination and providence.[12]

And insofar as it is manifold, it takes on various names.
X. Now the divine intellection consists in the contemplation (that is, the intuition) and the knowledge of these ideas, or rather, of this idea. And this

---

11. 1.7.15–17 in Ames, *Medulla* (1634), 27; idem, *Marrow* (1639), 24–25.
12. 1.7.19–22 in Ames, *Medulla* (1634), 27–28; idem, *Marrow* (1639), 25.

intellection takes on various names because of the creatures and its various relations to the creatures. Thus in respect to first principles, it is called *intelligence*, by which God in individual matters perceives each thing that is most fundamental; in respect to the truth that considers individual matters it is called *knowledge*, which from its breadth is called *omniscience*, and in regard to the being that things have in their own proper measure, it is called *foreknowledge*; in respect to the dependence of truths amongst themselves, it is called *wisdom*, by which he knows what is fitting to each thing as well as what is foreign to it; in respect to putting the entire order into practice, it is called *prudence*, by which he knows how to accommodate the most advantageous occasions to all things; and finally, in respect to the executing of the practice, it is called *art*, by which he knows how to effect all things most skillfully (Heb. 11:10). These terms are commonly employed in the Scriptures to explain the perfection of the divine intellect for the comprehension of those who have an especially imperfect intellect; yet by their own nature, they allow this distinction and not another. The words above are continually the words of Ames, in the place already cited.[13]

The perfection of the divine intellect arises from five qualities.
XI. From these things it remains clear that God knows all things, not in the things themselves, but in himself. And from this we see the entire perfection of the divine intellect, a perfection through which the intellect of God is: (1) independent, because he knows not from some other source, but from himself, and by beholding himself most perfectly. For there cannot be allowed in God either any accident or any idea different from his essence. This is the meaning the text intends when it removes every counselor from God. (2) Most simple, since in himself, at one glance, God perceives all things without any composition of homogeneous things or separation of heterogeneous things, without any discourse, abstraction, or other such ways of knowing that belong to creatures, ways that arise from their imperfection. (3) Immutable, since he does not understand one thing differently or more than he understands another thing, nor does he understand more before than he does now, or more now than he did before. This is so of course because he perceives all things in his immutable essence, and in his eternity, by which he coexists unmoved with all types of times, without any succession. For this reason all things are spoken of as laid bare and intimately open to his eyes (Heb. 4:13). (4) Eternal, since he neither begins nor ceases to understand, insofar as things known in themselves begin and cease to exist, or they become what they were not. And this is so of course because he understands not

---

13. 1.7.29–30 in Ames, *Medulla* (1634), 29; idem, *Marrow* (1639), 26–27.

through species that he has received, but through his own eternal essence, that is, through his eternal decrees (Acts 15:18; Eph. 1:4). (5) Infinite, since he alone knows not only himself and his own infinite mind, but also all the truths of all things, as well as their reasons, without any reception either of ignorance or of error. On this account his wisdom is spoken of as higher than the heavens, longer than the earth, broader than the sea (Job 11:8–9). These passages also prove the same truth: Psalm 139:6, Psalm 147:5, Isaiah 40:28, John 21:17, and so forth.

The divine intellect considered as an act is called omniscience.

XII. Knowledge (in the text, γνῶσις) is the act of the divine intellect (which we considered a little while ago as a faculty). And we have already called this knowledge, from the breadth of its object, *omniscience*, because to him all things are laid bare and intimately open. The sacred page asserts this knowledge for the divine intellect in many ways, when (1) in absolute terms, it says that he looks to the ends of the earth and perceives all things that are under heaven (Job 28:24), and thus that he is the God of knowledge (1 Sam. 2:3). These passages point to this same truth: 1 Samuel 16:7; 1 Kings 8:39; Psalm 94:2; Psalm 139:1, 3–4, 6, 12; Acts 15:18; 1 John 3:20. (2) In negative terms: "No thought is hidden from you" (Job 42:2; cf. Heb. 4:13). (3) In comparative terms, when he is called the light in whom is no darkness (1 John 1:5), whose eyes traverse the whole earth (2 Chron. 16:9), and who likewise numbers all our hairs (Luke 12:7). For this reason Augustine, commenting on Psalm 136, says, "God is all eye because he sees all things."[14] And it cannot but be so because he knows all things in himself, he who is, eminently, all things. Likewise, because he sustains and governs all things (as they have all proceeded from him), he confers upon them all whatever they have of knowledge and cognition. And if he were robbed of his knowledge of anything, he would not be most perfect, and thus he would not be what he is, that is, God.

The objects of divine omniscience

XIII. In particular, through his own omniscience God knows himself in himself, he knows his own mind (Rom. 11:34). Next, he also knows all other things: universal and singular, substantial and circumstantial, good and evil, thought, said, and done, past, present, and future, whether they are future by a necessary cause, that is, a cause determined to this effect by its own nature; or by a contingent

---

14. Cf. 1.2.10 §XVI, where it is cited as Ps. 36. This seems to be a comment on Psalm 94:9 in a letter by Jerome, *The Homilies of Saint Jerome*, 1:177.

cause, a cause not in itself determined to this effect; or by a free cause, operating by free choice. To reinforce all these things separately with separate passages of Scripture would be more lengthy than is necessary or useful.

Various distributions and denominations of divine knowledge
XIV. Meanwhile, God perceives all those things in more than one way, and thus the divine knowledge is divided into various descriptions. For there is his general knowledge, by which he is occupied with all things universally; there is his special knowledge, by which he knows his own individually (Rom. 8:29; 1 Peter 1:2). Furthermore, there is his theoretical knowledge, by which he simply knows; there is also his practical knowledge, by which he also works, and that with an affection that is either positive (Ps. 1:6) or negative (Rev. 3:15–16). And because of a lack of the former he sometimes says that he does not know (Matt. 7:23). And in respect to this diversity, God's knowledge is clothed in various names. In relation to past things, it is called recollection and reminiscence (Ps. 25:6–7), speaking by all means in a human way, according to an affection and an effective operation, not according to his knowledge simply speaking. In relation to present things, it is called vision and sight (Heb. 4:13).

Natural and free knowledge
In relation to future things, it obtains a double name. There is his natural knowledge or knowledge of simple intelligence, by which he knows purely possible things, perceiving their possibility in his own all-sufficiency and omnipotence. And there is his free knowledge or knowledge of vision, by which, first, he sees that universal order, long ago decreed from eternity to be applied to things in their own time, and afterwards actually applied to them in creation, the order through which all things are appointed to have such dependency and connection among themselves that from it God, although he never decreed certain things to happen in actuality, can foresee and foretell that they will happen (that is, given the proper prerequisites), for example, that dry straw, if it be brought close to fire, will burn. In this way God also foresaw and foretold that David, if he remained in Keilah, would be delivered by its inhabitants into the hand of Saul,[15] namely, because by the order that was decreed and concreated with things, an enemy delivers an enemy into the hand of his master or his friend to be destroyed. Second, he foresees that certain things, whether they are good or evil, will happen in actuality, and that from his decree alone, since a determined future event admits no other foundation and no other cause besides the divine decree alone.

---

15. 1 Sam. 23:12

The invented idea of a third knowledge, which they call middle knowledge, we will expressly refute in the elenctic part.[16]

Wisdom is the power of the divine intellect and knowledge.
XV. There remains to discuss the power of the divine intellect and knowledge, by which it is called *wisdom*; the power to which are attributed such "riches," that is, such abundance and fullness, that its judgments and ways are called "unsearchable and past finding out"; the power by which he is named the only wise God (Rom. 16:27; 1 Tim. 1:17), that is, wise preeminently and independently, and likewise, great in counsel (Jer. 32:19; Job 12:13), the one in whom concur wisdom and might (Dan. 2:20); the power by which his wisdom is unsearchable (Job 11:7; Ps. 147:5; Isa. 40:28; Ps. 139:18), by which it is compared with the abyss in depth, with the earth in breadth, with the heavens in height (Job 11:7–8; cf. Ps. 36:6; 92:5; 1 Cor. 2:7–9), so that the psalmist exclaims, "How manifold are your works! In wisdom you have made them all" (Ps. 104:24; cf. Ps. 136:5; Prov. 3:19; 8:30; Jer. 10:12; etc.).

What is the wisdom of God, and to what is it aimed?
XVI. This essential wisdom—for the personal wisdom which the Word is named (Prov. 8:1; Matt. 11:19) because in him lay hidden all the treasures of wisdom and knowledge (Col. 2:3), and who for that reason is called the wisdom and power of God (1 Cor. 1:24), is not our present business—is nothing but a certain peculiar power and perfection of the divine intellect and knowledge by which God knows what methods to use in the unfolding of his counsels and works to exalt his glory as greatly as possible. For which reason that essential wisdom is chiefly occupied and concerned (1) with the counsels, decrees, predestination, election, and reprobation of God, to which points the text's exclamation, "O the depth of the riches, both of the wisdom...!" (2) With the works of creation, conservation, and governance, concerning which the psalmist says, "In wisdom you have made them all" (Ps. 104:24; 136:5). And especially (3) with the formation of man, the microcosm[17] (Ps. 139:14–15). Likewise, (4) with the uniting and ordering of creatures so different from each other, because of which he is called the God of peace (1 Cor. 14:33), who does all things in their own time and measure (Eccl. 3:11), especially (5) in the marvelous work of redemption through the Son and Holy Spirit, because of which the Savior

---

16. §XX, below
17. Man is a "little cosmos" because in his being he reflects every part of the universe. Cf. 1.3.9 §IV.

is not only named the wisdom and power of God (1 Cor. 1:24), but also called the manifold wisdom of God (Eph. 3:10) into which even angels long to look (1 Peter 1:12). And moreover, (6) in the mysteries of the Christian faith, which the apostle calls the wisdom of God, distinguished from the wisdom of this world (1 Cor. 2:6). Furthermore, (7) in the gathering and defending of his church against the most cunning attacks of so many and such great enemies, whom by his wisdom he time and again catches in their own scheming (Ps. 59:12; 10:2). Finally, (8) in his most wise direction and governance particular to individual believers.

The Elenctic Part

It is asked: 1. Does the knowledge of God extend to each and every thing?

XVII. It is asked, first, whether the knowledge of God extends to each and every thing. Certain philosophers from the Peripatetics are said to have thought that the perceiving of individual things belongs to material potency or the senses alone; they stated that the knowledge of God does not extend to individual things but only to general things. The Pelagians are in harmony with them, to a certain point at least, when so that they may more easily support the idea of independent free choice in the matter of predestination, at least of a non-peremptory predestination, they acknowledge none but general decrees, for example, "I will to save those who believe and those who repent," because God does not know whether the human will will determine itself to believe or not. More openly with the crassest Pelagians, the Socinians, so that they might hold more firmly to the idea of the independence of indifferent free choice and the omnimodal contingency of things, state that God has no knowledge of free and contingent future things. We will examine them in their own section.[18] The Reformed state that through the infinite perfection of God's intellect, he knows all things, singulars as well as universals; indeed, it is more proper to say that he knows singulars than universals, because universals do not exist except through the abstraction of the human mind from singulars, and this abstraction, on account of the imperfection it implies, does not square with an infinitely perfect being. For this very reason they do not accept the idea of God's general decrees, and ascribe to the infinite perfection of the divine intellect the fact that he perceives future and free contingencies in perfect detail.

---

18. §XIX, below

It is proved from the Scriptures.
And they are taught these truths by Scripture, in which it is said that Christ, since he is God, knows all things (John 21:17), that all things are intimately open to God's eyes (Heb. 4:13), even singulars (Ps. 147:4; 56:9), even to the hairs of our head (Matt. 10:30), that he knows those who are his (2 Tim. 2:19), and in fact that he knows future and free contingencies (Ps. 139:1–6; Matt. 16:34–35).

And from reasons
But they are also taught these truths by right reason. For unless God knew all things: (1) he would not be infinitely perfect, insofar as knowing all things is, in the common opinion of all, more perfect than not knowing certain things. And particularly in regard to singular things: (2) Does he who created singular things not know them? (3) Is he who conserves and governs singular things ignorant of them? (4) Does he who knows himself, the most singular thing, and who in himself knows all things, not know singular things? (5) If man knows singular things, then will they evade the intellect of God? Moreover, (6) God does not, properly speaking, know anything but singular things, or at least he does not know in any way but singularly, because he does not know by abstracting from singular things, since that occurs through the imperfection and weakness of men, for they do not have a singular knowledge of all singular things, and from their knowledge of singular things, they form for themselves a general knowledge. Finally, (7) if he did not have an exact knowledge of singular things, he could not have a knowledge of general things, because general things arise from singular things. I need not mention the fact that (8) general things do not exist, and thus are nonentities, and thus he would have knowledge only of those things which do not exist. In particular, (9) if he did not have foreknowledge of future contingencies, he would not be omniscient, for those contingencies can be known, as is evident in a thousand prophecies. And it is no hindrance, as the philosophers object, that the divine intellect is immaterial, given the fact that it is occupied with singular material things immaterially (just as it is with spiritual, immaterial things). We will examine a little further on the objections of the Socinians against God's foreknowledge of future contingencies.[19]

2. Does God understand by reasoning? The thoughts of various factions
XVIII. It is asked, second, whether God understands by reasoning, by thinking discursively. The Anthropomorphites of old, because they found in the image of God the faculty and act of thinking discursively, also transferred the same to

---

19. §XIX, below

the prototype. Vorstius and the Socinians, so that they might more conveniently hold that God is dependent upon human choice as well as upon the objects he is to know, and especially so that they might hold to a conjectural knowledge which cannot be had apart from reasoning, state that God knows by reasoning, by thinking discursively, by drawing conclusions, progressing from the more known to the less known, as we humans do.

The opinion of the Reformed together with their reasons
The Reformed, although they acknowledge that God perceives in perfect detail human discursive thoughts and reasonings, even so deny that he does so by reasoning, but assert rather that he does so by intuiting. Because, they say, (1) God knows all things by intuiting, in such a way that all things are laid bare and intimately open to him; to his eyes, that is, to his intellect, nothing is hidden (Heb. 4:13). Now, what is understood by intuiting is not gathered by reasoning. (2) Because God knows all things, not in the things themselves, but in himself, and by intuiting his own decrees, thus (3) the intellect of God is independent: it does not receive its ideas from things, but is the exemplar of things. (4) God's intellect, indeed God's essence, is most simple, and for this reason it does not progress from the more known to the less known by thinking discursively or by reasoning. Likewise, (5) it is infinite, and accordingly nothing is unknown to it, nothing to which it would need to proceed by reasoning. (6) It is eternal: in it there is no change through which it proceeds by reasoning from one more known thing to another more unknown thing. Finally, (7) it is most perfect, entirely free of all ignorance, increment, process, and change from the more known to the lesser known, and of all the similar imperfections that discursive thinking implies.

An objection
It is also no hindrance to these truths to say that he understands human reasonings, since he understands them not by reasoning, but by intuiting our thoughts from afar (Ps. 139:2).

3. Concerning future and free contingencies, does God have only conjectural foreknowledge?
XIX. It is asked, third, concerning future and free contingencies, whether God has only conjectural foreknowledge. Long ago the crass Pelagians, because they feared that by the certain foreknowledge of God the contingency of things and the indifference of our free choice would be ruined, acknowledged only a conjectural foreknowledge in God. The Socinians, who follow them in every detail,

think the same thing, and do so based on the same hypotheses. Thus even Socinus, in his *Lectures*, openly professes that if the doctrine of the Reformed concerning God's certain foreknowledge of all future contingencies stands, the contingency of things cannot be defended, nor the liberty of our choice.[20] The result of all these errors is the ruin of eternal and immutable predestination, of the perseverance of saints, and of the certain persuasion of salvation. The Reformed judge that this idea of conjectural foreknowledge is opposed to Scripture and the divine nature.

From Scripture

It is opposed indeed to Scripture, since Scripture testifies that: (1) all God's works are known to him from eternity (Acts 15:18). (2) Nothing can happen, even and especially nothing contingent, unless by a prevenient divine decree (Lam. 3:37; Prov. 16:33). (3) God foresees even future contingencies (Ps. 139:1–2). Indeed also (4) he predicts them, even many centuries before they come to pass, as it is evident in a thousand prophecies: concerning the birth of the Messiah, concerning persecutions by Christ's enemies (Ps. 2:1–2; Ps. 22; etc.; cf. Acts 4:25–27). Thus Tertullian rightly says in book 2 of *Against Marcion*, "the foreknowledge of God has as its witnesses as many prophets as it has made,"[21] and also as many prophecies.

From reason

And in addition, conjectural foreknowledge is opposed to nature, not only to God's, but also to ours. Thus by nature we understand that (1) to a most perfect being belongs a most perfect knowledge, and no one would call perfect knowledge conjectural. (2) An independent being foreknows all things independently, and thus he knows not in things but in himself, and by certain and perfect intuition of himself. (3) No event can have any futurity except through the decree from eternity, and this decree is most perfectly known to God. (4) The immutable God foreknows immutably, and thus also infallibly. Finally, (5) he foreknows in eternity, and this eternity coexists with all types of time, truths we have taught

---

20. There are several instances where Faustus Socinus notes this point in various ways, namely in chs. 6–12. The most likely chapter most relevant here is chapter 8, "De Dei praenotione seu praescientia" in idem, *Praelectiones theologicae* (Raków: Sebastian Sternacius, 1609), 24–28.

21. See bk. 2, ch. 5, Tertullian, *Adversus Marcionem* in PL 2:290; idem, *Against Marcion* in ANF 3:301.

in their own places,[22] and thus he foreknows a thing as if it were present: he foreknows certainly and infallibly.

Objections

If they plead the fact that God is said to have been saddened (Gen. 6:6–7), to have tested the obedience of Abraham (Gen. 22:12), to have hoped for good grapes from his vineyard (Isa. 5:2), and similar such things they have gathered (Gen. 18:21; Ex. 16:4; Deut. 8:2; Ps. 81:10, 13–14), there is a ready response: These things are said in a human way and must be understood in a way worthy of God, according to the well-worn phrase of Athanasius.[23] Next, if they also plead that future contingencies do not have a determined truth, we say in opposition that indeed they do not have a determined truth in themselves, but nevertheless, they do in the decree of God, who does all things according to the counsel of his own will (Eph. 1:11).

4. Besides natural and free knowledge, is there a middle knowledge in God?
What do the Jesuits say?

XX. It is asked, fourth, whether besides natural foreknowledge, or the knowledge of simple intelligence, and free foreknowledge, or the knowledge of vision, there is in God some third foreknowledge, which they call middle knowledge. The Jesuits (whom the Remonstrants follow) and other semi-Pelagians, so that they can more conveniently protect God's certain foreknowledge of future free events against the Pelagians and Socinians but also hold intact an independent indifference of free choice, have contrived, besides natural knowledge, by which God from the all-sufficiency of his own nature knows possible things, and besides free knowledge, by which he from his decree knows future things, a certain third knowledge, by which God certainly foreknows future, free things, though not from his decree, but rather from the surrounding conditions, given which, the will determines itself to this or that thing. And this third knowledge they have baptized *middle knowledge* for two reasons: (1) because it is a knowledge that belongs neither to natural knowledge nor to free knowledge: not to natural knowledge because it has for its object not what is possible but what is future; not to free knowledge because it does not know from the decree. And at the same time (2) because it shares something from both: from natural knowledge because it does not know from the decree; from free knowledge because it is occupied with what is future. Two Spanish theologians, Peter Fonseca and

---

22. §XI, above; 1.2.11 §§IX, XI
23. Cf. 1.2.15 §XIX.

Luis Molina, contend for the glory of the paternity of this invention. The Reformed reject this novel invention as idle, false, and injurious to the divine perfection.

By what arguments is it toppled?

XXI. The Reformed do so chiefly by the following reasons: (1) because middle knowledge is superfluous, since every knowable thing is subject to the two received knowledges, natural and free. For if a thing is considered as merely possible, then undoubtedly it falls under natural knowledge. If it is considered as having a connection with various second causes, and thus as a thing that will occur if it should be construed with those second causes, even though it never actually will occur, it belongs to that latter knowledge that depends upon the decree, the decree that constituted at creation the order that would thereafter be applied to things, so that for example, dry straw would be burned if it were laid near a flame, even though God never did decree that it would be laid there or burned. And finally, a thing that will actually occur belongs to free knowledge. Next, (2) because God's idea, in the intuition of which we heard that his knowledge consists, can be considered only in two ways: either in an antecedent relation to his decree, under the notion of God's reason, and thus supplying his knowledge of simple intelligence, or in a consequent relation to his decree, and thus supplying his knowledge of vision. (3) Because by middle knowledge the intellect of God would draw its ideas from elsewhere, and thus it would depend upon creatures. And on the other hand, (4) the human will and its primary determination would be released from dependence on God. (5) The connection that exists between an event that will happen freely or contingently and the circumstances that surround it would, since it precedes the divine decree, not be subject to the divine will. From this (6) there will arise a concept of fate worse than that of Stoicism, a fate that God himself is entirely unable to turn, because that future event is reckoned antecedent to all of God's good pleasure. Furthermore, (7) neither will this knowledge have the right to be called knowledge, since it has no true object. For that which has no determined truth, whether in itself or in its cause, is also not knowable. So surely it would imply knowing what is not knowable. Accordingly, (8) it will be more correctly called conjecture than knowledge. Indeed, (9) even called error, for he who knows as certainly future what can happen or not happen, that is, what is not certainly future, undoubtedly errs. See Twisse, *On Middle Knowledge*; Rutherford, *Exercises Defending God's Grace*; and others.[24]

---

24. For books 2–3 of William Twisse (c. 1577–1646), directed against Francisco Suarez, see

The chief objections in favor of middle knowledge

XXII. Meanwhile in objection they bring up: (1) those passages in which God predicts under a future condition which he never decreed (e.g. 1 Sam. 23:11–12; Matt. 11:21; Jer. 26:2–3; etc.). I respond, God foresaw those things by his free knowledge, from the decree by which he decided to apply to all things in their own time that order through which, from this construction of things, such an event would follow, provided that the ordinary concurrence of God agreed. It was based on this order that he predicted that the Keilahites would deliver up David. For it is the order of things in this world that an enemy delivers up an enemy, if he can (cf. 1 Sam. 24:19). Other specific responses to the other passages can be found in many places, and so for the sake of brevity we leave them to their own authors. (2) That all things that occur have been set to happen from eternity, antecedent even to the decree of God. For one of two contradictories—either something will happen, or it will not—was true antecedent even to the decree. And God accordingly foreknew which one was true, not by his natural knowledge, which is concerned with purely possible things, and also not by his free knowledge, which follows his decree. Therefore he did so by a certain third or middle knowledge. I respond, We completely deny that one of two contradictories was, antecedent to the divine decree, to happen or not to happen determinately. Indeed logically, only one or the other of the contradictories could be true, but indeterminately so; that is, only one of the two, speaking disjunctively, could come to pass. And God held this fact in his natural knowledge. (3) That apart from this middle knowledge, there does not appear to be a way to reconcile the contingency of events, the liberty of choice, the certain foreknowledge of future contingencies, with the divine decrees, with providence, with the grace of conversion. I respond, That disagreement of free choice with the decrees and with divine foreknowledge, which this knowledge promises to take away, rests in nothing else than a perverse definition of free choice, according to which it is nothing but a faculty by which, given all the prerequisites for acting, you are able to act or not to act, and thus, entirely all certainty of futurity and dependence of free choice is excluded. But when this definition is replaced by a more correct definition (according to which free choice is nothing but the faculty of acting from counsel), all the disagreement ceases. For God has decreed many future things through contingent causes, many things through free causes, and his foreknowledge of vision takes nothing away from this fact. But these

Dissertatio de scientia media in tribus libris absoluta (Jacob à Biesius, 1639), 237–498. For Samuel Rutherford (1600–1661), see Exerc. 1, chs. 3–4 in *Exercitationes apologeticae pro divina gratia* (Amsterdam: Henricus Laurentius, 1636), 57–158.

things will recur in the chapters on the decrees, on providence, on free choice, and on conversion.[25]

5. Is the possibility of things not known by God except by his decree?

XXIII. It is asked, fifth, whether the possibility of things is not known by God except by the decree of the will by which he willed this or that thing to be possible or impossible. The Cartesians, because they want for that possibility to have a certain reality and for it to be able to have no reality except by the divine will, state that God cannot have any knowledge of this reality or possibility except from the will or decree by which he willed one thing to be possible, while he did not will another thing to be possible. You have the Cartesian opinion represented more distinctly in our *Gangrene of the Cartesian Innovations* (sect. 2, ch. 10, §2).[26] The Reformed, as they grant that every possibility of the creatures is founded in God, though not in God's will as we conceive it as different from God's all-sufficient essence, thus state that the possibility of things is founded not in God's will, indifferent to every creature, but in his all-sufficient essence, which we conceived of as antecedent by nature to his will, in a rational manner or order, that is, *in signo rationis*, as they say.[27] Accordingly, that they may consider the matter as distinctly as possible, they conceive in God: (1) that he can do something, from which the possibility of things results, (2) that he knows he can do it, from which his natural knowledge arises, (3) that he wills it to come to pass at some point, from which his decree and the thing's futurity flow, and (4) that he brings it forth through his executive power.

The reasons they have for this opinion are: (1) that from the hypothesis of their adversaries' opinion, possibles would have had reality, or what is the same thing, some kind of entity and essence, from eternity. And from this, eternity will not be an incommunicable attribute of God, such that from it we could solidly defend the deity of the Son and the Holy Spirit against the anti-Trinitarians. (2) The possibility of things would depend precisely upon the will of God, which implies many absurdities, for example, that God, if he willed, could cause contradictory things to be true simultaneously, since all possibilities depend upon his will: that God would exist and not exist, that God would be omnipotent and at the same time not, that man is man and not man, and so on in all things. By the same logic it would follow that God could, if only he willed, teach what

---

25. 1.3.1 §XXXI; 1.3.10 §XXXIII; 1.4.4 §§XXX, XXXI; 1.6.4 §XXVI

26. Mastricht, *Gangraena*, 253–54.

27. The distinction *in signo rationis* is a rational ordering rather than, for example, a temporal one. Cf. *in signo rationis* in Muller, *Dictionary of Latin and Greek Theological Terms*.

is entirely contrary to all those duties that he has prescribed to us, for example, that we would not have him for God, that we would not love him, indeed that on the contrary we would pursue him in hatred, that we would blaspheme, and it would also follow that these things would, if he had willed, have been good. And indeed, if the will of God is the cause of all possibility of truth and goodness, and if the will of God is indifferent to every good, so that *no* good can be formed, as they say, before God's will has determined itself to effecting that it be so, then even God himself will be good, wise, and just, and so forth, because he wills to be, and if he had willed not to be good or just, then he would not have been so. Furthermore, (3) if the possibility of things depends upon God's will or decree alone, then also the sufficiency and perfection of God will depend upon his will and decree, such that he would therefore be all-sufficient and perfect because he wills and decreed to be so. The reason is because his all-sufficiency and infinite perfection, as that which can be represented outside of God in infinite ways, parceled out as if bit by bit, are the foundation of all possibility. (4) From the hypothesis of this opinion, in place of the twofold division of the divine knowledge that has been heretofore received in the Reformed world, there will have to be adopted one that is not only threefold, as the Jesuits have recently contrived, but fourfold, as we have recently shown.[28]

The foundation of the Cartesian opinion consists chiefly in these two things: (1) on the one hand, they state that possible things, even though they are distinguished from God and from the divine ideas (which is hinted at clearly enough in the famous Wittich's *Peaceable Theology*, §200), have had from eternity some sort of reality or essence.[29] But eternity, as we heard so far from the Reformed, is proper only to God. (2) On the other hand, they state that this eternal reality of possible things ought to depend by necessity, not only upon God simply considered, but exclusively upon the will of God, indifferent to all things, the contrary of which we have so far demonstrated by its many absurd consequences. Therefore, the origin of this error is in this, that they do not distinguish between the essence and the will of God, and thus it happens that the possibility of things, which results from his essence, they refer to his will.

---

28. This was only "recently shown" if one attends to the citation contra Wittich in Mastricht, *Gangraena*, sect. 2, ch. 10, pp. 253–69.

29. Wittich, *Theologia pacifica* (1671), 160–61.

The Practical Part

The practice of divine omniscience: 1. The glorification of God

XXIV. So then, we proceed straight to practice. First, as the text shows, God's knowledge furnishes an outstanding argument for the glorification of God, namely that we might exclaim, "Oh the depth of the riches, both of the wisdom and knowledge of God!" and likewise, "To the only wise God be honor and glory forever" (1 Tim. 1:17). And we do so because (1) he is a being that is not irrational by nature, acting either from compulsion or rashly, but a being that is intelligent in the highest degree, (2) one who rejoices in an intellect that is independent, most simple, immutable, eternal, and infinite, and thus most perfect. And by it (3) he perceives in detail not many things, but all things, and all truths of all things, such that they are to his eyes as bare and uncovered (Heb. 4:13). Yet not only does he perceive things, but also, (4) he so wisely arranges all his judgments, ways, and works, that you may exclaim: "Oh how unsearchable are his judgments, and his ways past finding out!", and likewise, "How manifold are your works! In wisdom you have made them all" (Ps. 104:24). For if we celebrate man more than a beast because of his intellect (Ps. 32:9), if we make so much of a man who has some degree more of knowledge and wisdom than the common lot, or who shows some mark of outstanding wisdom and prudence, how much more will we make of God! For his wisdom is "higher than the heavens, deeper than the abyss, longer than the earth, broader than the sea" (Job 11:8–9). Especially if we think distinctly of his works—of creation, governance, redemption, and that ineffable counsel of peace, and the whole economy of the three persons concerning it—then surely we will burst forth with the psalmist, "I will celebrate you, Lord, for awesome are your works. Wonderful are your works, and worthy of wonder, and my soul knows it full well" (Ps. 139:14; 92:5; Jer. 10:12–13; 51:15–16). Therefore, we are supplied with a manifold argument for God's glorification from the knowledge and wisdom of God. But by what method should it be arranged? I respond, in such a way that: (1) we marvel at it with our heart (Ps. 139:14); (2) we celebrate it with our mouth, "I will celebrate you, Lord…," "Oh, the depth…!"; (3) we imitate it with our work, with an insatiable, and as it were, an infinite zeal for the divine knowledge and wisdom, a practice we will treat shortly below.

2. The humbling of man

XXV. Then conversely, second, it offers us an argument for being humbled by a comparison of our ignorance and folly with the infinite knowledge and wisdom of God, after the example of Asaph (Ps. 73:22) and Agur (Prov. 30:2–4).

It is this that opposes (1 Cor. 8:2) and takes away (2 Cor. 10:5) the spirit of natural knowledge, or rather, carnal knowledge. For you should see those who understand the least bit more than the common people, even in things of lighter moment, such as grammar, poetry, and even mechanics: how high they lift their head, how important they are to themselves, how important they want to be to others, how much they expect from everyone else, and how insolent they are if in their own opinion they do not obtain it. Here therefore, what will more effectively batter down our arrogance than to think how little there is that we know above others, indeed, how much there is that we do not know, especially when we compare our superficial wisdom with the abyss of God's knowledge and wisdom? What will more effectively invite us to humility? (Even if you should be more rich than many in your extraordinary knowledge and wisdom.) God inculcates this humility (Jer. 9:23), teaching us nothing but (1) to think that God is most wise, since he is the one who made us wiser than brute beasts (Job 35:11). Accordingly (2) to exclaim to ourselves, "What do you have that you did not receive? And if you received it, why do you boast as if you did not receive it?" (1 Cor. 4:7). Moreover, (3) to take what you have freely received above others and to render it to God with submissive gratitude, and in that way "to cast down thoughts and every high thing that exalts itself against the knowledge of God" (2 Cor. 10:5). And (4) to think about God's dreadful judgment upon the arrogance of worldly wisdom (1 Cor. 1:19–20).

3. Modesty

XXVI. From the two preceding practices, a third in particular emerges, an argument for modesty, whenever we are occupied (1) with the judgments of God exercised against others, (2) with the ways of his mercy toward us and others, (3) with the revealed[30] wisdom of God (1 Cor. 2:6–7), (4) with the Word of God and the wondrous things of the law (Ps. 119:18), especially (5) with things that are difficult, troubling, apparently contradictory, insoluble,[31] and (6) with the mysteries of the faith. Here, what will more effectively form us in modesty than a devout comparison of God's wisdom with our foolishness, that by it not only would we think, "the foolishness of God is wiser than men" (1 Cor. 1:25), and likewise, "Oh, the depth of the riches both of the wisdom and knowledge of God!", but also we would beware, more than a dog or snake, by our own wisdom: (1) to call the divine wisdom to account in the matters of God and faith, to confer with flesh and blood (Gal. 1:16), just like the Socinians and Scholastics

---

30. προφορικήν
31. δυσνόητα, δύσκολα, ἐναντιοφανῆ, ἄλυτα

do. For the natural man does not receive the things of the Spirit of God; indeed, he considers them as foolishness (1 Cor. 2:14). Much less (2) to strive against the divine wisdom (2 Cor. 10:5; 1 Cor. 1:21) by philosophy falsely so-called, or any kind of empty deceit (Col. 2:8). Or even (3) to raise ourselves beyond the wisdom of God so that we would be wise beyond what has been written (1 Cor. 4:6) or beyond what is proper, which was the sin of our first parents (Gen. 3:4–6) and of the Antichrist (2 Thess. 2:4), which could be called being high-minded (Rom. 11:20). Or finally, (4) in any way to despise the wisdom of God, whether more crassly by considering it to be foolishness (1 Cor. 1:18, 23; Acts 17:18), or more subtly, which is done by others who, disdaining the simplicity of scriptural wisdom, daily explore new meanings, forge new dogmas, or if they cannot, cast old things into new forms (as they call them), that at least they may seem to have invented something new, which is an epidemic disease in our age. On the contrary, (1) we should extol the wisdom of God, we should marvel at it, after the example of the psalmist (Ps. 104:24; 119:18; 139:6) and of the apostle (1 Cor. 2:7; Rom. 11:33). (2) We should willingly subject ourselves to it (Rom. 8:5, 7). And if at times (3) the mind of the flesh should try to resist, we should take its reasonings captive and drive them back to the obedience of Christ (2 Cor. 10:5), and sing to it that song of Zophar, "Will you find out a searching of God? And will you reach to the perfection of the all-sufficient one? It is higher than the heavens—what will you do? Deeper than hell—what will you know?" (Job 11:7–8).

4. Detesting sins

XXVII. Furthermore, fourth, it offers an argument against sins. First, against past sins, that (1) we may remember them (Rev. 2:5), that (2) we may sorrow over them (Jer. 31:18–19), that (3) we may confess them to God (Ps. 32:5), that (4) we may turn ourselves from them (Rev. 2:5), because the omniscient God sees all of them (Hos. 7:2), since he knows all our thoughts (Ps. 139:23), no matter how hidden in our inmost heart (2 Chron. 6:20), all our words (Ps. 139:4), all our deeds, with all of their circumstances (Ps. 139:3), and he maintains a most accurate memory of them (Ps. 109:14; Hos. 8:13; 9:9) and does not put them away except through and after our conversion (Jer. 31:34; Num. 23:21; Acts 3:19; Mic. 7:19; Ezek. 23:21–22). Next, against future sins, that we may seriously detest even those sins most trivial and most far removed from the sight of all creatures, because not only their witness, but also their judge and avenger, is the omniscient one, in whose sight they are committed, and the one who is the knower of hearts, in whose eyes all things are bare and intimately open

(Heb. 4:13). It helps here to consider these passages: Job 34:21–22, Psalm 94:7, and Job 22:14.

5. Sincerity in whatever duty

XXVIII. Again, fifth, it offers an argument for sincerity in all our duties, first toward God, whether offered publicly or privately, after the example of David in 1 Chronicles 29:17, "I know, my God, that you search the heart, and that you love uprightness. As for me, in the uprightness of my heart I have freely offered all these things," and of Paul in 2 Corinthians 1:12; and particularly in the exercise of all good works, because God, the most kind rewarder (Heb. 11:6), knows our works (Rev. 2:2, 13, 19; 3:8), and remembers them, as if they were set down in perfect detail in a book of remembrance (Mal. 3:16), and does this so that he may reward them (Acts 10:4; Neh. 5:14, 19; 13:10, 14, 22, 31; Isa. 38:3). Next, also toward our neighbor, that we should complete all our duties as if in the sight of God (Col. 3:22–23), who will both remember and commemorate them one day, at the last judgment (Col. 3:24; Matt. 25:34–35).

6. Confidence and consolation

XXIX. In addition, sixth, it offers an argument for confidence and consolation. First, in the public troubles of the church, when both Satan and the Antichrist, and the followers of both, by their schemes and plots, which seem all but unsearchable and past finding out, press so hard upon the church that there scarcely appears a crack through which to escape, then what will help us more effectively than the fact that to the eyes of God all things are bare and intimately open, that God laughs in the heavens at their counsels (Ps. 2:1–7), that he says, "Take counsel, and let it all be in vain" (Isa. 8:10)? Next, in the private afflictions of every believer, in disease, poverty, persecutions, dangers, that a merciful Father sees: "But," we say, "you do see, for you behold perversity and wrath…; the poor commits his cause to you; you are the helper of the orphan" (Ps. 10:13–14), and, "He sees" (Ex. 3:7; Rev. 2:2, 9; Isa. 49:15). Specifically, in poverty, where the means of living are lacking, what will more effectively support us than to hold on to the fact that God knows that you need earthly things (Matt. 6:31–32)? And so also in spiritual desertions, when we suspect that God has forgotten us (Ps. 13:1–2; 77:9–10; 88:5), then what help could you suggest and give that would be more effective than Isaiah 49:15, "Can a woman forget her little child, that she should have no compassion on the son of her womb? Even if these forget, yet I will not forget you," and likewise, "The Lord knows who are his" (2 Tim. 2:19)? Finally, in whatever strait and difficulty, by which we time and again are forced to such a point of necessity that no small crack appears through which we could escape (2 Chron. 20:12), so that we say, "Where shall I flee from your Spirit?" (Ps. 139:7), and likewise, "What shall we do, men and brethren?", then what will be more effective for us to remember than 2 Peter 2:9, "Thus God knows how to rescue his own," that he to whom there is no counselor will be to us a counselor (Ps. 73:24), and in addition that he gave his own Son, that by office he might be our Counselor (Isa. 9:6)?

7. Zeal for spiritual knowledge and wisdom. What sort of zeal is it?
XXX. Finally, seventh, it offers an argument inviting us to a zeal for knowledge and wisdom, that we may not be brute beasts who have no intellect (Ps. 32:9). I say for knowledge and wisdom, but not for just any sort: not (1) for imaginary wisdom, in which we are wise in our own eyes only, or we prefer to seem rather than to be (Prov. 3:7; Rom. 1:22; 1 Cor. 3:18). Nor (2) for false, carnal wisdom, or the mind of the flesh (Rom. 8:6), by which we consult with flesh and blood (Gal. 1:16), minding earthly things (Phil. 3:19). Nor (3) for deceitful wisdom or the wisdom of villainy (Luke 16:8). Much less (4) for that devilish wisdom of which James 3:15 speaks (cf. Gen. 3:1). Nor (5) for worldly wisdom (1 Cor. 2:6) and that deceitful and cunning philosophy (Col. 2:8), but for the true philosophy, which is the wisdom of God (1 Cor. 2:7), the wisdom from above (James 3:15), and the mind of the Spirit (Rom. 8:6); for spiritual wisdom, which the Holy Spirit teaches (1 Cor. 2:13), and indeed also for civil and political wisdom, like that of Solomon (1 Kings 4:29) and of Bezaleel (Ex. 31:3), but such as nonetheless is from God and according to God (James 1:5; 1 Cor. 3:19–20); but chiefly for theological wisdom, which is in a mystery (1 Cor. 2:7), the wisdom by which we spiritually discern the spiritual things of God (1 Cor. 2:11, 14). By this wisdom, we are separated (1) from brute beasts (Job 35:11; Ps. 32:9), (2) from unbelievers (Ps. 79:6; Isa. 1:3), and (3) from the foolish (Prov. 15:7). By it (4) we approach God and imitate him in one of his chief perfections, which is his wisdom and knowledge, in which imitation our perfection consists (Matt. 5:48). Thus, (5) in this alone may we boast (Jer. 9:24). Indeed, (6) upon it God makes to depend our justification (Isa. 53:11) and eternal salvation (John 17:3), while conversely, (7) upon ignorance he has pronounced his wrath and indignation (Ps. 79:6), and destruction (Hos. 4:1–6; 2 Thess. 1:8–9).

By what means must it be obtained?
And so that in our zeal we may pursue this divine knowledge and wisdom fruitfully, it is necessary (1) before all things, that we approach the fountain, that is, the depth of wisdom and knowledge, the Father of lights, the fountain of life, in whose light we enjoy light (Ps. 36:9), at whose feet we should place ourselves

most humbly. (2) That we solicit his instruction and illumination with most fervent supplications (James 1:5; Dan. 2:21), following the example of Solomon in 1 Kings 3:11. Furthermore, (3) that to his corrections we show ourselves compliant and teachable (Ps. 25:4; 143:10), that in this way we may come forth without doubt wiser than our enemies; indeed, even wiser than our teachers (Ps. 119:99). At the same time, (4) that we deny our own carnal wisdom (1 Cor. 3:18; Gal. 1:16; 2 Cor. 10:5). And finally, (5) as those who have gained spiritual and divine wisdom, that we constantly walk in it (Eph. 5:15).

CHAPTER FOURTEEN

The Truthfulness and Faithfulness of God

Will their unbelief render God's faithfulness useless? God forbid! Indeed, let God be true and every man a liar.

—Romans 3:3–4

The second perfection of the intellect is truth.

I. Just as the will, by its own nature, aims at the good as such, insofar as it is nothing but a rational appetite for the good as known, so the intellect, by its own nature, aims at the true. And since the perception of the intellect is only true logically when it perceives in accord with its object, so also the expression of the intellect is only true ethically when it accords with the perception of the intellect. And when this expression consists in promises, it is only called true when the fulfillment is consistent with the promises. Thus finally, from these things arise both God's truthfulness and his faithfulness, which two things we will subjoin to the divine intellect as its two qualities, because they come from his intellect, inasmuch as it cannot be deceived or deceive. We will build this topic on the words of Paul in Romans 3:3–4.

The Exegetical Part

It is constructed upon the exegesis of the text.

II. The apostle advances this text's apology against the difficulty that could have been brought against him from the unfaithfulness of the Jews, that in rejecting them contrary to the assurance he had given in so many promises, God seems to do violence to his own truthfulness. The apostle opposes this difficulty with:

    A. A certain anticipation of the objection, which brings forward the difficulty: μὴ ἡ ἀπιστία αὐτῶν τὴν πίστιν τοῦ θεοῦ καταργήσει; "Will their unbelief nullify the faithfulness of God?," that is, will their unbelief and rejection make void the trustworthiness of the divine promises? He opposes it here with:

1. The thing causing injury: ἀπιστία, the "unbelief" of the Jews. Namely, that by which they refused to receive Christ, who was offered to them in so many promises (John 1:11), and on this account were rejected by God (Rom. 11:1–2).

2. What was injured: πίστις θεοῦ, the "faithfulness of God," which denotes: (a) his αὐτοπιστία and ἀξιοπιστία, credibility in himself and worthiness of trust, on account of which he is fully most worthy to be believed most securely; (b) his constancy and immutability in his decrees (Num. 23:23; Prov. 30:5, 8); (c) his faithfulness in fulfilling what he has promised (2 Cor. 1:18, 20); and (d) his truthfulness in all that he has said (Jer. 10:10). In this passage, it especially designates his faithfulness.

3. The injury: καταργήσει, "will nullify," caused through the unbelief of the Jews. And something is said καταργεῖσθαι, to be nullified, if its force and effectiveness are taken away, which happens to promises when they are not fulfilled. And this seemed to occur in the unbelief of the Jews, since it seemed to be incompatible with the promises concerning an eternal covenant (Hos. 2:19; Jer. 31:33, 36). From this, furthermore, the faithfulness or trustworthiness[1] of one who promises also gradually erodes and vanishes, for whoever does not supply what was promised loses trust. Moreover, while Paul sets this forth interrogatively (μὴ...καταργήσει; "Will it nullify?"), he argues very strongly for the negative, calling all people, as it were, to witness that this would be most unjust, as if he were saying, Who will say that it is right for the faithfulness of God, supported by so many promises, to be undercut by the unfaithfulness of certain Jews?

B. A rhetorical answer, in which the difficulty brought forth is removed:

1. By a certain rejection of abhorrence: μὴ γένοιτο, "Let it not be," "Let it not be done," "God forbid," in Hebrew, חלילה, "far be it," a formula used by one who intensely recoils and with detestation denies that it is right for God to be in difficulties on account of human ungodliness.

2. By a certain choice of substitution: γινέσθω δὲ ὁ θεὸς ἀληθής, "On the contrary, let God be true," or "he shall be true" or "let him remain true." In it there occurs:

---

1. ἀξιοπιστία

a. On the one hand, the thing chosen: "Let God be true." Let him be constant and worthy of trust, let the pronouncements of God be in all things conformable to both the mind and the object, let him be faithful in all his promises.

b. On the other, the thing left remaining: "and every man a liar." Either in a comparative sense: even if all became liars or failed in their faithfulness; for it is better for the latter to be fulfilled than the former not to be. Or in an absolute sense, that every man is a liar, yet God will remain true. Here ψεύστης, "liar," does not denote such a person who has given himself over to lies, or in actuality is lying, but who could lie, which it is common to all people. And the γινέσθω, "let him be," in this portion of the sentence must be taken not imperatively, but permissively, so that the sense is, Let God remain true, and he will remain true, although every man is a liar and lies.

The Dogmatic Part

The universal truth and faithfulness of God is proved: By the Scriptures

III. The sacred page everywhere and in more than one way confirms this truth and faithfulness, which the text attributes to God alone, to be universal and undisturbed, whenever it expressly proclaims that (1) he is true (Jer. 10:10; 1 Thess. 1:9; 1 John 5:20); (2) he does not know how to be deceived or how to deceive (Num. 23:19; 1 Sam. 15:29; Titus 1:2; Heb. 6:18); and in particular, (3) in his words, he is truthful, and thus they are truth (John 17:17); and likewise, (4) in his works, and thus all the paths of the Lord are mercy and truth (Ps. 25:10; Rev. 15:3; 16:7).

And by three reasons

IV. And God cannot be otherwise, because (1) all falsehood and deception comes either from imperfection, that you do not know correctly, or from malice, by which you prefer not to tell what you know, or to tell it as you know it. But both of these are repugnant to the one who is the God of truth (Ps. 31:5), whose Son is truth itself (John 14:6), and the Spirit, who is the Spirit of truth (John 16:13). (2) There could not be any truth or anything true if God were not true and truthful, insofar as there cannot be a second truth which is not from the first. Therefore, either the creature would have what it had not received from God, or it would have received truth from one who did not have it, which is repugnant to the one who is himself essential truth (Ps. 100:5) and who in his own way is alone true (Rom. 3:4). Therefore also, by his truth he is distinguished from the false gods (2 Chron. 15:3; John 17:3). Thus Philo rightly said, "Each word of God is an oath,"[2] and Fulgentius called him truth without deceit, goodness without malice, and blessedness without misery.[3]

What is truth and how many kinds of it are there, in general?
V. Moreover, all truth consists in agreement: either agreement of the appearance with the thing, by which gold differs from brass, and this is customarily called metaphysical or transcendental truth (though perhaps it will be more accurately sought in agreement with the divine idea); or agreement of the mind with the thing, by which we understand a thing as it is, and this is called logical truth; or the agreement of words with the mind, by which we speak according to our understanding, which is called ethical truth. The first truth is opposed to pretense, the second to error and falsehood, and the third to lying, which is nothing but to proceed contrary to the mind.

What is the truth of God and how many kinds of it are there?
VI. Any of these kinds of truth is applicable to God preeminently, for (1) through his essence, he has whatever there is of true deity, without any pretense (John 17:3), and contrary to this essence, the false gods who bear nothing of the divine in themselves only feign its appearance, or obtain it in the brains of their worshipers (Ps. 115:5–6). Next, (2) his mind is most exactly congruent with things themselves, because he perceives all things in himself, and there is no creature hidden before him (Heb. 4:13). Furthermore, (3) his expression is congruent with his conception (although, to the one not paying close enough attention, it may at times not seem to be congruent, as in Genesis 22:2): (a) in narrations of every sort; (b) in predictions of future things (Gen. 49:10; Isa. 34:16); (c) in the explanation of saving dogmas (Ps. 19:8); (d) in the threat of punishments (Deut. 28:15; Rev. 19:11); and (e) in promises of benefits (Rev. 19:1; 2 Cor. 1:18, 20). Finally, (4) his operation is in all its forms congruent with his plan and

---

2. Mastricht: *singula Dei verba, sunt juramenta,* Philo: ἄλλως τε καὶ οἱ λόγοι τοῦ θεοῦ εἰσιν ὅρκοι καὶ νόμοι τοῦ θεοῦ καὶ θεσμοὶ ἱεροπρεπέστατοι, "Besides, even the mere words of God are oaths, and God's laws and institutions are most sacred." See Philo of Alexandria, *Legum allegoriae* (Νόμων ἱερῶν ἀλληγορίαι), bk. 3, ch. 72 in idem, *Philonis Alexandrini Opera Omnia,* eds. L. Cohn and P. Wendland, 3 vols. (Berlin: Georg Reimer, 1896), 1:158.

3. This phrase of Fulgentius of Ruspe is frequently cited in the period as "Fulgentius *ad Monimum* lib. 1," but has not been located. Cf. *PL* 65:151–78. The Lutheran theologian, Johann Gerhard, cites both this quotation and the previous one from Philo, and provides exact specificity on Philo's quote, but not that of Fulgentius (*lib. 1 ad monim.*); idem, *Loci theologici* (Jena: T. Steinman, 1610), vol. 1, locus 2, sec. 16, para. 286.

its expression. So then, God is called faithful (a) in his decrees (Isa. 14:24, 27), (b) in creation (1 Peter 4:19), (c) in redemption (Heb. 2:17), (d) in grace (John 1:17), and (e) in the protection and preservation of the church (Rev. 19:11).

The things contrary to the divine truthfulness
VII. In all things, this universal truthfulness and faithfulness of God excludes (as it does in the creatures, but even more so): (1) whatever is false, and whatever disagrees with things as they are (Prov. 6:19); (2) hypocrisy and any semblances of this sort (Ps. 15:2); (3) false speaking or lying (Titus 1:2; Heb. 6:18); (4) deceits, deceptions, and frauds (Prov. 14:25), and other things of this sort.

The Elenctic Part
1. Do the Reformed, by their arguments, undermine God's omnimodal truthfulness and teach that God pretends? The calumnies of our adversaries
VIII. It is asked, first, whether the Reformed, by their arguments, undermine God's omnimodal truthfulness and teach that God pretends. All of our adversaries, although by different hypotheses and in different degrees, agree in the affirmative. The Pelagians and all Pelagianizers—papists, Socinians, Remonstrants, and Lutherans—in order more effectively to denigrate the Reformed churches among their own people, and to remove and keep them from the Reformed communion, heap up such calumnies in cart loads. They observe, as it seems to them, that on the one hand God says in his own Word that he does not will the death of the sinner (Ezek. 18:23, 32), and that on the other hand the Reformed teach that he wills the death of the sinner and that he has determined it by an immutable decree of reprobation. Again, on the one hand God declares in his Word that he wills all to be saved (1 Tim. 2:4 ff), and on the other hand the Reformed teach that God does not will that all be saved. Furthermore, God offers all his own Son as the Redeemer, inviting them with excellent reasons to take hold of him as he is offered, with a living faith, and to repent of their sins, and yet meanwhile he does not will that all would believe, repent, and attain salvation, and thus, according to Reformed doctrine, he is a pretender. Consequently, God declares that he wills what he does not will, and thus he is not truthful in all things.

The true opinion of the Reformed
The Reformed, on the contrary, frankly testify publicly before God that they believe that God is truthful in all things, and that his words always correspond in perfect detail both to the things about which he has spoken and to his own

mind, and likewise that he always wills what he declares that he wills, but that he wills it in the way he wills. If he declares that he wills a futurity or an outcome, then that outcome will always occur. If he should declare that he wills something to be our duty, that we should do it, or do something else, or not do it, then that is always our duty, although it may not be done in actuality. On this point the Reformed distinguish the will of God into his legislative will, by which he wills and determines what we ought to do or not do, but only *de jure*, regarding the rule, and not regarding the outcome; and his decretive will, by which he wills and determines what he himself wills to do, either what will come to pass or what will not, but only *de facto*, regarding what actually happens, and not what ought *de jure* to be done or not. For this reason, God wills many things by his legislative will that do not occur *de facto*. For example, he willed that Pharaoh should let Israel go *de jure*, that is to say, God willed something to be the duty of Pharaoh that he did not will *de facto*. Conversely, he wills many things *de facto*, for example, all sins that are committed, that he does not will *de jure* or as our duty. We will present this again more distinctly, God willing, in the following chapter.[4]

The objections of our adversaries are quelled.

Based on this distinction, we respond to the objections in this way: (1) that God does not desire the death of the sinner is by his legislative will, since in earnest he wills that there be an inseparable connection between the conversion of a sinner and his salvation, and thus in earnest he invites all to conversion and in earnest promises life to anyone who is converted to him, even if at the same time he does not will this by his decretive will, that is, even though he did not decree from eternity to confer, by his own grace, faith and repentance upon all sinners, and so to save them in actuality. Thus the judgment of the Reformed is nothing other than that God in the will of his eternal decree does not will that each and every sinner be saved in actuality, something that I know not even our adversaries dare to say. But again they say (2) that God declares that he wills it. I respond: (a) The Reformed do not deny that God wills all to be saved, but they do deny that God wills each and every individual to be saved. They deny that God says this in his Word anywhere. He wills that all be saved, that is, all who believe and repent, from any nation or rank among men (Rev. 5:9; 7:9). Next, (b) God wills it by his legislative will, that is, he wills to prescribe faith and repentance for all (Acts 17:30), in earnest promising salvation to those who believe and repent, and willing in earnest to save them. However, he does not will this by his decretive will, that is, he has not decreed from eternity that all attain salvation in actuality.

---

4. 1.2.15 §§XXII–XXVI, XXX

And thus we proceed to the third objection, (3) that God is a pretender when he offers salvation to sinners by so many and such excellent arguments and yet does not will to confer it to them. I respond, God, according to the Reformed, does offer in earnest remission of sins and eternal salvation to sinners who believe and repent (Ezek. 18), although he never decreed from eternity to confer to each and every person to whom he offers it the grace of faith and conversion, and thus to save them. For this reason, in the opinion of the Reformed, he is not a pretender.

2. Can the divine faithfulness that is in God, and from that, the divine faith that is in us, be based on something false?[5]

IX. It is asked, second, whether the divine faithfulness that is in God, and from that, the divine faith that is in us, could be based on something false. We bring together two falsehoods. For since our divine faith, by which we believe, rests on nothing but the faithfulness of God, insofar as he is the first truth and entirely unshakeable, then if our faith could be based on something false, then so could the faithfulness of God, and vice versa. Neither should we believe something by divine faith unless God himself bears testimony to its truth, nor does God bear testimony except insofar as it is truthful. So then it cannot occur that the truth of the testimony borne by an omniscient witness might be separated from the truth of the thing, nor also that what we are obligated to believe by divine faith might not be true. This whole demonstration is manifestly confirmed by 1 Corinthians 15:14–15, "If Christ has not been raised, our preaching is vain, and your faith is also vain. Moreover, we are even found to be false witnesses, because we have testified about God that he raised Christ from the dead." That is to say, if the testimony is not true, then the witness is false. In addition, if the divine faithfulness could be based on something false, then the logical argument that is the strongest of all will not be valid in the least: "God has said it, therefore it is true." These arguments are from William Ames in his *Marrow* (bk. 2, ch. 5, §25),[6] with which one could compare his *Disputation on the Truth of Divine Faith*, where more arguments are offered and the objections are expressly struck down without much difficulty.[7] Indeed, because we have already considered

---

5. As throughout the chapter, here both "faithfulness" and "faith" are translations of the same Latin word, *fides*.

6. William Ames's discussion regards the formal object of faith, or *objectum quo*, which is "the trueness or faithfulness of God" (*Dei veracitas aut fidelitas*). The majority of Mastricht's argument in this section is taken almost verbatim from Ames. See his *Medulla* (1634), 2.5.25, pp. 227–29; idem, *Marrow* (1639), 2.5.25, pp. 223–24.

7. William Ames, "Disputatio repetita et vindicata de fidei divinae veritate" in *Opera* (1659), 2:357–96.

this controversy in chapter 1 of this book, §XXVII, here it will suffice simply to point it out again.

3. Could God deceive if he wanted?

X. It is asked, third, whether God could deceive if he wanted. Descartes, together with his followers, so that he might maintain that every possibility, every truth, etc., depends upon the will of God, believes that God could lie. There are many arguments on this ability that appear in his *Meditation* IV.[8] And in the "Response to the Second Objections" he affirms that God can advance *some sort of verbal lie*.[9] So also do others.

The arguments of the Reformed

The Reformed believe that God neither can deceive nor wills to deceive, and that the conclusion that he can do so if he wills is false and impious, because: (1) it is contrary to the Scriptures, in which it is impossible for God to lie (Heb. 6:18), from which he is said not to be able to lie (Titus 1:2; etc.). (2) It is contrary to the nature, not only of the first truth, but also of the very truth itself, even *to be able* to deceive, because without doubt there is greater perfection in a witness that cannot deceive than in one that can. (3) It is contrary to the nature of God, in whom by this rationale there would be "yes and no," which the apostle cries out against (2 Cor. 1:18). It would also be (4) against the goodness of the most merciful Creator to be able to deceive his own miserable creatures, which even baron Johann Ludwig von Wolzogen acknowledges: "For falsehood to proceed from truth, for deception to proceed from goodness, would be repugnant to his most perfect nature."[10] (5) By this hypothesis, all the trustworthiness of the whole sacred Book will be endangered, as it is sustained by nothing other than the immovable truthfulness of God, and when that has been taken away, it falls to ruin. (6) All the trust that we owe to God and to his word is endangered, for if God could deceive, provided that he wills it, and especially also if he could will to deceive—since, according to the Cartesians, the possibility of all things depends upon his will, by which he is from eternity indifferent to every possible thing—then we will never believe him very safely or securely. (7) The divine majesty itself will be endangered. For if he can deceive, provided that he wills it,

---

8. René Descartes, *Oeuvres de Descartes* (Paris: Vrin, 1896, 1996), 7:52–62.

9. The printing of Mastricht's original Latin is striking: *VERBALE ALIQUOD MENDA-CIUM Deum proferre posse, affirmat.* Cf. Descartes, *Oeuvres de Descartes*, 7:142.

10. Baron Johann Ludwig von Wolzogen (1599–1661), *De Scripturarum interprete adversus exercitatorem paradoxum* (Utrecht: Johannes Ribbius, 1668), 9.

he can also lie (God forbid such blasphemy!) if he wills, he can be imperfect if he wills, he can be not God if he wills.

Objections of the Cartesians

At the same time they allege to the contrary: (1) that theirs is an argument in favor of wisdom, of power, and thus of a sort of perfection, and such perfection ought not to be banished from the most perfect God. I respond: (a) In this way hereafter it will have to be counted among the praises, among the perfections and attributes of God, that he can deceive if he wishes. (b) By what argument will they demonstrate that this is the work of wisdom, power, and any sort of perfection? (c) At least up to this point, theologians and philosophers considered it as nothing but an argument in favor of crafty subtlety to say that God can deceive. (2) But, they counter, we do not say simply that he can deceive, but only if he wills it. I respond, In this way, the will of God seems to presuppose the possibility of a thing, which is contrary to the hypothesis of the Cartesians, to whom the will of God is the cause of all possibility (see Wittich, *Peaceable Theology*, §119).[11] From this it manifestly follows that if God is not willing, he also is not able, and conversely, that if he is able to deceive, he is also willing to do so, since to God nothing is possible unless he wills it in actuality, as the celebrated Frans Burman says in many places in his *Synopsis of Theology* (vol. 1, ch. 21, §§20, 24; ch. 25, §§9–10), adding that nothing is possible or has been from eternity, unless it exists in actuality (ch. 21, §§24, 26), from which it follows that if God can deceive, not only has he willed to do so from eternity, but also, this has occurred in actuality.[12] But they add, (3) He does not will to do so. But I will say, On what basis will it be certain for you that God does not will to deceive? If they should respond, It is sufficient that he said he does not will to do so, then I will press them, But what if he willed to deceive in saying that also? If Descartes should retort, Because being willing to deceive is without doubt a testimony of malice and weakness, I would oppose him, saying, According to Descartes, the will of God is the cause of entirely every truth, goodness, and possibility, and it is repugnant, according to him, to think that the will of God was not indifferent to all things from eternity (see Wittich, *Peaceable Theology*, §119).[13] From this, two conclusions come forth: (a) God from eternity could have willed, and even does will, to deceive. (b) If he had willed to deceive, then to will to deceive would

---

11. Wittich, *Theologia pacifica* (1671), 87–88.

12. Frans Burman (1628–1679), *Synopsis theologiae et speciatim oeconomiae foederum Dei*, 2 vols. (Utrecht: Cornelius Jacobus Noenardus, 1671–1672), 1:117–19, 145–46.

13. Wittich, *Theologia pacifica* (1671), 87–88.

by no means be a testimony of malice and weakness; in fact, on the contrary, it would be a good thing and a thing that showed power. See also our *Gangrene of the Cartesian Innovations* (sect. 2, ch. 12).[14]

The Practical Part

Upon the divine truth rests: 1. The infallibility of the divine Word

XI. In regard to practice, upon the divine truth and faithfulness rests, first, the entire certainty and trustworthiness of the divine Word, since it is the word of him who cannot lie (Titus 1:2), for whom it is impossible to lie (Heb. 6:18), and from this it is called the word of truth (Col. 1:5), more refined than all purest gold (Ps. 12:6). Furthermore, upon it rests all our religion, all our faith and observance, with all things they contain. Thus it is entirely incumbent upon us to devote ourselves to becoming more and more convinced of the truthfulness and faithfulness of God. We are formed in this way by diligently and devotedly comparing (a) God's words with his deeds, (b) the things God predicted with their outcomes, (c) his threats with his judgments, (d) his promises with his benefits, (e) his teaching with nature (Isa. 34:16; Josh. 1:3, 6, 14; 1 Kings 8:56). Thus by all these things we may be rooted more and more in the persuasion of God's universal truthfulness. And to them we should also add our prayers, that God himself would persuade us of it (Ps. 43:3).

2. The solution of faith

XII. In particular, second, upon it, as upon its final solution, rests all our faith (1 Cor. 15:14–15; Heb. 10:23). Specifically (1) in the articles of our faith (2 Tim. 1:12), (2) in the controversies of religion, (3) in especially abstruse mysteries (1 Tim. 3:16), (4) in things hard to understand and unsolvable, which we meet in our reading of Scripture. In all these things, in this one thing we can be secure, that the things we believe have been revealed to us by him who cannot lie, that faithful witness (Rev. 1:5), whose faithfulness no faithlessness can undermine, who will be true even if everyone becomes a liar. And by this one thing we can most effectively check whatever thoughts that exalt themselves against the knowledge of God, and whatever tricks, inventions, and explanations that come from the most cunning adversaries, provided that we depend upon the one Word of God, for, "A showy gloss has deceived many—lean upon the word of God, and you will be safe," according to that common proverb.[15]

---

14. Mastricht, *Gangraena*, 269–74.

15. This common proverb (*textus non fallit multos speciosa fefellit glossa; Dei verbo nitere tutus eris*) occurs mostly among Lutherans; e.g. Johann Möller, *Defensio Lutheri defensi, das ist*

3. All divine worship

XIII. And not faith only, but third, also on it rests all our divine worship, specifically: (1) the unmoved profession of the truth (Heb. 10:23; John 3:33); (2) all promptness in obedience (Rom. 4:19–21); (3) all confidence in prayers (Dan. 9:4; 1 John 1:9); (4) all constancy in adversities (1 Peter 4:19; 2 Thess. 3:3); and (5) all perseverance in faith (1 Cor. 1:8–9; 10:13).

4. Solid consolation

XIV. Furthermore, fourth, upon the divine truth and faithfulness rests solid consolation in all kinds of adversities. And that is because through it, all the many and great promises made to the afflicted (Heb. 13:5) will be yes and amen (2 Cor. 1:20). God will neither nullify his kindness by them, nor in them will he lie, against the assurance he has given (Ps. 89:33; Heb. 6:17–18). As Cyprian rightly says in *On Mortality* (ch. 4), "God is truthful, and his Word to believers is eternal and firm. If a venerable and praiseworthy man promised something to you, you would certainly have faith in him who promised, nor would you believe that you were being deceived and duped by him whom you know well to stand firm in his words and deeds. But now God speaks to you, and you, faithless, are restless in your mind?"[16] In particular, this comforting power shows itself throughout the Scriptures, in the case (1) of imminent persecutions of the church by any enemies (Rev. 18:5–6; 19:20); (2) of spiritual desertions (Heb. 13:5; Isa. 49:14–15; Matt. 11:28); (3) of doubts that our prayers will be heard (Matt. 18:19); or (4) that we will be set free from every evil (Ps. 23:4). In all these and a thousand other cases, what will restore our joy more sweetly than to think that: (1) God is altogether truthful, and particularly in his promises, he is faithful, to such a degree that his faithfulness cannot be rendered void by anyone's faithlessness (Rom. 3:3). Especially since (2) in addition, he has reinforced them by swearing an oath (Heb. 6:17; cf. Ps. 146:5–6). Indeed, (3) he has given so many and such great evidences of his faithfulness and truthfulness (2 Kings 20:9; 2 Chron. 21:7; Isa. 38:7; Jer. 32:22). And thus (4) the saints throughout all ages have clung so constantly to it in all uncertainties: Abraham (Rom. 4:18–19), David (2 Sam. 7:28), and so forth.

---

der Wolverhädigte Luther entgegen gesegt dem Unverthädigten Luther (Frankfurt: Zacharias Härtel, 1706), 99.

16. Cyprian, *De Mortalitate* in *PL* 4:586; idem, *On the Mortality* in *ANF* 5:470.

5. The avoidance and hatred of sin

XV. On the other hand, fifth, in the truthfulness and faithfulness of God is also (1) that which should draw sinners back from wickedness, as they reflect that God is altogether truthful and immovable in his threats, just as in his promises (Jer. 8:9–11; Rev. 2:5). We are given examples of this in the Israelites (Num. 14:21–38; cf. 26:65; Deut. 1:35), in the Judahites (2 Kings 24:2). (2) That on account of which they should not despise the divine threats, since they come from a most truthful God (Deut. 29:19; Ps. 139:7). In fact rather, (3) that on account of which they should tremble at them (Isa. 66:2), and also (4) because of them throw themselves down and humble themselves before God, after the example of the Israelites (Num. 14:39), of the Ninevites (Jonah 3:4–5), of Hezekiah (2 Kings 20:2; Isa. 38:2), indeed, even of Ahab himself (1 Kings 21:27) and of Simon the Magician (Acts 8:24), remembering that those who despise and scoff at the divine threats are condemned: Cain (Gen. 4:7–8), the Judahites (Isa. 5:18–19), the Israelites (Amos 6:3), Manasseh and his subjects (2 Kings 21:11–17).

6. And of false speaking, and so forth

XVI. Specifically, sixth, in the truth and faithfulness of God is that on account of which we should be on our guard (1) against any false speaking (Ex. 20:16; Prov. 6:12–15); (2) against all hypocrisy (Ps. 35:16; 10:7); (3) against all lying (1 Kings 22:22–23; Ps. 31:6; Prov. 6:17); (4) against all unjust equivocations and mental reservations (Prov. 26:24); (5) against all deceits and frauds (Prov. 14:25); (6) against any faithlessness and covenant-breaking (Ps. 15:4; Rom. 1:31); (7) against all hatred of the truth, that by which we strive against it (Rom. 1:18; 2 Tim. 3:8). For all these things (1) are most exceedingly abhorrent to the truthful and faithful nature of God, who is truth itself (John 14:6) and the God of truth (Ps. 31:5), because of which he thus cannot be false (1 John 2:21); and also to the character of the children of God. Indeed rather, (2) they incline toward the character of Satan, the pledged enemy of God, who is a liar and the father of lies (John 8:44; 1 Kings 22:21–22). Thus, (3) they shut off sinners from communion with God and participation in the heavenly kingdom (Rev. 21:27; 22:15) and (4) devote them to destruction (Ps. 5:5–6).

7. Zeal for truthfulness

XVII. Finally, seventh, in the truth, faithfulness, and sincerity of God is that on account of which we should labor (1) for truthfulness in all our words (Eph. 4:15; 2 Thess. 2:10); (2) for faithfulness in our promises, whether offered to God or to men (Ps. 15:2; 116:14, 18; Josh. 24:21–22); (3) for sincerity in our deeds, that is, "in simplicity and godly sincerity, not in fleshly wisdom" (2 Cor. 1:12). (4) We should render ourselves compliant to the truth (John 18:37; Rom. 2:8; 1 Cor. 13:7; Gal. 3:1). And (5) we should walk in the truth (2 John 4). Also, (6) we should be sanctified in the truth (John 17:19). For in this way, (1) we will to that extent become like God and be made partakers of the divine nature (2 Peter 1:4). And thus (2) we will receive the favor of the triune God: the Father, who is the God of truth (Ps. 31:5); the Son, who is truth itself (John 14:6), from which the truth is called the truth of Christ (2 Cor. 11:10); the Holy Spirit, who is called the Spirit of truth (John 14:17; 15:26; 16:13), who leads his own into all truth (John 16:13; Ps. 143:10), because of which truth is called a fruit of the Spirit (Eph. 5:9). And also (3) we will prove ourselves true and living members of the militant church, which is called the pillar and ground of the truth (1 Tim. 3:15; 4:3; John 18:37), and then after that (4) of the triumphant church also (Ps. 15:1–2). In this way (5) God will show himself truthful and faithful to us in his promises (2 Cor. 1:18, 20).

CHAPTER FIFTEEN
The Will and Affections of God

Our God is in the heavens; he has done all that he has willed.
—Psalm 115:3

The contemplation of the divine will

I. Among the rational faculties, we have drawn out the first faculty, which regards its object as true, namely, the divine intellect, with its qualities and virtues. Following that comes the second faculty, which is directed to its object as a known good. We will contemplate it: (1) as it is a faculty (according to our mode of conceiving), (2) as an act, and (3) as a virtue. In the first, we will present the nature and character of the divine will; in the second, its affections, which are nothing but acts of the will; in the third, its virtues: goodness, grace, righteousness, holiness, and so forth. In this chapter, on the will and affections, the psalmist will light the way in Psalm 115:3.

The Exegetical Part

It is constructed upon the exegesis of the text.

II. The text has a ready and honorific response to the skeptical and jeering question of the Gentiles in the preceding verse: they asked, "Where now is your God?" as if they were saying, You cannot show him and thus he is nowhere, and consequently, he does not exist at all. The prophet responds in the name of the Israelite church promptly and honorifically: "Our God is in the heavens, and he does all that he wills." At the same time, he supplies an honorific description of his God, in which occurs:

    A. The one described: וֵאלוֹהֵינוּ, "But our God…." Here the conjunctional prefix וְ, which ordinarily has a copulative force, is adversative, looking partly to the immediately preceding question, "Where now is your God?," to which he responds, "But our God is in the heavens," and partly to the following description of the false gods of the Gentiles from verses 4 to 9:

"Their idols are silver and gold...." He is described as אלהים, God, in the plural number, three in persons. He only is the true God: he is the God infinite in perfection and power, and each of his persons, Father, Son, and Holy Spirit, is infinite, in such a way that our God is thrice infinite, omnipotent, and perfect. The prophet adds the pronominal suffix of the first person plural, נו, "our," that is, the one who has chosen us out of the nations to be his people, his own possession, the one to whom we also have given back ourselves to be his people, the one who not only has given himself to us by the national covenant that he entered into with us, just as we in turn have given ourselves to him, but also has devoted himself in all that he is, by a personal covenant of grace to be the God of true believers, just as we believers in turn have given back our whole selves to him.

B. The description: "...is in the heavens, and he does all that he wills." These three things are attributed to him:

1. Existence, and the place of existing: He "is in the heavens," בשמים. He "is," not as your gods, who are not (1 Cor. 8:4), and are not anywhere except in your idol-temples; and he is "in the heavens," the most exalted, most glorious places, while your gods exist on the earth, imprisoned in narrow spaces. And he is in the "heavens," in the plural, which is to say, he is in all the heavens. This is not because he is imprisoned in them, as if he were not elsewhere outside of them, but because in them he makes his divine majesty manifest with a particular glory.

2. Will: חפץ, which denotes "to will," or to act from counsel and good pleasure. He has an intellect, he has a will, he sees, he hears, whereas your gods are silver or gold, gods who have eyes, and do not see, ears, and do not hear; that is, they understand nothing: they are lifeless and irrational.

3. Power and operation: "he does all that he wills." He is endowed with power, whereas your idols can do nothing. Indeed, he is omnipotent, he can do all things, and he also does do them, whereas your gods, confined to their own places, do nothing at all; in fact, he does what he wills, not as one coerced, but freely, from counsel, from rational complacency. As a result, all things that happen come to pass by his power and will alone. He does what he wills, and as a result, all things are accomplished by the command and consent of his will alone; it is no sooner said than done (Rev. 4:11; Ps. 33:9).

The Dogmatic Part

The will of God is affirmed by testimonies: first of Scripture, then of nature.

III. From the text, nothing is incumbent upon us in this chapter except the contemplation of the divine will. Scripture in an infinite number of places attributes will to God (e.g. Eph. 1:11; Rom. 9:18–19; Matt. 11:26; 26:39, 42; 1 Cor. 12:11). And so does nature, in more than one way, for: (1) "will" is without doubt a perfection, and one that does not connote any sort of imperfection. (2) It is communicated to the creatures from God, so then it is preexistent in him who communicates it. (3) He cannot operate in a way inferior to his own creatures to whom he has communicated a more perfect way of operating, that is, from counsel. So then, he cannot act either by nature, like the irrational creatures, or rashly, like foolish people; so then, he acts from counsel, which belongs to will. Otherwise, (4) nothing in the world would occur contingently. For a cause acting naturally acts to the limit of its forces, such that it is not able not to act, or to act in a different way. And from this, furthermore, (5) it would follow that no worship, no gratitude at all belong to God on account of his blessings, just as neither worship nor gratitude belongs to the sun, although it dispenses to us light and heat, by which we can do so many and such great things, since it dispenses them not by will but by nature. Indeed, (6) all sovereignty, grace, mercy, and righteousness must be removed from God, since they require a will. Finally, (7) nor would he be the cause that was absolutely first, independent and most perfect, most blessed in itself, or the cause of blessedness in others, for without a will, he could neither enjoy himself nor impart any enjoyment of himself to others. To affirm a will for God with more reasons than these is nothing but to light a candle for the sun.

What is the human will?

IV. We should rather investigate what, what sort, and how manifold is the will in God, what his acts are, and what its affections and virtues are. We will come to a knowledge of this matter in no way more helpfully than by setting up a comparison of our will with God's, so that it may be evident in what they agree and in what they differ. Let us take as our beginning the term *will*, which denotes three things: (1) that force of our mind which is the principle of will or the faculty of willing; (2) the act of that faculty, or the willing itself; finally, (3) the willed object. The first two belong most especially to this chapter. And thus, the will is that faculty of acting from free choice,[1] or from rational complacency, and its act is called the rational appetite. For there is natural appetite, by which

---

1. ἐκ προαιρέσει

vegetative things are directed to the good that is natural to them, though it is entirely unknown to them; sensitive appetite, by which brute beasts are directed to their object as it is known to them by their senses, seeking the good suitable to them and fleeing the evil adverse to them; and rational appetite, by which men and angels are directed to their object as known to them by their intellect, so that from this intellection, whether it comes before or together with the appetite, we speak of this appetite as rational, from counsel, and from rational complacency. And for it, at least as it is exercised concerning the means (for concerning the end as such, deliberation does not occur) the final judgment of the practical intellect is prerequisite, insofar as it shows rational creatures what agrees with their particular inclination and what is contrary to it. And here also, the rational appetite is not proper to man in such a way that it excludes the sensitive and natural appetites, but rather that it includes them, just as a larger number includes a smaller, and it also directs them.

What then are its acts?

V. Furthermore, the acts of this rational appetite as such are of two kinds: the elicited act, or the willing itself, and the commanded act, concerning the acts of any other faculty: of the intellect, of the senses, of the members. The first occurs either by willing what is consonant or by not willing what is dissonant. Moreover, it either wills (1) the end, from which a triple act arises: (a) love, by which it is simply inclined to that end as a good; (b) enjoyment, by which it is inclined to a good as already acquired and possessed; and (c) intention, by which it is inclined to a good as it is yet to be acquired. And this third act usually presupposes the end as obtainable, from which arises hope and desire, but if on the contrary it should consider the end as not obtainable, it produces willingness[2] and a wish, and this willingness is nothing but that imperfect act of will which lacks the power of obtaining. Or it wills (2) the means, and this again by a triple act: (a) the choice of suitable means, if several are available, from which we speak of free choice, to which it is proper to attribute liberty; (b) complacency, which is occupied with the means as chosen; (c) the use of the chosen means, which is commanded by the will, directed by the intellect, perfected by the other faculties through the commanded acts of the intellect, of the senses, of the members. From these things, conversely, what negative willing is can be inferred without any trouble.

---

2. *velleitas*

The object of the will is the good.

VI. In every circumstance, the will is brought to its end, as to its good, meaning what is agreeable to the inclination of him who wills, whether it is truly good or not, as long as it agrees with his inclination. Therefore, given this most brief sketch of the created will, in which appears a manifold dependency of the acts upon the faculty, upon the objects, and upon each other, a manifold composition and change, and thus a manifold imperfection, we see that will cannot belong univocally to God and to creatures.

To what extent is will not applicable to God?

VII. Therefore, it will be helpful in a few words to compare the above things with the divine will. (1) The objects and effects of the divine will are not called, except improperly, by the name *will*. (2) The faculty of willing in God does not in fact differ from the act of willing, since in him potency and act, perfection and imperfection have no place. (3) Neither does his liberty of willing or of not willing one thing over another argue (unlike in the creatures) that the faculty is in fact different from the act, or that the faculty needs to be actuated. Rather, it only denotes a natural indifference of a most simple act toward its object, an indifference by which it could be terminated or not on this thing rather than that thing. (4) Also, God entirely lacks a natural appetite, because a natural appetite is led to its own object as it is an unknown thing, and it is directed to its end more by something else than by itself, which is thoroughly abhorrent to the first and most perfect cause. (5) So also, due to his lack of senses, all idea of a sensitive appetite falls away from God, and with it, all passions and affections. (6) Therefore in God remains only a rational appetite, which is terminated on an object as it is understood.

What is will in God?

VIII. With these points touched upon, we have stated that the will in God is nothing but his most wise propensity toward himself as the highest end, and toward the creatures, on account of himself, as the means. It is called a propensity partly so that it may be distinguished from his intellect, which is only a simple intuition, and partly so that we may employ such an expression that is fit to connote all the acts of our own will. We also call it a most wise propensity so that we may distinguish it from a natural and sensitive appetite. We assign to it a twin object: himself as the primary object and the creatures as the secondary object, and they on account of him, insofar as they bear some image of his goodness and have been suitably designed to aim at him and his glory. And so that we may perceive these things a little more clearly, it must be further noted that

God's will has entirely the same reason for what it wills as his intellect does for what it knows. For the appetite is rational, and accordingly it is directed to its object in the way offered to it by the intellect. Therefore, just as the divine intellect does not know except through the intuition of his own most perfect essence, so also through his will, God does not arrive at the goodness of the creatures as it is in itself. For in that way in his willing he would necessarily depend upon the creatures and would exist by reason of them in a passive potency, and consequently would exist posterior to them. But just as eminently all the goodness of all creatures is contained in him, thus he is directed to his own immeasurable goodness, insofar as through his most free choice it is distributed analogically[3] among the creatures.

The independence of the divine will. Its four corollaries
IX. Thus far we have contemplated the nature and character of the divine will. We now proceed to its properties. By them God's will is, first, independent (Rom. 11:35–36), since it is his very essence, the first cause of things: "By your will they exist and were created" (Rev. 4:11). So then, (1) the fact that he operates *ad extra* does not presuppose some goodness in the object, but rather puts it there by his act of willing: "Because he willed he brought us forth" (James 1:18); "He has mercy on whom he wills" (Rom. 9:18). Just by this hypothesis alone, in the matter of predestination, the idea that the will of God would be dependent upon anything foreseen is destroyed.

(2) Neither by this independence does his will admit any cause, although it prescribes the dependence of cause and effect to things among themselves. So then it is certainly said rightly that God wills one thing to exist for the sake of another, yet it is said wrongly that the one thing is a cause, properly speaking, by which the will of God is internally moved to will the other thing. Thus God willed that the sun and stars exist for the sake of the generation, conservation, and corruption of terrestrial beings, yet the sun and stars are not causes by which God wills those beings to be generated, preserved, and corrupted. So it is in all things outside of God, which indeed through the divine will are causes and effects among themselves, but still are not causes of the divine will.

In fact, (3) by this independence, in God himself the willing of one thing is not properly called the efficient cause by which he wills another thing in himself. For example, the fact that he willed to confer faith to Peter is not properly called

---

3 *exemplariter.* God's goodness is the exemplary cause, or the original pattern, of created goodness.

the cause by which God willed in himself to confer salvation to him. For the efficiency of the cause upon the effect and the dependence of the effect upon the cause cannot happen to the divine will, which is God himself, willing all things truly and simply at one and the same time by a single act.[4]

Nevertheless it is true (4) what the Scholastics say, obscurely enough, that the passive attingency[5] of the will with respect to one thing is the cause, or reason rather, of the passive attingency of another thing. That is to say that, for example, the fact that Peter's faith is attingent upon the will of God is the cause or reason that his salvation is also attingent. Therefore, in this sense, it is rightly said that God wills one thing because he willed another.

The simplicity of the divine will

X. Second, the will of God is most simple because it is the willing God himself. So then, by one most simple act he wills each and every thing, the end and the means. Thus there are not many volitions in God; and there is not an order of the volitions with respect to God, but only with respect to the thing, and with respect to our conception of it. For as above we saw that the divine intellect, by intuiting itself in one most simple act, without any composition and division, or discursive reasoning, or any such thing, perceives at one and the same time all the truths of all things as well as their reasons, so now we say that the will of God, by most perfectly willing itself, by a single and most simple act, wills at one and the same time all the goodness of all creatures, insofar as that goodness has been conferred, or is about to be, through the most free act of the infinite, self-communicating goodness. Thus, the perfectly good will of God is the first source of every goodness which exists in the creatures, whether absolute goodness or the relative goodness that they have among themselves such that they become to each other causes and effects, ends and means. For this reason, we by no means allow many wills or several volitions, much less those that are adverse to each other, although we conceive of that one will of God in various modes because of its effects and objects, and thus we make distinctions in it, as we will teach more definitely as we proceed.

The immutability of the divine will

XI. Third, the will of God is entirely immutable (Mal. 3:6; 1 Sam. 15:29; Ps. 33:11), and thus, "He does not will first this, then that, but he wills all that he wills at one and the same time, and always. He does not will again and again, nor

---

4. Cf. 1.7.41 in Ames, *Medulla* (1634), 31; idem, *Marrow* (1639), 28.

5. *Attingency*: the effect or influence of one thing upon another.

does he will now this, now that, nor does he will afterwards what he did not will, or not will what he willed previously, because such a will is mutable. All that is mutable is not eternal, but our God is eternal." These are the words of Augustine in his *Confessions* (bk. 12, ch. 15).[6] This is to say that just as his intellect is immutable because of the very fact that in understanding he does not regard the creatures but himself, and in himself, all things, so his will, because he wills himself, and for the sake of himself, all things, is by that fact unchangeable (Mal. 3:6; Num. 23:19). "My counsel shall stand, and I will do all my will" (Isa. 46:10). By this observation the antecedent and consequent will of both the Pelagians and the Pelagianizers falls apart, as will be evident in its own topic.

The eternity of the divine will
XII. Fourth, the will of God is eternal (Eph. 1:4), for it is the willing God himself. For this reason neither does he begin to will what he did not will previously, nor does he stop willing what he willed previously. Nor does he will one thing prior to another, although based on the order that we observe in our will we conceive that God wills the end prior to the means according to the order of intention, and he wills the means prior to the end according to the order of execution.

The infinity of the divine will
XIII. Fifth, the will of God is infinite, because it is the infinite God himself. This is not of course to say that he wills all willable things to exist just as he understands all intelligible things, but that he wills himself, who is infinite, and on account of himself, he wills all things, partly that they may exist, partly that they may not. And it is beyond doubt that he does not will to exist all willable things for these reasons: (1) because by this reason they would exist in infinite act, and accordingly, God would not be alone infinite; (2) because the will of God is most free concerning extrinsic things, which does not belong to the intellect, and thus he wills these things by free choice. Therefore, although his will does not will all willable things as his intellect understands all intelligible things, yet this does not hinder it from being equally infinite, because there is no finitude in the one willing, but in the things willed, and the limitation of the things willed does not arise extrinsic to him, but it comes from the will of God itself. "For our God is in the heavens, and he does whatever he wills" (cf. Isa. 46:10; Rom. 11:19).

---

6. Augustine, *Confessiones* in PL 32:832; idem, *Confessions* in NPNF1 1:180.

The freedom of the divine will

XIV. Sixth, the will of God is free, and most free. For freedom is of the essence of the will. This freedom is either antecedent to the thing willed, as its principle, in which sense God freely wills only that which is different from himself: "By your will they exist" (Rev. 4:11). Or it is concomitant with it, in which sense God wills himself and all things. Furthermore, two things coincide with divine freedom, insofar as it concerns extrinsic things: indifference, and free choice, that is, counsel or rational complacency. By indifference I mean that by which the one willing neither has been determined by nature to one or the other thing nor is determined of necessity by the object. For when an active power has been determined by nature to one or the other of two opposites, or it is determined of necessity by the object, then freedom is banished. Since, for example, fire by nature cannot but burn, or a hungry ox with fodder before it cannot but eat, those acts are thus not said to be free. Moreover, we understand God's indifference not to be a passive indifference in which an indeterminate will could be determined from another source, which belongs to creatures with respect to their Creator, but an active indifference in which by nature he could will or not will this or that thing. Furthermore, this active indifference of freedom belongs to God not by way of privation, as if his will at some point existed fully indeterminate and afterwards determined itself, which kind of indifference the Socinians and Pelagians would want so that they might undo the eternity of the divine decrees; but only by way of negation, since the will of God has certainly never been indeterminate, though by its own nature it always exists indifferent and indeterminate with respect to his creatures. Nor by his own nature, for example, was God more determined to create than not to create, or to do so in one way or another.

Besides indifference, for freedom of the will is required counsel.

XV. Besides indifference, secondly, for freedom is required counsel or choice, in which the will, by nature indifferent to both of two things, is determined to one or the other. And this determination, in the created will, at least concerning means, comes from the last judgment of the practical intellect, when it shows to the will that this or that thing either agrees or disagrees with its own particular propensity and inclination (with which willing has an inseparable connection). Thus we see that the will was created free, not absolutely, but only secondarily, since it unchangeably wills that which agrees with its own propensity, whereas God's will or propensity in itself has no connection with any creature, though the creature receives such a connection from God's willing it. So then, God wills this before that not only freely, but most freely, while the creature wills dependently by divine predetermination. This is the most free choice by which a nature antecedently indifferent is determined to this or that thing.

The efficacy of the divine will

XVI. Seventh, the will of God is universally effective. For whatever he wills, and just as he wills, he brings into effect in its own time and in its own way. Nor is there anything, if he wills it, that does not occur, or that does not occur as he wills it. "For our God is in the heavens; he does whatever he wills." And Revelation 4:2 says, "By your will they exist and were created." But (what must be noted) it always occurs just as he wills: if he wills the outcome of a thing, it always occurs; if he wills that it only be our duty, that we should will it ourselves, then it is so. But one must also distinguish between his effecting will and his effective will. The effecting will is only toward things that are good, both physically and morally. The effective will also concerns moral evils, insofar as first, in the eternal decree he determined their futurity, although he did not will to effect the evil itself to come to pass as such, and second, he also wills the substrate of sin, although he does not will its lawlessness and defect.

What is God's negative will?

XVII. Knowing now what God's will is, it is worthwhile to see what his negative will is.[7] In us it is another elicited act of our will by which it is occupied with evil, or that which does not agree with its inclination. But this negative will in God is nothing other than that act of the will by which, most perfectly willing himself, he is averse to everything adverse to him and to his glory, which is the only end of all things. It is called an act of his will, but certainly not another act, or one different from the willing by which he is turned by nature toward the good, just as his intellect recognizes false and contradictory things by an act of understanding that is not different from the act by which it recognizes true and good things. So then, we also make the primary and immediate object (although not the formal object) of the divine negative willing his own goodness, just as the primary and immediate object of his intellect, when it knows something false and evil, is his immeasurable perfection, insofar as it represents most clearly, as in a mirror, the appearance of all truths; and in knowing his perfection most perfectly, by the same stroke he most thoroughly ascertains what is false, contradictory, or evil, in

---

7. *voluntas*: will; *noluntas*: negative will. The distinction between the infinitives *velle*, *non velle*, and *nolle* is a subtle one derived from scholastic Latin in order to differentiate a positive willing, a non-willing, and a negative willing. A classic example comes from Thomas Aquinas, *Summa theologiae*, IaIIae q. 6, a. 3 ad 2.

one and the same act. He does this so thoroughly, that by most perfectly willing his own goodness, he is also most perfectly averse to whatever is adverse to him. This is visible to some extent in the creatures also, since he who perfectly loves God, by that very fact, also perfectly hates all that he knows is adverse to him. But at the same time, the secondary and formal object of the divine negative will is that which is by its own nature evil, though not physically but morally evil. For the physical evil that exists, God wills, by a willing most properly so-called. His negative will is occupied with moral evil, not absolutely, but insofar as it is such by its own nature. For it can occur and often does occur, that what by its own nature is adverse to the divine goodness, tends, contrary to its own nature, or incidentally, by an omnipotent and most wise directing of it toward that goodness as if it were its end, and thus in that measure, that is, by reason of this direction that is preternatural to it, it strips its nature of evil and is changed, as it were, toward the good incidentally, that is, insofar as by virtue of this omnipotent direction, it becomes fit for an end that is truly good, though it nevertheless is and remains, by its own nature, and in respect to the creatures perpetrating it, most wicked. Thus, God's negative will is occupied with what is evil in its own nature, not only because it is adverse to the norm of acting set before it by God, but also because it could not be directed by the power of the creatures to a truly good end. The action by which this negative will of God is directed toward evil is aversion (Ps. 5:4), just as the action of his will toward good is appetite, and yet it certainly is not directed toward evil by affection, but rather by effective operation, that is, destroying, abolishing, and punishing it. Even if an evil does not exist, or never will, God is still adverse to it, as it is inimical to his nature, since he would abolish and destroy it if it existed, just as he loves a good that will never exist, because, as it is congruent to his own goodness, if it existed he would conserve it, cherish it, and so forth.

The object of the will is the good.

XVIII. The object of the will, as we have said, is the good, that is, whatever is agreeable to the propensity of the one willing, whether this good is truly good, that is, conducive to the health of the one willing, or not, as long as it agrees with his propensity, such that it stirs up his appetite. And moreover, the final judgment of the practical intellect shows it to be so. On the contrary, the object of negative will is evil, or that which is repugnant to that propensity. The object of the divine will, considered inwardly, is nothing but the infinite goodness of God as it most fully satisfies him, and considered outwardly, it is whatever agrees with that goodness, just as the object of his negative will is whatever is discordant with that goodness.

What are the affections in God in general?

XIX. Furthermore, these acts of the will, willing and negative willing, take up, according to the diversity of their objects and the different method of operating upon their objects, different names, being called both affections and virtues. Affections, then, in God are nothing other than the acts of the divine will insofar as they sustain such relations to the creatures, and set such operations in motion in the creatures, as the analogous affections in men sustain and set in motion. So then, according to the common saying of Gregory of Nazianzus, since these affections are attributed to God in a human way, they must be understood in a way worthy of God,[8] according to the effective operation rather than the affection. So that we can more easily understand this, five things must be distinguished in the affections of God: (1) the act of willing, for example, in his wrath, he wills to take away, to punish; (2) its object, namely, what is adverse to his will: the sin and the sinner, when it comes to his wrath; (3) the relation between the willing and its object, based on which we reckon the concept of an affection, or by which we name each particular willing, such as wrath; (4) the foundation of this relation, the agreement or opposition that exists in the creatures; and finally, (5) those operations which customarily result in the creatures from those affections: blessing or punishment. These operations are accompanied in the creatures by various sorts of change, disturbance, and alteration, in their very bodies: for example, in wrath, an agitation of the mind, and a boiling of the blood around the heart. And these things, because they involve imperfection, must be religiously kept separate from the most perfect being.

What are they in specific? 1. Love

XX. Thus, let us descend from the general to the individual affections. First, the love of God (John 3:16) is his willing that which agrees with himself, or that which is his own, so to speak, and his operating in regard to it just as the affection of love in man does: embracing union with it or embracing its presence, blessing it, and resting in its goodness. Concerning this, we will say more in its place.[9]

2. Hatred

On the other hand, second, his hatred (Ps. 5:4) is his willing, or negatively willing, what is repugnant to himself, and doing against it the same works that hatred does in the creatures; that is, obliterating and punishing it.

---

8. Cf. 1.2.13 §XIX.
9. 1.2.17 §VI

3. Desire
Third, his desire and expectation (Isa. 5:2) is his willing an absent good. If the good seems difficult and uncertain for the creatures, then that desire is also named hope (1 Peter 3:20). If it should seem easier for the creatures to obtain and less uncertain, then it is named expectation, and from the analogous operations that surround it, it is called care.

4. Avoidance
On the other hand, fourth, his avoidance (Ps. 5:5) is his willing, or negatively willing, an absent evil, as it is difficult and threatening. If its occurrence is more probable for creatures, but is still avoidable, it is called fear, which is attributed to God (Deut. 32:26–27; Gen. 3:22). Inclined to the same end is his jealousy, or fear of losing a most precious thing (Ex. 20:5; Isa. 9:7; 37:32). If the evil happens to the creatures unavoidably, it brings him despair (Isa. 5:4; Jer. 2:21). And with these should be joined the analogous operations of the creatures in their own such affections.

5. Joy
Fifth, his joy (Heb. 13:15–16; Gen. 8:21) is his willing a good that is present and that concerns himself. It looks either to a service obtained from the creature (Heb. 11:4) or to a blessing which God bestows upon the creature (Deut. 30:8–9; Isa. 62:5; Jer. 32:41).

6. Sorrow
On the other hand, sixth, his sorrow and displeasure (Isa. 63:10; Ps. 78:40) is his willing, or negatively willing, a present evil. And if it should arise from some deed that belonged to him, it generates penitence (Num. 23:19, Gen. 6:6–9; 1 Sam. 15:11), which implies a change not in the worker, God, but in the work (Jer. 18:8).

7. Wrath
Furthermore, seventh, his wrath (Rom. 1:18; Eph. 2:3) is his willing to spurn and to obliterate what is repugnant to himself, by punishing it. If he does so by more serious punishments, then it is called burning anger and also fury (Deut. 29:20). In addition to these affections, in the creatures there is also wonder, boldness, and so forth, which we do not read applied to God in Scripture.

What is virtue in God? 1. In general
XXI. Moreover, insofar as God, by his own will, according to right reason, operates most readily, he is said to be endowed with virtues. For a virtue is a

habit by which the will is inclined to acting well. Concerning these virtues, first, this rule must be generally observed: they must not be conceived in God as first acts or habits that are destined, by operations yet to be produced, to result in a second act, for a potency of this sort does not apply to one who is a most simple act; but rather, they are virtues only insofar as by them God operates most readily. Second, the virtues, so different in us, denote in God a single readiness in acting, which readiness coincides with his essence. Third, one must take heed that they do not suggest any imperfection; and by this rule, those sorts of virtues must not be attributed to God which designate reference to someone greater, such as faith, hope, obedience, humility; and likewise, those which arise from imperfection, such as modesty, chastity, and so forth; and finally, those that are occupied with moderating the affections, such as temperance. And fourth, those virtues that remain and involve no imperfection are to be left for God in such a way that we conceive of them with the highest eminence of perfection.

2. In specific

Moreover, the virtues in God are: first, goodness, which is as it were the general virtue; then second, grace, or goodness toward the creatures, which, according to various respects, is also called mercy, longsuffering, and clemency; third, righteousness, or goodness in rewarding and in punishing; and finally, fourth, holiness, or moral goodness. In the following chapters we will treat each of these individually.

The distribution of the divine will: The will of the sign and will of good pleasure
XXII. Now, nothing remains except that we should add a few things about the distribution of the divine will. By all means, the will of God is one and only one, yet it is distinguished by us into various modes, first on account of the different kinds of things that it wills, next on account of the different modes in which we see that it wills what it wills. Thus they distinguish the will of God, first, into the will of the sign and the will of good pleasure. The latter denotes the decree of God itself, either his effective decree of good or his permissive decree of evil: "He does whatever he pleases" (Ps. 115:3) and "Yes, Father, so it has pleased you" (Matt. 11:25–26; Luke 12:32). But the former generally denotes some sort of indication by which God wills something to be signified to us, either that it would be simply believed and acknowledged, to which pertains his prediction, fulfillment, and remembrance of things or deeds, or, that our actions would be obliged to it as a norm, to which pertains, first, his command, promise, exhortation, invitation, and persuasion; next, his prohibition, threatening, dissuasion, warning, and so forth. Specifically, however, in thus contrasting the former with

the latter, we customarily look to the commandment, that is, the sign command-ing or prohibiting a specific effect of the divine will, for which reason they also call the will of the sign the will of the commandment.

Secret and revealed will

XXIII. Furthermore, second, they divide God's will into his secret and revealed will, according to Deuteronomy 29:29. Understand by the word *secret* those things that God decreed either to do or to permit and that he has so far not revealed, either by their outcome or by a prophecy. Consequently, they do not supply to us a way to know our norm; indeed, modesty requires that in investi-gating these things we would not be too curious. But the things that have been revealed to us oblige us immediately to assent and faith, and the things in them that are commanded for our doing or prohibited for our avoidance require obe-dience on the spot, and thus, putting aside all curiosity, we must carefully study their observance.

Absolute and conditioned will

XXIV. They employ, third, the distinction between God's absolute and condi-tioned will, not of course with respect to the act of God who wills, for in that way all his will is absolute, but with respect to the things willed by God in this act. For God wills that some things occur absolutely but other things under a condition. Thus he wills regeneration, faith, and repentance in the elect abso-lutely, but in such a way that salvation comes to them under the condition of faith and repentance. But, seeing that this distinction is often stolen and used in a worse sense by the Pelagians and Pelagianizers (as we will teach on it a little further on),[10] it is generally disregarded by the orthodox.

Decretive and legislative will

XXV. But, fourth, the most accurate distinction of all is between God's decretive and legislative will, or his will of plan and will of precept. Of these, by the former he determines events, that is, what is to be or not to be *de facto*, whether it is good or evil. By the latter, he determines what is to be or not to be *de jure* only. Included under God's decretive will are: (1) predestination, election, reproba-tion, and preterition; (2) the covenant of grace, concerning the salvation of the elect, between the Father and the Son; (3) the absolute promises of regeneration, sanctification, faith, and perseverance; (4) the complements of these promises, by discriminating grace, and so forth. To God's legislative will or will of precept

---

10. §XXVII, below

belong precepts and prohibitions, promises and threats. Concerning this distribution, this must be carefully noted: just as the decretive will only determines the occurrence or futurity of a thing, but does not, however, determine its moral goodness and badness (for it determines promiscuously the occurrences of good and evil things), so the legislative will only determines the goodness and badness of the thing willed, while in the meantime it states nothing about the futurity or non-futurity of the same.

The double consequence

From this we evidently perceive (1) by what reckoning the will of God is always and universally effective: the former, that is, the decretive will, is so according to the event, and the latter legislative will is so according to our duty, while at the same time he wills in earnest by his legislative will many things that never occur, just as also many things occur by his decretive will that he does not will. And so we perceive from this as well (2) that there is nothing in these wills on God's part that is repugnant, since they do not will the same thing or in the same way.

The use of this distribution

XXVI. Therefore, when this distinction is neglected you will in no way escape the following difficulties: (1) there would be contrary wills in God, by which God wills and does not will the same thing. (2) Certain wills of God would be ineffective because they do not achieve his intent. Consequently, (3) the will of God would not be omnipotent, and (4) he would not be blessed in every way, because what he wills in earnest he does not achieve. On the contrary, when you rightly distinguish the efficacy of the one from the other, as we have said, not only will you entirely avoid conflict and ineffectiveness in the divine wills, but you will also most fittingly free him from the idea of pretending, about which our adversaries continuously growl at us, saying that God (in our opinion, that is) indicates that he wills many things that he does not in fact will, and thus he pretends. Without any trouble we will answer back that God always wills in fact what he indicates that he wills. But what he wills by his legislative will, although he wills its goodness, yet he does not immediately will its futurity, nor does he indicate it.

The Elenctic Part

It is asked: 1. Is there such a will in God that depends upon a condition
to be supplied by creatures?

XXVII. It is asked, first, whether there is such a will in God that depends upon a condition to be supplied by creatures. The crass Pelagians of old—whom now the Socinians join—out of a love for independent free choice, by which it could will anything without any predetermination of the divine will, stated that there is such a will in God that wills only if the creature wills, that desires, that chooses only as the creature wills, a will that is saddened, that is pained because the creature does not will what he wills. The semi-Pelagians, with whom the Jesuits, the Arminians, and others collude, out of a love for the same independent freedom, and so that they may suspend man's conversion on his free choice, although they profess some sort of dependence upon a general influence of God's providence, upon his concursus with the willing creature, upon his influence on what is effected, they notwithstanding want that first act of the creature's will, by which it determines itself, to be thoroughly independent, and thus they teach such a will in God that anticipates that first determination and depends upon it. The Lutherans, out of hatred for an absolute divine will, especially in the matter of reprobation, and out of a love for a universal salvation of each and every person, admit such a will in which he wills their salvation under a condition: if only they themselves will it. They all agree on this, that in many things God's willing is suspended upon a condition to be fulfilled in advance through the free choice of the creatures, and because this condition is not fulfilled, God is frequently frustrated in his intent. Thus, according to them, he wills, for example, that all his commandments be kept most exactly, if, that is, men will to do so. He likewise wills each and every one to be saved, if only they themselves will to believe in Christ, to repent from their sins, and to labor to do good works. Thus, in place of the absolute willing of God they admit nothing but a certain suspended willingness.

The Reformed, although they acknowledge a will in God that suspends this or that event upon this or that condition, for example, the salvation of Peter upon his faith, a will which likewise in this sense could be called conditioned, nevertheless do not acknowledge any will of God that depends upon any condition, because (1) Scripture, in the sense already spoken of, teaches only such a will of God that is absolute, the will by which "he does all that he wills" (Ps. 115:3): "My counsel shall stand, and I will do all my will" (Isa. 46:10). But a conditional will that depends upon the human will does not do anything, nor can it. (2) Scripture proclaims an absolute will, even in the things that presuppose man's free choice: "He gives to will and to do for his own good pleasure" (Phil. 2:13), "The heart of a man will plan his way, but Jehovah will direct his steps" (Prov. 16:9), and "The heart of the king is in the hand of the Lord; he will turn it to whatever he wills" (Prov. 21:1). (3) Scripture teaches an absolute will of God, specifically even in the things that respect predestination, election, and reprobation: "He has mercy upon whomever he wills, and he hardens whomever he wills" (Rom. 9:18), and, "It is not of him who wills or of him who runs, but of God who shows mercy" (Rom. 9:16; cf. vv. 19–22). (4) The will of God is the very essence of God, and the essence of God is entirely independent, as most all of our adversaries admit (though the Socinians dissent), while on the contrary, a conditioned will depends upon a condition. Thus, by this hypothesis, God will be dependent, that is, not God. (5) By this conditioned will, man's free choice would be independent, and thus it would be God. (6) The will of God, by this rationale, would be mutable, and thus the essence of God would be mutable, so then we would have a mutable God, contrary to the Scriptures (Mal. 3:6; James 1:17). (7) Through the same rationale, God would not be omnipotent, for he is not able to do what the creature does not will. (8) Nor would he be most wise, because he wills in earnest what, at least according to the semi-Pelagians, he foresees will never exist. (9) Nor would he be blessed in every way, inasmuch as he does not always achieve what he wills in earnest. (10) Nor would he be the most absolute Lord of all things, inasmuch as to him does not belong power over that condition upon which his will depends, particularly not over man's free choice and over all those things that depend upon that free choice.

The objections are resolved: Generally, by two observations.
XXVIII. To the things objected on the contrary, you will make a satisfactory answer without any trouble, if first you carefully distinguish between God's willing and what is willed, which two things meanwhile our adversaries confuse: what belongs to the thing willed they apply to God's willing, and thus, for example, they refer that condition, such as the faith upon which the will of God suspended the salvation of Peter, to the will of God. You will also answer the objections if, second, you remember that his will must be distinguished into his decretive and legislative will, and accordingly you refer the promises and threats, so often given conditionally, to his legislative will, which determines nothing concerning the occurrence of the things willed, but only concerning their rightness, and which thus does not indicate anything but the mere connection of the thing promised with the prescribed duty. So then to the passages of Scripture raised in objection—Psalm 81:13–14, "Would that my people had heeded me! I would soon have subdued their enemies," and its parallels (Isa. 48:18; Matt. 23:37; Isa. 5:4, 7; Luke 7:30), inasmuch as in them, God seems to have desired plainly enough a repentance and salvation of the Jews that he never achieved—the response is quite easy: in these and similar passages are contained encouragements to obedience and discouragements from sins, and these are fortified by promises and threats, which are illustrated in various ways, not only with similar things but also with examples, and thus, these encouragements and

discouragements pertain to the legislative will, which determines nothing concerning the occurrence of what has been willed, but only denotes the individual connection of the duty with its promise; and by these things, God wills nothing but that men be bound, under the promises and threats, to their prescribed duties.

Specifically

And this is evident, for example, in the adduced passage in Psalm 81, in this way: God exhorts the Israelites that they should heed him (Ps. 81:8–9), he adds promises (v. 10) and threats (vv. 11–12), and finally concludes (v. 13) with "Oh! If my people had heeded me," signaling that there was no other cause why he had not subdued their enemies and had not fed them with the "fatness of the wheat" than their own disobedience (vv. 14–16). It is a similar case in Isaiah 5:4, 7. The prophet's design is to call the Jews back from the vices that had been remembered in a lengthy catalog in the last part of this chapter, and to this end he employs, among other things, an argument from God's kindnesses, which are such that they cannot but clearly show how vigorously he approves of their obedience, which is drawn from them by so many kindnesses, and on the contrary, how he disapproves of their disobedience, which he willed to be connected with such great penalties. So also in Matthew 23:37, the Savior threatens the destruction of the Jews because they obstinately neglected the grace that he offered to them. Although they might also customarily respond in other ways to this passage: that Christ willed the salvation of the Jews, not as God but as man, in pious sympathy, or, if he also willed it as God, then he also achieved it in whom he willed, that is, among the sons of Jerusalem, although the Pharisees opposed him. Finally, in Luke 7:30, when he speaks of the counsel of God scorned by the Pharisees, he does not mean anything except the gospel, and by that, the salvation offered to them under the condition of faith.

2. Should the distinction of the divine will into antecedent and consequent will be sustained?

XXIX. It is asked, second, whether the distinction of the divine will into antecedent and consequent will ought to be tolerated. The first authors of this distinction seem to have been Chrysostom and John of Damascus, and from these the semi-Pelagians—as much the ancient ones as the modern ones, such as the Socinians, Jesuits, Remonstrants, and others—eagerly took it up so that they might more easily defend universal grace and independent human choice.[11]

---

11. On the good pleasure of God's will as a precedent will (εὐδοκία τὸ θέλημά ἐστι

By this distinction, God is believed to will something for the rational creature antecedent to one of its acts, something that consequent to the same act, he does not will. Thus they want God to will salvation for all men antecedent to faith or unbelief, though he does not will it for most, having foreseen their unbelief. Their distinction in this matter is this, that God is quite often frustrated antecedently, but never consequently. The cause of this reality is the free choice of creatures, which by its unbelief makes it to happen that, once God's prior will, which is good and best, and by which he wills a person's salvation, is abandoned, he proceeds to the other will, by which is decreed a person's eternal condemnation. Among the Reformed, there are not lacking great men—for example, Du Moulin in his *Untying of Most Weighty Questions*, Walaeus, Perkins, Twisse, and from the papists, Alvarez in his *On the Helps of Divine Grace* (bk. 5, disp. 34, no. 2)—who suppose that it can be tolerated in a wholesome sense, that is, if by *antecedent will* is understood that will of God by which he makes a connection between a certain antecedent and consequent, between a preceding condition (for example, faith and repentance) and some benefit, such that from this connection he promises that whoever believes will be saved, or, if Peter believes, he will be saved; and if by *consequent will* is understood the execution of the conditioned promise, for example, because Peter believes, he will be saved.[12] But indeed, in the Pelagian sense that we have presented, in which the will of God is understood as suspended upon a condition, this distinction cannot in any way be tolerated, for the reasons we argued in the preceding controversy. However, since in the preceding more wholesome sense the distinction is of meager importance and of equally meager use, and on the other hand, since there is a fairly great danger of abuse, it would be preferable not to allow it into the church. Moreover, to the extent that the sense is heterodox, it generally coincides with that which we considered in the two preceding paragraphs, and it falls apart by the reasons given there.

τὸ προηγούμενον), see Chrysostom on Eph. 1:5 in *NPNF1* 13:52; *PG* 9:13. On the explicit terms "antecedent will" (προηγούμενον θέλημα) and "consequent will" (ἑπόμενον θέλημα), see John of Damascus, *The Orthodox Faith*, bk. 2 chs. 29–30 in *NPNF2* 9:42–43; *PG* 94:969–72. John of Damascus argues that God's antecedent will originates in himself, whereas God's consequent will originates in us. The part of the consequent will that allows a sinner to be damned is "a concession to free-will."

12. Pierre Du Moulin (1568–1658), *Enodatio gravissimarum quaestionum* (Leiden: Elzevir, 1632), 315; Diego Alvarez, O. P. (1550–1635), *De auxiliis divinae gratiae et humani arbitrii viribus et libertate* (Rome: Stephanus Paulinus, 1610), 260.

3. Does God will, by his decretive will, that each and every person be saved?

XXX. It is asked, third, whether God wills that each and every person be saved. Once Origen supposed that God, by his decretive will, willed or had decreed from eternity that not only would each and every person at some point finally in actuality be saved, but even the demons themselves. That is, after they by the proper number of years, according to the proportion of the sins they committed, had paid the penalty in hell, they would at last be restored to eternal salvation. To this position came Francesco Pucci the Socinian, and Samuel Huber, a Swiss, who was at first a Reformed preacher, but due to his view of universal grace was removed from the ministry, and from there was supported by the Lutherans and promoted to the ministry, though when he began in their churches to propound with Origen the salvation of each and every person, he was ejected from the ministry all over again. These taught that each and every person would at last arrive at salvation. The Pelagians as well as the Socinians, as also the Jesuits and Arminians, that they might safeguard man's self-determined[13] choice, taught that God indeed wills that each and every person would be saved, but only by his conditioned or antecedent will, if they themselves should have willed to believe and repent. The Lutherans, although they do not profess that the choice is self-determined, nevertheless do profess such a kind of choice which can positively not resist the Holy Spirit as he gives birth, as it were, to conversion and faith in us. They likewise state that God wills that each and every person would be saved. The Reformed indeed do believe that God wills all to be saved, because Scripture constantly testifies to this (1 Tim. 2:4; Ezek. 18:23; 2 Peter 3:9), but they do not believe that he wills that *each and every person* would be saved,[14] because Scripture nowhere says this. Therefore, they admit that God wills that all be saved, that is, anyone, or with Scripture as our interpreter, from every generation, people, and nation (Rev. 5:9), namely, as many as Christ would purchase, as many as would believe; not, however, each and every person. Then they also admit that God wills all to be saved by his antecedent will, in that sense which we designated in the previous paragraph, namely, that God willed that between

---

13. αὐτεξούσιον. The earliest Christian Latin definition of this term occurs in Tertullian, *De Anima*, 21.6 where he translates it as *libera arbitrii potestas*, literally "the power of a free choice": *haec erit vis divinae gratiae, potentior utique natura, habens in nobis subiacentem sibi liberam arbitrii potestatem quod* τὸ αὐτεξούσιον *dicitur, quae cum sit et ipsa naturalis atque mutabilis quoquo vertitur, natura convertitur.* Cf. *arbitrii libertas* in *De anima*, 20.5. Cf. Origen, *De Principiis* 3.1–8. Among classical Greek philosophers, see Epictetus, *Disc.* 2.2, where in English translations the term is translated, "what is in your own power" or "what freedom belongs to you."

14. God wills *omnes*, "all" to be saved, but not *omnes et SINGULI*, lit. "all, and *each individually*."

faith and salvation there would be an inseparable connection by which each and every person who believes would not perish, but have eternal life (John 3:16), and from this connection, he wills to invite anyone, as much the elect as the reprobate, to faith, and under that condition, to offer salvation. But, since we already set aside that distinction of the divine will into antecedent and consequent in the preceding paragraph, we would prefer to state that God wills all to be saved by his legislative will, which determines nothing concerning its occurrence, that is, he has promised that whoever would believe would have eternal life, namely, due to the connection that we have already designated, and due to that connection he offers and promises salvation in earnest to all. He does not will, however, that each and every one will be saved by his decretive will, that is, he has not decreed that all would obtain salvation in actuality.

Arguments of the Reformed

And this, at last, is the true hinge of the controversy, such that if our opponents want to obtain anything against us, they ought to demonstrate that God has decreed that each and every person will be saved, something I know quite well that our adversaries will not undertake, because (1) Scripture expressly testifies that God does not will this—in fact, he wills the contrary (Prov. 1:24–29; Ps. 95:11; Matt. 20:18; John 17:9). (2) In this very business of salvation and predestination he expressly professes that he does not will that each and every person would be saved—in fact, he created the wicked for the day of punishment (Prov. 16:4), he hardens whom he wills (Rom. 9:18), he has prepared vessels of wrath for destruction (Rom. 9:22), and he has prescribed not a few for judgment (2 Peter 2:9). Furthermore, he testifies that (3) he denies the necessary means of salvation to the greatest number (John 17:9), and (4) he does not call each and every one to partake of grace (Ps. 147:20; Acts 14:16). In fact, (5) he forbids the gospel of salvation to be preached to many (Matt. 10:5; Acts 16:6–7). Also, (6) he does not will to give faith to each and every person (2 Thess. 3:2; Acts 13:48). So then it must be entirely denied that God, by his decretive will, wills that each and every person will be saved, unless (7) we wish (a) to lead the divine omnipotence into a most pressing crisis, inasmuch as it cannot achieve what it wills in earnest and intends would happen; (b) to establish contrary wills in God, of which one wills, for example, that Judas be saved, and the other does not; (c) to assert a mutable will for him who is in all things immutable, a will by which now he does not will what previously he earnestly willed; (d) likewise, to attribute an ineffective will to him who can do all that he wills; (e) to attribute to him a will that is dependent upon the creatures, and also temporary; and, in fact, (f) unless we wish to ascribe to the most wise being a fatuous will, a will by which he earnestly wills what he knows that he never will achieve.

4. Is the will of God the sole cause of every moral good? The difference of opinions XXXI. It is asked, fourth, whether the will of God, just as it is the sole cause of every reality and possibility, is also the sole cause of every moral good. Descartes, together with his followers, as we have already observed above in chapter 13,[15] thinks that the cause and root of every moral good is in God's will insofar as it is absolutely indifferent, willing this thing to be good and that thing to be not at all good. The Reformed (1) consider the will of God on the one hand in the identical sense (if I may use barbarous terms), insofar as it coincides with the very divine essence, and so accordingly it is as if you were asking whether the essence of God or God himself is the cause of every moral good; and in this sense, the Reformed do not answer in the negative. Or on the other hand, they consider the will of God in the formal sense, insofar as the divine essence is conceived by us as constructed with this or that relation: in this sense, the Reformed together deny that his will is the sole cause of all moral good. (2) They distinguish moral good into that which belongs to positive right—and this they acknowledge to depend upon the most free will of God: for example, resting from one's works precisely on the seventh day is a moral good, but one belonging to positive right—and into that which belongs to natural right, that which rests upon nature itself, either the nature of God or the nature of man, just as in his original righteousness he bears the image of the divine holiness and righteousness, that is, not from God's will, but from his very essence. (3) They think of any moral good either with respect to its essence or with respect to its existence. Thus, they confess that every good with respect to its existence is from the will of God, insofar as it is the commanding and executing principle in the production of all things (Rev. 4:11), but in respect to its essence, they hold that every natural moral good depends not upon God's will as such, as a positive good, but upon his nature, as he is God. So think all the Reformed together, if you exclude one or perhaps two who suppose that whatever is right and good is so because God wills it, and not that God wills it because it is right and good.

---

15. 1.2.13 §XXIII

The arguments of the Reformed

The reasons of the Reformed are that (1) Scripture testifies that God wills many things because they are good and right, which he therefore could not but will: "You will not also destroy the just with the unjust.... Far be it from you that you should do such a thing.... Shall not the judge of the all the earth do judgment," that is, "do right?" (Gen. 18:23, 25; Rom. 1:32), and, "It is a righteous thing with God to repay with affliction" (2 Thess. 1:6). In fact, evil things are of such a kind and so great that they are repugnant to the purity and holiness of his nature, or of his eyes, such that he *cannot* look upon these things (Hab. 1:13). (2) If all good depended upon his will, and that will were indifferent from eternity, he would have been able not to prescribe that we know him, love him, revere him, and so forth. In fact, (3) he would have been able to command what is entirely contrary, for example, that we hate him, blaspheme him, rebel against him, and so forth. Indeed, (4) all these things, if he had willed them, would be good and laudable. (5) I will not add anything regarding the ideas in God, which coincide with the nature of God and are infinitely perfect, such that they can be expressed in the creatures in an infinite number of ways, ideas that according to this reckoning would be mutable. Nor also will I add (6) that then not even God himself would be holy, just, good, and so forth, before his will had determined itself to it, and thus he would be holy, just, and good only because he wills to be such. (7) Nor would we in laboring for holiness and righteousness be shaped according to his natural perfection, but only his voluntary perfection, which Scripture argues against (Matt. 5:48; Luke 6:36; 2 Peter 1:4).

Objections

The foundation of our adversaries' opinion is in three things: (1) if all goodness were not by the will of God, then God would not be in all ways independent and perfect. I respond, It would be true if a good were given that did not depend upon God; but it is one thing to depend upon God and upon the nature of God, and another to depend precisely upon the will of God as such. (2) That otherwise we would have to say that objects have their essence through themselves and are prior, at least in their nature, to the divine will. I respond, Although several things do not depend upon the will of God as such, yet it is not that they do not depend upon God simply, for they depend upon his nature and essence as such. (3) That it would follow in this way that the divine will depends upon other goods, and thus is dependent. I respond, By no means, because those goods depend upon his most holy nature and not vice versa, that the nature of

God depends upon them. See also our *Gangrene of the Cartesian Innovations* (section 2, ch. 9).[16]

5. Do affections properly belong to God?

XXXII. It is asked, fifth, whether affections properly belong to God, or whether the affections in God are disturbances of the divine will properly speaking, by which the will of God either is conveyed to an object or flees from it, disturbances from which hatred, wrath, pleasure, avoidance, joy, sadness, and other human affections result. The Anthropomorphites will not hesitate to profess that God is endowed with human members and also human affections, nor also will they hesitate to profess the mere willingness of the Pelagians and semi-Pelagians, that is, a willing that is imperfect and suspended upon free human choice, a willing that is in fact nothing except a desire and wish, a willing from which, in addition, wrath, hatred, avoidance, joy, and sorrow are produced. The Socinians, because they hold that God is dependent upon human free choice, also openly assert for him a mutable will and the desire, fear, joy, sorrow, anger, regret, and other affections that arise from it. The Reformed, although they do not at all deny that words that express affections, just as words that express body parts, are employed to speak of God in the Scriptures, and although likewise they acknowledge that when every imperfection is removed from the affections, the substance of those words is in God, even so do not dare to allow in God these disturbances, in which almost the whole nature of affections consists.

Arguments

And this is because (1) Scripture expressly answers the question in the negative (Num. 23:19; 1 Sam. 15:29; Rom. 9:29). In these passages, what is taught concerning the regret of God must be applied by analogy to all affections. Because (2) nature or right reason does not tolerate in the most perfect being the many imperfections of human affections, for example, (a) imperfect willing; (b) the dependence of the affections upon their objects, by which they are influenced; (c) the impotence by which you are not able to do what the affections demand, and the affections are frequently overcome and fade away when they are not satisfied; (d) various mutations, and sometimes such as are quite ignoble, because of which they are customarily called passions. Because of (3) the infinite blessedness of God, which cannot be augmented by any increase of good, nor be touched and violated by any sense of evil, and much less be driven around in so many cycles of the affections.

---

16. Mastricht, *Gangraena*, 246–52.

Objections

Nor do our adversaries respond sufficiently when they claim that whatever there might be of imperfection in these affections does not injure God in the least because it is absorbed by the immeasurable abundance of good that is in him. Indeed, they affirm that even what is especially adverse to him is turned, by his most perfect wisdom and power, to his own good. Indeed, this sort of clever remedy might be able somehow to comfort people who are disturbed by the boiling of their affections, but it cannot take away from God the imperfection with which he cannot be God. For whatever happens, when adverse things fall upon him and they move him, they do not cease to be unpleasant, nor can they finally be crushed by the immense abundance of his felicity without a fight, such that at least some measure of dissatisfaction, wrestling, and as it were, fire and burning of the soul for some time takes its seat in God and disturbs his blessedness, until at last that storm subsides. And our adversaries do not have anything to allege for themselves except that frequently in the Scriptures the affections of love, hatred, regret, etc. are attributed to God, to which the ready response is that: (1) the attributed affections are also expressly removed from him elsewhere, for example, regret is attributed to him in Genesis 6:6 and Jeremiah 18:8, yet on the contrary, the same is removed from him in Numbers 23:19 and 1 Samuel 15:29. And this teaches that affections are attributed to him not without a grain of salt, namely, (2) not according to the affections, or the motions and disturbances of the soul, but only in relation to the effective operations that those affections customarily excite in creatures: that is, the affections that are attributed to God in a human way must not be understood except in a way worthy of God. To the customary places adduced to the contrary (Ezek. 33:11; 2 Peter 3:9; 1 Tim. 2:4), you will thus be able to make a satisfying answer without any trouble, if first you should show generally from the things already said that the discussion is not about the decretive will, but only about the legislative will, by which God wills by ordering that they should convert themselves and receive his reward, eternal life, or, that conversion is their duty and the reward of conversion is life. Moreover, the discussion is not about specific individuals, but about any sort of person. Then second also, it could be responded individually to the passages cited that in Ezekiel 33:11 it does not say that God does not will the death of any sinner, but rather of the one who converts himself: "I do not will the death of the sinner, but that he should be converted and live," that is, I do not will the death of him who is converted. So also in 2 Peter 3:9, the apostle does not say that God wills all altogether to be saved and none of them to perish, but only all believers: "He is patient toward *us*, not willing that any *of us* should perish." Nor is it said in 1 Timothy 2:4 that God wills for each and every person to be saved, but only "all," that is, every kind of person, that is, kings and magistrates as well as their subordinates, as the analogy of the context shows. Such a response, with the necessary adjustments, could be applied to a fair number of other Scripture passages.

The Practical Part

The will of God: 1. Is the basis of all Christian practice.

XXXIII. First, the will of God, as it is considered as a faculty, is not so much practical as the basis of all Christian practice. For (1) if God were not a voluntary and most free agent, how would he be worshiped and revered? How could we solicit any good things from him? How could we avert evil things by prayer? How could we give thanks for the benefits we have received? That is, if he should act no differently than the sun, forced to do all things by a necessity of nature. (2) How will his sovereignty, care, providence, and governance stand, on which our piety rests with all its weight? For what authority, what power, either to impose laws or to vindicate them once imposed, can there be for one who does all things by a necessity of nature, without any choice of the will? So then (3) what sort of obedience, worship, reverence, and so forth, would belong to him, if what he does, he cannot but do? Finally, (4) where also will the freedom of our will reside if not even God is able to exercise freedom of choice?

2. It shows the perfection of the divine authority.

XXXIV. In particular, second, the self-determination[17] of God's will commends the perfection of his authority, by which he is "in the heavens, and he does all that he wills." That is, as in the intellect there is counsel and wisdom, so in the will there is authority. For this reason, just as the will of God is (1) free and most free, (2) independent, (3) absolute and immutable, (4) eternal, (5) most efficacious, so also his authority is absolutely (1) most free, and through it, "he does whatever he wills," and for that reason, his will stands (cf. Matt. 20:15); (2) entirely independent (Rom. 11:35; Jer. 18:6); and so then (3) immutable and irresistible (Rom. 9:18) as well as (4) most efficacious: "he does whatever he wills" (cf. Ps. 33:9; Lam. 3:37; Isa. 14:14); and (5) most universal: he does all things he wills. This appears in particular: (1) in his creation of things (Rev. 4:11), (2) in his governance of things (Isa. 14:6–7), (3) in his dispensation of empires and kingdoms (Dan. 4:17; Jer. 27:5; Ezek. 28:17), (4) in his dispensation of wealth and fortunes (Ex. 3:22; 11:2), and especially (5) in his governing of human affairs, chiefly of

---

17. αὐτεξουσία

those which concern the eternal state: in predestination, election, reprobation, calling, and regeneration, concerning which we will soon say more. Therefore when it comes to this self-determined authority of God, (1) let us adore and celebrate it (Matt. 6:10, 13); (2) let us submissively arrange ourselves to his pleasure (Matt. 6:10), (3) whether it is a duty that must be done, or (4) a punishment that must be endured (1 Sam. 3:18; Acts 21:14; Matt. 26:39, 42, 44).

3. It checks the responses of the flesh in the business of predestination and of particular redemption.

XXXV. So then, third, it restrains the reckless rashness of those who suspend the divine will upon the foreseen works of the creatures in the business of particular predestination, election, reprobation, redemption, calling, and conversion, as well as those who ask why it elected this one and reprobated that one, why it redeemed this one and not that one, and so forth. As if it were not self-determined, and the will of the supreme Lord did not accordingly stand by every right, and he could not by right respond to these scorners, "Am I not permitted to do what I will in my own affairs? Is your eye evil because I am good?" (Matt. 20:15), and likewise, "Does not the potter have power over the clay, that from the same lump he may make one vessel for honor but another for dishonor?" (Rom. 9:20). Those people do not consider that the will of God is (1) independent: it is that from which, through which, and to which are all things, to which no one has given such that it is bound to repay him (Rom. 11:35–36); (2) most absolute: it has mercy on whom it wills and whom it wills, it hardens (Rom. 9:18); (3) free and most free; (4) most wise: "Oh, the depth of the riches, both of the wisdom and knowledge of God!" (Rom. 11:33). So then, crying out and responding back in this way is nothing but (1) calling the self-determined to account, (2) subjecting the independent to creatures, (3) stripping the most absolute of his sovereignty, (4) correcting the most wise. And what sort of person, finally, will do all these sorts of things with impunity?

4. It represses the will to sin.

XXXVI. And so, fourth, it restrains every will and longing for sin, such as those Peter points out in 1 Peter 4:3, in which (1) we do not will to submit ourselves to the divine will (Job 21:14; Ex. 5:2). No, but (2) we expressly set our own will against the divine will (Jer. 44:16–17), and (3) we do the will of the flesh (Eph. 2:3). Or (4) in whatever way, we do not acquiesce to the will of God, we murmur in protest, we respond against it (Num. 14:27, 29). Finally, what is all of this except (1) to subjugate the independent will; (2) to elevate our own will to independence; (3) to dispute the freedom and sovereignty of God; (4) to stir up the most efficacious will of God to work against us, that it would (5) make us subject to the will and desire of our enemies (Ezek. 16:27), or (6) give us up to our own desires (Rom. 1:24); indeed, (7) to reduce ourselves, who were created with freedom, to slavery to ourselves, to our own sins, and to Satan (John 8:33–34; 2 Tim. 2:26)?

5. It urges the denial of our own will.

XXXVII. On the contrary, fifth, it urges us that (1) we should deny our own will, at least insofar as it is opposed to the divine will (Luke 9:23), or even in any way that it varies from it (Acts 21:14; John 5:30; 6:38); (2) we should crucify (Gal. 5:24) and mortify (Col. 3:5) our lusts and carnal affections, subjugating them and leading them to the obedience of Christ (2 Cor. 10:5); (3) we should call our affections that cry out against God, reason, and will back to their own place and order, so that they may be subject to our will, that is, to our rational appetite, and in this way become acts of the will just as they are in God, so that finally the will of God alone may be by its own right independent and absolute. We will say more on this in its own topic, in the chapter on self-denial.

6. Zeal for fulfilling the divine will

XXXVIII. Also sixth, it urges zeal for fulfilling the divine will as promptly as possible. In this consists our observance, by which we fulfill the will of God for his glory, with submission, "as servants of God, doing from the heart what God wills, with good will serving the Lord" (Eph. 6:6–7). This zeal particularly includes that: (1) we should religiously inquire into the will of God, which is prescribed as our rule (Col. 1:19; Eph. 5:17; Rom. 2:17). (2) We should know the will of God and have it, as our one and only rule of living, continually before our eyes, indeed, continually in our heart (Ps. 40:8; 16:8). (3) We should carefully arrange the steps of our life according to it (Gal. 6:16; 1 Peter 4:2). And for this reason, (4) we should be conformed as much as possible to the divine will (Rev. 2:6), and that (5) with profound submission, as servants (Eph. 6:6–7; Acts 13:36), though at the same time also "from the heart, and with good will serving the Lord" (Eph. 6:6–7; 2 Chron. 15:15). We should be motivated by (1) the example of the Savior (Ps. 40:7–8; John 4:34; 5:30; 14:31); the fact that otherwise (2) we will not enter into the kingdom of God (Matt. 7:21), nor (3) be heard in our supplications (John 9:31), nor (4) be admitted into the honor of spiritual kinship with Christ (Matt. 12:50). And this duty of obedience to the divine will should be fulfilled specifically in the work of faith (John 6:29), repentance (Ezek. 33:11; Matt. 3:2), and zeal for total sanctity (1 Thess. 4:3; Heb. 10:36).

7. *It particularly shapes us in:* Humility

XXXIX. Seventh, besides these things, a pious meditation on God's self-determined will can shape us particularly in (1) zeal for humility, if at any time goods or gifts befall us, from which there could arise an occasion of being proud, that we may think that by the most free will of God that conferred them, they could be removed and transferred to another (1 Cor. 4:7; Rom. 11:21–23; Eph. 2:8–9; Deut. 7:7–8).

Mercy

(2) The practice of mercy toward an unfortunate neighbor, who by that most free will of God is afflicted with those evils from which we ourselves, by the same freedom of God, are immune (Matt. 9:11, 13).

Equanimity

(3) The exercise of reasonableness and equanimity, by which we should be far from all envy due to goods conferred on our neighbor and meanwhile denied to us, because the self-determined will of God allots all these things by its own most free choice (Matt. 20:15; 1 Cor. 12:11, 15). And so then, to strive against this allotment by envy is nothing but to kick against the goads, to erode the sovereignty and most free power of God, and to torture ourselves in vain.

8. *Zeal for conforming our will with the divine*

XL. Moreover, eighth, it especially summons us to zeal for conforming our will with the divine will, which the Savior commends (Rev. 2:6), and which is to be accomplished in these ways: (1) while we strive as much as possible to make our will resemble the perfections of the divine will. Namely, just as (a) the will of God is independent, ours also in the business of divine worship should be independent of any creature (1 Cor. 7:23; Matt. 15:9). (b) The most simple will of God is brought simultaneously by one act to its end and its means: thus our will, in the matter of salvation, should in godly simplicity be brought by the same act to its end and its means (Phil. 2:12). (c) The will of God is absolute and unlimited, recoiling from all idea of mere willingness: thus ours, in the business of worship and divine obedience, ought to be wholly absolute, not suspended upon any condition (Josh. 24:15; Matt. 8:21–22; Rom. 14:7–8), and also unlimited (Matt. 19:16, 21–22; Mark 6:20). (d) The will of God is most free: thus also ours, in the business of divine worship, should be spontaneous (2 Cor. 8:3, 5, 7, 10–11; Ps. 110:3), and accordingly free from all spiritual servitude to the flesh, sin, and the devil, a will that also pursues Christian liberty as eagerly as possible (Gal. 5:1). (e) The will of God is universally effective: thus also ours should not cling to idle purposes and wishes, but should result in work (Matt. 21:29–30; 7:21; Gal. 5:6). (f) The will of God is infinite: thus also ours, in divine duties, should be infinite, that is, insatiable (Ps. 73:25; Phil. 3:13–14). (g) The will of God is eternal: thus also ours, in its zeal for knowing and observing the divine will, should be interminable and eternal (Ps. 1:2; 119:44; 112:1). In addition, (2) our affections also should be conformed to the affections of God, which is accomplished especially in two things: (a) when our affections aim at the same object at which the divine affections aim, when we love, desire, bestow hatred upon, detest, and shun the same things that God does (Rev. 2:6; Ps. 139:21–22). (b) And when they are carried out according to the same reason, carried out, that is (as we have said) as acts of the will, as rational appetites that are subject to reason, not ruling over it, and not as the acts of animals and brutes (2 Peter 2:12; Jude 10). In addition (3) we should order our works according to the will of God, by willing the same thing that God wills (Matt. 6:10; John 3:21), and to the same end, his glory, so that thus we would, as it were, serve the divine will (Acts 13:36). Finally, (4) our passions also should be conformed to the divine will (Matt. 26:39, 42; cf. Phil. 2:7; Acts 21:14; 1 Sam. 3:18; 2 Sam. 15:26; 10:12).

Motives

By such a conformation of our will to the divine, (1) we will to that extent be made to resemble God and be rendered partakers of the divine nature (2 Peter 1:4; 1 Peter 1:14–15). And (2) this conformity of the will and of the affections will lay the foundation for a most pleasant familiarity and communion with God (Amos 3:3), while a discrepancy in them destroys it (Isa. 59:2). In addition, (3) such a harmony will procure for us a most pleasant tranquility of soul in whatever fortune, whether it be prosperous or adverse, that is, if always and everywhere you say and sense, "Your will be done." While on the contrary, (4) no fortune will satisfy if you are out of tune with the will of God. Indeed, not even heaven will satisfy you if there you should will something other than what God wills.

Supports

Moreover, several things are conducive for obtaining this conformity: (1) carefully searching for and seeking out the will of God, to which you labor to conform your own (Eph. 5:17; Col. 1:9); (2) denying, smothering, tearing out, crucifying, and mortifying whatever is in any way adverse to the will of God (Gal. 5:25; 2 Cor. 10:5); (3) striving with every effort that we may do those things that God wills to be done by us, that is, that we may stand complete in all the will of

God (Col. 4:12). Drexel in his *Heliotropy* has other things of this sort, which are quite helpful.[18]

9. Consolation and patience

XLI. Finally, ninth, it supplies consolation and builds patience in any adversities to reflect that (1) no matter what kind and how great those adversities are, they come to us neither contingently, with the Deity unaware and unwilling, nor by a necessity of fate, which not even God himself can resist, but by the most free good pleasure of the supreme arbiter, in whose most free, most just, and also most merciful dispensation it is entirely necessary and just that we rest, unless we wish, by an abominable sin, to thrust down the self-determined will of God beneath our fleshly mind. (2) Day by day we are to come back to God in our prayers, asking that his will be accomplished (Matt. 6:10; Acts 21:14). (3) We have need of endurance, that we might do the will of God and might receive the promise (Heb. 10:36). (4) Toward this very end is every evil sent to us by God, that we might be accustomed to his most free will and to his most absolute authority over us, and that we might rest in it (Job 1:12, cf. v. 21). Finally, (5) by humble submission and patience, the most free good will of God, at whose nod all these calamities are conveyed to us and can also be taken away or directed to our advantage, can be reconciled to us (2 Sam. 15:15). From this sort of devout meditation on the divine will, many have drawn solace in every most pressing adversity: Eli (1 Sam. 3:18), David (Ps. 39:9; 2 Sam. 16:10), and even the Savior himself (Matt. 26:39).

---

18. E.g. books 4 and 5 of this work address impediments (*impedimenta*) and aids (*adiumenta*) to conform the human will to the divine will. Also, the image on the title page explains the title: the sun (*voluntas divina*) shines upon flowers (*voluntas humana*), which in turn grow toward the sun. Jeremias Drexel, *Heliotropium seu conformatio humanae voluntatis cum divina* (1627), 548–69.

CHAPTER SIXTEEN

The Goodness of God

Why do you call me good? No one is good but one, God.
—Matthew 19:17

The theory of the divine goodness

I. Just as the truthfulness of God arises from the intellect because it tends toward the true, so also his goodness arises from the will because it is conveyed to the good. If it is considered absolutely as desirable and communicative, it is specifically called God's *goodness*. If it is considered as communicative of a good from pure propensity or good will,[1] it is designated as *love*, *grace*, and *mercy*. If it is considered in that communication as acting as if according to a certain rule, it is called *righteousness*. Finally if it is considered as corresponding to the rule of acting that it prescribed to rational creatures, it is denominated *holiness*. Each of these will be treated in the following chapters. The Savior asserts the goodness of God in Matthew 19:17.

The Exegetical Part

It is built upon the exegesis of the text.

II. These words contain the Savior's particular response to the address of a young man who had greeted him as good. In that response, the Savior endeavors, based on the young man's admission, to convince him to acknowledge that he is God. Here two things occur:

 A. A rebuke: "Why do you call me good?" Here occur two readings. One has it this way: τί με ἐρωτᾷς περὶ τοῦ ἀγαθοῦ; εἶς ἐστιν ἀγαθός, "Why do you ask me about the good?..." Thus read Beza, Grotius,[2] the

---

1. εὐδοκία

2. On Matt. 19:17, Beza, *Novum testamentum…Bezae annotationes* (1588), 86–87; Hugo Grotius, *Annotationes in libros evangeliorum* (Amsterdam: Johannes and Cornelius Blaeu, 1641), 331–32.

Latin interpreters, the more ancient and more corrected copies, likewise the Hebrew Gospel of Matthew,[3] with which the Vulgate agrees on many points, and among the church fathers, Origen, Chrysostom, Augustine, and others.[4] Thus the aim of the Savior was to rebuke the young man, not because he called him good, but because he was inquiring about the good, though there is nothing good in men, and accordingly, no one is legitimately called good. That is, because that young man acknowledged in Jesus nothing greater than a man, yet hoped that he, with Jesus guiding the way, would by his own strength arrive at the possession of his good, by which eternal life is supplied, as if all he lacked in that matter was a guide, he thus in this mind had greeted Jesus as a good teacher, that is, as a guide to the good. But Jesus, so that he might oppose this error and simultaneously furnish us with a pattern of modesty, says that there are not many sources of good, but only one, that is, God. At the same time he indicates that it is not enough for us to be guided to the good, unless the God who regenerates and converts should illuminate our eyes and furnish us with strength. The other reading has it thus: τί με λέγεις ἀγαθόν; οὐδεὶς ἀγαθός, εἰ μὴ εἷς, ὁ θεός, "Why do you call me good? No one is good but one, God." In this way the majority of Greek codices have it, and also the Greek interpreters—Euthymius, Theodoret, and Syrus. Thus it is read at Mark 10:18, Luke 18:19, and so Beza, Piscator, Diodati, and others.[5] It is as if he should say, You ought not to call me good, because you do not consider me to be God, who alone is good, that is, good independently, perfectly, through himself, and by his own nature, just as he alone is called immortal (1 Tim. 6:16). Therefore he does not spurn the title, or deny that he is good, as the Socinians desire out of hatred for the deity of Christ (for who would dare to deny that Jesus was good?), but he assesses the soul of the one greeting him, either because in his words he attributes to him what he

---

3. This is possibly a reference to a Hebrew translation and Jewish commentary on the Gospel of Matthew in the twelfth chapter of a manuscript by the fourteenth century Jewish polemicist, Shem Tov ben Isaac Shaprut (or Ibn Shaprut), *Eben Bohan* (c. 1380). Cf. G. Howard, *Hebrew Gospel of Matthew* (Macon: Mercer University Press, 1995).

4. Origen, *Commentarius in Matthaeum*, bk. 10, ch. 15 in *PG* 13:1281–82; Chrysostom, *Hom. LXXIII in Matthaeum* in *PG* 58:603–4.

5. On Mark 10:18 and Luke 18:19, Beza, *Novum testamentum…Bezae annotationes* (1588), 185, 302; Johann Piscator (1546–1625), *Analysis logica evangelii secundum Matthaeum*, 3rd ed. (Herborn: Christopher Corvinus, 1606), 452–53; for Matt. 19:17 in Giovanni Diodati (1576–1649), *La Sacra Biblia tradotta in lingua Italiana, e commentata*, 2nd ed. (Geneva: Pierre Chouet, 1641), 25.

does not believe belongs to him; or, if he does believe that it belongs to him, even so he does not believe that he is that one to whom alone it belongs, namely, God.

B. A correction: "No one is good but the one God." So then, if goodness applies to me, even by your testimony, by all means I am also God. Here the Savior:

1. Takes away a certain goodness from all creatures: "No one is good," namely, in that way, that is, the highest good, independent and from itself. If you should insist: But God saw all things that he had made, and behold, they were *very good* (Gen. 1:31), then there will be an easy response: No one and nothing is good by nature essentially, absolutely, infinitely, immutably, good from every perspective, the cause of all good. Every creature has its goodness communicated to it, and likewise has only its own goodness, not that of other creatures, and thus much more, does not have the greatest abundance of goodness. Nor can they communicate the goodness they have to others, unless it is roused by the influence of divine providence.

2. Claims this goodness for God and for him alone: "But the one God," namely: (1) through his essence, that is, originally, as the fount of goodness, while the creatures are good through participation, like streams from the fount; (2) through his efficiency, since he alone communicates himself, and independently can do good, while the creatures cannot do so unless they are roused and advanced through his influence; (3) through his existence, since he alone is the good existing by necessity, while creatures are only good contingently and exist by his will. The Gentiles acknowledged this, at least those into whom some sparks of barbarian philosophy had penetrated. Thus Plato said in his *Meno*, "Virtue is not in us by nature, and neither is human teaching, but it comes by divine providence."[6] And Seneca, "No mind is good without God."[7] And Porphyry himself recognized that human beings could not "become perfect" except "through the paternal mind."[8] Philo teaches us that the Jews likewise believed this

---

6. Plato, *Meno*, 100b. The citations in the remainder of this paragraph (Plato, Seneca, Porphyry, Philo of Alexandria, Macrobius, and Philo of Byblos) are taken verbatim from Grotius, *Annotationes in libros evangeliorum* (1641), 2:332–34.

7. Seneca, *Ep.* 73.16 in LCL 76:112–13.

8. Note Mastricht's identical phrasing in his citation, *non posse homines* τελειοῦσθαι *nisi* διὰ τὸν νοῦν πατρικόν, with Grotius, *Annotationes in libros evangeliorum* (1641), 2:332. Also, note

way: εἷς ἐστιν ἀγαθός, "One is good."[9] By them God is customarily called one, and also one without addition. Likewise also by the Assyrians, as witnessed by Macrobius, the highest and greatest god is called Adad, which means *one*.[10] Thus in Philo of Byblos we read of "Adod, king of the gods."[11] The word in Hebrew is אֶחָד *ehad*, "one" and the phrase in Job 14:4, לֹא אֶחָד, "Not one," the Aramaic translator interprets as, "but God."

The Dogmatic Part

That God is good: It is proved by the Scriptures

III. Therefore God is truly good, and most highly good, and alone good in his own way. Scripture intends this whenever it: (1) declares in clear terms that he is good (Ps. 25:8; 119:68) and (2) removed from all evil (Ps. 92:15; Deut. 32:4); (3) recounts in their degree, that is, preeminently, the riches of his goodness (Rom. 2:4); (4) testifies to all that he is the author of all goodness (Gen. 1:31); and (5) prescribes the loving, worshiping, and serving of him, which apart from his goodness would be done irrationally.

It is confirmed by four reasons.

IV. And nature teaches this when it acknowledges that God: (1) is a being, and therefore good (for being and good are transposed by philosophers), and the first and thus also the highest being. For this reason he is also the first and

---

that in bk. 10, ch. 28 (cf. 10.23), *De Civitate Dei*, in *PL* 41:307 (cf. 41:300) and *The City of God*, in *NPNF1* 2:198 (cf. *NPNF1* 2:194), Augustine attests to a work, no longer extant, by Porphyry, *De regressu animae* (*On the Regression of the Soul*), and notes in 10.23, *quem graece appellat paternum intellectum vel paternam mentem*, and then also in 10.28, ...*multa vitia per nullas teletas purgari dicis, sed per solum* πατρικὸν νοῦν, *id est, paternam mentem sive intellectum*...." Thus it seems Grotius reconstructed a citation of Porphyry from Augustine's Latin quotation, a Greek fragment which Mastricht cited. On the reconstruction of Porphyry's *De regressu animae*, see P. Hadot, "Citations de Porphyre chez Augustin," *Revue d'Etudes Augustiniennes et Patristiques* (1960), 6(3):205–44.

9. E.g. Philo of Alexandria, *On the Account of the World's Creation Given by Moses* in *LCL* 226:18–19.

10. Macrobius, *Saturn.* 1.23.17.

11. Philo of Byblos's Greek translation of the Phoenecian historian Sanchuniathon is no longer extant: only in Eusebius of Caesarea's *Praeparatio evangelica* are surviving fragments known to be preserved. For the phrase from Philo of Byblos, Ἄδωδος βασιλεὺς θεῶν, in English see bk. 1, ch. 10, Eusebius of Caesarea, *De praeparatione evangelica* in *PG* 21:84; idem, *Preparation for the Gospel*, 1:38; for a Greek critical edition, idem, *Eusebius Werke VIII/I: Praeparatio Evangelica*, ed. Karl Mras, series *Die Griechichsen christlicher Schriftsteller* (Berlin: Akademie-Verlag, 1954), 43:49. On the phrase "Hadad, king of the gods," see, E. Lipiński *Studies in Aramaic Inscriptions and Onomastics* (Leuven, 1975), 65n2.

highest good. (2) Is perfect, and therefore desirable and communicative, the one in whom the sum of goodness consists. (3) Is for all things the author of all their goodness (because nothing occurs that has its goodness from itself) and thus good from himself, for what you do not have, you cannot communicate. (4) Absorbs every species of good: the useful good, insofar as he disperses his own perfection and goodness in all things; the delightful good, inasmuch as all satisfaction of rest and joy consists in the possession, communion, and enjoyment of him (Ps. 16:11; 34:9); the honorable good, for by his own holiness, he as the exemplar offers the norm and origin of all holiness. Thus Augustine says in *On the Nature of the Good* that God alone is immutably good, he alone is the good of all good, he alone is the cause of all goodness for all things that are good.[12] Likewise in *On the Trinity* (bk. 8, ch. 3), after he recounts the different species of goodness in the creatures, he adds, "Take away this or that good thing, see the good itself if you can, and so you will see God, not as the good in some other good, but as the good of every good.... There would not be communicable goods unless there were an incommunicable good. When therefore you hear of this good or that good, goods that can otherwise be said to be also not good, if you can understand them without the things that are good by a participation in the good, you will at the same time understand the good itself when you hear of this or that good. If therefore you can, with those things taken away, perceive the good by itself, you will perceive God."[13] And also on Psalm 135, "The Lord is good, but good not as the things that he made are good—he made heaven and earth and all that is in them good. He himself is properly good, the good from which everything else is good, for he himself made all things good. He himself is good, he whom no one made; he himself is good by his own good, not by a good imparted from anywhere else; he does not need anyone by whom he might become good, but other things need him so that they might become good."[14] We have spoken of these things a bit more fully so that you may perceive the distance between created and uncreated good.

Objections against the goodness of God

V. Meanwhile it seems to stand against the divine goodness: (1) that it is not desired by all, indeed, it is shunned by most. I respond, Notwithstanding, it is by its own nature desirable, and it deserves to be desired by all, but that it is

---

12. Mastricht italicizes this statement as if it were a direct quote, however; it is not extant in current texts and thus appears to be a summary statement of ch. 1 of Augustine, *De natura boni contra Manichaeos* in PL 42:551.

13. Augustine, *De Trinitate* in PL 42:949; idem, *On the Trinity* in NPNF1 3:117.

14. Augustine, *Enarrationes in Psalmos* in PL 37:1740.

not desired by all is not because of a defect of God's goodness, but from the abundance of his avenging justice on account of which they think of him as the severe avenger of their sins. (2) That he does not bestow his goodness on all, not on the reprobate, yet he is a good that communicates itself. I respond: (a) He does bestow good upon all, but freely, whatever good and however much he wills. Indeed, (b) because he is good by essence, he must be averse to evil and to evil men, and for this reason he does not communicate himself to them. I need not add (c) that he is infinitely good to himself alone, for otherwise he would by nature necessarily save all men. At the same time, (d) he is good to all to the extent that he endures them, preserves them, and fosters them as long as they exist, and confers whatever they have, besides every defect of theirs. (3) That in Psalm 18:26, he is said to be perverse with the perverse. I respond, The consequent is denied, for the point is that God, through his righteousness, accommodates himself in his judgments to the perverse morals of the perverse, without any perversity.

What the good is in its idea

VI. Furthermore, the good in its idea sometimes denotes what agrees with the inclination of the one willing, whether it is truly good or not, as we saw in the preceding chapter.[15] But the true good (as even Aristotle judges, although not carefully enough) is that which all desire. More correctly, it is what on account of the perfection of its nature is desirable and deserves to be desired, and is communicative of itself. Thus in the good, three things concur: (1) a certain, essential perfection on account of which it deserves to be desired as good. (2) A faculty for communicating its perfection, on account of which it is called useful. (3) The relation of both to the desire, from which it is denominated as desirable.[16] Thus they enumerate a threefold good: (1) metaphysical or essential good, which every being obtains as it is a being, namely, that perfection which is conveyed to it from its cause, on account of which it can be desired. This perfection does not have any evil that is opposed to it. (2) Physical good, which it obtains as a being of such a sort that is destined for the use of another, namely, that perfection by which it is fit for its use, whether that use is universal, a use it offers to the whole universe, or particular, a use it can convey to this or that thing. Thus medicine is called good because it is conducive for health. To this is opposed what is useless and unfitting, or also what is harmful. (3) Ethical good, which it obtains as

---

15. 1.2.15 §VI
16. *appetibile*, from *appetitus*, "desire" or "appetite"

a rational being, to the extent that it arranges itself according to a rule. To this good is opposed vice and sin.

What the goodness of God is

VII. Specifically, the goodness of God is nothing but that perfection of his through which he can communicate himself and deserves to be desired, and must be. For this reason, it includes three things: (1) his infinite perfection, which is made known to us by all his attributes, the perfection through which he is אל שדי, El Shaddai (Gen. 17:1) and sufficient for all things, and that to infinite blessedness. By this perfection he is good in himself and goodness itself (Ps. 25:8; Ex. 33:19), in whom there is no evil (Deut. 32:4). (2) His faculty of communicating himself, when he wills and to the extent that he wills, from which he is said to be good and to do good (Ps. 119:68). By this faculty he distributes his goodness bit by bit, so to speak, to everything: to beasts, to men, to the elect, and so forth (Ps. 36:5, 10; 57:3, 10; 104:24; 119:64). (3) That relation which rests on the preceding two as upon its foundation, the relation through which he is desirable and must be desired or sought in every way (Ps. 42:2; 63:1; 9:10; 34:10; 69:6, 32; 119:2, 10).

The intrinsic or immanent goodness of God

VIII. Therefore, the goodness of God can be considered, on the one hand, as it is in God, that is, as immanent. And in this way his goodness is: (1) his essence itself, and essential, while the majority of the creatures' goodness is accidental, accessory, and separable. (2) Independent, from which he is called the source of life (Ps. 36:9), for he is good by his own goodness, while all the creatures are good by means of his goodness, namely, through participation, by mere favor (Ps. 144:2). (3) Most simple, from which he is called goodness itself (Rom. 11:22), pure, unadulterated goodness, without any mixture of any imperfection or wickedness (Ps. 92:16). (4) The light in which there is no darkness (1 John 1:5), while in the creatures, there is not goodness without wickedness, or at least without imperfection. (5) Infinite and unlimited (Ps. 57:10), without any capacity of increase or decrease, above all that we conceive or think (Eph. 3:18–19), while creatures are never so good that they could not become better. (6) Eternal (1 Chron. 16:34, 41; throughout the Psalms), without beginning, without flux, without end, while since the goodness of the creatures has beginning and flux, it has an end, or at least can have an end. For this reason (7) God's goodness is great, and most great (Neh. 9:25; Ps. 5:8), while whatever goodness the creatures possess is like a tiny drop (Isa. 40:15).

The extrinsic or transferred goodness of God

IX. On the contrary, the goodness of God can be considered as it exists in creatures, as his transferred goodness, his beneficence. And in this way, he is the cause of all created goodness: (1) the exemplary cause, insofar as he expresses himself and represents his own infinite perfection as if by parts, such that all irrational beings bear some vestige of it, and all rational beings bear an image of it (Gen. 1:26). (2) The efficient cause (Gen. 1:31), insofar as every creature bears all its own goodness as received from God (James 1:17). (3) The final cause (Prov. 16:4; Rom. 11:36), insofar as all creatures either strive toward him (Ps. 42:2) or are directed toward him (Ps. 19:1).

The different ways of communicating

X. Moreover, the goodness of God is transferred to the creatures in different ways: (1) in a universal way, to all creatures, by creating, bearing, governing, and equipping them (Ps. 36:6; 147:9). (2) In a common way, to men indiscriminately, to the elect as well as the reprobate (1 Tim. 4:10), in piling upon them various common kindnesses (Rom. 2:4; 1 Tim. 6:17). (3) In a special way, to the elect (Ps. 36:7; 73:1), in dispensing saving goods to them (Eph. 1:3; 1 Peter 1:3–4). For this reason, according to its various respects it takes on various names: love, grace, mercy, longsuffering, patience, clemency, and kindness (all which will be treated expressly in the next chapter).

The Elenctic Part

It is asked: 1. Are they not raving mad who devise an evil God?

XI. The goodness of God that fills heaven and earth is so well known that not only not among Christians, Jews, and Muslims, but not even among the most barbarous nations are there any who would dare defame it openly, for which reason, with respect to the elenctic part, we will be brief. It is asked, first, whether they are raving mad who devise an evil God. There are said to be those among the Indians who worship the devil so that he would not harm them, and by worshiping him, make him God. At one time, the Cerdonians, Marcionites, and Manicheans believed that there was some sort of independent principle of evil and likewise an independent principle of good, and they raved that the God who was the author of the law and the prophets was not good and was not just, and they also called that principle of evil "God" as much as they did the principle of good, as Augustine testifies in *To Quodvultdeus on Heresies*, 21.[17] The Reformed

---

17. Augustine, *De haeresibus ad Quodvultdeum* in PL 42:29.

judge all who speak of an evil God to be raving mad, because they are calling "God" one who is not God. For God is the most perfect being, and goodness is without any doubt a perfection. If they should say, You Christians acknowledge a principle of evil as well—Satan; I respond, Certainly so, but we do not acknowledge an independent principle of evil like the Cerdonians, Marcionites and Manicheans did, and accordingly, we do not acknowledge a principle of evil that is God.

*2. Do they not deny that God is God who do not acknowledge
that he is the highest good?*
XII. It is asked, second, whether they do not deny that God is God who deny that he is the highest good. The heathen philosophers, fighting tooth and nail among themselves about the highest good, sought the highest good with great variety: some sought it in goods of fortune, in wealth, honors, and desires, others in goods of the body, in good health, strength, and beauty, others in goods of the soul, in wisdom, virtue, and tranquility of soul, such that Varro numbered more than two hundred opinions about the highest good, among which there was none that acknowledged God as the highest good, no doubt on account of this, that blinded and made foolish by sin, they did not see that the highest good was God alone. And in the last account what is this except to deny in reality that God is God? What is this except to substitute wretched riches, fickle honors, vain desires, foolish wisdom, meager and sterile virtue for the highest good, and to raise them to the throne of God? Thus our apostle rightly declares regarding these men that knowing God and yet not glorifying him as God, thus they are discovered to be fools in these debates of theirs, and their foolish heart has been darkened such that they exchanged the truth of God for a lie (Rom. 1:21, 25).

*3. Do they not abuse the divine goodness who from this—that the one
God is called good—strive to deduce that Christ is not God?*
XIII. It is asked, third, whether they do not abuse the divine goodness most wickedly who from this—that the one God is called good—deny that the Son of God, Jesus Christ, is good, and thus God from eternity. The Socinians, so that they might by the testimony of the Son of God himself more powerfully cast him down from the throne of eternal deity, and thus in the same stroke undermine the Trinity and the satisfaction of Christ, twist the testimony of Christ against Christ. They assert that in the text Christ rebukes the man for calling him good, since no one is good except one, God, and that he accordingly denies that he is good, or at least the highest good, as God is. The Reformed think that this is a repulsive twisting of Christ's meaning against him. Christ does not deny

that he is good, nor that he is the highest good, nor does he rebuke the young man in that way. They argue using these reasons: (1) for if you should think of Christ as a man, he was so good that he did not know evil (2 Cor. 5:21), that there was no deceit in his mouth (Isa. 53:9); or as the God-man, he was even more good, and it would involve a contradiction for him not to be good—he was that good shepherd (John 10:11); or as God, he was most good, the highest good. (2) His most hostile enemies themselves, even when challenged, could not charge him with even one vice, at least not justly (John 8:46). Indeed, (3) in addition they even declare him a good man, a truthful man, who taught the way of God in truth (Matt. 22:16). Furthermore, (4) he is that very one through whom God dispenses every good (Eph. 1:4), outside of whom no good, no salvation can come to us (Acts 4:12). Moreover, (5) as the Socinians themselves acknowledge, he is the true God and eternal life (1 John 5:20). And such a one would rebuke the young man because he greeted him as good? Such a one would deny that he was good? At the same time they say, (1) He rebuked him because he called him good. I respond, He certainly rebuked him, not because he called him good, but perhaps because he called him good with a mind to flatter, or what is more likely, because he called him good as God alone is, while at the same time he did not believe that he was God. But, they say, (2) We do not say that he denied that he was good, but that he was God, because he is not good in the way that God is. I respond: (a) Christ rebukes the young man not because he announced that he was God, but because he greeted him as good though he did not consider him as God. And (b) if he rebuked him for this reason, that he considered him as God and as the highest good, though the young man did not say anything but "good teacher," from what source did the Savior acknowledge that he considered him as God and as the highest good, if he was not God? For God alone is the knower of hearts (Jer. 17:9–10), just as he alone is good. Since therefore he was God, and most highly good, as God is, by what right would he have rebuked the young man because he declared him as such? Consult what we have already considered on this topic in the exegetical part.

4. Does the goodness of God require that he will each and every person to be saved?
The difference of opinions
XIV. It is asked, fourth, whether the goodness of God requires that he will each and every person to be saved, and, to this end, to give his Son to each and every person as a redeemer. We have already considered in the preceding chapter the question whether God wills each and every person to be saved,[18] and we are not

---

18. 1.2.15 §XXX

undertaking any question now except whether his goodness requires this. The Pelagians and Pelagianizers, the Jesuits, and the Remonstrants (captivated by a perverse love of the dogma of the universal will of God to save everyone, the efficacy of which depends upon man's independent choice) affirm that it does.

The orthodox arguments

The Reformed deny it because: (1) God is good and communicative of himself in such a way that that notwithstanding, he remains a most free and wise being who most freely dispenses his goodness according to his own wisdom. (2) If by his goodness he necessarily willed that each and every person be saved, then through that same goodness he could not will the manifestation of his avenging justice in the just condemnation of some. (3) Through his own infinite goodness, God has dispensed and does dispense all good that all creatures—even the worst, down to the reprobate and the demons—possess, but by his goodness he is not strictly bound to dispense eternal salvation to each and every person. (4) Nor does it hinder the divine goodness that he dispenses his goodness in various ways and degrees among his own creatures and does not confer every good to every creature, that for example, the goodness he confers on angels he does not confer on men, and what he dispensed to man he does not cast to the beasts. Thus, it absolutely does not hinder the divine goodness that he does not dispense to dogs the good that belongs to his children (Matt. 15:24). Furthermore, (5) with his goodness not standing in the way, he wills to condemn most of mankind eternally (Prov. 1:26–27; Rom. 9:15, 18). I do not see anything by which our adversaries can demonstrate with any plausibility an inseparable connection between the goodness of God and the will to save everyone. Consult the preceding chapter on the will of God as well as the subsequent chapter on his grace.[19]

5. *Do the Reformed, by their doctrine concerning absolute reprobation*
and so forth, erode the goodness of God?
XV. It is asked whether the Reformed, by their doctrine concerning the absolute decree, reprobation, the election of the few, the decree of the fall of our first parents, and so forth, erode the infinite goodness of God. We pose this question especially due to the Lutherans, who so that they may more easily justify the schism they have made and denigrate our churches, have nothing more frequently in their mouth than the opposition between God's love for men and

---

19. 1.2.15 §XXX; 1.2.17 §XXXII

Calvin's hatred for them.[20] So then, they respond to the question by affirming it; the Reformed by denying it. The occasion for their false accusation is (1) first generally, in the absolute and immutable decree by which God wills evil upon men. But our adversaries should have paid attention to these two things: (a) that the decree of God is his immanent operation, which does not touch the creature by bringing either evil or good upon it, and thus it injures no one. (b) If they should say that nevertheless he wills evil upon man, which is contrary to his goodness, then I will retort, He does not will to confer evil on him except on account of his sin, as the meritorious cause of that evil. The foundation of their false accusation is (2) in the absolute and immutable reprobation by which he destined man to eternal damnation. But (a) reprobation, as it is a decree, does not touch or injure anyone. (b) He has not predestined to inflict damnation upon anyone except on account of his unbelief and unrepentance, as the meritorious cause of damnation (Prov. 1:26–27). Furthermore, (3) in the fact that we state that God has elected few. But the Savior stated the same thing as we do (Matt. 20:16), and I know that our adversaries will not say that he is therefore hateful toward men. In addition, (4) that by the absolute and immutable decree, we make God the author of sin. But (a) the decree does not operate outside of God, for which reason it is not the cause of sin, which is surely outside of God. (b) It is not the cause of sin, but only of its futurity, between which there is the greatest difference. For the futurity of a thing is from eternity, for whatever is in time was future from eternity, while the future thing occurs in time. The futurity is from God by the decree, the future thing is from the creatures: the futurity is good, the sin evil. (c) God did not decree sin as such, except to permit it. In addition, (5) that we say that God by his providence influences the sinner and his sins, and therefore necessitates that the sinner sin. I respond: (a) Sin consists in lawlessness alone (1 John 3:4). God does not influence that lawlessness, but only its substratum, that in which the lawlessness exists (Acts 17:28). Next (b) by his influence, predetermining the will to that in which lawlessness exists, he does not necessitate, but leaves to man the faculty of determining himself, under God, from free choice, from counsel, from rational complacency, in which the true freedom of our choice consists. Finally, (6) that we teach that God from eternity decreed the fall of our first parents. I respond, He decreed the futurity of the fall, which would be procured only by the abuse of human choice, and he did so for this end, that from it he would have an opportunity for demonstrating his own glory, as much the glory of his mercy as the glory of his avenging justice.

---

20. ἀντίθεσιν *inter* φιλανθρωπίαν Dei et μισανθρωπίαν *Calvini*

It will suffice to have mentioned in this place these things that will be spoken of more fully in their own places.[21]

The Practical Part

The goodness of God stirs us up: 1. To love God

XVI. Now for practice. If God is truly good, most highly good, and all good, then first, we should love him analogously, that is to say, preeminently (Ps. 18:1–2; 116:1, 5), for good and loveable are reciprocal, such that what is not loved should not be considered as good. Wherefore, if you love a meager ray of divine goodness in the creatures, if you so greedily desire a tiny drop from this fountain, will you not love the sun itself, and the continually flowing fountain of all good? As Anselm says in *Prosologion* (ch. 25), "Love the one good in which all good things exist, and it will be sufficient for you."[22]

The acts of love

Let us love him, I say: (1) by desiring, panting after, and diligently seeking the presence, possession, union, communion, and enjoyment of him (Ps. 42:2; 63:1), so that we may be as it were cemented to him (Ps. 63:8; 1 Cor. 6:17), just as he desires and seeks us (Ps. 119:176). (2) By hanging all our good on him (2 Cor. 8:5). (3) By removing all the evil of sin from his sight (Isa. 1:16), that we may please him (Rom. 12:1–2; 14:18), and that he may make all his goodness pass before our face (Ex. 33:19), and that by his goodness he may remove every evil from us (Ps. 103:3). (4) By resting in his infinite goodness, as in our sole and entire good (Ps. 16:5–6; 73:25–26), that thus we might not desire him to be more good or less just, for in both we would deny his infinite goodness (Ex. 34:7).

The affections of love

In all these things, let us love God: (1) truly and sincerely, with our heart and not only with our mouth or motions—love from a pure heart, and from faith unfeigned (1 Tim. 1:5; 1 John 3:18)—that is, as God is truly good. (2) Superlatively, from our whole heart, from our whole thought, with all our strength (Matt. 22:37), above all things that are in heaven and on earth (Ps. 73:25); that is, just as he is the highest good, exceeding every good. (3) Solely, with neglect and contempt of all other goods (Ps. 73:25; Song 8:7), at least to the extent that they are adverse to this one good (Phil. 3:7–8); that is, as he alone is good. (4) Independently, on account of him alone, not on account of any other thing

---

21. 1.3.1 §XVII; 1.3.4 §XI; 1.3.10 §XXXII
22. Anselm, *Proslogion* in *PL* 158:240.

(John 6:26); that is, just as he is the independent good that has done all things on account of itself (Prov. 16:4), from which and to which are all things (Rom. 11:36). (5) Constantly and immutably, not only for a time (Rev. 2:4; 2 Tim. 4:10); that is, as he is the good that is eternal, immutable, and always the same. (6) Efficaciously, not lazily, but energetically (Gal. 5:6; Song 8:7), not in word, nor in tongue, but in deed and truth (1 John 3:18; Matt. 7:21); that is, just as he is the good that in all things is communicative of itself.

The incentives of love

Moreover, conducive for kindling and inflaming this love is: (1) striving with every effort, that more and more we may be rooted in faith and the persuasion of this infinite goodness of God (Col. 2:7), so that rooted and grounded in love we may have the strength to comprehend with all the saints what is the breadth and length and depth and height, and to know the surpassing love of Christ (Eph. 3:17–19). (2) Being frequent and deep in the contemplation of that infinite goodness and perfection which is intrinsic to God, that we may as it were taste and see it (Ps. 34:8), just as a greedy man in the contemplation of gold is inflamed to love for it. Especially (3) being assiduous in meditation on that goodness which is extrinsic to God, which Psalm 17:7 proclaims to be marvelous, which fills the earth (Ps. 33:5) and reaches to heaven (Ps. 57:10), which is visible in the creation, sustaining, and governance of this universe (Ps. 36:6–8), and par excellence in the work of human redemption, in the face of our Lord Jesus Christ (Titus 3:4; 2 Cor. 4:6).

2. To seek every good in God

XVII. Second, in God and in his infinite goodness is that in which and from which we should seek for ourselves every good. I say "in which" namely because his goodness is all-sufficient (Gen. 17:1), a sun and shield (Ps. 84:12), an exceedingly great reward (Gen. 15:1); and "from which" because, as he is the fount of life, in whose light we enjoy light (Ps. 36:9), so also from him comes every good gift (James 1:17). He is the one who blesses us with every blessing (Eph. 1:3). And if therefore we should lack: (1) delightful good, he through his goodness fills our hearts with food and gladness (Acts 14:17). By his goodness he abundantly offers us all things to enjoy (1 Tim. 6:17), and he crowns us with goodness and mercies (Ps. 103:4; 84:12). If we should lack (2) useful good, and good necessary for sustaining this life, he gives heed to heaven, and heaven to earth, and earth to the grain, and it to Jezreel (Hos. 2:21–22; Ps. 104:10–16). Indeed, he is the one in whom we live, move, and have our being (Acts 17:28). If we should lack (3) honorable and saving good—faith, hope, love, piety, and so forth—he is the Father of lights, from whom comes every saving good (James 1:17), who blesses us with every spiritual gift (Eph. 1:3). These things are so if only (1) we, in pursuing any good, do not dig for ourselves wells that hold no water (Jer. 2:13), and we do not say, Who will show us any good? (Ps. 4:6); (2) we wrench that good, as it were, from the highest good by our most ardent prayers (James 1:5; Matt. 7:7–8); (3) and do so by faith in his Son Jesus (John 16:23), in whom all his promises are yes and amen (2 Cor. 1:20); and in addition, (4) with filial reverence for his name (Ps. 34:9–10); and also (5) by a godly resting in that good which the highest good has deigned to dispense to us (Phil. 4:11–13; 2 Cor. 12:9); and (6) we do not consider any earthly goods to be anything but corollaries (Matt. 6:33–34).

3. To seek the remedy of every evil in the goodness of God
XVIII. Third, in the infinite goodness of God is the remedy for every evil, and from this he is called a healer (Ex. 15:26), as he is the one who heals all our diseases (Ps. 103:3). Therefore, should we be pressed: (1) by evils of fortune, by poverty, he through his goodness will be for us our portion and inheritance (Ps. 16:5–6), and also from his treasury as much as we need will be supplied (Matt. 6:32; 2 Cor. 9:10; Ps. 23:1–2). Should we be pressed by the wickedness and ferocity of our enemies, he by his goodness will be our stronghold, high place, shield, and strength (Ps. 18:1–2). Should we be pressed (2) by evils of the body, by disease, he by his goodness will heal all our infirmities (Ps. 103:3; 6:2–4; 38:8–9, 22). Should we be pressed (3) by evils of the soul, by sins, he forgives all our iniquities (Ps. 103:3) and does so according to his goodness (Ps. 51:1; Isa. 43:25). Should we be pressed (4) by impotence in resisting sins, his grace will be sufficient, his power will be made perfect in weakness (2 Cor. 12:9). Should we be pressed (5) by spiritual desertions (Ps. 77:7–9), Jehovah is good, slow to anger, abounding in goodness; he does not keep his anger forever (Ps. 113:8–10; Isa. 54:7–10). Indeed, in all evils entirely, however many and whatever sort they are, the remedy is supplied for us from the infinite goodness of God, that is to say, the Lord is good, our strength in difficulty (Nah. 1:7), the one who also is able to take care that all evils work together for us for good (Rom. 8:28). These things are so if only (1) we seek our remedy in him alone (Isa. 55:6–7); (2) we place our hope in him alone, for the Lord is good to those who wait for him, to the soul that has sought him (Lam. 3:25; Nah. 1:7), inasmuch as he is the one who for the sake of his own goodness sends any evil upon us (Heb. 12:6–7), who for the sake of his own goodness restrains it (Ps. 23:4), who by that same goodness promises his presence and help (Ps. 91:15), who by that same goodness keeps his promises (Heb. 10:23). If only (3) we remove the evil of our sins from

his sight (Isa. 1:16; 55:7), for they alone separate us and the God who is most good (Isa. 59:1–2).

4. To acknowledge the wickedness of sin

XIX. Fourth, in the infinite goodness of God is that in which we should acknowledge the wickedness of sin, namely because (1) it alone cries out against his infinite goodness and, as much as it can, labors to cast down the most good God from the throne of his deity, and for this reason it is called by the Fathers *deicide*.[23] (2) By it we abandon the highest good (Jer. 2:13; Deut. 32:15); and (3) on account of it we are abandoned by the highest good (Isa. 59:1–2) and will be abandoned eternally (Matt. 25:41; 2 Thess. 1:9). (4) It renders our very soul, which was made so good by the good God, according to his own image, so evil and unfit for any good. (5) By it the true and infinite goodness of the Creator is placed below the imaginary goodness of the creatures. (6) By it we repay the highest good, from which all good is supplied to us, with nothing but evil (Deut. 32:6). (7) By it we despise the treasury of divine goodness (Rom. 2:4).

In what manner

And in all these things, let us acknowledge the wickedness of sin in such a way that the goodness of God would draw us (1) to repentance (Rom. 2:4); (2) to profound sorrow for past sin (Lam. 5:16); (3) to avoidance and detestation of every future sin (Ps. 97:10); (4) to seek sin's remedy in the goodness of God alone, which is in Christ Jesus (Ps. 51:1, 7).

5. To imitation

XX. Fifth, in the infinite goodness of God is what we should imitate. Psalm 119:68 offers the prototype in summary: "You are good, and do good."[24] He is good: good in intrinsic and immanent perfection, by which he is lovable and is loved by himself, by which he is communicative of himself, by which he is desirable and to be desired by all. He does good: he pours out goodness and distributes it to creatures, indeed to all creatures, the good and the evil, although in different ways and degrees.

---

23. E.g. Petrus Chrysologus, Sermo CLXXI in *PL* 52:647; Chrysostom, *Adversus Judaeos* in *PG* 48.

24. תוב ומתיב

Being good. Motivating reasons. Supports

Therefore we should strive that according to his example we become good and do good. First, we should become good, that is, apt for the use for which we were created—and that use was that we would acknowledge, love, glorify, and live blessed with the Creator forever (Isa. 43:7). The aptitude for this use is in the image of God and its original righteousness, that is, in the wisdom of the intellect (Col. 3:10), the holiness and righteousness of the will (Eph. 4:24). Deprived of this original righteousness by sin, we are inept for our use, as unprofitable servants (Luke 17:10), and for that reason, entirely evil (Gen. 6:5, 12–13; 8:21). Accordingly, the business of imitation requires before all things that (1) we should be restored by God to that lost goodness, which is accomplished by regeneration to life, by conversion to faith in God and Christ, by sanctification to the restoration of the divine image (John 3:5; 1 Cor. 6:11). (2) Restored and renewed by God, we should renew ourselves more and more (Rom. 12:2), wash ourselves, remove our evil from the sight of God, learn to do good (Isa. 1:16–17).

Doing good

Then second, we should do good, according to the use for which, by the goodness of our creation, we were intended. We should do good, that is, toward God, by acknowledging, loving, glorifying, and faithfully serving him (Rom. 1:9), and toward our neighbor, by pouring out our goodness upon all, even the wicked and our enemies (Rom. 12:17, 19–21; Matt. 5:44–45), although in diverse ways and degrees (Gal. 6:9–10).

By this imitation of the divine goodness: (1) we will become like God in one most perfect property of his, and we will be rendered partakers of the divine nature (2 Peter 1:4), in which the chief perfection of the rational creature consists (Matt. 5:48). (2) We will show ourselves to be children of God—"that you may be children of your Father who is in the heavens" (Matt. 5:45)—since we by spiritual generation have been made partakers of his goodness. (3) We will have an argument within us upon which we can build a certain assurance of our restoration to the image of God (2 Thess. 1:11; Eph. 5:9; Gal. 5:22; Col. 3:12).

6. To seek blessedness in God

XXI. Sixth, in the infinite goodness of God is that in which we should seek and obtain our blessedness: "Who will make us to see good? Lift up the light of your countenance upon us, O Jehovah" (Ps. 4:6). Here the "light of the countenance" is nothing but that good which is sought, in which is the fullness of joys before the face of God (Ps. 16:11), in whom is the vein of life, and in whose light (goodness) we enjoy light (Ps. 36:9–10) while we taste and see how good the Lord is (Ps. 34:8).

The manner

Specifically, in God's goodness we should perceive, first, our objective blessedness, or that good which renders us blessed, that is, not any created good, as the ancient philosophers raved, but the good that is uncreated, independent, highest, and infinite, which for this reason is called "the fountain of life" and also "our portion" (Ps. 16:5–6), since it can avert every evil like a solid shield and offers every good like the sun (Ps. 84:11), all the way to perfect fullness, and it abundantly compensates all our labor and effort, as our exceedingly great reward (Gen. 15:1). Second, in God's goodness we should perceive our formal blessedness, namely in the possession, union, communion, enjoyment, and delight in the highest and infinite good. By this blessedness we have that good—"Whom have I in the heavens besides you?" (Ps. 73:25)—and our God is God: "Blessed is the nation whose God is Jehovah" (Ps. 33:12). By it God expends his goodness upon us, he communicates it to us (Ps. 33:22; 36:10; 42:5). By it we enjoy that same goodness (Ps. 59:10; 17:7), we delight in it (Ps. 63:3; 69:16), and in it we rejoice and exult (Ps. 31:7; 36:7). In this way the infinite goodness of God shows what this blessedness is and where it can be found.

Motives for seeking it

But it does not only show it; indeed, it also invites us to seek it. For as seeking blessedness is innate to all, and seeking it from elsewhere is innate to carnal men, accordingly the following motives urge us to seek it in the goodness of God alone. (1) Because in him is the highest end of our life (Matt. 6:33), without which all that we do will be done rashly and in vain. (2) Because by our consideration of this end all our actions ought to be directed, and of our actions, those alone are upright which tend in an upright line, so to speak, to that end: all other actions are curved and distorted. Therefore whoever lives without concern for this blessedness, for this end, is like one who shoots an arrow without a target or commits a ship to the waves without a compass.[25] For this reason in the Scriptures such persons are said to go astray (Isa. 53:6; Ps. 119:176), likewise to turn aside, and to become useless, and not to practice what is good (Rom. 3:11–12). (3) Because

---

25. William Ames uses almost exactly the same metaphors in the same order: "Therefore, whoever lives without regard to this highest goal acts just like someone who shoots arrows without aiming. Or he lives like someone who commits a battleship to the waves or winds when he has disregarded the North Star or all concern for a safe haven where he ought to land." *A Sketch of the Christian's Catechism*, trans. Todd Rester (Grand Rapids: Reformation Heritage Books, 2008), 6.

the highest good has the highest dignity and excellence, and thus deserves the first and primary place in our thoughts and pursuits (Matt. 6:33; Phil. 3:13–14). Therefore those who, neglecting this good, are distracted by any other are just like infants, considering the most important matters of little moment and occupied with worthless things (Ps. 62:10; Prov. 23:5).

And the means of finding it

Nevertheless, it is not sufficient to seek blessedness unless we also find it. And this will happen if we seek it: (1) in its own place, not in the world and worldly things, in wine and grain (Ps. 4:7; 17:14), but in God alone (Ps. 73:25). (2) By the proper means, by knowledge and faith in God and the Mediator (John 17:3; Acts 4:12; John 14:6). Also (3) by a righteous struggle, seeking it first (Matt. 6:33), and neglecting other things (Phil. 3:13–14). And if (4) we join to our seeking a zeal for good works (2 Peter 1:5, 11). And (5) in all these things we are pure in heart (Ps. 73:1; Matt. 5:8). We will relate more things of this kind in another place.[26]

7. To glorify God

XXII. Finally, seventh, in the infinite goodness of God is that on account of which we should glorify him, following the perpetual example of the saints, and especially of David (Ps. 135:3; 106:1), of Moses (Ex. 34:6), of Asaph and his sons (2 Chron. 5:13), and of the Levites (Ezra 3:11). For the goodness of God is: (1) that property by which he most greatly pours himself out and commends himself to creatures. For this reason Augustine says on Psalm 135, "Because God is good and made all good things, and he who made them is much better than these things he made, you will not find anything better to say of him than, 'The Lord is good,' if, that is, you understand that he is properly good, the good by which everything else is good."[27] (2) That property which especially touches us and thus compels us to celebrate it, for which reason Bernard says, "Just as there is no moment in which we do not enjoy the goodness of God, thus there should be no moment in which we do not have him present in our memory."[28] (3) That in the celebration of which is the most pleasant business of the saints, as Augustine says in the passage already cited: "I am possessed by an indescribable sweetness when I hear 'The Lord is good,' and when I have surveyed all things to be considered which are outside of him, I do not praise those things without that one, but

---

26. 1.2.23 §XIV
27. Augustine, *Enarrationes in Psalmos* in *PL* 36:1740.
28. Bernard of Clairvaux, *De interiori domo* in *PL* 184:511–12.

I find him perfect without them, not lacking, not changeable, not seeking good from anything that he might be increased, not fearing evil from anything that he might be reduced. If then whatever other thing we praise, we praise because it is good, there can be for you no greater cause, none better nor more firm, wherefore you should praise God, than the fact that he is good."[29] And so that we may be more unencumbered for this business of glorification, three things are profitable: (1) that we know (a) what his goodness is, what his immanent goodness is, what his transferred goodness is; (b) what its qualities are, and its weight, that it is independent, immutable, eternal, most high, and infinite; (c) what its effects are, in creation, providence, redemption, and beatification. To reflect on these things distinctly greatly makes for promptness in celebrating him. (2) That we sense, taste, see, and marvel at it: "How great his goodness, and how great his beauty!" (Zech. 9:17). (3) That what we sense in our heart, we pour out with our mouth, and rouse others to do the same: "Confess to the Lord, for he is good, for his goodness endures forever" (Ps. 106:1). "Praise the Lord, for he is good; sing to his name, for it is pleasant" (Ps. 135:3). "Bless the Lord, O you his angels, bless the Lord, all his hosts, bless the Lord, all his works, bless the Lord, O my soul!" (Ps. 103:8, 11, 20–22).

---

29. Augustine, *Enarrationes in Psalmos* in *PL* 36:1740.

CHAPTER SEVENTEEN

The Love, Grace, Mercy, Longsuffering, and Clemency of God

The Lord, a God merciful and gracious, slow to anger,
abundant in kindness and faithfulness.
—Exodus 34:6

The goodness of God

I. The goodness of God that we called his transferred goodness operates either by giving or by directing, and the latter either by prescribing or retributing. From this latter directing it is designated *righteousness*. From the former giving it is, according to the diverse way of reckoning, first the things given and then the giving itself, designated as (1) *love*, which is nothing except goodness as it is communicative of itself; (2) *grace*, which is nothing but love that is not owed; (3) *mercy*, which is nothing but grace toward the miserable; (4) *patience*, which is nothing but mercy toward a sinner; (4) *longsuffering*, which is nothing but patience that is long-lasting; and (5) *kindness*, which is nothing but longsuffering with beneficence. And these are the affections of the gracious God, about which Moses speaks in Exodus 34:6.

The Exegetical Part
It is constructed upon the exegesis of the text.

II. In these words is contained a certain celebration of gratitude, wherein, so that Moses would return thanks that his prayers were heard and that he was given an opportunity to glimpse God, Jehovah shows him an example and, as it were, prescribes a specific formula. In it, two things are noted:

    A. The one who is celebrated: יהוה, Jehovah, which according to the rabbis of the Hebrews is the name of grace. They note this appositely and suitably in this present celebratory task, insofar as by this name, the virtues contained here—love, grace, mercy, and so forth—grow immeasurably strong, since, for example, his love is thus celebrated as truly existing, independent from everything, as immutable, always the same and self-consistent, as most simple, without hypocrisy, as infinite, without limit or measure, as eternal, without end, and so forth, since all these things are involved in the one name *Jehovah*. Compare what we have considered in its own place concerning this name.[1]

B. The celebration, representing by the amassing of titles his:

1. Love and mercy: רחום אל, "A God merciful." If the words should be taken in the nominative case, then from common usage the substantive verb "is" should be implied, so that this sense emerges: "Jehovah is a merciful God." If the words should be taken in the vocative case, then it will be an address of praise from God himself, directed to himself and offered to Moses as an example and formula. Furthermore, אל, "God," is the subject to be applied to all the following titles, so for example, רחום אל, חנון אל "God is merciful," "God is gracious," and so forth. אל denotes the strong God, who will distribute his strength into all the following attributes, and thus it presents us with a powerful love and mercy, which nothing at all can resist. רחום, "merciful" is from the verb רחם, which only occurs once in the Qal, namely, in Psalm 18:1, where David uses it for his own love toward God, intending to signify his intimate and most intense love for God. It occurs frequently in the Piel, meaning, besides love, the affection of mercy, or love toward a miserable person, with sympathy. It is commonly and frequently used for the love of God toward miserable men, but never for the love of men toward God. At the same time, it repeatedly expresses his common love. It derives either from רחם, "womb" such that it denotes that love which a mother has toward a child in her womb (cf. Isa. 49:15), or from רחמים, "compassion," the singular of which is not found, which, as Piscator observes on Psalm 18, is because there are many works of mercy.[2] From the same idea comes the noun σπλάγχνα, "inward parts" (Col. 3:12) and the verb σπλαχνίζομαι, "I am inwardly moved" (Matt. 15:32). It denotes love, not an ordinary love as אהבה does, but an intimate, most tender love, arising from the bowels themselves, such a love by which, in addition, the entrails are strongly moved. And it is this sort of love that belongs to God when he considers the miserable. For this reason not only is

---

1. 1.2.4 §VIII
2. See "Scholia in Psal. XVIII" in Johann Piscator, *In librum psalmorum commentarius* (Herborn: Christopher Corvinus, 1611), 100.

he designated in the text אֵל רַחוּם, "strong," "vigorous," or "robust in love," but also, in Psalm 51:3, a multitude of mercies is asserted for him: כְּרֹב רַחֲמֶיךָ, "according to the multitude of your mercies."

2. Grace: חַנּוּן, "gracious," and supplying אֵל, "strongly gracious." It means doing something *gratis*, that is, freely, by pure, unadulterated good pleasure. It is opposed (a) to the payment of a price and the recompense of wages (Gen. 9:15; Ex. 21:11); (b) to justice (Ps. 35:7, 19); and (c) to merit (1 Sam. 19:5). Thus, Noah is said to have found grace before God (Gen. 6:8), as well as Moses (Ex. 33:13). In the New Testament the corresponding verb is χαριτόω, "I show favor" (Eph. 1:6).

3. Longsuffering: אֶרֶךְ אַפַּיִם, "long in nostrils." Here אֶרֶךְ means "long-extended," and it is used for the cloud above the tabernacle (Num. 9:19), which extended itself and covered every part of the tabernacle. אַפַּיִם denotes nostrils and anger. Thus אֶרֶךְ אַפַּיִם denotes that he is slow to become angry and to inflict punishment. For those who are wide in nostrils more easily blow out the spirit of anger boiling in their breast and are more easily placated. In anger, the blood around the heart boils and the heart itself is warmed beyond its limit, but those who have narrow nostrils also draw less cold air for cooling it down. They also give way more quickly to the fumes rising from the heart, and blow them out more slowly due to the narrowness of their nasal passages. Hence Spaniards speak of the flaring nostrils of those who get angry. Moreover, patience is included under longsuffering, as it is only different from it by a degree of duration. In the New Testament, the corresponding word is μακροθυμία, "longsuffering" (Rom. 2:4).

4. Clemency, or kindness: רַב חֶסֶד, "abounding," or great, "in clemency." חֶסֶד denotes, besides piety (because kindness is a work of piety), kindness and benefit (Deut. 5:10; Ps. 106:1). It denotes every kindness that is conferred upon others, whether living or dead, whether miserable or not miserable, whether deserving or undeserving, whether conferred justly and rightfully or liberally and kindly, as Nikolaus Serarius observes in his second book on Joshua.[3] רַב signifies a

---

3. Nikolaus Serarius, S. J. (1555–1609), "Liber Secundus qui ipsum Josuae librum explicat," col. 373, in the compilation, *Commentarii in sacros Bibliorum libros, Josuae, Judicum, Ruth, Tobiae, Judith, Esther, Machabaeorum* (Paris: Edmund Martin, 1611). The original sentence Mastricht cited translates, "It is evident in the Scriptures that the Hebrew word חֶסֶד, in its widest sense, is

surpassing amount and a very high degree of anything, whatever it might be. Among the prophets, for the most part, חֶסֶד denotes a kindness that is exercised toward someone to whom absolutely nothing is owed, according to Maimonides in *The Guide of the Perplexed*.[4] Paul Fagius also adds that it denotes a kindness that is not common, but extraordinary, eminent, rare, and one that is done gratuitously, without respect to compensation.[5] In that sort of kindness, God is predicated as רַב, abundant, great, and thus πλούσιος χρηστότητος, "rich in kindness" (Rom. 2:4).

The Dogmatic Part

That there is in God a certain benevolent and beneficent propensity toward his creatures. It is proved by the Scriptures.

III. Therefore, according to the whole text, there is in God a certain benevolent and beneficent propensity toward his creatures, which, according to its various objects and its various modes of acting with regard to those objects, is now called love, now grace, now mercy, now patience and longsuffering, now clemency and kindness, insofar as that one propensity absorbs preeminently the perfections of all these virtues in men. This is said in Scripture, in general, whenever good pleasure of the will[6] is attributed to him (Matt. 11:26; Eph. 1:5), and in specific, whenever love, grace, and mercy are ascribed to him, just as we will show individually in their own places.

It is proved also by reasons.

IV. Speaking of the same propensity are: (1) the will of God, insofar as it is nothing but a propensity toward good. (2) His goodness, insofar as it is communicative of itself. His operations speak of it: (3) creation, whereby he showed a propensity toward the existence of the creature; (4) preservation, for the

---

every kindness that embraces and includes anyone, whether living or dead, whether wretched or not, whether deserving or not, whether it is conferred justly and rightfully or liberally and generously."

4. *Moreh Nebuchim*. Moses Maimonides, *The Guide of the Perplexed*, trans. S. Pines, 2 vols. (Chicago: Chicago University Press, 1963, 2010), I.54.64b–67a, 1:124–28. For a widely available early modern Latin translation with commentary on Rabbi Samuel Aben Tybbon's Hebrew translation from the Arabic, see Johannes Buxtorf, Jr., *Rabbi Mosis Maimonidis liber* מורה נבוכים *Doctor perplexorum* (Basel: Genathius, 1629), I.54, 86–90, esp. 87.

5. Mastricht appears to summarize Fagius's list and comments on Exodus 34:6–32: Paul Fagius, *Thargum, hoc est, paraphrasis Onkeli Chaldaica in sacra biblia: Pentateuchus*, vol. 1, foll. r5 recto–r7 recto.

6. εὐδοκία τῆς θελήματος

permanence of the same; and (5) governance, whereby he directs the creature toward goodness and its use. His operations toward men especially speak of this propensity, operations such as (6) election, whereby he shows a propensity to decree salvation for the miserable, and (7) redemption, whereby he shows a propensity toward the restoration of the lost, and so forth. I will say it in a word: whatever operation of his you please, it argues for that propensity of which we have spoken.

This propensity is declared.

V. That propensity is called *benevolent* when considered intrinsically and *beneficent* when considered extrinsically. In itself generally considered, it is love; insofar as it is independent, free, and is not owed, it is grace; insofar as it considers the creature as miserable, it is mercy; insofar as it considers the offending sinner whom it endures, it is patience; insofar as it endures him a long time, it is long-suffering; insofar as it also does good to him, it is clemency and beneficence.[7] Accordingly, so many virtues in creatures do not designate anything in God except his one propensity, measured in various ways. For the sake of brevity, I mention it this once, so that I am not compelled to recall the same thing again in each individual case, and the reader can recall it as the need arises.

Love in God: That it is

VI. Therefore, the propensity to good generally considered is designated *love*, which is taught by all that we have already brought forth in §§III–V, and is also quite emphatically taught in 1 John 4:8–10: "God is love. Through this the love of God was made manifest among us, that he sent his only begotten Son into the world so that we might live. In this is love, not that we loved God, but that he loved us." Here this propensity is distinctly denoted, intrinsically, as benevolent, and extrinsically, as beneficent. The passages in Romans 5:5, John 3:16, and Deuteronomy 33:3 may also be added.

What it is

VII. Love is nothing but a propensity of the will toward a thing, just as hatred is an aversion from a thing. It is a propensity of the will, not such that it is something

---

7. Here and elsewhere, some of the close connections among the Latin word pairings are lost in translation. For example, to the *miser*, "miserable," God's goodness is *misericordia*, "mercy," or literally, "misery of the heart" (cf. §XXI); when it *benefacit*, "does good," or gives *beneficia*, "benefits" or "kindnesses," to the sinner, it is *beneficentia*, "kindness" or "beneficence," and is called *benefica*, "kind" or "beneficent"; similarly, when it wills good, it is *benevolentia*, "good will" or "benevolence," and is called *benevola*, "benevolent."

different from God, but it is his will itself, and it is not properly an affection, as we observed above.[8] Although, it could be considered as an affection, and thus single and uniform in respect to all creatures; or as an effective operation, and thus diverse, according to the variety of the goods which it dispenses, as we will teach in its own place.[9]

Its three ingredients

As an affection or propensity immanent in God, it includes: (1) an appetite for union, which in us is a longing,[10] the sort that the Savior expresses in John 17:24, "I desire that where I am, they also will be with me," a longing by which he, as it were, seeks us (Ps. 119:176). The apostle points to the same reality in Ephesians 2:4: "With great love he loved us," compared with verse 13, "As you who were once far off have now been brought near." This longing does not exist in God from some lack, as it does in us, but from an abundance of goodness that is communicative of itself (Job 22:2–3). (2) The aim of doing good, which is called *benevolence*, whereby he makes one good, or better, beloved. And accordingly this love precedes all the goodness of the one who is beloved, seeing that he confers it. From this we perceive how God could love the elect who were still sinners, devoid of faith and of every good, how he loved them: (a) before all their spiritual life, before faith and every good of the same kind (Eph. 2:5; John 3:16; Rom. 5:8); (b) before all their natural life (Rom. 9:11); (c) before his Son was offered to the world (John 3:16); indeed, (d) before the world was created, from all eternity past (Eph. 1:4; 2 Tim. 1:9); and God did this, namely, that by this benevolence he might confer to them life, faith, his Son, and all things. If you should say, How could he love the workers of iniquity? (Hab. 1:13; Ps. 5:4–5), then I will say, He loved the workers while he hated their works; he loved them by his love of benevolence, not by his love of complacency[11] (Ezek. 16:5). (3) The joy of acquiescence, by which God is pleased in all his people, namely, in sinners on account of his Son apprehended by faith, that is, in the Beloved (Eph. 1:6). By it (a) his own are precious to him (Ps. 116:15); (b) he frequently commends them (Song 5:2); (c) he very frequently visits them with his grace (Luke 1:68; Rev. 3:20), a grace by which (d) he opens secret things to them (John 15:15) and (e) suffers with them in adversities (Isa. 63:9; Heb. 4:15).

---

8. 1.2.15 §XXXII
9. §IX, below
10. *concupiscentia*
11. *Complacentia*, "complacency," means good pleasure and approval.

The objects of divine love

VIII. In his love God is first and foremost occupied with himself, insofar as he is the highest good, on account of which he has made and does make all things (Prov. 16:4). And in this love the divine persons are occupied with each other: the Father with the Son (John 3:35; 5:20; 10:17; Matt. 3:17; 17:5), the Son with the Father (John 14:31). Finally, on account of himself, God is in this love occupied with all things, namely because he has rendered them suitable for promoting his own glory (Prov. 16:4; Rom. 11:36), especially with men (Isa. 43:7), and among these, chiefly and most tenderly with the elect (Eph. 1:5–7); and with all things, not in themselves, but in himself, because his love is independent.

The threefold love of God toward his creatures

IX. From this emerges a threefold love of God, that is, toward his creatures: (1) a universal love (Ps. 104:31; 145:9), through which he created, conserves, and governs all things (Ps. 36:6; 147:9). (2) A common love, extending itself particularly to men, certainly not to each and every individual, but yet indiscriminately to anyone, as much the reprobate as the elect, of which kind is also the love that dispenses the benefits that are mentioned in Hebrews 6:4–5 and 1 Corinthians 13:1–2. (3) A love proper to the elect, by which he dispenses saving benefits to them, benefits that accompany salvation (Heb. 6:9), which accordingly are different from nature and natural benefits. For it is most terrible to confuse nature and grace. This love is again on the one hand called an objective love, by which such goods are dispensed that indeed concern man and are aimed at him, but yet do not enter him: of such kind are the goods of election, redemption through the satisfaction of Christ, and calling to salvation through the proclamation of the gospel. Or on the other hand, it is a subjective love, which, so to speak, enters man himself, as regeneration, conversion, sanctification, and union and communion with Christ. Both of these are especially particular and proper to the elect (Rom. 8:29–30; John 1:12). Compare what we will teach on this topic a little further on from here, concerning grace, in §§XV–XVII.

The properties of divine love

X. And finally, this love is: (1) free and most free (Hos. 14:4), not arising from any worth, whether foreseen or existing, in those who are beloved (Ezek. 16:8); (2) firm and immutable (Rom. 5:8, 10; 1 John 4:10; John 13:1); (3) infinite and eternal, never to be changed (John 3:16), never to cease (Ps. 27:10), and never to be diminished (Song 8:7), much less interrupted (Rom. 8:35); (4) effective and most fruitful, pouring itself out in all sorts of blessings (Ps. 34:9–10), as much spiritual (Eph. 1:3; 1 John 3:1–2; Cor. 1:20) as corporeal (Matt. 6:32–33);

(5) pure and sincere, thoroughly lacking all hypocrisy, hatred, and perverse intention, for it is a love that does not love except on account of itself (Deut. 7:6–8; 1 John 4:8), and one that loves so that it may bestow itself on its own (Isa. 63:9; Rev. 4:8), not so that it may take or receive anything from them (Job 22:2); and finally, (6) ardent and fervent (Jer. 31:20; Rom. 5:5, 8; Song 8:6–7), and thus whenever he pours out his love into their hearts, he does so that he might make them, in their own way, like him, and transform them into his own image (2 Cor. 3:18; 2 Peter 1:4).

Hatred in God: That it is, What it is

XI. Yet there is (as we taught above in chapter 15)[12] also in God a hatred or aversion, first to sinners (Rom. 9:13), then to sin (Ps. 5:4–5). Its affection is nothing but an adverse will (Hab. 1:13; Isa. 1:15), and its effective operation, withdrawal (Isa. 59:2), punishment (Ps. 5:5–6), and all that commonly flows from the affection of hatred in men, but without disturbance or change in God. Therefore, it considers the sinner, and him alone, especially the obstinate sinner, inasmuch as in his torment and destruction, God is said to rejoice (Deut. 28:63; Prov. 1:26). It considers him on account of sin alone, because sin is repugnant to God's nature, his law, his honor (Ps. 45:7). And thus, finally, it considers the sinner to this end, to torment him (1) in general, by all his judgments (Deut. 28:15), all the way to the end (Ps. 11:5–6); in specific, (2) by horrors of conscience (Prov. 17:22); (3) by every sort of death (Gen. 3:3; Rom. 5:14); indeed (4) by the cursed death that fell on his own Son (Gal. 3:13; Rom. 8:32); and finally, (5) by the eternal condemnation of the reprobate sinner himself (Heb. 10:26–27). But because hatred in God concerns his avenging justice, in this topic it will suffice to have touched upon it.

Grace in God: It is proved that it is

XII. From love is perceived what grace is in God, the grace from which the text says אֵל חַנּוּן, "God is gracious," and likewise רַחוּם, "merciful." Nor is anything in Scripture more frequently on the tongue than the grace of God (e.g. Ps. 85:10; 111:4; 112:4; Eph. 1:6; 2 Cor. 13:14, where it is specifically attributed to the Mediator; and a thousand other places). It cannot but belong to God because goodness belongs to him, and a will that is freely and independently communicative of itself, and so also love, or the benevolent and beneficent propensity which, as it dispenses good things freely and independently, and thus *gratis*, is called *grace*.

---

12. 1.2.15 §XX

What it is, as far as the word

XIII. In regard to the word *grace*, it denotes either that on account of which God is gratifying to us, namely the whole of his gracious perfection (John 1:14), or that through which we please God (Eph. 1:6). Again, it denotes either favor in God, which is in Greek χάρις, or its fruits in us, χαρίσματα (1 Cor. 12:4, 11). Accordingly, *grace* designates either (1) the grace that gives freely (Matt. 11:26; Eph. 1:6), that is, the gratuitous favor of God; or (2) the grace that is given freely, namely, any good that comes to any creature, specifically those common goods that come even to unbelievers, though on account of them they are not even a whit more pleasing to God; or (3) the grace that also makes one gratifying (Ps. 84:11), namely, saving gifts, faith, hope, and love, through which we please God.[13] And so the divine favor that dispenses such things to men is commonly called grace.

What grace is, as far as its substance

XIV. Grace, if you consider its substance, is nothing but undeserved love. Since it is called love, everything we have already said about love applies to it. Insofar as this love is undeserved, or entirely free and independent of all worth and merit of the creature, it is specifically called grace (Rom. 11:6), such that the whole rationale of his dispensing it, according to the Scriptures, is in the good pleasure of his will (Matt. 11:26, Eph. 1:5). This grace accordingly considers each and every creature, all the way up to the blessed angels, for whatever they have, they have it by the pure and unadulterated grace of God, for who before him has given to him that he might be repaid? (Rom. 11:35) At the same time, those things are specifically attributed to grace which are different from nature. For nature must not be confused with grace, because natural things, since they are owed as it were from the benevolent constitution of God to every creature, if not individually at least insofar as it belongs to a species, are not customarily considered as grace, inasmuch as grace, being added to nature, is by all means un-owed.

What is universal grace and what sort is it?

XV. Now we would not repeat concerning grace what we just above taught concerning love, if a manifold controversy, one that has been in every age most vexing, did not urge us to do so. There is, then, first, universal grace, by which God dispenses natural things to each and every creature and is thus named the Savior of all (1 Tim. 4:10), the one who saves beasts and men (Ps. 36:6) and

---

13. These three things that the term *gratia*, "grace," designates are, in Latin, (1) *gratia gratis dans*, (2) *gratia gratis data*, and (3) *gratia gratum faciens*.

takes cares that his sun rises over the field of the just and the unjust (Matt. 5:45), concerning which see above.[14] This grace particularly confers to man his free choice and whatever sort of strength he has for natural good, and also stirs up and encourages that strength by its influence. And all these things, although they come forth from the gratuitous love of God, and thus from grace, yet in the use of Scripture, and also of all ancient orthodoxy, rarely and less properly are they called grace. For the latter tradition cautiously distinguished nature from grace against the Pelagians.

What is common grace and what sort is it?

XVI. There is, second, common grace, by which he dispenses moral goods, particularly to men, but indiscriminately, to the elect and the reprobate. To this kind of grace belong the virtues of the intellect, such as ingenuity, wisdom, and prudence (Ex. 31:3), as well as the virtues of the will, the ethical virtues (Luke 18:11), of which kind are all the virtues of pagans and unbelievers. In this number should be reckoned those things that appear more closely to approach saving things, such as are mentioned in Hebrews 6:4–5, Isaiah 58:2, and 1 Corinthians 13:1. To this pertains external calling to participation in Christ through the proclamation of the Word (Ps. 147:19–20; Matt. 20:16), and also internal calling through some sort of illumination, and all those good things which are conspicuous in temporary believers (Matt. 13:20–21).

What and what sort of grace is proper to the elect?

XVII. Finally, there is, third, the singular grace by which he dispenses saving goods (from which it is called "the grace of God that brings salvation," Titus 2:11), the goods that accompany salvation (Heb. 6:9), to the elect alone (Rom. 8:29–30). For this reason these things are called the goods of the elect, the gladness of the people of God, and the glory of his inheritance (Ps. 16:5). In this grace are particularly included: (1) election (Eph. 1:5; Rom. 11:5), which therefore must not be sought from works, from faith, or from anything else that is foreseen. For if it is by grace, then it is no longer from works, otherwise grace is no longer grace (Rom. 11:6). Accordingly, it is not of him who wills or of him who runs, but of God who shows mercy (Rom. 9:16). (2) Redemption through the satisfaction of Christ, inasmuch as it is throughout the Scriptures restricted to the people of God (Matt. 1:21), to the sheep of Christ (John 10:15), to those who were committed by the Father to Christ (John 17:9). For although the blood of the Son of God (1 John 1:7) is of infinite value, and in that respect satisfaction

---

14. §IX

can be called universal, nevertheless, because it was neither the intention of the Father nor of the Son to devote that blood to all so that they might be saved, satisfaction must be referred entirely to singular grace. (3) Effectual calling (Rom. 8:29) or conversion to faith in Jesus Christ (John 3:3), and that faith itself (2 Thess. 3:2; Acts 13:48). For this reason, neither conversion nor faith are the fruit of free choice (2 Cor. 3:5), but the fruit of the Holy Spirit (Gal. 5:22), who produces them not only by persuading as men do (1 Cor. 3:5–7), but also by effecting them (Phil. 2:13), by creating them (Ps. 51:10), by taking away the heart of stone and putting in its place a heart of flesh (Ezek. 36:26–27; Jer. 31:33; 32:39). (4) Justification (Rom. 3:24), which is accordingly not from works (Eph. 2:8–9; Gal. 2:16). Finally, (5) eternal salvation, that is, with respect to the right we have to it, "For by grace you have been saved through faith, and that not of yourselves; it is the gift of God" (Eph. 2:8), although its possession by the grace of God is in addition suspended upon zeal for good works (Matt. 25:21, 34–35).

Things opposed to grace: 1. Nature; 2. Merits
XVIII. Things that strive against divine grace, at least in this business of salvation, are, first, nature, inasmuch as by it we are children of wrath, dead in sins (Eph. 2:1, 3), carrying around a heart of stone (Ezek. 36:26); and also free choice, inasmuch as by it the natural man does not perceive the things of the Spirit, indeed, he considers them as foolishness (1 Cor. 2:14), and he does not subject himself to the divine law, and he also cannot (Rom. 8:7). Second, all merits and works in the matter of justification (Rom. 3:24; Gal. 2:16), for grace is undeserved love.

3. Wrath: That it is, What it is, and What sort it is
XIX. Especially, third, wrath, which is attributed to God throughout the Scriptures (e.g. Ex. 4:14; 2 Sam. 24:1; Ps. 90:7; Rom. 1:18; 2:8–9; etc.), not according to an affection of disturbance, as we have taught above in chapter 15,[15] but according to the effective operation of vengeance, namely that by which God conducts himself toward the sinner as an irate man does toward his offender. Therefore, wrath is in God nothing but his avenging justice, or his inclination to strike those who have struck him by their sins. This inclination comprehends three things: (1) the purpose or desire for vengeance (John 3:36; Rom. 1:18; 9:22); (2) declarations of this purpose by threats (Hos. 11:9; Jonah 3:9); (c) the execution of the purpose and threats through all kinds of judgments and vengeance (Eph. 5:6; Ps. 6:1; Rom. 3:5; Matt. 3:7). The striking of God, whereby

---

15. 1.2.15 §XIX

his wrath is stirred up, comes from sin alone, and every sin, for by sin is violated: (1) his legislative authority (James 4:12; cf. 2:9–10); (2) his attributes: his holiness (Hab. 1:13; Ps. 5:7; Isa. 1:13) and his glory (Isa. 42:8); (3) his good gifts and kindnesses (Hos. 2:8–9; Rom. 8:20–22). But yet sin strikes God in various ways, that is, more heavily or more lightly (John 19:11), and for this reason there also arise various degrees of divine wrath, insofar as it grows strong and becomes a burning, and even more, a fury (Ps. 6:1)—speaking, that is, in a human way, insofar as he dispenses his judgments as if he were man raging in wrath. At the same time, all the wrath of God is (1) terrible, whereby God is said to be "one who has wrath"[16] (Nah. 1:2), since his wrath, like himself, is infinite (Ps. 90:7, 11), in its intensiveness, like a consuming fire (Heb. 12:18), and extensiveness, reaching to all evils whether corporeal or spiritual, to life, to death, to persons, families, kingdoms (Jer. 18:9), continuing eternally, an unquenchable fire (John 3:36). (2) Irresistible, for which reason it is compared to a whirlwind (Zeph. 1:14–15; Zech. 7:14). The rest of this line of thought concerns God's avenging justice, with which the wrath of God in fact coincides.

That mercy belongs to God is proved: by the Scriptures
XX. Moreover, just as it is perceived from love what the grace of God is, so furthermore, from grace, it is perceived what mercy is. This mercy is asserted for God throughout the Scriptures in more than one way, and indeed to a preeminent degree, when in the text God is called רב חסד, "full" or "copious in mercy," just as elsewhere he is called the Father of mercy (2 Cor. 1:3) and rich in mercy (1 Peter 1:3; Eph. 2:4), the one in whom there is a multitude of mercies (Ps. 51:1), who is tender in mercy (Ps. 25:6, Luke 1:58), in whom there are bowels of mercy (Ps. 40:11), from which he is called רחום, "merciful," and in the New Testament, σπλάγχνα, "inward parts" are attributed to him (Luke 1:78), and these parts wrench from him his use of the verb σπλαγχνίζομαι, "I am inwardly moved" (Matt. 15:32; Mark 8:2; cf. 1:41; 6:34; etc.).

And by reasons
And because to him belongs goodness, which is communicative of itself, love, which is a propensity toward a thing, grace, which is undeserved love, as the preceding sections have proven, who would say that mercy does not belong to him, a mercy that, as we will say, is nothing but grace toward the miserable, since the miserable especially need his goodness, love, and grace? I will not add that when it comes to men, mercy is among the perfections, among the virtues in which the

---

16. בעל חמה

majority of the more generous spirits especially excel; in fact, they excel in it by a communication of it from him, as from the Father of mercy: therefore, who would deny mercy to him?

Objections against the mercy of God

XXI. If you should say: (1) It involves an imperfection because it involves sorrow, since from its root it is, as it were, a misery of heart[17] that comes from the sense of another's misery, I will grant that in respect to this affection, it does not belong to God except insofar as that affection denotes knowledge, just as in the case of his patience, and insofar as that affection produces an effective action of liberation or consolation: in these ways it entirely belongs to God. Anselm insightfully says the same in chapter 8 of the *Proslogion*: "You are merciful, O God, according to us and according to yourself, according to our sense and according to your sense: when you regard us in our misery, we experience the effect of your commiseration; you do not experience the affection of commiseration."[18] If you should add, (2) It cries out against justice insofar as it calls for a certain relaxation of it, then I will deny this because mercy is conjoined with justice, not opposed to it (Ex. 34:7), because he never shows mercy contrary to justice, just as he never exercises justice contrary to mercy; indeed, he never exercises justice without any mercy, although in showing mercy, he does, so to speak, exceed justice, in which sense mercy is said to boast against judgment (James 2:13), just as he who remits five hundred florins to one who owes him a thousand, or who gives him as a gift the same amount he owes, is not said to act contrary to justice but to exceed or surpass it.

What the mercy of God is

XXII. Moreover, mercy is, with respect to its root, a misery of heart from the sense of another's misery, with a promptness in giving aid to the miserable; and with respect to its substance, at least in God, it is nothing except grace toward the miserable. I say "grace," so that at this point we may bring into this section what we have already said about love and grace. I say "toward the miserable," first so that we may leave aside the angels, as much the good angels, in whom there is no misery, as the evil angels, whom he gave over entirely to his justice and shut out from all mercy (2 Peter 2:4), and next, so that we may point out the operations by which the divine mercy pours itself out. For since misery is twofold (at least of human beings, since for the sake of brevity we are not concerned

---

17. *miseria cordis*, and thus *misericordia*, "mercy." So also in §XXII.
18. Anselm, *Proslogion*, in *PL* 158:231.

with God's mercy toward brute beasts, Ps. 36:6), the shameful misery of sin and the sorrowful misery of punishment, the divine mercy gives aid in the case of both, in a way proper to each. In the case of sin, God gives aid through mercy, partly (1) by reconciling sinners to himself through the blood of his Son (2 Cor. 5:18), (2) by giving as a reconciler for them his very own, only begotten Son (John 3:16), (3) by surrendering his Son to misery and to a most disgraceful death (Rom. 5:6–8), (4) by granting them faith in the reconciler (Phil. 1:29); and partly by subjugating the tyranny and dominion of sin (Rom. 6:12), so that they may conquer it and triumph over it (Rom. 7:25). Again, God gives aid to a sinner through mercy in the case of punishment (1) by bearing with the sinner (Rom. 9:22; 3:25; Isa. 1:9; Lam. 3:22), in which consists the patience and long-suffering of God, concerning which we will soon speak; (2) by punishing his sins not according to their worth and guilt (Ps. 103:10); (3) by pointing him to the remedy for imminent penalties, that is, faith and repentance (Matt. 3:7; Jer. 18:7–8); (4) by movingly inviting him to embrace that remedy (Jer. 2:14); (5) by receiving those who embrace it into his grace (Luke 15:20); (6) by forgiving them all their sins (Ps. 103:3; 51:1); (7) by consoling and upholding those who have been appointed for paternal chastisements, persecutions, and other adverse things (2 Cor. 12:9–10; 2 Cor. 1:3; Heb. 2:17–18).

The properties of divine mercy

XXIII. From all these things and several others, divine mercy receives different descriptors, when it is called (1) great and ample (2 Sam. 24:14; Ps. 57:1; 103:11; Neh. 13:22); (2) incomparable (Jer. 3:1); (3) certain and infallible (Isa. 55:3); (4) eternal and ceaseless (Ps. 25:6); and (5) free and most free (Matt. 11:25–26; Eph. 1:11). For although the virtue of mercy is present to him by nature, nevertheless its dispensation depends upon his pure and unadulterated good pleasure. And this must be carefully noted, so that (a) by mercy we would not injure his power and dominion, as if on account of mercy he could not constitute a creature in whose just condemnation he would manifest the glory of his justice, against the testimony of Paul (Rom. 9:15–18, 20–22). So that we would not oppose mercy (b) to reprobation, as if on account of mercy he could not pass over a sinner according to his pleasure, denying to him the means of salvation, and thus condemning him on account of his sins (Rom. 9; Acts 14:16). Nor (c) to particular redemption, as if on account of mercy he could not apply the blood of his Son to certain persons without applying it to all persons (Matt. 1:21; John 17:9). Nor (d) to particular calling, as if it were not in his power to call whom he willed. That which could be said concerning the distribution of divine mercy into universal, common, and proper to the elect is more than adequately evident from what has been said concerning love and grace.

Opposed to divine mercy in its own way is severity in the exercise of his judgments.
XXIV. Opposed in its own way to the mercy of God is his severity (Rom. 11:22) in exercising his judgments against those who offend him (James 2:13), judgments of which mention is made most frequently in the Scriptures (e.g. Isa. 26:9; 5:16; Ezek. 14:21; 39:21; Rom. 2:3; Rev. 14:7; 15:4; etc.), and of which a great number of examples stand out, such as those upon Satan (Gen. 3:15), our first parents (Gen. 3:15), the ancient world (Gen. 7:17, 21), Pharaoh and the Egyptians (Ex. 14:27), Korah, Dathan, and Abiram (Num. 16:31–33, 35), Achan (Josh. 7:25), Abimelech (Judg. 9:53), Adoni-bezek (Judg. 1:6), Judas (Matt. 27:5), Ananias and Sapphira (Acts 5:5, 10), Herod (Acts 12:23), and a thousand others. From these things it is gathered that the judgments of God that he exercises through his severity are nothing but the particular punishments exercised upon particular sins.

The meritorious cause and the penalty of the judgments
Thus concerning judgments, these five things should be considered: first, the meritorious cause, sin, not just any sin, but the particular sin, which is usually gathered from the analogous penalty (Judg. 1:6; 1 Sam. 15:33; 2 Sam. 12:9–10; Isa. 3:24; 5:8–13), and second, the penalty, not the common penalty but the particular or extraordinary penalty, namely, the one that corresponds to the sin (cf. the above texts).

The ends of the judgments
Third, the reasons or ends of the judgments to be dispensed: (1) the glorification of God, insofar as the judgments show that God is just and holy (Ex. 7:5, 17; Lev. 10:3; 1 Sam. 4:8; Isa. 2:11, 17; Ezek. 7:4, 9, 27); (2) the conversion of men, first of those afflicted by judgments (Rev. 2:21–23), and next of those who look on at them (Rev. 11:13; Job 34:23, 26); (3) the derision and insulting of the impious (Job 12:16–19; 27:23; cf. Ezek. 14:8), as in the example of the Jews (1 Kings 9:8; Jer. 18:16), the Moabites (Jer. 48:39), and the Babylonians with their king (Isa. 14:4–18).

The species of judgments
Fourth, the species of judgments, for they are either spiritual (Amos 8:11–12; Rev. 2:5; 2 Thess. 2:10–12) or corporeal (Deut. 28:15–68); again, either private, for individuals, such as disease, poverty, and insults (Rev. 2:21–23), or public,

epidemics and endemics (Jer. 18:7), such as famine (Lev. 26:26), plague (Ps. 91:3), war (Lev. 26:25), drought, floods, and storms (Hag. 1:11; Ezek. 14:21).

For what causes they are sent

These judgments are usually sent on account of egregious sins against: (1) God, such as, preeminently, (a) ingratitude (Isa. 1:3; 2 Chron. 32:25); (b) contempt for the divine Word (Isa. 42:24; 2 Kings 22:13); (c) despising of his ministers (2 Chron. 36:16); (d) covenant breaking (Josh. 23:16; Ezek. 16:59); (e) idolatry (Isa. 2:8; Jer. 2:13); (f) pride (Isa. 2:11; Ezek. 33:28). (2) Our neighbor, such as (a) deceit (Jer. 9:5; Hos. 4:1); (b) neglect of widows and orphans (Isa. 1:23; Jer. 5:28); (c) oppression of the poor (Isa. 3:14; Ezek. 45:9); (d) biting usury (Ezek. 33:15); (e) cruelty to the miserable (Ezek. 16:49); (f) defrauding of wages (Jer. 22:13). (3) Our own persons, such as (a) haughtiness in dress (Isa. 3:18); (b) extravagance in feasts (Isa. 5:12; Amos 6:1–4); (c) abuse of the benefits of God (Isa. 5:4); (d) perjuries in our oaths (Hos. 4:1–2); (e) avarice (Isa. 5:8); (f) hypocrisy (Isa. 10:6; 2:6). Nevertheless, it must be observed here that the judgments of God are not continually sent when these sins are present, but when they are committed (1) by all the people (Jer. 5:1; 6:13), (2) shamelessly (Isa. 3:9; Jer. 3:3), (3) after various admonitions and rebukes (Ps. 95:10–11; 2 Chron. 36:15–16), and (4) after having spurned the judgments of God exercised upon others (Jer. 3:8; Isa. 1:5).

The properties of the judgments

Fifth, the properties, by which his judgments are: (1) just (Ps. 119:75, 137; Ezek. 7:3, 8, 27; Rev. 15:4; 16:5–7; 19:2, 11); (2) unsearchable (Rom. 11:33; Prov. 25:2); (3) plainly astonishing (Isa. 29:14), insofar as they are poured out not only on sinners themselves but frequently also on their offspring (2 Kings 10:1–14; Ps. 109:12–15; 119:73), insofar as they are poured out not only on the ungodly but also on his own (Ps. 6:1; 2 Sam. 24:12–13), indeed insofar as he sometimes passes over the wicked and assails his own (1 Peter 4:17), and further, insofar as he sometimes assails the wicked through the wicked (2 Chron. 33:24–25); (4) dreadful, even to the godly themselves (Heb. 10:31; Ps. 119:120; Isa. 6:5; Jer. 4:19); (5) unalterable (Jer. 15:1; Ezek. 14:14; Ex. 32:33). Although these things properly concern God's avenging justice, it seemed good to bring them over to this chapter, so that contrary things might be juxtaposed and shed more light on each other.

It is proved that patience and longsuffering belong to God.

XXV. Furthermore, from mercy it is easy to perceive the innate character of the patience and longsuffering that are very often attributed to God (Ex. 34:6; Ps. 103:8; Job 21:7–9; Nah. 1:3; Isa. 30:18; 1 Peter 3:20; 2 Peter 3:9, 15; Num. 14:18, Neh. 9:17). And no one will take away these attributes from God who has thought carefully upon: (1) how much offense to God there is in every sin, inasmuch as by it the sinner prefers himself, his own desires, and all the creatures to God, and as much as in him lies casts down God from the throne of his deity, for which reason sin is frequently called *deicide* by the Fathers. (2) How much holiness there is in God, how much aversion, how much repugnance to sin (Ps. 5:4–6, 10; 7:11). Furthermore, (3) how much power there is in him to punish, a power by which no one can prevent him from suddenly striking down an offender with one little word (Ps. 50:22; Amos 9:1–2). In addition, (4) how great is the abundance of the sins that are perpetrated moment by moment, how great their filthiness and disgrace, such that if it should happen that a human being, no matter how longsuffering and mild, were allowed to see it all at once, as God does, he would not even bear with the world for an hour (Jer. 32:31). And in light of these things (5) how great, in addition, is God's effort to call the sinner to repentance, that his destruction may be averted (2 Cor. 5:19–20). And finally, (6) how great also are the kindnesses that, without respect to any demerit, he repeatedly piles upon even the worst people (Ps. 73:3–12). I say that he who has put together all these and other things will, I am sure, acknowledge how much patience there is in God, how much longsuffering!

What patience and longsuffering are and what their acts are in God

XXVI. Patience, with respect to creatures, differs from longsuffering because in the former we frequently cannot pay back the evil of the one who offends us, whereas in the latter, we do not want to. In God, however, it differs because in the latter, God overlooks more numerous and more serious offenses, and also for a longer time. It is said from these things that God is "long of nostrils" and longsuffering,[19] that is, slow and long to anger. This patience is nothing but his mercy insofar as for a long time he postpones vengeance or does not pay back evil to the one who commits it (Matt. 17:17). It occurs (1) by forbearing for a time or by not immediately paying it back, indeed by waiting for a long time: for days (Jonah 3:4), for years (Luke 13:6–9), for a century or more (Gen. 6:3); (2) by forewarning, by calling to repentance, that by it, if possible, the penalties may be avoided (Matt. 23:37; Luke 19:41–44; Matt. 3:10); (3) by showing forth, as an

---

19. ארך אפים *et* μακρόθυμος

example, his judgments exercised upon others (Jer. 7:12, 14; Luke 13:4); (4) by foreshadowing total destruction in milder misfortunes (Ps. 7:11). For example, compare the Sodomites of Genesis 14 with chapter 19, and consider Pharaoh in Exodus 6–14, and the Israelites in Amos 7:1–12. (5) It occurs by not punishing in proportion to merit (Ps. 103:9–10; Lam. 3:22; Job 11:6; Ezra 9:13); and moreover, (6) by doing good to offenders (Rom. 2:4; Isa. 5:2). Finally, (7) in the very destruction, by saving a remnant (Isa. 1:9): for example, Noah with his family in the universal flood (Gen. 6:17–18; Matt. 24:37–38; 2 Peter 2:5); and in the destruction of Jerusalem (Ezra 9:8, 13).

The causes and reasons of the divine longsuffering and patience
XXVII. The causes and reasons of such great patience and longsuffering of God are: (1) his good and beneficent nature, more prone to doing good than to destroying (Lam. 3:33; Jer. 31:20). (2) The manifestation of his own glory (Rom. 2:4–5), as in the example of Pharaoh (Ex. 9:16; Isa. 48:9–11). (3) The promise made to the godly and their seed (1 Kings 2:1–4, 2; cf. 2 Sam. 7:14–15). (4) The godly that are mixed among the ungodly (Gen. 19:22; 2 Kings 22:19–20; 2 Chron. 34:28). (5) The still to be completed number of the saints (Rev. 6:10–11). (6) The not yet complete measure of sins (Gen. 15:16). (7) A desired conversion and repentance (1 Kings 21:29; 2 Chron. 32:26; 2 Kings 20:19). Accordingly, (8) the goal of postponed punishments is: (a) so that there may be time for repenting (2 Peter 3:9, Rom. 2:4); (b) so that sinners may be rendered more and more without excuse (Rom. 1:20); and (c) so that those who do not repent may be punished more severely (Ps. 50:21; Eccl. 8:11–12; Rom. 2:4–5).

It is proved that a desire for vengeance belongs to God, from
the Scriptures and from reasons.
XXVIII. Opposed to patience and longsuffering in its own way is the desire for vengeance, by which God is said to be jealous, a punisher, an avenger, one who has wrath; and to punish his enemies; and to store up wrath (Nah. 1:2; Ex. 20:5); likewise, to be an avenger (1 Thess. 4:6), to whom belongs vengeance (Deut. 32:35; Rom. 12:19; Heb. 10:30; Ps. 94:1; Jer. 50:15); likewise, to come in vengeance (Isa. 35:4) and to put on vengeance (Isa. 59:17). And thus we see that he is patient (1) not as one who is compelled through impotence, but as one who is knowingly and willingly so, inasmuch as he does not will his own patience to be profaned with impunity (Rom. 2:4); (2) not through ignorance, as we ourselves suffer things to happen of which we are ignorant (Jer. 50:28); (3) not through a defect or neglect of justice, for which reason justice is frequently conjoined to longsuffering (Ex. 20:5–6; Nah. 1:2–3; Jer. 18:7, 9); (4) not

through sluggishness or a defect of purity and holiness (Ps. 10:11–12; 94:6–7; 50:21–22).

The acts of vengeance
Moreover, God exercises his vengeance when (1) he suddenly punishes (Jer. 18:7), examples of which stand out in Genesis 7:21–22 and 19:24, and Leviticus 10:2. (2) He punishes extremely heavily and severely, frequently on account of a sin that is (in appearance) trivial (Gen. 3:16–17; Lev. 10:2–3; 1 Sam. 13:9–14; 6:19; Acts 5:5–10). (3) He punishes inexorably and unswervingly (Ps. 50:22; Jer. 15:1; Ezek. 14:14; Ex. 32:33). (4) He punishes not only sinners but also their children, family, and relatives (Ex. 20:5; Num. 16:31–32; Josh. 7:24–25). Finally, (5) he punishes eternally (Matt. 25:41, 46; 2 Thess. 1:9). It should suffice, from the law of opposites, here to have touched upon these things that concern his avenging justice.

The clemency of God is proved and explained.
XXIX. It remains for a word to be said about the clemency or beneficence of God, from which he is called חסד רב, "abundant in kindness" in the text (cf. Neh. 9:17). Scripture throughout claims this kindness for him with extraordinary descriptions, when it celebrates his χρηστότης, "kindness" (Eph. 2:7), his χρηστότης καὶ φιλανθρωπία, "kindness and love toward man" (Titus 3:4), the fact that he has shown his marvelous clemency (Ps. 31:22), that he is great in clemency (Ps. 145:8), that his clemency excels all the way to heaven (Ps. 36:5) and is precious (Ps. 36:7), that he is abounding in clemencies and goodness (Isa. 63:7), in eternal clemency (Isa. 54:8), from everlasting to everlasting (Ps. 103:17). For clemency is nothing other than mercy that does good to a sinner, whereby (1) it operates in a humane, sweet, and mild way with sinners, from which it is denominated φιλανθρωπία, "love for man" (Titus 3:4; Prov. 8:31). (2) It draws and allures sinners to repentance (Isa. 5:26; Hos. 2:14; Matt. 11:28; Isa. 55:1; Song 2:10; Rev. 3:20). (3) It heaps upon them all kinds of benefits (Rom. 2:4), in which it coincides with the goodness of God (which is treated expressly in the preceding chapter). Opposed to this clemency in their own way are severity, harshness, and hardness (Matt. 25:24).

The hardness of God
By this hardness, (1) he acts extremely rigidly, severely, and inhumanely with sinners, especially the impenitent, by afflicting them with disgraces (Deut. 32:19–26; Matt. 3:7; 16:4), by turning his face from them (Isa. 1:15), as if by driving them away from his face (Isa. 1:12–13). And even with his own, (2) by

deserting them (Ps. 13:1–2; 77:7–9) and (3) by piling all sorts of evils upon them (Ps. 88:3–18), all the way to the end, (4) by casting them away from his face into the outer and eternal torments (Matt. 18:32, 34; 22:13; 25:41, 46).

The Elenctic Part

It is asked: 1. Is the love of God alone sufficient for reconciling a sinner, without any satisfaction of Christ?

XXX. It is asked, first, whether the love of God is alone sufficient for reconciling a sinner, without any satisfaction of Christ. The Jews, besides the love of God in which a sinner may be reconciled to God, require nothing except repentance, and at one time, the use of sacrifices, but now only the observance of the remaining ceremonial worship, without any satisfaction of the Messiah. The Socinians most wickedly abuse the love of God by which he gave his Son for the sinner, such that they exclude the satisfaction and merits of Christ from the mysteries of religion, because by this love God was already reconciled to the world, and nothing is required by him except obedience to the commands of Christ, indeed because the grace of this love also rigidly excludes all satisfaction of Christ. The Reformed, although they acknowledge that love of benevolence by which God gave his Son to the world, nevertheless do not allow that by his love of complacency the world was reconciled to him. Thus they admit that to this end of reconciliation, the satisfaction of Christ was necessary.

Arguments

They do so because (1) Scripture expressly declares that there are, notwithstanding this love of God, those who are enemies of God (Rom. 5:10) and children of wrath (Eph. 2:3). (2) It expressly says that God hates, even loathes sinners (Ps. 5:5–6). (3) The father who loves his son can,[20] on account of sin his son committed, become so angry with him that he would have to be reconciled to him: and there is an example of this in David and Absalom (2 Sam. 13:39; cf. 14:24, 28, 32–33). (4) The God who loves the world reconciled it to himself through Jesus Christ by not imputing their offenses against them, and also, by making him who knew no sin to be sin for us (2 Cor. 5:18–19, 21). (5) We do not intend the satisfaction of Christ and the reconciliation procured by it to point to the idea that God, in terms of an affection, became loving after being unloving, but rather that, in terms of an effective operation, he removed from the sinner

---

20. Emended from the original "cannot" (Latin, *non possit*; Dutch, *niet zoude konnen*) because of context. Cf. the same argument in 1.5.2 §XVIII.

that on account of which the affection of love cannot pour itself out on him for salvation.

Objections

If they should say: (1) But at the same time there is in God love, which is nothing but a propensity to beneficence, that is, to do good, and a love that is effective, indeed, that love whereby he gave his only begotten Son to the world: could this flow forth from an angry, hostile heart? I respond: (a) There is in God a universal or common love by which he is inclined to do good to every creature, and so then also to man (Ps. 36:6; 1 Tim. 4:10), by external and common benefits (Ps. 17:14), and there is also a special, saving love by which he dispenses the benefits that accompany salvation, which have an unbreakable connection with salvation (Heb. 6:9). The love of God does not dispense these things unless there has previously been reconciliation through satisfaction. (b) That effective love by which he gave his Son to the world, was not for the world, except so to speak objectively, a love that by itself did not touch man such that it would render him, without other things intervening, better. So then it is not strange that this love could be present before reconciliation and satisfaction. But a subjective love, which enters into the one loved such that it confers salvation upon him, presupposes reconciliation through the satisfaction of Christ. (c) There is the love of benevolence, by which God wills for those who are beloved such things on account of and through which they can one day please him, the love by which, for example, he elected them from eternity, he redeemed them in time, he daily grants them faith and repentance, and this love precedes reconciliation through satisfaction. And there is the love of complacency, by which in addition we please him and he has made us acceptable to himself: he has "made us accepted in the Beloved" (Eph. 1:6). And this love at last requires in advance a reconciliation through the satisfaction of Christ so that it may be "in the Beloved." If they should say, (2) that we, through the love of God, are justified freely by his grace (Rom. 3:24–25), and likewise, our sins are remitted to us and are pardoned through the same love, and thus not on account of a payment or satisfaction, I respond: (a) But in that text there is added, "through the redemption" (the kind that is procured by a redemption price) "that is in Christ Jesus," that is, a redemption by his blood, and that "for a demonstration of his righteousness." By this redemption (b) we are justified freely, and also our sins are remitted and pardoned, insofar as God freely accepts the satisfaction of Christ for us, and likewise freely imputes this satisfaction to one sinner and not to another. In addition, (c) we are justified freely, insofar as man confers nothing for his own justification, nothing for the remission of his sins. If they should press further that if there must be a payment, whether through you or through another, it is not remission or pardon, then I will oppose them: (a) Here it is not by a true and proper name a payment, which does exclude all grace, but a satisfaction, which involves grace in many ways. Next, (b) it would perhaps be possible for us to have substituted ourselves as our own expromissor and satisfaction, but not when the creditor himself, and indeed without being asked, substituted for his debtor one who would satisfy, and he freely accepts that one's satisfaction for his debtor. More on this controversy will occur below, in the chapter on the impetration of salvation.[21]

2. From the love by which God elects us, is it solidly concluded
that election is from foreseen faith?

XXXI. It is asked, second, whether from the love by which God elects us it is solidly concluded that he elected us from foreseen faith, since God could not love a sinner who is not established through faith in Christ. The Remonstrants, the Jesuits, and others, so that they may hold that the grace of God is equal toward all, a grace that is determined by and has its efficacy from our free choice, suspend election upon free choice, such that a person, according to his own pleasure, determines himself to believe. And so that they may obtain this, they state that God, by his justice, exercises electing love toward no one who is not in Christ, in whom no one can be except through faith. The Reformed acknowledge that for the love of complacency, by which we are pleasing to God, it is a prerequisite that we be in Christ and so also that we have the faith by which we are in Christ, but that for the love of benevolence, by which he elects us, these are not prerequisites, since: (1) even that faith by which we are in Christ does not begin except by the love of God, inasmuch as it is called the gift of God (Phil. 1:29). (2) That same faith flows forth from the love of election (Acts 13:48; Eph. 1:4). (3) That love of benevolence, by which he elected us, by which he gives the Redeemer to us, calls us to him, and confers faith in him, is conceived as different from the love of complacency, by which we please him only after or through faith (Heb. 11:6), from which one can respond to the basis of the opinion of our adversaries without any trouble. More things of this kind will occur in the chapter concerning election.[22]

3. Does the saving grace of God extend equally to each and every person?

XXXII. It is asked, third, whether the saving grace of God extends equally to each and every person. The Pelagians, Socinians, Jesuits, Remonstrants, and

---

21. 1.5.18 §§XIX, XXXIV
22. 1.3.3 §§X, XVII

others state that the saving grace of God extends equally to each and every person, that it is sufficient for believing, for repenting, and so forth, and that it ought to be determined by independent choice alone. They state this so that they may hold that free choice is indifferent and independent from anything, even from God, such that it can determine itself according to its own pleasure to believe and to repent, if only this duty is proposed to it and it is persuaded to accomplish it. The Dominicans among the papists agree with their own Jesuits on this, that free choice could—at least through sufficient grace, which belongs to each and every person—determine itself to believe and repent, but they believe that for it to result in an act of believing, repenting, or doing any good works requires a certain grace that is not only moral, a grace that is accomplished by persuading, but in addition physical, a grace that predetermines a person's will to believe,[23] while the Jesuits want a moral, persuasive grace to be sufficient for this, a grace to which the choice can determine itself at its pleasure.[24] The Reformed universalists distinguish between objective and subjective grace: they make the former universal and state that the latter is proper only to the elect.[25] For an express treatment of them, see the following controversy. The Lutherans likewise teach a universal grace that is saving, although they suspend the production of faith, repentance, and so forth, not upon a person's free choice, but upon the physical operation of the Holy Spirit; yet meanwhile, they attribute to free choice that it is able positively not to resist the Holy Spirit as he brings forth faith, expressly concerning which see also the controversy a little further on.[26] The Reformed commonly acknowledge a universal grace concerning natural things and a common grace concerning moral things, but saving grace concerning things that accompany salvation they do not allow, except as a grace proper to the elect: they acknowledge no saving grace that extends equally to each individual, not even that grace that they call objective. And they do so for these reasons: (1) our adversaries—especially the Pelagians and the Pelagianizers—are compelled to state that there is grace without grace. For what is grace except a

---

23. E.g. On the effects of divine government on individuals, see Domingo Báñez, O. P. (1528–1604), *Scholastica commentaria in primam partem…S. Thomae*, 4 vols. (Douai: Petrus Borremans, 1614), 3:503–25.

24. E.g. on the concursus of God with the act of the human will, see Francisco Suarez, S. J. (1548–1617), *Opus de divina gratia* (Lyon, 1651), 2:147–50; on whether sufficient grace is given to all human beings, elect and reprobate, 2:263–67, 2:314–19.

25. E.g. Moises Amyraut (1596–1664), *De libero hominis arbitrio* (Saumur: Jean Lesnier, 1667); another form of Reformed universalism is represented by John Davenant (1572–1641), *Dissertationes duae, prima de morte Christi…altera de praedestinatione et reprobatione* (Roger Daniel, 1650).

26. §XXXIV

privilege, or that which belongs, so to speak, to private law, according to Isidore of Seville (in Gratian, *Decretum*, dist. 3, ch. 3)?[27] And what privilege is there that is universal, that does not distinguish? (1 Cor. 4:7). They are compelled (2) to confuse nature with grace, when the powers natural to human choice, powers that determine universal grace, so to speak, and the remnants of natural light and the common notions[28] found in those who have heard nothing spoken about Christ, they refer to grace. They are compelled (3) to distinguish sufficient grace, which is common to all, from efficacious grace, and thus to call sufficient a grace that cannot produce an effect without the addition of efficacious grace, that is, a sufficient grace that is insufficient, and indeed, what is worse, to claim that the efficacy of grace is from free choice. They are compelled (4) to advocate middle knowledge as a reinforcement for this universal grace, a knowledge whereby before the decree God foreknew who would be willing or not, which we have dispatched in its own place.[29] They are compelled (5) to assert a will of God that decreed that each and every person would be saved, which does not differ by much from the universal election of Origen,[30] Pucci,[31] and Huber,[32] which we have expressly dispatched in the chapter concerning the will of God.[33] They are compelled (6) to state that there is a willing of God that has been suspended upon a condition, that is, a willingness that is dependent, temporary, ineffectual, and mutable by the hour, which we have rejected above.[34] They are compelled (7) to teach a redemption in which it can happen that none of the redeemed will be saved, and in which the greatest part of the redeemed will in fact perish. They are compelled (8) to make the object of predestination man who has been redeemed, called, and equipped with sufficient strength to believe. They are compelled (9) to confuse the proclamation of nature and of the Word, so that they may retain the idea that even those who have had no opportunity to hear the Word are called to be saved. They are compelled (10) to state that a grace that is

---

27. Isidore of Seville defines *privilegium* etymologically as *quod est quasi privatae legis*, idem, *Etymologiae*, lib. 5, ch. 18 in *PL* 82:2020; cf. Gratian's *Decretum*, dist. 3, capp. 1–3.

28. κοινὰς ἐννοίας

29. 1.2.13 §§XX–XXII

30. E.g. *PG* 39:248. Origen is associated with a broader doctrine of apocatastasis, signifying a universal return to an original state, which also had implications for universal salvation.

31. Francesco Pucci (1543–1597), *De Christi Servatoris efficacitate in omnibus et singulis hominibus, quatenus homines sunt, assertio catholica* (Gouda: Joannes Zassenus Hoenius, 1592).

32. Samuel Huber (1547–1624), *Compendium thesium de universali redemptione generis humani facta per Christum Jesum, contra Calvinistas* (Tübingen: Georg Gruppenbach, 1590).

33. 1.2.15 §XXX

34. 1.2.15 §§XXVII–XXVIII

sufficient for salvation has come to those who have had no opportunity to know Christ. And thus (11) they are compelled to admit that without any knowledge and faith in Christ salvation can be acquired. These things are all of such a character that to have touched upon them is to have refuted them. We quelled the objections formerly when we treated the will of God.[35]

4. Is at least objective grace universal? The thoughts of the Reformed universalists
XXXIII. It is asked, fourth, whether at least objective grace is universal. Those Reformed who accept universal grace (perhaps for this end, that on the one hand they might not entirely withdraw from the received opinion of the Reformed, and that on the other hand they might more closely approach the opinion of the Lutherans and the Arminians, and more powerfully entice them, and lay out a path to ecclesiastical harmony and peace) to some extent deny that grace is universal and to some extent affirm that it is. In order to do so, they distinguish between objective grace and subjective grace. Objective grace is a grace that a person relates to only as an object, and to them this includes the grace of satisfaction, of calling, to which they add a strength, restored by grace, whereby someone can yield and believe, if only he wills, and this grace they assert is universal. Subjective grace is a grace that a person relates to as a subject, and according to them this includes the grace of regeneration, conversion, faith, and repentance. They do not want this latter grace, however, to be universal, but proper to the elect. They agree with the Pelagianizers in acknowledging that some saving grace is common to each and every person. However, they differ chiefly in these points: (1) While the former teach a kind of universal grace that excludes particular grace, the latter teach both a universal and a particular grace. (2) While the former extend their universal grace equally to individuals, the latter extend theirs unequally insofar as they refer more grace to the elect than to the reprobate. (3) while the former refer to free choice the strength by which you can yield and believe, a strength that remained in it after sin because that strength was either entirely uninjured by the fall of our first parents or at least not thoroughly extinguished, the latter refer that strength to grace, by which the strength extinguished by sin is restored. (4) While the former teach a universal grace by which each and every person can yield, believe, and repent absolutely, the latter teach a universal grace by which every person can do these things under a condition, if they should will. (5) While the former teach a universal sufficient grace whose efficacy depends upon free choice alone, the latter suspend the efficacy of their own universal,

---

sufficient grace upon the superabundant grace by which God confers not only the ability, if they should will, but the willing itself, of that for which they have the ability. It seemed good to consider this matter in a little more detail so that we may know how different the genuine currency is from the counterfeit,[36] and not consider these Reformed to be in the same place with the Pelagians.

And of the Reformed with their reasons
The Reformed, in whatever way they may acknowledge a universal grace concerning natural things and a common grace concerning moral things, even so commonly they acknowledge no universal grace concerning saving things, whether that grace be objective or subjective, because: (1) Scripture teaches no saving grace that is universal, as will be evident in dealing with the objections. (2) Even the grace of election is objective, though it is especially particular, as our brethren of the opposite opinion acknowledge with us; and also, vice versa, the strength by which all are able if they should will does not belong to objective grace but to subjective grace. (3) The grace of redemption, satisfaction, and calling, in the same way as the grace of election, is throughout the Scriptures particular and proper to the elect, just as we will show specifically in their own places.[37] (4) From this hypothesis of our brethren, there is now no person who is not able to yield to the God who calls, to believe in Christ, and so forth, an idea that Scripture speaks against throughout (Jer. 13:23; Rom. 8:7; 1 Cor. 2:14). (5) From their hypothesis one or the other of the following must by necessity be acknowledged by our brethren: either that strength which has been restored to each and every person does not result from the grace of regeneration, conversion, and sanctification, or if it does so result, then regeneration, conversion, and so forth, are universal. And which of these two is more indigestible, I surely do not know.

Objections of the universalists
The reasons whereby our brethren fight for their opinion are supplied: (1) from the universal redemption of Christ, which Scripture teaches throughout, for example in 1 Timothy 2:4, 6, "Who gave himself as the price of redemption for all," and so forth. I respond, He certainly did so for all, but not for all individually, which is required to argue for universality. "For all," means for anyone (Rev. 5:9), especially since the Savior expressly excludes the world (John 17:9).

---

36. *qui distent aera lupinis*, cf. Horace, *Epistulae*, 1.7 v. 23.

37. 1.5.18 §XXXIX on the procurement of redemption; 1.6.1 §XVII on its application in general; and 1.6.2 §XVIII on calling in particular.

(2) From universal calling, which Scripture teaches (Rom. 1:19–20; Ps. 19:1, 3, 4; Acts 14:17). I respond, Those passages do not teach a universal calling to Christ, that each and every person may receive him by faith, which is the question of this argument, but a calling to God, that they might seek him, if perhaps they might by feeling their way toward him, find him, worship him, and so forth (Rom. 1:21; Acts 17:27). (3) From the idea that through grace each and every person is restored to that state from which they fell through the sin of our first parents, the state in which they could have yielded to God if they had willed. I respond, It has not yet been proved, nor can it be proved, that each and every person through grace is restored to that state from which they fell in our first parents, for in that way, each and every person would be restored to original righteousness, to immortality, and to dominion over the creatures of earth and the blessedness of paradise.

5. Could someone still unregenerate, by the strength of his free choice,
without grace, not resist the Holy Spirit? A comparison of opinions
XXXIV. It is asked, fifth, whether someone still unregenerate can apart from grace, by the strength of his free choice, if not cooperate with the Holy Spirit as he seeks to work faith and repentance, at least positively not resist him. That is, as the Holy Spirit seeks to bring in the light of grace, can someone remove the barriers for him, so to speak, by frequenting holy things, by pouring out prayers, by using the sacraments, and other such things? The Jesuits, in favor of the idea of an independent choice, teach that when the free choice in its own strength alone, apart from the predetermining grace of God, has begun to determine itself to believe and to repent, God cooperates with it by a concursus of his grace, so that faith, with all that follows it, springs into action. The synergists among the Lutherans think that the free choice cooperates with the Holy Spirit as he works faith and repentance. The rest of the Lutherans, because they press for a universal sufficient grace—and so that on the one hand they might not retreat too far from their god-man Luther,[38] who in his own treatise *The Bondage of the Will* entirely destroyed the strength of free choice in the business of conversion and elsewhere,[39] and also so that on the other hand they might not leave to the unregenerate person nothing at all that would render universal, sufficient grace effective—state that the unregenerate, by the strength of free choice, can at least positively not resist, that is, he can, by diligently hearing the word of God,

---

38. *a Luthero Theandro suo*

39. Luther, *De servo arbitrio* (Wittenberg, 1525); idem, *The Bondage of the Will*, trans. J. I. Packer and O. R. Johnston (Grand Rapids: Baker Academic, 2012).

by praying, and so forth, remove the barriers for the Holy Spirit as he seeks to bring in the light of grace.

The opinion of the Reformed with their own reasons
The Reformed indeed acknowledge that an unregenerate person, without saving grace, is able not to resist the Holy Spirit negatively, just as happens in sleep, for example, and that he likewise can in some sense listen to holy things, outwardly pray, take the sacraments, and so forth, but they add that this is not done by the strength of his free choice alone, but by the common grace of God, which also works in the unregenerate whatever moral good exists in them or is produced by them: for example, whatever natural skill was in Bezaleel (Ex. 31:2–3), whatever moral good was in these who are said to have been enlightened by the Holy Spirit, to have tasted the good Word of God and the powers of the age to come (Heb. 6:4–5). The Reformed think this way chiefly for these reasons: (1) Scripture suspends every good work, even down to a good thought, upon some grace of God (2 Cor. 3:5). (2) The man who is "natural" or unregenerate does not perceive the things of the Spirit; indeed, he considers them foolishness and cannot understand them (1 Cor. 2:14). Therefore, how could he turn himself to the Holy Spirit who is about to work the saving grace of faith and repentance, and remove the barriers for him, so to speak, as he brings the light of grace into him? (3) The fleshly mind, which is the only mind that exists in the unregenerate, does not submit itself to the divine law; indeed, it cannot (Rom. 8:7). How therefore would it give aid, so to speak, to the Holy Spirit as he seeks to work faith? (4) On the contrary, it fights against the Holy Spirit (Isa. 63:10; Acts 7:51), and such are all of us by nature, that is, before regeneration (Eph. 2:3). How therefore would we remove the barriers, so to speak, for the Holy Spirit as he seeks to bring the light of grace into us? (5) One who would remove the barriers for the Holy Spirit ought at least to know that the Holy Spirit produces faith and repentance, but from where will an unregenerate person acknowledge that, especially since he is darkened in his mind, and in addition, alienated from the life of God (Eph. 4:17–18), indeed, entirely blind (Rev. 3:17)? Moreover, how would such a person be a midwife for the Holy Spirit? Finally, (6) positively not to resist the Holy Spirit is nothing other than to show oneself compliant and obedient to him, but how could an unregenerate person do this by the strength of his free choice?

The objection of the Lutherans
I do not see what they could show in favor of this their Helen—set on fire as she was by their own Luther, and also thoroughly condemned by his hypotheses

in his *Bondage of the Will*,[40] though the modern Lutherans, every time we have to contend with them on this issue, are desperately in love with her and kiss her passionately—except that experience itself shouts that those who are still unregenerate, equipped with nothing but their free choice, can attend to holy things, pour out prayers, and use the sacraments and other external things. But (1) we do not deny that such things can be performed by the unregenerate; rather, we deny only that this can happen by the strength of their choice, since such things are done by the aid of common grace. Next (2) we deny that this can be done by the unregenerate with the result that they do not resist the Holy Spirit. For this is nothing other than to show oneself compliant to the Holy Spirit, to desire or to embrace the grace of regeneration, which cannot come from one who is dead in sin.

6. Do those who suspend election upon foreseen things not weaken
the grace of election? A comparison of opinions
XXXV. It is asked, sixth, whether all who think that election is made from foreseen things, whether faith or good works, do not weaken the grace of election. The Pelagians and Socinians, who do not recognize a certain foreknowledge of future contingencies, state that election (at least a personal and peremptory election) is made not from grace but from faith and repentance as they exist now, that is, in the moment of death or even after death, so that they may hold to a free choice that is entirely indifferent, independent, and mutable by the hour. The semi-Pelagians, Jesuits, and Remonstrants, who allow a certain foreknowledge of future contingencies, so that similarly they may retain an independent choice through which faith and repentance do not depend upon the grace of election, but election upon faith and repentance, state that God elected not from pure grace but on account of foreseen faith, or as the papists say, on account of foreseen good works. Although the Lutherans do not want to appear to suspend faith and repentance upon the strength of the free choice, nevertheless, so that choice may not confer nothing in which the efficacy of universal sufficient grace can be found, they ascribe to its strength a non-repugnance, and from this, they suspend election upon foreseen faith.

---

40. On the allusion to Helen, note that not only was Helen alluringly attractive, but the result of an improper love for her was preventable war. In part 1, section 12 and part 2, section 1 of *De servo arbitrio* (lit. "On the enslaved choice"), Martin Luther mentions the destruction of Troy in connection with commitment to free choice.

The arguments of the Reformed

The Reformed think that all these, though in different ways and in different degrees, weaken grace, or at least disparage it, and preceding them in this opinion are: (1) the apostle, in Romans 11:6, "For if by grace, it is no longer from works; otherwise grace is no longer grace; if from works, it is no longer grace." (2) The very nature of grace, since grace is undeserved love, that is, a love that is independent and most free, as we taught above.[41] For this reason, however much is suspended upon nature, or the strength of one's own choice, is also not suspended upon grace, especially when it is suspended upon independent choice. That which could be alleged to the contrary comes from those passages of Scripture which seem to suspend election upon faith, to which we will respond, God willing, in the chapter on election.[42]

7. Do those who suspend justification on good works not weaken
the grace of justification? A comparison of opinions

XXXVI. It is asked, seventh, whether those who suspend justification upon good works do not weaken the grace of justification. The Socinians, so that they may not state that our justification depends only upon the righteousness of Christ given to us, that is, on his satisfaction and merits to be received by faith alone, suppose that we are justified on account of our good works, certainly not our legal works but our evangelical works, that is, on account of works offered in obedience to the law of Moses to the extent that it has been corrected and augmented. The Remonstrants, so that we may not be justified by the righteousness of Christ alone, imputed to us by pure, unadulterated grace, but instead by works, teach that we are certainly justified by faith, but only insofar as that faith works through love, in good works, or insofar as faith, by divine acceptilation,[43] is counted as a full obedience that agrees with the law. The papists enumerate two types of merit: one that applies to the works that were accomplished before conversion, a merit that comes not from righteousness but from congruity, and another that belongs to good works after conversion and comes from righteousness and from condignity. In merit from congruity there is, according to them, some liberality of God, but a liberality that still depends upon the congruency of the works. Merit from condignity excludes all grace, inasmuch as in it there is some sort of payment. The Reformed judge that all these in various ways weaken the grace of justification, for the same reasons which we noted in the preceding

---

41. §XIV
42. 1.3.3 §§X, XVII
43. *acceptilatio.* See footnote in 1.2.1 §XXIV.

controversy, and for others that we will mention in the chapter on justification, where in addition we will expressly examine the arguments in favor of justification from works.[44]

8. Do they not abuse the mercy of God who state that not only all people, but even devils, will at some point be saved? A comparison of opinions

XXXVII. It is asked, eighth, whether they do not abuse the mercy of God who state that by it not only each and every person, but even the devils themselves, will at some point be saved. We have touched upon this controversy in the elenctic part of chapter 15, book 2, §XXX. The Pelagians and semi-Pelagians, ancient as well as modern ones (that is, the Socinians, Jesuits, and Remonstrants), in favor of independent choice, state that God wills that each and every person be saved under a condition: if they should will to believe and repent. Long ago Origen, on account of the mercy of God, admitted no compensatory or satisfactory punishments at all for sins, however great and serious those sins were, and no matter what creature committed them, but allowed only the punishments of purgatory by which sinners would be rendered suitable to enter heaven. Thus sinners, in proportion to their sins, were for a certain period of time to be tormented and purged, and after these things, each and every sinner, the devils as much as man, were to be received into grace and to be let into the kingdom of God. Augustine testifies to Origen's views in *On Heresies, to Quodvultdeus* (ch. 43).[45] Francesco Pucci, an Italian Socinianizer, and the Swiss Samuel Huber, a Lutheran who had been a Reformed minister, taught on account of the mercy of God that each and every person, at least among human beings, would in actuality be saved.[46]

The opinion of the Reformed with their own reasons
The Reformed think that all these shamefully abuse the mercy of God, contrary to: (1) the Scriptures, which remind us of a judgment without mercy (James 2:13), eternal flames (Matt. 25:41, 46), an unquenchable fire that will never be extinguished, and a worm that will never die (Isa. 66:24); (2) the avenging

---

44. 1.6.6 §§XX, XXII, XXVI

45. Augustine, *De Haeresibus ad Quodvultdeum* in *PL* 42:33–34.

46. Francesco Pucci, *De Christi Servatoris efficacitate in omnibus et singulis hominibus*; Samuel Huber, *Compendium thesium de universali redemptione generis humani facta per Jesum Christum, contra Calvinistas.* Cf. against Pucci's views, Franciscus Junius, Sr., *Catholicae doctrinae de natura hominis jacentis in peccato, et gratia Dei ex peccato evocantis omnes communiter, et suos excitantis singulariter, collatio cum doctrina nova libelli…cuius inscriptio De Christi Servatoris efficacitate in omnibus et singulis hominibus* (Leiden: Franciscus Raphelingus, 1592).

justice of God (2 Thess. 1:8–9); (3) the nature of sin, which from the infinite majesty of God that has been wounded, contracts a guilt of infinite punishment, and because a finite sinner cannot receive an intensively infinite punishment, he by necessity requires one that is extensively infinite, that is, infinite in duration, or eternal; (4) Scripture's doctrine of reprobation, inasmuch as the doctrine of the universal salvation of all takes it utterly away, right out of the midst of Scripture; (5) its doctrine of election, for when reprobation has been taken away, election is taken away by the same stroke. For when there is no reprobation, there is also no election.

Objections

I do not see what, at least with any plausibility, our adversaries could allege in favor of the universal salvation of all, other than: (1) that it is repugnant to the infinite mercy of God to punish eternally a creature that sins for a brief period of time. I respond: (a) The divine attributes, mercy and avenging justice, by no means fight among themselves, and therefore from this, the fact that avenging justice is given in the Scriptures (Rom. 1:32; 2:6ff.; 2 Thess. 1:6–11; Gen. 18:25) is not taken away by his mercy. (b) Although the mercy of God is infinite and natural to him, such that he can have mercy on whom he wills (Rom. 9:15), yet his dispensation of it depends upon his most wise choice: he has mercy on whom he wills and also hardens whom he wills. (2) That it is also repugnant to divine justice, which demands proportion between the offense and the penalty, and so accordingly, demands that a finite sin should not be punished with an infinite penalty, and that what was perpetrated in a short space of time should not be chastised with a penalty of infinite duration. I respond: (a) Although justice punishes every sin with an eternal punishment, yet it does not neglect proportion in the degrees of punishments (Luke 12:47). (b) The gravity of the offense must not be estimated from its duration alone, but also from its object, just as to kill a king is more serious than to kill a beggar (2 Sam. 18:3). So then, to kill an infinite God, which is the end to which every sin, as much as in it lies, gives its full effort, contracts a guilt of infinite punishment, and because a finite creature does not allow an intensively infinite punishment, it by necessity requires a punishment that is infinite in duration, or eternal.

The Practical Part

The practice of this chapter is zeal: 1. For procuring for ourselves the benevolent and beneficent propensity of God

XXXVIII. In the delineation of the practice we will say less than the worthiness of this argument might require on account of the fact that most of the things that we observed already concerning the goodness of God can, with the proper changes made, be easily applied to this chapter, because goodness, to the extent that it is communicative, coincides with love. But at the same time, the specific practice of this chapter could be zeal, first for procuring for ourselves and inclining to ourselves, so to speak, that propensity of God in which we find the sum of all love, grace, mercy, longsuffering, and clemency.

The motivating reasons
And we should have this zeal because: (1) in that propensity, all perfection of love, grace, mercy, longsuffering, and clemency found in all the creatures is absorbed, as in an abyss, for which reason it is compared to a most tender or paternal propensity (Ps. 103:8, 11, 13). Indeed, (2) it is exalted infinitely many degrees above it (Isa. 49:15–16). (3) It is the source and sum of all felicity of all the creatures, inasmuch as through it he lavished his only begotten Son upon the world (John 3:16), and with him, all things (Rom. 8:32). (4) In particular, from it redounds to us election, redemption, calling, regeneration, conversion, justification, adoption, sanctification, glorification, and whatever other things that accompany salvation, just as we taught in the dogmatic part (cf. Eph. 1:2–4; 2 Peter 1:2–3). (5) It alone is sufficient for us (2 Cor. 12:9); it is sufficient for all things (Phil. 4:11–13), and so necessary that without it we are nothing (1 Cor. 15:10). Thus (6) from it, not only is he called rich in grace (Eph. 2:4), great in mercies (Ps. 51:1), in those same mercies, most tender, even to our offspring (Ps. 25:6, Luke 1:50), and likewise eternal (Ps. 25:6), and immutable (Isa. 54:10); but also the Father of mercies (2 Cor. 1:3). Wherefore (7) the saints were always concerned to find grace in the eyes of the Lord (Gen. 18:5; Ex. 33:12, 13, 16–17; Num. 11:15; cf. Ps. 119:41; 90:14). And also (8) grace forms the prow and stern in the majority of the apostolic epistles (Rom. 1:7; 16:24; 1 Cor. 1:3; 16:23; 2 Cor. 1:2; 13:14; Gal. 1:3; 6:18; Eph. 1:2; 6:24; and so forth). Indeed, (9) the whole business of the apostles and of the gospel is in this: to make known, to offer, and to confer the grace of God to men, for which reason it is denominated the word of grace (Acts 14:3; 20:32) as well as the gospel of grace (Acts 20:24).

The means of procuring it
But lastly, by what supports will we procure for ourselves this benevolent and beneficent propensity of God? I respond: (1) Surely not by a foolish attempt to bend God, or to change the unchangeable one from being unloving to being loving, but rather (2) by committing this business in its entirety to the Mediator, in whom the Father was well pleased (Matt. 3:17; 17:5), who has reconciled us to the Father, not by changing the Father, but by removing from us whatever

obstructed his grace, as it were, and rendered us unfit to receive the saving streams of divine grace (Col. 1:20–21; Eph. 2:12–17; 2 Cor. 5:19–21), by tearing up, as it were, the record of debt (Col. 2:14), so that we may now be those who have found grace in the Beloved (Eph. 1:6), and from his abundance we can draw grace upon grace (John 1:16). For this reason the grace of our Lord Jesus Christ, the love of the Father, and the communion of the Holy Spirit (2 Cor. 13:14) are arranged in such a way that the first place is for the grace of our Lord Jesus Christ. So then (3) our duty, whereby we should procure for ourselves the love of the Father, is to strive that we may be imbued with the grace of Christ, which will happen by a true and living faith in him (John 14:23; 1:12; Rom. 3:24; Eph. 2:8; cf. John 14:6; Acts 4:12). Let us add (4) a love for God and for the Mediator, by which we might at least be confirmed in a reciprocal love (Deut. 7:9; John 14:23; 1 John 4:10). And so also, (5) let us carefully compose ourselves to the commandment of his will and word (Gal. 6:16). Finally, (6) let us remove from his sight whatever could turn his soul away from us (Isa. 1:15–16; 59:2).

2. Zeal for taking heed that we not turn the propensity of God away and rouse his loathing against us

XXXIX. Second, zeal for taking heed that we not obstruct this propensity of love, grace, mercy, patience, and clemency toward us, that we not turn it away from us, and on the contrary that we not rouse his loathing, hatred, wrath, severity, vengeance, and judgments against us (2 Sam. 22:23–26), which occurs (1) by every sin (Rom. 1:18; Ps. 5:4–6; Isa. 1:15–16), and particularly: (2) by hatred for God (Deut. 5:9; Ex. 20:5); (3) by abuse of the divine grace, patience, and longsuffering (Rom. 2:4–5); (4) by cruelty and hardness toward our neighbor (James 2:13); (5) by idolatry (Deut. 6:14–15; 7:4; Jer. 8:19); (6) by vanities and lies (Deut. 29:19–20); (7) by unbelief and disobedience (John 3:36); (8) by unrepentance (Rom. 2:4–5); and (9) by other such things that the apostle mentions (Eph. 5:5–6; Col. 3:5–6). That we might avoid these and other such crimes, it will help us to think often and much, on the one hand, upon the weight of felicity and blessedness that there is for us in the love, grace, mercy, patience, and kindness of God, and on the other hand, upon the burden of misery that there is in his hatred, wrath, severity, vengeance, and judgments. Arguments in particular will be supplied from the dogmatic part.

3. Zeal for exploring the propensity of divine love, grace, and mercy toward us. The motives

XL. Third, zeal for exploring, if we observe some propensity of God toward us, some love, grace, or mercy, whether is it only that universal propensity which is inclined to beasts as well as men (Ps. 36:6), or that common propensity which is inclined to the reprobate as well as the elect. For since (1) such great affinity is at times discerned between nature and grace, an affinity by which, in the external exercise of religion and virtues, nature frequently exceeds grace, as it is evident not only in certain of the more honorable pagans—Plato, Cato, Aristides, Scipio, Seneca, and others—but also in the church, for example, in the Pharisee and the tax collector (Luke 18:10–14); since also (2) between common and saving grace there is sometimes such great agreement, as is evident by examples (Isa. 58:2; 1 Cor. 13:1); since (3) in these things, so many and such great men have deceived themselves, and myriads of pseudo-Christians still day by day deceive themselves, taking a more agreeable and humane nature for the grace of regeneration, and common gifts for signs of saving grace (James 1:26–27; Luke 18:11; Rev. 3:17), and (4) they have not deceived themselves without danger, indeed, not without eternal destruction—for all these reasons, there is nothing more necessary than to distinguish here the things that are excellent (Phil. 1:9–10) and to make our calling and election sure, and our every saving grace (2 Peter 1:10).

The distinguishing marks

But finally, by what indications will we certainly acknowledge and discern that propensity, specific to the elect, which dispenses election, redemption, calling, and union and communion with Christ? I respond, (1) We will not seek the distinction in the affection of God itself, inasmuch as it is uniform in respect to all, but rather in the effects by which it differs, specifically in those effects that are declared to be gifts of grace,[47] fruits of the Holy Spirit, and things that accompany salvation. These sorts of things are: (2) faith, not just any faith, but saving faith, which we have elsewhere distinguished from common faith.[48] For this faith is expressly attributed to special grace (Phil. 1:29; John 3:16), and included in the greater gifts (1 Cor. 12:31; cf. 13:13), and attributed to the Holy Spirit as his fruit (Gal. 5:22), and thus he is called the Spirit of faith (2 Cor. 4:13). And especially, (3) our love toward God offers us a prominent argument for his love toward us (1 John 4:19; Rom. 5:5), and particularly that love which is similar to the divine love in its own way, such that it furnishes a sort of ectype of it, from which we can more evidently gather the prototype. We will delineate this love a little further on from here.[49] Next, (4) love toward the brethren (1 John 4:7–8, 11–12, 20; 1 Cor. 13:1), and not just any sort, not a love in words and tongue,

---

47. χαρίσματα
48. 1.2.1 §§V, XL–XLIII
49. §XLII, below

but in deed and truth (1 John 3:18). It is a love such as that of God toward us, and a love by which we love our neighbor on account of God. Furthermore, (5) grace, mercy, patience, and longsuffering toward all, that is, as the elect of God, holy and beloved, let us be clothed in bowels of mercies,[50] kindness, modesty, gentleness, mildness, bearing with one another, and forgiving each other (Col. 3:12–14). Finally, (6) all those things by which election, redemption, regeneration, conversion, and union and communion with Christ are recognized and discerned, as by the fruits and marks of divine love, things that will be discussed each in its own place.[51]

4. Zeal for using the propensity of divine love, grace, and so forth

XLI. Fourth, zeal for using the propensity. For to what end does God expend this propensity, his love, grace, mercy, longsuffering, and clemency? So that they may be idle? But if they are idle, will they not be in vain? This is why the apostle gives such a serious warning in 2 Corinthians 6:1: "We exhort you that you would not have received the grace of God in vain," if indeed only in vain (Gal. 3:4) and not also to the aggravation of the divine hatred, wrath, vengeance, and judgments (Rom. 2:4–5; James 2:13). And we will use this propensity (1) as an opportunity for humiliation, because whatever goods we possess above others we have not by our own efforts, by our merit and worthiness, but by the pure, unadulterated propensity of God, by God's love, grace, mercy, longsuffering, and clemency (1 Cor. 4:7; Eph. 2:8–9; Rom. 3:24, 26–27). Next, (2) as an opportunity for comfort, for God is the Father of mercies and the God of all comfort (2 Cor. 1:3). For generally, in all adversities, as much corporeal as spiritual, what at last can be more efficacious to raise us up and to sustain us than devout thought upon the love, grace, mercy, longsuffering, and clemency of God, so often and with so much affection recalled to mind by the saints (Ex. 20:6; 34:6; Ps. 103:3, 14)? And specifically (a) in evils of the body, in diseases (Ps. 6:2); (b) in evils of fortune, in poverty (Ps. 34:8–10; 147:9, 11), in the hatred and persecutions of enemies (Ps. 23:4–5; 84:11); and especially (c) in evils of the soul, in the anguish of sins (Ps. 51:1), in spiritual desertions (Isa. 54:7–8; Ps. 147:3), in our conscience and in the sense of our unworthiness (Luke 18:13; Matt. 8:8; Luke 8:44)—for love is pure grace, entirely free and independent (Rom. 11:36)—and in the multitude, weight, and lasting continuation of sins, that God is abundant, great, and infinite in mercies, as we have shown above.[52] Furthermore,

---

50. σπλάγχνοις miserationum
51. 1.3.3 §XXIII; 1.5.18 §XLVIII; 1.6.3 §XXXVII; 1.6.4 §XXXVIII; 1.6.5 §XXIV
52. §XX

(3) as an opportunity for trust in the face of every fortune, as much adverse as favorable. For he who has placed his trust in Jehovah, mercy shall surround him (Ps. 32:10). And thus we can cling secure to God, not turning in the least away from him, either from fear of evil or from hope of good, because he who is a sun and shield will give grace and glory, and no good thing will he withhold from those who walk perfectly (Ps. 84:11). Finally, (4) in this very use of grace, we should beware of contempt of it (Rom. 2:4–5) and abuse of it—whether in impudence (Jude 4) or in carnal security and sluggishness (Rom. 6:1; cf. 3:8).

5. Zeal for imitating God's love, grace, and so forth

XLII. Fifth, zeal for imitating the love, grace, mercy, patience, longsuffering, and clemency of God (Matt. 5:43–45, 48): (1) by love toward God, who loved us, not only with a universal and common love, but also with that precious love by which we are made drunk with the fatness of his house and the river of his delights (Ps. 36:7–8). This is the love John urges in 1 John 4:19. And not only by any sort of love, but by a love that is as similar as possible to the divine love, (a) a love that is pure and without hypocrisy (1 Tim. 1:5), which does not stay in the mouth and tongue (1 John 3:18), but streams forth from the heart, and from the whole heart (Matt. 22:37), that is, just as the love of God is toward us. (b) A love that is free and independent, arising not so much on account of God's benefits or something that proceeds from him (John 6:27) as on account of him alone, that is, just as his love or grace toward us did not arise from any grace or worthiness in us. (c) A love that is not idle, but effective (Gal. 5:6), that is, as the love and grace of God is toward us. (d) A love that is superlative, above all dearest things (Matt. 10:37, 39), that is, just as God loved his own above all things, indeed in a certain sense, above his very own and only begotten Son (Rom. 8:32; 5:5–8; John 3:16). (e) A love that devotes all things to God (Song 8:7; Phil. 3:7–8), that is, just as he devoted to us, besides his Son, himself, his attributes, and all things (Rom. 8:32; 1 Tim. 6:17). Compare what we considered in chapter 16, §XVI. (2) By love and grace toward our neighbor, in which we do good freely, without any respect to worthiness or repayment, just as God does (Matt. 5:45–46). (3) By mercy, in which we are ready to console and assist those found in any misery, just as God is (Luke 6:27; 10:30, 37). (4) By patience and longsuffering, in which we are inclined to bear long and much with an offender (Matt. 17:17), to forgive offenses, no matter how serious (Matt. 18:21–22), just as God does (Matt. 6:12, 14–15; 18:35), to reconcile after offenses (Matt. 5:24–25), just as God does (2 Cor. 5:18). Finally, (5) by clemency and kindness, in which we conduct ourselves mildly and humanely, even with the greatest offenders (Gen. 45:4–5; 50:19–21), and in addition, heap benefits upon offenders and enemies, just as God does (Matt. 5:44–46; Rom. 12:20–21). Arguments for expanding on all these things will be abundantly supplied from the dogmatic part.

6. Zeal for glorifying and giving thanks

XLIII. Finally, sixth, zeal for celebrating God and giving thanks to him for all these attributes. We are pointed to this practice by (1) the so oft-repeated aggregation of all these attributes in doxologies (Ex. 34:6; Neh. 9:17; Ps. 103:8). And to this practice (2) as to its ultimate goal, every grace of election aims: to the praise of his glorious grace (Eph. 1:6; Rom. 9:23), of redemption (Eph. 2:4, 7), of calling (Eph. 1:9, 12), of regeneration (Titus 3:4–5; 1 Peter 1:3), of justification (Rom. 3:24, 26), of adoption (1 John 3:1; Eph. 1:18), of sanctification (Rom. 6:15, 17), of glorification and eternal salvation (Eph. 2:6–7), and of all his benefits (Ps. 23:5–6). That we may be more prompt in this task of thanksgiving and glorification, it will help us to think often and deeply upon: (1) the God who is inclined to us in love, grace, and mercy, who alone is sufficient for himself, and who does not take, and cannot receive, any benefit from us (Gen. 17:1; Ps. 16:2; 50:9–14). (2) The human beings to whom he is inclined in love: What is man that you remember him? (Ps. 8:4). A thing of nothing (Ps. 39:5–6), a drop from a bucket and dust on the scales, nothing, and less than nothing (Isa. 40:15, 17), even transgressors, and his enemies (Rom. 5:10). (3) The propensity by which, in such perfection, and in so many ways—in love, grace, mercy, longsuffering, clemency—the all-sufficient God pours himself out to miserable sinners (Ex. 34:6) and so tenderly embraces them too (Jer. 31:20). Finally, (4) the benefits of this propensity, so many and so great, natural, moral, and saving benefits, such great riches of kindness, forbearance, and longsuffering (Rom. 2:4). Let us continue to think long and earnestly upon these things, until: (1) in our heart, we grasp in some measure, with all the saints, what is the breadth, and length, and depth, and height, and know his surpassing love (Eph. 3:18–19). (2) With our mouth, we break forth, "Bless Jehovah, O my soul...Jehovah is merciful and kind, slow to anger, and abundant in mercies" (Ps. 103:1–8). And (3) we pay him back, as much as is in us, by our work (Ps. 116:12), which will be accomplished in particular, as we have said, by an eager imitation of these attributes.

CHAPTER EIGHTEEN

The Righteousness of God

Righteous are you, O Lord, and upright in your judgments.
—Psalm 119:137

The contemplation of the divine righteousness

I. We have said that the goodness of God can be considered either as it is communicative of itself, a goodness whereby he makes other things good, or, as it is desirable in itself. In the prior way it is a property that is, as it were, physical or natural, insofar as its communication occurs through love, grace, mercy, patience, longsuffering, and clemency, and thus we have considered it so far. According to the latter way it is a property that is, as it were, ethical or moral. And again it can be considered in this way: either relatively, according to a fixed rule to which it fits most exactly, and thus it is denominated *righteousness*; or absolutely, insofar as it abhors all moral impurity, and conversely, is prone toward every moral good, and thus is designated *holiness*. We will ponder righteousness in this chapter and holiness in the next. Through his righteousness, God is disposed to act according to the uprightness of his nature as its eternal rule. By that same righteousness he prescribes to his creatures a rule, or a manner of acting, that is, a law, and also, for the creatures' obedience or disobedience, recompenses either good or bad. The prophet presents this righteousness in Psalm 119:137.

The Exegetical Part

It is constructed upon an exegesis of the text.

II. The text has a certain doxological address, or a certain celebratory acclamation, with its argument taken from righteousness. In it, two commended things occur, namely:

   A. The person: "Righteous are you, O Lord." Here, there is:

   1. The person commended: "Lord," יהוה. From this name the description of commendation, "righteous," increases exceedingly in strength,

insofar as this phrase signifies, according to the nature and emphasis of the name יהוה, that the righteousness of God is independent, immutable, most simple, infinite, and eternal.

2. The argument of commendation: literally, "Righteous you," צדיק אתה. In Hebrew usage, אתה stands for the copulative substantive verb "you are," such that the phrase means, "You are righteous," although in addition here it is emphatic: "You, you are righteous," that is, preeminently and independently, "you alone." And this emphasis also increases in strength in some measure from the construction whereby the adjective "righteous" is set before the pronoun "you": "Righteous you are, you Jehovah, nor is anyone righteous, that is, righteous in the same way, besides you." Furthermore, צדיק, "righteous," either refers to words, and thus speaks of one who is truthful, who acts according to what he has said as if according to a rule, both in promising and in threatening; or it refers to things and actions, namely, speaking of one who acts, according to his nature and constitution, in one way with the righteous and in another way with the wicked, that is, either in rewarding the former or in punishing the latter, and in this way it denotes equity and decency.

B. The judgments: וישר משפטיך, "and upright in your judgments." The copulative ו connects the righteousness of his nature with the righteousness of his judgments or operations, because he who is upright also acts uprightly, just as he who does not act uprightly is not upright or righteous. ישר could either be taken substantively, "Your judgments are something upright, or uprightness," emphatically, "not only are they upright, but they are also uprightness itself," such that it denotes an eminence of uprightness, above all that is upright; or it could be taken adjectivally, "Your judgments are something upright," or, "Your judgments are upright," that is, each one of your judgments, such that it denotes a universality of uprightness in each and every one of your judgments, in your proceeding according to the uprightness of your nature, according to the truth of your words, whether your promises or your threats, according to the constitution of their objects, whether good or evil, by dispensing to each different things, either rewards or punishments.

1. The thing commended: משפטיך, "your judgments." משפט is polysemous, for it denotes: (1) a custom, a manner, a mode of acting

(Jer. 30:18; 1 Sam. 8:9), for if in the latter text it denoted right[1] or righteousness, then what is right for tyrants would be right for kings; (2) law, namely forensic law, according to which they administered and enforced the right in the Israelite republic (Ezek. 20:11). Furthermore, (3) the pronouncement of a sentence, a *jurisdictio*, a "speaking of the right," as it were (Deut. 1:16; Judg. 16:31; Job 9:15). In addition, (4) the execution of the sentence by rewarding or by punishing (Num. 20:12; Ps. 51:4), which is the same thing as the Greek κρίνω, "I judge" (Rom. 3:4; Heb. 10:30, from Deut. 32:36). And because subordinated things do not disagree, all of these meanings can be joined together easily enough. From this we gather that the word in the plural, מִשְׁפָּטִים, means that all his manners and modes of acting, all his laws, his pronouncements, and the executions of his sentences, whether they occur by rewarding or punishing, are upright.

2. The argument of commendation: יָשָׁר, "upright." It is opposed to crookedness, by which something strays from its own rule, and thus it coincides with צַדִּיק, "righteous." In moral things, crookedness is the same thing as sin or lawlessness (1 John 3:4; cf. Ps. 125:5), in which an act departs from its rule, and יָשָׁר describes that which is congruent with it (Eccl. 7:29). Therefore, it means that God is righteous not only in himself, but also in all his judgments and operations.

The Dogmatic Part

That God is righteous in himself and in all his works is proved:

From the Scriptures

III. So then, by the testimony of the psalmist, God is righteous in himself and righteous in all his works. And with his testimony Scripture concurs in many places and in many ways, when: (1) it expressly declares that he is righteous, upright, and holy (Ps. 25:8; 11:7; Deut. 32:4; Ex. 9:27; Jer. 12:1; Dan. 9:14). (2) It removes from him everything that is contrary: injustice, iniquity, respect of persons,[2] greed for bribes, and all the causes, effects, and adjuncts of all injustice (2 Chron. 19:7; Rom. 3:4; 9:13–14; Heb. 6:10; Deut. 32:4; Job 8:3). (3) It attributes such affections to him which require righteousness in the creatures:

---

1. *jus*: law as a universal principle of right or justice, translated below as "right," "the right," or "a principle of right." Cf. Justinian, *Institutes*, 1.1.3, "The precepts of right (*juris praecepta*) are these: to live honorably, not to wound another, and to render to each his own." The principle "to each his own" (*suum cuique*) is repeated throughout this chapter.

2. προσωπολημψίαν

hatred, wrath, severity, vengeance, judgments, and punishments. As we have shown in their own place, all these are nothing in God but an immutable act of righteousness.[3] (4) It declares that he renders to each according to his work and thus gives to each his own (Job 34:11–12).

And from reasons

Nor is he able not to be righteous, because: (1) he is absolutely perfect, so then for this reason he cannot lack this perfection, which involves no imperfection. (2) He is the Lord, the governor, the director of the whole universe, who without righteousness would degenerate into a tyrant. (3) He is the Judge of all the earth (Gen 18:25): without righteousness, how would he pronounce judgment? (4) And if God were not righteous, where would any righteousness come from? In that case either there would be no righteousness, or a righteousness that did not proceed from God, or that proceeded from him in whom it does not exist, and which of these is more or less absurd?

What righteousness is in general and in specific

IV. Moreover, righteousness is, generally, agreement with its own right and rule, and thus it coincides with uprightness, to which is opposed any crookedness or variance from its norm, as we said in the exegetical part. So then, righteousness (1) involves the right (from which it is denominated), that is, what belongs to each person (Rom. 1:32; Luke 20:25), which is the norm of acting, and (2) an agreement with this right, which is the form of righteousness, just as a discrepancy from this right is unrighteousness. The result is that righteousness is predicated relatively[4] and therefore differs from holiness, which consists in a quality.[5] Thus the former does not admit of degrees, and is perfect, or there is not any, for it agrees with its rule or it does not, whereas the latter admits of degrees. Individually, the righteousness of God also consists in this agreement, just as it does for the creatures, except that God himself is the principle of right and norm of acting for himself, whereas the creatures acknowledge that their principle of right and norm of acting have been prescribed from another source, and for this reason, divine right and human right are distinguished. Although at the same time, divine right, insofar as it is natural, in fact coincides with human right, moral and decalogical right, for God provided a certain image of it in the original

---

3. 1.2.17 §§XI, XIX, XXIV, XXVIII, XXIX
4. ἐκ τοῦ πρὸς τί
5. ἐν ποιότητι *seu qualitate*

righteousness of man. Therefore, when God works in a way congruent to this divine right, although not dependently, he is said to act righteously.

What and how manifold the righteousness of God is

V. Therefore, this righteousness is observed distinctly: (1) in the will of God. And thus it is defined as the constant will of rendering to each his own,[6] which, since it coincides with his essence, denominates God himself as righteous. (2) In what he says. And from this righteousness he is denominated as truthful, faithful, and constant, not declaring anything but what agrees with the uprightness of the divine nature, which has been discussed expressly above.[7] (3) In what he does. And this righteousness, again, is either (a) a righteousness of governing, or a dominical righteousness, whereby as the *dominus*, Lord, who is independently righteous,[8] he governs all creatures with utmost equity, or in a way congruent with that uprightness which in some measure he expressed in the original righteousness of human beings. Thus Psalm 33:4–5 says, "The word of the Lord is upright, and all his work is done in faithfulness. He loves righteousness and judgment." And no one may cry out against this that so many perverse, unjust, and most wicked things happen in the world, for God by his right permits those things and does not commit them, and he does this that in those very things he may one day make known his righteousness. Or, it is (b) a righteousness of jurisdiction, a judicial righteousness, whereby he prescribes his right to the rational creatures in particular, and in that way governs them in a way suited to their own particular nature. This is accomplished in part by legislating in precepts and prohibitions, that is, in prescribing a duty under a reward or punishment, according to his own holiness or eternal law—"There is one lawgiver, who is able to save and to destroy" (James 4:12; Rom. 10:5; Deut. 27:26; Gal. 3:10)—and in part by sanctioning the law with promises and threats (Deut. 30:15).

The retributive justice of God[9]

VI. This is also accomplished in part by fulfilling that sanction (Jer. 32:19), first by rewarding the fulfillment of duties according to his free promise (Ps. 18:23–25; Rom. 2:6–7; 2 Thess. 1:5–7; 2 Tim. 4:8). But the justice of this reward is

---

6. This is a paraphrase of the first line of Justinian's *Inst.*, bk. 1, tit. 1, ln. 1: *Justitia est constans et perpetua voluntas jus suum cuique tribuens*, "Justice is the constant and perpetual will that renders each one his due right."

7. 1.2.14 §§III–VII

8. αὐτοδίκαιος

9. Here and below, "justice" translates *justitia*, the same word elsewhere translated "righteousness."

nothing other than purely *ex pacto*, by covenant, without any condignity (Luke 17:10; Rom. 11:35–36), because from his abundance of goodness, he refuses to be worshiped for nothing (Isa. 45:19), and instead chooses, by promising, voluntarily to make himself a debtor (2 Tim. 2:13). He fulfills the law's sanction, second, by afflicting, or by sending evils, indeed on the occasion of sin, but not in repayment of the same. And he does this, either (1) so that sin might be, on the one hand, corrected, emended, averted, and prevented (Heb. 12:5–11; 1 Cor. 11:31), or on the other, restrained in the elect who are not yet born again (Acts 9:3–5, 9), and that steps may be laid down toward their conversion; or (2) so that some hidden good might be brought forth, to which end exploratory afflictions aim (Deut. 8:2; 13:3; Judg. 2:22; 3:4), or so that some visible good might be exercised and increased (Ps. 26:1–2; 66:10; Rev. 2:10). These afflictions are directed not by justice but by fatherly love (Heb. 12:5–7; Rev. 3:19). He fulfills the law's sanction, third, by punishing transgressors, repaying with sorrowful evils the shameful evils committed against him. This justice is called by different names: hatred, wrath, burning anger, severity, vengeance, and judgment, just as we expressly taught in the preceding chapter.[10]

Avenging justice is essential to God and its execution is entirely necessary.
VII. It can no more be doubted that this avenging justice is essential to God than that goodness is, for it coincides with it, insofar as it is nothing but goodness driving evil back into line, just as grace is goodness promoting virtue. But this is so such that the execution of punitive justice is not equally free, given sin, as grace is, given virtue, because God is not a debtor of any benefit to the creature except by his own gratuitous promise (Luke 17:10; Rom. 11:35), whereas the creature, due to sin, remains a debtor to divine justice, for its penalty (Rom. 1:32). Therefore, the punishment of sin is unavoidable and necessary in many ways: (1) from God's decree (Isa. 14:24, 26–27; Rom. 9:21–22); next, (2) from his threatening (Gen. 2:17; 3:3); furthermore, (3) from the natural hatred of God toward sin and the sinner (Ps. 5:4–6), which does not denote anything but his will to punish them; (4) from the intrinsic merit of sin itself (Rom. 1:32; 6:23); in addition, (5) from the nature of law, which prescribes a duty to man under a penalty, and which otherwise would be no different than advice (James 2:10; Gal. 3:10); and finally, (6) from his very own and only begotten Son, who was punished (Rom. 8:32). From all these things that have been amassed, it cannot but be concluded without doubt that sin must be punished, especially because Scripture expressly declares this (2 Thess. 1:6; Hab. 1:13; Ps. 5:4).

---

10. See n. 3, above.

The properties of divine justice

VIII. Finally, the justice of God: (1) is no respecter of persons, showing no partiality (2 Cor. 5:10) and not sparing the multitude when it sins (Jer. 18:7), nor indeed the whole first world,[11] nor any dignity and excellence of person, nor even kings (Isa. 14:4–5), in fact, not even those conjoined to him by covenant, no matter how closely (Amos 3:2), as is evident in the examples of Moses, David, and so forth. It is (2) inexorable (Ezek. 14:14, 18, 20; Jer. 15:1). It is (3) universal, to such a degree that not even one sin can be forgiven without being rigidly punished, either in the sinner or in a surety (Gal. 3:10).

The Elenctic Part

It is asked: 1. Can righteousness obtain in God, and how?

IX. Regarding the righteousness of God, various points are either brought up as problems or are controverted. It is asked, first, whether and how righteousness can obtain in God. The reason for doubt on this point is that, since righteousness consists in conformity to one's rule, God does not have a principle of right or a rule prescribed for him according to which he might order himself during his acting. I respond, He certainly does not have a principle of right or a rule different from the uprightness of his own nature, nor one that is prescribed for him from somewhere else, nor one to which he is forced to order himself, and yet he does have a most righteous and holy nature, which has customarily been called the right or the eternal law. Indeed, he has that law of nature which he prescribed in the Decalogue to rational creatures, to which he voluntarily orders himself in his governance of the creatures. Besides these points, we have sufficiently demonstrated that there is righteousness in God, from the Scriptures and from reasons, in §III.

2. Should the government of God be called righteous in every respect?

The reasons for doubting it

X. In particular, second, concerning the righteousness of government, it is asked whether the divine government should be called righteous in every respect. The reason given for doubting this is, on the one hand, that: (1) such manifold and great injustice in the world is observed under his governance, which seems inconsistent with an omnipotent, most wise, and most just ruler. (2) He dispenses terrible things to his own, that is, to the godly (1 Cor. 15:19), and to his enemies, that is, to the ungodly, he dispenses excellent things (Ps. 73:3–9; 17:14;

---

11. That is, the world before the flood.

Jer. 12:1). (3) He is a respecter of persons in the business of predestination: he dispenses to equals unequal things, forming from the same lump one vessel for honor, another for dishonor; to some he shows mercy, others he hardens; to this one he lavishes grace, to that one he denies it, without any distinguishing reason in the objects, but by his own pure, unadulterated choice (Rom. 9:11–24). (4) He punishes the sins of parents in their children (Ex. 20:5). (5) He punishes, for the guilty, his own innocent Son: for the sake of us who were most wicked, he made him to be sin who knew no sin (2 Cor. 5:21).

Responses to the objections

But on the other hand, righteousness is a perfection, and indeed one which implies no imperfection, and for this reason it cannot be banished from the one who is most perfect. We therefore respond that through all things God is righteous in his government of this world, just as we demonstrated in §III. (1) To the first objection, we say that God permits that injustice justly, according to his own sovereign authority,[12] and indeed he does so to this end, that he may make his avenging justice manifest in punishing the guilty. (2) To the second, we respond: (a) God never sends upon his own, upon the godly, anything truly evil, or upon his enemies, upon the ungodly, anything truly good (Isa. 3:10–11), but only apparent good. (b) That evil which he sends upon his own is in fact good, just as the good which he confers upon his enemies is in fact evil, because for the godly their evil is beneficial (Rom. 8:28), just as for the ungodly their good is harmful. To the former, it is a fatherly chastisement whereby he removes their sin, the highest and only evil, or it is an exploring and exercising of their faith, patience, prayers, and so forth. (c) Even if we should grant (though we do not) that what he sends in this life is truly good for the ungodly, just as it is truly evil for the godly, even so God will afterward compensate the godly for their evil more than a thousand times over (2 Cor. 4:16–17), and will likewise compensate the ungodly for their good (Luke 16:19–26). (3) To the third, we say: (a) In his government, God is by no means a respecter of persons, since a respecter of persons is called, and is, someone who, though he owes to equals equal things by a prescribed rule, yet dispenses to them unequal things; but God neither acts from a prescribed rule, nor does he owe anything to anyone, for who has given anything to him that it might be repaid to him? From him and through him are all things (Rom. 11:35–36). Next, (b) predestination is a divine decree, which is nothing but an immanent action of God that produces nothing beyond itself; consequently, it does not dispense anything good or evil, although it is

---

12. *pro sua potestate* αὐτοκρατορικῇ

the norm according to which his providence dispenses all things. And (c) if you should consider this providence that dispenses salvation and condemnation, it does not confer unequal things to equals, but to those who are unequal—that is, to believers and unbelievers—it confers unequal things: to believers, on account of Christ, salvation; to unbelievers, on account of their sins, a most just condemnation. Finally, (d) God acts with his creatures as a most absolute master, who arranges their affairs according to his own choice (Matt. 20:15). He has mercy on whom he wills and hardens whom he wills; from the same lump he makes a vessel for honor or for dishonor (Rom. 9:18, 20–21). He uses the former for the glorification of his mercy and the latter for the glorification of his avenging justice, in the way that a master arranges the affairs of his slaves, devoting this one to more honorable work and that one to less honorable work, with no respect of persons. (4) To the fourth we say that God never punishes the sins of parents in children who are innocent. For as to the sin of the first parents, their children committed that sin in their parents by virtue of the covenant of nature. And as to the subsequent sins of proper or closer parents, those are never punished in their children except either as they are prone to the sins of their parents or as they also imitate those sins. (5) To the fifth we say that he did not punish his Son as one who was simply innocent, but as one who was guilty from his eternal expromission, although in himself he was innocent.

3. Does all righteousness depend upon the will of God alone?

XI. Furthermore, third, concerning legislative righteousness, it is asked whether all righteousness depends upon the divine will alone, that is, whether something is righteous because God wills it to be righteous, or whether on the contrary God wills something because it is righteous. From this another question also results, whether God through his righteousness could have prescribed things entirely contrary to what he commanded. I respond: (1) God is by all means the one who is righteous before all others, indeed righteous in himself, but from this the will of God, as such, is not immediately the cause of all righteousness, since we conceive certain things to be righteous antecedent to the will of God, although they are not righteous antecedent to his nature. So then (2) certain things are righteous because God wills them, namely, those things that belong to positive right, and certain things God wills because they are righteous, namely, those things that belong to natural right, insofar as they are congruent with the holiness of his own nature, or with the nature of man insofar as he bears the image of God. Therefore (3) God could not have commanded things contrary to what he commanded except insofar as they belong to positive and discretionary right. For he could not have prescribed, for example, blasphemy, idolatry, disobedience, and other such things, although he was, for example, able to abrogate the Old Testament ceremonial worship and substitute for it another. We have considered this question in the chapter on the will of God, §XXXI.[13]

4. Can God, without violation of his righteousness, obligate man
to do impossible things? A comparison of opinions
XII. It is asked, fourth, whether God can, without violation of his righteousness, obligate man to do impossible things. The papists and other perfectionists, so that they may more securely hold that man can be morally perfect in this life, that is, that he can observe the whole divine law, state that God cannot, without violation of his righteousness, obligate man to do impossible things. The Socinians and Remonstrants, in favor of their idea of uninjured free choice, by which a person can do whatever is prescribed to him by the divine law, state that God, by his righteousness, cannot constrain man to do impossible things. The Reformed distinguish between (1) things that are simply impossible, that are impossible for the whole human species, or that exceed the strength of the whole human race, things for which it never received strength from God, for example, for flying— on this point they acknowledge that a human being cannot be bound to do such kinds of impossible things without a violation of the divine righteousness—and (2) things that are relatively impossible, things for which, in his creation and original righteousness, man did receive strength from God, though he lost it by his own recklessness. God is altogether able, without violation of his righteousness, to oblige man to do these kind of impossible things, for example, to keep his law perfectly, although this is impossible for a sinner. And this is so because God cannot, through the sin of man and through the fact that man has squandered his strength to offer what is prescribed, be deprived of his right to require what is owed to him. On this point we will say more elsewhere.

5. Is God by his own justice equally bound to reward obedience and
to punish disobedience? The opinion of the Romanists
XIII. It is asked, fifth, regarding remunerative justice, whether God is by his justice equally bound to reward obedience as he is by that same justice bound to punish disobedience. The papists state that God by his justice is equally bound to reward good works as he is to punish evil ones. They do so that they may more effectively support their merits: both merits that come from congruity, which belong to works performed before conversion, works that, though they presuppose some sort of liberality of God, nevertheless merit from congruence and

---

13. 1.2.15 §XXXI

accordingly are owed from divine justice some sort of wages, insofar as justice requires that even those who merit from congruity be rendered their own due; and also merits that merit from condignity, namely, works performed after conversion, to which wages are owed by strict right.

The opinion of the Reformed with their reasons
The Reformed, although they acknowledge that God is obliged by his free promise to give the promised reward, since every promise results in a debt, nevertheless think that good works merit absolutely nothing and that God, by his promise, does not so much become a debtor to good works, or to those who work them, as to himself, the one promising; so then, from his justice he does not reward good works as much as punish evil works, to which a penalty is owed by their own nature. Their reasons are chiefly that: (1) Scripture refers all reward to grace, that is, to love that is not owed (just as we have shown in the chapter on love, grace, and so forth, §XXXVI),[14] and not to justice. (2) Our works originate from him, for which reason the apostle says, "Who has first given to him that it should be repaid to him? From him, through him, and to him are all things" (Rom. 11:35–36), and thus they are more God's works than ours. How therefore could he owe anything to us on account of them? (3) They do not affect God (Ps. 16:2; Job 22:2; 35:7; Ps. 50:9). What therefore would he owe to us on account of them? (4) They proceed from us as from slaves (Luke 17:10), and a master owes nothing to a slave.

Objections
If they object: (1) that they are called wages—we respond, We must think of these wages as paid not from a debt but from grace (Rom. 4:4). (2) That worthiness is asserted for them—Yes, but a worthiness that comes not from the value of the works but from agreement with the free promise of God (Eph. 4:1; Phil. 1:27). (3) That reward is referred to his justice (2 Thess. 1:6–7; Heb. 6:10)—Yes, but a reward that results not from the merit of the work but from the free promise of the rewarder.

6. Are those sorrowful evils that come upon justified believers in this life sent to them by the avenging justice of God? A comparison of opinions
XIV. It is asked, sixth, concerning the afflicting justice of God, whether those sorrowful evils that in this life meet those who are truly believers and justified, evils including their death itself, are sent upon them by the avenging justice

---

14. 1.2.17 §XXXVI

of God. The celebrated Cocceius, so that he might hold to a greater division between the Old and New Testament, and to the idea that those true believers who lived under the Old Testament did not have forgiveness of their sins, that they were under guilt until the actual satisfaction of Christ, stated that they were under the wrath of God, under his curse, under the fear of death, and so forth, and that therefore all the evils that met them in this life were sent upon them on account of their own guilt, through divine avenging justice.[15] A certain theologian, Reformed by profession, since with his own ideas, and with his own clear and distinct perceptions (which for him as well as for all the Cartesians are the norm of all truth), he could not reconcile these temporal evils with the fatherly love of God which chastises his own for their salvation, stated that these evils arise from the punishing or avenging justice of God, because Christ did not satisfy for them. The papists, so that they might more effectively assist their proper satisfactions of believers for the temporal penalty of sins, and likewise their purgatory and indulgences, state that Christ satisfied only for the eternal penalties of sins and left paying the temporal penalties to them, and thus that those temporal penalties are sent upon them by the avenging justice of God.

The opinion of the Reformed with their reasons

The Reformed certainly acknowledge that these evils are not sent without justice or contrary to it, because all things which God does are just; they also acknowledge that they are sent on the occasion of their sins, so that they may be prevented and averted, and thus turn out for their salvation. However, they do not grant that they are sent by the avenging justice of God, but by the fatherly love of God: so then, they are not punishments properly speaking, but fatherly chastisements. Between those chastisements and punishments they observe a manifold distinction, since: (1) punishment is inflicted by a judge, chastisement by a father; punishment by avenging justice, chastisement by fatherly love. (2) Punishment tends to the detriment of the punished, chastisement to his advantage. (3) Punishment inclines toward repayment for a past offense, chastisement toward avoidance of future sin. And their reasons are chiefly that: (1) Christ satisfied for believers' sins most perfectly and exactly, and took away all their guilt, and thus avenging justice cannot exact any penalty at all for those sins. Moreover, Scripture teaches everywhere that he most exactly satisfied for

---

15. E.g. Johannes Cocceius (1603–1669), *Summa doctrinae de foedere et testamento Dei* (1648), §58. Cf. W. J. van Asselt, "The Doctrine of the Abrogations in the Federal Theology of Johannes Cocceius (1603–1669)," *Calvin Theological Journal* 29 (1994): 101–16; idem, *The Federal Theology of Johannes Cocceius (1603–1669)* (Leiden: Brill, 2001).

them (John 1:29; 1 John 1:7; 2 Cor. 5:21; Isa. 53:4–5, 11), such that by his one offering of himself he has perfected all believers (Heb. 10:14), and that the justified have all their sins forgiven (Rom. 4:7–8; Ps. 103:3). Next, (2) there is now no condemnation for those who are in Christ Jesus (Rom. 8:1), and he who punishes when there is no guilt, no condemnation, acts unjustly. Furthermore, (3) the apostle denies that the elect of God can be accused, because God justifies, or that they can be condemned, because Christ has died (Rom. 8:33–34). In addition, (4) God does not see iniquity in Jacob, nor wickedness in Israel (Num. 23:21), much less does he punish them. Besides, (5) if God would punish the justified with temporal punishments, Christ would not save perfectly, "to the uttermost," those who come to God through him, which is the opposite of what the apostle teaches (Heb. 7:25). And not least that (6) the evils that are sent upon believers are said to proceed from the love of God (Heb. 12:11–12; Rev. 3:19; Ps. 119:71; 1 Cor. 11:32), and thus not from his avenging justice. Finally, (7) they are sent upon them to their advantage (Rom. 8:28; Ps. 119:71), and thus they are more rightly called benefits than punishments. I need not add that (8) their death itself is nothing but a deliverance from sins (Rom. 6:6; 7:25; 8:10; 2 Cor. 4:10) and a passage into life, from which, for believers, it is numbered among good things (1 Cor. 3:22; Rom. 14:8), and they are pronounced blessed who die in the Lord (Rev. 14:13). Thus death is even embraced by believers, with such great desire (Phil. 1:21; Rom. 8:25).

An objection

The chief thing which they object to this is that in the Scriptures God sometimes more severely censured believers who sinned more seriously, such that they bore the wrath of God (Mic. 7:9); in fact, he is said to have avenged their sins, in the case of Moses and Aaron (Ps. 99:8), and he is revealed to have acted in the same way with David, Solomon, and others. I respond: (a) To censure more severely for more serious sins does not necessarily mean to punish, as is evident in the case of David, on whom he inflicted such serious affliction after forgiveness (2 Sam. 12:13–14). (b) He inflicted more serious things for more serious sins, not to the end that he might repay their offense and satisfy his justice, but that he might reveal his holiness, his hatred toward sin, and his impartiality, for an example to others, as is evident in the chastisement of Moses and Aaron: "You were a forgiving God to them, and yet an avenger of their evil deeds" (Ps. 99:8). In this sense also (c) the church is said to have borne the wrath of God and his vengeance, that is, materially, not formally, as they say.

7. Can God without violation of his justice afflict an innocent creature?
The difference of opinions

XV. In addition, seventh, it is asked concerning the same afflicting justice whether God can without violation of his justice afflict an innocent creature, at least with an eternal affliction. The Arminians, so that God would not be able to have reprobated a rational creature that was not yet created and not yet fallen, apart from its foreseen sins, affirm that it is against the justice of God to afflict an innocent creature. The Socinians do affirm that God can afflict an entirely innocent creature, but by perverse hypotheses, that is, so that they might maintain that Christ, who was entirely innocent, was not punished on account of our sins, and thus did not satisfy for us by his sufferings and by his death, though he was afflicted. Thus they state that it is not repugnant to the justice of God to afflict the innocent.

Reasons for the common opinion of the Reformed
Several among the Reformed, for example, the famous Twisse, think that God not only can afflict the innocent but also can afflict them with eternal torments. The rest acknowledge at least that he can afflict them simply but he cannot afflict them with eternal torments, such as are in the eternal torments of the damned. They prove that he can indeed simply afflict the innocent: (1) by the testimonies of Scripture (e.g. Matt. 20:15; Jer. 18:6; Rom. 9:21–22). And next, (2) because his authority over his creatures is infinite, and thus that authority extends even over the innocent. Furthermore, (3) to him belongs at least as much authority over innocent rational creatures as belongs to men over innocent beasts, that he may even kill them. In addition, (4) because God can by his own authority, as I believe all acknowledge, at least lightly wound the finger of an innocent creature with a needle. If this is granted, why could he not, by the same authority, take away its whole finger? And why not even its temporal life? Add (5) the passage in John 9:2–3, when to the disciples who ask for what reason congenital blindness was brought upon this man, whether it was on account of the sin of his parents or on account of his own sin, the Savior responds that it was neither on account of the sin of his parents or on account of his own sin, but so that the works of God might be made manifest in him. Indeed, he does not intend to deny that both he and his parents have sinned, but only to affirm that this blindness was sent upon him without respect to sin but for the glorification of God. I will add (6) that all those evil things which are sent upon true believers and the justified by God are sent upon those who are in a certain sense innocent. For although they are sinners in themselves, yet in Christ through justification, on account of the gifted and imputed righteousness of their surety, they can be called, and are

called by God, innocent: "If your sins are as scarlet, they will become white as snow, and if they are red as crimson, they will be as white as wool" (Isa. 1:18). And the reason is given: "The blood of Jesus Christ cleanses us from all sin" (1 John 1:7). Yet I would not dare to determine that God can afflict the guiltless with eternal torments, because not only are these eternal torments destined for those damned on account of sin as their penalty, as torments due to them from the justice of God (2 Thess. 1:6, 9; Matt. 25:41–46), but chiefly because these eternal torments, if destined for some other purpose than the punishment of the damned, can convey nothing to the glorification of God's mercy or avenging justice, and if something does not incline to the glory of one or the other of these, it seems that God, in such matters, is not able to do it.

An objection

It is not valid to use as a contrary argument the reprobation of as yet only possibly created and fallen creatures, because that reprobation, inasmuch as it is an immanent action, neither afflicts nor punishes, nor does God punish the damned according to its prescription, as it were, except after their sin has been committed.

8. Can God without violation of his justice not punish sin?

A comparison of opinions

XVI. Finally, eighth, it is asked concerning avenging justice whether God can without violation of his justice not punish sin. That he can punish sin if he wills is without controversy among all, from Romans 1:32 and the continuous tenor of Scripture. However, that he is able not to punish, or even that he wills not to punish, is what the Socinians state out of hatred of the satisfaction of Christ. And they do so by various hypotheses, namely, that: (1) to punish sins does not concern the justice of God or his nature, as if punishing justice were natural to him, but rather (2) his hatred and severity, which are different from his justice; accordingly, it must be referred not to his justice but to his accidental severity, and therefore, in not punishing sins his justice is not injured. The celebrated Twisse, with a number of others, such as Grotius and others, state that indeed God is able, from his absolute power, leaving aside his decree to the contrary, not to punish sins, but that he does not will such.[16] The majority of the Reformed think that he neither is able, nor wills, not to punish sins. There are those who

---

16. William Twisse, *A Treatise…clearing certain doubts concerning predestination* (London, 1646); idem, *Vindiciae gratiae, potestatis ac providentiae Dei*, 2nd ed. (Amsterdam: Johannes Janssonius, 1648); Hugo Grotius, *Ordinum Hollandiae ac Westfrisiae pietas* (I. Patius, 1613); idem, *Defensio fidei catholicae de satisfactione Christi* (Maire, 1617).

pursue a middle way and think that it does not show a due consideration of the absolute authority of God to say that through it he cannot pass over with impunity even the least sin, because (1) this seems to them to verge upon rashness, that a creature should undertake to determine what the infinite God, through his own infinite authority, can or cannot do. And (2) it is not prudent enough, for it is odious and exposed to the calumnies of our adversaries, to wish to defend the idea that God cannot, through his absolute and infinite authority, dismiss unpunished even the least sin. And (3) there comes quite a difficult burden of proof to demonstrate solidly and clearly that God cannot do this through his absolute power.

The arguments for the orthodox opinion
Therefore, they think that it is entirely sufficient for conquering our adversaries to state that God cannot do this, arguing not from the doctrine of his absolute authority, but from many other facts gathered and joined together, namely: (1) from his eternal decree, in which he determined that he willed not to hold the guilty to be not guilty (Ps. 50:21; Ex. 20:5). Next, (2) from the threat by which he has declared a penalty for the sinner (Gen. 2:16–17), the truth of which threat demands the penalty. Furthermore, (3) from his natural hatred toward the sinner (Ps. 5:4–6), from which they infer that God is not able not to hate sin and the sinner, because otherwise he would also be able to love them, from the nature of contraries, and thus sin would not then be sin, for whatever God loves is not sin. Now, moreover, to hate sin and the sinner is in God nothing other than to will to punish them. In addition, (4) from the nature of law, for by it he prescribes a duty to the rational creature under an express or tacit threat upon its transgression. Otherwise, law would degenerate into advice or simple direction, the sort that belongs, for example, to doctors toward the sick. Now if God is not able not to prescribe a law to a rational creature, because otherwise he would not be the most absolute Lord, then he is not able not to threaten a penalty to a transgressor, and if he is not able not to threaten, then he is also not able not to inflict the threatened punishment, without violation of his own truthfulness. Moreover, (5) from the intrinsic demerit of sin, by which it is worthy of death (Rom. 1:32; 2 Thess. 1:6). Finally, (6) from the death of God's very own, only begotten, most beloved Son, from which they gather that if God could have spared sin and the sinner, then of course he would have spared his only begotten Son, but he did not spare him (Rom. 8:32); therefore, he is not able to spare sin and the sinner. From all these things put together they conclude finally that God is not able to dismiss a sinner unpunished. Also from these things, Scripture declares that he is of purer eyes than that he could look upon vexation (Hab. 1:13), indeed

that he loathes the sinner (Ps. 5:5). That middle and more modest way seems especially satisfactory to me. Accordingly, against the Socinians, we acknowledge that: (1) the punishment of sin is referred by the Scriptures to the hatred, wrath and the severity of God, but those things, through his simplicity, are not accidents or different from his nature, nor properly affections, but his very will to punish, which coincides with his avenging justice. Meanwhile, (2) the exaction of penalties or the exercise of punishment is referred in the Scriptures not only to his hatred, wrath, and severity, but also to his justice itself (2 Thess. 1:6; Neh. 9:33; Ps. 11:6–7; 129:4; Lam. 1:18; Dan. 9:14; Rev. 16:5). And from this he is denominated a defender of justice (Ps. 9:4), one who has a day of just judgment (Rom. 2:5) and exercises just recompense (Heb. 2:2), and just condemnation (Rom. 3:8), and who is also an avenger (1 Thess. 4:6).

Objections

To these things, if it should be objected: (1) That anyone can renounce his own right, then we will respond: (a) Whatever the creature can do is not immediately something the Creator can do: for example, he cannot abdicate his own dominion. (b) God is the Judge of the whole earth, who is not able not to exercise his right (Gen. 18:25; Rom. 3:4–6), who does not care for his own right, but the right of the whole republic. Accordingly, if he should give it up, he would give up not his own right, but that of another. (2) That the actions of God, however many they are, are most free. I respond: (a) His free actions are those that do not imply something opposed to his holiness and justice, and they are free only to that extent. (b) So also for punishment: in relation to circumstantials—what penalty, when, where, and to what degree it is to be inflicted—it pertains to the most free choice of God, while the essential part of punishment pertains to his justice and holiness. (3) He can mitigate, defer, and transfer penalties to another. I respond, He can, provided that he does not entirely remove them and as it were collude with the sinner (Ps. 50:21). But even then, all these things concern the circumstantials of punishment, in which to him as the most absolute Lord belongs freedom of dispensation. (4) At least sins against his positive laws are not opposed to the divine nature (since those laws flow from his choice alone), but only to his good pleasure, and accordingly, they also can be taken away by that good pleasure alone, by his mere forgiveness. I respond, It is still sin, and thus it has violated God's just will and wounded his infinite majesty, and because of these things it has made the sinner guilty of treason against God, and naturally comes to be punished by his justice, especially since whoever strikes against any one point becomes guilty of breaking the whole law (James 2:10).

The Practical Part

The righteousness of God supplies: 1. An argument for glorification

XVII. In practice, the divine righteousness first furnishes an argument for divine glorification, from which we observe how familiar it is for the saints to sprinkle the divine righteousness into their doxologies (e.g. Ps. 7:17; 48:10; 71:24; 145:7; 51:14; Rev. 19:1–2; Isa. 26:7; Dan. 4:37). For "Jehovah Sabaoth will be exalted through judgment, and God will appear to the saints as holy through righteousness" (Isa. 5:16). Thus the heavens and heavenly beings are said to tell of God's righteousness (Ps. 50:6; 147:6). Indeed, God himself is said to declare his righteousness before the eyes of the peoples (Ps. 98:2). In particular, arguments for worship are supplied by his: (1) governing righteousness, by which he directs everything so exactly according to its nature and character, by rendering to everything its own, so that all his works are called pure righteousness (Ps. 119:75; 111:7; Isa. 9:6). (2) Judicial righteousness, by which as the Judge of the whole earth, he judges the nations, and judges the earth with righteousness (Ps. 96:1, 10, 13), and righteousness is called the support of his throne (Ps. 89:14; 97:2). (3) Legislative righteousness, by which he prescribes laws so just in every part (Deut. 4:8; Rom. 7:12). (4) Remunerative righteousness, by which he does not will to be worshiped for nothing (Isa. 45:19), and repays even a hundredfold (Matt. 19:29; 25:34–35) every duty, no matter how small (Matt. 10:42). (5) Chastising righteousness, by which he rigidly censures the sins even of his own people (Lam. 1:18; Isa. 42:24). (6) Avenging righteousness, whereby he also does not dismiss, nor can dismiss, even the least little sin (Hab. 1:13; Jer. 50:15, 28; 2 Thess. 1:6, 8–9), but in fact censures them with so many and such great judgments. In all these things (7) he does so with such great rigor of righteousness, a righteousness that is unavoidable and inexorable, for which reason it is compared to the mountains and to a great deep (Ps. 36:6), and called high (Ps. 71:19) and eternal (Ps. 103:17; 111:3). And so that we would be more unencumbered for the task of this celebration, it will help (1) to observe diligently the way and works of God, so that we may everywhere acknowledge God's righteousness (Ps. 119:75); (2) to recall to mind his past judgments (Ps. 71:19; Mic. 6:5). (3) We should never disparage or criticize the divine judgments upon others or upon ourselves, even when they are exercised upon the church, but rather acknowledge their utmost righteousness, and in that righteousness rest peacefully (Lam. 1:8; Mic. 7:9; Ps. 39:10; Jer. 12:1; Job 40:3–5).

2. An argument for terror, contrition, and humiliation

XVIII. Second, the righteousness of God offers an argument to sinners for terror, horror and trembling, humiliation, and contrition, because: (1) it is chiefly by his righteousness and judgments that God is called great and terrible (Dan. 9:4; Deut. 7:21; Nah. 1:5; Job 37:22). (2) Every sin deserves eternal execration (Gal. 3:10), and every man has committed such a great abundance of so many sins (Ps. 28:5); indeed, all the righteousness of all people is like a menstrual rag (Isa. 64:6). (3) God is so rigidly just that he does not will to pass over even one sin, even the most trifling, and also cannot (Hab. 1:13; Ps. 5:4–6). (4) God's righteousness rages, as it were, against sin in so many ways: with implacable hatred (Ps. 5:4–6), with wrath, rage, limitless fury (Ps. 90:11; 2:12; Deut. 32:22), with unavoidable vengeance (Nah. 1:2, 4–5, 6), with judgments to be feared even now (Heb. 10:27, 30, 31). The things that we spoke about individually in the preceding chapter a little more broadly can be brought to bear here.[17] (5) The Judge who is omniscient, the knower of hearts, and most severe, has by his righteousness set a certain day on which he will examine and judge each and every person, as well as every thought, word, and deed of each and every person (Rom. 2:5–6, 8, 9; 2 Cor. 5:10; Matt. 12:36). All these points, and others carefully joined with them, should surely wrest from the most hardened the exclamation, "Woe to us, for we have sinned so greatly!" (Lam. 5:16), likewise, "Wretched man that I am! Who will deliver me?" (Rom. 7:24), and similarly, "Men and brethren, what shall we do?" (Acts 2:37).

3. It compels us to seek the Christ who satisfied for sin, to take hold of him, and so forth.

XIX. So then, third, the righteousness of God supplies a tutor to Christ,[18] for in him God willed to declare his righteousness (Rom. 3:25), and therefore gave him to us to be our righteousness (1 Cor. 1:30; Jer. 23:6), and made him to be sin for us, that we might become righteousness in him (2 Cor. 5:21). His righteousness is for this reason called the righteousness of God (Rom. 10:3). Accordingly, (1) this righteousness convicts us of the necessity of satisfaction, as there is no righteousness sufficient for us that by it we might stand before his tribunal (Ps. 130:3; 143:3), and our righteousness, however great it is, is nothing but a menstrual rag, and we cannot stand in the judgment, except by God's righteousness (Ps. 1:4–6; 5:4–6). So then, one of two things is necessary, without a middle option: either the satisfaction of another intercede, or we perish for eternity.

---

17. See n. 3, above.
18. *paedagogum ad Christum*. Cf. Gal. 3:24.

(2) It makes the Redeemer precious to us (1 Peter 2:7), and the blood of redemption precious (1 Peter 1:19). Thus, let us count those things which were gain as loss, that we might not have our own righteousness, but that which is through faith in Christ (Phil. 3:7–9). (3) Let us promptly, by whatever laws we may, take hold through faith of the Christ who has been offered to us (John 1:12), that we might be justified by faith in Christ (Gal. 2:16). (4) When we have taken hold of Christ, let us securely rest in him (Isa. 50:20), for he has himself provided for us the righteousness of the law (Rom. 8:4), and being delivered up for our offenses, he was raised again for our righteousness (Rom. 4:25). (5) Let us deny all else, only that we would not lose him (Matt. 16:24–25).

4. It draws us to the fear and reverence of God.
XX. Meanwhile, fourth, the severe and rigid righteousness of God rouses us that we might walk with all reverence and filial fear in his sight, just as with a consuming fire (Deut. 4:24). Thus, (1) let us carefully take heed to ourselves that we might not at any time offend such a righteous God, even in the smallest matter (Job 37:23–24; Heb. 12:28–29). (2) Let us carefully take heed to ourselves against all opinion of our own righteousness, and all arrogance before God, the sort shown by the Pharisee (Luke 18:11–12), and the Laodicean church (Rev. 3:17), and the Jews (Rom. 10:3; cf. Ps. 130:3; Job 9:3). (3) Let us never rush into the presence of the most righteous Deity in the unrighteousness of our sins (Isa. 1:12–13), nor without any pious concern for offending him (Eccl. 5:1–2; Isa. 8:13; Gen. 28:17). Indeed, (4) let us not pour out our prayers before the most righteous Deity in the unrighteousness of our sins, because not only does he not hear sinners (John 9:31), but he also drives them from his sight and abhors them (Isa. 1:14–15; Prov. 15:8). Finally, (5) let us sinners not have any dealings with God without the Mediator between us (1 John 2:2), without the Advocate who appears before the Father for us (Heb. 9:24), who repairs the deficiency of our own righteousness by his abundance, that we might be complete in him (Col. 2:10), the one who for this reason is said to have been given by God for us as righteousness (1 Cor. 1:30). Therefore, let us never approach our holy exercises except in his name (John 16:23; Heb. 4:15–16; cf. 9:14).

5. It draws us back from sins. In general
XXI. Also, fifth, the most exact justice of God draws us back from every sin, because God: (1) as the Lord, governs us with such great justice and equity. (2) As the Lawgiver, he has prescribed laws so just, so fitted to our usefulness and well-being, laws which he prescribed with such just promises and sanctioned with such just threats, and thus in every sin it is the essence of injustice and

iniquity to transgress. (3) As the Judge, "on the day of his wrath and the revelation of the righteous judgment of God" (Rom. 2:5), he will exact from everyone a most strict accounting for everything that has been done (2 Cor. 5:10–11). And (4) what is the head of the matter, as the just and severe Avenger, he will attack with his hatred, wrath, severity, vengeance, and judgments every sin, here and hereafter, unto all eternity, and thus it is the essence of madness to provoke such a God by our sins.

In specific

Particularly, God's justice draws us back: (1) from all injustice, fraud, or deceit in contracts and commerce with our neighbor (Jer. 22:13; Prov. 19:5, 9), and likewise from all respect of persons and greed for bribes in judgment (Amos 5:12; Ps. 82:2, 5). (2) From all murmuring, by which we call into doubt the justice of God in his divine judgments, we tear it down, we kick against it (Job 10:2–3, 15–16; cf. Matt. 20:11, 13, 15). (3) From all hypocrisy, by which we wrap up with external piety the unrighteousness hidden inwardly in our hearts (Matt. 23:14, 25–29), because a deceitful heart is an abomination to God (Ps. 5:6; 15:2). Finally, (4) from all Epicurean security, by which, because the day of vengeance, wrath, and judgment is far off (Amos 5:18), indulging in all injustice we treasure up for ourselves wrath against the day of wrath and of the declaration of the just judgment of God (Rom. 2:5).

6. It rouses us to a zeal for righteousness.
XXII. Conversely, sixth, God's righteousness calls us to a zeal for righteousness, first for acquiring it, then for exercising it to acquire it, so that we may be righteous, and for exercising it, so that we may act righteously. I say for acquiring righteousness, speaking of that righteousness of Christ that is imputed (concerning which see above, §XIX), which comes through (1) a denial of our own righteousness (Rom. 10:3); (2) a desire for the righteousness of another (Phil. 3:9); (3) faith in Christ (Rom. 5:1); (4) justification through faith (Phil. 3:8–9). But I am speaking as well of that righteousness that is inherent, and particularly: (1) original righteousness, which we received by creation (Eccl. 7:29), we lost through the fall of our first parents (Rom. 5:19; Ps. 51:5; John 3:6), and we recover by regeneration, conversion, and sanctification (Eph. 4:24–25). (2) Actual, or rather, habitual righteousness (1 John 3:7; Mic. 6:8; Phil. 1:11), by which we, in general, dispense to each what should be rendered to him, according to the divine command (Ezek. 18:5, 21; Prov. 21:15; 20:7). On the other hand, a zeal for exercising righteousness concerns (1) God, that we should give to God what is God's (Matt. 22:21), for example, our very selves (1 Cor. 6:20), and

likewise, his own love, honor, worship, and obedience (Deut. 6:5, 13; 10:12–13; etc.); (2) our neighbor, that we should faithfully offer to him whatever belongs to him by the divine law (Rom. 12:7–8). This happens partly by rendering to each his own, which is distributive justice, in which by a right discrimination of things and of persons, and by an appropriate comparison of things to things and of persons to persons, with a geometric proportion observed, without any respect of persons we faithfully deliver to each person whatever belongs to him (Rom. 12:7–8). Likewise, it happens partly by recompensing, either evil things to the evil, which is avenging justice, committed to the magistrate alone (Rom. 13:4), or good things to the good, which is remunerative justice (Rom. 13:4). Likewise, it happens partly by doing commerce, in contracts, purchases, and sales (Luke 3:14; 1 Thess. 4:6), which is called commutative justice. And in specific, this righteousness is exercised, after the example of God: (1) in ruling, by superiors toward inferiors (Col. 4:1), without violence or oppression (Isa. 5:8; Hos. 5:10–11); (2) in prescribing laws (Eph. 6:9; Lev. 25:43), by not exacting things that are unjust or impossible (Ex. 1:13–14); (3) in judging (Deut. 25:1; Prov. 17:15); (4) in remunerating (Rom. 13:3–4); and finally, (5) in punishing (Rom. 13:3–4).

Motives
And, so that we would be more prompt in the exercise of righteousness, it will help to consider that (1) in this righteousness is a great part of the divine image (Eph. 4:24), and through it we are rendered partakers of the divine nature (2 Peter 1:4) and thus made perfect, just as our Father in the heavens (Matt. 5:48). (2) In this way we will be partakers of all of those blessings which have been promised to the righteous (Prov. 3:33; 10:2; Isa. 3:10; 32:16–17). Also, (3) God then will repay us according to our righteousness (Ps. 7:8; 18:20, 24). Finally, as the righteous judge, he will reward us with the crown of righteousness (2 Tim. 4:7–8), by which the righteous will shine in the kingdom of their Father (Matt. 13:43).

7. It consoles us in all adverse circumstances.
XXIII. Finally, seventh, the righteousness of God offers us solace: (1) in all afflictions and judgments of God, even the heaviest, to consider that (a) God is righteous, and righteous are his judgments, and we have deserved all of them by the unrighteousness of our sins (Mic. 7:9; Neh. 9:33; Dan. 9:7). Also (b) God is afflicting us so far beneath what we deserve (Lam. 3:22; Isa. 1:9). (c) He does not afflict from the heart (Lam. 3:33), and not from hatred, but from fatherly love (Heb. 12:6–8; Rev. 3:19), and (d) not so that we would perish, but so that we would not be condemned with the world (1 Cor. 11:32). Then in particular,

(2) whenever we are pressed by the persecutions of enemies, by liars and the calumnies of men, whoever they may be, whenever violence prevails over justice (Hab. 1:2–4), there is in the heavens a righteous Judge to whom we can call out, and he is the God of our righteousness (Ps. 4:1; 7:8; 43:1), he will reward us for our righteousness (Ps. 18:20, 24), and he will care for us, so that at length our righteousness will come forth as the light of noon day (Ps. 37:6, 28; Isa. 59:14, 16); indeed, one day he will, for the sake of his own justice, take vengeance on those who afflict us unjustly (2 Thess. 1:5–7). Also, (3) in even those anxieties we suffer for our sins, we can raise ourselves by meditation upon the divine justice, which, since it was satisfied by the cursed death of the Son, cannot again exact penalties for our sins, because for our sake he made him to be sin who knew no sin, so that we might become righteousness in him (2 Cor. 5:21), so that we can now boast, "Who will condemn? Christ has died" (Rom. 8:33–34). Finally, (4) in the noble contest of faith against the insults of so many enemies, both spiritual and fleshly, that we can promise to ourselves the crown of righteousness, which the righteous Judge will more certainly than certain give to us at length (2 Tim. 4:7). And, that he will take vengeance through his justice on our enemies, so that we can exult with lifted voice, "Your wrath has come, and the time of the dead, that they may be judged, and you may give a reward to your servants and destroy those who destroy the earth" (Rev. 11:18); "Hallelujah! Salvation and honor and glory and strength be to the Lord our God, for his judgments are true and righteous" (Rev. 19:1–2).

CHAPTER NINETEEN
The Holiness of God

You shall be holy, for I Jehovah your God am holy.
—Leviticus 19:2

We proceed to the holiness of God.

I. We have contemplated the goodness of God as metaphysical goodness, by which he is desirable, and likewise as physical goodness, by which he is communicative, first by bestowing good through love and grace, then by ruling and rewarding good through righteousness. Now remains his moral goodness, by which he is most especially imitable, and it is called *holiness*. Yet here another distinction must be observed between the righteousness of the preceding chapter and the holiness of the present one: righteousness denotes a relative goodness, by which God acts according to eternal right, as if according to his own rule, whereas holiness expresses an absolute goodness, by which God is inclined to all moral purity and recoils from all impurity of sin. Moses is commanded to impress this holiness of God upon Israel, both as a motive and as an example for zeal for holiness, in Leviticus 19:2.

The Exegetical Part
The doctrine is built upon the exegesis of the text.

II. In these words a precept is contained, wherein Moses is commanded to impress upon the Israelites a zeal for holiness, and its argument is taken from the holiness of the Lord their God. In it two things occur:

    A. The duty commanded: "You shall be holy." Here, there is:

        1. A certain virtue, holiness: קְדֹשִׁים, "holy," from קָדַשׁ, a verb meaning, "he has been separated from common use," that is, consecrated, sacred, holy, pure, unpolluted, clean, and chaste. From this verb comes קִדֵּשׁ in the Piel, "he prepared, he appointed." The noun קֹדֶשׁ, "holiness," commonly denotes, not a holy thing, not the sanctuary

or the temple, but either the city of Jerusalem, as Rabbi Kimchi observes, or rather the stronghold of Zion, as Boate thinks (*Sacred Observations*, bk. 2, ch. 9).[1] Nevertheless, it sometimes does denote the tabernacle or temple (Ps. 29:2; 96:9), sometimes its entrance room (1 Kings 8:8), sometimes its sacrifices (Neh. 10:33), sometimes angels (Deut. 33:2), sometimes holy people (Lev. 10:10), and sometimes holy land (Ex. 15:13; Ps. 78:54), because all these things have been separated or should be separated to a holy use. In this passage, קדשים denotes not only being separated from every profane thing, but also being intrinsically averse to all impurity of sin and devoted to every form of moral purity.

2. The zeal and exercise of holiness, תהיו, "you will be," or "you shall be," that is, take care that: (1) you become holy, that you may be sanctified (Ex. 19:10), either by an extrinsic holiness such as there was in the washing of clothes and in other Levitical or ceremonial purifications, or by an intrinsic holiness, through the purification or sanctification of the Spirit: "in the sanctification of the Spirit, for obedience and sprinkling of the blood of Jesus Christ" (1 Peter 1:2), which happens in the exercise of faith and repentance, and in zeal for holiness. (2) You continue in it more and more, and advance in holiness. And that (3) you act in a holy way, and become holy in all your life, a holy one of Israel.

B. A twin argument for the command, namely:

1. The attribute of God: "for I am holy." I am holiness itself (Isa. 63:15), the source of all holiness, the one who sanctifies you (Ezek. 20:12), the idea and pattern of all holiness. It is fitting therefore in every way that you also would be holy, that you would seek and obtain this from me, from holiness itself, and that you would compose yourselves entirely to my holiness as to your pattern.

2. The mutual relationship or covenant between God and his people: "your God," the one who has as it were sanctified and dedicated myself to you as your God, and the one to whom you have entirely sanctified,

---

1. Arnold Boate (Latin: Arnoldus Bootius; Dutch: Arnold De Boot; 1600–1653), *Animadversiones sacrae ad textum hebraicum Veteris Testamenti* (London: Richard Bishop and Jacob Junius, 1644), 2.9.10–13, pp. 215–18. On the phrase בהדרת קדש, which is commonly translated "in the beauty of holiness," Boate prefers "in the magnificent and beautiful holy place" (*in sanctuario magnifico et decoro*). Boate evaluates several translations but spends more time on the views of Kimchi on Psalm 29:2, who concludes the referent is to the *arx Sionis*, or the stronghold of Zion.

separated, and dedicated yourselves as my people through the covenant of grace. Accordingly, it is entirely necessary that you should be holy. Therefore, here is presented, on the one hand, the holiness of the creature as the image, and on the other hand, the holiness of the Creator as the pattern. And thus, since the infinite holiness of the Creator is inaccessible to you (at least as it is in itself), you should gather the holiness of the Creator, as much as can be done, from the holiness of the creature, as from its image.

The Dogmatic Part

It is proved that God is holy: From the Scriptures

III. Consequently, no one can doubt that God is holy par excellence, because throughout Scripture he is called the Holy One (Isa. 40:25; Hos. 11:9; Job 6:10; Hab. 3:3); and the Holy One of Israel (although I hold the opinion that this is speaking specifically about the Son), in more than thirty instances (Isa. 41:20; 43:14); the Holy One of Jacob (Isa. 29:23); the most Holy One[2] (Dan. 9:24, which is speaking about the Messiah); the thrice Holy One (Isa. 6:3), in whom, so to speak, a triple holiness converges, for which reason to him is attributed the description in the plural with a singular pronoun, אלהים קדשים הוא, meaning as it were, "He is the holy Gods" (Josh. 24:19). Moreover, it is also without doubt that in the three persons there is one essential holiness, which therefore is attributed individually to each: to the Father (John 17:11), to the Son (Dan. 9:24; Ps. 16:10), to the Holy Spirit (Rom. 1:4). Thus by this argument it is not at all foolish to infer the Trinity of divine persons from the angelic trisagion (Rev. 4:8). For all these reasons, he obtains his name from his holiness (Luke 1:49); indeed, he is named the only Holy One (1 Sam. 2:2).

And from reasons

IV. If he were not holy: (1) how could he be most perfect, when without doubt holiness is a perfection which connotes no imperfection? (2) How could he be perfect in any perfection, when holiness is the basis of all perfection? For without holiness, what would his wisdom be except cleverness? His sovereignty, except tyranny? His power, except violence? His grace, except recklessness and negligence? Indeed, (3) without holiness, how would he behave properly toward himself? How would he behave properly toward the creatures? That is, how

---

2. *Sanctus Sanctorum*

would he govern in a holy manner? I also add, (4) if God is not holy, where does any holiness come from? How could God, the source of holiness, not be holy?

What holiness is in creatures

V. In order that we more easily understand what the holiness of God is, since it is inaccessible to us as it exists in him, it is necessary that we should contemplate that holiness in its image, that is, in the imaged holiness of creatures. Therefore, generally, holiness is nothing other than the moral goodness of a rational being. For there is goodness of essence, through which a creature is desirable, and there is goodness of use, through which it is called useful: this twofold goodness is common to all creatures. Then there is moral goodness, by which it is fitted with morals that are becoming to God, and this goodness is particular to rational creatures. Specifically, this holiness in creatures is either (1) covenantal holiness, by which the saints are set apart as the special possession of God for devotion to holiness (Num. 15:40; Deut. 7:6), by which they profess it and, by the judgment of charity, on account of this profession, are considered as saints. By this holiness the whole race of Israelites were once holy to God, and also by this holiness all the infants of Christians are considered holy (1 Cor. 7:14). Or, it is (2) habitual holiness (under which we also include actual holiness), which consists in an intrinsic purity of the will and of the affections, through which we are fitted to live in a way becoming to God. By this holiness we are properly addressed in Greek as ὅσιοι and in Latin as *sancti*, "holy ones" or "saints." Or, it is (3) relative holiness, by which places, times, and other things are called ἱερά and *sacra*, "sacred," because (a) they are made God's own, (b) they serve for producing and promoting habitual holiness, and also (c) in their own way, they convey a comeliness that is agreeable to God and to the divine worship. In the prior twofold signification, which applies especially to this chapter, holiness embraces: (1) a separation to divine use, in which sense the Mediator is said to have been sanctified (John 10:36), and Paul separated (Rom. 1:1; Gal. 1:15). Next, (2) a dedication by which you have devoted yourself and all that is yours to the glory, will, and cause of God (2 Cor. 8:5; Rom. 12:1; Lev. 21:6).[3] Furthermore, (3) an exhibition of divine holiness, in which the interior things of the heart together with the exterior things of the body in their own way display the purity of the divine law (Ps. 51:10; 1 Thess. 5:23). Finally, (4) a detestation of and fleeing from all impurity (2 Cor. 1:12).

---

3. Dutch: *aan de ere, heerlykheit, wille, en zake van Godt opdraagt en toeëigent*

What holiness is in God

VI. From this image of holiness, it is easy to gather in some way what the innate character of divine holiness is. Namely, it is his moral excellence, through which (1) he is separated from whatever is common and profane, just as the Mediator is called "holy, innocent, undefiled, separated from sinners, and exalted above the heavens" (Heb. 7:26). Next, (2) he is devoted to himself, doing all things on account of himself (Prov. 16:4), seeking, in all things and above all things, himself, and his own glory and good pleasure (Eph. 1:11). Furthermore, (3) in all his thoughts, words, and deeds, he is exactly in conformity to the holiness which he has expressed in his own law, and thus throughout Scripture he invites people everywhere to the imitation of his own holiness (Lev. 19:2; 11:44; Matt. 5:48), even while, without doubt, he does not invite them to some other holiness than that which is set forth in the law. Finally, (4) he is pure, and most absolutely contrary to everything evil, iniquitous, and base that he proscribes in his own law (Hab. 1:13; Ps. 5:4–6), indeed, from these things he shrinks back, as it were, in utter horror (Deut. 25:16; Rev. 21:27).

God reveals his holiness in various ways.

VII. Furthermore, God reveals his holiness in various ways. (1) In his works (Ps. 145:17): (a) in the decrees, predestination and election, "that we should be holy and blameless before him" (Eph. 1:4); (b) in creation, when he created man upright, according to his own image (Eccl. 7:30), in holiness and righteousness (Eph. 4:24); (c) in providence, especially in moral providence, when he prescribes the law to rational creatures by commanding and forbidding, sanctions it by promising and threatening, carries out the sanction by rewarding and punishing (Ezek. 20:11–12); when he contracted the covenant of works with them (Deut. 30:15–16); (d) in redemption, when he sanctified the Son (John 10:36) so that he might for our sake sanctify himself (John 17:19), that he might sanctify us to God (Eph. 5:26; Heb. 2:11); when he punished his very own, only begotten Son by a cursed death, that he might show his own holiness, whereby he cannot look upon evil (Hab. 1:13; Rom. 3:25); (e) in calling, insofar as he calls with a holy calling (2 Tim. 1:9), not to impurity but to sanctity (1 Thess. 4:7), that we might be those called to be saints (Rom. 1:7; 1 Cor. 1:2); (f) in sanctification, insofar as he regenerates, converts, and sanctifies us entirely, that our whole spirit, soul, and body may be preserved blameless (1 Thess. 5:23); and finally (g) in glorification, when he will present the church to himself, not having spot or blemish or any such thing, but holy and blameless (Eph. 5:26–27). But also, God reveals his holiness (2) in his own Word, in Scripture, which for this reason is called holy (Rom. 1:2; 2 Tim. 3:15), in the truth by which he sanctifies us (John 17:17), and especially in his own law, which is called holy: "The law is holy, the command-ment holy, just, and good" (Rom. 7:12), because in it he reveals some shadow[4] of the divine holiness, to the extent that it can be imitated, for which reason it is likened to a mirror (James 1:23–25). Furthermore, he reveals the same holi-ness (3) in the worship, rites, sacrifices, sacraments, baptism and the Supper, which everywhere are called holy because they tend toward holiness (James 1:27; Rom. 12:1). In addition, he reveals the same holiness (4) in his people, in his subjects, who are called throughout Scripture a holy people (1 Peter 2:9), in his church and house, whose chief beauty is holiness (Ps. 93:5). Moreover, he reveals it (5) in his ministers, who for this reason are called holy men of God (2 Peter 1:21), who are ordered to bear on their forehead קדש ליהוה, "holiness of the Lord" (Ex. 28:36), because God wills to be sanctified among those who come near to him (Lev. 10:3). Also, (6) in his train of angels, who for this reason are throughout the Scriptures called holy (Luke 9:26; Matt. 25:31). Finally, (7) in all those things which sustain some sort of relation to God, such as holy places (Ps. 11:4; 20:2) and holy times (Ex. 20:11). By all these things and many others, God reveals that he is holy, and that he is the one who will sanctify his own (Lev. 21:8).

How holiness belongs to God

VIII. Accordingly, holiness belongs to God: (1) not as some kind of accessory, but as his very essence, for the one who in Isaiah 45:23 is said to swear by himself says in Psalm 89:35 and Amos 4:2 that he has sworn by his holiness. And (2) not as something received from another, but as the source of all holiness in all things (Lev. 20:8; 21:15; Ezek. 20:12; 1 Thess. 5:23). And (3) not in a certain measure, but without measure, in an infinite degree, a holiness that for this reason cannot be augmented or diminished, for it is his essence, although it can be declared more and more, and ought to be (Matt. 6:9). And (4) not according to the holi-ness of his law or of whatever imaged holiness, but as the idea and pattern, and the norm, of all holiness (1 Peter 1:15; Eph. 4:24). And (5) not so much as a cer-tain particular attribute of his, but as a universal affection,[5] affecting, as it were, every other attribute of his, and thus his power, or his arm, is called holy (Isa. 52:10; etc.). And finally, (6) not some common affection of his, but the one that is chief by far, the one by which he is celebrated even by the angels themselves, not once, but three times and in the same breath, as it were: "Holy, holy, holy is

---

4. ἀποσκιμάτιον
5. *affectio*, usually "property"

Jehovah Sabaoth" (Isa. 6:3; Rev. 4:8), which is nowhere read regarding any other attribute of his.

The Elenctic Part

It is asked: 1. Do the titles "Most Holy" and "His Holiness" belong to any mortal?

IX. Those things which we have said about the holiness of God are so evident to all that no controversy can be stirred up by anyone, even by God's enemies. But at the same time, it is asked, first, whether the titles "Most Holy" and "His Holiness" belong to any mortal. The Roman pontiff, so that he might have titles agreeable to his absolute rule, wishes to be addressed as "Most Holy Father," even "His Holiness," to which, not without reason, an offended bishop at the Council of Trent wisely remarked, "If God alone is called holy, how can his vicar be called most holy?" The Reformed hold the opinion that these titles in no way belong to any mortal, and especially not to the pope, because: (1) God himself, although he is in fact most holy, even holiness itself, is nevertheless rarely or never called most holy or holiness itself; on the contrary, the name designated for him is "holy" (Ps. 111:9). (2) The Savior Jesus, although he himself is also most holy, and in fact is holiness itself (it is he whose vicar the pontiff deceitfully claims to be), is frequently called the Holy One of Israel (Isa. 10:20; Ps. 78:41)—the name of our Redeemer is Jehovah of hosts, the *Holy One of Israel* (Isa. 47:4), the one whom the Father sanctified (John 10:36)—and is nowhere designated as most holy, or as holiness itself. And also (3) Peter, whose successor the pope commends himself to be, indeed was and was called holy, and he designates himself as a fellow elder,[6] but he is never named "Most Holy," and much less "His Holiness." For this reason (4) by this very fact he reveals himself to be the Antichrist, as the one who exalts himself above all that is called God or *holy* (2 Thess. 2:4). And especially since (5) to be most holy and holiness itself coincides with the most holy essence of God itself, and thus it is God himself, who is holiness itself. No sinner—and all acknowledge that the pope himself is a sinner—is or can be called most holy, or holiness itself, and (6) especially the pontiffs, who are in fact the Antichrist, among whom in addition some were heretics, such as Liberius the Monothelite, and others even prostitutes, such as Pope Joan,[7] sodomites, and pederasts, those who are called קָדֵשׁ, "holy male prostitute," by antiphrasis, and קְדֵשָׁה, "holy female prostitute," by euphemism (Deut. 23:17;

---

6. *compresbyterum*, συμπρεσβύτερον (1 Peter 5:1)

7. The assertion of a female Pope Joan has been discredited in modern accounts of the history of the popes since the seventeenth century, but it persisted in Protestant polemical works as late as the middle eighteenth century.

22:21; see Selden, *On Natural Right*, bk. 5, ch. 4, p. 575).[8] I need not mention (8) that on account of a similar arrogance, Herod was once devoured by worms (Acts 12:21–23). I do not see what the pope's sycophants can plead, at least with any plausibility, for these blasphemous titles. If they should say that they are political titles, then I will respond that they either belong and are attributed to him truly, and thus introduce blasphemy by all the preceding reasons, or they do not belong to him, and thus are falsely attributed to him, and blasphemously as well.

2. Does not papal canonization, in which by many rites mortals are pronounced saints, and it is declared that they must be considered as saints by everyone, detract from God and his holiness? The opinion of the Romanists

X. It is asked, second, whether papal canonization, in which by many rites mortals are pronounced saints, and it is declared that they must be considered as saints by everyone, does not detract from God and his holiness. The papists, not content to have made their pope most holy, in fact holiness itself, in order that they might extol this "Most Holy One" of theirs even more, say not only that he is of such a rank, but also that he can, by a certain solemn rite and decree, raise other departed people to the level of saints, such that thereafter (1) they are publicly considered and called by all, in an extraordinary way, "saints"; (2) they are invoked in the public prayers of the church; (3) temples and sanctuaries are dedicated to God in their memory; (4) sacrifices are offered to God publicly in their honor; (5) feast days are celebrated in their honor; (6) their images are painted with a certain kind of light, and are placed in a distinguished place for veneration in the churches; (7) their relics are enclosed in cases and publicly honored (see Bellarmine, *Disputations*, tom. 2, controv. 4, *On the Church Triumphant*, bk. 1, chs. 7–9).[9] Bellarmine adds that it must be believed that the pope does not err in this canonization, yet there are those who deny this: Cajetan in his *Treatise on Indulgences*,[10] Aquinas in his *Quodlibetal Questions* (Q. 9, qu. 8),[11] and Melchior Cano (tom. 1, bk. 5, ch. 5), in these words: "The judgments of the church, which proceed from uncertain testimonies of men, are weak grounds for certain and confirmed faith, and such is that judgement whereby it decides that some holy

---

8. John Selden, *De jure naturali et gentium juxta disciplinam Ebraeorum* (Strasbourg: Endter, 1655), 575.

9. Robert Bellarmine, S. J., *Disputationes de controversiis Christianae fidei*, 4 vols. (1610), 2:868–73.

10. See Tommaso de Vio Cajetan (1468–1534), *De indulgentiis* in *Opuscula omnia* (Antwerp: Johannes Keerberg, 1611), sigs. 63 v–75 r.

11. Thomas Aquinas, *Quaestiones de quolibet* in *Opera Omnia iussu Leonis XIII* (1996), 25/1.

person should be enrolled in the catalogue of saints."[12] And furthermore, the pope's sycophants call this canonization an apotheosis.

And the opinions of the Reformed with their own arguments

The Reformed, although they gladly admit that those who are truly saints from the declaration of Scripture should be received as such, and even venerated by civil worship, even so call such canonizations and apotheoses impious, superstitious, and idolatrous, because (1) there is neither feather nor footprint of them found in the Scriptures, and therefore they are superstitious, for they are a plant which the Father has not planted, and thus must be uprooted, according to the judgment of the Savior in Matthew 15:13; they are a doctrine of men, condemned in the same chapter, verse 9, and by Paul in Colossians 2:18, 20, 22. (2) This canonization commands the invocation of creatures, which Christ claims for God alone (Matt. 4:10) and God claims for himself alone (Isa. 42:8), so then it is idolatrous and injurious to God. (3) It attributes infallibility to the Pope, which belongs to God alone, since every man is a liar (Ps. 116:11). For they cannot demonstrate a promise of infallible direction. For this reason, in the judgment of Cajetan and Cano, a damned person could be canonized and invoked as a saint. "Nor is there a difference," adds Cano, "whether you worship the devil or a damned human being."[13] (4) The man of sin, that lawless one, can sanctify, that is, declare a person a saint, who perhaps is in the catalogue of the damned, who in his life was nothing but a wandering beggar, like Francis of Assisi, or who perhaps in reality never existed. I need not add that (5) most of the requirements for this canonization belong only to the divine holiness, for it alone can examine the heart and inward parts, and thus pronounce with certainty who is in fact a saint.

Objections

Bellarmine does not have anything in favor of this canonization that is of any significance. He says, for example, (1) that God willed that the holy writers note in particular the saints' glorious life and death. Therefore it is believable that God wills that it should thereafter be done in the same way. I respond: (a) As if there were no distinction between this notation and the canonization already described. (b) In the whole of Scripture, those seven honors of canonization already mentioned are never noted to have been either decreed or conferred upon any mortal. (c) The papists do not usually confer those honors upon all

---

12. Melchior Cano, O. P. (1509–1560), *Opera* (Madrid: Gazeta, 1776), 1:362.
13. Cano, *Opera*, 1:362.

those whose glorious life and death are noted in the Scriptures. (2) That unless we know who in fact are saints and who are not, we cannot worship them as is proper, we cannot be roused to imitate them, we cannot rejoice together with the saints, nor give thanks to God for their glory. I respond: (a) We should not worship them religiously. (b) We know in particular those whom we should imitate because we see them imitating Christ (1 Cor. 11:1). (c) Therefore, either the papists do not do what they ought, or they have a particular knowledge of all the saints who are in glory and are obligated to canonize them all.

3. Do merits from condignity not detract from the most pure holiness of God?

XI. It is asked, third, whether merits from condignity do not detract from the most pure holiness of God. The papists, lest we should attain eternal life from the merits of Christ alone, and so that papal authority may be supported and lifted up by good works, especially those, as they say, of "charity"—the endowments of temples and monasteries—suppose that the good works of believers merit eternal life from condignity, and accordingly deny that these merits detract from the divine holiness. The Reformed on the contrary affirm that they do, because: (1) God is most pure in eyes, and he cannot look upon our sinful defects (Hab. 1:13); he is thrice holy, that is, most holy (Isa. 6:3). (2) Moses is commanded to take off his shoes because even the place where he was standing was holy from the presence of God.[14] (3) Those who are mindful of the most strict divine holiness pray with such concern for deliverance from his tribunal (Ps. 130:3; 143:2), because no one can stand before him. (4) He is so holy that he finds blemishes even in the holy angels (Job 25:4–5).[15] (5) Even the cherubim before God cover their faces and their feet with their wings, crying out, "Holy, holy, holy is Jehovah Sabaoth" (Isa. 6:2–3). On the other hand, even the best works of the saints are like a menstrual rag (Isa. 64:6). Surely the man who tries to merit eternal life by his own works, and indeed to merit from condignity, from the strictness of God's justice—surely, I say, that man does not adequately realize the severity of the divine holiness. It will suffice here to have touched on these things which will be treated more fully, God willing, in another place, in the chapter on justification.[16]

---

14. Cf. Ex. 3:5.
15. Cf. Job 4:18; 15:15.
16. 1.6.6 §§XX, XXII

*4. Does the Reformed religion by its hypotheses erode the holiness of God
by establishing that he is the author of sin?* A comparison of opinions

XII. It is asked, fourth, whether the Reformed religion by its hypotheses erodes the holiness of God by establishing that he is the author of sin. The enemies of the Reformed religion, however many there are—Socinians, Arminians, Anabaptists, papists, and especially Lutherans—by misrepresenting us on this point, compete as if for a prize to denigrate our religion more, and thus they answer in the affirmative. The Reformed on the contrary deny that by their own hypotheses God is the author of sin, because: (1) the hypotheses of the Reformed religion in all things coincide with the hypotheses of Scripture, for which reason, if Scripture does not erode the holiness of God, then neither does the Reformed religion. The antecedent will be evident through the responses to the objections. On the contrary, (2) the hypotheses of the Reformed religion, since they coincide with Scripture, as much as possible tend toward amplifying the wisdom, power, righteousness, and holiness of God, for to decree the futurity of sin, to permit sin, to withdraw grace from the sinner on account of sin for the holiest reasons, to offer good opportunities to people that they abuse for the purpose of sinning, all show his wisdom, power, righteousness, and holiness, as will be evident by our responses to the objections of our adversaries.

Objections

For if they should allege, according to the Reformed, (1) that God decreed future sins, we will respond that (a) Scripture teaches the same thing (Acts 2:23; 4:27; cf. Acts 15:18; Eph. 1:11). (b) He decreed not to bring the sin into effect, but only to permit it (Ps. 81:12; Acts 14:16). (c) The decree is only the cause of futurity, not of the future sin itself, for that is produced by creatures through the abuse of their own free choice, as is evident in Pharaoh, Judas, and others. (d) He decreed them by his most wise counsel: "Your hand and counsel predetermined" (Acts 4:27–28), and the counsel of the most wise is certainly most wise. And he did so to this end, that by the permitted and predetermined sin he might provide himself an opportunity to illustrate the glory, first of his mercy in the free redemption of the sinner, in which his wisdom and his goodness alike are evident, and next of his justice in the just punishment of the sinner, in which is his holiness. (2) That he ordained man to sin. I respond: (a) Scripture also teaches this (Ex. 9:16; Rom. 9:37; cf. Jude 4; 1 Peter 2:8; Rom. 9:21–22). (b) He ordained to leave man to himself and to his own choice (Acts 14:16; Rom. 1:24), that he might make manifest his avenging justice (Rom 9:22), in which his holiness is evident.

(3) That God compels man to sin.[17] I respond, He does not compel man, but has decreed that the sinner bring forth sin by counsel and rational complacency[18] (in which the liberty of our choice properly consists), and he only acts in this such that the futurity and event arise certainly and infallibly according to the decree. (4) That he wills sins. I respond: (a) Scripture also says this, and it does not make God the author of sin (Acts 4:27–28). (b) He does not will them by his legislative will or will of precept, but only by his will of decree: he wills that the futurity and event of the sin which the sinner freely perpetrates would infallibly arise. (5) That according to the Reformed, he commands sins, impels men to them, hardens men, blinds them, and gives them over to a reprobate sense. I respond: (a) Only in the same sense in which Scripture says in 2 Samuel 16:10 that the Lord commanded Shimei to curse David; in 2 Samuel 24:1, "He incited David against them"; in Exodus 9:12, "He hardened the heart of Pharaoh" (cf. Ex. 14:17); in Isaiah 6:10, "Make the heart of this people fat, and make their ears heavy, and shut their eyes, lest they see"; in Romans 1:28, "God gave them over to a reprobate mind"; and in 2 Thessalonians 2:11, "God will send to them an effectual working of error, that they should believe a lie." Therefore, if in all these things Scripture does not make God the author of sin, then neither do the Reformed. (b) They do not teach that God commands sins, properly speaking: not by his law, in which he forbids them, but by his providence, insofar as he efficaciously permits and directs them. Nor do they teach that he impels men to sins, properly speaking, that is, unwilling, but rather by withdrawing his grace on account of sins, by abandoning them to their own lusts. Nor do they teach that he hardens or blinds them by infusing blindness or hardness into them, but by justly punishing them with blindness or hardness on account of the sins they committed. (6) That the Reformed attribute the same evil actions to God and to the impious. I respond: (a) Only in that sense in which Scripture does in 2 Samuel 12:11–12: "You did it secretly, but I will do it publicly" (also 2 Sam. 24:1; cf. 1 Chron. 21:1; Gen. 45:8). (b) Indeed, they attribute the same actions, but not in the same way, for the same end, according to the dictum, "When two things do the same thing, it is not the same thing" (cf. Gen. 45:8).[19] (c) Nor do they, properly speaking, attribute the same thing to both, for they attribute the futurity and the event of sin to God, but the sin itself to man: to God, only

---

17. Latin: *Quod (3) necessitet hominem*; Dutch: *Noch eens (III) werven zy tegen dat Godt den mensch noodzaakt en dwingt*, "Yet they raise against [the Reformed Religion] that God necessitates and forces man."

18. Latin: *complacentia rationalis*; Dutch: *redenmagtig welbehagen*

19. Latin: *duo cum idem faciunt, non est idem*; Dutch: *wanneer twee een en hetzelfde doen, is 't echter niet hetzelfde*.

the subject in which is the lawlessness or sin; to man, the lawlessness or sin itself. Compare what we have said on this matter in chapter 16, §XV and perhaps will speak about in the chapters on the decrees, reprobation, providence, and elsewhere.[20]

The Practical Part

The holiness of God rouses us that: 1. We should strive to be sanctified by God.

XIII. In practice, the holiness of God stirs us up that, first, we should strive with every effort to be sanctified by God, which is what the Savior desires for the elect (John 17:17) and Paul desires for his hearers (1 Thess. 5:23), with such great affection, that is, since we are all by nature unclean and profane, (Job 14:4), and our righteousness itself is unclean (Isa. 64:6), and likewise we are impure in our lips and heart (Isa. 6:5).

Ways

We should strive that God, who is thrice holy, holiness itself, and the source of all holiness, would sanctify us entirely, that is, that he would confer upon us that holiness which we discussed in §V, in the following ways: (1) in redemption, by sprinkling and washing us as it were in the blood of the Son (Ps. 51:7; 1 John 1:7; Heb. 10:22; 1 Peter 1:2), who sanctified himself for us to that end (John 17:19). Then, (2) in regeneration through the Spirit (John 3:3, 5), by taking from us the heart of stone, by substituting a heart of flesh, by inscribing his law on our hearts (Ezek. 36:25–27; Jer. 31:33–34), by making us spiritually alive who were dead in our sins (Eph. 2:5–6). Next, (3) in conversion (Jer. 31:18–19), by leading us to faith in Jesus Christ, by which we are united with him, and thus are crucified and resurrected with him (Gal. 2:20; Rom. 6:5). Finally, (4) in renewal (Eph. 4:24; Rom. 12:2), by restoring in us little by little the purity of the divine image (2 Cor. 4:16), by subduing the old man and raising up the new one, so that we may become new creatures, in whom the old things have passed away and all things have become new (2 Cor. 5:17).

Means

That sanctification is a work of God alone (John 6:44) although it is accomplished by the ministry of the Word (Acts 26:17–18). There are no other parts for us to play at this point except: (1) to observe and to learn of the excellence, utility, and necessity of sanctification (John 3:5), that thus our yearning for it

---

20. 1.3.1 §XXVII; 1.3.4 §XI; 1.3.10 §XXXII; 1.4.3 §XXV

might grow. (2) To beseech God that he would create in us a clean heart and renew a right spirit within us (Ps. 51:10). At the same time, (3) to give our diligent and constant attention to the means which God customarily uses in this sanctification—the reading and hearing of the Word, conversation with the godly—and by these things to wait (Ps. 27:14) until at last it seems good to God, who commanded the light to shine out of darkness, to shine in our hearts (2 Cor. 4:6).

2. Having been sanctified, we should sanctify God. The acts of sanctifying God
XIV. Next, second, having been sanctified by God, we should reciprocally sanctify God (Ex. 29:43; Lev. 22:32; Isa. 8:13; 29:23; Matt. 6:9; 1 Peter 3:15), not of course by making him more holy, as God sanctifies us, but (1) by acknowledging, admiring, and venerating the holiness of God in our heart (1 Peter 3:15; 1 Sam. 6:20; Isa. 8:14); (b) by praising the same with our mouth (Ps. 71:22; Isa. 6:3); (c) by expressing it in our deeds, while we are engaged in divine worship, its individual parts, and all things that are dedicated to God or that concern him in whatever way, doing so never without singular reverence, concern, and devotion (Ex. 19:22; Lev. 11:44), as God has in some way communicated his holiness to those things; (d) by taking careful heed with concern lest we profane the most holy name or worship of God by contempt, temerity, negligence, apathy,[21] sluggishness, and other such things that are proscribed in the third commandment.

The motivating reasons
For (1) God desires to be sanctified by those who hasten to him (Lev. 10:3). (2) God sanctified us for himself to this end, that we might sanctify him (1 Peter 2:9). And (3) unless we have sanctified him by virtue, he will sanctify himself in us by punishments and judgments, as is evident in the case of Nadab and Abihu (Lev. 10:2–3), the men of Beth-shemesh (1 Sam. 6:19), Uzzah (2 Sam. 6:7), Uzziah (2 Kings 15:4–5), and others (Ezek. 28:22; 38:22–23). Compare what is said by commentators on the third commandment and the first petition of the Lord's Prayer, and what we said above in chapter 4, in the practical part.[22]

3. Sanctifying God, we should abhor every profanity.
XV. Third, sanctifying God, we should abhor every profanity, impurity, and impiety that is enumerated in Matthew 15:9, Galatians 5:19–21, and Ephesians 5:3, whether it is of the body or of the spirit (2 Cor. 7:1), whether it internally

---

21. Latin: *acedia*; Dutch: *traagheit*
22. 1.2.4 §XX

lurks within the heart (2 Cor. 4:2; Eph. 5:12) or is externally evident in deed (Isa. 3:9), whether in us or in others (Ps. 139:21), because (1) the most holy one abhors all these things (Hab. 1:13; Ps. 5:4–6); and accordingly (2) they separate us from God (Isa. 59:2; 1:13; Ps. 11:5; 101:3); (3) he sanctified his own Son that he might destroy these works of the devil (1 John 3:8); (4) they will eternally separate us from heavenly beatitude (Rev. 21:27; 1 Cor. 6:9–10). For these reasons: (1) we should earnestly detest them (Rom. 12:9; Heb. 1:9; Jude 23); (2) we should strive to be purged from them and on account of them strive to be reconciled to God through the blood of Christ (1 John 1:7; 1 Peter 1:18–19); (3) we should wash ourselves from them (Isa. 1:16; Jer. 4:4, 14; 2 Tim. 2:21); (4) we should deny all ungodliness (Titus 2:12).

4. Abhorring these things, we should pay attention to holiness.
XVI. On the contrary, fourth, having been purged from every profanity, we should also pay attention to holiness, that is, that we might be holy, because our God is holy. This means that (1) we should separate ourselves more and more from every common, polluted, and worldly thing (Ezra 6:21; Rev. 18:4; Rom. 12:2), to which end the Nazirite vow and all the Levitical purifications pointed. (2) We should dedicate, consecrate, and resign ourselves more and more to God (2 Cor. 8:5), that is, as a holy sacrifice (Rom. 12:1). (3) We should pay attention to the inward heart, and to the purity of all our affections (Ps. 51:10; Matt. 5:8; 1 Tim. 1:5). (4) We should give ourselves to holy works, the sort which (a) flow from a holy and pure heart (Ps. 51:10; Matt. 5:8; 1 Tim. 1:5); (b) tend toward the sanctification or glorification of the divine name (1 Peter 2:9; 2 Tim. 2:21); and (c) are arranged according to the most holy will of God (Rom. 12:1–2). We should be stirred up to all these things because (1) God, our God, is holy, most holy, holiness itself, and the one who desires that we be holy. (2) Holiness is his chief and universal perfection, for which reason he is called thrice holy, and thus by a zeal for holiness, we are made like him in his chief perfection. (3) From all eternity past, God has been so eager for establishing and restoring holiness by predestination, redemption, calling, and so forth, just as we taught in particular above in §VII. Indeed, (4) each Person, in the work of sanctification, has taken his own particular part, and the Holy Spirit in particular obtains from this work his office as well as his name. Finally, (5) without sanctity we will never see God (Heb. 12:14; Matt. 5:8). It will suffice to have touched on these things which will be spoken of more extensively, God willing, in the chapters on regeneration, conversion, and sanctification.[23]

---

23. 1.6.3 §XXXIX; 1.6.4 §XXXVIII; 1.6.8 §§XXXI–XXXVIII

5. Let us attentively test our own holiness.

XVII. Meanwhile, fifth, in this zeal for holiness, let us frequently test ourselves, that we may approve what is excellent, that we may be pure (Phil. 1:10; Heb. 5:14), and that deceit may not pass for truth, form for power (2 Tim. 3:5), more sensible reason for religion, more reputable education for a sanctified conscience, a graver demeanor or the theatrics of the Pharisees for true piety, a seditious or schismatic impetus for zeal for holiness, or a ceremonial, ritual, and external holiness for a real holiness, and that none of these external things may creep up against what is internal, but rather that we may be renewed in true holiness (Eph. 4:24). From what has been said, this holiness will be discerned without much great labor. Namely, it is a true holiness, (1) which not only to some extent, on this or that point, separates from the world and from worldly matters, but rather, entirely (Rom. 12:2; Titus 2:12); (2) which consecrates and sanctifies the whole man, in soul as well as body, to God (1 Thess. 5:23; 1 Cor. 6:20; Rom. 12:1), by completely denying itself (Luke 9:23), by taking nothing away from God and reserving nothing for itself, unlike Ananias and Sapphira (Acts 5:2) or the young Pharisee (Matt. 19:21–22), by devoting all things to him (Matt. 19:27), even up to life and death itself (Rom. 14:7–8; Matt. 16:25–26); (3) which strives for internal rather than external holiness (Ps. 51:6, 10), as opposed to Pharisaical holiness (Matt. 23:23–27); (4) which, in the sight of God rather than of men (Matt. 6:1–6), abstains (5) not only from this or that impurity, as the Pharisees did (Luke 18:11), but from every worldly lust (Titus 2:12), from every pollution of the world (2 Peter 2:20–21), hating even the garment defiled by contact with the flesh (Jude 23), indeed, from all appearance of evil (1 Thess. 5:22); (6) a holiness which, conversely, gives itself not only to one good work or another, like Pharisaical holiness (Luke 18:12; Matt. 5:20; Phil. 3:6), nor even one that gives itself only in many things, like Herod (Mark 6:20), but in everything, in all things desiring to live honorably (Heb. 13:18; Phil. 4:8); and finally, (7) which endures not only for a time (Gal. 3:3), but to the end, and indeed, increases more and more (Rev. 12:11; 1 Cor. 15:58).

6. It makes for consolation.

XVIII. So then, sixth, when it is clear that we have some sincerity of holiness, there comes forth consolation even in our impurity. If at any time we should have to cry out, "Woe is me, for I am a man of unclean lips!" (Isa. 6:5), likewise, "We are all as one who is unclean, and all our righteousnesses are like a filthy garment; we all fall down as a leaf, and our iniquities, like the wind, drive us away" (Isa. 64:6), and likewise, "Who will deliver me from this body of death?" (Rom. 7:24), then at that time, what more effectively raises us up than to think that God is holy, most holy, holiness itself, the source of all holiness, the one who sanctifies us (Ezek. 20:12), who blots out our transgressions like a cloud, who dissipates our sins like a cloud (Isa. 44:22), who sanctified the Son that he might sanctify us, who gave him to us as sanctification (1 Cor. 1:30), who offered himself for us, that he might sanctify us, and cleanse us with the washing of water by the word (Eph. 5:25–26), who promised to us on account of the covenant that he will write his laws on our mind and heart, will take away our heart of stone and replace it with a heart of flesh; that he will sprinkle clean water upon us so that we may be cleansed from all our filth; that he will give us a new heart and a new spirit so that we may walk in his commandments; that he will cleanse us from all our iniquities (Ezek. 36:25–27, 33)? Then also in whatever adversities, it will console us that God will be good to those who have been clean in heart (Ps. 73:1), that they shall one day see God (Matt. 5:8), and that those whom he has sanctified he will more certainly than certain also glorify (Rom. 8:30), and finally, that the holy one will lead us into his holy place, so that we may sing to him, "Holy, holy, holy is Jehovah Sabaoth" (Isa. 6:3).

7. Finally, it makes for the glorification of God.
XIX. Finally, seventh, in this is the last and highest use of the divine holiness, that by the example of the holy angels (Isa. 6:3) and the heavenly saints, we might be duly accustomed to celebrate God by his holiness, because not only is he most holy, and holiness itself, but also, he has shown that he is holy from all eternity past, he shows it even now, and he will show it, that he might reveal that he is the God who sanctifies us, without doubt to the end that we would see and celebrate that he is holy. And thus in this celebration we rightly place the end of election, of redemption, and thus of every saving grace.

CHAPTER TWENTY

The Authority and Power of God

Now, to him who is able to do exceedingly abundantly above all that we ask and that we think, according to the power that works in us, to him be glory in the church.

—Ephesians 3:20–21

The chapter on the authority and power of God

I. From the attributes by which God is conceived by us to work, after life, intellect and will, and the virtues analogous to them—truthfulness, goodness, love, grace, righteousness, and holiness—we proceed to authority and power,[1] whereby the preceding working attributes immediately achieve their work, as it were. And this authority and power the apostle marvelously outlines in Ephesians 3:20–21.

The Exegetical Part

It is built upon the exegesis of the text.

II. In these words is contained a most expressive doxology, with its argument taken from the omnipotence of God. In it, three things occur:

A. Δυνάμενος, the one "able" or "powerful," to whom the doxology is devoted: τῷ δὲ δυναμένῳ, "and to him who is powerful," that is, to God. Here, the article τῷ seems to have a distinctive force: it distinguishes the God who is powerful from any other who is powerful; in fact, it rather declares him to be the only one who is powerful, for any sort of omnipotence is denied to the creature. It is as if he should say, "to him who alone is powerful," for a creature can do nothing without God, and God can do all things without the creature, for which reason

---

1. Latin: *potestatem et potentiam*; Dutch: *Magt en Kracht*. In this chapter *potestas* is always translated as "authority" and *potentia* always as "power." See Mastricht's own distinction between *potestas* and *potentia* in §§II.B and V, below.

he is called the one powerful above all, and μόνος δυνάστης, "the only Potentate" (1 Tim. 6:15).

B. Δύναμις, or the power[2] through which he is δυνάμενος: κατὰ δύναμιν, "according to his power." Δύναμις expresses strength, ability, vigor, force; sometimes, the strength to work wonders (2 Thess. 2:9), and sometimes abundance or opulence (Rev. 18:3), the kind of power the apostle attributes to the divine wisdom in Romans 11:33, "Oh the depth of the riches, both of the wisdom…." So it is also among the Hebrews: חיל (e.g. Ruth 4:11) denotes power as well as all that in which power seems to consist, such as armies and wealth. Whenever δύναμις is applied to the Spirit, it denotes a certain strength that is greater than usual. Furthermore, power is either a productive power, from which magistrates are sometimes called powers[3] (Rom. 8:38), just as angels are called authorities[4] (Eph. 3:10; Col. 1:16), and it is perhaps in that sense that we hear of the powers of the heavens (Matt. 24:29). Or, power is a produced power, and thus miracles are called powers (Matt. 7:22; Mark 6:2, 5; Luke 10:13; Acts 8:13; etc.), because in them shines forth a divine power that is clearly infinite, without which true miracles could not be performed; and in addition, the strength that produces miracles is also called powers (Mark 6:14; 1 Cor. 12:10). But, what should be chiefly observed in this passage, there is a power by which you can act *de jure*, that is, ἐξουσία, authority or moral ability;[5] and there is a power by which you can act *de facto*, otherwise called strength, force, or physical power, and in this narrower sense it is called δύναμις. In the creatures these two are not only distinguished, but are also separated, such that authority may belong to a person to whom power does not belong, and vice versa; but in the Creator they coincide, for he can do nothing *de jure* that he cannot do *de facto*, and vice versa (Jer. 18:6; cf. Rom. 9:20–22; Matt. 20:15). For this reason we see "the kingdom," to which authority belongs, and "the power" joined together in Matthew 6:13. But even so, we will be occupied with each distinctly in this chapter.

C. Δυνατόν, what the power can do, or rather, the working of divine power, concerning which is explained:

---

2. Latin: *potentia*; Dutch: *de kracht of magt*, power or might. *Potentia* also signals power as ability, and thus elsewhere the Dutch translation uses *Almagtigheit Godts* for *omnipotentia Dei*.

3. *virtutes*, δυνάμεις

4. ἐξουσίαι, *potestates*

5. *auctoritas, seu facultas moralis*

1. The act, in the word ποιῆσαι, to effect, to produce. "He effects whatever he wills" (Ps. 115:3). This power of effecting can be considered either insofar as he is simply able to effect even what he never wills to effect (Matt. 3:9; 26:53), which they call his absolute power, whereby he is considered as the simply powerful one.[6] Or, this power can be considered insofar as in addition, what he is able to do, he does, which is called his ordained power and executive power, whereby what he knows he is able to do he also wills to do, and puts into effect (Ps. 135:6).

2. The work, the product of the power, or what it will produce, which is commended:

   a. From the universality of the object: "all." Namely, all things that are not repugnant to his nature or to the nature of things (Luke 1:37; Phil. 3:21; 2 Chron. 20:6).

   b. From the preeminence of the power through which it is produced, which is explained in:

      i. Absolute terms: "exceedingly abundantly." The formula is a clear example of rhetorical amplification, a manner of speaking in which we see the apostle take delight (2 Cor. 3:9; 7:15; Phil. 1:9; 1 Thess. 4:1, 10; etc.).

      ii. Comparative terms: "what we ask and think." His power is denoted as absolutely infinite, a power greater than which none can exist, be thought of, or be sought.

The Dogmatic Part

The infinite power and authority of God is proved: From the Scriptures

III. It is evident from this that an unlimited and infinite power belongs to God, a power because of which he is called Lord (Ps. 136:3) and King of kings (Dan. 2:47; 4:37), the great King (Ps. 48:2; Matt. 5:35), to whom belong kingship and power (Matt. 6:13). And from this power, he is throughout Scripture named אביר, mighty (Job 34:20), שׁדי, almighty or omnipotent (Gen. 17:1; 49:25; etc.)—from שׁדד, as if he were a destroyer who could, according to his pleasure, just as he produced all things from nothing, also destroy and reduce them to nothing—גבור, the mighty one (Deut. 10:17), אמיץ כח, mighty in strength (Job 9:4), כביר, strong (Job 36:5), παντοκράτωρ, almighty (2 Cor. 6:18; Rev. 1:8),

---

6. αὐτάρκης, *simpliciter potens*

μόνος δυνάστης, the only Potentate (1 Tim. 6:15). Not only is he adorned with these descriptions, but in addition, it is expressly declared that he can do all things, even bring forth offspring for Abraham from stones (Matt. 3:9; 19:26; Mark 14:36; Luke 18:26). Indeed, there is nothing that he cannot do (Rom. 9:19), because by his arm, by his outstretched right hand, he stretched out heaven and earth (1 Chron. 29:12; Jer. 32:17). Thus, from all these things, it is by no means unreasonable that the apostle extols the exceeding greatness of God's power (Eph. 1:19).

And from reasons

IV. And who at last will doubt this? For (1) the first being does not allow any prior being that would limit his authority and power. (2) Authority and power are undoubtedly among the perfections that involve no imperfection. (3) Through his simplicity, his authority and power coincide with his infinite essence; thus they are also necessarily infinite themselves. (4) All things either do not have their own authority and power, or they have them from the first cause, who cannot but have in a preeminent measure that which he communicates.

What the authority of God is

V. From all these titles and arguments we are taught, first, his authority and then next, his power. These sometimes appear as separate things in creatures, such that you might do by power what you cannot do by right. But in God these coincide, for whatever he can do by authority, or by right, he can also do by power or strength, and vice versa. Nevertheless, they are distinguished in this way: first, the authority of God is his right and universal dominion, independent and most absolute, over all creatures, to make decisions concerning them entirely according to his own judgment. For this right belongs to him (Rom. 1:32; 9:20–21; Matt. 20:15), a right by which all things are his own, as much with respect to their ownership as to their use:[7] heaven and earth (1 Chron. 29:11–16), the earth and all its fullness (Ps. 24:1), the beasts of the field (Ps. 50:10–11), gold and silver (Hag. 2:9), and chiefly man (Rom. 14:8), and in particular, his body and his soul (1 Cor. 6:20; Ezek. 18:4).

Its foundation and titles

VI. The foundation of this right is in the preeminence of deity alone, by which he stands a thousand leagues above all things (Isa. 40:17, 22–23), and thus has them as if under his feet (Isa. 66:1). For given this preeminence alone, it is manifest

---

7. *tam* κτήσει *quam* χρήσει

that his right and authority are even over things that are not yet manifest, that is, to make them exist according to his will, and to exist at the time and with the qualities that he appoints. Meanwhile, the titles he has to this authority can be plural, namely, (1) creation, by which he obtains a right over all things, as an artisan over his work (Jer. 18:6); (2) preservation, and every kindness, by which he obligates the creature to gratitude to him (Deut. 32:6); furthermore, particularly in rational creatures, (3) redemption (1 Cor. 6:19–20; Titus 2:14); (4) covenant, by which we give ourselves to God (2 Cor. 8:5; Rom. 12:1; Ps. 116:16); and even (5) sin, on account of which he certainly does not receive the right to punish, but exercises it (Rom. 1:32)—this right is also called the righteous requirement of the law (Rom. 8:4).

Its objects

VII. The authority of this right extends itself to everything: (1) to possible things, such that whichever of them he wills are brought to pass (Ps. 115:3)—indeed, they come to pass exactly in the way he wills (Jer. 18:6)—and the rest remain as merely possible to him (Lam. 3:37); (2) to all things that exist (1 Chron. 29:11–16), all the way to kingdoms and empires (Dan. 2:21); (3) to rational creatures, which he guides not only by physical motion where he wills, without their knowledge, as he does with the irrational creatures (Prov. 21:1), but also by moral motion, prescribing the things that must be done and avoided, so that with knowledge and willingness they might comply (Rom. 6:6); and especially (4) to the elect (John 17:9–10), by acquired right, so to speak.

Its exercise and action

VIII. God exercises the right of this authority over all these things, first in general, by making decisions concerning them entirely according to his own judgment (Ps. 115:3; Matt. 20:15), and yet in different ways: (1) in the case of possible things, when from them he brings to actuality the ones he wills, and just as he wills, even by making from the same lump a vessel for honor or for dishonor (Rom. 9:21). (2) In the case of existing things, when he sustains them as long as he wills (Ps. 90:3), he destines and applies them to the use that he wills (2 Tim. 2:20), he transfers kingdoms and wealth to whom and in what way he wills (Dan. 2:21; Ex. 11:2), he fixes the boundary of life and death (Job 14:5) and prolongs life according to his pleasure (Isa. 38:5). (3) In the case of rational things, when he chooses, reprobates, redeems, calls, regenerates, converts, justifies, sanctifies, glorifies, and condemns whom he wills (Eph. 1:5; Rom. 9:18, 21; Matt. 11:25–26), and furthermore, when he prescribes them laws, sanctions those laws, and once sanctioned, exhibits and executes them as he wills; indeed, when he reckons children as standing in their parents and imputes the sins of parents to their children (Rom. 5:12, 14, 16–19; Ex. 20:5; Lam. 5:7), just as also when he grants the righteousness of one to many (Rom. 5:12). (4) In the case of the elect, when he dispenses his gifts as he wills (1 Cor. 12:8–11).

Its properties

IX. Finally, this authority is: (1) independent and eternal, because it rests upon his deity, and does not receive anything from the creature that it might be repaid to it (Rom. 11:35–36). Although the exercise of authority sometimes implies a prerequisite, as punishment implies sin, yet from this prerequisite there is nothing added to increase the authority of God, just as crimes do not increase the authority of a judge, though that authority presupposes a criminal. Indeed, whatever authority there is, whoever obtains it does not obtain it from any other place than from this source of authority (Rom. 13:1; Col. 1:16; James 4:12). So then, it is (2) infinite, unlimited, most absolute, and entirely autonomous.[8] For who would limit or restrict the absolutely first being (Rom. 9:19)? Who would speak against him (Rom. 9:20; Matt. 20:22–23)? And it is also (3) unique to God and incommunicable, because it rests in the preeminence of his deity, although he has handed over mediatorial and economic authority, as it concerns the church, to the Son (Matt. 28:18; Eph. 1:20–23).

What the power of God is

X. Second comes power, or strength, by which he is able to work the things he does not will, and he does work all the things he wills. Accordingly, to him belongs not a power by which he is passively worked upon (for he would be worked upon by another being that would be, for that reason, prior to him, and he also would be mutable), but a power by which he works or produces something. Nor does power belong to him insofar as it is distinguished from act,[9] as if by working he should turn from being idle to being busy, for he is most pure act, but rather, insofar as the creature, which before did not undergo the working of God, now by his will does undergo it, with no change from this arising in the worker, but rather in the work. Just as in the case of the sun, which warms a man whom it did not warm before, no change occurs except in the man, who before did not undergo the sun's rays and now does undergo them. Nor also does a power belong to God that is in reality different from his will, although it

---

8. αὐτεξούσιος

9. When *potentia*, "power," is contrasted with *actus*, "act," it is sometimes also translated as "potency" or "potential."

is distinguished from it in our thought. For we conceive of a power that precedes his will, a power by which he is simply able to do things, and this coincides with the sufficiency of his essence (Rom. 11:23), and also of a power that follows his will, which in its own way is posterior to his sufficiency and looks toward his efficiency, insofar as what he wills, he executes (Ps. 115:3; 135:6). Thus we should conceive of it in this order: we think that God first can, then knows he can, next wills what he knows he can, and last, powerfully effects what he wills, and accordingly, what he wills does not differ in reality from his power. And this is taught by the syllogism of faith in Matthew 8:2–3, "'Lord, if you will to heal, you can.' 'I will,'" and therefore it was done, where an argument is made from the will that accedes to power.[10]

It extends to all things.

XI. This power of God extends to all things, from which he is called omnipotent or almighty (2 Cor. 6:18; Rev. 1:8), since he can do all that he wills (Ps. 115:3) and more than he wills (Matt. 3:9; 26:53), such that no one and nothing can resist him (Rom. 9:19). And he can do all these things without difficulty or weariness (Isa. 40:28), indeed, even things that are impossible for nature (Matt. 19:26). Yet the things that are impossible *by nature*, God cannot do through his omnipotence, for it implies that God can cause to be done what cannot be done. Moreover, what is impossible by nature involves a contradiction, and whereas such a contradiction cannot be a being, it also cannot be a work of power. Moreover, a contradiction is involved either on the part of God, when a work would speak of an imperfection in the most perfect worker, as when he were said to be able to lie or deceive; or on the part of the thing, when the thing would overturn itself, as would a triangle that did not have three angles. Both kinds of contradictions are impossible to God, for they imply that by which God would deny himself (2 Tim. 2:13), or say that he was not God. For if, for example, he should lie, he would be implying that he was not the most perfect being, and thus not God. Not only must this be accepted concerning the prior kind of contradiction, but also concerning the latter kind. For if God made a triangle which did not have three angles, he would have another idea of a triangle than he has, and thus he would be otherwise than what he is, and consequently he would be implying that he is not the same as he used to be, and since he was God then, he would be implying that he is not God now.

---

10. *a voluntate arguitur, ad potentiam accedente.* Cf. §XX below. The *voluntas accedens ad potentiam* "accedes to power" in the sense that it immediately precedes and undertakes to do a particular act of power.

What is the root of impossibility?

XII. Accordingly, that God cannot do impossible things does not result from some lack of power, but rather from an abundance of it. For if he could do impossible things, such as lie or sin, he could be non-omnipotent. For this reason we say that God is unable by his power, that is, most powerfully unable, not unable through infirmity. And we say even more accurately that a thing cannot be done that God cannot do. Moreover, a thing cannot be done because it is repugnant either to the divine nature and perfection, or to the divine will and decree, or to the divine majesty, or to itself. Moreover, we say that God is able to do by his power what is possible, not as if it were by nature possible prior to God's ability to do it, for in that way, the power of God would depend upon it, but rather because a thing is possible based on the fact that God can do it. In the same way, vice versa, God cannot do this or that, not because it is impossible; rather, it is impossible because God cannot do it. Thus the root and foundation of possibility and impossibility is not in things but in the power of God.

Absolute and ordained power

XIII. Even though power is one and most simple in God, for it is his essence itself, we nevertheless customarily distinguish it into absolute power, insofar as we conceive it as preceding his will (Eph. 3:20; Mark 5:27); and ordained power, insofar as we conceive it as following his will. Through the latter, not only is he already able if he wills, but also, he effects what he wills (Ps. 135:6).

The properties of divine power

XIV. Finally, from what has been said, the power of God is: (1) his very essence or powerful deity, for in God, there is not one thing and another thing. From this, it is (2) infinite, not only in itself, insofar as it is the omnipotent God himself (Gen. 17:1), nor only from the perfection of its working, insofar as whatever it works, it works by a mere nod (Ps. 33:9; Isa. 40:28; Eph. 1:19; Phil. 3:21), but also from its object (Luke 1:37), insofar as it extends to all possible things (in the same way as God's intellect, on account of its infinity, extends to all intelligible things). Nor does God ever effect so much through his power without being able to effect more (Eph. 3:20). For although all things that he can do cannot exist simultaneously, because in that way something infinite in actuality would exist besides him, and his power would be emptied, as it were, and accordingly he would not be infinite, nevertheless, God does not lack the power by which he could produce such infinite actuality, if its existence were not repugnant to the nature of things. It is (3) independent, such that he can work through means, without means, and against means (1 Sam. 14:6). Lastly, it is (4) eternal

(Rom. 1:20), for even though from eternity he did not work beyond himself, nevertheless, he had power from eternity, and he had the same power by which, when he willed, he worked to make the world. And by this power, he could have produced a world from eternity, if only the world could have existed from eternity.

The Elenctic Part

It is asked: 1. Is the foundation of divine authority in the eminence of deity alone?
The opinion of the Remonstrants
XV. It is asked, first, whether the foundation of all divine authority over human beings is creation, covenant, kindness, and sin. The Remonstrants, that they might more effectively reject the eternal reprobation of not yet created or fallen man, affirm that all the authority of God over man rests either in creation, through which, just as a potter, he has authority over the clay (Jer. 18:6; Rom. 9:20); or in covenant, by which man binds himself to God; or in sin, by which man made himself guilty; or in kindness, because of which he is obligated to gratitude. And since none of these obtain from eternity, they claim that God also had no authority to reprobate a person.

And the opinion of the Reformed with their reasons
The Reformed distinguish between authority itself and its exercise, in such a way that God has authority from the infinite eminence[11] of his deity, or because he is God, and the supreme Lord of all things, whereas for the exercise of this authority there are various prerequisites, namely, the existence of an object through creation, of sin so that he may punish it, of kindness so that it may express gratitude, and a covenant so that it may claim what is promised. But the authority of God does not result from any other thing than from his deity, which is evident from these reasons: (1) because Scripture testifies that God had authority over Jacob and Esau when they were not yet created, not yet existing, not yet covenanted to him, not yet liable to sin, before the boys had been born or had done anything good or evil; he had authority over them, indeed an authority to elect or reject them (Rom. 9:11–13), and likewise to show mercy or not show mercy, or even to harden (Rom. 9:15, 18), that is to say, just as a potter has authority over the clay, to make from the same lump a vessel for honor or for dishonor (Rom. 9:21). Next, (2) if he should receive authority from something, he would not be independent, nor infinite, and thus there would be in God something

---

11. ἐξοχῇ

dependent, something finite, which would day by day grow stronger and become greater. And since (3) authority and power are, through God's supreme simplicity, God himself, his powerful essence, it would follow that the divine essence could admit increments. Also, (4) from eternity he had authority to decree, from infinitely many possible things, these things rather than those, that they might pass into futurity. Finally, (5) in the civil forum, the judge does not receive authority to punish the criminal from the criminal or from the crime, but rather, only opportunity for the exercise of his authority, the right of which he already had before.

The objections of the Remonstrants

Nor is it valid to argue on the contrary that: (1) a son, for example, may surpass his father in learning, wisdom, virtue, or strength, and yet from these it does not follow that he has authority over his own father, and in the same way, God does not obtain authority over man from the preeminence of deity alone, apart from his creation of man, man's sin, etc. For there is a different reason for this authority: the father has an authority over the son that is derived from his paternity, and the son cannot take it away from him by any of his own prerogatives. In the same way, (2) assume that in an aristocracy or democracy there is a person who surpasses all his fellow citizens in wisdom, honesty, and the other virtues; even so, he does not by this fact obtain the authority to command his fellow citizens. For the reason for the difference is in this, that the authority of commanding is conferred by God (Rom 13:1–3). Although at the same time, if those citizens have authority to elect the magistrate, then from the divine precept, they are bound to choose the best and most suitable person to rule (Ex. 18:21). Furthermore, (3) though to the angels belongs an excellence and eminence beyond all mankind, nevertheless there does not belong authority over man, because God did not confer such authority upon angels. In particular, (4) authority does not accrue to God from creation, because then he would have created infinitely more things so that his authority would be rendered greater, although the authority which he had from eternity, which he possessed from the eminence of his deity, he could not exercise in actuality unless an object first existed through creation. (5) The evil or sin of the creature does not procure for the Creator the authority to punish, just as it does not procure it for the civil judge, although it is the demeritorious cause of the punishment. And (6) nearly the same can be said regarding the covenant, for it does increase the obligation of the one who is covenanted to render what he promised, but it does not establish the authority of God over the one who promises. Finally, neither is it valid to argue that (7) God by his reprobation does injury to the reprobate who does not yet exist when he destines him for the glory of his avenging justice, especially since he does not punish him except because of his own intervening sin and demerit.

2. Can God through his authority decree unequal things for equal persons?
XVI. It is asked, second, whether God through his authority can, without respect of persons[12] or hint of injustice, decree unequal things for equal persons. The Remonstrants, Lutherans, and others, that they might more easily suspend the whole business of election and reprobation upon foreseen faith and unbelief, and find in foreseen things a certain inequality according to which God has decreed unequal things, deny that he can.

The arguments of the Reformed
The Reformed affirm that he can because: (1) Scripture affirms it (Rom. 9:11–23; Jer. 18:6). (2) Both those who are equal and those who are unequal compared to each other, are in equal measure his possession, concerning which he can make decisions according to his choice (Matt. 20:15). (3) The authority of God is infinite and most absolute, and neither the equality nor inequality of creatures can limit it (Rom. 9:20–21). Especially since (4) he is not subject either to a law or legislator by which his power may be restricted (James 4:12). And (5) to decree something, since it is an immanent act of God,[13] does not affect the creature either for good or for evil, inasmuch as from eternity it does not yet exist (Rom. 9:11), nor does he dispense evil except after sin has been committed.

Objections of our adversaries
If they should say, (1) In such a decree there is a respect of persons, we will say that a vicious respect of persons is nothing other than conferring unequal things upon the sort of equals to whom you are bound by the command of a superior to confer equal things. But God does not acknowledge a superior who commands him, nor is he obligated in any way whatsoever to confer equal things (Rom. 11:35–36). If they should say, (2) There is injustice in this, if to whom equal things belong you should render unequal things, we will say that injustice is when you do not render to each what is his own, but the creature, in respect to its Creator, properly has nothing that is his own (1 Cor. 4:6; John 3:27; James 1:17–18). Compare what has been said on this topic in chapter 18, §X.

---

12. προσωποληψίας
13. An immanent act (*actus immanens*) is typically contrasted with a transient act (*actus transiens*), the difference being that an immanent act has its terminus in the subject whereas a transient act has its terminus in the object. Cf. 1.3.1 §VII.

3. Can God through his authority punish the sins of parents in their children?
The thought of our adversaries and of the Reformed, with their reasons
XVII. It is asked, third, whether God through his authority can punish the sins
of parents in their children. The Pelagians and Pelagianizers, who do not accept
the imputation of the first sin, such as the Socinians of our day, simply deny
that he can. The Reformed distinguish between the first sin of our first parents
and the subsequent sins that have been committed by our near parents or by
parents of prior generations. Now the first sin God certainly can punish in all
posterity, and also does actually punish, because of the fact that it was the sin
of the whole human nature. But the subsequent, or personal, sins God does not
indeed always punish in the children, though nevertheless, he can, and then especially when the children either are prone to the same sin of their parents, when
they approve of it, or when they in some way make themselves participants in
it. Yet at the same time, he never punishes, on account of parents' sin, children
who are entirely innocent. The Reformed affirm that God can do this because
(1) Scripture expressly speaks this way in Exodus 20:5, "…visiting the sins of the
parents on the children to the third and the fourth generation of those who hate
me." Whether you should refer that hatred to the parents or to their generations,
there is at least attributed to God an authority to visit, that is, to punish, the sins
of the parents in their children. The same is said in Exodus 34:7. (2) The first
sin of the first parents is the sin of the whole human nature, and it came into the
world, and death through it (Rom. 5:12). (3) The independent, most absolute
authority of God extends as much to children as to their parents, and then especially when they imitate the sins of their parents, or approve of them, or show
that they are prone to the same thing. (4) Children are just as much sinners as
their parents, and thus are liable to infinite punishment, and from this, according
to our adversaries themselves, the authority belongs to God to avenge in them
the sins of their parents also. I will also add (5) that children, according to the
thought of those skilled in law, are parts of their parents, and therefore parents
may be punished in their children.

Objections

It does not help our adversaries (1) that God declares that he does not will
to punish the sins of the parents in their children (Ezek. 18:20). For it speaks
(a) through this whole chapter about innocent children (18:14–18), whom God
does not will to punish on account of the sins of the father, although from his
most absolute authority, he could. It speaks (b) about the personal sins of parents, which God ordinarily does not will to punish in their children, but not
about the first sin, which is a sin of the whole human nature. It speaks (c) against

the calumny of the Jews, who accused God of injustice, saying that they were being punished on account of their parents' sins alone, and not on account of their own sins.[14] God responds that he does not have need to punish them on account of another's sins: there is a sufficient weight of sins in them on account of which they may be justly punished, and accordingly he does not will to punish the sins of the parents in them. However, he does not say that he could not do so if he so willed. (2) That it seems to breathe of injustice to punish the sin of one in another, since justice renders to each his own. For it breathes injustice only when the one punished is entirely innocent, but not when through his own sins he is already liable to God's avenging justice, and that for infinite punishment. We already dealt with other questions considering the authority of God in chapter 18, on the righteousness of God,[15] to which the authority of God is at least closely related, if not the same thing, insofar as authority is nothing but the faculty of acting according to right.

4. Does passive power occur in God?

XVIII. It is asked about the power of God, fourth, whether passive power occurs in God, a power by which he could suffer good or evil from the creatures.[16] Conrad Vorstius and the Socinians, that they might have a God who depends upon human choice and is changed hour by hour according to its pleasure, affirm that it does. The Reformed deny that it does, because (1) Scripture denies that God can receive anything from the creatures, whether good or evil (Ps. 16:2; Job 22:2; 37:7; Ps. 50:9–11; Rom. 11:35; Zech. 7:5), because (2) in that way he would have someone prior to himself by whom he would suffer, and thus would not be the absolutely first being (Isa. 44:1; Rev. 21:6). (3) He would not be independent, and accordingly, not God. (4) He would not be immutable, for that which suffers is changed. (5) He would be corruptible, since he who suffers is changed into either something better, or something equally good, or something worse, in which case he is corrupted. And as there is nothing better than God, nor anything equally good, nothing would remain but for him to be changed into something worse, and thus, to be corrupted. Nor is it valid to argue on the contrary that he is served by virtue and offended by sin, for neither virtue nor vice touch his essence so that it suffers, but rather they touch his law, and only in that sense do they touch the Lawgiver. But these controversies belong to the

---

14. Ezek. 18:2
15. 1.2.18 §§IX–XVI
16. See n. 9, above.

chapter on the immutability of God, where we have considered more questions of this sort.[17]

5. Is the power of God infinite in itself or only with respect to us?
The thought of the Socinians
XIX. It is asked, fifth, whether the power of God is infinite in itself, excluding all limits, or only with respect to us. Vorstius and the Socinians—because they teach a finite God, who as far as his essence does not extend beyond heaven, and whom we cannot define—state that the power of God is called infinite, not because it has no limits, but because it has limits that exceed the power of creatures, and we cannot attain to its limits with our mind.

And of the Reformed with their reasons
The Reformed teach that the power of God is in itself infinite, and absolutely and simply so, inasmuch as (1) not only can it do above all that we ask or think (Eph. 3:20–21), but also, it can simply do all things (Phil. 3:21; Luke 1:37), as he is the Almighty (2 Cor. 6:18; Rev. 1:8; 4:8), which does not describe one who is unable to do something. And for this reason he is called the only Potentate (1 Tim. 6:15) and the mighty God (Isa. 9:6; cf. §III). (2) It is the "exceeding greatness of his power," to which belongs "the working of the power of his might" (Eph 1:19). (3) It coincides, by God's omnimodal simplicity, with his essence, which we have demonstrated in chapter 9 to be absolutely infinite.[18] (4) If it were finite in itself and simply, then surely someone would exist who had limited it, and he would be prior to and more powerful than God himself. And surely, (5) all with one voice agree that it is more perfect to be able to do all things simply than only relatively, and likewise to have an absolutely infinite power than a limitedly infinite power, infinite only with respect to us, and thus the latter cannot belong to the most perfect being. Not to mention that (6) if we should conceive of a power that is not infinite in itself and simply, it could not be said that he has power so infinite that it exceeds our mind and understanding.

Objections
Nor is what they object to the contrary valid: (1) that the power of God is constrained and restricted by his will, since (a) not his power itself, but rather its exercise with respect to objects, is restricted through his most free will (Ps. 33:9; 115:3), and it must be restricted, lest there arise two infinite things, and

---

17. 1.2.7 §§VI–VIII
18. 1.2.9 §§III, VI

consequently, none. And thus (b) the power restricted by his will is not the power by which he is simply able, which the question for us here concerns, but the power by which he operates, that is, his executive power. (2) That the intellect of God exceeds his power, insofar as he knows more than he can produce: for example, he knows himself, and he knows infinite things that he cannot produce. I respond: (a) God's intellect and power, on account of his supreme simplicity, are on God's part one and the same, though his intellect extends itself to more objects than his power. (b) Just as his intellect extends to all knowable things, so also his power extends to all possible things, without any disparity. (c) Although God's ordained power, seeing that it is restricted by the divine will, does not extend to all possible things, even so his absolute power does extend to all possible things, which are infinitely many. (3) That God cannot do contradictory things—he cannot deny himself, he cannot lie, and so forth—and accordingly his power is not simply infinite. I respond, All those things are not objects of some power, but rather objects of impotence. For to be able to lie, to sin, to deny himself, and so forth, do not speak of power and perfection, but rather of impotence and defect. Accordingly, the power of God would by no means be infinite if it could do those things. So judges Augustine in *On the Creed* (ch. 1): "God, because he is omnipotent, cannot die, cannot be deceived, cannot lie. For if he could die, he would not be omnipotent; if he could lie, deceive, be deceived, behave iniquitously, he would not be omnipotent. For if these things were in him, he would not be worthy to be omnipotent."[19] See also our chapter on the infinity of God.[20]

6. Does God will to do anything through his omnipotence
that he does not bring into effect?
XX. It is asked, sixth, whether God wills many things to happen that through his omnipotence he does not do. The Pelagians and Socinians, because they uphold the independence of free choice and the idea that its strength was entirely uninjured by the first sin, so that they might obtain that God earnestly wills the perfect observance of the law and the eternal salvation of each and every person, if only they should will it, state that not all that God wills to be done through his omnipotence is actually done. The semi-Pelagians, and likewise the Jesuits, Arminians, and all others who uphold an antecedent and conditioned will, or willingness, of God, and likewise the idea that the strength of free choice was

---

19. Augustine, *De symbolo ad catechumenos tractatus IV*, bk. 1 in *PL* 40:629; idem, *On the Creed* in *NPNF1* 3:369.
    20. 1.2.9 §VI

certainly wounded but not extinguished by the sin of our first parents, so that they may hold that notwithstanding God earnestly wills that each and every one be saved, state that he wills many things through his omnipotence that he never brings into effect. The Lutherans, although they acknowledge that the strength of free choice for spiritual good has been entirely extinguished, yet because they state that men can through the strength of their own choice at least positively not resist the Holy Spirit as he brings forth faith and repentance, by frequently attending holy things, by praying, and so forth, likewise think that God wills many things to happen that by his omnipotence he does not bring into effect.

The opinion of the Reformed together with their reasons
The Reformed, on the contrary, though they hold that God, by his legislative will, or will of precept, wills many things which according to his decretive will he does not bring into effect, state that whatever God wills in order that it might happen, that is what he brings into actual effect by his own omnipotence. They do so since (1) Scripture everywhere testifies that God does whatever he wills (Ps. 115:3). Thus, Paul says in Romans 9:18, "He has mercy on whom he wills, and whom he wills he hardens," and adds also in verse 19, "Who will resist his will?", and likewise in verse 22, "God, willing to show his wrath and power...on the vessels of wrath fitted for destruction." And (2) this is the force of that syllogism of faith which is in Matthew 8:2–3, "'Lord, if you will, you can.' 'I will,'" and therefore it was done. In it the argument proceeds from the will that accedes to power,[21] and from there to the effect. So then (3) the will that accedes to power is the effectual *principium* of the created world: "By your will they exist and were created" (Rev. 4:11); he commands, and whatever there is comes to be (Ps. 33:9). (4) If he did not bring about what he earnestly wills, naturally there would be something resisting and impeding his will, which Scripture denies: "In your hand there is strength and power, and no one is able to withstand you" (2 Chron. 20:6; Rom. 9:19). (5) If anything resisted or impeded his will, there would be, with manifest contradiction, one more powerful than the most powerful. In addition, (6) the independent one would depend upon a dependent one. Also, (7) the dependent one would become independent, and in addition, (8) infinite power would be made finite. (9) The most blessed one would not be blessed in every way, since he could not enjoy his will. And (10) the most perfect one would not be fully perfect, because in the opinion of all, it is more perfect to accomplish what you will than not to accomplish it.

---

21. Cf. §X, above.

Objections

If they should charge to the contrary: (1) "I willed to gather your children…but you were unwilling" (Matt. 23:37), I will respond: (a) The text speaks concerning the will of Christ as a man, not about the will of God, or of Christ as God. (b) Even if it speaks concerning the divine will of Christ, he did also gather children of Jerusalem, even though the Pharisees and all sorts of others were not willing. If they should say, (2) He willed that Pharaoh let Israel go, I will respond, He willed to command, he willed from his command, that it be the duty of Pharaoh, but he did not will that it would be done. If they should charge, (3) He does not will the death of the sinner, but that he turn and live (Ezek. 33:11), I will respond, He does not delight in the death of the sinner in general or in the idea, but rather delights in the conversion of the sinner, and his life. He does so, that is, by his legislative will, insofar as he wills to command repentance for the sinner and to promise him life. If furthermore they should say, (4) He wills that all people would be saved and come to a knowledge of the truth (1 Tim. 2:4), which nevertheless is not done, I will respond: (a) He does not say "all individually," which is the very question, but only "all," that is, "any kind," just as in Luke 11:42 and Mark 1:5, from every lot of persons, as much kings, for whom he orders prayer, as subjects. (b) He wills to prescribe to all the knowledge of the truth, and to that end he promises salvation by his legislative will, but not by his will of decree, such that it would happen in all men, for in that way no one would be damned, contrary to the sentence of Christ (Matt. 20:16).

7. Can God through his absolute power do contradictory things?
XXI. It is asked, seventh, whether God through his absolute power can do contradictory things. The Socinians, so that they may hold that the power of God is not in itself and simply infinite, deny that he can do contradictory things (cf. §XIX). The Weigelian fanatics, on the contrary, hold that because God is omnipotent he can do even those things that are contradictory.[22] Descartes and his followers, because they suspend all possibility and impossibility upon the will of God, distinguish between something contradictory on the part of God and on the part of the thing; they appear to state that the first is entirely impossible; concerning the latter they refrain from determining anything (Descartes, *Responses*, 6 §6; Wittich, *Peaceable Theology*, §§199–201).[23] The Reformed

---

22. E.g. Valentin Weigel (1533–1588), *Theologia Weigelii das ist Oeffentliche Glaubensbekändtnüss* (Frankfurt: Samuel Müller, 1699). For a recent translation of some of Weigel's thought, see Valentin Weigel and Andrew Weeks, *Valentin Weigel: Selected Spiritual Writings* (New York: Paulist Press, 2003).

23. Descartes, *Oeuvres de Descartes*, 7:431–33; Wittich, *Theologia pacifica* (1671), 158–62.

conclude that God cannot do any contradictory things. For (1) if, from their own concession, God cannot do things that are contradictory on his part, or things that are repugnant to his nature, then neither can he do those things that are contradictory on the part of the thing, because by this rationale the mind of God, which coincides with his nature, would hold contradictory ideas, for example, the idea of a man who was not a man. Therefore, things that are contradictory on the part of the thing are also such on the part of God. So then (2) if he could do contradictory things, he would deny himself, contrary to the apostle (2 Tim. 2:13), for he would be what he is not. Also, (3) he could lie, contrary to the Scriptures (Titus 1:2; Heb. 6:18). For if he could do contradictory things, he could also say contradictory things. And finally, what is it to lie except to sustain contradictory things, whether words that contradict the mind, or a mind that contradicts reality? The apostle explains such contradiction in 2 Corinthians 1:17: "that with me there should be yes and no." Indeed, he also expressly places the faithfulness of God and of Christ in this: "For as God is faithful, our word to you was not yes and no. For the Son of God, Jesus Christ…was not yes and no" (vv. 18–19). I will add that (4) by this rationale, contradictory things could also be true, through which all the force of reasoning would fail, inasmuch as it rests wholly on this, its own first principle: the same thing cannot be and not be at the same time. I need not say that (5) it would also happen, as a result of that opinion, that we would be bound to believe by divine faith those things which are "yes and no," or contradictory.

Objections

If our adversaries should say on their own behalf (1) that the will of God is the cause of every reality, every true thing, and every good thing, we rejected this idea when we dealt strongly with another like it in chapter 18, §XI. Now we also add that in a contradiction and in contradictory things, there is no reality, but rather the negation of all reality, for we do not demonstrate the falsity of some opinion more solidly than by showing that it involves a contradiction. If they should say (2) that the infinite power of God extends to all reality, (a) we have already denied that there is any reality in a contradiction and in contradictory things; (b) if there is, Weigel and his enthusiasts succeeded when they attempted to conclude from the infinite power of God that God can do contradictory things. If they should say (3) that a finite creature cannot and ought not determine what God through his infinite power can or cannot not do, we will answer them: (a) So also our adversaries could not and ought not determine that God cannot do the things that are repugnant to the nature of God, or which imply a contradiction on the part of God. (b) The finite creature cannot and ought not determine what God can or cannot do through his infinite power, unless God and the nature of God have determined it already, for example, to deny himself and to lie. Whoever desires more of this sort of arguments can refer to our *Gangrene of the Cartesian Innovations* (section 2, ch. 11), and especially also the *Rationale theologicum* of Vedel (bk. 3, ch. 8).[24]

8. Can God through his power produce a body infinite in mass?
The thought of the Cartesians and of the Reformed, with their reasons
XXII. It is asked, eighth, whether God through his power can produce a body infinite in mass. The Cartesians, so that they may hold that the universe is indefinite, that in this way it might be uncertain whether it is infinite or not, do acknowledge that God could not produce a thing infinite in perfection, but they entirely affirm that he could produce a thing infinite in extension and number. The Reformed deny that God can produce a thing infinite in any way, because (1) by this rationale, there would exist more than one infinite, and thus none, for either one would have the infinity of another and thus they would make only one infinite, or it would not have that infinity, and thus no infinite would exist. (2) By this rationale, infinity would not be an attribute proper to God, contrary to Jeremiah 23:24, nor from that infinity of Christ by which he was simultaneously in heaven and on earth (John 3:13) would we rightly infer that his deity is consubstantial[25] with the Father. (3) By this rationale, it could happen that the flesh of Christ is infinite and omnipresent, and therefore the arguments of the Reformed asserting the contrary against the Ubiquitarians are vain. (4) Through this hypothesis, God would have formed something to which nothing could be added, and therefore by one infinite thing his omnipotence would have been exhausted. (5) By the same rationale, whatever the Cartesians cry out to the contrary, God also could make a thing infinite in perfection, for since extension, mass, and body are without doubt a certain sort of perfection, it could not but be true that a thing infinite in mass is also infinite in perfection. (6) It is incompatible for something to be created and yet in some way infinite, for when it is created, it is made finite. And thus what is not finite is not created. For this reason, if there can be several infinite things, whatever sort they are, there also can be several uncreated things, and thus likewise several independent things, yet none of which is the absolutely first being and, consequently, none of which is God.

---

24. Mastricht, *Gangraena*, 257–69; Nicolaus Vedel (1596–1642), *Rationale theologicum* (Geneva, 1628), 620–54.
25. ὁμοούσιον

Objections

The bases for the contrary opinion are generally: (1) that the will of God, from eternity indifferent to anything, is the cause of all possibility, from which it cannot but follow that if God had willed or would will that a thing infinite in extension or number actually exist, that thing would by that very fact have been possible. We have already rejected this basis in chapter 18, §XI. We do not add anything except this: What if we should say the same about a thing infinite in perfection? If God had willed it to be possible for something infinite in perfection to exist alongside of himself, then would it not then have been made possible? And thus there could be two or even more things that are infinite in perfection. (2) That the same will of God, indifferent from eternity, is the cause of everything true, as Descartes holds in *Responses*, 6 §6.[26] Thus it would occur that although something were most contradictory or repugnant to the nature of God, if only God had willed it or would will it, it would not be contradictory or repugnant to the nature of God. (3) That God can, through his absolute power, do what is repugnant to the nature of things and thus, what is contradictory. Therefore it would occur that even though a thing infinite in extension or number were especially repugnant and contradictory, even so, God could do it. All these hypotheses we have already routed (cf. *Gangrene of the Cartesian Innovations*, ch. 7).[27]

9. Can God deceive if he wills?

XXIII. It is asked, ninth, whether God can deceive if he wills. This question can have various proper places, namely, in the chapter on the truthfulness of God, insofar as it is repugnant to him to deceive; in the chapter on the will of God, insofar as it regards the condition, "if he wills"; and in the chapter on the power of God, insofar as it speaks of his being able under this condition. But seeing that we have aired this question in both its parts in the chapter on the truthfulness of God,[28] there is no use in occupying ourselves with it in this place again; it will suffice to point out that it also applies here.

10. Can the authority and power of God be communicated to the creature?

XXIV. It is asked, tenth, whether the authority and power of God can be communicated to the creature. The Ubiquitarians among the Lutherans,[29] so that

---

26. Descartes, *Oeuvres de Descartes*, 7:431–33.

27. Cf. *TPT* 1.2.18 §XI; 1.2.15 §XXXI. Mastricht, *Gangraena*, 82–91.

28. 1.2.14 §X

29. E.g. Johannes Brenz, *De majestate Domini nostri* (Morhart, 1562). The Würtemberg Confession and its adoption at the Synod of Stuttgart (1559) became a major confessional symbol of the Ubiquitarians until the Formula of Concord.

they may hold that the body of Christ is present in the bread of the Eucharist, state that through the hypostatic union of the two natures in Christ, there has been communicated to his human nature, besides omnipresence, also the divine omnipotence and authority, and since they acknowledge that the human nature is a creature, they state in the same stroke that the authority and power of God can be communicated to the creature. The Reformed deny that the authority and power of God can be communicated to creatures, or that it was communicated to the human nature of Christ, because (1) the authority and power of God are his very essence, which the Lutherans acknowledge, and consequently, the very essence of God would be communicated to the creature and to the human nature of Christ, and through this, the creature and the human nature of Christ could be God, for that which has the essence of God is God. (2) Christ as a man acknowledges one more powerful than himself when he asks to be sustained in his sufferings (Ps. 16:8, 10–11; 22:1–2; Matt. 26:39, 42, 53; Heb. 5:7), and likewise when he, about to perform miracles, turns to the Father with prayers (John 11:42; etc.). (3) He was under passive power with respect to his human nature, which does not square with omnipotence. (4) There would have been communicated to him either an omnipotence different from God, and thus there would be two omnipotences, or the omnipotence of God itself, and thus not only through another's omnipotence would Christ as a man have been omnipotent, but also his human nature would have performed divine operations, insofar as his human operations—eating, drinking, walking—would have been operations of omnipotence. I need not add (5) that from this hypothesis the human nature of Christ would be God, for anyone who works by the same power as the Father is God, from the teaching of Christ (John 5:18–20). Nor is it valid to argue on the contrary (1) that he testifies that all authority in heaven and on earth has been given to him (Matt. 28:18). For he is not speaking about divine omnipotence but about the mediatorial authority by which he is able, in those matters which regard the church, to do all things in heaven and earth, which is evident from the words immediately following: "All authority has been given to me…. Go therefore and teach all nations…." (2) That as head of the church, he ought to be omnipotent according to his human nature, because otherwise he could not defend her against the gates of hell and the world. For to this end it is sufficient that his whole person is omnipotent. (3) That he performed miracles according to his human nature. For the whole omnipotent person performed miracles, not properly the human nature.

11. Do those who deny that God can make a body infinite and omnipresent
deny or abridge the omnipotence of God? A comparison of opinions
XXV. It is asked, eleventh, whether those who deny that God can make a body infinite and omnipresent, or existing in separate places simultaneously, deny or abridge the omnipotence of God? Weigel and his enthusiasts, or fanatics, because they state that God in his infinite power can also do contradictory things, when they hear our theologians resist this, cry out that we deny the omnipotence of God, just as we mentioned in §XXI. Descartes, since he states, as we have said elsewhere, that everything possible and impossible, true and false, good and evil, depends upon the indifferent will of God, states that God can do contradictory things; and when they hear our theologians assert the opposite, Cartesians are forced by their hypotheses to conclude that we insult the infinite power of God. The papists, so that they may more securely hold that the body of Christ is present in all their masses, though separated by the distance between so many places, thus take refuge in the omnipotence of God when they hear our theologians resist this view because it involves a contradiction: they likewise snarl that we insult the omnipotence of God. The Ubiquitarians, so that they may hold that the body of Christ is present in the elements of the Lord's Supper, think that his body, from the personal union of his two natures, is omnipresent; when they hear that this view involves a contradiction and various absurdities which we will show in book 7, chapter 5, §§XXI–XXII, they take refuge in the omnipotence of God and, immediately seeking to denigrate our theologians who deny that God can do this because it involves a contradiction, cry out that they either deny or insult the omnipotence of God. And, what is a quite manifest indication of a hopeless cause, Johann Gerhard, in his *Loci theologici*, states, "Those things that imply a contradiction and cannot be done with respect to human power and knowledge do not immediately imply a contradiction and are not immediately impossible with respect to divine power."[30]

The opinion of the Reformed
The Reformed frankly acknowledge God's infinite power, and that by it he can do everything that does not imply a contradiction. When they deny that he can make a body omnipresent or simultaneously present in several separate places, because these things connote a contradiction, they do not deny or insult the omnipotence of God. For even our adversaries themselves, the Lutherans and the papists, commonly acknowledge that God cannot do contradictory things,

---

30. Johann Gerhard, *Loci Theologici*, ed. E. Preuss (Berlin: Gustavus Schlawitz, 1863–75), 1–2:335–36.

if perhaps you leave out Arnoldus Veronius among the papists and Mentzer or Chemnitz[31] among the Lutherans. And if someone else should state that God can do things that are contradictory, he is stating either that the things that are contradictory according to reason are not always contradictory according to God and Scripture, or that a judgment of contradiction does not belong to reason in the mysteries of the faith, concerning which one can see Vedel in his *Rationale theologicum* (bk. 3, ch. 7–8).[32] Therefore it must not be shouted that we deny or insult the divine omnipotence, but rather, it must be shown that an infinite body, or a body that simultaneously coexists in different places, does not connote a contradiction.

The Practical Part

The authority and power of God: 1. Urges us to acknowledge it,
in particular over ourselves.

XXVI. The practice of this chapter urges that first we should more and more strive to acknowledge the authority and power of God, in particular over ourselves, and to be persuaded of it. For to this end God teaches his authority and power over everything in general (Ps. 24:1; Ezek. 28:4) and in particular presses upon his people to reflect upon his authority over them (Deut. 32:6, 9–10), just as Paul presses it upon the Corinthians (1 Cor. 6:20), and the psalmist does upon himself (Ps. 116:16). I say that we should strive to confess promptly and frankly (1) that God cannot for any cause whatsoever, except for his own gracious promise, be a debtor to us for any kindness, because we and all that we have are his (Luke 17:10; Rom. 11:35). (2) That God, in deciding concerning us whatever he may, does not do us any injury, because however much we are, we are his own possession (Jer. 18:6; Matt. 20:13–14). For this reason, we will be (1) more prompt to give thanks in favorable circumstances (Rom. 11:35–36; 1 Cor. 15:10); (2) more patient in adverse circumstances (Ps. 39:9; 1 Sam. 3:18); (3) more confident in whatever future event, whether it be favorable or adverse (Ps. 27:7; 130:6; Job 13:15). And this will be so, namely, if we should think that to him belongs at least as much—nay, infinitely more—power over us than to a potter over his clay (Jer. 18:6; Isa. 45:9; Rom. 9:20–21), or than belongs to us over the brute beasts, over little worms.

---

31. Balthasar Mentzer (1565–1627), *Disputationes theologicae*, 9 vols. (Giessen: Hampnel, 1610–1671); Martin Chemnitz (1522–1586), *Loci theologici*, 8 vols. (Frankfurt: Tobias Mevius and Elerdius Schumacher, 1653), 38–41.

32. Vedel, *Rationale theologicum*, 554–653.

2. It forms us to patience.

XXVII. In specific, second, the divine authority and power forms us to patience, silence,[33] and acquiescence in God: (1) if we are vexed by the public fortune of the church, her most unjust lot, the multitude of her enemies, their power, and their insolence, to consider that (a) to God belongs a most absolute right over the church, which is his kingdom, his people, and his own possession. (b) He will not be sluggish or negligent in caring for the things that are his own (Ps. 121:3–4). Accordingly, (c) when it seems to him appropriate and fitting, first for his own glory and then for the church, he is able with no trouble by his omnipotence to give her aid, to change her lot, to scatter all her foes, however many and however great (Ps. 81:14–15). And at the least, (d) by his omnipotence he never will permit his own possession to be brought to utter loss, or wholly subjugated to her foes, as if the gates of hell should boast over her (Matt. 16:18; Ps. 46:1; 110:1–2). (2) If any private calamity, disease, lack, or persecution presses hard upon us, what helps bring us more effectively to silence and to solace than to think that (a) he is our Lord, under whose authority we are, as clay under the authority of the potter (Jer. 18:6), and he can make decisions concerning us, as his possession, based entirely on his own judgment (Ps. 39:10; Lev. 10:3)? But also that (b) he is the Father Almighty, who can change our fortune if only he should will (Matt. 8:2–3), and no doubt he shall will, when once the proper time has come, once it is fitting first for his own glory, then for our salvation (John 2:4; Ps. 27:14)? (3) If there is a lack of necessary strength in matters bodily as much as spiritual, what will benefit us more effectively than to think that God our Father is almighty, and his grace is sufficient for us (2 Cor. 12:9–10; Phil. 4:12–13)? And in particular, (4) if the power of spiritual enemies, considered in light of our infirmity, should vex us, what will sustain us more effectively than the omnipotence of the Father, whose own possession we are (John 10:28–29; Eph. 6:10)? And last, (5) if in all things, our affairs seem to have come to utter loss and to despair, what will console us more effectively than to think that God, whose own possession we are, is able to do with infinite overabundance beyond what we ask or think (Eph. 3:20; 1:19; Rom. 4:20–21)?

3. It forms us to self-denial.

XXVIII. Third, it forms us to self-denial to think that through the most absolute authority and power of God, (1) there is on earth no absolute dominion and right of ownership, because all men themselves depend on God, nor is there anything that we, according to its whole, have brought forth from nothing

---

33. ἐχεμυθίαν

(Ps. 24:1; Hag. 2:8–9). (2) The dominion and right of ownership that we have is only derivative, like that of stewards and treasurers,[34] and communicated by God (Hos. 2:8; John 19:11). And (3) it is communicated, certainly not that we might enjoy it for the sake of our passion, as our own possession, but that we might use it, as we use instruments, for the sake of God and his affairs, like laborers and stewards who will give account to God of the tools entrusted to them. So then (1) more than any other sin we must beware lest we believe that we are our own by right (1 Cor. 6:19), and perfect masters of our own affairs (Ps. 12:4). And also (2) we must beware lest we spend ourselves and our possessions, whatever they may be, upon ourselves and for our own honor, desire, and convenience, which, according to the Scriptures, is to live for ourselves (2 Cor. 5:15; Rom. 14:7). (3) In addition, we must beware, no matter how well-off we are, lest we squander the least of our goods, or spend them in vain, because they are God's goods and not our own (Hos. 2:8–9). On the contrary, (4) let us deny ourselves (Luke 9:23) and crucify the flesh and its desires (Gal. 5:24; Col. 3:5).

It rouses us: 4. To surrender ourselves and our goods to God
XXIX. On the other hand, fourth, the infinite authority and power of God moves us promptly to surrender and devote our whole selves and all our goods to God, whose they are (2 Cor. 8:5). Not because this confers anything for augmenting or establishing God's right, but because it makes for our advantage if we freely own this right of God by our consent. Indeed all men, down to the worst (John 1:11), and even down to unclean spirits, belong to God, and bend their knees to him (Phil. 2:10), though unwilling; believers alone freely and promptly acknowledge and declare it (Song 2:16; 6:3; Ps. 116:16), and having entered into covenant with God, receive, as it were, his name (Ezek. 16:8; Mal. 3:17). Specifically, let us devote to God (1) our body (Rom 12:1), (2) our soul (Prov. 23:26), which are (3) both our essential parts (1 Cor. 6:20), and let us expend all the faculties of both, our life and death, for the divine glory, such that if we live, we live for the Lord, or if we die, we die for the Lord, because whether we live or die, we are the Lord's (Rom. 14:7–8). And not only ourselves, but (4) let us also take all that is ours—our talent, power and authority, families, subordinates, fortunes—and lay it before God (Matt. 21:3, 7–9), and use it for his glorification. But let us not expend all our possessions in one and the same way—neither all on the poor, nor all on the Republic, nor all on the church and churchly worship—but let us in whatever way nonetheless expend all things for God, and apply them to the uses that he has prescribed for us, that thus we may possess none of these things

---

34. Latin: *oeconomorum et quaestorum*; Dutch: *huishouders en rentemeesters*

merely for ourselves. Indeed, (5) let us expend all our efforts, studies, labors, not for ourselves, but for God (Ps. 115:1), that thus we may always be engaged in the affairs of our Lord, and if asked at any time whose work it is that we do, we can honestly respond, "It is my Lord's work that I do" (Rom. 1:9; 1 Cor. 10:31). Moreover, (6) let us expend all these things for our Lord in such a way that we hold absolutely nothing back from him, unlike Ananias and Sapphira (Acts 5:2), and unlike the young Pharisee (Matt. 19:21), or exercise in any way restraint or limit—whether we live or whether we die (Rom. 14:7; Phil. 1:20–21)—or suspend our service upon any condition (Matt. 8:21–22), or stipulate anything as a reward besides communion with God himself (Luke 17:10; Matt. 19:27–28; Gen. 15:1; Ps. 73:25).

Supports
So that we may do all these things more promptly, the following will help us do this expending frequently and devotedly: (1) that most absolute right that we have asserted above for God from his deity, creation, redemption, and so forth; and accordingly, how great a sacrilege it would be to remove from God the things that are in so many ways his own. (2) That he stamped us as his own possession in creation with his own image, and after it was lost, he restored it by sanctification (Eph. 4:24), and what is more, he sealed us, so to speak, by the blood of his own Son (Rev. 7:3; 9:4; 14:1; Ezek. 9:4). To what end did he do these things, except that we might render to God those things that are God's (Matt. 22:20–21)? (3) That we have quite often dedicated ourselves to God by solemn covenanting: in baptism, the Lord's Supper, diseases, and judgments, and so forth (Josh. 24:15, 21–22; Ps. 22:11). I need not add (4) that he has bound us to him and made us his own by so many and such great kindnesses (Rom. 12:1; 1 Cor. 6:20).

5. To submit ourselves promptly to God
XXX. In addition, fifth, God's authority, by which he can prescribe laws for us at his pleasure and ratify the prescribed laws by promises and threats, and God's power, by which he can apply and execute those promises and threats, spur us on that: (1) we should submit promptly to his powerful hand (1 Peter 5:6), that is, with spontaneous consent, we should become his subjects and servants (Ps. 116:16). In this way we deny the inner parts of our soul themselves—the intellect and reason (2 Cor. 10:5), the will, and likewise the affections (Matt. 26:39, 42)—so that we may be prepared to undertake every command of God without exception (1 Sam. 3:9; Jer. 42:5), whatsoever the mind of the flesh cries out to the contrary (Gal. 1:16). Next, (2) when this universal subjection is

accomplished, we should swiftly execute what has been prescribed for us by him (Ps. 40:8; 143:10; 1 Thess. 4:3; 1 Peter 4:1–2; Col. 4:12). And (3) when we faithfully render this duty, we should promise ourselves more certainly than certain what comes in its train, the promises (Heb. 10:36), because he who promised is faithful and omnipotent (Rom. 4:21). Just as on the contrary, (4) if we should oppose him, from his same omnipotence it is more certain than certain that we may imagine for ourselves all those curses that he has pronounced against the rebellious (Deut. 28:15; 27:26), namely, "Since," according to Augustine in some place, "he is the God of immeasurable authority, and thus there is neither a place in which one can hide, nor a time when one can escape, nor an authority by which one can resist him."

6. To revere him and flee from our sins

XXXI. So then, sixth, a reflection upon the divine authority and power moves us to reverence and fear (Mal. 1:6; Isa. 8:13), for he is the one and only Lawgiver, who is able to save and to destroy (James 4:12). It moves us to fear, not a fear by which we flee from him as from an enemy, but a fear by which we revere him as Father (Heb. 12:28), by which we carefully take heed lest in any way we offend him by some sin (Gen. 39:9), and especially by sin that strives with full purpose, as it were, against the divine authority and power in particular, sin such as (1) haughtiness and pride, in which we spurn the legislative authority of God (Ex. 5:2) and high-handedly offend him (Num. 15:30; Ps. 19:13), and we spit, as it were, upon his authority as well as his power (Jer. 44:16–17), we exalt ourselves against Jehovah (Jer. 13:15), we break his yoke and bonds (Jer. 5:5; Ps. 2:3), and provoke him to wrath as if we were stronger than he (1 Cor. 10:22). (2) Testing God, in which we attempt to place limits upon his authority and power (Ps. 78:18–19, 41). (3) Desperation, in which when we are placed in extremity, we imagine that the hand of God is shortened (Isa. 59:1; Num. 11:21–23). (4) Carnal security, or the imagination of impunity (Ps. 10:5–6, 11; 50:20–21), as if God were powerless and could not avenge an injury brought against him, just like an idol (Zeph. 1:12).

7. To recline upon him

XXXII. Seventh, a devout reflection upon the divine authority and power builds a solid confidence in which we securely commit ourselves, our goods, all our fortune, efforts, and undertakings, to God, because (1) through his authority and dominion, we are the special possession of him who obtained us for himself by creation and redemption (1 Cor. 6:20), to whom we have devoted ourselves and our goods with full will (2 Cor. 8:5), who has taken us for his own possession, and accordingly will also take up the care of his own possession, a care in which we will be able to rest, just as David says, "I am yours, save me" (Ps. 119:94), speaking as one who has experienced this salvation (Ps. 116:16). (2) Not only is there nothing at all impossible for him; there is also nothing difficult (Ps. 78:19–20; Isa. 40:28). (3) No enemy can prevail against him (John 10:29; 1 John 4:4; Rom. 9:19), indeed, not even a united front of enemies, the gates of hell (Matt. 16:18; Ps. 3:6–7; 68:1–2), because he is our omnipotent Lord *Sabaoth*, "of hosts" (Ps. 46:11; Ps. 89:8). (4) Through his omnipotence, he can do all things, through means however weak, without means, and against means (1 Sam. 14:6; Rom. 4:17; Dan. 3:17). Finally, (5) he alone has power (Ps. 62:11), and without him we all can do nothing (John 15:5), inasmuch as he is the one who works all things in all things (Rom. 11:36).

8. To glorify him for his authority and power

XXXIII. Finally, eighth, the divine authority and power furnishes us with an argument for glorifying God (Eph. 3:20; Matt. 6:13), and thus in glorifying him (1) let us inwardly marvel at the greatness of his authority and power (Eph. 1:9), the wideness of his reign (Ps. 24:1), and the power of his administration (Jer. 32:17–19). (2) Let us openly extol and celebrate it (Neh. 9:32; Ps. 147:5; 99:2; Rev. 15:3; 1:8). (3) In our own way, let us imitate (a) his independent authority, that right over all things which God confers upon us (1 Cor. 3:21–22), by submitting to God alone (1 Cor. 3:23), and by not suffering to be brought, as regards our conscience, under the authority of anything (1 Cor. 6:12), standing in this liberty (or right) which Christ acquired for us by his own blood (Gal. 5:1), and not concerned with anything more than that we may not abuse that authority (1 Cor. 10:23) or use it in a way that makes others stumble (1 Cor. 8:9). (b) His power, by which we also are powerful and strong (1 Cor. 16:13), powerful in the power of God (Eph. 6:10), indeed, in our own way, omnipotent: "I can do all things through Christ who strengthens me" (Phil. 4:13).

CHAPTER TWENTY-ONE

The All-Sufficiency or Perfection of God

I am the mighty God who is sufficient. Walk before me and be perfect, and I will make my covenant….

—Genesis 17:1–2

Among the attributes that are, so to speak, derivative, the first is all-sufficiency.[1]
I. From the attributes that are, so to speak, primitive, which have been recounted up to now, three attributes emerge that are, so to speak, derivative: all-sufficiency and perfection, whereby he is most perfectly sufficient for himself and all things; majesty and glory, whereby he is such that he is most worthy to be praised and celebrated; and blessedness, wherein he is in every way most blessed. God himself teaches his all-sufficiency in Genesis 17:1–2.

The Exegetical Part

It is built upon the text.
II. The argument of the text is a most effective exhortation toward life with God and sincerity, with a promise of covenanting. In it is set forth:

    A. The foundation of the exhortation, in the all-sufficiency of God: אני אל שדי, "I am the mighty God who is sufficient." In it there is presented:

        1. The all-sufficient one: אני, "I," that is, Jehovah, who is named in the words immediately preceding. For in this name, or rather in the one named, is the foundation of all sufficiency. For by it, he truly is and exists: he is from himself, independent; he is immutable, always the same; he is most simple goodness and perfection; he is infinite essence and goodness, or all goodness and perfection; he is eternal and unending essence and perfection, and so forth. Of such kind is this "I."

---

1. *omnisufficientia*

2. The all-sufficiency: שַׁדַּי אֵל, *El Shaddai*, with "am" understood by ordinary Hebrew ellipsis. This all-sufficiency is expressed in two descriptions, that he is namely:

a. אֵל, *El*, "the mighty God," from אֱיָל, "might, strength" (Ps. 80:2). It properly means "mighty" (Ezek. 31:11), and through antonomasia,[2] the God who is the mightiest of all (Gen. 14:22; 21:33), for which reason it is commonly translated by Franciscus Junius and Immanuel Tremellius as *Deus fortis*, "the mighty God."[3] The Septuagint interprets the word in Psalm 7:12 as ἰσχυρός, "strong, mighty."[4] And from this word comes אֵלִי, "my God" (Matt. 27:46) and *Eloi* (Mark 15:34), unless you prefer that those words come from *Elohi*, and thus אֱלוֹהִי. The result is that here, as a fulcrum for the divine all-sufficiency, is meant not only that he is God, but also that he is the mighty God, whom no one and nothing can resist: "I am he who can supply the fullest goods that I will promise you, and thus accordingly, most blessed are they who are covenanted with me."

b. שַׁדַּי, *Shaddai*, which has three or four derivations: (1) as if it were שַׁדְדַי, from שָׁדַד, "to destroy," as if he should say, "I am the one who, just as I have created all things, can also destroy them, the one who can destroy all your enemies." (2) From שַׁד, "breast," because he nourishes all things: "I am the one who can nourish you and look out for you in all things necessary for your nourishment." Nor are there lacking some who (3) derive it from the Arabic שָׁדַד, which means "to strengthen, to bind," as if you should call him πάντα κρατῶν, "the one holding all things." Sanchuniathon, the author of the history of the Phoenicians, mentions a certain god whom his translator, Philo of Byblos, calls Ἀγρός, "Farm," and Ἀγρότης, "Farmer," as if he had in mind that the name שַׁדַּי was from שָׂדֶה,

---

2. That is, the use of a description or title in place of a proper name.

3. Ps. 7:12, *Testamenti Veteris Biblia Sacra*, eds. and trans. Immanuel Tremellius and Franciscus Junius, 6 vols. (London: Henry Middleton, 1581): *Deo vindice justi, et Deo forti detestante hodie*, "God the defender of the just, and the mighty God detesting [the wicked] today"; cf. Ps. 7:12 in the Sixto-Clementine Vulgate (1592): *Deus judex justus, fortis, et patiens, numquid irascitur per singulos dies?*, "God the just judge, mighty, and patient, is he not angry every day?"; Ps. 7:11, KJV (1611) reads: "God judgeth the righteous, and God is angry with the wicked every day."

4. Ps. 7:12 (LXX), ὁ Θεὸς κριτὴς δίκαιος καὶ ἰσχυρὸς καὶ μακρόθυμος μὴ ὀργὴν ἐπάγων καθ᾽ ἑκάστην ἡμέραν.

"field."[5] Aquila translated it as ἱκανός, "competent" and in another place ἄλκιμος, "brave."[6] Thus Drusius.[7] Elias Levita, in his *Tishbi*, says that the majority explain that it means "mighty" and "victor," as if he should say, "I am the one who wills and is able to protect you," such that he is not boasting of what remains concealed for himself, but is revealing his sufficiency for his people.[8] But (4) the origin that seems most correct to me is that the word is composed from ש, the demonstrative pronoun אשר, "who," and די, "sufficient," which according to Drusius is Plato's ἀνενδεής, "without need,"[9] such that God is saying that he is that one who is sufficient, namely,

---

5. This Greek translation of the Phoenecian historian Sanchuniathon (Σαγχουνιάθων) by Philo of Byblos (also known as Herennius Philon) is not extant, with only fragmentary evidence via Eusebius of Caesarea's brief summary, paraphrases, and occasional quotations. For Mastricht's citation, cf. bk. 1, ch. 10 in Eusebius, *De praeparatione evangelica* in PG 21:80; idem, *Preparation for the Gospel*, 1:40. For Ἀγρός and Ἀγρότης in Philo of Byblos, see *Philo of Byblos: The Phoenician History*, trans. and eds. H. W. Attridge and R. A. Oden, Jr., in Catholic Biblical Quarterly Monograph Series (Washington D. C.: Catholic Biblical Association of America, 1981), 2.12.; cf. idem, *The Phoenician History of Philo of Byblos: A Commentary*, in *Études préliminaires aux religions orientales dans l'Empire romain*, vol. 89 (Leiden: Brill, 1981).

6. Aquila Ponticus of Sinope (fl. 130) up to the early modern period was referred to as both Aquilas (עקילס) and Onkelos (אונקלוס), in contrast to modern scholarship which generally views these as two different individuals. The Aramaic commentary on the Pentateuch associated with Aquila Ponticus is known as the *Targum Onkelos*. On *El-Shaddai* as *Anah Chiulah Sapukah*, "I am the Mighty, the Sufficient," Syr. *El Shaddai Aloha*, see *Pentateuchal Targumim: the Targums of Onkelos and Jonathan Ben Uzziel*, trans. J. W. Etheridge, 2 vols. (1862–65), 1:66n6. For the Aramaic text and English translation, see M. Aberbach and B. Grossfeld, *Targum Onkelos to Genesis* (New York City: Ktav, 1982), 100–101.

7. Mastricht seems to cite Philo of Byblos and Aquila Ponticus directly from ch. 45 on Gen. 16:1 in Joannes Drusius, *Ad loca difficiliora Pentateuchi, id est quinque librorum Mosis commentarius* (Franeker: Fredericus Heynsius, 1617), 62–63. On Drusius's life and works, see *BWDN* 4:359–63; *Biographischwoordenboek van protestantsche godgeleerden in Nederland*, 6 vols. (Utrecht, 1907–1949), 2:620–29.

8. For Elias Levita (1469–1549) on "שדי" and "Schadai" see Elias Levita and Paul Fagius, *Opusculum recens Hebraicum a doctissimo Hebraeo Eliia Levita Germano grammatico elaboratum, cui titulum fecit* תשבי *id est, Thisbites* (Isny, 1541), 235–36. The most common title was the edition entitled *Lexicon Hebraicum utilissimum* (Basel, 1547). For biography and bibliography, see "Levita, Elijah" in Isidore Singer et al., eds., *Jewish Encyclopedia* (New York City: Ktav Publishing House, 1901–1906), 8:46–48. The Hebrew text of this lexicon frequently utilizes Hebrew letters to transliterate German words, e.g. in this entry *Almechtiger*, "the Almighty," is אלמעכתיגר.

9. Drusius states that Plato described God as "ἀνενδεής" (i.e. *nullius indigum*, lacking nothing) in his *Ad loca difficiliora Pentateuchi*, 62; lacking a definite citation, clearer sources are Clement of Alexandria, *Strom.* 2, *Paed.* 3.1; Philo of Alexandria, *On the Virtues*, LCL 341:168–69, "For God has no wants (ἀνεπιδεής), He needs nothing, being in Himself all-sufficient to himself (ἀλλ' αὐτὸς αὐταρκέστατος ἑαυτῷ)...."

for all things, for perfect blessedness, παναρκής, "all-sufficient," both for himself and his people, and that from himself, that is, αὐτάρκης, "self-sufficient." It is as if he should say, "I am the one who is sufficient for you for all things." So then, שדי denotes nothing other than the perfection of God by which he has enough for himself and for all things, and especially for his own, for their omnimodal blessedness.

B. The duty of the exhortation: "Walk before me and be perfect." There are two parts, as it were, to this duty, unless you prefer to call it a twofold duty, namely:

1. Life with God: התהלך לפני, "walk in my sight." התהלך is from הלך, "he walked, he went forward." In the Hitpael it denotes "he walked continuously, unceasingly," "he lived." Verbs of this conjugation designate vehemence and frequency (Isa. 38:3), and this verb is used metaphorically for life, morals, and actions (Ps. 1:1; 119:1; etc.). In this passage it does not mean anything but to abide with God, to live for God, for his glory, according to the prescription of his will and law. לפני means "before God," "in the sight of God," "as if with God present," so that in walking, we should continually have God right before our eyes, just as reciprocally, as we walk, God has us before his. The same is described otherwise as walking with God, after God, in the ways of God. We have expressly delineated the nature and practice of this life with God in our *Prodromus* (Specimen 3, "The manner of life with God"),[10] and we will perhaps delineate it in the ascetic part.[11]

2. Integrity: והיה תמים, "and be perfect." Here תמים means "whole, perfect," from תם, "complete," (Gen. 25:27), which signifies someone not astute at deceiving, as Rashi thinks on that passage.[12] It is used concerning sacrificial victims, which ought to be perfect and

---

10. Specimen 3, "De Conversatione cum Deo" in Mastricht, *Prodromus*, 173–201, where Mastricht considered Genesis 5:24, "And Enoch walked with God...," explaining that *conversatio* involves knowledge of God, love, and worship. The duties of love are: (1) an *amor concupiscentiae*, that is a desiring and seeking after God; (2) an *amor acquiescentiae* that is, communion with him and confidence in him, which is a walking and *conversari cum eo*; (3) an *amor benevolentiae*, that is, obedience, repentance, and reformation of life.

11. 3.2.4. Cf. below, §XV.

12. See Rashi on Gen. 25:27 in *Pentateuch with Targum Onkelos, Haphtaroth, and Rashi's Commentary on Genesis* (Jerusalem, 1973).

unblemished, and it is also attributed to the holiest persons, such as to Abraham, Noah (Gen. 6:9), David (Ps. 18:23), Job (Job 1:1). It denotes someone sincere, whole, without guile, without pretense, and according to the Vulgate, simple.[13] Aquila in Genesis 20:5 also translates it ἄπλαστον, that is, unfeigned. Symmachus renders it ἄμωμον, without reproach. In Paul it seems the same is meant by ἄρτιος and ἐξηρτισμένος, complete and thoroughly equipped (2 Tim. 3:17).[14] Therefore, God does not require from Abraham an omnimodal perfection of degrees, as the papists want, but only that he endeavor to walk genuinely, without pretense, in every part of his law.

C. The motive of the exhortation, namely, the promise of the covenant: ואתנה בריתי, etc., "and I will make my covenant between me and between you." בריתי, "my covenant," certainly does not mean that covenant of nature which was made between God and our first parents, but the covenant of grace in the blessed seed. And by it God intends to signify both that the divine all-sufficiency will not be beneficial to him at all without this covenant, and that he cannot enter that covenant without walking before God, and without sincerity and genuineness. We will deal expressly with this covenant in its own place.[15]

The Dogmatic Part

The all-sufficiency of God is proved: From the Scriptures

III. And so God is that perfect one who is sufficient, that is, not only for himself, but also for us, and that not for this or that thing, but for all things. Therefore, (1) שדי, *Shaddai*, is included in his names, and by it he is designated, and is, "God" (*Deus*, derived from די). (2) He is expressly called perfect (Matt. 5:48) and תמים דעים, "perfect in knowledges" (Job 37:16). And (3) he lacks nothing at all, nor is he in need of any counsel, help, power, or kindness (Job 22:2–3; Ps. 16:2; 50:12; Isa. 40:14; Rom. 11:34–35). Indeed, (4) he communicates all things to all things (Rom. 11:36; Acts 17:28; Ps. 145:16).

---

13. *simplicem*, ἁπλοῦν. E.g. Vulgate Job 8:20; 9:21; Matt. 6:22. Cf. 1.2.6 §XXVII.
14. Cf. 1.1.2 §II.B.3.b.ii.
15. 1.5.1

And from reasons

IV. Nor can he be other than perfect and all-sufficient, for he is: (1) the absolutely first being (Rev. 1:5, 8), and thus the one whose sufficiency and perfection nothing could have restricted, for otherwise it would have existed prior to the first being. (2) Being par excellence, the highest entity, ὁ ὤν, יהוה, and thus the one for whom there can be no lack of existence, perfection, or sufficiency, for otherwise entity would be devoid of entity, and the highest being would not be highest. (3) Infinite essence, which cannot be limited by a lack of any perfection, by which he would not be sufficient, either for himself or for others. (4) Most simple essence, which admits of nothing heterogeneous by which he might be perfected, and from which he might be more sufficient for himself. (5) Eternal, the one who, since there existed nothing besides him to perfect him, was alone sufficient for himself, and who even now requires nothing by which he might be perfected or become more sufficient. Indeed, (6) he has conferred to all things outside himself whatever sufficiency they have, and thus he had it all, and has it now, eminently; otherwise, he would not have conferred it. "With you is the fountain of life, and in your light we enjoy light" (Ps. 36:10). Namely, "As the sun is always seen in its fullness and is never diminished," unlike the moon, "so God exists perpetually perfect, full of power, wisdom, immortality, and all other good things," as Theophilus says in his *To Autolycus*.[16] Wherefore also in John of Damascus, *On the Orthodox Faith* (bk. 1, ch. 5), not only is he called "perfect," but also "exceeding and preceding all perfection."[17]

Some objections against the perfection and sufficiency of God

V. Nor do the following oppose these truths: (1) that he created all things, and created them on account of himself (Rom. 11:36; Prov. 16:4). For he did not create so that he might be perfected by created things, but so that he might perfect them, and pour out, as it were, his perfection upon them, such that when it is received it may be acknowledged and celebrated by those who receive it. (2) That he exacts duties from the creatures. For he does not do this so that he may be perfected by the duties offered, but so that those offering them may be perfected for him, and so that in the offering, they may procure for themselves eternal blessedness. But still, you will insist, he expects glory from them. I respond, Yes, but that glory is the recognition and celebration of this perfection

---

16. Theophilus, *Ad Autolycum* (Πρὸς Αὐτόλυκον) in *PG* 6:1077–78; idem, *To Autolycus* in *ANF* 2:100.

17. τέλειος...ὑπερτελής, καὶ προτέλειος, *super-perfectus, et ante perfectus*. John of Damascus, *Expositio accurata fidei orthodoxae* (Ἔκδοσις ἀκριβὴς τῆς ὀρθοδόξου πίστεως) in *PG* 94:801–2; idem, *NPNF2* 9:4.

which he already had from eternity (John 17:5). And this celebration does not result as much in his perfection as in ours. (3) That he seeks his ends by the work of instruments. I respond, Not from necessity, but from liberty; not from a defect of virtue, but from an abundance of goodness, so that the dignity of some efficiency may be bestowed to the creatures, and his own efficiency in the creatures may be rendered more perceptible. (4) That he lacks the perfections of the creatures, such as sight, hearing, and other such things. I respond, To the extent that these are perfections, he does not lack them, but to the extent that they connote imperfections, then once those are taken away, that which remains of pure perfection is in him as in the idea, representatively, and as in the cause, eminently (Ps. 94:9; Rom. 11:36). For there cannot be in the effect what in no way was in the cause.

The nature of perfection and divine sufficiency is explained.
VI. Moreover, the perfection and sufficiency which we have asserted for God is not understood to be limited in a certain kind and for some certain use, the sort of perfection that belongs to all the creatures and excludes only privative imperfection. Rather, it is a universal perfection and sufficiency which includes every good, in every kind, and is sufficient for all creatures for all things, all the way to infinite blessedness, and which accordingly also excludes negative imperfection. From this perfection, in Greek he is called, insofar as he has enough in every way, ἐξαρκής, "fully sufficient"; insofar as he has enough for all creatures for all things, παναρκής, "all-sufficient"; insofar as he has enough, not from another source, but from himself and in himself, αὐτάρκης, "self-sufficient." In particular, (1) he has enough for himself, since he does not desire and cannot receive more than he has, because he is infinite (Ps. 50:9–13; 16:2), which is made abundantly clear from the world, created as it was not from eternity, but only in time, and by his own will. (2) He has enough for all things different from himself, inasmuch as he gives to all life, and breath, and all things (Acts 17:25), and through him, in particular as human beings, we live, and move, and have our being (Acts 17:28). But especially (3) he is sufficient for his covenanted people (Ps. 23:1): (a) for dispelling from them all evils, for which reason he is called their shield, rock, strength, and deliverer (Ps. 18:2; 84:11); (b) for conferring to them all goods, as much spiritual as bodily (Eph. 1:3), from which he is called a sun (Ps. 84:11); (c) for abundantly compensating them for all their hardships, troubles, and miseries undertaken for his sake, from which he is called their exceeding great reward (Gen. 15:1). If he should offer them none of these things, if only he should offer himself, he would offer them all things, and thus they rightly rest in him alone (Ps. 16:5; 73:25).

His perfection and all-sufficiency results: From all his perfections
VII. This perfection and all-sufficiency, according to the nature of the attributes
that are, so to speak, derivative, arises first from the attributes of essence that we
have enumerated so far, such that if he lacked even one of those attributes, he
would not deserve to be called either perfect or all-sufficient. Thus, for example,
(1) through his independence he is perfect, and has enough for himself and for
his own from himself, such that in the blessing of his own people he cannot be
impeded or limited. (2) Through his immutability he is perfect, and has enough
for his own without variation, increase, or decrease, such that in this they have
a solid foundation for their blessedness. (3) Through his simplicity, he is pure,
unadulterated perfection and sufficiency, from which they can fear no hint of
imperfection or defect in him. (4) Through his infinity, there belongs to him an
unlimited and illimitable perfection, by which he alone can satisfy the infinite
appetite of his own. (5) Through his eternity, he never was, is, or will be not perfect and all-sufficient, and he can bless his own eternally. (6) Through his life, all
his perfection is active[18] for him, and sufficient for his own for whatever life there
is—natural, spiritual, and eternal. (7) Through his intellect, he is conscious of
his own perfection, and he perceives the necessities and desires of his own, so
that he may supply them. (8) Through his will, he enjoys his own perfection, and
to his own he wills to communicate, from his satiety, all that is enough for them.
And thus (9) through the rest of his attributes, just as we showed individually in
their distinct contemplation.

From the Trinity of persons
VIII. There is also, second, another point from which the perfection and all-
sufficiency of God arises: the subsistence of the three persons. From it that
perfection and all-sufficiency strengthens, if it were possible, in intensity, by
being reflected as it were from person to person, since the Father is most fully
satisfied in the Son, as in the most absolute image of himself, in the brightness
of his glory, in the express image of his hypostasis (Heb. 1:3; Matt. 3:17; Prov.
8:30), the Son in turn in the glory which he possessed from eternity with the
Father, and in their mutual glorification (John 17:5, 1), and the Holy Spirit in the
love and fellowship of both (2 Cor. 13:14). But this perfection and all-sufficiency
is also brought to us by the distinct persons distinctly, when the Father by his
love, the Son by his grace, and the Holy Spirit by his communication pour out
the perfection and all-sufficiency of God upon us (2 Cor. 13:14). It is as if the
perfection and sufficiency of one divine person were not sufficient to bless pitiful

---

18. Latin: *actuosa*; Dutch: *werkzam en werkdadig*

little man, and it were necessary for the three, each of which is God, perfect and all-sufficient, to cooperate for this end, just as we will show more clearly in the chapter on the Trinity.[19]

The Elenctic Part

1. Do the Socinians by their hypotheses not thus effectively take away the omni-modal perfection and all-sufficiency of God?

IX. Indeed, those who intentionally by arguments presume to impugn God's omnimodal perfection and all-sufficiency will scarcely be discovered, and not even scarcely. But those among our adversaries who do not indirectly erode the same by their hypotheses, although they do it by various degrees, will also scarcely be found. And those who do this the more openly are first the Socinians, then the Pelagians. Therefore it is asked, first, whether the Socinians by their hypotheses, through trickery, do not thus effectively take away the omnimodal perfection and all-sufficiency of God. Conrad Vorstius in his *Treatise on God* and his notes on the same, and with him the Socinians throughout their writings, because of their desperate love for independent choice and their implacable hatred for the eternal deity of Christ, the Trinity, the satisfaction of Christ, and our justification on account of the righteousness of Christ alone, are compelled to teach, and do teach, various things that are incompatible with the infinite perfection and sufficiency of God.[20]

The affirmative is proved

The Reformed prove this is so in the following way. (1) The Socinians wholly remove from him such things which, by the unified consent of all, connote perfection, and which ought to be possessed by the one who is perfect in the highest degree, and without which he cannot be perfect in that way. Such things include (a) independence, when they teach that he depends upon human choice; (b) immutability, when for the sake of the variability of that same choice, he changes his decrees as if by the hour; (c) simplicity, when they teach that he has been composed in more than one way, for example, composed of subject and accident, essence and attributes, virtues, and so forth; (d) infinity, insofar as they speak of him as restricted to heaven; (e) omniscience, when they desire to hide future contingencies from him; (f) omnipotence, when they deny that he

---

19. 1.2.24 §§I, XI–XIV, XXIV

20. Cf. Conrad Vorstius, *Amica collatio…super notis hujus…ad illius tractatum de Deo…ubi variae quaestiones theologicae explicantur: maxime quae divinam praedestinationem et quaedam Dei attributa concernunt* (Gouda: Caspar Tournaeus, 1613).

can bend the will of man; (g) avenging justice, when they deny that it necessarily demands punishments for sinners; and (h) others, just as we have shown in their own places. (2) On the other hand, they attribute to him such things that breathe of manifest imperfection: for example, affections or passions of the soul, desires, mere willingness, repentance, and other things that are unworthy of the most perfect being. (3) They reject the satisfaction of Christ, through which his holiness and righteousness, wounded as it were by human sins, receives what it is due. (4) They slander the most holy Trinity, from whose most blessed fellowship results immeasurable perfection, as we will show in its own place.[21] We could pile up more things of this kind if the things adduced were not sufficient, or if they had not already been adduced through the individual chapters.

2. Do the Pelagians and semi-Pelagians deride and undermine the perfection and all-sufficiency of God?

X. It is asked, second, whether, with the Socinians, the Pelagians and semi-Pelagians deride and undermine the omnimodal perfection and sufficiency of God. The Pelagians and semi-Pelagians, the Socinians, Jesuits, Remonstrants, and others, stricken by the same perverse love of independent choice, and with various pretexts constructed for it—of obtaining harmony between the foreknowledge and providence of God, a harmony among liberty of choice, the contingency of things, and the holiness of God, by which he might be immune from responsibility for sins—pose such things through which the omnimodal perfection and all-sufficiency of God cannot but fall to ruin.

The affirmative is proved

They do so namely, (1) when they attribute to God a will that depends in more than one way upon human choice and upon other conditions, by which his will is made to be conditioned, and by the same stroke his perfection of independence, which is the source of all of his other perfections and properties, topples to the ground. (2) When God, according to the fancy of human choice, is changed and disturbed in his own counsels, and is subjugated to a master, as it were. (3) When there is alleged for him a willingness, or an imperfect willing, by which he earnestly wills what he never achieves, and is by that reason impotent, for he cannot produce what he wills, and likewise unhappy, inasmuch as he does not have what he desires. (4) When they attribute to him that he earnestly wills, in particular, that each and every person be actually saved, and since the majority escape this wish, he is sufficient neither for himself and for his own wish, nor for

---

21. 1.2.24 §§XXIII, XXVIII

those for whom he wills this salvation. (5) When they deprive him of authority and power over man's free choice, by which he can neither achieve his wish nor convert men, unless they are willing and thus convert themselves. (6) When they suspend predestination upon things foreseen in the creature, and thus deprive him of both independence and self-sufficiency. These things should suffice for a specimen.

The Practical Part

The perfection and all-sufficiency of God: 1. Convinces us of the vanity of all things.

XI. As far as practice is concerned, the perfection and all-sufficiency of God, first, convince us of the imperfection, insufficiency, and vanity of all creatures (Eccl. 1:2). For if God alone is absolutely perfect and all-sufficient, then naturally every creature is in itself imperfect, empty, and vain, since: (1) from itself and in itself, it has entirely no perfection by which it might be sufficient either for itself or for others (Jer. 2:13). And (b) if it should have something conferred to it by God, it is plainly idle and useless unless it is excited and applied by God, as by the prime mover, and likewise unless it is commanded by the all-sufficient God to deliver, as it were, the received perfection to this or that person (1 Kings 17:4, 6). And if there is no perfection and sufficiency present in creatures, then there is also no reason for us (1) to love any things inordinately (1 John 2:15–16; James 4:4); (2) to place our trust in them (1 Tim. 6:17; Ps. 62:9–10); (3) to fear excessively or bear reluctantly the loss of any earthly thing (Ps. 73:25).

2. It comforts us in all adversities.

XII. Second, they provide us a foundation for our comfort. If we are not sufficient for ourselves, and the whole universe is not sufficient for us, since our soul by nature is endowed with an appetite that is entirely insatiable, then let us reflect upon the fact that God is most all-sufficient, both for himself and for us (Ps. 73:25). In particular, (1) if there are lacking any goods of the soul, such as force of judgment (James 1:5), uprightness of will, faith, hope, love, and moderation of the affections; or of the body, such as health, strength, and good temperament; or of fortune, such as necessary resources, honors, and the favors of men. (2) If there threaten dangers which we are no match to ward off. (3) If there press against us any enemies, whether spiritual—Satan, the world, sins, and consciousness of sins—or corporeal, our consolation can be: (1) that God is all-sufficient and most all-sufficient, *El Shaddai*, a shield and sun (Ps. 84:11; Gen. 15:1), the one who is sufficient for himself, all the way to infinite blessedness, and accordingly is much more sufficient for us, who do not require such and so great a perfection. And (2) the one who, in addition, has promised, by so many promises and with such solemnity, that he will be all things for his own, and in all things, a sun and shield (Ps. 91:15; 84:11; 5:11–12; Heb. 13:6). (3) And what is more, he has demonstrated in reality to his own in so many ways, always and everywhere, on every occasion, that he is most all-sufficient. Meanwhile, so that we may more certainly enjoy this all-sufficiency of God, and by it be more solidly raised up according to our need, it is altogether necessary that: (1) we be covenanted to God through faith: "I am the mighty God who is sufficient.... I will establish my covenant" (Gen. 17:1). For he is not all-sufficient for all people indiscriminately, but only for his own. (2) We frequently call upon that all-sufficiency in our prayers (Ps. 91:15; John 16:23; Ps. 27:8).

3. It rebukes those who in practice neglect the all-sufficiency of God.
XIII. Third, they rebuke all those who, as much in word as in deed, deny this all-sufficiency and perfection of God, or at least erode it. This is done: (1) by those who are openly impious, who when they have abandoned God and been delivered over to themselves and their own worldly things—wealth, honors, pleasures, and indeed sins—perceive all sufficiency to be in those things, and none in God (Jer. 2:13; Mal. 3:14). (2) By secret hypocrites, who recognize some sort of sufficiency in God, and therefore also bring him something, and sometimes even much, especially in the external duties of religion, yet do not recognize all sufficiency in him, and thus also do not desire constantly and in all things to cling to him (Matt. 13:20–21). This is the obvious reason why they do not trust that in God they will have all things which they view as necessary or useful for themselves, from which they conclude that certain things must, whether by right or by wrong, be sought for them from creatures (Hos. 2:4–5, 12). Indeed, (3) even by those who have been truly regenerated, as can be seen in Moses's refusal (Ex. 3:11–12), in Abraham's lie (Gen. 20:2), and in other failures of the saints, that is, those who were not sufficiently persuaded that God could sufficiently enough relieve them in their necessities and imminent dangers. Specifically, the all-sufficiency of God is destroyed or eroded by: (1) desperation or distrust (Num. 11:21; 2 Kings 7:2); (2) vain confidence in creatures, by which in reality we are promising ourselves something from creatures that God either cannot or does not will to confer upon us (Ps. 62:8–11); (3) inordinate love of creatures, by which we actually suppose there is something present in the creatures that is not in God, for which reason covetousness is called idolatry (Eph. 5:5); (4) frauds and devices, when we strive to obtain by tricks what we despair of obtaining by legitimate means in God, or from him, as in the example of Jacob (Gen. 27:6ff.; cf. Ps. 125:5); and finally, (5) all sins, insofar as in them is a

turning away from God and a turning toward creatures (Jer. 2:13), which certainly would not occur except by expecting from the creatures something that is not in God.

The gravity of these sins
Accordingly, (1) those sins, and whatever others, involve idolatry as well as apostasy, insofar as we defect from God to the creatures, because we attribute to them things which are not in him. And from this fact shines forth the shamefulness and gravity of sins (Heb. 3:12). (2) This obstructs the favor and kindness of God to us, so that from that omnimodal sufficiency of God we can promise ourselves nothing at all, as the divine threats show (Matt. 17:19–20; 21:21–22; 13:58; Mark 6:6). Indeed, (3) such sins make us liable to the most weighty judgments of God, as can be seen in that captain in 2 Kings 7:17, who through his distrust in God denied God's all-sufficiency; and indeed, in Moses himself, who for the same reason was with his brother Aaron most strictly excluded from the possession of the land of Canaan (Num. 20:12).

4. It awakens a zeal for various virtues.
XIV. Fourth, the contemplation of the divine sufficiency can raise us up as needed to one or the other of the following virtues: (1) the glorification of God (Ps. 96:4; 145:3). For if every perfection and sufficiency provides us an opportunity to celebrate the creatures, how much more that highest and infinite perfection and sufficiency of God, by which he is sufficient for himself and for us, all the way to infinite blessedness, and which is the foundation of all his majesty and glory? (2) Love, by which we embrace him above all things, as he alone is sufficient for us for all things—"I will love you, O Lord, my strength…my rock, my fortress…" (Ps. 18:1–2)—a love by which we desire and seek him with all zeal (Ps. 73:25), we rest in him, we rejoice in him alone (Ps. 16:5–6; 4:6–8). (3) The constant placing of our trust in him alone, as he alone is sufficient for us for all things, that is, he is all in all (1 Cor. 13:10),[22] perfect light to the intellect (Ps. 27:1), goodness to the will, life to the whole soul (Ps. 36:9), righteousness to the affections, joy to the heart, health, splendor, and immortality to the body, and so forth. "Whatever will be loved will be present, and what will not be present will not be desired" (Augustine, *On the Trinity*, bk. 13, ch. 7).[23] (4) The raising up of hope and patience in whatever adversities (Ps. 27:13–14; 77:10, 13, 14; 73:25). (5) The offering of obedience and worship to him, as from this

---

22. Cf. 1 Cor. 12:6; 15:28.
23. Augustine, *De Trinitate* in *PL* 42;1020–21; idem, *On the Holy Trinity* in *NPNF1* 3:172.

he will be to us a shield and an exceeding great reward (Gen. 15:1; Ps. 84:11). (6) The humiliation of ourselves, namely, that because of his highest sufficiency, we might acknowledge, feel, and confess our deepest need, and because of his omnimodal perfection, our imperfection (Gen. 18:31). We often seem perfect to ourselves, in our own eyes, but if we would compare ourselves with the highest perfection and sufficiency of God as our norm and example, then we at last will say, "Shall man be justified in comparison with God? Behold, some among his servants have not remained faithful, and in his angels is discovered foolishness. How much more those who dwell in houses of clay?" (Job 4:17–19). "Our very righteousness, brought under the examination of the divine righteousness, is unrighteousness; it is filthy in the indictment of the Judge, though it glitters in the estimation of the worker" (Gregory, on Job 3).[24] Then, in each of these, if they should be described individually as in a sermon, the following could be explained as needed: (1) the singular force and efficacy of the divine all-sufficiency and perfection, by which it flows into us to form, nourish, increase, and confirm these virtues in us. (2) The motivating reasons which, from the consideration of the divine all-sufficiency, impel us to zeal for these virtues. And finally, (3) either the means by which we fruitfully attain the habit of these virtues, or the manner in which their operations are directed.

5. It draws us to walk with God.

XV. Fifth, a persuasion of the divine perfection and sufficiency draws us to walk with God, just as God himself invites Abraham to this duty in our text. First, generally, it embraces all godliness, and especially all those virtues which we designated in the previous section. Then, particularly, it is (1) to have God present to us always and everywhere, as if at our right hand (Ps. 16:8; 26:3). (2) To strive with God for the same end, to aim with him at the same goal, everywhere to seek and to pursue the same thing that God does, to will and not to will the same thing with God (Rev. 2:6), and indeed to do it for the same thing, that is, for the glory of God (Rom. 11:36). And (3) in the same way as well, which is in Scripture "to walk in the ways of God" (Deut. 19:9; 28:9). What then are these ways of God? They are the ways of holiness (Ps. 77:13), of goodness and truth (Ps. 25:10). Thus, to walk in the ways of God is nothing other than to go forward in the law of God (Ex. 16:4; Neh. 10:29), in the precepts of God (1 Kings 6:12), in the statutes and judgments of God (Lev. 20:8), to cling constantly in these things to God (Deut. 4:4), and to turn aside from him neither to the right

---

24. See bk. 5, ch. 11, sec. 21 on Job 3:26, Pope Gregory I (d. 604), *Moralia, sive expositio in Job* in PL 75:690; idem, *Morals on the Book of Job*, trans. J. H. Parker, 3 vols. (Oxford, 1844), 1:257.

nor to the left (Deut. 12:32). Furthermore, (4) in walking, to grasp as it were the hand of God (Jer. 31:32), and not to let it go (Gen. 32:26; Luke 24:29), that is, as babies who would walk with their parents join hands with them, we also should join hands with God, that is, we should depend upon him wholly through all things: and this at last is to walk in the name of God (Mic. 4:5). In addition, (5) in walking, to vary and inflect our steps, as it were, with God, that is, so we might cling constantly to him. This at last is to walk with God, or after God (Deut. 13:4). This happens when, as he walks with us in the ways of his judgments, we follow him in repentance, humiliation and reformation, prayers, and patience (Lam. 3:40–41), and as he walks in the ways of kindness, we follow him in joy, gratitude, and praises (Ps. 103:1–3). Furthermore, (6) in all these things, to have ourselves continually as under the eyes of God, in all sincerity of conscience: "I am the mighty God who is sufficient. Walk before me and be perfect," that is, sincere (Gen. 17:1).

Motivating reasons

And we should do so since God is all-sufficient, not only for himself, but also for us: in warding off all evils, as a shield; in summoning and pouring out upon us all good things, as the sun; in compensating all our labors and losses, as our exceeding great reward: in a word, since he alone can be all in all for us, so let us also in him alone be wholly fixed in heart, let us inseparably cling to him, and let us never, either in fear of any evil or in hope of any good, allow ourselves to be torn from him. In this way at last, God will be perfect and all-sufficient not only for himself, but also for us, by repairing all our defects (Ps. 103:3–4) and satisfying all our desires (Ps. 103:4–5; 20:4; 6:10).

6. It inflames us with zeal for covenanting with God.
XVI. Sixth, it inflames us to strive with every effort to be covenanted with the most perfect and all-sufficient God. God reveals this use of his all-sufficiency in the words of our text: "I am the mighty God who is sufficient. Walk before me and be perfect, and I will establish my covenant with you."

The motivating reasons

For by this covenanting (1) the all-sufficient God becomes our God (Jer. 31:33); (2) without it, this all-sufficiency, however great it is, will not profit us in the least (Isa. 65:13); indeed, (3) it will rather stand against us (Isa. 65:13; Ps. 34:15–16).

The manner
Moreover, this covenanting is done (1) through Christ, the one who for this reason is called the messenger of the covenant (Mal. 3:1), in whom all the divine promises are yes and amen (2 Cor. 1:20); (2) through faith (Hos. 2:19) in Christ, who is the way to the Father (John 14:6), "in whom we have boldness and access with confidence through faith in him" (Eph. 3:12).

7. It provides an example that we should imitate: (1) His perfection
XVII. Finally, seventh, it provides an example that we should imitate: (1) the perfection of God—"Be perfect" (Matt. 5:48)—indeed, even his essential perfection: for example, his independence, that with respect to our conscience we also might be independent, though not from God (1 Cor. 7:23); his immutability, that we also might be such in the pursuit of good (1 Cor. 15:58); his simplicity, that we also might be simple (Matt. 10:16) and sincere (2 Cor. 1:12); and in this way through the rest of his attributes, just as we observed throughout in their distinct contemplation. Yet it is the moral perfection of God that especially provides an example for our imitation, and to this end he has represented this perfection in his law, concerning which Paul speaks (Phil. 3:15; Col. 4:12; cf. James 3:2).

(2) His sufficiency
(2) The sufficiency of God, by which, first, we should be sufficient for ourselves, under God (2 Cor. 9:8), so that (a) we may be far from covetousness (Heb. 13:5), by which we seek sufficiency in wealth; (b) we may not be anxious much concerning the things that pertain to this life (Matt. 6:25ff.); nor (c) quite anxiously go round after a supply or abundance of earthly wealth (1 Tim. 6:9); and (d) we may be content with any lot (Phil. 4:12). And then, we should also promptly bestow our sufficiency upon others, just as God does (2 Cor. 8:7, 14), persuaded that (a) in this manner we are made in some way like unto this divine perfection (Matt. 5:48), in which likeness our highest perfection consists; (b) the divine all-sufficiency will that much more tenderly watch over us and our necessities (Matt. 6:26, 30).

CHAPTER TWENTY-TWO
The Majesty and Glory of God

I am Jehovah: this is my name, and my glory I will not give to another, nor my praise to graven images.

—Isaiah 42:8

I. The intrinsic excellence of the perfection and all-sufficiency that we discussed, insofar as it scatters a certain splendor by which it might be acknowledged and celebrated, supplies the second of the attributes which are, so to speak, derivative, namely, majesty and glory, which God himself most magnificently claims for himself in Isaiah 42:8.

The Exegetical Part

II. In the text is contained a certain declaration or solemn promulgation of three of his own royal characteristics, as it were, which he wills to be peculiar to himself alone, among which:

A. The first is in his essence: אֲנִי יְהוָה, "I Jehovah." Supply from the missing Hebrew the substantive verb "am," as is done in Isaiah 43:12. This is the mark, and as it were, the familiar signature by which God customarily subscribes and confirms his precepts, as he does throughout Leviticus (18:2, 30; 19:2–4, 10, 12, 14, 16, 18, 25, 28, 30–32, 34, 36, 37). It can be referred either to the preceding things, such that it is like a confirmation of the preceding prophecy concerning Christ, from the nature of the God who calls, and from the truth of the preceding promises (cf. Isa. 42:9); or to God, such that after the absolute prediction concerning Christ has been made, it returns back to the purpose and contends that Jehovah is the only true God. Moreover, Jehovah is the name of God's essence, in which all his perfections are comprehended: independence, immutability, simplicity, immensity, omnipresence, eternity, omnipotence, omniscience, grace, and so forth, as we have taught in their own places. In this essence, accordingly, all his internal glory is grounded. Accordingly, this name is especially proper to him, and is altogether incommunicable, for which reason it is also called his memorial (Ex. 3:15; Ps. 135:13; 102:12; Hos. 12:5).

B.　The second is in his name: הוא שמי, "This is my name." Supply again the ellipsis "is." הוא, "this," by kabbalistic interpretation, is to many Jews the very name that God gives to himself: "my name is הוא," but because it has not yet been solidly proved that הוא is among the names of God, it will more appropriately mean "this" and be referred to the preceding "Jehovah," with the resulting meaning, "This, that is, 'Jehovah,' is the name especially proper to me, by which I am distinguished from the gods of the Gentiles, which in no way belongs to any creature, neither in a full nor in a diminished sense, as with my other names." This is so at least in the nominative or vocative case, although, in the oblique cases, and in composition with other words, it can in some way belong to creatures, just as it seemed good to the ancients to sprinkle a small part of the name Jehovah, because it was the name of grace, into their own names, as is evident in the names Jonathan, Jozadak, and others. We taught these things elsewhere against the Socinians.[1]

C.　The third is in his glory and praise: "And my glory I will not give to another, nor my praise to graven images." Here God takes away:

1.　Glory, from all universally: וכבודי לאחר לא אתן, "And my glory I will not give to another." Here there is:

a.　The thing taken away, or what he takes away: וכבודי, "and my glory." It means either the glory of the name of Jehovah in particular, that is, "I will not suffer that anyone in heaven or on earth will arrogate to himself this glorious name or the glorious essence signified by it"; or, "my glory" in general. He does permit the creatures to have glory, but he prohibits them from having his own glory, "my glory," that is, religious worship. Moreover, כבוד is from כבד, "to be heavy," either in quantity or quality, in magnitude or multitude, in weight or number, in wealth, in glory, from which we read of the "weight of glory" (2 Cor. 4:17). It differs from honor and praise, because honor belongs to common dignity (Rom. 12:10), and praise to greater dignity, but glory to the greatest

_____

dignity, namely, heroic dignity. And thus it belongs preeminently to the Best and Greatest.

b. The person from whom it is taken away: לְאַחֵר, "to another," for example, to Bel, to Nebo, to Merodach,[2] and to any other who is not by nature God, or who is a foreign god (Mark 16:17; Ps. 16:4).

c. The taking away itself: לֹא אֶתֵּן, "I will not give," that is, "I will not suffer my glory to be diminished or transferred to another." Or, by litotes, it means that he will avenge himself most severely on those who ascribe his name Jehovah, or his glory, to another.

2. Praise, from graven images: וּתְהִלָּתִי לַפְּסִילִים, "and my praise to graven images." Supply "I will give." It is as if he should also say, "I will not suffer even my praise, although it is lesser than glory, to be transferred to graven images." Here again there is:

a. The thing taken away or prohibited: תְּהִלָּתִי, "my praise," that is, "the praise that belongs to me alone." תְּהִלָּה, "praise," is from הָלַל, "it shone, it gleamed, it was bright, it glittered" (Job 29:3), from which comes the name הֵילֵל, *Lucifer*, "the light bearer," the morning star, because nothing appears more shining and full of light (Isa. 14:12). In the Piel, it means "to praise," because he who praises someone makes him shine, as it were, and scatters his light.

b. The object from which it has been taken away: לַפְּסִילִים, "to graven images." פְּסִיל or פֶּסֶל denotes an image, but one that has been graven or hewn from wood, stone, etc. The Greeks render it as εἴδωλον, "image," and γλυπτόν, "graven image," "statue"; the Chaldeans, as "image." Because the Gentiles believed that something of the divine or of deity was present in their idols, statues, and images, and on account of this would bestow divine praise or religious worship upon them, just as the Romanists also do, God therefore forbids the bestowing of any religious worship—whether it be called glory (*latria*) or praise (*dulia* or *hyperdulia*)—either upon living things and false gods, or upon things bereft of life: idols, statues, or any sort of images.

---

2. Cf. Isa. 46:1; Jer. 50:2.

The Dogmatic Part

The majesty and glory of God is proved: From the Scriptures

III. And so, our God has a majesty and glory entirely peculiar to himself, which Scripture teaches: (1) whenever it declares that God is great, that is, not in mass, but in the majesty of perfection (Deut. 7:21; 10:17; Neh. 1:5; 4:14; 9:32; Ps. 47:2 and throughout the Psalms; Isa. 12:6; Jer. 10:6; Dan. 11:45; cf. ch. 9 on the infinity and greatness of God). (2) Whenever it declares that he is glorious and marvelous (Deut. 5:24; 11:2; Ps. 8:1, 9). (3) Whenever it declares that he is the Most High (Gen. 14:18; Num. 24:16; Deut. 32:8; Ps. 7:18; Lam. 3:38). (4) Whenever it makes mention of his great and terrible deeds, as witnesses of his majesty (Deut. 10:21; 2 Sam. 7:21–23; Ps. 71:19; Acts 2:11). (5) Whenever it extols his magnificence above the gods (Ps. 135:5). (6) Whenever it says also that he is praiseworthy and greatly to be praised (Ps. 48:1; 96:4; 113:3; Ex. 15:11). (7) Whenever it extols the honor of God and shows that we must extol it, as much in precepts as in examples (Isa. 6:3). By all these things he is declared to be the God of glory (Acts 7:2).

And from reasons

IV. And if majesty and glory did not belong to him, (1) for what reason would he have created, nourished, and governed the world? For the creature could not have moved him to do these things, as it did not yet exist, nor could any hope of gain by which he might one day be perfected by what was created, for he has been sufficient for himself from all eternity. So then, there is no reason left but the recognition and celebration of that infinite perfection which he has had from eternity, and in this consists his glory (Prov. 16:4; Rom. 11:36). (2) For what reason would he have created the creatures, and would they stand forth in this theater, other than that they might declare how great an artisan he was, how great his power, wisdom, and goodness? To this end are the heavens said to tell the glory of God (Ps. 19:1; cf. 8:3, 9; Rom. 1:20). (3) For what could be the highest end of all things, in which all ends might rest subordinate, if not the glory of God? For the end to which the universe was created is presupposed to be more excellent than the universe itself, and what then is more excellent than the universe, other than God alone? And how can God be an end, except that he may be glorified? Finally, (4) he made many of his creatures glorious: the Messiah (Isa. 42:21), the sun and stars (1 Cor. 15:41), David (Ps. 21:5), Solomon (Matt. 6:29), and so forth, so shall not he himself be more glorious?

Four ingredients of the divine glory are enumerated:

1. The infinite eminence of his essence and attributes

V. Moreover, the glory of God is nothing other than the brightness, so to speak, of his infinite eminence, which is to be acknowledged and manifested. Thus, these four things come together in glory: first, a certain infinite eminence. For just as honor belongs to whatever is good, and praise to whatever is more excellent, so glory belongs to that which is most eminent. Moreover, this eminence belongs to God, first from his essence, insofar as he is Jehovah (Ex. 33:18–20; Isa. 42:8), and next from his attributes, inasmuch as from them, as if from various parts, comes forth that eminence of the divine majesty, just as we have shown throughout in our individual contemplation of them. This eminence is the foundation of all the divine glory, for which he deserves to be esteemed and celebrated by us, and also for which he is celebrated as the God of glory (Acts 7:2), the King of glory (Ps. 24:8), the Father of glory (Eph. 1:17), and for him is asserted the eminence of glory (Eph. 3:14–16).

2. The brightness of this eminence

VI. Second concurs the brightness, so to speak, of that perfection and eminence (Isa. 35:2), from which his glory is said to be shining, as it were, and thus the Son is denominated the radiance of his glory (Heb. 1:3), and the glory of the Lord is said to have shined around the shepherds (Luke 2:9), as also the light from heaven around Paul (Acts 9:3; Matt. 17:2). Thus he is said to dwell in light inaccessible (1 Tim. 6:16). This brightness does not so much dazzle the eyes of the body—as did the glory of Solomon (Matt. 6:29), of the sun (1 Cor. 15:41), and of the morning star (Isa. 14:12)—as it does the eyes of the mind, although sometimes an external splendor is also joined to it, as if for a symbol, as is evidenced from adduced passages (Luke 2:9; Acts 9:3; Ex. 33:18, 19, 23; Ezek. 1:26–28; 3:12; 43:1ff.; and others).

3. The recognition and estimation of the same

VII. From this, third, arises the recognition of this eminence, whereby it is called the face of God (Ex. 33:20), the face of glory (Jude 24–25), and likewise, his name (Matt. 6:9; Ex. 20:7), since the majesty and eminence of a thing is made known from its face and its name. This recognition, at least that which is perfect in all accounts, belongs to God alone, who from it is said to dwell in light inaccessible, whom no man has seen (1 Tim. 6:16; John 1:18). Nevertheless, a more imperfect recognition, from revelation, from his attributes, from his operations, also comes to the creatures: the angels (Isa. 6:1; Matt. 18:10), Moses (Ex. 33:23; Num. 12:8), the shepherds (Luke 2:9), the apostles (John 1:14), Paul (Acts 9:3), and others. Nevertheless, this recognition is not without degrees, since now we see and know "through a mirror, dimly," but one day, "face to face" (1 Cor. 13:12). And these three things, eminence, brightness, and recognition, constitute the internal glory that is coeternal with God.

4. The celebration or manifestation of the same

VIII. Finally, fourth, in glory comes the celebration or manifestation of the eminence recognized through its brightness, which is more properly called glorification than glory. By it the inward eminence that has been recognized, together with its proper estimation, is made public and extolled. And this is done: (1) by God himself, as he glorifies himself, when he makes manifest the ineffable and incomprehensible preeminence of his essence in his attributes and operations (Num. 14:21; Ps. 72:19; Lev. 10:3). (2) By the divine persons themselves, among themselves: thus the Father glorifies the Son (John 17:1), the Son in turn (as the radiance of his glory, Heb. 1:3) glorifies the Father (John 17:4; 8:49), and the Holy Spirit glorifies the Son (John 16:14) and the Father, and thus he is called "the Spirit of glory and of God" (1 Peter 4:14). (3) By angels and men, when they make manifest their recognition, experience, and estimation of the divine glory, and amplify and extol, as much as they can, that very eminence of God (Isa. 6:3; Luke 2:14; Ps. 8:1; Rev. 4:10–11). (4) By the Word of God, and especially the Word of the gospel, which accordingly is called the glorious gospel (2 Cor. 3:7–8), since it makes known to us the glorious attributes of God—his power, wisdom, grace, righteousness—and the glorious Son of God (Phil. 2:11). (5) By the works of God (Ps. 90:16; 111:3): of creation, preservation, and governance (Ps. 8; 19:1; 104:24, 31); especially by those exceptional works which we call miracles, inasmuch as in them the glory of the divine omnipotence appears more splendidly. But chiefly (6) by the operations of grace, in which he is concerned with his church. That entire counsel of peace, in which he decided to save the church, and that most wise economy, which he has brought forth in his governance: to what end do they point other than the glorification of God? "That every tongue should confess that Jesus Christ is Lord, to the glory of God the Father" (Phil 2:11)? Accordingly the angels declare, "Glory to God in the highest!" (Luke 2:14). In particular, (a) the glory of mercy and of avenging justice shows itself in the eternal business of predestination (Eph. 1:5–6; Rom. 9:22–23). (b) The glory of wisdom, in his seeking out a way of deliverance that is harmonious with both justice and mercy, and indeed in distributing as it were the task that each person of the Trinity assumed to himself in this business of redemption, all because of which Paul exclaims, "Oh, the depths of the riches both of the wisdom and knowledge of God!" (Rom. 11:33), and the Savior is denominated the wisdom and power of God (1 Cor. 1:24). Again, (c) the glory of love and grace toward the world (John 3:16; Rom. 5:8). Furthermore, (d) the glory of holiness, by which he could not even tolerate our sins in his own Son, and thus rigidly punished them (Rom. 8:32). In addition, (e) the glory of avenging justice, by which he did not spare his own Son (Rom. 3:25). Therefore, for these and other reasons, the gospel is called the glorious gospel of the blessed God (1 Tim. 1:11), and the light of the glorious gospel of Christ is said to shine (2 Cor. 4:4).

The celebration of God is chiefly accomplished by religious worship.
IX. Meanwhile, this celebration or manifestation of the divine eminence is chiefly performed by rational creatures in their religious worship, inasmuch as in it combine the praises of Israel (Ps. 22:3), and the voice of thanksgiving (Ps. 26:7; 35:18; 99:3), and not least, supplications of every kind (1 Tim. 2:1), all in which the omnipotence, omniscience, and unexhausted goodness of God are acknowledged and extolled.

The Elenctic Part
X. Because the infinite perfection and all-sufficiency of God are the basis and foundation of all glory and divine glorification, it is clear that all who erode the perfection and all-sufficiency of God by the same stroke also injure, obscure, and take away the glory of God. Accordingly, in this chapter recur the Socinian and Pelagian controversies from the preceding chapter.[3]

It is asked: 1. Do the Socinians by their hypotheses not weaken and obscure the glory of God? The affirmative is proved.
It is therefore asked, first, whether the Socinians by their diverse hypotheses do not egregiously weaken and obscure the glory of God. The Socinians, as we said in the preceding chapter, out of a perverse love for independent free choice and a hatred for the holy Trinity and the eternal deity and satisfaction of Christ, violate and obscure the glory of God in more than one way, when: (1) they remove those perfections from God—independence, immutability, simplicity, infinity, omnipresence, omniscience—on account of which God deserves to be glorified by us. (2) They assert for him imperfections—mere willingness,[4] repentance, longings, and so many disturbances of the affections—on account of which he deserves to be vilified, or at least more frigidly glorified and celebrated, just as we taught in the preceding chapter, §IX. (3) They dispute and deny the glory

---

3. 1.2.21 §§IX, X
4. *velleitas*

of eternal deity to the Son of God and to the Holy Spirit, notwithstanding the fact that the Son is expressly called the brightness of the Father's glory (Heb. 1:3), and that he asks that the divine glory which he had with the Father from eternity be conferred upon him (John 17:5). (4) They transfer the glory of religious worship, which in the text Jehovah asserts for himself alone, as does the Savior (Matt. 4:10), to Christ as a mere man. (5) They deprive him of the glory of avenging justice, by which he is of purer eyes than to be able to look upon evil (Hab. 1:13; Ex. 34:7), and they all but make him like a sinner (Ps. 50:21). (6) They deny to the Son of God the glory of satisfaction, by which he redeemed the human race by his own blood, although the Father, on account of this glory, gave to the Son the name above every name, that at his name every knee should bow (Phil. 2:7–9). (7) They take away from the Son of God the glory of our justification, insofar as it proceeds from his righteousness alone, imputed and granted to us, on account of which, namely, "when he had by himself made purification for our sins, he sat down at the right hand of the throne of the majesty on high" (Heb. 1:3). (8) They take the glory of this justification, withdrawn from the Son of God, and place it upon themselves, as it were, since they try to acquire it for themselves by their own works, against the apostle: "Lest any man should glory" (Eph. 2:8–9); "Where is glorying then? It is excluded…by the law of faith" (Rom. 3:27). We will not heap up more things of this kind.

2. Do the Pelagians, ancient and modern, by their opinions not attack and obscure the glory of God?

XI. It is asked, second, whether the Pelagians, ancient as well as modern—the Socinians, Jesuits, and Remonstrants—by their opinions do not obliquely attack and obscure the glory of God. We have affirmed and demonstrated this in the preceding chapter, §X, by showing on the one hand how they absolve God of various perfections—independence, immutability, infinity, omniscience, omnipotence, infinite blessedness—because of which he could and should be glorified, and by which he is glorified throughout the Scriptures, and on the other hand how they heap upon him various imperfections: for example, they heap upon him dependence, ignorance, impotence, and so forth, from which the glory of God is made worthless and obscure. But because we have already examined these things in the place cited, we will not add more here.

3. Do the Romanists, against the command of God, not give the glory of God to another, and his praise to graven images?

XII. It is asked, third, whether the Romanists, against the declaration of God, do not give his glory to another, and his praise to graven images. We will not linger over the self-condemned pagans, who are indifferent to the authority of Scripture and of God himself, since of the two crimes, theirs, by which they gave the glory of God to their false gods, Jupiter, Mercury, and the like, and the praise of God to graven images, in which they believed there was some deity and divinity, was an idolatry of a lesser rank. But on the other hand, the crime that the papists commit, they who in their words acknowledge the authority of God and Scripture, but only for this end, that without God, without Scripture, indeed against God and Scripture, they might more highly exalt the legislative authority of their pontiff, who commands the universal Christian church to do such things—who should endure this?

The affirmative is proved

They obscure the glory of God in more than one way: (1) obliquely, as it were, through various hypotheses, when namely (a) they diminish and obscure the grace of gratuitous justification with their twofold merit, from congruity and from condignity (Rom. 3:24, "By grace…"; v. 27, "Where is glorying…?"; 4:2, 4, 16; 11:6, "If it is of works, then it is no longer of grace, otherwise grace is not grace, and if it is of works, then it is not grace.") (b) Against the same grace, they urge satisfactions for venial sins, by which they restrict the glory of Christ, such that he is not a perfect Savior who can save "to the uttermost" (Heb. 7:25). (c) Against the same grace, they urge the intercessions of the heavenly saints, as if the intercession of Christ were not sufficient for them (1 John 2:1–2; Isa. 63:16). (d) To the detriment of grace, they excessively extol the strength of free choice (2 Cor. 3:5–6; cf. 1 Cor. 15:10). But (2) more directly, they erode and obscure the glory of God when: (a) on one hand, they give the glory of God or religious worship to others—that is, to the blessed Virgin, the angels, the heavenly saints, and the Roman pope—against the express declaration of our text, "My glory I will not give to another." (b) On the other hand, they bestow upon pictures and graven images, and likewise upon the bread of the Mass and relics of the saints, religious worship, the same which belongs to their prototypes, against the same declaration, "I will not give 'my praise to graven images.'" Likewise, they exchange the glory of the incorruptible God for an image formed like mortal man (Rom. 1:23). In addition, they serve those which by nature are not God (Gal. 4:8). As a cover for their sacrilege they have carefully sought out I know not what slender distinctions between *latria*, *dulia*, and *hyperdulia*, distinctions which Jehovah the Lawgiver does not know in his Word, or which he sufficiently rejects by contrary hypotheses he has laid down, as will be clearly seen, if God wills, in its own place.[5]

4. Do the Lutherans by their hypotheses not erode the glory of God?

XIII. It is asked, third, whether the Lutherans by their hypotheses do not erode and obscure the glory of God. The Lutherans, especially those who, so that they might more effectively fight for the ubiquity of the flesh of Christ and its presence in the symbols of the Holy Synaxis, and for universal redemption, obscure the glory of God in more than one way. They obscure (1) his infinite power, by which he can make decisions as he wills regarding what belongs to him (Matt. 20:15) by appointing from fallen sinners certain ones that he wills, that in them he may reveal the glory of his avenging justice through their just condemnation on account of their sins (Rom. 9:13, 15, 17, 18, 20–23). (2) His saving grace, by which (they say) he bestows just as much grace to the reprobate as to the elect, by willing that each and every person actually obtain salvation, from which it follows that grace is not grace, because grace is a privilege of some. (3) His independence, insofar as he depends (they say) upon man's free will, which as it pleases can positively not resist the Holy Spirit. But especially (4) when they teach that his glorious perfections, on which all his glorification is founded, are given to another, that is, to Christ insofar as he is a man or creature, perfections such as immensity, omniscience, omnipotence, power to give life, and others. This is diametrically opposed to the declaration of our text. See Johann Gerhard (loc. 2, §304), who even when this text is objected against him, answers not a syllable.[6] And moreover, he also twists the request of the Savior in John 17:5, "Father, glorify me with yourself with the glory which I had with you before the world existed," insufficiently considering that (a) the Savior does not seek a new glory for himself as a man, but a glorification or manifestation of that glory which he already had from eternity, which had been so greatly hidden by his emptying of himself (Phil. 2:6–9). And next, that (b) the Savior seeks to be glorified by the Father just as he himself had glorified the Father: "as your Son has glorified you" (John 17:1, 4). Accordingly, just as in glorifying the Father the Son has not communicated new glory to the Father, but only manifested that which he had, so also the Father, in glorifying the Son, has not communicated any new glory to him, but only manifested that which he already had from eternity. And

---

5. Mastricht does not revisit this point; however, see also 1.2.6 §XI, 1.2.8 §IX, and 1.2.12 §XI.

6. Johann Gerhard, *Loci theologici* (1863–75), 1–2:367–68.

thus accordingly, (c) his words are not about his human nature, that it should be blessed with a certain new glory, but rather the person of the God-man, that his divine glory may be manifested.

The Practical Part

The majesty and glory of God: 1. Shapes us for humility.

XIV. As far as practice is concerned, first, God's majesty and glory, just as in his essence, attributes, and operations, is beautifully represented in the Word (Isa. 40:15–17, 21; Jer. 10:6–7, 10, 12–13; Amos 9:5–6; Mic. 1:3–4; Hab. 3:3; Job 26:6–14; 34:13; 35:5; 40:4ff.). When devoutly deliberated upon and compared with our worthlessness (Isa. 24:23), it (1) suppresses our pride (Gen. 18:27; Ps. 8:1, 4); (2) produces reverence and fear of God (Isa. 2:10, 19, 21; Jer. 10:6–7, 10; Ps. 111:9; Isa. 59:19), and (3) a denial of all our own honor and glory (Ps. 115:1).

2. It draws us back from any profaning of the divine glory.

XV. Second, it restrains the madness of those who (1) hold this infinite majesty of God as of no consequence in their heart (Rom. 2:4; Mal. 2:2; Ex. 5:2); (2) blaspheme it with their mouth (Isa. 52:5; Ezek. 36:23; 1 Tim. 6:1; Titus 2:5); (3) and disparage it in their work, either (a) by teaching such things which agree little with the glory of his independence, grace, righteousness, and omnipotence (see elsewhere),[7] (b) by doing such things by which the glory of God is injured (Rom. 2:24; Titus 2:5), (c) by abusing the glory of God as a pretext for sins (1 Sam. 15:15), (d) by preferring their own glory to the divine glory (John 12:43), or (e) by despising the name or worship of God, by neglecting it, by treating it irreverently, or by profaning it in any other way, against the third commandment of the Decalogue.

Motivating reasons

For (1) by all these things the majesty and glory of God is violated, his name is profaned, his face is spat upon as it were, and at the least, he is provoked (Isa. 3:8) and debased (Ezek. 13:19); (2) against them God will more certainly than certain reassert his claim upon his own majesty, according to the threats (Ex. 20:7) and the examples of divine judgments: "Among those who are near me I will be sanctified, and in the sight of all the people I will be glorified," that is, by my judgments (Lev. 10:2–3; cf. 2 Sam. 12:14).

---

7. §§X–XIII, above

3. It calls us to the glorification of God. What is this glorification?

XVI. Third, the majesty and glory of God calls us to glorify his name (1 Cor. 6:20), which is done: (1) in our heart (Ps. 103:1–2; Luke 1:46), by acknowledging, esteeming (Mal. 1:14), and revering the infinite eminence of God, which he has displayed in his attributes, in his works, in his Son, and in his Word (2 Cor. 5:11; Jer. 10:6–8). (2) In our mouth (Ps. 40:16; 145:5), by celebrating it among his other perfections and virtues (1 Peter 2:9; 1 Chron. 29:11–14), the argument for which the whole Psalter will supply, and hence it is called תהלים, "praises"; and by awakening all things, that in this work of celebration they might join hands with us, inasmuch as we are not equal to the task alone (Ps. 103:20–22). (3) In our work (John 15:8); and this (a) by denying all our own honor, that God's honor might be preserved more unimpaired for him (Ps. 115:1; Matt. 3:11). (b) By bravely enduring on account of it whatever dangers, losses, reproaches, and torments, all the way to death (Phil. 1:20; Luke 9:26; Ex. 32:32; Rom. 9:3). (c) By religiously abstaining from all things by which the glory of God could be injured, diminished, or blasphemed (Ex. 20:7; Titus 2:5; Rom. 2:24). (d) By constantly doing those things which look toward the glory of God (Matt. 5:16). These sorts of things are especially (i) gratitude for whatever benefits have been received, as much corporeal as spiritual (Ps. 50:23; 1 Thess. 5:18); (ii) profession of his name and of evangelical truth (Matt. 10:32; Phil. 1:7, 20); (iii) payment of vows which have been offered on whatever occasion, in baptism, the Lord's Supper, in sicknesses, and so forth (Ps. 116:18; 50:14); and especially (iv) a holy manner of life (John 15:8; Phil. 1:11). (e) By surrendering our entire selves, body and soul, to divine glorification (Acts 15:26; 1 Cor. 6:20): in all our efforts and operations, as much as can be done, by expressly striving for the glory of God (1 Cor. 10:31), and at least in general, by devoting all our resources to the glory of God (Rom. 14:7–8), and by undertaking nothing at all which by its nature does not incline toward the glory of God, or which could in any way hinder it, however much in itself it might be an adiaphoron (1 Cor. 8:13; 9:15).

The motivating reasons

Commending this universal glorification of God are: (1) the highest equity of the matter itself, namely that to the one to whom belongs the highest eminence, indeed infinite eminence, all glory should be brought, that is, we should render to God what is God's (Matt. 22:21). (2) Examples of every kind to light our way: God glorifying himself, the persons of the Trinity mutually glorifying themselves, the angels doing the same night and day (Isa. 6:1–3), the heavenly saints, all the works of God (Rev. 4:8), and heaven and earth, as we have proved individually above. The fact (3) that for this end all things were created by God, and we, together with the angels, were created for this end alone (Rom. 11:36; Prov. 16:4; Isa. 43:7). (4) That in this glorification is all our perfection, excellence, and usefulness, through which we are suited for our use, that is, for the highest end of our creation (2 Tim. 2:20–21), and likewise the highest end of our redemption (1 Cor. 6:20; 1 Peter 2:9; Titus 2:14). And without it we are called unprofitable (Rom. 3:12). (5) That accordingly in this is our chief honor, and in addition, God has promised that he will honor those who have honored him (1 Sam. 2:8, 30). On the contrary, (6) that he will pour every disgrace, both here and hereafter, upon those who do not do this, and who despise him (1 Sam. 2:30); indeed, that he will curse them, and even curse their blessings (Mal. 2:2; Num. 20:12). Finally, (7) that we will be eternally glorified for this end, so that we may glorify him eternally with the blessed angels, day and night singing to him ceaselessly their threefold "Holy, holy, holy!" (Isa. 6:3; Titus 2:13). Compare what we have already observed concerning the sanctification of the divine name in chapter 4,[8] and concerning the glorification of God in our discussion of most of God's attributes.

4. It shows in what way we must strive for glory.

XVII. Fourth, the majesty and glory of God shows from where it must be sought and in what true glory must be located—namely, from God, and in God, who is the ocean as it were of majesty and glory (Jer. 17:14; Ps. 109:1)—and by what supports it is be obtained in God and from God, namely: (1) by contempt and disdain for worldly honor (John 12:43). "For if," as Chrysostom says, "you desire glory, despise glory, and you will be more glorious than all"[9] (cf. James 4:16; Heb. 11:25–26). (2) By humility (1 Sam. 2:30; James 1:9–10; 1 Peter 5:5–6). (3) If something of his honor, glory, authority, and wealth falls to us, by submitting and expending it to the divine honor and glory (Rev. 4:10; Prov. 3:9–10). Furthermore, by those virtues to which God himself in particular attributes glory, such as (4) the knowledge of God (Jer. 9:23–24), (5) patience and martyrdom (Rom. 5:3; Rev. 2:10), (6) zeal for sincerity (2 Cor. 1:12), (7) the glorious struggle for the faith and zeal for preserving a good conscience, inasmuch as for this the righteous Judge will award the crown of righteousness (2 Tim. 4:7–8), (8) fidelity

---

8. 1.2.4 §XX

9. *Si enim gloriari cupis , gloriam despice, et omnibus eris gloriosior*: John Chrysostom, Homily 4 on Matthew 1:17 in *PG* 57:51, Εἰ γὰρ δοξάζεσθαι βούλει, καταφρόνει δόξης, καὶ πάντων ἔσῃ λαμπρότερος, *Nam si gloriam consequi vis, gloriam contemne, et omnium gloriosissimus eris.*

and constancy in evangelical work (1 Thess. 2:19; Dan. 12:3), and any other such virtues that may be found in the Scriptures.

5. It stirs up our appetite for eternal glory.
XVIII. Fifth, the majesty and glory of God rouses us that we would pant and strive to be partakers of eternal glory, about which the apostle speaks: "We all with unveiled face, beholding as in a mirror the glory of the Lord, are transformed into the same image from glory to glory" (2 Cor. 3:18).

What this eternal glory is
So then, this glory is called (1) the glory of God (Rom. 5:2), and likewise the glory of Christ (2 Thess. 2:14); and (2) the exceedingly exceeding eternal weight of glory (2 Cor. 4:17); (3) the crown of glory (2 Tim. 4:8); and (4) the crown of life (Rev. 2:10; 3:11; 4:4), and the unfading crown of glory (1 Peter 5:4). By this glory (5) the righteous will shine like the sun in the kingdom of their Father (Matt. 13:43; Dan. 12:3). (6) The bodies of believers will be transformed so that they may be conformed to the glorious body of Christ (Phil. 3:21), and what is sown here in dishonor will rise again in glory (1 Cor. 15:41–43). (7) The souls of believers, cleansed from all disgrace of ignorance, as regards the intellect (1 Cor. 13:9–10, 21–22), and from all depraved concupiscence of the will and of the affections (that is, made like the angels, Matt. 22:30), will be transformed into the image of God. (8) The whole man will be constituted glorious, without spot or wrinkle or any such thing, holy and blameless (Eph. 5:27). And all this (9) in a glorious place, in the very dwelling of divine glory, the heavenly Jerusalem, whose glory is described in Revelation 21:1ff. And (10) with a glorious fellowship and society (Heb. 12:22).

Where it comes from
This glory (1) God the Father, by his eternal predestination, has prepared for his own (Matt. 25:34; Rom. 9:23; 1 Cor. 2:7), and (2) God the Son has acquired and will one day confer (Heb. 2:10; 2 Thess. 2:14; Rom. 15:7; John 17:22). Into this glory, (3) the Holy Spirit, the Spirit of glory (1 Peter 4:14), will at the proper time transform us (2 Cor. 3:18).

Means
Moreover, we will obtain this glory for ourselves by (1) a zeal for regeneration or conversion (1 Peter 1:3–4; John 3:5); (2) true and living faith (John 1:12; cf. Rom. 8:17, 21); (3) sincere love for God (1 Cor. 2:9); (4) assiduous zeal for good works (Rom. 2:7, 10), namely, the works of charity (Matt. 25:34–40);

(5) the noble contest for faith and a good conscience (2 Tim. 4:7); (6) patient tolerance of whatever adversities, for God and the Mediator (Rom. 8:17–18; 2 Cor. 4:17; Luke 24:26); (7) heavenly conversation (Col. 3:1; Phil. 3:20–21), in which we look not at the things that are visible, which are vanishing away, but at the things that are invisible (2 Cor. 4:18), and in all these things, (8) we endure to the end (Rev. 2:10; 2 Tim. 4:7–8).

6. It offers solace in whatever disgrace.
XIX. At the same time, sixth, while we live in exile from this glory, the majesty and glory of God offers solace in whatever disgrace, especially that which is sustained on account of God and Christ (Rom. 15:13; Ps. 69:7; 1 Peter 4:14), and even in the dishonor of death itself (1 Cor. 15:43).

By these arguments
In these things it offers solace to consider that (1) God alone is owed honor and glory (Ps. 115:1), whereas, on account of our sins, we are owed nothing but disgrace and trouble (Dan. 9:7–8). (2) The reproach of Christ itself is better than all the treasure of Egypt, as Moses judged (Heb. 11:26). (3) We can serve the interests of the divine glory, according to the divine will, not only in honor and glory, but also in contempt, from the analogy of 2 Timothy 2:20–21. (4) This is God's usual way of acting, that whom he wills to glorify, he first humbles (1 Sam. 2:7–8; Luke 24:26; Heb. 2:7). Finally, (5) he will one day repay every disgrace with that exceedingly exceeding eternal weight of glory (2 Cor. 4:17), when our body that was sown with disgrace will be raised with glory (1 Cor. 15:43).

CHAPTER TWENTY-THREE
The Blessedness of God

With your face is fullness of joys; at your right hand are pleasures forevermore.
—Psalm 16:11

The last attribute of God is his blessedness.

I. There remains the third of the derivative attributes and the last of all God's attributes, the one whereby he rejoices in and enjoys himself, his perfections, and all things, and communicates himself to his own that they might have fruition of joy. This attribute is called *blessedness*, and Psalm 16:11 describes it.

The Exegetical Part
It is built upon the exegesis of the text.

II. In these words the Psalm is concluded with a certain periphrastic description of a twofold divine blessedness, namely:

A. His own proper blessedness, or the blessedness of the divine face: "With your countenance is fullness of joys." I do not intend to deny that according to most interpreters, these words can be taken regarding the blessedness of creatures, which they enjoy before the divine face and in its sight; but notwithstanding, there is still no obstacle that would prevent us from taking these words as regarding the blessedness of God, since undoubtedly he cannot communicate to the creatures what he himself does not already possess preeminently, and especially since blessedness is expressly attributed to him (1 Tim. 1:11; 6:15). Meanwhile, there occurs here:

1. The blessedness that is attributed: שֹׂבַע שְׂמָחוֹת, "the fullness of joys," where שֹׂבַע denotes abundance, plenitude, indeed also fullness, because blessedness is not completed by any one good, but by the confluence of all goods. For this reason is added שְׂמָחוֹת, "joys," in the plural: by this word are designated both those goods that make one

blessed, and the repose and joy that arise from the possession and enjoyment of those goods. By both is meant that there is in God such a great abundance of perfection and glory, arising from so many and such great attributes, that he has enough, that he is full, as it were, and indeed that he overflows, having enough not only for necessity, but also for delight. And thus he cannot possess more, or desire to have more.

2. The essence of God, to which is it is attributed: אֶת פָּנֶיךָ, "With your face." The little word אֵת, Johannes Drusius says in his *Sacred Observations* (bk. 9, ch. 7), is not only a simple marker of cases, but one that at the same time also indicates the very substance of a thing.[1] In this passage, it could signify either "with," "at," or "in," such that it designates the blessedness that is in God or in the essence of God; or, it could signify "from" or "by," such that it denotes the blessedness which flows from God to the creatures. Perhaps it implies both. Moreover, "the face of God" seems to designate his very essence (Ex. 33:20), such that the aim of the phrase is that in the essence of God there is fullness of perfection, joy, and blessedness.

B. Communicated blessedness: נְעִמוֹת בִּימִינְךָ, "at your right hand are delights." Here again I do not deny that the words can be employed regarding the blessedness of God, but nevertheless, they can also be employed regarding the blessedness participated in by the creatures. Accordingly, there is also here:

1. The blessedness that is communicated: נְעִמוֹת, "pleasures," unless you wish from the preceding phrase to supply שֹׂבַע, and thus, "fullness of pleasures," or an abundance and assemblage of every honorable and pleasing good.

---

1. See book 9, chapter 7, "De ambiguitate particulae ETH: locus ex Genes. 4.1 adductus et declaratus" in Johannes Drusius, *Observationum sacrarum libri XVI* (Franeker: Radaeus, 1594), 191. There is no difference between the 1584 and 1594 edition on this point. Mastricht seems to be paraphrasing and interpreting here. In the passage cited, Drusius does not actually speak of the "very substance of a thing" (*ipsissima rei substantia*) but rather explains how אֵת may be, according to context, either the accusative case marker or a preposition meaning "with." "*Eth* is a Hebrew particle that sometimes is an article of the fourth case and is sometimes a preposition; when it is a preposition it has the same force as עִם, that is, 'with.' Thus, when you say *Eth Elohim*, it is an ambiguous expression whether you intend to say 'God' or 'with God,' but the circumstances of the passage remove the ambiguity most of the time." *Eth particula Ebraica modo quarti casus articulus est: modo praepositio. Cum praepositio est, tum idem valet quod* עִם, *id est, cum. Itaque cum dicis Eth Elohim, ambiguus est sermo utrum Deum an cum Deo velis dicere. Sed circumstantia loci hanc ambiguitatem plurimum tollit.*

2. The right hand of God, from which this blessedness is possessed as well as communicated: בימינך, "at your right hand." The right hand (as opposed to the left, which is commonly among men the weaker and more ignoble) to the Hebrews is the hand of faith and love, from which it seems to many that the word is derived from אמן, "to confirm," since the first root letter א is expressed in Isaiah 30:21. To the Hebrews, an especially beloved son is called the "son of the right hand" (Ps. 80:17). Here is signified that fullness of pleasures, or blessedness, will be communicated to the elect by the faithful and gracious power of God.

C. The duration of both forms of blessedness: נצח, "eternally," "irresistibly," "invincibly." And this is the perpetual adjunct of blessedness, which would not be blessedness if it were not eternal and unending.

The Dogmatic Part

It is proved that God is blessed and the source of all blessedness:

From the Scriptures

III. From this it is evident that God is not only blessed in himself, but also the source of all blessedness for his own. For this reason (1) he is expressly called μακάριος, "blessed" (1 Tim. 1:11; 6:15), and (2) שדי, *Shaddai*, "all-sufficient" (Gen. 17:1), and perhaps also (3) εὐλογητός, "blessed" (Rom. 9:5; 2 Cor. 11:31), unless you prefer to refer this description to his glory. (4) He cannot receive any good from another (Ps. 16:2; 50:12). And (5) he is the light in which there is no darkness (1 John 1:5), since blessedness and joy are frequently represented in the Scriptures by light (Ps. 112:4; Isa. 50:10). For this reason (6) it is said that he confers blessedness to his own (Ps. 16:11; 27:13), that he is their light (Ps. 27:1), and at last that in his light they see light (Ps. 36:9).

And from reasons

IV. Certainly: (1) he who rejoices in so many and such great perfections, which we have spoken of individually so far, and who cannot either have or desire more and greater perfections—is he not surely blessed? (2) He who from all these perfections is called, and is, all-sufficient for himself and for all his own (as we showed in chapter 21)—would he not be blessed? (3) He who exists as the cause of all blessedness for all things, such that they have nothing that they did not receive, and that they did not receive from him—would he himself not be blessed? What he has granted others, would he not have? Therefore, either there is no blessedness, though every creature, and especially every rational creature, cries out in desire for it; or, God is blessed. As Augustine rightly says in *The City of God* (bk. 9, ch. 2), "With the true God alone, and in him alone, and from him alone, the human soul, that is, the rational and intellectual soul, is blessed."[2] (4) He who alone lives from himself, exists from himself, and is good in himself,[3] who alone is goodness and perfection itself—would he lack the perfection of blessedness? And (5) he whose every perfection is always actualized, indeed, he who is one pure and unadulterated act—would this one not be blessed?

What is blessedness?

V. Blessedness, in Hebrew אשׁרי, in the plural, denotes the confluence of every good, which happens in the highest good. In Greek it is μακαρισμός, as if from μέγα χαίρων, "rejoicing much or greatly," or from the phrase μάλιστα χαίρειν, "to rejoice most vigorously" or (according to Favorinus) from μή, "not," and κήρ, "death," and thus as it were, μήκηρ, "not exposed to death or fate," from which, according to Erasmus, it speaks of immunity to corruption.[4] With regard to the thing it signifies, it is nothing other than the absence of all evil, and the possession and enjoyment of good in the highest good. And thus for blessedness the following are required: (1) the absence of all evil, (2) the possession and presence of all good in the highest good, and also (3) the enjoyment of it, that is, the sense of it and a repose and joy in it. From this it is clear that the possession of the highest good is insufficient for blessedness, as is evident in believers who are spiritually deserted, but that in addition there is required an enjoyment of that possession, that is, a recognition of it in the intellect, and likewise a repose in it, as well as a delight and joy in it, in the will. From this it is evident that objective blessedness (as they say), by the possession of which we are rendered blessed, is the highest and universal good, as we taught in chapter 16;[5] and that subjective blessedness, or the act by aid of which we enjoy that highest good, is partly the intellect, that is, the vision of God (John 17:13; Job 19:26), and partly the will, that is, the repose and delight in that highest good (Ps. 16:11), as we will demonstrate more fully in its own place.[6]

---

2. Augustine, *De Civitate Dei* in *PL* 41:257; idem, *City of God* in *NPNF1* 2:167.

3. *Qui solus est* αὐτοφυής, αὐταυτός, καὶ αὐταγαθός

4. For the citation of Favorinus and Erasmus together, see Μακάριος in Edward Leigh, *Critica sacra*, 2 vols. (Amsterdam, 1679), 2:200; Erasmus did not mention this specific etymology or a reference to Favorinus, but only mentions Homer: Desiderius Erasmus, *In novum testamentum annotationes* (Basel, 1540), 682.

5. 1.2.16 §XXI

6. §XIV, below. Cf. 1.8.4 §X; 3.2.3.

What is the blessedness of God?

VI. This blessedness of God involves, in its own way, the same things: the absence of all evil and imperfection, for he is the light in which there is no darkness (1 John 1:5), as well as the perfect enjoyment of his own self, from which there is said to be fullness of joys with his face (Ps. 16:11). In it is contained not only an exact knowledge of his own self, a knowledge proper to him alone (Rom. 11:34; 1 Cor. 2:11), but also a fullness, repose, and joy in himself, in the communion of the persons, and in all his works (Prov. 8:30; Matt. 17:5). But it is not just any sort of enjoyment of his own blessedness that is sufficient for God, but an enjoyment that is perfect in every way. That is, it is a blessedness (1) such as arises for him not from this or that good only, a good limited from some cause, such a blessedness as creatures have, but rather, one that arises from every good that can be imagined or can exist, whether he possesses it formally or eminently (Ps. 24:1; Eph. 1:20–21). (2) Which he possesses not from another, by begging it, but from himself and in himself, such that it is a blessedness that is essential, namely, "with his face," since a blessedness that is adventitious is also more imperfect, and separable. (3) Which he has always and immutably, for a blessedness that once was not, or that is able not to be, is passing away, and accordingly is not most perfect. (4) Which he has not through succession, passing from habit to act, or through composition, from the confluence of multiple goods, or from formal and objective blessedness, but a blessedness he possesses by a single, most pure, most simple act. Finally, (5) which he has not for himself alone, but which he can communicate, has promised to communicate, and also will communicate to his own, according to his own will, and their capacity (Ps. 4:6–7; 36:9; 84:11). But who at last might represent this infinite blessedness of God? For even our blessedness, in some sense finite, no eye has seen, nor ear heard, nor mind perceived (1 Cor. 2:9).

Difficulties against the blessedness of God are removed.

VII. Nor do the following hinder this blessedness: (1) that God does not possess all the goods that he bestows upon his creatures. For they imply imperfection, and thus if he did possess them he would be less blessed; and those that do not imply imperfection he does possess, if not formally, at least eminently, such that by them his own blessedness can in no way be increased. (2) That not all things which he wills are done, and in fact by far the greatest part is not done. Since whatever he wills to be done is always done, and accordingly, whatever is not done he also did not will to be done (Ps. 115:3); but the things that he willed only by commanding he willed only to be our duty, and to the extent they are not done, by punishing he obtains the glory of his own justice, by which he is well pleased. (3) That he is offended, exasperated, and incited to anger by his creatures. For God is, properly speaking, not injured, offended, or exasperated by sins, but this speaks of that by which a creature would be injured and offended, and by which God, if possible, would be offended, and by which his commandment is injured and violated. Finally, (4) that he is said to wait in vain, to wish, and to repent. For this happens, as we have explained elsewhere, only in a human way, according to the effective action, not the affection. In explanation of the divine blessedness could be compared what we have already taught on the goodness, all-sufficiency and perfection, and majesty of God.[7]

The Elenctic Part

1. Did the pagans frankly acknowledge the divine blessedness?

VIII. It is asked, first, whether the pagans frankly acknowledged the divine blessedness. Indeed, they hailed their own gods as μάκαρες, "blessed." The Epicureans, in order that they might consider God blessed, even deprived him of providence, so that he would not cease to be blessed, fatigued by cares and troubles from the universal preservation and governance of all things. Perhaps they even acknowledged some true blessedness in their gods, but the blessedness that was truly divine they never frankly acknowledged.

It is proved that they did not.

This is evident because: (1) they taught polytheism, which is inconsistent with divine blessedness, that is, infinite blessedness, for the infinite cannot be but one. (2) They cherished human gods, who, from their finitude, labored under many defects, and likewise, (3) gods who were lifeless, devoid of life, sense, and intellect, in their images and statues, a graphic delineation of which you have in Psalm 115:4–7. (4) In such a great variety of opinions about the highest good, there was none that located man's highest good in God, just as we already observed in chapter 16, §XII. (5) True blessedness cannot come to man except from such a good that is (a) absolutely highest, in which there is no admixture, whether of evil or of imperfection, which would destroy blessedness; (b) universal, in which nothing is lacking that deserves to be desired, a good that is sufficient for all things; (c) proper, a good that truly can be called our own, or a good not so much adhering to us as inhering in us; (d) constant and immovable, always like unto itself, indeed the same continually and eternally; and (e) infinite, a good that can satisfy the insatiable appetite of man. Now if you should compare these things

---

7. 1.2.16; 1.2.21; 1.2.22

that are required of the highest good, that it might be truly said to be blessed and to make one blessed, with all the things in which the pagan philosophers sought the highest good through so many circuitous routes, you will discover that there is nothing in all of them that can bear the honor of the highest good, by whose possession you could be called blessed.

2. Does he who seeks blessedness in anything besides God acknowledge that God is blessed?

IX. It is asked, second, whether he who seeks blessedness in anything besides God acknowledges that God is blessed. Epicurus sought blessedness either in external and carnal delights, or in inner tranquility of soul, or in both at once; Muhammad sought it in all sorts of external delights; and neither of the two sought it in the possession, communion, enjoyment, and glorification of God. By that fact neither acknowledges that God is sufficient to make him blessed, nor consequently that God himself is blessed. But since these things pertain to the chapter on glorification, at present we will put them aside for consideration there.[8]

3. Do the Pelagians and Pelagianizers not by their hypotheses disturb the blessedness of God?

X. It is asked, third, whether the Pelagians and the semi-Pelagians, both ancient and modern, do not by their hypotheses disturb the infinite blessedness of God in various ways. We have already observed in the two preceding chapters that the Pelagians and the semi-Pelagians, ancient and modern—Socinians, Jesuits, Remonstrants, and others—by their hypotheses erode the infinite perfection and all-sufficiency of God, and also his glory, which arises from them,[9] when (1) they strip God of certain perfections; (2) they attribute to him various imperfections; (3) they assert for him mere willingness and longings, by which he is frustrated in pursuing his own end. But now, if even one perfection should be lacking in him, and even one imperfection should belong to him, he will not be able to be called infinitely blessed, and if he does not possess that which he earnestly desires and would will, how could he be blessed, or be declared to be? It will suffice to have touched upon these things, so that we might know what can be disputed concerning the blessedness of God.

---

8. 1.6.9 §§IV–V. Cf. 1.8.4 §X.
9. 1.2.21 §X; 1.2.22 §XI

The Practical Part

The blessedness of God: 1. Supplies an argument for divine glorification.

XI. The practice of this chapter offers us, first, an argument for doxology, that God is not only blessed and most blessed, for which reason he is celebrated (Ps. 16:11; 1 Tim. 1:11; 6:15), but also the source of blessedness, in whose right hand is fullness of joys, the fount of life in whose light we enjoy light (Ps. 36:9). Considered individually, that (1) he who is all-sufficient and most blessed for himself offers blessedness to the miserable: "What am I, that you...?" (2 Sam. 7:18; Ps. 8:5). (2) He who is most blessed offers this blessedness most freely, not moved by any hope of repayment (Rom. 11:36). (3) For the sake of conferring blessedness upon his own, he cast his very own Son into extreme misery (Rom. 8:32). (4) By the misery of the Son he restores a greater blessedness to his own than they had when they were blessed in our first parents (Rom. 5:17); indeed, (5) a blessedness even greater, in its own way, than that of the angels, insofar as he has raised them to the blessedness of sons (John 1:12; 1 John 3:1; cf. Heb. 1:5). From all these things, there is surely supplied to us abundant reason on account of which: (1) we should bless God inwardly in the heart, and rejoice in his blessedness (Ps. 103:1–2). (2) We should bless the blessed one with the mouth, by celebrating him (Eph. 1:3). (3) We should be zealous to increase his blessedness, as much as in us lies, by religiously fulfilling his will and desires (Ps. 81:13; Isa. 5:2). And at the least, (4) we should carefully take heed lest in offending, exasperating (Isa. 63:10), and grieving him (Eph. 4:30) by our sins, we disturb, as much as in us lies, his blessedness.

2. It marks the madness of sin.

XII. Second, it marks the madness of every sin, for it labors not only to strip the most blessed one of his blessedness by offending, provoking, and grieving him, but also the sinner himself of the hope of his own blessedness, by utterly stripping it away. For if God himself is not perfectly blessed through us, how will he render us blessed? And if we ourselves try to despoil him, as it were, of his blessedness by our sins, how will he be willing to confer blessedness upon us?

3. It rebukes the foolishness of those who seek blessedness outside of God.

XIII. Third, it also rebukes the foolishness of those who disregard the true vein of all blessedness and pursue their own blessedness in any sort of things, in wealth, honors, and delights, those whom Psalm 4:7 marks out. For all these things, (1) however great they are, or seem to be, do not even make a man good, much less blessed, given that they usually fall upon the worst, and thus also the most miserable (Ps. 73:3ff). Indeed, (2) they very frequently offer an occasion for sin and eternal misery, and shut men out from blessedness (Matt. 19:23–25). I need not mention that (3) there is nothing in all these things that can bless or satisfy the chief part of us, our soul (Matt. 16:26), and nothing that we are not commanded to deny in order to obtain blessedness (Luke 14:33). Indeed, since (4) in all these things there is hardly any that does not fall upon the brute beasts themselves, and they are ignorant of blessedness (2 Peter 2:12). And thus, (5) it makes for perfection, glory, and blessedness also to despise all these things, and for that reason, they are considered more perfect and more blessed who make the least of them.

4. It draws us to seek blessedness in God.
XIV. On the contrary, fourth, (1) it convinces us that the blessedness of the rational creature is possible, because not only is God most blessed, and thus able to communicate his blessedness, but he has also endued rational creatures with an appetite for blessedness, and certainly he did not do so in vain (Ps. 4:6). (2) It shows us where to seek true blessedness: (a) in the union or possession of the most blessed one (Ps. 73:25; 16:5; 33:12; 144:15); (b) in communion with God (1 John 1:3; 2 Cor. 13:14), by which he is with us, in us, for us, and, as our God, devotes himself and all his attributes to us and to our blessing (Rom. 8:32); (c) in the enjoyment of God, which embraces, first, the perfect knowledge (and as it were the vision) of God (John 17:3; 1 Cor. 13:12; Job 19:26–27), and of our blessedness as well, in union and communion with God (2 Cor. 3:18; 4:6), and second, a perfect repose and joy arising from this union and communion, together with our knowledge of it, that is, a perfect fullness of joys and pleasures with God's face, and at his right hand (Ps. 16:11; 1 Cor. 2:9; Ps. 84:11); and (d) in the sweetest glorification of God (Isa. 6:3; Rev. 4:8, 10–11; 5:9ff.).

Motivating reasons
(3) It draws us to seek blessedness, because (a) as we said, it can be obtained, since God is blessed and most blessed, and no one and nothing can restrain or impede him if he should will to confer it; since the rational nature is capable of blessedness; since so many have obtained and do possess it; since God delights in the blessing of his own, and to that end established that whole council of peace. (b) Blessedness is greatly desirable, just as misery is greatly abominable. For there is no one who does not desire his own blessedness. (c) It is desirable in that it renders everything else desirable, for nothing is desirable apart from blessedness; indeed, nothing is desirable except for the sake of blessedness. For why do people desire wealth, honors, pleasures, and so forth, except for the

sake of blessedness? And likewise, why do we turn from and avoid every adversity, except that they impede and disturb our blessedness? (d) Blessedness alone can satisfy the human appetite, for it is like the center of the soul, which rests nowhere but in blessedness. It is the whole of man (Eccl. 12:13). (e) Blessedness is so necessary for us that apart from it not even the whole world can profit us (Matt 16:26).

Its supports

(4) It supplies us supports for obtaining blessedness: that we (a) acknowledge and feel our extreme misery as long as we are destitute of God and are the enemies of him who is the source of all blessedness (Isa. 59:2; Eph. 2:12). (b) Pursue reconciliation with God with all our effort, through faith in the blood of the Mediator (2 Cor. 5:19–20; Col. 1:20), that we may be freed from all evil, which is the first part of blessedness. (c) Strive for union with Christ, that at the same time we may be united with God, in which is the foundation of blessedness for all, for blessedness comes through faith (Phil. 3:9; John 14:6). (d) Strive with all our effort for uniformity with God and with his will (Rev. 2:6; Ps. 40:8), which best procures his friendship. (e) Yield ourselves in covenant with God by receiving the conditions of the covenant offered to us, that namely God should become our God (Gen. 17:1), in which every point of our blessedness consists (Ps. 33:12). (f) Walk with God in the light, and thus we will have communion with him (1 John 1:3, 6–7). (g) Zealously employ those means by which we are brought closer to God: faith, hope, love, repentance, prayers, and the duties of public and private worship (James 4:8). Compare what we considered above in chapter 16, §XXI.

5. It consoles us in any adversity.
XV. Finally, fifth, the blessedness of God is profitable for consolation: (1) for the vacillating, the spiritually deserted, the doubting, and those all but despairing of their blessedness (about whom speak Isa. 50:10; Ps. 77:7–9; 88:3–4; etc.). Whenever within them they observe nothing but sin, guilt, death, and corruption, slithering as it were through all the corners of their soul; whenever outside them nothing meets them but confusion and destruction, and a certain murk of gloom, misery, death, and who knows not what evil; whenever it seems to them that all things threaten eternal damnation, lost salvation, that heaven is closed up, that God has withdrawn from them, to such a degree that they wrestle with despair and all but think of hanging themselves—at that time what will bring them more effective help than the fact that God is blessed and the source of all blessedness, and thus blessedness is at least possible even for them, especially

since so many have actually acquired it, and that nothing can impede God from conferring it even to them; and not only that it is possible, but also probable, since the most blessed God is the highest good, and thus communicative of his blessedness, and especially since he has offered so many and such great proofs by which he has demonstrated his propensity for blessing the miserable: he gave his very own and only begotten Son to the world for this end; he gave him over to death, and to a cursed death; he takes such anxious care to call forth miserable sinners to sharing in this blessedness (Matt. 11:27–28; Isa. 55:1–2; 2 Cor. 5:19–20). If at last by all these things there finally is found a certainty of blessedness, how great will be the comfort! But (2) to those who are confirmed in communion with God, and certain of their own blessedness, how great a joy there is supplied! How great a solace! That God is not only blessed in himself, but also more certainly than certain will be for them the fount of every blessedness. Now come diseases, come poverty, persecution, death, and any great evil, they will say, "If God be for us, who can be against us?" (Rom. 8:31). Those things may take away the verdure and the foliage of blessedness (which they possess in hope and in some way in reality), yet they will never rip out root and trunk. They will exult in triumph with the apostle, "Who shall separate us from the love of Christ?… I am persuaded that neither death, nor life, nor anything, shall separate us from the love of God which is in Christ Jesus our Lord" (Rom. 8:35; 38–39).

The conditions of consolation

This is so if only (1) they truly and without hypocrisy have been reconciled to God (Rom. 5:1). (2) They truly enter into the covenant of grace between themselves and God (Gen. 17:1–2). (3) According to the formula of this covenant, they have truly reciprocated to God, so that there is a mutual communion between them (Song 2:10). (4) Through the regeneration, renovation, and sanctification of the Holy Spirit, they have truly been made partakers of the divine nature, that they might be fit for there to be communion and conversation between them and God. (5) They discern in themselves a sincere and honest zeal for walking constantly with God (Gen. 17:1–2). These things provide the chief marks and indicators of the infallible blessedness that is to be received from the blessed God.

CHAPTER TWENTY-FOUR

The Most Holy Trinity

The grace of the Lord Jesus Christ, and the love of God, and the communication of the Holy Spirit be with you all. Amen.
—2 Corinthians 13:14

The mystery of the most holy Trinity

I. We taught above that the faith by which we rest in God for eternal life and blessedness rests on two foundations: that God is sufficient and that he is efficient. Moreover, he is sufficient on the one hand through his essence and essential attributes, whereby he exists as אל שדי, *El Shaddai*, and on the other hand through his subsistence, whereby the three persons of the deity each fulfill their own economic task in the blessing of man, as the apostle teaches in 2 Corinthians 13:14.

The Exegetical Part

It is built upon the exegesis of the text.

II. In these words is contained a prayer, in which the apostle entreats the individual persons of the deity that each would deign his own economic benefit to be imparted upon his beloved Corinthians. This prayer specifically considers:

  A. The Son: "the grace of the Lord Jesus Christ." In putting the Son before
     the Father he is not considering the order of subsisting in the persons
     as much as the order of the conferring of saving benefits, that is, as far
     as execution, where the redemption of the Son is first, although with
     respect to intention the election of the Father comes first. By the same
     phrase is also signified the essential equality of the persons, whereby the
     Father, although prior to the Son in the order and mode of subsisting, is
     still not superior to him in essence. Here there occurs:

1. The benefit which is prayed for: "grace." Not that natural grace common to the whole Trinity, concerning which we spoke above,[1] but personal grace, which consists in the redemption of the miserable, a grace peculiar to the Son according to economy, and in which is contained every benefit arising from Christ. Moreover, this task of redemption is called "grace," first because he freely undertakes it in the counsel of peace, and second because he dispenses it by love that is not owed, on whom and by what laws he wills.

2. The benefactor, represented:

    a. By his authority: "of the Lord." There is a triple lordship evident in the Scriptures: (1) a lordship of the divine nature equally common to all the persons, when God throughout the Scriptures is called "Lord." (2) A lordship of person, which belongs particularly to the Father, as he is the Creator, Lawgiver, and Judge (Mal. 1:6). (3) A mediatorial lordship, acquired by the blood of redemption (Rev. 1:5, 8; 1 Peter 1:19). It is this lordship that the apostle attributes in this passage to the Son in particular. For although with respect to his Father, because he took our guilt unto himself, he is a servant (Isa. 53:11), nevertheless, with respect to us whom he would redeem and did redeem, he is Lord (Acts 2:36). For this reason it belongs to him to dispense grace according to his own pure, unadulterated good pleasure.

    b. By his proper name: "Jesus," whereby he is designated Redeemer by office. For although both the Father and the Holy Spirit also devote their own work to the deliverance of the sinner, yet they do not do so by office, as does the Son.

    c. By his appellative name: "Christ," whereby he is designated the one anointed and called to the mediatorial office.

B. The Father: "the love of God." Here again occurs:

1. The benefit: "love," ἀγάπη. The love understood is the love of election, which the apostle derives from foreknowledge (Rom. 8:29). It is the love of foreloving,[2] of the giving of the Son (John 3:16), which arises from God's simple propensity toward the elect, a propensity, moreover, whereby he delivered the Son over to death for them (Rom. 5:5–9). Accordingly, this love is not only the love of benevolence,

---

1. 1.2.17 §§XII–XV
2. *praedilectionis*

which precedes redemption and faith in the Redeemer in the order of nature, but also the love of complacency, which follows faith (Heb. 11:3), the love by which, now reconciled, he embraces them on account of the grace of the Son. Thus it is not only the love of benevolence, by which he gave the Son as Mediator (John 3:16), by which he accepts the price of his blood, which love precedes the grace of Christ, but also the love of complacency, by which he embraces those redeemed and reconciled, the love that follows the grace of Christ, which is indicated to be the whole economic office and benefit of the Father.

2. The benefactor: "God," namely the Father, who is God not only by nature, which is common to all the persons, but also as it were by office. For in the economy, in which he is Lord, Creator, Lawgiver, and Father of the household,[3] the Father is throughout Scripture called "God" by appropriation. Moreover, he is God not only with respect to men, nor only with respect to Christ as man or as the Mediator, the God-man, but also with respect to Christ as the Son, by reason of the order of subsisting, and especially with respect to the redemptive office, by which in the counsel of peace he was made a debtor to the Father for the guilt of the elect, and thus subject to him, as to God.

C. The Holy Spirit: "the communication of the Holy Spirit," where again are noted:

1. The benefit: κοινωνία, "communication,"[4] which designates the whole economic office and benefit of the Holy Spirit, insofar as in sanctification and glorification, the Holy Spirit actually communicates the grace of Christ and the love of the Father.

2. The benefactor, who is called:

a. "Spirit," that is, not with respect to essence, for in that way the Father and the Son are also Spirit, but with respect to subsistence, insofar as he subsists through spiration (John 20:22).

b. "Holy," because he sanctifies by office, for which reason he is called the Spirit of holiness (Rom. 1:4).

---

3. *Pater-familias*, also "head of household" or "father of the family." In Mastricht's use *familia*, "household," includes the nuclear family but speaks more broadly of the whole household establishment, including its *famuli*, "household servants." Throughout the chapter he draws on the close connection of *familia* to *oeconomia*, "economy" or "household management." Cf. 1.2.25 §II.

4. Mastricht here translates κοινωνία as *communicatio*, "communication" or "sharing," rather than *communio*, "communion" or "fellowship," thus emphasizing the Spirit's work over its result.

The Dogmatic Part

That God is triune: It is proved from the Scriptures.

III. Therefore because, as all admit, this prayer contains adoration (which is proper to God, Matt. 4:10), adoration of the one God and adoration of the three, uniform adoration of the three, and adoration on account of a triple economic benefit, it cannot but be that in the one God there are three distinct persons, persons who also differ in their office and economic benefits. This is what the Scriptures teach whenever, first, they mention more than one who are God, which occurs: (1) in all those passages where God speaks to himself or about himself in the plural number (Gen. 1:26; 3:22; 11:7; cf. Isa. 6:8). For we should not tolerate the more recent Jews, who want this to mean that either the angels, or heaven and earth, or the elements were called to participate in creation, or who mock that God is speaking about his one self in the custom and style of magnates. For neither could the angels, or any creature, be called to participate in creation, as it is a work of infinite strength, nor is that style of great modern men consistent either with the Scriptures, or with the character of the Hebrew language, or with the customs of easterners, and only lately has it been received among westerners; nor is Scripture consistent enough with the style of great modern men, for no one says "we the kings of France" or "we Louises," in the way Scripture speaks about God, but rather, "we the king of France." (2) In those passages in which Jehovah is distinguished from Jehovah (Gen. 19:24; Ex. 34:5; 2 Sam. 12:24–25; Ps. 45:7; Hos. 1:7; Ps. 110:1; cf. Matt. 22:43–44; Dan. 9:17). For Jehovah is distinguished from Jehovah neither by essence, since there is but one Jehovah (Deut. 6:4), nor by accidents, which do not occur in Jehovah, so nothing remains except that they differ as persons. (3) In those passages in which the name of God is repeated by different turns in the same sentence, which you should not dare say occurs by tautology (Num. 6:24–26; Deut. 6:4; Ex. 3:15; Josh. 22:24; Ps. 67:5–7; Dan. 9:19; Isa. 6:3; 33:22; Zech. 1:3). (4) There could be added, if not as an apodictic argument, at least as a dialectic one, those passages in which adjectives, nouns, or verbs in the singular number are associated with Elohim in the plural (Gen. 1:1; etc.). Although, this argument is exposed to not a few exceptions and difficulties, since (a) the same structure is also employed for purely singular things, for the gods (Judg. 16:23–24), for one man (Ex. 4:16), and also (b) for one person of the divinity (Ps. 45:7). (c) By force of syntax, from it there could be conceived no less rightly three essences as three persons. (d) That mode of speaking is not utterly abhorrent to the character of the language, as is evident in the word "owner" (בעלים, Ex. 21:29; Isa. 1:3) and "lord" (אדונים, Gen. 40:1; 42:33), which name also belongs to God, from which he is called "Lord of lords" (אדוני האדונים, Deut. 10:17; cf. Mal. 1:6). For this reason, Calvin thought that in conflicts with the anti-Trinitarians this kind of argument should be put aside,[5] although I judge that once the mystery of the Trinity is sufficiently proved by other testimonies, it can be quite usefully applied for confirmation, since the aim of the syntax employed is undoubtedly the Trinity of persons.

Likewise, the Scriptures more clearly teach the same thing when, second, they mention three in God, by way of limitation: Psalm 33:6; Isaiah 61:1; 63:7, 9, 10; Matthew 3:16–17, from which comes that adage of the ancients, "Go to the Jordan and you will see the Trinity";[6] Matthew 28:19, since we cannot be baptized in the name of one who is not God (1 Cor. 1:13), nor were the Israelites said to be baptized in the name of Moses, but rather "into Moses," that is, according to the Syriac Peshitta and the Arabic, "under Moses" (1 Cor. 10:2); 2 Corinthians 13:14; 1 John 5:7, which passage is read in Cyprian and others before the time of Arius, and indeed by the Socinians themselves in their German version of the Racovian Catechism, printed AD 1630.[7] These passages also may be added: John 14:16; 15:26; 1 Corinthians 12:3; Galatians 4:6; Ephesians 2:18; 3:14, 16; 1 Peter 1:2; Titus 3:5–6; Revelation 1:4–6.

It is confirmed by scriptural reasons.

IV. Confirming the same are reasons supplied from the Scriptures: that (1) everything divine is attributed in the Scripture to three who are distinct, since to each individually are attributed the divine names, attributes, operations, and religious worship, under which heads everything divine is comprehended, which we will show regarding each person in the subsequent chapters.[8] (2) Salvation and life cannot be restored to a sinner if there is not more than one person in the one God, insofar as satisfaction (apart from which there can be no reconciliation), since it takes away the morally infinite evil of sin and acquires the

---

5. E.g. John Calvin on *Elohim* in Gen. 1:1, *Opera quae supersunt omnia*, ed. Edouard Cunitz et al. (Brunsvigae: C.A. Schwetschke, 1863–1900), 23:15; idem, *Calvin's Commentaries*, 1:70–71.

6. *Abi ad Jordanem et videbis Trinitatem*: This saying was variously attributed to Augustine, Athanasius; or to "the ancients," as a retort to the Arians, *Abi, Ariane, ad Jordanem et videbis Trinitatem* in Turretin, *Institutio theologiae elencticae*, pt. 1, loc. 3, q. 25 §7.

7. Mastricht is citing the so-called "Johannine Comma," found in 1 John 5:7–8 in some editions of the New Testament. Commenting in his *Annotationes* on 1 John 5:7–8, Hugo Grotius supposed it was inserted by the Arians, idem, *Opera omnia*, 4 vols. (Basil: Thurneysen, 1732), 3:1143. For the German version of the Racovian Catechism, see Smalcius, *Catechismus der Gemeine derer Leute* (1608).

8. 1.2.25 §IV; 1.2.26 §§VIII–XII; 1.2.27 §§VII–X

infinite good of union with God, cannot come but from the infinite God, and yet one and the same person does not make satisfaction to himself. Other reasons are supplied from the economic office peculiar to each person in the work of our salvation, which we will treat in their own places.[9]

Natural reasons are excluded.

V. At this point you will await demonstrations from nature in vain, because mystery exceeds nature, and thus here is especially valid the saying, "We believe the things of art by art, the things of nature by nature, but the things of God by God."[10] Yet we do not deny similarities by which its possibility might be declared in some manner once a demonstration has been made from the Scriptures, although we do not judge this worthy of indulgence here. Nor also do the testimonies of the pagans, drawn perhaps from the Scriptures or from the tradition of believers, say the same thing, but only similar things. See Johann Gerhard, *Loci theologici*, on the Trinity (locus 3, §28), and Balthasar Meisner, *Sober Philosophy* (pt. 1, sect. 4, ch. 9, q. 2), and others.[11] Therefore also, reason should not be listened to, from Scripture or from the creature, when it cries out against the Trinity, a doctrine that exceeds its capacity.

The chief terms of this topic are explained.

VI. And this at last is what the ancients, from the very beginnings of Christianity, desired to be designated by *Trinity* (a word certainly unwritten as to its syllables, but most evidently written as to its meaning, 1 John 5:7): by it they understood one divine essence, common to the three persons, the Father, the Son, and the Holy Spirit, who differ according to three modes of subsisting. And by *essence* they intended what elsewhere Scripture calls substance (תוּשִׁיָּה, Prov. 8:14),[12] nature (φύσις, Gal. 4:8), the form of God (μορφὴ θεοῦ, Phil. 2:6), the divine nature (θειότης, Rom. 1:20), the deity (θεότης, Col. 2:9). Or, it is that through which God is God, for that by which something is what it is, is called its essence. And while this essence is in act, or is outside of its own causes, it is termed *existence*;

---

9. 1.2.25 §VII; 1.2.26 §XIII; 1.2.27 §XI

10. τῇ τέχνῃ τὰ τεχνικά, τῇ φύσει τὰ φυσικά, ἀλλὰ τῷ θεῷ τὰ θεῖα πιστεύομεν. Cf. pseudo-Justin (Martyr), Ἐρωτήσεις Ἑλληνικαὶ πρὸς τοὺς Χριστιανούς (*Quaestiones Graecae ad Christianos*) in PG 6:1485–88.

11. Johann Gerhard, *Loci theologici* (1863–75), 1–2:380. Gerhard cites Balthasar Meisner (1587–1626) specifically here. Cf. Balthasar Meisner, *Philosophia sobria, in qua problemata lexica et logica in controversiis papisticis subinde occurrentia, succincte discutiuntur*, 3 vols., 6th ed. (Rintel, 1626), 1:600. Gerhard silently corrects the reference in Meisner, as Meisner's numbering scheme skipped from part 1, section 4, chapter 8 to chapter 10.

12. Cf. *essentia* in 1.2.3 §XVIII.

and insofar as that existence belongs to accidents, it constitutes *inexistence*;[13] insofar as on the other hand it belongs to singular substances, *subsistence*; and insofar as that subsistence is present in rational, complete, and incommunicable substances, it is called *personality*. Thus from this term, a person is nothing other than a rational, incommunicable substance. This is the force of the terms of this topic.

The communion of the three persons
VII. We will perceive the thing designated by these terms when, as by its parts, we have explained first the agreement or communion of these three, then second, their difference, and finally third, their economic office in the business of human salvation. Therefore the three persons agree: (1) in essence, from which they are called *unum*, one thing (1 John 5:7) and they constitute one God in number (not in species). And this happens differently than in created persons on account of the fact that the divine essence is infinite, and therefore communicable to more than one person. So then, (2) in all the essential attributes—eternity, omniscience, omnipotence—which coincide with the essence. Namely, (3) in essential aseity, by which the Son and the Holy Spirit is each as equally *a se*, from himself, as is the Father, although in addition to this there is in the Father a personal aseity peculiar to him (John 5:26). In addition, (4) in religious worship, which is equal to each (John 5:23). Finally, (5) in emperichoresis, through which one person is said to be in the other (John 14:9–11) due to the identity of essence.

The distinction of the persons from the essence
VIII. A twofold difference occurs. The first difference is that through which a person differs from the essence: certainly not a real difference, in which they differ as one thing and another thing, for God is most simple; nor a difference by mere reason, or only in our conception, for they differ as one from three; but by reason which has its reason for distinguishing in the thing itself. For although the divine essence is equal to the three persons taken together, yet it is broader than each of them. Wherefore essence and person differ (1) as broader and narrower, because the essence is common to the three persons. (2) As communicable and incommunicable, since the essence exists as common to the three persons. (3) As restricted and restricting, for the person restricts the essence in its own way. (4) As abstract and concrete, for person connotes essence, which essence does not do. See Maresius, *Systema* (loc. 3, §§14–18).[14]

---

13. *inexistentia*, the existence of an essence *in* its accidents

14. Samuel Maresius (Desmarets, 1599–1673), *Collegium theologicum sive systema breve universae theologiae* (Geneva: Johannes Antonius and Samuel de Tournes, 1642), 40.

What kind of distinction is there among the divine persons?
IX. The other difference is that among the persons themselves. Concerning which, first and foremost we must carefully avoid on the one hand Sabellianism, which admits of no difference among the persons other than a difference of reason and name, insofar as one person is called from his different operations now Father, now Son, now Holy Spirit; and on the other hand, the tritheism of Valentine Gentile, which imagines three eternal and unequal spirits, of which the first is the *essencer* and the rest are *essenced*. Some who intend to avoid Sabellianism say the persons differ really, but that seems to tend toward tritheism. And again others who intend to avoid tritheism state that the persons differ modally, as one mode from another, not indeed by reasoning alone, but in reality, which they express with the two words conjoined, by saying that they differ really-modally,[15] that is, as one mode from another, not by reason only, but in reality. And this indeed satisfies me the most. Nevertheless, there are those whom none of these please; instead they judge that it must be said that the persons differ personally. But what is this to say except that the persons differ as persons, while nothing is said about how one person differs from another? And yet if someone cannot walk in these scholastic stilts,[16] let him say that he has been taught from the Scriptures to believe that the persons differ as three (1 John 5:7), but by what kind of distinction he does not know, since Scripture does not disclose this; or that they differ supernaturally, not naturally.

In what do the three persons differ among themselves?
X. Whatever may be the case, at the least they differ: (1) in the hypostatic properties—subsisting entirely from himself; subsisting from a certain other one, and subsisting from two—which cannot coincide in any one person without contradiction. But concerning the properties specific to each person, we will deal specifically in the contemplation specific to each person.[17] (2) In the order of subsisting, in which the Father is the first person, since he subsists entirely from himself; the Son the second, inasmuch as he descended from the Father; the

---

15. *realiter modaliter*
16. *cothurnis hisce scholasticis*: A *cothurnus*, from the Greek κόθορνος and often translated "buskin," was a set costume piece of Roman tragedy to elevate main characters above secondary characters. It had a rectangular boot with a six or seven inch heel. Not only were these boots heavy, but according to classical references, quite clunky and cumbersome. Actors are also described as having to descend or get down from them. Cf. Ovid, *Amores* 2.18; Lucian, *Saturnalia* 19; *Anacharsis* 23.
17. 1.2.25 §VI; 1.2.26 §§V–VII; 1.2.27 §VI. Likewise for the following sentence.

Holy Spirit the third, as he proceeds from two, which we will teach individually in their own places. (3) In the mode of operating, which imitates the manner of subsisting and of order, insofar as, outside himself, the Father works from himself, through the Son and the Holy Spirit; the Son from the Father, through the Holy Spirit; and the Holy Spirit from the Father and the Son, through himself. In this the operative force indeed is only one, common to three, but the order of operation, and also its terminus, is diverse. And from this there is appropriated to the first person the first work, creation; to the second, the second, dispensation and redemption; to the third and last, the last, consummation and sanctification.

The economy of the three persons

XI. And thus upon this communion of three distinct persons rest a certain economy, economic offices of the persons, economic properties, economic worship, and indeed even economic sins. It is worth dealing with these things more distinctly, inasmuch as they occur less frequently in common places. There is therefore: (1) a certain economy common to the three persons: for in it there is the Father of the household, and there is as it were a common emissary, the Spirit. There is one who begets, the Father; there is one who is begotten, the Son; there is one who proceeds from the two, the Holy Spirit. The Father loves the Son (John 15:9; 5:20); delights in him (Prov. 8:30) as in the perfect image of himself (Col. 1:15), in the brightness of his glory and the express image of his person (Heb. 1:3); rests in him (Matt. 3:17); and glorifies him. The Son in turn honors the Father (John 8:49; 17:4). The Holy Spirit searches the depths of both (1 Cor. 2:10), and glorifies both (John 16:14–15). And all this without any loss of either independence (John 5:26) or equality (John 5:23). Into this household's fellowship[18] (2 Cor. 13:14; 1 John 1:3), and as if into its society, in time he received the church, which for this reason is called the house of God (1 Tim. 3:15; 2 Tim. 2:20), in which God is said to dwell, and to have his own fire and hearth, as it were (Isa. 31:9), and likewise the city and kingdom of God (Matt. 6:10, 13), from which the members of the church are denominated throughout the Scriptures as sons and daughters (2 Cor. 6:18), and likewise servants (Rom. 1:1), friends (John 15:15), members of the household, citizens (Eph. 2:19), and subjects.

---

18. *in huius familiae* κοινωνίαν

The economic offices of the three persons

XII. The persons undertook the government of this household by entering into counsel, as it were (Zech. 6:13), or by forming a pact between them (Isa. 53:10–11), whereby, according to the order of subsisting peculiar to each, each person undertook, so to speak, a certain task or economic office, through which the first person, as the Father of the household, acts as Lord and director, the one who sketched out, as it were, the whole business of future governance in predestination (Eph. 1:11; Acts 4:28), and in addition as Creator (Gen. 1:1; Ps. 33:6), lawgiver and judge (Gen. 18:25), and also avenger of the law (Rom. 1:18; Nah. 1:2), and accordingly, as God, not only theologically but also economically, that is, not only by nature and essence (which is common to all the persons), but also as if by economic office, for which reason the name "God" throughout the Scriptures is attributed by appropriation to the Father, as we saw in the exegetical part (2 Cor. 13:14; cf. 5:19; 1 Tim. 2:5). Again, the second person, as the middle person, undertook the task of mediator (1 Tim. 2:5), of surety (Heb. 7:22), of *goel*, "kinsman-redeemer" (Job 19:25; 17:3; Isa. 38:14), of the redeemer who would give himself as the sacrifice (Isa. 53:10). Finally, the third or last person adopted the province of emissary, the one who was sent as if by breathing (John 20:22; 14:26), that in order to consummate the work of redemption already begun he might, according to his own name, act as sanctifier (Rom. 1:4), teacher (John 14:26), leader (Ps. 143:10; John 16:13), and comforter (John 14:16). Yet this distribution of the economic task requires a twin caution: (1) that it be understood to have been made without any dependence or essential inequality, as we have already taught from John 5:26;[19] (cf. v. 23; Phil. 2:6–7), though we do see that a sort of economic inequality results from it (John 14:28). And thus (2) each person has this economic office of his own not by excluding the other persons. For which reason not only the Father, but also the rest of the persons, are Creator (Psalm 33:6), and not only is the Father called Judge (Gen. 17:25), but also the Son (John 5:22–23; 2 Thess. 1:7–8). Therefore, the *ad extra* operations, on account of the fact that they flow from the essence, are undivided, and they are worked only in a mode or order that is diverse.

The economic turns in governing for the persons

XIII. According to this diverse economic task, each person has his own turns, so to speak, in governing, such that the manner of the Father's governing in creation, in the covenant of works, in the protevangelium, in appearances, in

---

19. 1.2.12 §II.B.1, 4

addresses, was especially conspicuous before the Sinaitic giving of the law. Then came the dispensation of the Son (that Angel who bore the name of God within himself, Ex. 23:20–21), in leading the church through the desert (Ex. 23:20–21), in delivering to her the law from the Father (Gal. 3:19)—not indeed as a covenant of grace (at least not with respect to the Decalogue, which had nothing but the material of the covenant of works, though set forth with an evangelical goal and arguments), except perhaps with respect to the ceremonial law, which had the gospel of the Old Testament—by which law the church was directed all the way to the death and ascension of Christ. Finally, the governance of the Holy Spirit began to become evident, from his solemn outpouring (Acts 2:1ff.; 13:2) all the way to the end of the age (John 14:16–17), in sending forth ministers, in qualifying them for their tasks (Acts 2:4; 1 Cor. 12:7–11), in working with them by signs and miracles, in prospering the Word declared by them (Rom. 15:19), in spiritually vivifying the dead through regeneration (John 6:63), in converting hearts to receive the Mediator by faith (2 Cor. 4:13), in renewing the image of God in them, in illuminating the mind, correcting the will, ordering the affections, leading into all saving truth, and comforting in adversities. Accordingly, this diversity of dispensing will endure all the way to the end of the world, when the Son will present the kingdom to the Father and there will be established a common administration, in which God is all in all (1 Cor. 15:24–28). Yet, these things must be taken perpetually in such a way that the governance of no person is ever excluded: for the *ad extra* works are undivided for the entire Trinity, because they flow out of one and the same essence.

The economic attributes of the persons

XIV. Furthermore, to this economic governance correspond economic attributes: (1) when to the Father as the Lord, as the head of the household, as the first to sketch out the whole task of its care through predestination, is attributed authority (Rom 9:21–22; Matt. 20:15); when to him as the Creator, strength and power (Matt. 11:25; John 10:29; Heb. 1:3); when to him as the legislator and avenger, justice (Gen. 18:25; 2 Thess. 1:6); when to him as the Father of the household, love (2 Cor. 13:14), fatherly love, that is (Ps. 103:13), and motherly love (Isa. 49:15). Again, (2) when to the Son as the Word, as the steward, is attributed wisdom (Prov. 8:1ff.); when to him as sponsor and redeemer, grace and mercy (2 Cor. 13:14; Eph. 5:2). Finally, (3) when to the Holy Spirit as the consummator is attributed power (Luke 1:35), when to him as the communicator, sanctifier, teacher, leader, and comforter, communicative goodness (Ps. 143:10). There are those who are pleased by these economic attributes: power to the Father, wisdom to the Son, goodness to the Holy Spirit, whereby the triune God is most great, most wise, most good, to which correspond being able, knowing, and willing. And these attributes, since they truly differ objectively in some way, and yet on God's part constitute one and the same thing, if they do not explain the Trinity, at least demonstrate it, and from them, the Father is the creating person, the Son the redeeming person, and the Holy Spirit the sanctifying person. Yet this concept I dare not adopt, because other attributes also in the same way both differ amongst themselves and coincide with the essence, and thus more than three persons would have to be admitted in God, contrary to the Scriptures.

Economic worship

XV. There is in addition, analogous to these economic offices of the persons, economic worship. In it, (1) from each person those benefits are anticipated and sought that are analogous to his economic office (2 Cor. 13:14; Isa. 63: 7, 9–10): from the Father, election, the giving of the Redeemer, justification, remission of sins; from the Son, redemption, satisfaction; from the Holy Spirit, regeneration, conversion, sanctification, and comfort. Indeed, (2) we seek whatever benefits from each in that order in which they subsist and operate (Eph. 2:18; 3:14–16), for example, redemption from the Father through the Son and through the Holy Spirit, and so forth. Also (3) for every benefit, we give thanks to each of the persons according to their order, and also in our praises, we ordinarily make mention of the individual persons (1 Peter 1:2–3, 17, 19, 21–22; Rev. 1:4–5). Concerning this we will perhaps say more in the proper places.[20]

Economic sins

XVI. There are, finally, also economic sins which particularly cry out against the economic offices of each person (Matt. 12:32; John 8:55). And indeed sins against the Father are seen throughout the Scriptures, sin against the Son is brought to mind (Heb. 6:6; 10:29), and sin against the Holy Spirit (Matt. 12:31; Heb. 10:29; Acts 7:51; Eph. 4:30; Isa. 63:10). But we will speak, Lord willing, more fully about the specific economic office, benefits, worship, and sins, of the individual persons, each in his own particular theory.

---

20. 1.2.25 §§XIII–XVIII; 1.2.26 §§XXIII–XXVI; 1.2.27 §§XXI–XXIII

The Elenctic Part

It is asked: 1. Is there an essence one and the same in number common to
Father, Son, and Holy Spirit? A comparison of opinions
XVII. It is asked, first, whether there is an essence one and the same in number
common to the Father, the Son, and the Holy Spirit? The infidels, pagans, modern Jews, and Muslims are ignorant of the Father, the Son, and the Holy Spirit,
or even pursue them in hatred, and accordingly they allow no communion of
essence at all among those three. Among the pseudo-Christians, the Simonians,
the Cerinthians, the Merinthians, the Ebionites, and others—in whom, while
the apostle John was still living, the anti-Christ was already working—by denying the eternal deity of the Christ, were also by the same stroke denying the
identity of essence among the three persons. Macedonius, from whom the Pneumatomachi arose in the course of the fourth century, in stating that the Holy
Spirit was the chief among created angels, denied the same identity of essence.
In the same century, Arius was declaring that Christ was not of the same substance with the Father, but rather of a similar substance.[21] Photinus, at almost
the same time, in teaching that Christ was a mere man who before his birth from
the blessed Virgin did not exist, rejected the communion of essence between
the Father and the Son. The Tritheists at the beginning of the seventh century,
whose founder was John Philoponus, an Alexandrian philosopher (as witnessed
by Nicephorus, bk. 18, ch. 49),[22] and also the Peratae, asserted that according to
the number of the three persons there are also numbered three essences. Following these, last century Valentine Gentile disseminated among the Swiss that in
God there are three eternal spirits, each in turn subordinate to the other, such
that the Father is the *essencer* and the Son and Holy Spirit are *essenced*. The
Anabaptists also seem to admit three essences in God, which, according to the
number of the three persons, agree in operations, in righteousness, holiness, virtues, and benefits. The Socinians think that the Father and the Son differ in their
entire essence, as Creator and creature, and that the Holy Spirit is not even a
person, but only an accidental force of God.

The opinion of the Reformed with their reasons
The Reformed, against all these, teach that to the Father, the Son, and the
Holy Spirit belong a divine essence that is one and the same, not in species,

---

21. *Christum Patri non* ὁμοούσιον *sed* ὁμοιούσιον
22. Nicephorus Kallistos Xanthropoulos of Constantinople (c. 1320), *Ecclesiastica historia*
in *PG* 147:429–34.

but indivisibly, that is, one and the same in number. And they do so because (1) Scripture teaches this, as if in so many words, in 1 John 5:7: "There are three who testify in heaven: the Father, the Word, and the Holy Spirit, and these three are *one*," that is, in essence. And thus (2) "Jehovah," by all means the name of the essence, who is אלהינו, "our God" in the plural, is called יהוה אחד, "one Jehovah." (3) Although Scripture teaches one God, and one alone, that is, one essence, notwithstanding, it teaches that the Father is that one God, and so is the Son whom he sent (John 17:3). And (4) it makes all the divine attributes, which coincide with the divine essence, common to the Father, the Son, and the Holy Spirit, just as we will show separately in the contemplation of each of the persons.[23] (5) Though it commands us to worship religiously only one God (Matt. 4:10; Isa. 42:8), nevertheless it also commands us to present the Father, Son, and Holy Spirit with religious worship (2 Cor. 13:14; Rev. 1:4–5), which we will demonstrate distinctly concerning each of them in their own place.[24] (6) They are mentioned throughout Scripture as equals, for example, in the institution of baptism (Matt. 28:19), in the heavenly witness (1 John 5:7), in the prayer for the Corinthian church (2 Cor. 13:14), likewise in the prayer of John for the seven churches of Asia (Rev. 1:4–5). Therefore, since they are brought together equal to each other, in such a dignity that cannot but point to one divine essence, it is evident that this one divine essence is common to the three persons.

Objections

And there is not anything that our adversaries may allege to the contrary except: (1) that every person requires his own essence, and indeed an essence peculiar to himself, from which they conclude that an essence the same in number cannot be common to three persons. To which we respond that to every human person there does indeed belong his own peculiar essence because of the fact that the essence of human persons is finite, and accordingly it cannot be common to more than one; but one must think differently concerning the divine essence, which from its infinity is altogether able to be common to three persons. (2) That a person is nothing but a singular intelligent substance, and so according to the number of the persons, singular intelligent essences are required. But we respond that for the constitution of a person, a singular intelligent essence is not sufficient, because this also belongs to a separated soul, which even so is not a person, but that in addition for the constitution of a person it is desired that it be

---

23. 1.2.25 §IV; 1.2.26 §X; 1.2.27 §VIII
24. 1.2.25 §IV; 1.2.26 §XII; 1.2.27 §X

incommunicable. And since this is not true of the divine essence, which from its infinity is common to the three, it cannot be a person. (3) That if the three divine persons agreed in one essence, then they would also agree among themselves, and thus they would make one person. I respond, They certainly do agree, but only in one third thing,[25] that is, the essence; but by that very fact they do not agree in the same personality. And thus they are not *unus*, one person, but only *unum*, one thing, according to that statement of John, "these three are *unum*," one thing (1 John 5:7).

2. Are the Father, Son, and Holy Spirit distinguished as persons?
The separation of opinions
XVIII. It is asked, second, whether the Father, Son, and Holy Spirit are distinguished among themselves as persons. The Triformians (whom we spoke about in ch. 8, §VIII) once stated that they differed as parts of the one deity, and thus they stated that God was a composite, as it were, of three parts, of which the Father had one, the Son another, and the Holy Spirit the third. In this way not only will there exist composition in God, but in addition, neither the Father, nor the Son, nor the Holy Spirit will be the whole God. The Tritheists, ancient and more recent, among whom is Valentine Gentile, wanted them to differ as so many deities, and thus from this arise three gods. Approaching these in their own way are the Socinians, when they say that the Father and the Son differ as things as far apart as heaven and earth, as Creator and creature, and moreover that the Holy Spirit differs from both of these as a force or accident differs from its subject. The Sabellians think that the persons are distinguished by so many denominations, by which one and the same person, from the various modes of operating, is named now Father, now Son, and now Holy Spirit. The Tetratheists indeed distinguished them as three persons, but added to these the essence, which formed a fourth person (cf. what we considered above in the place cited).[26]

---

25. *in uno tertio*, a reference to the law of logic that two things agreeing in some way with a third thing also agree in that way with each other. Cf. Aristotle, *Elench.* 6.8, idem, *Topics* 7.1 §6. On the law of proportion, see §272 in Dionysius van de Wynpersse, *Institutiones logicae* (Groningen: Hajo Spandaw, 1767), 95, "Whatever two things agree with one certain third thing, to the same extent they agree amongst themselves; however, when one of the two agrees with the third thing, and the second is incompatible with it, also to the same extent they are incompatible amongst themselves." *Quae duo conveniunt cum uno quodam tertio, eatenus conveniunt inter se; quando autem duorum unum convenit cum tertio, et alterum huic repugnat, repugnatque quoque eatenus sibi invicem.*
26. 1.2.8 §VIII

The opinion of the Reformed with their reasons

The Reformed state that in the one common divine essence they differ as three persons, because (1) the Father, Son, and Holy Spirit are truly persons, inasmuch as they are endowed with all the personal prerequisites. For each of them is a singular, intelligent, incommunicable substance, conspicuous in its personal operations, as we will demonstrate individually when considering each one.[27] (2) They are numbered as *tres*, three persons, not as *tria*, three things, and as persons who are *unum*, that is, one thing (1 John 5:7), and moreover, (3) as *alius et alius*, one and another, not *aliud et aliud*, one thing and another thing (John 14:16). (4) The Father and the Son without doubt are persons, and when the Holy Spirit is numbered with them (Matt. 28:19; 1 John 5:7), he is numbered as a person. (5) In the Scriptures, to the individual persons are assigned their own characteristic properties—subsisting from himself, subsisting from one, and subsisting from two—which cannot all square with any one person, and which are in addition such properties as argue for persons—generating, being generated, and proceeding from two. In addition, (6) in the Scriptures to each of them are attributed such operations as belong only to a person, operations we will show individually when considering the individual persons. Therefore, (7) they do not differ as equal parts, because the essence of God through simplicity does not allow parts, as we have taught in its own place;[28] and if it did admit of parts, by this hypothesis no person would have the whole deity and thus be the whole God. (8) Nor do they differ as divine essences or deities, because not only are they called one (1 John 5:7), and not only have we demonstrated in the preceding paragraph that there is an essence one and the same in number common to them, but the contrary, three gods, would stand to us against the tenor of Scripture. (9) Nor do they differ as Creator and creature, because each is a divine person, just as we will soon demonstrate regarding each one individually.[29] (10) Nor do they differ only in denominations arising from the diversity of operations, but by the characteristic properties which cannot all occur in any one person without contradiction. With these arguments all set forth in this way, I do not see what could be objected to the contrary, at least with any appearance of truth.

---

27. 1.2.25 §V; 1.2.26 §V; 1.2.27 §V. So also for (6).
28. 1.2.6 §XXIII
29. 1.2.25 §IV; 1.2.26 §§VIII–XII; 1.2.27 §§VII–X

3. Is it not a dogma of Scripture that God is one in essence and three in persons? A comparison of opinions

XIX. It is asked, third, whether the dogma of God as one in essence and three in persons is not a dogma of Scripture. Indeed, the anti-Trinitarians deny it, saying it is false, except that certain more recent Socinians, in order that they might avoid the universal hatred of Christians for the Socinian denial of the Trinity, cry out until they are hoarse that we have thrust this upon them by misrepresentation, since they acknowledge that God is one in essence and nevertheless acknowledge that Father, Son and Holy Spirit are called God. Although when they are asked more distinctly whether they acknowledge that that one divine essence is common to those three, they reply that this does not appear in Scripture. Certain papists, because the word *Trinity* does not appear in Scripture, refer the dogma to traditions.

The opinion of the Reformed is proved.

The Reformed state that it is altogether a dogma of Scripture, because (1) through the preceding controversies we have already demonstrated from the Scriptures that there is one and the same essence common to the Father, Son, and Holy Spirit, and that nevertheless they are distinguished among themselves as so many persons. (2) Also in the dogmatic part (§§III–IV) we demonstrated from the Scriptures of both Testaments that it is taught in the Scriptures. (3) Upon it is built the whole faith of Christians, who for this reason are baptized into God the Father, Son, and Holy Spirit, and long ago were not admitted into the communion of the Christian church before they had professed their faith concerning this dogma.

Objections

Now nothing remains except that from these hypotheses laid down we should briefly resolve the common objections of all those who are opposed to the Trinity. They allege: (1) that from the infinity of each person are inferred three infinite beings. But they do so unjustly, because through the unity of the essence there also belongs to the three one infinity, inasmuch as it coincides with the essence. (2) That from the Trinity of persons conjoined with the unity of essence results a quaternity. They allege this wrongly, because essence and persons do not differ in reality but only in reasoned reason.[30] For neither can any essence really

---

30. *ratione ratiocinata*, that is, by reason that takes its reasons not from itself but from rational analysis of its object. Cf. §VIII, above.

differ from its own subsistence. (3) That since there is acknowledged only one singular divine essence existing through itself, there is only one person, since a person is nothing other than an individual substance endowed with reason. But a singular substance, although endowed with reason, does not immediately constitute a person unless there is added incommunicability, as is evident in a separated soul. (4) That every person requires for himself his own essence, and thus according to the number of three persons there are constituted three essences. I respond, By all means every person in the concrete requires an essence, but not a different one or one peculiar to himself, since the one essence, through its infinity, is sufficient for the three persons. (5) That three divine persons constitute three gods just as three human persons constitute three men. I respond, By no means, since to three human persons belong three essences in number, while common to the three divine persons is the same essence in number. (6) That since three persons agree in one and the same essence, they also agree among themselves and thus constitute only one person. I respond, They surely agree, but not except in one third thing,[31] which is the essence, and thus they are *unum*, one thing. But they do not agree in the same personality in number, wherefore they are not *unus*, that is, one person, but *unum*, one thing. (7) That the Trinity implies various absurdities, for example: (a) that the Son is the Father, for the divine essence, they say, is the Father; the divine essence is the Son; therefore, the Son is the Father. I respond, Besides the fact that there is a paralogism in the expository syllogism—since the middle term "essence" is indeed something singular, but yet also something common, which the laws of the expository syllogism do not tolerate, for in it is required a middle term that is not only singular but also incommunicable, otherwise it would imitate a universal—it is also false to say that the divine essence is either the Father or the Son, although both the Father and the Son do have the same essence in number. (b) That if the Father is true God, the Son cannot be true God, which they attempt to conclude in this way: the Father is true God; the Son is not the Father; therefore, the Son is not true God. I respond, The fallacy of this expository paralogism will be apparent if it is resolved into its analogous direct syllogism: whatever the Father is, the Son not; but the Father is true God; therefore, the Son is not true God. For the major premise is true only with respect to personality, not simply, nor with respect to essence, and thus it implies only that the Father is not the same person as the Son, and not that the Son is not true God, on account of the essence common to both.

---

31. See n. 25, above.

4. Is the dogma of the Trinity necessary to believe? The difference of opinions
XX. It is asked, fourth, whether the dogma of the Trinity, for the Christian church, indeed for each of its members, is necessary to believe. The anti-Trinitarians, because they deny its truth, are compelled to disown its necessity, and indeed its utility. The Remonstrant Apologists, although they dare not openly deny its truth, lest they seem to have crossed publicly into the camp of the Socinians, nevertheless undermine it evidently enough through their devices, and nevertheless openly deny its necessity. They do this so that they might be able to admit Socinians into the communion of their churches.

The opinion of the Reformed is proved.
The Reformed, although they do not state that a distinct knowledge of it, by which you clearly perceive its nature, is necessary for salvation, nevertheless judge that a knowledge of the fact of it,[32] which is most clearly taught in the Scriptures, is altogether necessary, or at least that those who entirely deny it cannot be saved. And they do so because: (1) Scripture expressly teaches that in this is eternal life, that we know that the Father is "the one true God, and Jesus Christ, whom he has sent," namely, that he also is the one true God.[33] (2) Nor does anyone acknowledge the Father who does not acknowledge the Son (1 John 2:23). (3) Nor does anyone honor the Father who does not honor the Son (John 5:23). (4) No one can either seek or find salvation by the love of the Father, and by the grace of the Lord Jesus Christ, and in the communion of the Holy Spirit, who has not acknowledged the Trinity (2 Cor. 13:14). (5) No one can be admitted into the communion of the Christian church who has not professed his faith in the Father, the Son, and the Holy Spirit (Matt. 28:19). (6) No one can pursue his own salvation in the satisfaction of Christ who does not receive Christ's deity, inasmuch as that satisfaction cannot stand apart from his deity (1 Tim. 2:5). (7) No one can believe the majority of the mysteries of the Christian religion who does not acknowledge the Trinity, inasmuch as they are built upon this mystery.

Objections
In vain will they object to these things: (1) that believers of the Old Testament were saved without belief in the Trinity. I respond: (a) This must be proved by our adversaries. (b) The testimonies of the Old Testament that we stated in §III

---

32. κατὰ τὸ ὅτι
33. John 17:3. Cf. Mastricht's explanation of this passage in 1.2.25 §X.

solidly refute this. And (c) if they had not acknowledged the Trinity, they would have neither acknowledged nor worshiped the true God, and accordingly would have been idolaters—indeed, atheists. For whoever does not acknowledge and does not worship that one who is truly God is an atheist. (2) That the article of the Trinity does not have any use for the practice of piety. I respond: (a) If it were granted—though it is not conceded—that it does not have its own particular use, nevertheless it is the basis and foundation of all Christian practice, without which no practice, or at least no Christian practice, can stand. And then (b) that it also has its own particular use was already taught in the dogmatic sections on the economy of the Trinity,[34] and the practical part of this chapter will amply teach the same. (3) That the majority do not understand this mystery, but they should not therefore immediately be excluded from a participation in salvation. I respond, Although they may not understand its nature, *how* God is one in essence and three in persons, yet they can understand from the most clear revelation of Scripture its truth, *that* God is so.

5. Can the dogma of the Trinity be obtained by the power of reason?
A comparison of opinions
XXI. It is asked, fifth, whether the dogma of the Trinity can be obtained by the power of reason. Theophrastus Paracelsus and his chemists attempted to demonstrate it from their three natural principles of body, that is, salt, sulfur, and mercury. Several Scholastics tried to conclude it from the nature of the understanding God, in roughly this manner: reason teaches that God understands, that from this understanding is born an idea or image, and that when the thing understood is something good, there arises love. Since, however, that image and its love as well are not accidents in God but substance, it cannot occur but that one substance is in the one understanding, the one understood, and the one loved. And thus they said that the Father is God understanding, the Son is God understood, and the Holy Spirit is God loved. Others among them, such as Scotus (on bk. 1 of the *Sentences*, distinctions 2, 9, 10),[35] tries to evince the Trinity from production, in this way: producing is a certain perfection which implies nothing of imperfection, and therefore it belongs to the most perfect being, and that from eternity, before the production of this universe; and since eternal production stipulates an eternal product, and since this also implies no imperfection in its concept, there must also be received an eternal product; and because producing

---

34. §§XII–XVI, above
35. John Duns Scotus, *Opera Omnia*, 12 vols. (Hildersheim: Georg Olms Verlagsbuchhandlung, 1968), bk. 1, dist. 2, qq. 6–7, 5.1:299–380; bk. 1, dist. 9–10, 5.2:823–71.

and being produced also involves a perfection without any imperfection, this also must be admitted in the most perfect being. From this it results that the Father is God producing, the Son is God simultaneously producing and produced, and the Holy Spirit is God produced only. Gabriel Biel pursues the same argument (on bk. 1 of the *Sentences*, dist. 10, q. 1),[36] as well as Raimundo de Sabunde in his *Natural Theology* (ch. 46–55),[37] and several of the Cartesians (though others of them cry out against it): for example, Johannes Clauberg in his *Disputations* has adopted the same argument and laboriously pursues it at length in a number of disputations.[38] Not a few of his followers add other arguments, saying for example that there is no possession of any good that is pleasant without a companion, and because in God there has always been a most pleasant possession of the highest good, it is easily concluded that God has never been without a companion. Thomas Aquinas in his *Summa theologiae* (pt. 1, q. 32, art. 1) cries out against the Scholastics, stating that such an attempt detracts from faith in more than one way.[39] Others among the Scholastics state that in all creatures there is some vestige of the Trinity, but in the human soul there is an image of it, insofar as "the mind remembers itself, understands itself, loves itself: if we discern this, we discern a trinity; we do not yet discern God, but the image of God," which they cite from Augustine, *On the Trinity* (bk. 14, ch. 8).[40] Nor are there lacking from our own theologians those who attempt, if not to demonstrate the Trinity, at least to declare it from the three primary attributes of God—power, wisdom, goodness—such that the Father is as it were God the powerful, the Son God the wise, and the Holy Spirit God the good.

The reasons of the Reformed

The common opinion of the Reformed is that the Trinity cannot be either searched out by natural reason or solidly demonstrated, though at the same time it can be declared and, with respect to its possibility, proved with similar things and *a posteriori* reasons. And they hold this opinion because: (1) it is a mystery, which all acknowledge who know its truth, if only you leave out those who in

---

36. Gabriel Biel, *Super primo Sententiarum* (Basel, 1508) sigs. RR iii (verso) – RR iv (recto); idem, *Collectorium circa quattuor libros Sententiarum*, eds. W. Werbeck and U. Hofmann, 4 vols. (Tübingen: Mohr Siebeck, 1973–1992), 1:348–56.

37. Raimundo de Sabunde (c. 1385–1436), *Oculus Fidei, theologia naturalis sive liber creaturarum* (Amsterdam: Petrus van den Berge, 1661), 38–49.

38. For his twelve disputations on the Trinity, see Johannes Clauberg (1622–1665), *Disputationes selectae* (Duisburg: Francois Sas, 1665), 13–97.

39. Thomas Aquinas, *ST*, Ia q. 32, art.1.

40. Augustine, *De Trinitate* in *PL* 42:1044; *On the Holy Trinity* in *NPNF1* 3:189.

fact acknowledge no mystery, but only those things that are clearly and distinctly perceived. That it is a mystery is taught by the thing itself: for if there is in the Christian religion any mystery, it is certainly that the one is three, which the apostle also signifies well enough in Colossians 2:2: "to the knowledge of the mystery of God, both of the Father and of Christ" where the polysyndeton "both… and" shows clearly enough that Paul's words concern plural persons in God—the Father and the Son—though for his own reasons he does not make express mention of the Holy Spirit. Therefore is not what he calls "the mystery" surely the Trinity, or at least the plurality of persons in God? (2) As Aquinas teaches, it detracts in more than one way from the dignity of this dogma, through which it concerns matters unsearchable to reason, and from the faith itself, to the extent that the anti-Trinitarians believe we construct such a great matter upon this sort of sorry little reasons. Add that regarding this mystery, "In faith, to seek reasoning is to spread a parasol before a weak eye so that it may not be struck by a more extraordinary light," as Richard of St. Victor says (*On the Trinity*, bk. 1, ch. 1).[41] (3) None of the philosophers, not even all philosophers together, by all the acumen of their reason, ever attained to the knowledge of it. (4) The dogma of the Trinity is the basis of the entire Christian faith, and thus if that may be resolved into natural reason, nothing will hinder the whole Christian religion from being resolved into reason, and thus it would degenerate from faith into philosophy. (5) No natural reason can be produced to solidly conclude that therefore the God who is one in essence is three in persons.

Objections

And this is evident by induction. For if (1) with the Paracelsists you should say, In any body there is salt, sulfur, and mercury, at best you will have that there is in any body some likeness to the Trinity. You will nevertheless not have what would solidly conclude that therefore in the one God there are three persons. If (2) you should say with the Scholastics that nature teaches that God understands, and that from this understanding arises an idea or image, you will likewise have (a) a similitude or some sort of vestige of the Trinity, but you will not have an argument concluding that in God there is a Trinity. You will say (b) that understanding is a characteristic act, peculiar to the Father alone,

---

41. Richard of St. Victor (d. 1173), *De superdivina Trinitate* (1510), 7 recto–7 verso. Here Richard refers to faith as "the superior way of knowing" (*superior cognoscendi modus*) to reasoning, and also notes, "Therefore, the one who can consider (*intueri potest*) these things which belong to faith without reasoning knows and understands them by far more manifestly than the one who demands and investigates…."

and accordingly the Son and Holy Spirit do not understand, and thus lack this perfection, and consequently, are not infinitely perfect, and thus not God. Or (c) if should you say that both the Son and the Holy Spirit also understand, you will say that from this understanding of the Son again arises a certain idea, and a love, and accordingly there are three persons in the Son, and likewise in the Holy Spirit. And thus instead of three, you will have nine divine persons. If (3) you should allege with Scotus, the Scotists, and the Cartesians that nature dictates that producing, being produced, and simultaneously producing and being produced are perfections in God, the difficulties raised by the preceding argument will recur, *mutatis mutandis*. If (4) with others you should attempt to infer the same from the three primary attributes of God—power, wisdom, goodness—you will fall into the same trap. Nor can any other natural reasons be represented which are not liable to the same or similar difficulties, just as we have amply demonstrated in our *Gangrene of the Cartesian Innovations* (sect. 2, ch. 17). If finally (5) you should object that certain heathen philosophers held to it, as recognized by Philippe du Plessis Mornay (*On the Truth of the Christian Religion*, ch. 6),[42] Juan Luis Vives (*On the Truth of the Christian Religion*, bk. 2 ch. 2),[43] and others; if namely you should try, with Marsilio Ficino (on bk. 6 of Plato's *Republic*),[44] to demonstrate that Plato held to it, or likewise with Scaliger (*Exoteric Exercises on Subtlety*, exercise 365, sect. 3),[45] that Aristotle held to it, and also with Plotinus (on Aristotle's *On Heaven* in the *Second Ennead*),[46] and so forth, I will retort that either these acknowledged only a likeness and vestige of the Trinity, or they held to it from the writings of Moses and the prophets, or from interaction with the Jews, as Eusebius witnesses (*Preparation for the Gospel*, bk. 9, ch. 3).[47] At the least, the ancient Greek philosophers had gone to the Egyptians, Chaldeans, Phoenicians, and the Hebrews in order to learn from them, as the following teach with unanimous agreement: Diodorus Siculus (*Library of History*, bk. 2, last chapter),[48]

---

42. Phillippe du Plessis Mornay, *De la verité de la religion chrestienne* (1581), 95–130; idem, *De veritate religionis Christianae* (1583); idem, *A woorke concerning the trewnesse of the Christian religion* (1587).

43. Juan Luis Vives, *De veritate fidei Christianae* (1551), 130–36.

44. Marsilio Ficino (1433–1499), *Opera* (Basel: Heinrich Petrus, 2 vols. 1561), 1:942–43.

45. Julius Caesar Scaliger, *Exotericarum exercitationum liber XV, de subtilitate* (Hannover: Daniel and David Aubrius, 1620), 1067–68.

46. Cf. Plotinus, *Enneads* in *LCL* 441.

47. Eusebius, *De praeparatione evangelica* in *PG* 21:681–88; idem, *Preparation for the Gospel*, 3:404–8.

48. Diodorus Siculus, *Bibliotheca historica*, ed. Ludwig Dindorf, 5 vols. (Leipzig: Teubner, 1866–68), 2.60.1–4, 1:226; idem, *LCL* 303:80–84.

Diogenes Laertius (*Lives of Eminent Philosophers*),[49] Eusebius (*Preparation for the Gospel*, bk. 10),[50] Cyril of Alexandria (*Against Julian*, bk. 1),[51] Justin Martyr (*Apology*, 2),[52] Origen (*Against Celsus*, bk. 1),[53] Augustine (*City of God*, bk. 18, ch. 36),[54] Lactantius (*Divine Institutes*, bk. 4, chs. 6–7),[55] and so forth.

The Practical Part

The mystery of the Trinity: 1. Shows the atheism of the anti-Trinitarians.

XXII. The practice of this chapter first opens to us the profanity and atheism of all those who do not accept the Trinity. These our Savior notes when from his consubstantiality with the Father indicated in John 5:19 ("Whatever the Father does, these things the Son also does") he concludes that the Jews do not honor the Father, because they do not honor the Son (John 5:23; 1 John 2:23). For this reason Paul, from the fact that the Gentiles were without Christ, concludes that they were atheists (Eph. 2:12). And he does so with reason, for (1) is not he an atheist who denies religious worship to the one who is the true God (Rom. 1:21)? Or, (2) if someone should bring religious worship to him whom he does not believe to be God, is he not an idolater (Gal. 4:8; Matt. 4:10)? Furthermore, (3) what sort of grace of our Lord Jesus Christ, what sort of communication of the Holy Spirit is there when the honor of deity that belongs to them is sacrilegiously removed from them? Indeed, what sort of love of the Father is there when the honor of deity is disputed for his beloved Son and for the Spirit of his mouth? And at last what religion can exist when the grace of Christ, the love of the Father, and the communion of the Holy Spirit are banished? Finally, (4) what sort of confidence of remission of sins is there without satisfaction? Or satisfaction without the deity of the one who satisfies? What sort of regeneration for a man dead in sin, what sort of conversion and sanctification, without the communication of the Holy Spirit? Or communication without

---

49. Diogenes Laertius, *Lives* 1.1 in *LCL* 184:24–29.

50. Eusebius, *De praeparatione evangelica*, PG 21:765–843; idem, *Preparation for the Gospel*, 2:460–506.

51. Cyril of Alexandria, Πρὸς τὰ τοῦ ἐν ἀθέοις Ἰουλιάνου (*Adversus Julianum*) in PG 76:509–32.

52. Justin Martyr, Ἀπολογία δεύτερα ὑπὲρ Χριστιανῶν (*Apologia secunda pro Christianis*), PG 6:457–462; idem, *Second Apology*, ch. 10 in *ANF* 1:191–92.

53. E.g. bk. 1, ch. 13–18, Origen, Κατὰ Κέλσου (*Contra Celsum*) in PG 11:679–94; idem, *Against Celsus* in *ANF* 4:401–3.

54. Augustine, *De Civitate Dei* in PL 41:582–83; idem, *City of God* in *NPNF1* 2:382; cf. *Confessions* 8.3, *City of God*, 10.23.

55. Lactantius, *Divinae institutiones* in PL 6:461–65; idem, *Divine Institutes* in *ANF* 7:100–6.

deity? And finally, what sort of religion is there without the confidence of remission of sins, without regeneration, conversion, and sanctification? Therefore, in place of religion there cannot thrive among the anti-Trinitarians anything except horrendous atheism, base idolatry, vain presumption of salvation, and most certain desperation.

2. It supplies an argument for glorification.

XXIII. Second, the holy Trinity supplies us an argument for divine glorification, with the example going before us of the seraphic doxology in Isaiah 6:3, repeated in Revelation 4:8 and signified also in Romans 11:36 and Revelation 1:4–5. For in the most blessed society of the three persons shines forth exceedingly: (1) the infinite perfection of God, insofar as the infinite power, wisdom, and goodness of the three most perfectly comes together in the one (John 17:23). (2) His immeasurable blessedness, in the most sweet fellowship of the persons, the unanimity[56] in their joint counsels, by which the persons most perfectly know and love each other, rest in each other, and reciprocate their own perfection to each other, which these passages support: Proverbs 8:30; Matthew 3:17; 17:5; John 17:21–22. Furthermore, (3) their mutual glorification, by which the Father glorifies the Son, the Son the Father, and the Holy Spirit the Father and the Son, as we have shown above from John 17:4–5, 22 and 16:14.[57] I do not add (4) that whole argument for glorification which is supplied to men from the most wise economy of the persons in the business of their salvation, concerning which we spoke in the dogmatic part.[58] Nor also do I add (5) the argument for gratitude and glorification which is supplied to us from the revelation of this great mystery, inaccessible to reason, unknown to the most sagacious philosophers, the revelation of that "wisdom in a mystery, the hidden wisdom…which none of the rulers of this age knew…but God has revealed to us through his Spirit" (1 Cor. 2:7, 8, 10). And indeed (6) that argument supplied to us from communion with the most holy and blessed Trinity, concerning which we will speak below.[59] Based on all these arguments, nothing was more customary for the primitive church than during their sacred rites to sing hymns and praises to the most holy Trinity, which hymns have been gathered by Josse Clichtove in his *Elucidatorium*

---

56. ὁμονοία
57. §XI. So also for the next sentence.
58. §§XII–XVI
59. §XXV

ecclesiasticum, and likewise Georg Cassander in his *Liturgies*.[60] See also Voetius, *Select Disputations* (pt. 1, p. 483).[61]

3. It commends the excellence of man.

XXIV. Third, it exceedingly commends the excellence and blessedness of elect man, inasmuch as for his blessedness just any one was insufficient, as it were, though infinitely powerful, wise, and good, and instead three, each of which is such, acted in harmony for that blessedness.

What this excellence includes

Specifically, that (1) each of these three, in this business of this blessedness, took to himself his peculiar task, so to speak: the first that he might decree and prepare this blessedness; the second that he might acquire it; the third that he might apply and confer it, as will be evident in each particular theory of the persons.[62] (2) Each also confers a specific benefit to man: the first, love; the second, grace; and the third, communion (2 Cor. 13:14). (3) Each of these expends, as it were, by his undertaken office, his entire self and all things that are his, as great as they are, for this blessedness. Indeed (4) they also introduce the sinner into their economy, household, and society, so that he is not only a servant, friend, and member of the household, but also a son of the household,[63] on account of that one and only natural and indeed firstborn Son (Heb. 12:23). Moreover, (5) as a sign of this introduction, they will that baptism be conferred and their own name of the Trinity be invoked and poured out upon him (Matt. 28:19).

To what end it aims

From all these things the most holy Trinity commends to man his own excellence: (1) not to this end, that he may boast—for, "What is man that you are mindful of him?" (Ps. 8:5)—that is, as if this had come on account of his

---

60. E.g. "Tu trinitatis unitas" in Josse van Clichtove (Judocus Clichtoveus, d. 1543), *Elucidatorium ecclesiasticum ad officium ecclesiae pertinentia planius exponens* (Paris: Jean Petit, 1540), 11r; Georg Cassander (1513–1566), *Liturgica de ritu et ordine Dominicæ coenæ celebrandæ* (1558); e.g. "O Trinitas laudabilis" and "Qui nos creas Pater Deus" in idem, *Hymni ecclesiastici* (Cologne: 1556), 218–19.

61. Gisbertus Voetius, *Selectae disputationes theologicae* (1648–1669), 1:483. Here Voetius specifically mentions hymns by, in order, Ambrose, Bede, and Paulinus, which is the exact same ordering of the first authors in the table "Auctores Hymnorum" in Cassander, *Hymni Ecclesiastici*, 1. Also, Voetius specifically names, for example, "Tu Trinitatis unitas," found above in Clichtove, *Elucidatorium* (1540), 11r.

62. 1.2.25 §VII; 1.2.26 §XIII; 1.2.27 §§XI–XIV

63. *filius-familias*; cf. *Pater-familias*, n. 3 above.

innate merit, and not from the pure grace of the Trinity. But rather so that (2) he might gratefully acknowledge the grace of the most holy Trinity. And that (3) he who has been exalted by the grace of the Trinity to such great dignity might not in his living cast himself down below the reprobate, indeed below the herds of cattle. Moreover, that (4) because the most holy Trinity has freely taken such great care for his salvation, he might not negligently disregard his own salvation.

4. It entices us to zeal for communion with the holy Trinity.
XXV. Fourth, it allures us that by every effort we might embrace the communion of the most holy Trinity (John 17:21–23). That this communion with the holy Trinity does come to man is evident, first, from many testimonies of Scripture in which is asserted either a common communion with the three persons (2 Cor. 13:14; Eph. 2:18), or a specific communion of us with the Father and the Son (1 John 1:3; John 14:23), with the Son alone (1 Cor. 1:9; Rev. 3:20), or with the Holy Spirit (Eph. 4:3–4).

Motivating reasons
It is also evident, second, from reasons, in which one and the same benefit of God is sought from two, such as grace and peace from the Father and the Son (Rom. 1:7; 1 Cor. 1:3; 2 Cor. 1:2), or from the three together (Rev. 1:4–5); or when the same benefit is in different passages of Scripture distinctly asserted for the three persons. For example, our teaching or instruction is distinctly attributed to the Father in John 6:45; it is attributed to the Son in Matthew 23:10; it is attributed to the Holy Spirit in John 14:26 and 1 John 2:27. Thus, as our instruction is common to the three persons, so also is every saving benefit, although it belongs to each in his own specific way, that is, to the Father in original authority, to the Son in accomplishment, to the Holy Spirit in communication. To the Father, I say, on account of original authority, from which it is said that thus it was his good pleasure, and because he wills, he makes us alive (John 5:21; James 1:18); to the Son by right of merit, insofar as he acquired by his own blood that we may now receive from his fullness grace upon grace (John 1:16); to the Holy Spirit through immediate efficacy of application (Rom. 8:11). Therefore it is to seek this communion with all zeal that the most holy Trinity invites us, because (1) in it consists all our excellence and blessedness (1 John 1:2–3). For what thing more excellent for man could be desired than communion and fellowship with the most blessed Trinity? (2) Upon this depends our every blessing and salvation. For which reason God formerly willed the solemn benediction of the priest to be made by a distinctly invoked triad (Num. 6:23–27), and Paul seeks

grace, love, and communion from the Trinity. Therefore, signifying this, we are also initiated in baptism to the Father, Son, and Holy Spirit.

Means

Moreover, let us strive for communion with the most holy Trinity, and let us happily attain it: (1) by zeal for the reconciliation of ourselves with God, for our sins separate us from God (Isa. 59:2) and alienate us from him (Eph. 2:12; 4:18), such that there can be no greater communion between us and God than between light and darkness (2 Cor. 6:13; Amos 3:3). Next, (2) by true and living faith in the Son of God, whereby united with him who likewise partook of our flesh and blood (Heb. 2:14), we might achieve the communion of the same Father and Spirit (John 20:17), and he might ask his Father that he give to us his Spirit (John 14:16), and thus we might have communion with the three. Finally, (3) because communion is mutual, let us on account of the benefits communicated or to be communicated to us by the most holy Trinity render back our duties to the Trinity (Rom. 12:1).

5. It urges the worship of the holy Trinity.
XXVI. Accordingly, fifth, the most holy Trinity urges that we religiously reciprocate to him the communion of worship: (1) let us in holiness keep the faith given to him in baptism, let us give back our whole selves to the Father, Son, and Holy Spirit into whose covenant and fellowship we have been received in the solemn sacrament, let us offer ourselves faithful to that covenant and fellowship (Matt. 28:19–20). (2) Let us expect every benefit and saving blessing from all the persons, inasmuch as by counsel and as if by office they came together equally for our salvation (Num. 6:24–27), and yet do so observing the order of conferring, so that we seek it from the Father, through the Son and Holy Spirit (Eph. 2:18). At the same time, (3) let us specifically request that benefit which is, by economic office, specific to each person, so to speak: grace from the Son, love from the Father, and communication from the Holy Spirit. And in turn (4) let us faithfully repay the economic office specifically belonging to each person: for example, let us offer to the Father reverence and obedience; to the Son, faith and love; to the Holy Spirit, obedience; and to all, gratitude and glory, just as we will teach specifically in the specific contemplation of the persons.[64] Finally (5) in all our prayers, hymns, doxologies, let us as much as can be done make distinct remembrance and commemoration of the three persons, following the custom of the primitive church, just as we have taught above in §XXIII. By all

---

64. 1.2.25 §§XIII–XVIII; 1.2.26 §§XX–XXVI; 1.2.27 §§XXI–XXIII

these things we will as it were oblige the grace of the Lord Jesus Christ, the love of the Father, and the communion of the Holy Spirit to come upon us.

6. It dissuades from sins.

XXVII. On the contrary, sixth, let us carefully take heed that we by no means offend any person by any sin, because (1) when one person has been offended, we offend all three, who are equally God, omnipotent, good, and just. (2) When one has been offended, we cannot experience the favor and grace of any. Indeed, (3) when one has been wounded, we incite against ourselves three most harsh avengers (Isa. 63:9–10). But those sins that strike against each divine person particularly we will indicate in their own place.[65]

7. It invites us to the communion of the saints.

XXVIII. Finally, seventh, the most blessed unity of the three persons, their unanimity and mutual love, invites us to imitation, namely that we who, by the bond of one Spirit, by the one faith, with the same Son of God and through him, are united with the same Father, should strive to keep inviolate the same body of Christ and the unity of the Spirit (Heb. 13:16).

Reasons

For (1) in this manner we are in our own way made to be like the most holy Trinity: "That they all may be one, just as you, Father, are in me, and I in you" (John 17:21). In this unity consists our highest glory: "The glory which you have given me I have given them, that they may be one, just as we are one" (John 17:22). (2) We cannot have communion with the sacred Trinity apart from this communion with the saints: "That they may be one *in us*" (John 17:21). Accordingly, (3) this mutual communion among ourselves offers an infallible argument for convincing the world that Christ was sent for us: "That the world may believe that you have sent me" (John 17:21). Finally, (4) in this union consists the chief perfection of the mystical body of Christ: "I in them and you in me, so that they may be made perfect in one" (John 17:23). This is surely no departure from reality, for as the chief perfection of the holy Trinity consists in the most perfect fellowship and communion of the divine persons, when the infinite perfection of God, by reflecting as it were from person to person, grows immeasurably strong, so also from the unity and communion of the saints, when so many and such great gifts not only come together in the same mystical body, but also reflect from one member to another (when you communicate your gifts to another,

---

65. 1.2.25 §XX; 1.2.26 §XXVII; 1.2.27 §XXV

when another communicates his to you, and when you entreat God for another for the gifts necessary to him, and another for you for yours, Rom. 12:4–6; 1 Cor. 12:12–13; Eph. 4:15–16), it grows immeasurably strong. The remaining things that make for the practice of this topic will be supplied, God willing, in the specific consideration of each person. One can also consult Gijsbert Schevichaven on knowing, loving, and praising the Trinity, and likewise Jean de Lorin in his *Commentary* on Wisdom 7:22–23. They are cited by the celebrated Voetius in his *Select Disputations* (pt. 1, p. 485), though I have not seen them.[66]

---

66. Gijsbert van Schevichaven, S. J. (1558–1622), *De ecclesiasticorum vita, moribus, officiis libri tres* (Mainz: Balthasar Lippius, 1621); cf. "Schevichaven, Gijsbert van" in *NNBW* 2:1284–85; Jean de Lorin, S. J. (1559–1634), *Commentarii in Sapientiam* (Cologne, 1624), 115–20; cf. Gisbertus Voetius, *Selectae disputationes*, 1:485, "I would have liked to run quickly through the Jesuit Gijsbert van Schevichaven's book on knowing, loving and praising the Trinity that was once available, but now there is not space for me to do so.... Lorin brings together the attributes of the Holy Spirit that could supply much for the practice of godly meditations and one's use in sermons."

CHAPTER TWENTY-FIVE

God the Father

I bow my knees to the Father of our Lord Jesus Christ, from whom the whole family in heaven and on earth is named.
—Ephesians 3:14–15

The consideration of the Father

I. So then we come straight to the individual consideration of the individual persons, and certainly first to the consideration of God the Father, whose prosopography, that is, the description of his person with respect to his deity, personality, and distinction from the rest of the persons, the apostle teaches quite exactly in the words above.

The Exegetical Part

It is built upon an exegesis of the text.

II. In them is contained a portion of that prayer or invocation that the apostle pours out for his beloved Ephesians from verse 4 all the way to the end of the chapter, such that in the words above, this portion has:

A. The invocation: κάμπτω τὰ γόνατά μου, "I bow my knees," which nearly coincides with the Greek προσκυνεῖν and the Hebrew השתחוה, both meaning to prostrate oneself in worship. It denotes a manner of praying in especially anxious circumstances (Luke 22:41; Acts 7:60; 9:40; 20:36). At the least it means two things: a religious worship of adoration, which, because from Matthew 4:10 such is fitting for none but God alone, argues that the invoked Father is God; and the subjection which is economically specific to the Father as to the head and Lord of the household.[1] Although at the same time, it is attributed to the Son (Phil. 2:10), namely as the Father's steward, the master of the house

---

1. *capiti et Domino-familias.* And thus below, *Pater-familias,* "Father of the household," and *Filius-familias,* "Son of the household." See 1.2.24 §II.B.2, n. 3.

(Jude 4) by the will and grant of the Father, and thus it is signified that he is God.

B. The one invoked, whom he represents under the relation he bears to the economy. Belonging to this economy is denoted here:

1. The Father of the household: "to the Father," πρὸς τὸν πατέρα. By all means not speaking essentially, as occurs in 1 Corinthians 8:6, but hypostatically, as occurs throughout the Scriptures, as often as he is distinguished from the Son; and moreover, economically, insofar as in the economy the Father is the governor, lawgiver, judge, and avenger of the laws, and in addition insofar as he is the benevolent caretaker of the whole household, insofar as he is the begetter of his very own and only begotten Son, and finally insofar as on account of the Son he is the adoptive Father of believers.

2. The Son of the household: "of the Lord," and "of our Lord." That is, Lord not through essential lordship, from the deity common to the three persons; nor through personal lordship, which is specific to the Father from the economy; but rather through mediatorial lordship proper to him by title of purchase (1 Cor. 6:20) and of redemption (Heb. 2:5). The text designates him with two names:

   a. His proper name: "Jesus," the Redeemer and Savior, by which is expressed his economic office.

   b. His appellative name: "Christ," by which is indicated the inauguration of his economic office through the anointing made by the Holy Spirit.

3. The household, πᾶσα πατριά, the universal economy (Eph. 1:10), that is, "every" or "the whole" πατριά, "paternity," or "parentage," or "kindred," or "family"; in Hebrew, מִשְׁפָּחָה, "clan" (2 Sam. 14:7; Est. 9:27) or בֵּית אָבוֹת, "fathers' house" (Ex. 6:25; 12:3). Moreover, a household is a people that has one common father of the household, or who belong to the same house (cf. Luke 2:4). Concerning this household are noted:

   a. The heavenly household: "in heaven," ἐν οὐρανοῖς. Or as it is commonly called, the "household above" as distinguished from the one below. Under it is comprehended the Father of the household; the Son of the household; the Holy Spirit, the common emissary of both (John 15:26); the angels, the ministering spirits (Heb. 1:14); and the blessed inhabitants of heaven (Heb. 12:22–23).

    b. The earthly household: "on earth," ἐπὶ γῆς. This means the church militant on earth, which is called the house of God (1 Tim. 3:15), members of the household of God (Eph. 2:19) and of the household of faith (Gal. 6:10); it is the church scattered throughout the whole globe.

    c. The origin of both: ἐξ οὗ ὀνομάζεται, "from whom is named." To be named is the same thing as to exist (Luke 1:32; Rom. 9:26), and likewise to be celebrated because of someone's name (1 John 3:1).

The Dogmatic Part

In the heavenly economy the first person is the Father.

III. From this it is clear that in the heavenly economy the first person is God the Father, since: (1) in every economy the Father is first. (2) Especially in the heavenly economy, the whole family is from the Father, and he is from himself, as much with respect to subsistence as to essence. (3) He is the font of all deity and of all the persons; from which (4) he is throughout Scripture (though not always) named first, for economic reasons (Matt. 28:19; 1 John 5:7; Rom. 1:7; 1 Cor. 1:3).

His deity

IV. That the Father is God from eternity is so undoubted by all that the enemies of the Trinity leave eternal deity to him alone. But at the same time, lest you doubt, not only is he named God throughout Scripture (John 17:3), but all divine things are attributed to him, such things as (1) divine names: God (John 3:16; 8:54), Jehovah (Ps. 33:6; Isa. 61:1); (2) attributes: independence, eternity (John 5:26; Rev. 1:4; Acts 17:28), and lordship (Matt. 11:25); (3) works (Acts 4:24–30); and (4) worship (John 17:1ff., Phil. 2:11; Matt. 11:25).

His personality

V. Likewise that he is a person is equally beyond doubt, for not only is he expressly called a person (Heb. 1:3), but also all personal attributes—life, intellect, will, personal operations—are attributed to him throughout Scripture (John 5:26; 6:57; Matt. 11:25–27).

His distinction from the rest of the persons

VI. Moreover, Scripture openly teaches that he is a person distinct from the rest (John 14:16; Matt. 3:16–17). And his personal or characteristic properties confirm this, properties such as: (1) aseity, not the essential aseity common to the three persons, but personal aseity, in which he has his essence *a se*, from himself, and lacks an origin from another, the aseity by which he is said to have life in himself and to have granted the Son to have the same life in himself (John 5:26), and is called among the ancients unbegotten.[2] (2) The active generation of the Son (Ps. 2:7), from which the Son is called his own and only begotten Son, through which generation he communicated to the Son his own same essence, in a manner entirely supernatural and not to be held to any laws of physical genera‑ tion. (3) The active spiration of the third person, common to the Father with the Son, in which they provide the joint principle[3] of the Holy Spirit, who accord‑ ingly is said to be sent by both (John 15:26). Furthermore, (4) personal primacy of order in subsisting, for which reason from him the whole family is named (Eph. 3:15). Finally, (5) personal primacy in operating: first *ad intra*, insofar as he is said to send the Son (John 3:16–17; 10:36; 16:28), and likewise to send the Spirit of his Son (Gal. 4:6), and the Son to send the Spirit from the Father (John 15:26); and second *ad extra*, insofar as he is said to have made the world through the Son (Heb. 1:2; Ps. 33:6) and the Holy Spirit is said to search the deep things of God (1 Cor. 2:10). By this primacy the Father works from himself, through the Son, and through the Holy Spirit.

His economic office
VII. From this order of subsisting and working, according to economic office the Father is: (1) Lord (Matt. 11:25; Eph. 4:5), inasmuch as he is the one who built the house (Heb. 3:4). So then it was his task by eternal predestination to prepare the governance of the future household, to arrange the end and order of the means (Rom. 9:22–23), namely so that they might all be managed according to the counsel of his will (Matt. 11:26; Eph. 1:11), to elect those to be accepted into the household, with the rest passed by (Eph. 1:3–4). He is (2) the Creator of the world (Ex. 20:11), such that he built the house (Heb. 3:3–4), planted the seeds of the household, of the family (Eph. 3:15), became proprietor of the household (Rom. 9:20), and thus could make decisions concerning all things based entirely on his own judgment, according to his good pleasure (Matt. 20:15). He is (3) the lawgiver (James 4:12) who furnished the man he created with the law of nature by creating him upright in his own image (Eccl. 7:29), and with positive law (Gen. 2:17), and sanctioned that law with a threat and promise, entering into a certain covenant with man. He is (4) the avenger of the law that was given, sanctioned, and violated (Rom. 12:19), who pronounced upon fallen man and all

---

2. ἀγέννητος
3. *principium sociatum*

his posterity as a punishment every kind of death, as much temporal as eternal, to be inflicted either upon the sinner himself or upon his surety. Finally, he is (5) the merciful Father (Ps. 103:13), who according to the eternal counsel of peace chose, sent, anointed, and gave to sinners the Mediator (Isa. 42:1; John 3:16–17; Isa. 61:1), tormented him for their sins with every kind of punishments (Isa. 53:1–6; 2 Cor. 5:18–19) so that he might redeem them, in addition sends the Holy Spirit (Gal. 4:6) that he might through faith apply the acquired redemption, regenerate, convert, and sanctify, and finally through the ministry of the Word calls to participation in redemption, justifies the called through faith, adopts the justified, and sanctifies and glorifies them. All of which are found throughout the Scriptures (Rom. 8:29–30). From all these things, the Father is particularly called God (2 Cor. 5:18), that is, not so much on account of his divine essence, which is common to all the persons, as on account of his economic office.

Economic attributes

VIII. Furthermore, from these economic offices there also belong to the Father certain economic attributes: for example, to him as Lord belongs authority (the sort which he also has communicated to the Son, Matt. 28:18), independence, liberty of acting according to his pleasure (Matt. 11:26; 20:15; Eph. 1:11); to him as lawgiver, judge, and avenger belongs justice (Gen. 18:25; 2 Thess. 1:6); to him as Father, love and mercy (John 3:16; Rom. 5:5, 8; 2 Cor. 13:14). For which reason all things which we have said concerning these attributes in their own places should be referred, not of course to the Father alone, but even so particularly to the Father, according to his economic office.

The administration of the Father before the law

IX. The household administration[4] of the Father was chiefly conspicuous first in the constituted state, in establishing the covenant of nature which was violated, and afterward in the destitute state, through the entire Old Testament period, and yet especially under the patriarchs in the promulgation of the protevangelium, the repeated promise of the blessed seed, in the deliverance of his household from Egyptian slavery, in the Sinaitic giving of the law. Concerning these things we will deal expressly in their own place.[5]

---

4. διοίκησις
5. 1.3.12; 1.5.1; 1.8.1; 1.8.2

The Elenctic Part

It is asked: 1. Does it belong to the Father alone to be God by
nature, the highest God?

X. This head of theology has not been so exposed to the darts of enemies, since all confess that the Father is a person, is likewise God, and is also distinct, at least from the Son. Yet so that we may know what can be controverted concerning this head of theology, it is asked, first, whether it belongs to the Father alone to be God by nature, the highest God. The anti-Trinitarians do acknowledge that the Son and the Holy Spirit are God, true God and eternal God, who will endure for eternity, and yet they do not acknowledge that they are God by nature, but are such artificially: the Father alone is God by nature, and accordingly they call him the highest God distinctively, not only with respect to magistrates, but also with respect to the Son and the Holy Spirit.

The opinion of the Reformed with their reasons

The Reformed say that not only the Father is God by nature, but also the Son and the Holy Spirit, and accordingly, at least with respect to essence, they are the highest God, just as the Father. We have already demonstrated this more generally in the preceding chapter, and Lord willing we will demonstrate it specifically in the following two chapters concerning the Son and the Holy Spirit, from which it will be evident that the three are by nature one and the same God, and indeed the highest God.[6]

Objections

Here we will only examine those things which can be pleaded to the contrary: (1) they allege the passage John 17:3, "That they may know that you (the Father) are that one true God." But (a) they do not add what is added by the Savior, "and Jesus Christ whom you have sent," supplying the words, "that he is that one true God," without which supplement the sense will be incomplete and disconnected. (b) They do not observe that it is indeed said that the Father is that one true God, but that it is by no means said that the Father alone is the true God, for thus it would exclude the Son, whom John (1 John 5:20) expressly calls true God, and whom even the adversaries declare to be such. (c) Nor do they observe that by the exclusive "only," persons of the same substance[7] are not excluded, but rather any other things of a different substance.[8] They allege (2) the passage

---

6. 1.2.26 §XVIII; 1.2.27 §XVIII
7. *personas* ὁμοουσίους
8. ἑτερούσια

1 Corinthians 8:6, "For us there is one God, the Father, from whom are all things."
I respond: (a) In the same way as Jesus is one Lord, not excluding the Father, so
also the Father is one God, not excluding the Son, whom "today he has begotten"
(Ps. 2:7), who is equal to God (Phil. 2:6), but rather excluding only any sort of
other things. (b) That is, as the Son is one Lord with respect to his mediatorial
office, so also the Father is one God with respect to his economic office. Unless
you prefer that (c) here not only the first person of the deity is called "Father," but
the whole Trinity, such that it should be understood that the one Trinity is the
Father of all things, e.g., through creation, providence, and so forth.

2. Did the Father beget the Son from eternity?
XI. It is asked, second, whether the Father begot the Son from eternity. Several
anti-Trinitarians, such as the Tritheists, do admit an eternal generation, but not
the sort by which the Father has communicated his own same essence to the
Son. The Socinians indeed acknowledge no eternal generation, although they do
not reject a generation made in time, first in regard to Christ, whom the Father
as it were begot in the resurrection of the Son, and next in regard to adoptive
sons, or all believers, whom he as it were begets through regeneration. They
think this way for this end, that they might shut out the eternal existence of the
Son. Among the Reformed rationalists, there is not lacking one or another who
cannot from clear and distinct perception reconcile with his own ideas a generation which consists in the communication of one and the same essence, and
therefore denies it (this issue will appear in the next chapter).[9] Otherwise the
Reformed commonly distinguish between the supernatural generation which
communicated the same essence in number from eternity to the Father's very
own and only begotten Son, the natural generation which in some way communicates the nature of God to believers (2 Peter 1:4), and finally the common
generation which has its place in corporeal things. They flatly reject the last one
in divine affairs, the second they admit in the sense posited, but the first they
guard against all anti-Trinitarians, because (1) active generation is expressly
asserted for him, and it is asserted to have been done from eternity (Mic. 5:2).
Next, because (2) a generation is asserted for the Father by which the Son is his
very own (Rom. 8:32) and only begotten (John 3:16), and thus equal to God,
namely to the Father (Phil. 2:6), a generation that cannot but be one by which he
made his own same essence common to him. (3) Through generation he bestows
to the begotten one a deity to which belong all the requisites of the God who

9. 1.2.26 §XVI

exists from eternity: for example, the divine names, attributes, operations, and worship, just as we will see distinctly in the next chapter.[10]

Objections
Now if they should object that a generation of this sort implies: (1) a diversity of essences; (2) a change in the one begetting as well as the one begotten; accordingly, (3) more than one imperfection in both; furthermore, (4) a transition from potency into actuality; (5) that the one begetting loses something from his own essence, namely that which he communicates to the begotten; and finally, (6) that generation from eternity cannot happen because a begotten presupposes that he did not exist before his generation; all of which—even from our very own hypotheses—cannot agree with God, there will come an easy response: All these things apply only to natural and corporeal generation, but they do not by any means apply to supernatural generation, which together with the Scriptures we assert for the Father.

3. Does the Father differ really from the Son and Holy Spirit?
XII. It is asked, third, whether the Father differs really from the Son and Holy Spirit, that is, whether he differs from the Son as the Creator from a creature, and from the Holy Spirit as a powerful one from his power, or as a subject from an adjunct. The anti-Trinitarians indeed all want the Father to differ really from the rest, as an essence from an essence, that is, as the creating essence from a created essence.

The opinion of the Reformed with their reasons
The Reformed think that he by no means differs really, as an essence from an essence, but only personally, as a person from persons, because: (1) there exists only one divine essence, which is equally common to the three, just as we demonstrated in the preceding chapter.[11] (2) If there were several essences in God, there would have to be acknowledged dependency, composition, and finitude in God, which because they connote imperfection we have barred from the divine essence, in their own places.[12] (3) We will assert in the next two chapters the same essence in number for the Son and the Holy Spirit.[13] They cannot object anything else except the unity of the divine essence, which cannot but belong to the Father (John 17:3), to which we have already responded in §X.

---

10. 1.2.26 §§VIII–XII
11. 1.2.24 §XVII
12. 1.2.3; 1.2.6; 1.2.9
13. 1.2.26 §XVIII; 1.2.27 §XVIII

The Practical Part

The practice of this chapter regards: 1. The duties which are owed to
God as Lord, which are: Honor

XIII. The practice of this chapter consists in the duties of economic worship specific to the Father, among which, first to the Father as Lord, master, and head of household belongs honor, which we also owe to earthly parents according to the divine command (Ex. 20:12), and which God laments has been denied to him by his own (Mal. 1:6), an honor which his natural Son brings to him (John 8:49; 17:4), and which the Father himself, in most wisely arranging and planning the business of our salvation by eternal predestination, has pursued as his sole aim (Rom. 9:23; Eph. 1:5–6). See also chapter 22 on the glory of God, §§VIII, XVI.

2. Submission

XIV. Second, to the same as Lord belongs submission, in which we endure every fortune, no matter how hard, which he himself has decreed or allowed for us, not only with a calm mind (1 Sam. 3:18), but also with thanksgiving (Job 1:21), just as his natural Son did (Matt. 26:39, 42). For it is not unusual for fathers of households to chastise their children—should we not much more be subject to the Father of spirits and live (Heb. 12:6–11)? See also chapter 20 on the power of God, §XXVI.

3. The duties which belong to the same as Creator

XV. Third, to the same as Creator—from whom the whole family is named, and from whom we are, whatever we are and have (1 Cor. 15:10)—belong: (1) the humble gratitude which the law requires toward any parent (1 Tim. 5:4) and which God laments has been denied to him by his own (Deut. 32:6), and which the natural Son repays to him (Matt. 11:25), namely on account of (a) the natural life conferred to us (Acts. 17:25, 28), (b) the spiritual life conferred and restored to us (Eph. 2:1), and (c) the eternal life to be conferred to us (1 John 1:2). (2) The rendering and resignation of our entire selves and of all our abilities to the Father as our Creator and proprietor, without reserving anything, because all things are his (1 Cor. 6:20; cf. ch. 20 §XXIX). (3) Faithfulness in the use and administration of all our possessions, as those that are good belong not to us, but to our Father and Creator. For among the duties of children toward their parents, and of servants toward their masters, is faith (Prov. 28:24; Titus 2:10; Col. 3:22–23). By this faithfulness we should promptly devote ourselves and all we have to our Father and Creator, and to his glory, as well as to the advantage of our common household (1 Cor. 6:20; 10:31; 1 Peter 4:11).

4. The duties which belong to the same as lawgiver, judge, and avenger
XVI. Fourth, also to him as a lawgiver, judge, and avenger belong: (1) an entire and most prompt obedience, which from the will of God we owe to our earthly parents (Eph. 6:1; Prov. 6:20–22), and servants owe to their lords (Col. 3:22)—how much more to the heavenly Father, the Lord of lords (1 Peter 1:14; Acts 5:29; Deut. 5:33)? (2) Reverence and fear, which we bestow upon our earthly parents (Mal. 1:6; Eph. 6:2–3), which servants bestow upon masters (Rom. 13:5, 7), and which subjects bestow upon judges and avengers of laws (James 4:12; Gen. 18:25, 27; Isa. 66:1; 2 Cor. 5:11).

5. The duties which are owed to the same as Father
XVII. Fifth, to him as our Father and benefactor belongs superlative love (Matt. 10:37), the sort by which he himself is concerned with us (2 Cor. 13:14; John 3:16; Rom. 5:5, 8), namely that there might be a mutual and reciprocal love by which we have communion with him in love. And this happens while we bestow upon God our Father not only a love that is sincere and perfect (Matt. 22:37), but also the sort of love which in its own way is analogous to his fatherly love toward us. But of what sort then is that fatherly love of God toward us that we should imitate? (1) It is free and entirely independent, first from all dignity of merit on our part, and next from all hope of gain on his part (Rom. 9:11–12; Titus 3:5; James 1:18), purely for his own sake. Thus our love should also be such, existing not because of any advantage to us from God or because of some reward arising from God, but purely on account of him (John 6:26). (2) The love of God toward us is eternal, from eternity to eternity, always the same and immutable (Hos. 2:16; Rom. 11:29; Isa. 54:9–10). Thus our love should also be eternal toward him, if not eternal on the before part (as they say) at least on the after part; it should be constant and immutable (Rev. 2:10). (3) It is a distinguishing love: God loves and preserves all his works (Ps. 36:6), but in a different manner and degree (Rom. 9:13). He loves them as the works of his hands, but he does not love them as sons. And thus our love toward God should also be a distinguishing love: we should love all things on account of God, as the works of God, as the image of God, but God on account of himself, above all things (Ps. 73:25).

6. Filial dependence
XVIII. But sixth, to him as our Father belongs from us a confident dependence upon him, by reason of his provision of nourishment, clothing, and anything else in whatever way necessary (Matt. 6:26, 32; 7:11), because he bears a fatherly care for his own (Ps. 103:13), and a motherly care (Isa. 49:15). Thus, toward him belongs to us access with boldness (Heb. 4:16).

7. From God the Father we are supplied an argument for consolation.
XIX. Furthermore, seventh, from God the Father we are supplied an argument for consolation in any adversities, that all those adversities come to us (1) from the Father (Matt. 10:29–31; Ps. 27:10; 1 John 3:1); (2) from the omnipotent Father who is able to help us (2 Tim. 1:12); (3) from the merciful Father who wills to help us (Ps. 103:13; Lam. 3:22; Heb. 13:5); (4) from the Father who is most highly good, who can turn even our worst to our good (Rom. 8:28); (5) from the Father who has already demonstrated his fatherly heart toward us in greater ways (Rom. 5:8; John 3:16); and (6) from the Father who will by no adversities be separated from his love toward us (Rom. 8:38–39).

8. It invites us to seek adoption from the Father.
XX. Finally, eighth, the fatherhood of God invites us to strive with every effort for adoption with him, motivated by the excellent privileges and benefits of this sonship, such as: (1) a most noble lineage, that is, a heavenly and divine lineage (John 1:13; 3:5; 2 Peter 1:4); (2) an illustrious family, when God is our Father (Matt. 6:9; 2 Cor. 6:18) and Christ our brother and bridegroom (Matt. 12:50; Heb. 2:11; 12:22–23); and (3) a rich inheritance: "heirs of God and joint heirs with Christ" (Rom. 8:17); and others.

The means of obtaining it
Moreover, let us obtain this adoption: (1) by faith in the natural Son of God (John 1:12), by which we will be united with him, and, once united, will with him obtain the same God and Father (John 20:17). (2) Through the Holy Spirit, who is the Spirit of adoption, whom the Father sends so that we may obtain adoption (Gal. 4:5–6). (3) By faithfully observing the duties of children toward our heavenly Father, duties we have explained thus far. (4) By carefully abstaining from every impurity of sins (2 Cor. 6:17–18), and especially of those which are particularly repugnant to his paternal dignity and our filial duty, such as rebellion and faithlessness, which commits treason against[14] him as the Lord of

---

14. *laedere*, thus the *crimen laesae majestatis*, the crime of treason.

ourselves and all of our possessions (Isa. 63:10; Jer. 4:17; Ezek. 2:3; 20:8; Hos. 5:7; 6:7); disobedience (2 Kings 17:14–15, 40), which injures God as the lawgiver; despising him (Deut. 8:11), which is contrary to the fear that belongs to him as judge; hatred (Ex. 20:5), which is repugnant to his love; distrust (Num. 11:21–23), which is repugnant to his fatherly care; impatience and other such things (Ex. 15:24; 1 Cor. 10:10), which are repugnant to his fatherly chastisements. It will suffice to have pointed out these things: arguments for amplification will be supplied from the chapters on the mutual duties of parents and children, and on adoption.[15]

---

15. 3.3.9; 1.6.7 §§XXI–XXVI

CHAPTER TWENTY-SIX

God the Son

I will tell the decree: You are my Son; today I have begotten you. Ask of me,
and I will give you the nations for your inheritance.

—Psalm 2:7–8

The contemplation of the Son

I. Following the Father in the divine economy is the Son. For just as the Father, because he subsists from himself, is the first person, so also the Son, because he subsists from the Father and has his essence communicated to him from the Father, is the second. Accordingly, just as we have contemplated the Father, so now we will also contemplate the Son. He relates his personal description and economic office from the economic covenant in the words above from Psalm 2:7–8.

The Exegetical Part

It is constructed upon an exegesis of the text.

II. In these words are contained the promulgation of the eternal covenant contracted between the Father and the Son concerning the mediatorial office of the Son. In it is presented:

A. The economic covenant between himself and the Father: "I will tell the decree," אספרה אל חק. There is abruptly introduced a second person speaking, certainly the same King about which verse 6 speaks. Such alternations of speech are not rare in the Song of Solomon and other poetic writings. And thus the Son is introduced, presenting to his enemies and promulgating that covenant whereby he has been constituted King, anointed over Mount Zion, that is, over the whole church. In the type the words can be understood as regarding David, for whom and for whose posterity was established the kingdom recently taken from Saul, after Ish-bosheth was removed (2 Sam. 5:3). In the antitype, the eternal

covenant is conferred upon Christ and promulgated to his members. חק,
"decree," denotes a statute which was established in the eternal counsel
of peace between the Father and himself, and likewise a commandment,
since like a law he intends it to be promulgated to all: it is an edict to
be published, an eternal and immutable decree. אל is put in place of את
(as in Judg. 7:25; Isa. 38:19; Jer. 4:23; 10:2). There are some who want
אֶל here to be the same as the Arabic particle אַל, which frequently is
a mark of the accusative case. For others it denotes "into," such that it
means "into statute" or "into law," "which I will carefully promulgate, so
that it may pass from me into custom," as it were. For others it denotes
"of," "I will tell of the decree" as in Job 42:7, "You have not spoken rightly
אֵלַי, of me," (thus Ps. 69:26; Jer. 27:19; Ezek. 21:28; etc.). For others, it
is "according to," that is, "according to the statute," such that it denotes
a congruency of one thing with another, as if he were saying, "My tell-
ing will be according to the decree." Others join it with the preceding
words in this sense: "I have established the King so that he might tell out
the decree." There are also some who point it אֵל with the Masoretes in
Génébrard,[1] such that it means "the statute of God"—thus the Septuagint interpreters and the Targum, both the Arabic and the Ethiopic, and
the Vulgate—but thus it should have been placed after the חק, instead
of being placed in front of it. It could also be emphatic: "I will tell the
very decree of my Father, which will be constant and inviolable before
everyone." אספרה, from ספר, is to count something as if by numbers,
to recount it in detail (2 Sam. 24:10; Ps. 119:13). Whatever may be the
case, there is indicated a statute, a decree, and an economic covenant
that exists between the Father and the Son, the same that is expressed
in Isaiah 53:10, and is called in other words "the counsel of peace,"
from Zechariah 6:13. Through it, as the Father undertook the office of
Lord, lawgiver, judge, and avenger in the work of human salvation, so
the Son undertook the office of expromissor, steward, and Redeemer.

---

1. Latin: *in Gen.* This reference, entirely omitted in the Dutch translation, seems to be
to the prolific professor of Hebrew at the University of Paris, Archbishop Gilbert Génébrard,
O. S. B. (1537–1597), who argues for this pointing in *Psalmi Davidis variis calendariis et commentariis genuinum sensum et Hebraismos aperientibus* (Cologne: Antonius Boëtzer, 1615), 6: *Ubi
observa* אל *El, posse esse nomen Dei, ut a Masoretis notatum sit perverse per segol, loco tsere. Vel, si sit
praepositio Latine vacare, Narrabo praeceptum (ejus), (ut) narrem statutum (ejus) sum constitutus Rex
ab ipso. Nam non tantum Rex, sed et Sacerdos.* "Observe here that אל, *El*, can be the name of God,
and thus it was wrongly noted by the Masoretes with a *segol* instead of a *tsere*. Or, if it should be
that the preposition is useless in Latin, 'I will tell the command' (of him), or, (so that) 'I would
tell the statute' (of him), 'I was constituted King by him.' For not only is he King, but also Priest."

And it was precisely from the tenor of this covenant that he said to the Son, "You are my Son."

B. The person of the Son, as the household manager: "You my Son," supplying "are." This is the address of the Father to the Son which Paul mentions in regard to the priesthood (Heb. 5:5), as does David in regard to the kingship (Ps. 110:1). It alludes to the establishment of men, when they promote those chosen to some dignity and office, and as it were they consecrate them by set words, by which they signify what is conferred on them, for what reason, and to what end. Moreover, there are distinctly noted:

1. The one who says, Jehovah: יהוה אמר, "Jehovah said." The word *Jehovah* is taken personally and economically here for the Father, as throughout the Scriptures (Psalm 33:6), just as what is added, "You are my Son," evidently confirms. For it belongs to a father to have a son, and to decree an inheritance for him. אמר, "He said," that is, in the counsel of peace. "He said," that is, "to me," as the Septuagint translators have it. When did he say this? Many supply "in baptism" (Matt. 3:17) or "in the transfiguration" (Matt. 17:5), but this is spoken concerning a past time, not a future one. Some think more carefully that it is not necessary to inquire scrupulously about the time of this statement, since with regard to the decree it was before all time, and with regard to the execution it is in time: "He said, he says, and he will say."

2. The thing said: "You are my Son; today I have begotten you. Ask of me, and I will give you," and so forth. Here regarding the second person is noted:

   a. His sonship: בני אתה, "You my Son," supplying "are." אתה, "you," is not in the vocative, "O my Son," as Grotius, serving his own anti-Trinitarian hypotheses, wanted it.[2] Indeed אתה is not here a bare address, but a witness of a clearly exceptional matter. Hence no paraphrase takes it in the vocative sense: all are suspicious of an emphasis on this address itself. בני, You are "my Son": not through creation, as Adam (Luke 3:38) and the angels (Job 38:7), nor through adoption, which is common to all believers (John 1:12; 1 John 3:1), but by nature and generation. From this is evident, first

---

2. Grotius, *Opera omnia* (1732), 1:221.

the deity of the Son, and then the personal distinction between the Father and the Son.

b. His eternal generation, as the foundation of his sonship: "Today I have begotten you," אֲנִי הַיּוֹם יְלִדְתִּיךָ. Here there is:

i. The one begetting: אֲנִי, "I," that is, Jehovah the Father, who was speaking in the previous hemistich (see also Prov. 30:4). It is placed here emphatically: "I, not anyone else."

ii. The time of the begetting, as it were: הַיּוֹם, "today." It can be taken in a twofold manner: (1) properly, concerning eternal generation, "Today I have begotten you," where "today" is an adverb of present time denoting the continued existence of the generation without succession, but "I have begotten" is a verb of past time denoting perfection and consummation. Generation is also referred to "today" insofar as eternity coexists present with all types of time (Ps. 90:4; cf. 2 Peter 3:8). For it is the procession of the Son which generation designates, a procession from eternity (Mic. 5:2; cf. Prov. 8:22; John 1:1). God is called the Ancient of Days[3] (Dan. 7:9), whose days do not pass away, but remain (Ps. 102:27). Therefore just as eternity in divine things is signified through time, thus also the "day" of eternity is signified by a "today" in which there is no variation or succession: with God in eternity there can be neither yesterday nor tomorrow, but only today. From these things, eternity is signified by "today," as in Isaiah 43:13: "Even from today, I am," that is, "from eternity," which accordingly the Septuagint translators render ἀπ᾽ ἀρχῆς, "from the beginning," by which eternity is also customarily designated (John 1:2). Less properly (2) the words are taken concerning a demonstration today of eternal generation. Thus taken there will be denoted a manifold time for that demonstration, namely, as often as God said to him, "You are my Son, I have begotten you," that is, "I have testified that I have begotten you." Moreover, he testified this both in word and in deed (John 5:36). Certainly he testified in word, partly in his baptism (Matt. 3:17) and partly in his transfiguration (Matt. 17:5)—others add in his nativity, although this is not as clearly read to have happened. It did happen at the

---

3. *permanens dierum*

least in the resurrection (Acts 13:33; Rom. 1:4). Yet others extend this generation to the whole exhibition of Christ, which began in his nativity and was consummated in the resurrection, because it is expressly taught that the Messiah would be the Son of God, and this is that great manifestation made to the fathers, to which the apostle refers them back, inasmuch as it was most manifest to the Jews (Acts 13:33).

iii. The act of begetting: יְלִדְתִּי, "I have begotten." Some with the Socinians refer this to the resurrection alone; others more correctly to the eternal communication of essence; and others to both, but primarily the communication of essence and secondarily to the manifestation made partly in baptism and partly in the resurrection, as we have said. Whatever may be the case, at the least is signified an eternal generation whereby he is denominated the Father's own, only begotten, and firstborn Son.

iv. The one begotten: "you." The Socinians and the Socinianizers, Grotius, the Jews, and others want this to be David; others want it to be David as a type of Christ; and others Solomon (2 Sam. 7:14). But in what way can it be said that God begot David and Solomon? They most correctly perceive it who think the Messiah alone is understood, because: (1) in the New Testament, this is only explained as concerning Christ (Acts 13:33; Heb. 1:5; 5:5). (2) Here there is no discussion about some adoptive son, but about God's own Son (Rom. 8:32), the only begotten (John 1:14; 3:16), who is in the bosom of the Father (John 1:18), and with the Father, who is himself God (John 1:1–2). (3) Here the discussion is about that Son of God for whom in the context is asserted omnipotence, omniscience, and divine worship.

c. His inheritance, arising from sonship, but based on a certain economic pact: "Ask of me, and I will give you," and so forth. Here there is:

i. The economic stipulation of the Father: "Ask of me," in which is contained the stipulation that the Son would render what from the mutual pact was incumbent upon him to render, namely that he would give himself as a sacrifice for sin (Isa. 53:10), and then by this his right he would ask his reward from the pact, the inheritance of the nations.

    ii. The reciprocal promise: "I will give you the nations for your inheritance." There is denoted a mediatorial lordship to be conferred to him, from redemption, over the nations—in fact over this whole universe (according to Matt. 28:18; Phil. 2:9–11).

The Dogmatic Part

In the economy of the Trinity, the second person is the Son.

III. Therefore, just as the Father in the heavenly economy obtains the first place, so the Son obtains the second, because: (1) in any household, especially where the mother is absent, the son is closest to the father, and then especially when he is the firstborn and only begotten son, he is so also by right of primogeniture. And in this economy such is the second person, who also for this reason is called the firstborn from the dead (Col. 1:18; Rev. 1:5), and simply the firstborn (Heb. 1:6). Next, (2) just as the Father, because he subsists from himself, is first; and the Holy Spirit, because he subsists from the Father and the Son, is third; so the Son, because he subsists from the Father alone, is rightly thought of as second. Furthermore (3) just as the Holy Spirit, because he subsists from the Son, or from two principles,[4] is the third person, so the Son, as a principle of the Holy Spirit, inasmuch he sends the Spirit, and the Spirit is sent in his name by the Father (John 15:26; 16:7; 14:26), is therefore without doubt prior in order, and thus is the second person. (4) From all these things, in Scripture he is most often enumerated second (Matt. 28:19; 1 John 5:7), although for economic reasons, and in specific for avoiding any disparity of essence, he is now and then recounted as first (e.g. 2 Cor. 13:14).

What is the Son? With respect to the name

IV. Moreover, he is denominated "the Son" in the Old Testament (Ps. 2:7, 12; Prov. 30:4), the אָמוֹן, "one brought up," who is in the bosom of the Father (Prov. 8:30; John 1:18), and throughout the New Testament "the Son of God," and indeed "in power" (Rom. 1:4), such that this is his "more excellent name" (Heb. 1:4). Just as we indicated in the exegetical part, he is not a son from creation, as are Adam and the angels, nor through adoption, as are believers (John 1:12; 1 John 3:1), nor through the temporal generation which occurs in regeneration, whereby believers in their own way are rendered partakers of the divine nature (2 Peter 1:4), but rather, through eternal generation (Ps. 2:7), from which his procession is said to be מִקֶּדֶם מִימֵי עוֹלָם, "from of old, from days of eternity"

---

4. *principia*

(Mic. 5:2), whereby from the Father he has the same essence in number. From this the Son is called his own (Rom. 8:32), πρωτότοκος, "firstborn" (Heb. 1:6), indeed μονογενής, "only begotten" (John 3:16), to whom there is none second: "For to which of the angels did he ever say, 'You are my Son, today I have begotten you'?" (Heb. 1:5).

And with respect to its substance

Therefore, the Son is for us the second person of the Trinity, begotten of the Father from eternity (Mic. 5:1), the personal image of the Father (Heb. 1:3), the one who together with the Father spirates the Holy Spirit. In his personal description, the following four items come for our consideration.

1. The personality of the Son

V. First his personality, which all certainly acknowledge with one voice, but not with one mind, since all anti-Trinitarians say that he is a created person, and Catholics that he is an uncreated person. We believe he is an uncreated person because: (1) he is called the Son of God. (2) He is begotten by God. (3) He is commanded to ask for an inheritance. (4) He is anointed God's King over Zion, (5) the one whom kings and anyone else must kiss and honor with all religious worship, (6) the one in whom they are bound to place their confidence, under the promise of blessedness. All these things and others Psalm 2 supplies in favor of the divine personality of the Son. Let there be added that (7) he is called the express image of the Father's hypostasis (Heb. 1:3), and likewise the image of the invisible God, namely, of the Father (Col. 1:15). And (8) to him in Scripture are attributed all the prerequisites of a person: (a) he is a substance, an hypostasis, endowed with (b) life (John 5:26); (c) intellect (Matt. 11:27), from which he is also called the Word (John 1:1); (d) will (Matt. 26:39), and personal operations (John 5:17, 19).

2. The distinction of the Son from the Father and the Holy Spirit

VI. Second, his distinction from the Father and the Holy Spirit. That they are distinguished, all who profess Christ certainly acknowledge with one voice, but not with one mind or in one sense. At the least they do not differ as Creator and creature, nor as God and God, but (1) as divine person and person, because they differ as Son from Father, the begotten from the one begetting. The Son differs (2) as the second of three persons. He differs (3) by his personal or characteristic properties, without a doubt from the Father through passive generation, and thus through procession from one principle. And because this cannot apply to the Father, it evidently distinguishes the Son from him, although he is the same in essence (John 10:30), and with respect to the mode of subsisting most similar and near to him, for which reason he is described as "being in the form of God," as "equal to God" (Phil. 2:6; John 5:18), and likewise the "image of God" (2 Cor. 4:4; Col. 1:15), the "express image of his person," namely, the Father's person (Heb. 1:3). And he differs from the Holy Spirit through active spiration, common to him with the Father, whereby with him he is the principle of the third person, communicating his own essence to him, who from this is denominated the Spirit of the Son (Gal. 4:6), and the Spirit of Christ (Rom. 8:9), who sends the Spirit from the Father (John 15:26), so that he may receive from him what belongs to the Son (John 16:14). For a sign of this spiration, when he was about to communicate the Holy Spirit to his disciples, he breathed on them (John 20:22). The Son differs (4) in the order of subsisting, from which he is second in the Trinity (Matt. 28:19; 1 John 5:7), that is, after the Father, inasmuch as he subsists from him (John 5:26), and before the Holy Spirit, as the one whom he sends (John 15:26). He differs (5) in the order of operating, in which just as the Father operates from himself, so also the Son operates from the Father (John 5:17; 19–21), and just as the Father operates through the Son (John 5:22; 1:3), so also the Son operates through the Holy Spirit (Rom. 8:11). Finally, he differs (6) in external operation, through which just as creation belongs to the Father, so dispensation or redemption belongs to the Son (1 Tim. 2:5–6; Rom. 3:25), just as consummation, communication, and sanctification belong to the Holy Spirit (2 Cor. 13:14; 1 Cor. 6:11).

The eternal generation of the Son

VII. Among these characteristics, since generation has the primary place, it deserves to be considered by us a little more distinctly. That there is an eternal generation with God we presuppose here from Ephesians 3:14–15 and Psalm 2:7, passages already expressly set forth, and we confirm it from Proverbs 8:22: "The Lord acquired me," that is, by begetting, "the beginning of his way, before his works," that is, so that I would be the beginning of his operations, "from then, from forever, מעולם, I had my origin, from the head, from the commencement of the earth." "When there were still no depths, חללתי," which the Septuagint translators render γέγενά με, "he had begotten me."[5] Aquila and Theodotion translate it even more meaningfully as ὠδινήθην, "I was brought forth in labor pains."[6] The word חללתי is used in Psalm 51:5, where the Septuagint translators

---

5. Cf. LXX Prov. 8:25. This particular reading of Mastricht's is difficult: (1) The perfect form of the verb should be either γέγονα (active) or γεγένηται (middle or passive); however, (2) in Prov. 8:25 the LXX and Origen's *Hexapla* actually read γεννᾷ, the present active of γεννάω.

6. See Origen, *Hexapla*, 2 vols. (Oxford, 1875), 2:326–27.

render it συνελήμφθην, "I was conceived."[7] In Micah 5:2 it is said of Christ according to his human nature that he was born in Bethlehem. And because he has an even higher nativity, there is added, "His goings forth are from of old, and from the days of eternity." Rabbi Haccados in *Galei Rezaya* gives the reason for the plural number of מוצאתיו, "his goings forth": "because there are two goings forth of the Messiah, one of divinity, the other of humanity."[8] To these others, add the passage Psalm 72:17, "His name shall endure forever; to the face of the sun" (that is, before the sun). "His name ינין, *shall be filiated*, and all nations shall be blessed in him," and so forth. The whole Psalm speaks about Christ, of whom Solomon was a type. This eternal generation is confirmed by his titles, by which: (1) he is simply named the Son of God (Mark 1:1; Matt. 16:16; Mark 14:61–62; 2 Peter 1:17; Matt. 3:17); (2) the Son begotten from God (Ps. 2:7, which is applied to Christ in Acts 4:25–26 and Heb. 1:5); (3) his own Son (Rom. 8:32; cf. John 5:18–19); (4) the firstborn (Heb. 1:6; Col. 1:15–18); and (5) the only begotten (John 1:14, 18; 3:18). Moreover, what is this generation? Several answer that it is an eternal production of the Son from the substance of the Father. In place of "production" you should perhaps have said more carefully that it is the communication of the same essence in number. The mode of this generation[9] is anxiously inquired into by many, but in vain, because it is ineffable and "beyond our thought, reason and comprehension," as Justin says.[10] Thus the ancients represented the secret of this generation by four adverbs, saying that it happened: (1) ἀκαταλήπτως, incomprehensibly; (2) ἀχρόνως, without vicissitude of time (Prov. 8:22–23; Mic. 5:2; Col. 1:17); furthermore, (3) ἀχωρίστως, inseparably (John 1:1; 14:10–11); and finally, (4) ἀπαθῶς,

---

7. Hebrew Ps. 51:7; LXX Ps. 50:7

8. Rabbi Haccados and the pseudopigraphical work, *Galei Rezaya* (*Secretorum Revelator*), (Rome, 1487) are figments of Paul de Herédia, published under the name Judah Ha Nasi, and presented only through citations. The supposed work presented Kabbalistic teachings as Trinitarian and captivated many Hebrew scholars throughout the early modern period. Cf. Robert J. Wilkinson, *Tetragrammaton: Western Christians and the Hebrew Names of God* (Leiden: Brill, 2015), 204–5. For Mastricht's reference, the most likely source is Pietro Galatino, *Opus de arcanis catholicae veritatis, hoc est in omnia difficilia loca veteris testamenti ex Talmud* (Basel: Joannes Heruagius, 1561), 157: *Dicit propheta Egressus, numero multitudinis, quia duo sunt Messiae egressus. Unus divinitatis, quae est aeterna, et ideo dicit ab aeterno; alter humanitatis, quae in suae matris substantia extat, quae ab hora creationis mundi creata est.* The verse in Hebrew is Mic. 5:1.

9. γεννησίας

10. ἄρρητος, καὶ ὑπὲρ νοῦν, ὑπὲρ λόγον, καὶ ὑπὲρ κατάληψιν. Cf. pseudo-Justin, Ἔκθεσις τῆς ὀρθῆς ὁμολογίας (*Expositio rectae confessionis*) in *PG* 6:1235–36, ...ὅτι ὑπὲρ νοῦν, ὑπὲρ λόγον, ὑπὲρ κατάληψιν κτιστῆς φύσεως, "...that is above the thought, reason, and understanding of our created nature."

without any passion or change, either in the Father or in the Son. You will have the various opinions of our adversaries in the elenctic part.[11]

3. The deity of the Son

VIII. Third, his deity, from which he is God, not only true God (1 John 5:20) and eternal God (Isa. 9:10)—eternal not only on the posterior part (as they say) but also on the anterior part (Mic. 5:2; Heb. 7:3)—but indeed also ὁμοούσιος, consubstantial with the Father, from which there is asserted for him deity (Col. 2:9) and the form of God, which is no doubt one, and thus through it he is equal to the Father (Phil. 2:6). We invincibly conclude such deity with this one general argument: the one to whom all divine things belong is undoubtedly the true God from eternity and consubstantial with the Father, for not even impudence itself will say that the one to whom all divine things belong is not God. Now to the Son belong all divine things, none excluded, because in Scripture are asserted for him the divine names, attributes, works, and worship, under which all divine things are embraced: therefore he cannot but be the true God, eternal and consubstantial with the Father.

Because there belong to him: (1) Divine names

IX. Therefore, once the minor premise has been demonstrated, the matter will be concluded. We will demonstrate it individually. First, that the divine names belong to him is evident because he is called: (1) Jehovah (Hos. 1:7; Jer. 23:5–6; Isa. 6:5; cf. John 12:40–41; Num. 14:2; 21:5–6). In the latter two passages the one who was tested by the Israelites, and who therefore sent fiery serpents upon them, is said to have been Jehovah; the same one is said to have been the angel of his face (Isa. 63:9–10) and also expressly Christ (1 Cor. 10:9). Again, in Psalm 102:16, 25–26 without a doubt the subject is Jehovah, but there the subject is the Son (Heb. 1:10–12); likewise in Psalm 68:18, which Paul teaches is said about the Son (Eph. 4:8–9). But this name Jehovah belongs to the highest God alone, which we have demonstrated above in chapter 4.[12] (2) Elohim (Ps. 45:6–7; 68:7–9, 18–19). (3) אל גבור, mighty God (Isa. 9:6). (4) אדני, Lord (Ps. 110:1; cf. Matt. 22:43; Mal. 3:1). (5) θεός, God, not only attributively (Rom. 9:5; 1:3–4; Titus 2:13; Jude 4; 1 John 5:20), but also subjectively (John 1:1; cf. John 4:24; Acts 20:28; 1 Tim. 3:16; John 20:28). (6) κύριος, Lord (Luke 1:16–17; 2:11), to which corresponds the name Jehovah. (7) Lord of lords (Rev. 17:14; 19:16). (8) The Lord of glory (1 Cor. 2:8), to which corresponds "the King

---

11. §XVI, below
12. 1.2.4 §XIV

of glory," whose name is Jehovah (Ps. 24:7–10). So then, there is not one divine name that is not claimed for the Son.

(2) Divine attributes

X. Second, Scripture teaches that divine properties belong to him: (1) a spiritual, most simple, immutable essence, attributed to him in Psalm 102:26–27 (cf. Heb. 1:12); (2) independence (Rev. 1:8, 17; 22:13); (3) eternity (Isa. 9:6; Rev. 10:6; Heb. 7:3; 9:14; Mic. 5:2; John 17:5); (4) omnipresence (Matt. 18:20; 28:20; John 3:13); (5) omnipotence (Rev. 1:8; Phil. 3:21; Heb. 1:3); (6) omniscience (John 2:24–25; 21:17; Rev. 2:23); (7) equality with the Father (Phil. 2:6; John 16:15; Col. 2:9). So then, neither is there one attribute that belongs to God that is not attributed to the Son.

(3) Divine works

XI. Third, divine works (John 5:17, 19), namely, the works of: (1) creation (John 1:3; Col. 1:16; Heb. 1:2; Ps. 33:6); (2) providence (Heb. 1:3; Col. 1:17); (3) miracles (John 5:21; 11:43–44; 2:19, 21; 10:17–18; Rom. 1:4); (4) redemption, such works as election (Matt. 24:31; John 13:18), redemption (Matt. 1:21), justification (Isa. 53:11), remission of sins (Matt. 9:6), sanctification (Heb. 10:10), spiritual vivification (Eph. 2:1), the institution of the sacraments (Matt. 28:18–19; 1 Cor. 11:23), the sending of the Holy Spirit (John 16:7, 13, 14).

(4) Divine worship

XII. Finally, fourth, divine worship (John 5:23; Phil. 2:10–11; Rom. 14:10–11), the sort that is: (1) in adoration (Heb. 1:6; 1 Cor. 1:2; Acts 7:59; 9:14; 2 Cor. 13:14); (2) in baptism, which is instituted in his name as well as the Father's (Matt. 28:19; 1 Cor. 1:13), and in the Lord's Supper, which is to be administered in remembrance of him (1 Cor. 11:24–25). (3) Because he is called the author of our salvation (Heb. 2:10), such that salvation is in his name alone (Acts 4:12). (4) Because we are commanded to place our faith, hope, and confidence in him (Heb. 12:2; John 14:1; Ps. 2:12; Rom. 10:9–11, 14; 1 Cor. 15:19). Therefore since all these things are so, what finally is lacking that he should be less than God from eternity, consubstantial with the Father?

4. The economic office of the Son

XIII. Finally, fourth, the economic office which the Son, consubstantial with the Father, tells in our text from the economic decree, and which he took up from the counsel of peace between the persons. Through this he was established as: (1) the steward or household manager, inasmuch as he is the one to whom all

authority is given (Matt. 28:18), that he would be faithful to him who established him, just as Moses was in all God's house (Heb. 3:2), that through him
God would create the world (John 1:3), and sustain it once created (Heb. 1:3),
so that his household servants would have a dwelling place in the world. (2) The
sponsor or expromissor (Heb. 7:22), the surety (Isa. 38:14), the Redeemer (Job
19:25), that he would take upon himself the cause and the entire guilt of the
sinning members of the household and give his own soul for them as an offering for sin (Isa. 53:10), that he would be made sin for them so that they might
become righteousness in him (2 Cor. 5:21). (3) The Mediator between God and
the sinning members of the household (1 Tim. 2:5; 1 John 2:1), that he as the
middle person in the economy of the Trinity would intercede as the middleman
between God and the sinner, that as God and man together he would promote
the cause of both, that as the Son by nature he would make sons of the household through adoption (Gal. 4:5–6). (4) The Redeemer (such as Moses is called
in the type in Acts 7:35–36), that having assumed the nature of sinners he would
free the household from sin (Matt. 1:21) and give himself as a ransom for many
(Matt. 20:28). (5) The ambassador of the Father, the interpreter, the Word (Mal.
3:1; John 1:1), that he would reveal to his own the Father, whom no one sees or
can see (John 1:18), that through him the Father would speak to men (Heb. 1:2),
that he would tell the statute of the Father (Ps. 2:7), that he would show the way
of salvation, from which he is called the way, the truth, and the life (John 14:6).
(6) The head of the church (Eph. 1:22–23). (7) The judge of the living and of the
dead (Rom. 2:16; John 5:22, 27).

His economic attributes
XIV. From these economic offices there also belong to him economic attributes,
such as: (1) wisdom, inasmuch as this is especially desired in a steward, ambassador, and interpreter. From it he is also denominated wisdom itself (Prov. 8:1;
1 Cor. 1:24). (2) Faithfulness, the chief virtue of a household manager (1 Cor.
4:2), which the apostle commends in Christ (Heb. 3:1–2), by which he seeks
not himself or his own, but those things which are his Father's (John 5:30; 8:29,
49–50). (3) Power (1 Cor. 1:24), inasmuch as through him the Father created all
things (Ps. 33:6) and sustains them, as by the word of his power (Heb. 1:3). And
especially (4) mercy (2 Cor. 13:14), by which he so loved us that he gave himself
for us (Eph. 5:2, 25–26; cf. Rom. 5:7–8).

The period of his economic administration
XV. Equipped with these economic attributes, the Son managed his own economic province, indeed from the beginning, insofar as through him "God also

made the worlds" (Heb. 1:2); and under the patriarchs, to whom he frequently appeared (Gen. 18:1; 32:29–30); but especially when by Moses he led his household from Egyptian slavery through the desert into Canaan (Acts 7:36), as a foreshadowing of future spiritual deliverance; when at Sinai he gave his law (Gal. 3:19), moral as well as ceremonial, by which his household would be directed all the way until he himself should come to his temple (Mal. 3:1); and finally, when by assuming flesh as the God-man, by announcing, accomplishing, and sealing salvation, in order that he might confer it by his Spirit, he consummated his economic period (Heb. 1:1; 1 Tim. 3:16; Gal. 4:4). The remaining things which pertain to the economic worship and to economic sins we will put aside for the practical part.

The Elenctic Part

1. Is Christ the Son of God from eternal generation alone?

The differences of opinion

XVI. It is asked, first, whether Christ is the Son of God from eternal generation alone. The ancient Jews in the time of Christ, however exceedingly degenerate in faith, nevertheless still acknowledged that their Messiah would be the Son of God, and indeed in such a way that he would be God's own Son, and from this, equal to God, as is evident from John 5:18, Matthew 26:63, and without a doubt from Psalm 2:12; but whether he would be the Son from generation is not clear. The modern Jews go further and deny that he would be the Son of God, for this reason: that they may more easily deny that he is true God and consubstantial with the Father. Cerinthus and Carpocrates did not even acknowledge that he was the Son of God due to his temporal nativity, as Irenaeus testifies (bk. 1, ch. 25–26; bk. 3, ch. 4), as well as Eusebius (*Ecclesiastial History*, bk. 3, ch. 28) and others.[13] Arius, an offspring of the previous, so that he might more strongly guard his own ὁμοιούσιον, "of similar substance," against the Catholics, indeed confessed that he was the Son of God, but not through generation, but rather through creation, much less through eternal generation; that he was a mere creature, though at the same time endowed with gifts and virtues surpassing every nature, both of men and angels, and who as a result deserved to be called the Son of God, though at the same time he was created from that which did

---

13. Irenaeus, Ἔλεγχος καὶ ἀνατροπὴ τῆς ψευδωνύμου γνώσεως (*Contra haereses*) in *PG* 7:680–87, 855–57; idem, *Against Heresies*, ANF 1:350–52, 416; Eusebius, Ἐκλησιαστικὴ ἱστορία (*Ecclesiastica historia*) in *PG* 20:273–76; idem, *Ecclesiastical History* in NPNF2 1:160–61.

not exist, and was different in substance from the Father.[14] He was condemned in the Nicene Council in the year 325, by 318 bishops. Paul of Samosata and Photinus likewise acknowledged that he was the Son of God, but through his nativity from the blessed Virgin, before which he did not exist. Muhammad in his Qur'an (which he wrote in the year 610 in the time of Heraclius, with his agents, a certain monk Sergio and John the Antiochian, a Jew) denies that he is the Son of God. Valentine Gentile, last century, acknowledged with the ancient Tritheists and Peratae that he was the Son of God, and indeed by eternal genera-tion, but not God in essence, but rather a created offspring of the essence. The Socinians, who do not differ one whit from Samosata and Photinus, so that they might more forcefully exclude his eternal deity and thereby his equivalent satis-faction for our guilt, and so that they might at last obtain that we are justified by our own works, do acknowledge that he is the Son of God, but by no means from eternal generation, but rather from his birth from the blessed Virgin, insofar as he was conceived in an entirely extraordinary way by the Holy Spirit, who in this work took the place of the begetting man and admixed a certain extraordinary substance with the seed of the woman, and likewise because by grace there was communicated to him a certain likeness with God, when (1) he was sanctified by the Father and sent into the world (John 10:34–36), (2) through his resurrec-tion from the dead he was begotten, as it were (Acts 13:32–33), (3) through his exaltation he was elevated to the right hand of God (Heb. 1:4–5). Others either add or substitute other causes of this sonship. Abraham Calov in his *Socinianism Overthrown* recounts eleven reasons, with eternal generation alone excluded.[15] The Remonstrant Apologists agree with the Socinians in this, that they approve the above four Socinian causes of sonship, but they differ in this, that they seem to add generation from the Father, although they do not admit that from it he is consubstantial with the Father (Episcopius, *Institutes*, bk. 4, sect. 2, ch. 35).[16] The Reformed state that on account of his eternal generation alone he is the Son of God, although this eternal sonship was made manifest in his sanctification and sending into the world, as well as in his resurrection and exaltation.

---

14. *creatum ἐκ μὴ ὄντων* [Rom. 4:17], *Patri ἑτερούσιον*

15. See Abraham Calov (1612–1686), *Socinismus profligatus, hoc est, errorum Socinianorum luculenta confutatio* (Wittenberg: Johann Borckhard, 1668), sect. 4, art. 2, controv. 10, pp. 208–12.

16. Simon Episcopius, *Institutiones theologicae* in *Opera theologica* (London: Moses Pit, 1678), 340–44.

That he is called the Son of God on account of his eternal
generation from the Father

Accordingly it is incumbent upon us here to demonstrate three things: first,
that the true cause of this sonship is the eternal generation of the Son from the
Father, which we will obtain in this way: (1) he is called the Son of the living
God (Matt. 16:16), the true Son (1 John 5:20), his own Son (Rom. 8:32), the
only begotten (John 1:14, 18), the beloved of the Father, in whom he rests (Matt.
3:17). (2) He is the Son equal to the Father (Phil. 2:6; John 5:17–18), indeed
the same in essence with the Father (John 10:30, 33, 36; 1 John 5:7), and God
consubstantial with him, which we have already demonstrated from the divine
names, attributes, operations, and worship. (3) He is expressly said to be begotten of the Father (Ps. 2:7) through communication of essence (John 5:26), and
that from eternity (Prov. 8:22–24; Mic. 5:2; John 1:1–2), from which he is called
the firstborn (Col. 1:15; Heb. 1:6). (4) He is celebrated as the essential image of
the Father, the effulgence of his glory and the express image of his person (Col.
1:15; Heb. 1:3). (5) He is the Son in such a way as is no creature, either visible
or invisible, in heaven or on earth, insofar as he is the Son neither through creation, by which the angels are sons of God (Job 38:6–7), nor through power,
by which magistrates are sons of God (Ps. 82:6–7); indeed, he is Son of God
in a way in which not even the angels, the most excellent of creatures, are (Heb.
1:4–5). Accordingly he cannot but be the Son through eternal generation. And
what they allege to the contrary, that this generation is in many ways derogatory
to God, we have already shown in the preceding chapter is only valid concerning
natural generation, but not, however, concerning supernatural generation.[17]

That he is not called the Son of God from any other causes

Then second, it must be demonstrated that he is the Son of God not on account
of a gracious communication of holiness or exaltation to the right hand of God
(as the Socinians want), because: (1) he was the Son of God before he was conceived by the Holy Spirit and before the things spoken were communicated to
him (Ps. 2:7; Mic. 5:2; Prov. 8:23–24). (2) In this way he would be the Son of
God according to his human nature, which Scripture resists as often as: (a) it
calls him the Son of God in a way opposed to his human nature (Rom. 1:4; 9:5);
(b) he is called the Son of Man undoubtedly according to his human nature
(Matt. 16:13, 16). (3) Nor are these three or four Socinian ideas all individually
total causes of this sonship, for thus one would suffice and the rest would be
superfluous; nor likewise are they partial causes of it, for thus from his conception

---

17. 1.2.25 §XI

he would have become the Son of God by degrees, and not have been the full Son of God before his session at the right hand of God, which is absurd. I will not add that (4) from the Socinian opinion he would be the same kind or species of son of God as believers, only in a different degree, against which Scripture cries out in Hebrews 1:4–5, and as often as it calls him alone God's own and only begotten Son.

An objection

Moreover, the fact that his sonship is referred to his conception by the Holy Spirit (Luke 1:35), to his sanctification (John 10:36), to his resurrection from the dead (Acts 13:32–33), to his exaltation (Heb. 1:4–5), does not therefore mean that these are causes of this sonship, but rather that they are indicators of its manifestation. For this reason elsewhere it is said that he was manifested in the flesh (1 Tim. 3:16), and that from his conception by the Holy Spirit he would be called the Son of the Most High (Luke 1:35), and likewise that his glory has been seen (John 1:14).

That he is not the Son of God partly on account of generation and partly on account of a gracious communication

Finally third, it must be shown that he is not called the Son of God conjointly, that is, partly on account of eternal generation and partly on account of a gracious communication of existence, holiness, power, and glory, as the Remonstrants, in favor of the Socinians, state in order to weaken eternal generation. This is so because: (1) Scripture distinguishes a twofold sonship in Christ in such a way that according to the flesh he is called the Son of Man and according to the Spirit, or the divine nature, he is called the Son of God (Rom. 1:3–4). (2) By this rationale he would be the Son of God equivocally from different causes, which Scripture resists when it calls him God's own and only begotten Son. (3) By this rationale he could be called according to the human nature the adoptive Son of God, and thus in no way would he be "without father" (Heb. 7:3).

2. Does the generation of the Son consist in the communion of essence in his eternal coexistence with the Father, and in his economic manifestation in the flesh? The origin and state of the controversy

XVII. It is asked, second, whether the generation of the Son consists in the communion of essence in his eternal coexistence with the Father, and in his economic manifestation in the flesh. Regarding the nature of this generation we have already represented and defeated various opinions of various adversaries in the preceding sections. The occasion for this question is provided by a certain

Dutch theologian,[18] who since he could not reconcile with his own ideas the received opinion of the Reformed concerning a generation that communicated to the begotten God's same essence in number, nor clearly and distinctly perceive how God, who was nothing but mere thought, could communicate his own thought to another without dependency and mutability, without the loss of eternity and other incongruities of the Socinians, stated at first that this generation does not consist in anything but his eternal communion in the same essence and his coexistence with the Father. But afterwards when he observed that this coexistence alone was certainly not sufficient for the idea of generation, he added the economic manifestation of the Son in the flesh through generation from the blessed Virgin, excluding all communication of essence.[19] This opinion has been proscribed and condemned by almost all the synods of the Dutch churches, and its author has been prohibited by the authority of his supreme magistrate from propagating this opinion, a prohibition also received by him.[20] Meanwhile, most synods have decreed that ministerial candidates must be examined on this

---

18. This is a thinly veiled critique of the Cartesian Herman Roëll (1653–1718), whose "controversial appointment [to the faculty at Utrecht in 1704]…was the reason the city requested Mastricht to live in 'peace and friendship,'" Adriaan Neele, *Before Jonathan Edwards: Sources of New England Theology* (Oxford: Oxford University Press, 2019), 48–49, esp. 49n101; cf. Brannon Ellis, *Calvin, Classical Trinitarianism, and the Aseity of the Son* (Oxford: Oxford University Press, 2012), 127–37. For accounts of the controversies, see Jean-Henri Samuel Formey, *Abrégé de l'Histoire Ecclésiastique*, 2 vols. (Amsterdam: J. H. Schneider, 1763), 2:350–52, esp. 352, note (a); idem, *An Ecclesiastical History: From the Birth of Christ to the Present Time*, 2 vols. (London: J. Newberry, L. Davis, C. Reymers, 1766), 2:220–22, esp. 222 note (a); Johann Georg Walch, *Einleitung in die Religions Streitigkeiten ausser der Lutherischen Kirche*, 5 vols. (Jena: Johan Meyers Wittve, 1733–39), 3:866.

19. On Roëll's early views on the generation of the Son, see idem, *Theses theologicae de generatione Filii et morte fidelium temporali quae…praeside Hermanno Alex. Roell…respondente Stephano Foccoma* (Franeker: Johannes Gyselaar, 1689), 3–5. And his later positions in idem, *Dissertatio theologica altera de generatione Filii et morte fidelium temporali, opposita epilogo...Campegii Vitringa* (Franeker: Johannes Gyselaar, 1690); idem, *Kort en Eenvoudig Berigt van het Verschil over de Geboorte des Soons, en Tydelicke Dood der Geloovige* (Amsterdam: Gerardus Borstius, 1691); his posthumously published treatment of *Heidelberg Catechism*, Q. 33 in *Explicatio Catecheseos Heidelbergensis opus postumum* (Utrecht: Gijsbertus van Paddenburg, 1728), 259–71. Mastricht interacted here most closely with Roëll's *Dissertatio theologica altera*.

20. This controversy began on two fronts with Roëll: in 1686 on the role of natural reason and in 1689 on the question of the eternal generation of the Son. See the historical account by the theological faculty of Leiden in 1723 for a list of synodical actions between 1690 and 1722, Johannes á Marck et al., *Judicium ecclesiasticum quo opiniones quaedam Cl. Herm. Alex. Röell, synodice damnatae sunt, laudatum* (Leiden: Samuel Luchtmans, 1723). For the contents of these declarations between 1690 and 1722, see *Documenta Reformatoria: teksten uit de geschiedenis van kerk en theologie in de Nederlanden sedert de Hervorming*, ed. J. N. Bakhuizen van den Brink et al., 2 vols. (Kampen: J. H. Kok, 1960).

opinion, and that anyone who holds to it must not be admitted to the ecclesiastical ministry.[21]

The opinion of the Reformed with their reasons
Therefore, the Reformed state that for the eternal generation of the Son of God is required communication of essence with the image or likeness of the one communicating it. Accordingly, communion of essence conjoined with coexistence is not sufficient, nor also is his economic manifestation in the flesh. On this point the arguments in §VII and the paragraph just before it are valid and sufficient, with necessary changes being made, to maintain that for our doctrine of generation a communication of essence is necessary. Here we must only demonstrate that coexistence in communion of the same essence, and likewise economic manifestation in the flesh, and even both conjoined, are insufficient to ground sonship and generation. We will strive to this end distinctly, in the following way.

First, we endeavor to maintain that coexistence in the communion of essence is not sufficient, in this way, because: (1) coexistence in the same human essence (for example, that of Peter with Paul) is not sufficient such that on that account Peter would be called the son of Paul, unless there should be in addition a communication of essence. (2) This coexistence is more effective for grounding a relation of brotherhood between them. (3) By the hypothesis of this coexistence the first person would be Son just as much as the second because of the fact that the Father coexists just as much in the same essence with the Son as the Son does with the Father. The same could be said about the Holy Spirit. Hence (4) through this hypothesis the characteristic or personal properties are taken away, and by the same stroke, the Trinity of persons. (5) In this coexistence is implied at least a double or triple existence of God, and since in God existence differs not at all from essence, by the same stroke there will need to be acknowledged a double or triple essence in God.

Second, that the economic manifestation of the second person in the flesh is also not sufficient to this end is likewise evident, since: (1) to be manifested in the flesh is by no means to be or to become a son of God. For the three men who appeared to Abraham, among whom stood the one Jehovah (Gen. 18:1–2), did not constitute or argue for three sons. And the Holy Spirit especially under the New Testament was rather frequently manifested to the church, and yet he did

---

21. For a sample of the questions to the ministerial candidates, see *Judicium ecclesiasticum…
laudatum*, 17–18.

not by that fact immediately become a son. If you should take exception that the Holy Spirit was not manifested in the flesh and did not bear the visible image of God, I will oppose you by asking, Who will say that to be manifested in the flesh or to become man is to become a son of God? By what reason is a divine person who manifests himself in the flesh to be called the Son of God more than one that manifests himself in any way without or beyond the flesh? Next, (2) if manifestation in the flesh is the foundation of sonship, what will be the foundation of paternity? For to be a son and to be a father are correlated, but manifestation in the flesh has the same relation to the Holy Spirit which it has to the Father. Furthermore, (3) the second person existed as the Son of God before he was manifested in the flesh (Ps. 2:7; Prov. 30:4), indeed from eternity (Prov. 8:25). He already was the Son of God when he was sent into the world (Gal. 4:4).

The objections of our adversary

As for the reasons of our adversary, it must be observed that in favor of the coexistence in which alone he placed the eternal generation of the Son he proffers no argument at all, either from Scripture or from reason, to conclude that the generation of the Son of God consists in that coexistence. Thus, by inferior thinking he rouses all his strength to maintain, presupposing this coexistence, that generation consists in the economic manifestation of the Son of God in the flesh. For this matter he urges: (1) that the word *generation* in the Scriptures repeatedly denotes manifestation (Prov. 17:17; 2:7; Song 8:5).[22] The force of this argument proceeds thus: if the expression of generation repeatedly denotes manifestation, then the generation of the Son consists in his manifestation in the flesh; but the prior is true, so therefore also is the latter. I respond: (a) There is no connection to the major premise. (b) It must be proved that something or someone who is manifested is generated in such a way that he is a son. (c) Granted that something which is manifested is said to be generated in an improper sense, even so nowhere is it customary that something manifested without any communication is called a son. For example, when in Proverbs 17:17 it says, "a brother is born," or manifested, "for adversity," to whom then is this brother in adversity a son? (d) Say that one who is manifested is in some way called a son, which will never be proved: surely from this it would not with just reason be concluded that the Son of God, his own Son, the firstborn, the only begotten, to whom the Father communicated life, that is, essence, is called such due to his manifestation. As for the minor premise, (e) we deny that any passage of Scripture can be produced through which being generated as a son consists in manifestation without any

---

22. Cf. §§27, 58, 64, Roëll, *Dissertatio theologica altera.*

relation of communication. Not Proverbs 17:17, for that speaks of a metaphorical generation of a *brother*, not a son. Nor Proverbs 27:1, "You do not know
what tomorrow will bring forth," for it speaks not about manifestation but about
production. Nor Song of Songs 8:5, "Under the apple tree I roused you: there your
mother with sorrow produced you," for it does not speak about manifestation,
but about production, and indeed with the sorrows of childbirth. He urges
(2) that the Son of God in the Scriptures is frequently said in economic matters
to have been declared the Son of God (1 Tim. 3:16; John 10:36; Acts 13:32–33;
Rom. 1:4; Matt. 3:13, 17; and so forth), for example in his baptism, his resurrection, and so forth.[23] But nowhere is he said by these economic matters to have
been begotten or made, since a declaration presupposes a pre-existing son. He
urges (3) that the third person is called the Holy Spirit from economic matters;
why therefore would he not also be named the Son from an economic matter?[24]
I respond: (a) Indeed he is named "the Spirit of sanctification" (Rom. 1:4)—
unless you prefer to refer this passage with most commentators to the divine
nature of Christ—and from this comes "the sanctification of the Spirit" (1 Peter
1:2). But this must be carefully distinguished from his denomination "Holy
Spirit," insofar as the latter is his distinctive name, whereas the former is only
a title, and many such titles are attributed to the Holy Spirit that are partly
economic and partly personal: in the prior is "the Spirit of life," "the life-giving
Spirit," "the Spirit of truth"; in the latter are, for example, "the Spirit of God"
(Matt. 3:16) and "the Spirit of Christ" (Rom. 8:9). (b) Although the denomination "holy" might be economic, yet by that fact the name "Holy Spirit" will not be
entirely economic. Accordingly the Spirit is named not from his economic operation but from his mode of subsisting, from which he is also called "the Spirit of his
mouth" (Ps. 33:6; 2 Thess. 2:8), "the Spirit of the Almighty" (Job 33:4), because
he proceeds as through an ineffable spiration, which is what John 20:22 intends
to signify. He urges (4) the passage Hebrews 7:3, asserting that the Word of God
prohibits him from thinking that Christ with respect to his divine nature (about
which this text speaks) has been begotten.[25] I respond, The text speaks about
Melchizedek in a figure, and about the Son of God in emphasis, saying that he
is "without father, without mother, without genealogy" because with respect to
the human nature he was without father and with respect to the divine nature
without mother and without genealogy, or because that divine nature lacks a

---

23. Cf. §§68–69, Roëll, *Dissertatio theologica altera*.

24. Cf. §74, Roëll, *Dissertatio theologica altera*.

25. Mastricht's Latin: *Verbum Dei inquit mihi prohibet cogitare quod Christus respectu divinae suae naturae de qua loquitur sit genitus*: Cf. Roell, *Dissertatio theologica altera*, 112: *Denique XII. expresse Scriptura cavisse videtur, ne secunda persona Deitatis proprie genita esse putetur.*

carnal father and mother. Finally, he urges (5) from reason (which in such great a mystery he should have held in subjection, 2 Cor. 10:5) that generation properly so-called is incongruous with his eternity and independence. I respond, This was once the argument of the Arians and is even now the argument of the Socinians, yet he might have easily taken away these troubles by distinguishing between natural generation, which alone urges these inconveniences, and supernatural generation, which by no means does so. The celebrated Campegius Vitringa, Sr., handled this controversy against his own colleague as carefully as possible in his writings, both in Latin and Dutch.[26] We have been more copious concerning it on account of its moment as well as its recentness, and because nowhere else does one come across it in the common places.

3. Is Christ God from eternity, and coessential with the Father?

XVIII. It is asked, third, whether Christ is God from eternity, and consubstantial with his Father. Long ago the Tritheists and Peratae, and in the last century Valentine Gentile, acknowledged the Son was God from eternity but not that he was consubstantial. The Arians acknowledged at least that he existed before the world, but not from eternity, nor consubstantial with the Father. The Samosatians and Photinians together with the modern Socinians believe that he did not exist from eternity, nor before his own nativity from the blessed Virgin, nor that he is consubstantial, but only a mere man, although they do not deny that he is both true God and even eternal, on the posterior part. For this reason they assigned him divinity and not deity, according to Smalcius,[27] which differ as finite from infinite. The Reformed teach that Christ, with respect to his divine nature, existed from eternity and is consubstantial with his Father. We spoke about the reasons for this doctrine in §§VIII–XII. Nothing remains now except that we should meet the objections of our adversaries. They allege: (1) that Christ himself says

---

26. Campegius Vitringa, Sr. (1659–1722), *Epilogus disputationis…de generatione Filii et morte fidelium temporali* (Franeker: Johannes Gyselaar, 1689); idem, *Korte verklaringe van het Gelove der Algemeene Kercke aengaende de geboorte des Soons, ende de tydelicke Dood der Gelovige* (Franeker: Johannes Gyselaar, 1691). On the debate between Vitringa and Roëll, see C. K. Telfer, *Wrestling with Isaiah: The Exegetical Methodology of Campegius Vitringa (1659–1722)* (Göttingen: Vandenhoeck and Ruprecht, 2016), 30–31.

27. θειότητα, *non* θεότητα. This is a summary statement of Smalcius, *Refutatio disputationis de persona Christi quam Albertus Grawerus...habuit anno 1612* (Rakow: Sternacianus, 1615), e.g. 10–11, that the Father is God by nature and Christ is God by a gift or grant of God; 21, that Christ has all things *ex dono Patris* and "so then it necessarily follows that he is not by nature the same God that the Father is"; 22, that Christ is equal to God because he does the works of God, but he does not do them *a se* or *ex se* but *secundum divinam naturam*, the divine nature that is given; 26, "we say that Christ is equal to God the Father, not *simpliciter*, that is, absolutely, but *secundum quid*, relatively."

that he is God as magistrates are gods (John 10:35), namely by reason of office, not by reason of essence. I respond, Christ had said in verse 30, "I and the Father are one," and from this the Jews gathered that he was a blasphemer, because by this very statement he had made himself God. Our Savior responds from the lesser to the greater: If magistrates on account of their office are called gods, why not I who have been sent by the Father? But after doing this he says that he is true God and consubstantial with the Father: "that you may know that the Father is in me and I in the Father" (John 10:37–38). (2) He was made Lord (Acts 2:36; John 1:27; Heb. 1:4; 3:2), therefore he was also made God. I respond: (a) To be Lord and to be God are not synonymous: there are many lords who are not by that fact gods. (b) There is a twofold lordship in Christ, a mediatorial lordship according to which he was made Lord, and an essential lordship which belongs to him insofar as he is Jehovah, which all kinds of translators render by the word κύριος, "Lord." Consider for example Jeremiah 23:6 and 33:16, when they render the words of the latter, with Glass and other learned men, "The one who will call" (or who will call together and will unite together through the Word) "her" (that is, Jerusalem) will be "Jehovah righteousness" (cf. Hos. 1:7).[28] With respect to this essential lordship, he is by no means made Lord. They allege (3) that the Son is lesser than the Father (John 14:28), subject to the Father (1 Cor. 15:28). I respond, He is said in another place to be equal to the Father, namely insofar as he was in the form of God (Phil. 2:6), from which there belongs to him equal honor with the Father: "that all should honor the Son *just as* they honor the Father" (John 5:23). From which one may easily gather that in different respects the Son is both equal to the Father and lesser than the Father: he is equal to him with respect to the form of God, or with respect to his essence; he is lesser not only with respect to his human nature, but also with respect to his economic office, insofar as in the eternal counsel of peace, by acting as expromissor he took upon himself all the guilt and all the cause of the sinner,[29] and in that was made subject to the Father, as a debtor and slave—unless you prefer that he is called lesser than the Father with respect to the relation of sonship, through which also in human affairs a son is said to be lesser than his father, although with respect to the essence of humanity and

---

28. Salomon Glass (1593–1656), *Biblia das ist die ganze H. Schrifft Altes und Neues Testaments* (Nürnberg: Endter, 1679), Jer. 23:6, p. 640; Jer. 33:16, pp. 650–51.

29. Cf. 1.5.1 §XXXIV. An *expromissor* is a surety that assumes the total debt of a debtor regardless of ability to pay, whereas a *fidejussor* is a surety only for the delinquent amount after the debtor's resources have been exhausted. On the question of Christ's satisfaction, Gisbertus Voetius and Petrus van Mastricht held that Christ was an expromissor for the elect whereas Johannes Cocceius held that Christ was a *fidejussor*.

also with respect to gifts, wisdom, goodness, he shows himself equal to him, indeed greater than him. They allege (4) that the Father is the one and only true God (John 17:3). I respond, In another place the Son is also called the true God (1 John 5:20), and if he is the true God he is also the one God. And in John 17:3 the Father alone is not called the one true God, but the Father is called the one and only true God, "That they may know you to be the only true God," and there is also added, "and Jesus Christ whom you have sent," namely, that they may know him be the one true God. They allege (5) that he is everywhere called a man and the Son of Man. I respond, But this does not occur such that it excludes his eternal deity, inasmuch as we have already demonstrated that more clearly than the sun, but because God was manifested in the flesh (1 Tim. 3:16), because the Son of God was in time born of a woman (Gal. 4:4). They allege (6) that he calls the Father his God. I respond, He calls the Father his God not only by reason of his human nature, but also by reason of his economic office, as we taught under the third objection. They allege (7) he is said to have all that is his from the Father. I respond, As he has certain things from the Father through eternal generation, as the Word—such as life, essence, and all the essentials of deity (John 5:26; cf. Ps. 2:7)—and other things through the grace of personal union, as the God-man, so none of these derogates from his deity whatsoever, but rather confirms it. They allege (8) that the Father alone is called our God in 1 Corinthians 8:6; therefore the Son is not God. I respond, Just as in saying that the Son alone is our Lord, the text does not deny that the Father also is our Lord, so in saying that the Father is our God, it does not deny that the Son also is our God. Therefore the intention of the text is nothing other than to seclude the so-called gods (1 Cor. 8:5) from both deity and lordship.

4. Is the Son God from himself?

XIX. It is asked, fourth, whether the Son is *autotheos* or God from himself. The Tritheists, Valentine Gentile, the Arians, the Samosatians, Photinians, and the Socinians, that they may more strongly deny that the Son is consubstantial with the Father, deny it. The papists, because Calvin and Beza, when disputing against Gentile (who stated that Christ was God *essenced*) call him *autotheos*, shout that they are undermining the Trinity by asserting that the characteristic property of the Father, by which he is from himself, belongs to the Son also; the papists even invent a new heresy, that of the *Autotheans*. The Remonstrant Apologists, in agreement with the Socinians, intending to undermine the Trinity through trickery, likewise deny it. The Reformed distinguish between essential and personal aseity: indeed they affirm essential aseity, in which the deity communicated to the Son and the Holy Spirit is *a se*, from itself; however, they deny personal aseity, insofar as the deity which the Son and the Holy Spirit possess, they do not possess from themselves but from the Father. The basis of this thought Christ himself sets forth in John 5:26: "Just as the Father has life in himself, so he has granted the Son to have life in himself." And if the deity which the Son and the Holy Spirit have is not from itself, it will not be true deity. Accordingly, although the Son and the Holy Spirit are *autotheos*, God from himself, even so they are not *autoprosopa*, persons from themselves. In this sense Bellarmine, Génébrard, and all who genuinely receive the consubstantiality of the persons admit that the Son is *autotheos*. Meanwhile Arminius misrepresents us that this opinion leads either to Tritheism, because it is stated that the three have their essence collaterally from themselves, or Sabellianism, because the aseity through which the Father is distinguished from the Son is made common through this independence of the Son.[30] But neither is true: for neither does it lead to Tritheism, because we have not stated that there are three essences collaterally from themselves, but one only, common to the three persons; nor does it lead to Sabellianism, for although the essential deity is made common, even so personal aseity remains proper to the Father. Therefore insofar as this question is argued between us and the anti-Trinitarians, it has been determined in the preceding paragraph; insofar as it is argued between us and the papists, it is nothing but a mere word-battle, which Ames demonstrates in *Bellarmine Enervated* (bk. 2, ch. 1, §1);[31] and finally insofar as it is argued between us and the Remonstrants, it has already been adequately determined. If you should want more, consult Alting, *New Elenctic Theology*.[32]

The Practical Part

The person and economic office of the Son: 1. Supplies an argument for glorification.

XX. The person and economy of the Son of God supplies for us, first, an argument for glorification and gratitude toward God, who by an eternal and immovable decree, induced by pure philanthropy, gave to his church not some outstanding man, or even an angel, but his Son, his own and only begotten Son, as steward, expromissor, Mediator, Redeemer, ambassador, and judge, that he would govern her, take her guilt upon himself, intercede as the middleman between him and her, redeem her by his own blood, open to her his will for

---

30. *per hanc Filii* αὐτοθεότητα

31. William Ames, *Bellarminus enervatus*, 4 vols. (Amsterdam: Johannes Janssonius, 1630), 1:81–82.

32. *Alting Elench. Nov. Loc. III. prob. 32:* This is most likely locus 3, third type of controversy, the first question, cf. Heinrich Alting, *Theologia elenctica nova, sive systema elencticum* (Amsterdam: Joannes Janssonius, 1654), 149–86.

obtaining eternal blessedness, guard her against all enemies, and finally confer to her the crown of righteousness. This philanthropy God himself commends (Rom. 5:5–8), and thus not even the Son can marvel at it enough (John 3:16), and according to the will of his Father he tells the decree of it as something outstanding (Ps. 2:7). Thus, here you rightly should exclaim with the apostle, "Behold what great love the Father has given to us!" (1 John 3:1). In this glorification of the divine philanthropy is the highest goal of the entire evangelical mystery (Eph. 1:6; Rom. 9:23).

2. It kindles a desire to know the Son.
XXI. Second, it kindles a desire more and more to know this Son, who from the decree of the Father tells himself to us. In this God the Father has established our justification (Isa. 53:11) and the Son our eternal life (John 17:3), from which the apostle made so much of "the excellency of the knowledge of Christ Jesus," such that he counted all things as loss and dung so that he might gain this Christ alone (Phil. 3:8). Moreover, he must be known: (1) as the steward to whom all authority has been given (Matt. 28:18), so that we bow the knee of our heart (Phil. 2:10–11), a steward such as Joseph once was, first in the house of Potiphar (Gen. 39:4, 8–9), then in the whole of Egypt (Gen. 41:40–41). In addition, (2) as the expromissor, so that once we have wholly renounced all our own righteousness we seek in him alone the defense of our cause (Phil. 3:9–10). Furthermore, (3) as the Mediator, without whom we should never try to approach the Father's throne (Heb. 4:14–16; John 14:6). Also (4) as the Redeemer, in whose ransom we should set all our hope and all our salvation (Acts 4:12). In addition, (5) as the interpreter and ambassador of the Father, to whom in all things we should most carefully listen (Deut. 18:15; Matt. 3:17).[33] Moreover, (6) as the head of the church, whom we should reverence (John 5:23). Finally, (7) as the judge, whom we should fear (2 Cor. 5:10–11), and long for as well (Luke 21:28), namely for different reasons.

3. It commends the sufficiency of our Mediator to us.
XXII. So then, third, it commends to us the sufficiency and perfection of our Mediator, from which it is said that all fullness dwells in him (Col. 1:19), and he fills all in all (Eph. 1:23), so that from his fullness we can draw grace upon grace (John 1:16); indeed, in him we are made complete (Col. 2:10). This sufficiency arises on the one hand (1) from the dignity and excellence of his person, by which he is not just any man, not an angel, not some most outstanding creature,

---

33. Cf. Matt. 17:5.

but the natural, very own, firstborn, and only begotten Son of God, in whom the fullness of deity dwells bodily (Col. 2:9–10). He is the brightness of the glory and the express image of the person of the Father, whom he constituted the heir of all things (Heb. 1:3–4); who for this reason can be and offer anything to his own, since he is omnipotent, the one to whom all authority in heaven and earth belong (Matt. 28:18); who knows the necessities and desires of his own, together with the means and methods of assisting and satisfying them, because he is omniscient, wisdom itself, the one in whom are hidden all the treasures of wisdom (Col. 2:3); who also wills to be all in all for his own, because he is most highly good and merciful (2 Cor. 13:14), the one who loved his church and gave himself for her (Eph. 5:2). Next, this sufficiency arises (2) from the statute of the Father which the Son tells to us in Psalm 2:7, from the counsel of peace (Zech. 6:13), through which it was the Father's good pleasure that in him all fullness might dwell (Col. 1:19), through which he has been constituted head over all things (Eph. 1:22), through whom the Father dispenses all things, and thus has now committed all judgment to the Son (John 5:22) by establishing him over all his house (Heb. 3:2). Finally, it arises (3) from his economic office, through which, as we have said, by the economic counsel of the Trinity he undertook the office of steward and universal Lord, of expromissor, Mediator, Redeemer, ambassador, head, judge, through all of which he has been made for us wisdom from God, righteousness, sanctification, and redemption (1 Cor. 1:30), such that in him alone is all salvation (Acts 4:12); he is the way, the truth, and the life, apart from whom no way is open to the Father (John 14:6), the one in whom God has blessed us with every blessing in the heavenly places (Eph. 1:3). For this reason in the Scriptures he is likened to all good things, when he is called our life (Col. 3:4), our nourishment (John 6:55), our physician (Matt. 9:12), our consolation (Luke 2:25), our protector (Isa. 32:2), a bundle of myrrh (Song 1:13), the fountain of salvation (Zech. 13:1), the Sun of righteousness (Mal. 4:2), our glory (Luke 2:32), and all in all (Col. 3:11).

4. It entices us that we may kiss the Son.
XXIII. Fourth, it entices us that we may kiss the Son (Psalm 2:12), that is, as a sign of the homage that was customarily conferred upon princes and their appointed governors (see Gen. 41:40, where the verb יִשַּׁק, "shall kiss" is used). In our opinion, to kiss the Son generally means nothing other than promptly to receive him as the King constituted by the Father, and as his governor, under all his economic offices, to adore him, and to offer to him all the worship that belongs to him. Specifically, it especially embraces the following three things: (1) that we depend entirely upon him, which is as if to kiss his hand; to promise

ourselves, to expect, and to wait for all things from him alone, inasmuch as to him as the supreme steward all things have been handed over, that they might be handed over to men (Eph. 4:8). (2) That we promptly submit ourselves to his authority and lordship (which is as if to kiss his feet), that we serve Jehovah (Ps. 2:11), bow our knees to him (Phil. 2:10), promptly heed and perform his commands (Matt. 3:17), readily lay all we have before him, and devote it to his glory (Matt. 21:2–3; 6–7). (3) That we love him frankly and above all things (Matt. 10:37)—this is as if to kiss his lips. This kiss of homage must be conferred upon him faithfully: (1) so that we may turn aside the wrath of both the Father and the Son: "lest he be angry"; (2) so that we may flee destruction: "and you perish in the way, when his fury is kindled but a little"; (3) so that we may obtain blessedness from him: "Blessed are all who hope in him" (Ps. 2:12).

5. It persuades toward faith in the Son.
XXIV. In particular, fifth, it persuades us that we should believe in him. For, "This is the work of God, that we believe in him whom he has sent" (John 6:29). We should believe, I say, not only *that* he is the one whom the Father has sent, the Messiah (Matt. 16:16), and not only *him* (Matt. 3:17), but also *in him*, so that by believing we receive him in our heart. For, "As many as received him, to them he gave authority to become sons of God, those who believed in his name" (John 1:12). And to this end: (1) the Father gives and sends him to us: "That he gave his only begotten Son, that whoever believes…" (John 3:16). To this end (2) the Son himself comes to us (John 1:11). To this (3) he invites us with so many arguments and promises (Matt. 11:28–29; Rev. 3:20; Song 5:2; Hos. 2:14–15). By this (4) we gain Christ, with all his benefits (Phil. 3:8–9). Without this, (5) the Son and all his offices, together with all his economic benefits, will not profit us one whit (Rom. 10:3–4; Gal. 3:2, 5–7). Indeed, (6) he will even be against us (Ps. 2:12; John 3:36). See also book 2, chapter 1, on faith.[34]

6. It urges that we should make the Son of God most great.
XXV. Furthermore, sixth, (1) let us extol the Son greatly and above all things (Matt. 10:37; Song 1:2). (2) Let us gain him for ourselves at the cost of anything else (Phil. 3:7–8; Matt. 13:46). (3) Let us calmly rest in him, as our most sufficient portion (Ps. 73:25), regardless of what things we should have to lack (Hab. 3:17–18). (4) Let us devote ourselves and all we have to his glorification, and let this be our alpha and omega, the first moving cause and the final end of all of our actions (Phil. 1:20; Rom. 14:7–8; 2 Cor. 5:15). (5) Let us seek all

---

34. 1.2.1 §§XXVIII ff.

things necessary for us, whether in body or in soul, from his hands alone: if we lack faith, hope, love, if we lack strength to resist temptations, if we lack solace in adversities, let us seek these things from him alone (Mark 9:24), because he can supply them all for us (Phil. 4:13), and it would be shameful to him if having passed him by, you should seek them from another (2 Kings 1:3). Finally, (6) whatever we undertake and do, let us undertake it all in the name of this Son, and in his strength (Eph. 5:20; Col. 3:17).

7. It rouses us to place our hope of salvation in him.
XXVI. In addition to these things, seventh, it rouses us that we should place our hope and confidence of eternal life in the Son (Ps. 2:12), for which reason he is called our hope (1 Tim. 1:1), and Christians are said to hope in Christ (1 Cor. 15:19; 1 Thess. 1:3); and from which he is also named the hope of Israel (Acts 28:20), insofar as specifically: (1) he as the expromissor and Mediator has endured in himself and taken away all that which could exclude us from the hope of salvation, namely, the guilt of our sins (Eph. 2:12–13; 1:7). (2) As the Redeemer, he acquired the right of eternal life by his own satisfaction and merit (Eph. 1:14). (3) As the righteous Judge, he will one day allot the crown of righteousness (2 Tim. 4:7–8). Only: (1) with living faith let us take hold of that anchor of salvation (Heb. 6:19); and (2) with zeal for an unblemished conscience (Acts 24:15–16), (3) let us devote ourselves to the continued emendation of our life (2 Cor. 7:1), just as, "Everyone who has this hope in him" (Christ) "makes himself holy, even as he is holy" (1 John 3:3).

8. It frightens us away from economic sins against the Son.
XXVII. Finally, eighth, it warns us that we should beware, more than a dog or snake, of all those sins which specifically and economically resist the Son: (1) the neglect and despising of him, whereby we do not receive him as he comes to us and offers himself to us (John 1:11; 5:43–44), and we despise him (Matt. 22:5; Acts 13:46; 28:24); next, (2) rebellion and resistance (Ps. 2:1–3; Acts 4:26–27; Luke 19:27); furthermore, (3) denial of him once received (Matt. 10:33; 26:70–71); in addition, (4) whatever lack of trust and unbelief (John 3:36); and finally, (5) malicious rejection of him, which coincides with the sin against the Holy Spirit, in which we trample underfoot the Son of God and count the blood of the testament polluted (Heb. 10:29).

CHAPTER TWENTY-SEVEN
God the Holy Spirit

*But the Paraclete, the Holy Spirit, whom the Father will send in my name,
he will teach you all things and recall to your memory all that I have said
to you.*

—John 14:26

The transition to the contemplation of the third person
I. In the economy of the Holy Trinity, the Holy Spirit has the third place insofar as he not only with reference to the order and mode of subsisting subsists from the two, the Father and the Son, but also with reference to the mode of operating, whereby just as he subsists, he also operates from the Father and the Son. From these truths, to him belongs by economic office the consummation of things, namely regeneration, conversion, sanctification, and so forth. We will build his personal description upon the words of our Savior which are in John 14:26.

The Exegetical Part
An analysis and exegesis of the text
II. These words contain a prophecy, or rather a promise, regarding the Holy Spirit's person, office, and economic benefits. In it we especially note these three points regarding the Holy Spirit:

    A. His person, or the benefactor, who is designated with a twofold name:

        1. An appellative name, from his economic office: ὁ παράκλητος, "the Paraclete." The article ὁ here is emphatic, designating someone who is Paraclete par excellence, and even more, who alone in the Trinity is Paraclete by office. Παράκλητος is a word frequent among the Jews in the Aramaic version and the Talmud, not as a "comforter," but as one who takes up the cause of another, and indeed for his benefit. It derives from παρακαλέω, "I call," such that it means an advocate,

one called to defend someone in judgment, or to assist with counsel in a decision, or to teach in unknown matters, or to intercede and entreat before another, or to lift up the soul in adverse circumstances, or to stir up the lazy and drive on the sluggish. From all these things, Paraclete means a defender of a cause, a teacher, comforter, exhorter, and intercessor. Therefore the Holy Spirit is so named because in the eternal counsel of peace he was called as it were by the Father and the Son to consummate the work of the Trinity in the cause of human salvation, a work decreed by the Father and accomplished by the Son, by teaching, leading, comforting, interceding, and exhorting, and thus to serve by office as the teacher, patron, comforter, and intercessor of the elect. Therefore by this one word is indicated both the appointment of the Holy Spirit through the economic pact, and his universal office.

2. A proper name: τὸ πνεῦμα τὸ ἅγιον, "The Holy Spirit." The two words, "Holy Spirit," form only one thing, the name of the third person; but it is a composite name, not a twofold name, proper and appellative. And although for the sake of brevity and abbreviation it is repeatedly expressed with the one word "Spirit," yet it always presupposes the other as implied. Meanwhile the article τὸ is prefixed to each of its parts distinctly, such that the first τὸ distinguishes the third person from the preceding two persons within the Trinity and the latter distinguishes the Holy Spirit from any other spirit that is impure and created. There are distinctly given two parts of the composite name, and by them he is called:

a. "Spirit," πνεῦμα. That is, not so much from the immaterial essence common to all the persons of the Trinity, or from some economic operation by which he makes men spiritual, as instead from the mode of subsisting, that he subsists through an ineffable spiration, from which he is designated "the Spirit of his mouth," "the Spirit of Jehovah," that is, of the Father, and "the Spirit of the Son," just as we will say more fully in the dogmatic sections.

b. "Holy," ἅγιον. That is, not so much from holiness, the essential attribute common to all the persons, as from sanctifying, insofar as that work has been committed as it were by the other persons to the third person as his economic office. Likewise regarding this more things will come in the dogmatic and practical sections.

B. His sending by the economic pact: ὃ πέμψει ὁ πατὴρ ἐν τῷ ὀνόματί μου, "whom the Father will send in my name." By these words two things in general are meant, namely the twofold principle from which he is sent, then the sending arising from both principles. These points are spoken of more particularly in the text with these three things:

1. The one sending: ὁ πατήρ, "the Father." Namely, the first principle of the Holy Spirit, neither proceeding nor sent by another, but simply from himself, concerning whom we have philosophized expressly in chapter 25.

2. The sending: πέμψει, "will send." The procession of the Holy Spirit is signified, insofar as he is from another. Moreover, the procession is twofold: one procession is eternal and personal, wherein he proceeds from the Father, from which he is called the Spirit of the Father (Matt. 10:20), the Spirit of God (2 Cor. 3:3), and the Spirit who is from God (1 Cor. 2:12); and from the Son, from which he is called the Spirit of the Son (Gal. 4:4) and the Spirit of Christ (Rom. 8:9), because he is also sent by him (John 16:7); and the other procession is temporal and economic, according to his economic office, through which he is the Paraclete.

3. The mode of the sending: ἐν τῷ ὀνόματί μου, "in my name." That is, partly from me as the second principle from whom he proceeds, as we have already said, and partly on account of me (Gal. 4:4), inasmuch as I am the one who obtained that Spirit for my own people by my merit and intercession. About this we will hear more as we progress.

C. His twofold economic benefit, namely:

1. Teaching, which respects the mind or intellect, as it confers to it a knowledge of things as yet unknown: ἐκεῖνος ὑμᾶς διδάξει πάντα, "he will teach you all things." Here there is noted:

   a. The teacher: ἐκεῖνος, "he." In the masculine gender, which from ordinary grammatical analogy hardly corresponds to a noun of the neuter gender. It is signified that the Holy Spirit will be not an accidental power of God, but a person, and such indeed to whom all things are evident, or who will be omniscient, that is divine.

   b. The ones being taught: ὑμᾶς, "you," that is, not only the apostles and others inspired by God,[1] but also all of the elect throughout

---

1. *aliosque* θεοπνεύστους

all ages of the world (Isa. 54:13; John 6:45; Jer. 31:34), although in different degrees and ways. Indeed the former in a more excellent and infallible degree, but the latter in an inferior degree, as much as is sufficient for their salvation.

c. The teaching, or the act of teaching: διδάξει, "he will teach," externally through the Word inspired by him, through the ministry; internally by the illumination of the mind, first extraordinarily and infallibly, which happened in extraordinary men, the patriarchs, prophets, and apostles, then ordinarily, in all that will be saved. He will teach not only the truth but also the goodness of the teachings; not only by urging but also by persuading them to walk in the truth. At the same time, in this one word "to teach" is comprehended by synecdoche every economic act of the Holy Spirit, that is, the act of directing, comforting, rebuking, and exhorting, which are required for procuring eternal life.

d. What is to be taught: πάντα, "all things," that is, which are necessary for salvation; and not necessary only for the being of Christianity, but also for its well-being.

2. Remembrance, which concerns the memory, that those things which are forgotten may return and extend their effectiveness. Here there is noted:

a. The remembrance, or the act of remembering: ὑπομνήσει, "he will recall to memory." In the Vulgate, Erasmus, and others it is "he will suggest." "Indeed not a bad translation," says Beza, "but one with a dangerous ambiguity, for things are also said to be suggested which you have not yet heard before. But here it concerns understanding and recalling to the memory things that have been heard. Accordingly, he will not only teach necessary and useful things for the first time, but he will also remind you of those things that you already possess."[2]

b. The things to be remembered: πάντα ἃ εἶπον ὑμῖν, "all that I have said to you." Namely, as Christ illuminated the teaching of Moses, so also the Spirit illuminated the teaching of Christ; and he did not, at least in the essentials, set forth anything new or different from it (John 16:13–14; Matt. 28:19).

---

2. Beza, *Testamentum Novum…eiusdem Th. Bezae annotationes* (1588), 402.

The Dogmatic Part

The Holy Spirit is the third person in the heavenly economy.

III. There is therefore among the divine persons one subsisting with the Father and the Son and distinct from them in various ways, who is called the Holy Spirit. All these things, written as it were by a ray of the sun, are set forth in the text, where: (1) he is called the Holy Spirit in as many syllables; (2) the ἐκεῖνος, "he," indicates that he is a person, and likewise his sending and his personal operations, "he will teach" and "he will recall to memory"; (3) the words "whom the Father will send in my name" convey his distinction from the Father and the Son; and finally, (4) the whole context argues that he obtains among the divine persons, when it speaks about God and the divine persons of the Father and the Son, and about the divine emissary of both. Other passages confirm this (Ps. 33:6; Isa. 61:1; Matt. 28:19; 1 John 5:7; etc.), and we see that it is demanded by the method of procuring salvation according to the eternal counsel of peace. For just as among the divine persons there is the Father, who outlined the work of redemption by eternal predestination, just as there is the Son, who accomplished the same, so also there is the Holy Spirit, who applies the accomplished redemption, and consummates the work by regeneration, sanctification, and so forth.

The names of the Holy Spirit

IV. The name "Holy Spirit" is employed (at least disjunctively) sometimes for God essentially (John 4:24) because each of the persons is both an immaterial essence and holy; and sometimes in particular for signifying the deity of the Son in contradistinction to his human nature (Rom. 1:4; 1 Peter 3:18; Heb. 9:14; Mark 2:8; 1 Tim. 3:16). When it is employed for the third person, it denotes either the person, as occurs in our text, or his benefits, both ordinary (Joel 2:28) and extraordinary (John 7:39; Acts 19:2; 1 Cor. 12:9–10), which are indeed carefully distinguished from the person (Acts 2:38; 10:45; 1 Cor. 12:4, 8, 11), but nevertheless also connote the person as their cause. For this reason he is called "the seven spirits" in Revelation 1:4, or "the septiform Spirit" according to the ancients.[3] Furthermore, the person in particular is called the Spirit because he subsists through an ineffable spiration, for which reason he is called the "Spirit

---

3. Mastricht is most likely referring to a common phrase in hymns found in Latin Christian liturgics. For example, the ancient hymn *Veni Creator Spiritus*, variously ascribed to Charlemagne, Ambrose of Milan, Rabanus Maurus, or Gregory the Great, among others, includes the line: *Tu septiformis munere*, lit. "you who are sevenfold in your office," frequently translated "sevenfold in thy grace." See also pseudo-Justin Martyr, ὁμοίως γὰρ ὥσπερ οἱ ἱεροὶ προφῆται τὸ ἕν καὶ τὸ αὐτὸ Πνεῦμα εἰς ἑπτὰ πνεύματα μερίζεσθαί φασιν, "For just as the holy prophets say that

of his mouth" (Ps. 33:6; 2 Thess. 2:8), a sign of which the Savior supplies to the disciples in John 20:22. And he is called Holy because by office he sanctifies (Rom. 1:4). There are also other names by which he is marked out, when he is called the good Spirit (Ps. 143:10), the Spirit of adoption (Rom. 8:15), the Spirit of grace (Heb 10:29), as well as the Spirit of prayers (Zech. 12:10), the Spirit of willingness (Ps. 51:12), the Spirit of promise (Eph. 1:13), the Spirit of truth (John 14:17; 15:26), the Spirit of glory (1 Peter 4:14), the Spirit of life (Rom. 8:2), the Spirit of bondage (Rom. 8:15), the Paraclete, and other more metaphorical names.

That the Holy Spirit is a person

V. That he is a person is evident from the fact that: (1) he is throughout the Scriptures counted with the other persons (Matt. 28:19; 1 John 5:7). (2) He offered himself to be seen under the figure of a substance (Matt. 3:16; Luke 3:22; Acts 2:3–4). (3) Πνεῦμα, "Spirit," in the neuter gender, is construed with a pronoun in the masculine gender, ἐκεῖνος, "he" (John 14:26). (4) He is said to be sent and to come (John 14:26). (5) All things personal belong to him, according to the Scriptures: (a) substance (Matt. 3:16), (b) life (Rom. 8:2), (c) intellect (1 Cor. 2:10), (d) will (1 Cor. 12:11), (e) personal operations such as regenerating, converting, sanctifying, teaching, comforting, leading, commanding, and sending ministers—passages proving this fact are found throughout the Scriptures; (f) that he is said to be affected with pain, to be grieved (Isa. 63:10; Eph. 4:30), to be sinned against (Matt. 12:32). (g) Unbegottenness,[4] which certainly is common with the Father, but also different from the Father in this respect, that in addition to it the Father begot, but the Holy Spirit by no means begot. Therefore, by his unbegottenness he is chiefly distinguished from the Son.

That he is a person distinct from the Father and the Son

VI. That he is also a person distinct from the Father and the Son is evident not only from the fact that he is numbered with the other two persons as the third (Matt. 28:19; 1 John 5:7; 2 Cor. 13:14); and that (2) he is expressly called *alius*, "another" (John 14:16–17), although not *aliud*, "another thing" with respect to his essence, as Vincent of Lérins says in his *Against Heresies*: "In the Trinity there is one and another, not one thing and another thing: in the Savior one thing and another thing, not one and another. How is there in the Trinity one

---

one and the same Spirit is divided into seven spirits...," Λόγος παραινετικὸς πρὸς Ἕλληνας (*Cohortatio ad Graecos*) in PG 6:299–300, *Hortatory Address to the Greeks* in ANF 1:287.
    4. ἀγεννησία

and another, not one thing and another thing? Because there is one person of the Father, another of the Son, another of the Holy Spirit, not one nature and another nature, but one and the same nature."[5] But especially that (3) personal and characteristic properties are attributed to him that are incommunicable to the other persons, namely: (a) passive spiration, or procession through spiration, from which he is called the Spirit as well as the Spirit of God, the Spirit of the mouth of Jehovah, speaking in a human way (Psalm 33:6; Job 33:4), and as a symbol of this the Savior, when he was about to communicate the Holy Spirit to his own, breathed on them and said, "Receive the Holy Spirit" (John 20:22). Accordingly the Father gives and sends him in the name of the Son (John 15:26) and through the Son (Titus 3:6); through this spiration he differs from the Father, who does not proceed from another. (b) The particular order in subsisting, by which he subsists from the Father and the Son, indeed as the one proceeding from them, and thus is numbered third in the economy (Matt. 28:19; etc.). Finally, (c) the particular order in operating, through which he acts from the Father and the Son, insofar as he operates as the one proceeding from them and sent by them; and accordingly he is said not to speak from himself but to receive from the others (John 16:13–15). By this he differs from both of the preceding persons, insofar as the Father operates from himself but through two others, the Son operates from another and through another, and the Holy Spirit operates from two others, but through himself.

That he is a divine person is proved: From his divine names
VII. That he is also a person who is not created but divine, coeternal and consubstantial[6] with the Father and the Son, is manifest not only from the fact that he is constantly grouped together with the divine persons as one with them (1 John 5:7), but also that all divine things are asserted for him as well as for the Father and the Son, namely, first the divine names, for he is called Jehovah, as is evident from a comparison of passages (Isa. 6:9 with Acts 28:25–26; Ex. 17:1, 7 with Ps. 95:7–8; Heb. 3:7, 9; 4:3, 7, 8; likewise Lev. 16:2 with Heb. 9:7–8; Jer. 31:31 with Heb. 10:15–16). He is called θεός, God (Acts 5:3–4; 1 Cor. 3:16–17 with 6:19). He is called κύριος, Lord (2 Cor. 3:17), by which in the majority of instances the Septuagint translators render the Tetragrammaton.

---

5. Vincent of Lérins (d. ca. 445), *Commonitorium adversus haereses* in PL 50:855.
6. ὁμοούσιον

From his divine attributes

VIII. Second, divine attributes, which coincide with the divine essence, attributes such as: (1) eternity (Heb. 9:14); (2) immensity (Ps. 139:7); (3) omniscience (1 Cor. 2:10–11, where he is said to search, that is, most accurately to know, the depths of God; cf. Jer. 17:10–11); (4) omnipotence and independent authority (1 Cor. 12:4, 6, 11; Luke 11:20 with Matt. 12:28).

From his divine operations

IX. Third, divine operations such as: (1) creation (Gen. 1:2; Ps. 33:6); (2) the working of miracles, the resurrection of the dead (Matt. 12:28; Rom. 8:11), the gift of miraculous healing, powers, tongues, and prophecy (1 Cor. 12:9–10); (3) the anointing of Christ (Isa. 61:1; Luke 4:18); (4) regeneration or spiritual vivification, renewal, conversion, sanctification, the strengthening of Christians, and the infallible leading of the prophets and apostles into all truth. These, with other similar things, will be shown in their own places.

From the divine worship that belongs to him

X. Fourth, divine worship, on account of which believers are called temples of the Spirit (1 Cor. 3:16–17; 6:19), because they are dedicated to his worship. Also, in his name we are baptized (Matt. 28:19) and pray (2 Cor. 13:14; Rev. 1:4–5), although more rarely, because he composes and forms our prayers rather than accepting and terminating them, and rather invokes, that is, makes and teaches us to invoke, than being himself invoked. He is religiously obeyed (Ps. 95:7 with Heb. 3:7, 9), and he is also particularly sinned against (Matt. 12:31–32).

The economic office of the Holy Spirit

XI. As far as economic office, the Holy Spirit is as it were the emissary of the Trinity, sent to bring about the things that have been decreed, for which reason in creation he is said to have brooded over the waters (מרחפת, just as a hen over her eggs, Deut. 32:11; Gen. 1:2; Ps. 33:6). For this reason he is also called the power of God (Luke 1:35; Rom. 15:13, 19), likewise the finger of God (Luke 11:20 with Matt. 12:28), who brings about miracles. Likewise he is the Paraclete, the advocate of the Trinity, called to bring to completion the cause of human salvation, which the Father designed and the Son accomplished. That is to say, just as the Son chiefly takes up the cause of man before God (1 Tim. 2:5), by offering himself for man (Eph. 5:2), so also the Holy Spirit chiefly takes up the cause of God before man, by leading man to faith in God and the Mediator, and by sanctifying and strengthening him, so that the salvation that was destined for him by the Father and accomplished by the Son might be applied, for which reason communication is attributed to him (2 Cor. 13:14).

The acts of the economic office: Teaching

XII. This office the Holy Spirit accomplishes chiefly by a threefold operation: first, by teaching (John 14:26), which is accomplished by sending forth teachers (Acts 13:2), by equipping the ones sent, and preparing them with the necessary gifts (Acts 2:4), by working with the ones equipped (Rom. 15:19), by inspiring the Word to be spoken (2 Peter 1:21), by concurring with the Word spoken by the inward illumination of minds (Heb. 6:4), and by efficacious leading (Ps. 143:10). For all these reasons, he is called the Spirit of truth (John 14:17).

Sanctifying

XIII. Second, by sanctifying, from which he is called the Holy Spirit. In its broader meaning this embraces: (1) regeneration (John 3:5) and renewal (Titus 3:5), in which the first act of the spiritual life of the soul is conferred, from which the operation is named vivification, and the one operating, the Spirit of life (Rom. 8:2); (2) conversion, by which the one made alive is led to the act of faith, for which reason he is called the Spirit of faith (2 Cor. 4:13); (3) sanctification (1 Cor. 6:11), through which the fruits of faith are brought forth (Gal. 5:22); (4) strengthening in truth and practice (2 Cor. 1:21–22); (5) raising up and rousing to every good thing (Rom. 8:14), whereby fervor and vigor are brought to them, for which reason he is compared to fire and a mighty wind (Acts 2:2–3).

Comforting

XIV. Third, by comforting (whereby he is particularly called the Paraclete), which occurs: (1) by interceding for believers with unutterable sighs (Rom. 8:26), namely that the grace of hearing and of comfort may be wrested from God, that is, by raising unutterable sighs in their hearts to this end. (2) By strengthening believers against the attack of any adversities (Rom. 8:26); (3) by making them certain in all adversities of the immovable favor of God toward them, for which reason he is said to be a witness (1 John 5:7) and to witness with our spirit (Rom. 8:15–16), to seal and anoint us, as a guarantee (2 Cor. 1:21–22; Eph. 4:30), to pour out the love of God into our hearts (Rom. 5:5), and by all these things to bring it about that we might be able to glory in oppressions (Rom. 5:3), and that there might be peace and joy in our hearts through the Holy Spirit (Rom. 14:17).

The economic attributes of the Holy Spirit

XV. From all these economic operations and benefits, to him in particular belong: (1) holiness, from which he obtains his name; (2) goodness (Ps. 143:10); (3) grace (Heb. 10:29; Zech. 12:10); (4) power, that is, the strength of God that accomplishes all things (Luke 1:35); (5) glory (1 Peter 4:14), for he is the one who leads believers to immeasurable and eternal glory.

The economic period of the Holy Spirit

XVI. There are also economic offices which belong to the Holy Spirit, certainly not with the other persons excluded, but to him for a singular reason, namely as they emerge from his particular operation, and likewise from his economic benefits. In addition, there are economic sins militating against the Holy Spirit, which, Lord willing, we will speak of in our practical part.[7] The Holy Spirit conducted his economic office indeed from the very beginnings of the world (Gen. 1:2), and under Moses in the desert, leading the church of God (Isa. 63:10; Acts 7:51–52), but he was especially promised in the time of the New Testament (Joel 2:28; Isa. 44:3), and at last took up his task upon the departure of the Son of God into heaven (Acts 2:1–6, 17), according to the previous and frequently repeated promises of the Son (John 14:16–17, 26; 15:26; 16:7). He will fulfill this task to the end of the age, ever to remain with his own and in them, lest they be left from the departure of their Savior as orphans, that is, until the Son delivers the kingdom to the Father, that God may be all in all (1 Cor. 15:24, 28), and even all the way to eternity (John 14:16).

The Elenctic Part

It is asked: 1. Is the Holy Spirit a person?

XVII. It is asked, first, whether the Holy Spirit is a person. The Pneumatomachi of old, the Macedonians, and in our time the Englishman John Biddle, acknowledged indeed that the Holy Spirit is a person, but only a created person, namely the Prince of Angels;[8] against these we will dispute in the subsequent question. The rest of the Socinians state, "In no way can the Holy Spirit be called a person, unless we wish to say all things that are present in God are persons distinct from

---

7. §XXV

8. John Biddle (1615–1662), *XII arguments drawn out of the Scripture, wherein the commonly-received opinion touching the deity of the Holy Spirit is refuted* (London, 1647), "I believe the holy Spirit to be the chief of all ministering spirits...so that as there is one principal spirit amongst the evil angels known in the Scripture by the name of Satan...there is, I say, one principal spirit amongst the good Angels," sig. A5 v.

God," as Smalcius says in his *Refutation of Grawer's Theses on the Holy Spirit*.[9] They assert in particular that he is some medium between the Creator and the creature, he is the accidental force of God, he is the divine breath, he is the gospel, he is the pious motions in man. For they dispute as Cadmean brothers,[10] and having deviated from the truth they do not find anywhere to set their feet. See the celebrated Hoornbeeck, *Socinianism Confounded* (vol. 1, p. 417).[11] The Reformed on the other hand state that he is a true person, (1) with Scripture, as we demonstrated above in §V; (2) with right reason, because: (a) since by common consent God is the absolutely most perfect being, how can there be admitted in him, apart from a contradiction, the imperfection of dependence, essential to an accident, whose existence is inexistence and dependence upon its subject, and which in addition is by its own nature more imperfect than a substance? (b) To form some medium between God and the creature is to form a medium between dependent and not dependent, finite and not finite, omnipotent and not omnipotent: in a word, a medium between contradictories. (c) By this rationale, in God there is something that is partly God, partly not God. (d) They fight amongst themselves: for if he is an accidental force of God, and thus in God, how would he be breath, which is outside of God? The whole argument by which we invincibly demonstrated in §V that the Holy Spirit is a person, namely that all personal characteristics are attributed to him by Scripture, we will not repeat.

Objections against the personality of the Holy Spirit.
We will only briefly refute objections. They allege: (1) that all those personal characteristics belong to the Holy Spirit through mere personification, such as when we read that Scripture foresees, the law speaks, sin seduces, and so forth. I respond, In personification one and perhaps another personal attribute is indeed ascribed to something which is not a person, but it is not evident, even by one example, where all personal characteristics are asserted for something that is not a person; indeed, it tells of a manifest contradiction to state that something which has all personal characteristics is not a person properly speaking. (2) That

9. Valentinus Smalcius, *Refutatio disputationis de Spiritu Sancto, quae hoc anno in academia Jenensi habita est, praeside Alberto Gravero* (Rakow, 1613), 6. Cf. Albert Grawer (1575–1617), *Grauerus redivivus, hoc est, praelectiones academicae in Augustanam Confessionem* (Jena: Johannes Ludovicus Neuenhanius), 191–204.

10. A reference to the army of warriors sprung from dragon's teeth sown by Cadmus, the mythical founder of Thebes. After he threw a rock into their midst, they fought and killed each other until only five remained.

11. Johannes Hoornbeeck (1617–1666), *Socinianismus confutatus*, 3 vols. in 2 (Utrecht, Amsterdam: Johannes á Waesberg, 1650), 1:417.

such things are attributed to him as do not belong to persons: for example, being given and poured out upon men, being baptized in him, anointed by him, filled by him, being given in measure. I respond: (a) It hinders one's being a person not at all for several things to be figuratively attributed to him; for example, God is called love (1 John 4:8), Christ the way, the truth, and the life (John 14:6), and likewise the resurrection,[12] propitiation (1 John 2:2), and the one who was made sin for us (2 Cor. 5:21). So then (b) all these things are indeed predicated of the Holy Spirit, but not except by reason of his charismatic gifts, in which sense the words "the Spirit" and "the Holy Spirit" frequently occur in the Scriptures (e.g. 2 Kings 2:9; Num. 11:17; Joel 2:28; John 7:39; etc.). (3) That the Holy Spirit is frequently not numbered with the other persons, the Father and the Son (e.g. John 17:3; 1 Cor. 8:6; 1 Tim. 5:21; Luke 9:26; John 8:16). I respond, This does not hinder his personality. As a matter of fact, sometimes when there is mention made of the Father and the Holy Spirit, none is made of the Son (1 Cor. 3:16). So also the Holy Spirit is joined with the Son, with no mention made of the Father (John 1:33; Rom. 9:1). It is sufficient that he is conjoined with the other persons, and not rarely (Matt. 28:19; 2 Cor. 13:14; 1 John 5:7), although for certain reasons known to God this is not always done. (4) That willing is even attributed to the wind (John 3:8). I respond, But without intellect, without the rest of all the personal properties which are attributed to the Holy Spirit. (5) That operations are also attributed to accidents, for example to love (1 Cor. 13:4–7) and to sin (Rom. 7:11). I respond: (a) Neither to love nor to sin are all personal characteristics attributed. And (b) the operations which are attributed to love and to sin are not personal, such as those asserted for the Holy Spirit. (6) That he is called the power of God, through which God works (Luke 1:35). I respond, He is not the accidental power of God, which cannot obtain in the most perfect being; nor God's instrumental power, because by his work God created the world (Ps. 33:6), in which an instrument cannot obtain; rather, he is God's personal or economic power, because the Father consummates the *ad extra* works through the Son and the Holy Spirit, as we taught above.[13] (7) That he is called breath (John 20:22), and is compared to wind and fire (Acts 2:2–3). I respond, He is compared for the purpose of indicating first his personal procession, as we saw above,[14] and next his economic operation, just as he is said in another place to have been in the wind (1 Kings 19:11–13).

---

12. Cf. John 11:25.

13. 1.2.24 §X

14. §VI

2. Is the Holy Spirit a divine person, from eternity consubstantial with the Father?

XVIII. It is asked, second, whether the Holy Spirit is a divine person, from eternity consubstantial with the Father. The Tritheists and Peratae of old, with whom Valentine Gentile does not differ one whit, did acknowledge that he was God, and that also from eternity, but yet denied that he was consubstantial with the Father. The Jews speak variously about the Holy Spirit: for he is now the force of God, now the magnificent gift of God, now heroic motions, sometimes the presence of the divine majesty in the Temple, which they call שכינה, *sheki-nah*, other times the lowest degree of prophecy, by whose influence the Writings of Scripture were set down.[15] Macedonius, and from him the Macedonians in AD 360, think that he is the prince of the created angels, the attendant of God, and the servant of Christ. The Englishman John Biddle has recently called this opinion back from the dead, and the celebrated Cloppenburg most solidly restrained him in his specific treatise, *Vindication of the Deity of the Holy Spirit against Biddle.*[16] Biddle attempts to build his invention upon these hypotheses: (1) he presupposes that in the Scriptures "Holy Spirit" and "good angel" are synonyms just as "impure spirit" and "evil angel" are, whether the discussion is about common angels or about an archangel. But he does so apart from Scripture, in which the Holy Spirit is never called a good angel, nor are good angels called holy spirits. (2) That in Psalm 51:12, רוח נדיבה, πνεῦμα ἡγεμονικόν, "commanding Spirit," according to the translators of the Septuagint, is the principal angel, or the prince and head of the created angels. But רוח נדיבה is variously rendered by translators: either concerning the spirit of David, a noble spirit such as befits a prince, or concerning the Holy Spirit, who makes him noble and adorns him with the spirit worthy of a prince; but that it is used concerning the Spirit as the prince among the created angels is still to be proved by Biddle. (3) That the Savior reduces him to a position beneath God by naming him the Paraclete, and thus attributing to him the ministry of an advocate. But that he is reduced by this name Biddle neither has proved nor tries to prove. For what is signified is his economic office, which he freely undertook in the counsel of peace, for which reason perhaps he is named רוח נדיבה in Psalm 51:12. (4) That he is distinguished in essence from God as the Spirit of God. But Biddle neither has proved this nor ever will prove it, for the word "God" is employed

---

15. *Hagiographa*, cf. 1.1.2 §VIII.

16. Mastricht offers an overview of Johannes Cloppenburg's (1592–1652) work, which is directly addressed to Biddle's twelve arguments, in *Vindiciae pro deitate Spiritus Sancti adversus pneumatomachum Johannem Bidellum Anglum* in *Opera omnia*, 2 vols. (Amsterdam: Gerardus Borstius, 1684), 2:451–97. Cf. Cloppenburg's more general refutations of Socinianism and his historical account of it in *Compendiolum Socinianismi confutatum* in *Opera omnia*, 2:319–441.

here hypostatically, such that it signifies the person of the Father, or even of the Son, just as is frequently done in Scripture. Therefore, until he has proved these four things from the Scriptures, he will have nothing—but he will never prove them.

A response is made to the objections.

We have already proved, however, that he is a divine person with this one invincible argument: that all divine things are attributed to him. Nor then does anything remain except that we should dispatch the chief objections of the Pneumatomachi. Biddle alleges (1) that he differs from God as his spirit. I respond, Certainly, but not as an essence from an essence, but as a person from a person. (2) That the one who gave the Holy Spirit is Jehovah alone (Neh. 9:6, 20). I respond, The sense of the words is, "You, O Triune Jehovah, Father, Son, and Holy Spirit, you are that Jehovah alone." (This occurs with the same intention and almost the same syntax in Deuteronomy 6:6, "Jehovah our God, Jehovah is one.") "You have made heaven…and you gave your good Spirit," and also in the same way you gave your Son to the world (John 3:16). So then, the whole Trinity and each of its persons are that Jehovah alone, "the only true God", and so is "Jesus Christ whom you have sent" (John 17:3). (3) That one who does not speak from himself (John 16:13) is not God. I respond, The Holy Spirit does not speak from himself insofar as he does not subsist from himself, but from the Father and the Son, not however because his essence is not from itself and so does not speak from itself, as we showed in the dogmatic part.[17] (4) That he hears from another (John 16:13), and thus is taught from another. I respond, Hearing from another and being taught from another are not totally synonymous, although they do coincide sometimes according to circumstance, as occurs in John 8:26–27, 21. Thus the Holy Spirit's listening to the Father must be taken in a way worthy of God, insofar as it denotes speaking from another, that is, according to his own order of subsisting and operating. (5) That in John 16:14 he receives from another, and thus depends upon another. I respond, Here also it is wrongly presupposed that receiving from another and depending upon another are synonymous. Thus he receives from another just as he subsists and operates from another, namely, not through dependence but through his own particular manner of subsisting, which we have taught above. His claim labors under the same defect when he alleges (6) that the Holy Spirit is sent, and so he serves. I respond, Although sometimes it happens that he who is sent serves, yet this is not universally true, nor can it be true concerning one to whom all divine things belong. (7) That he is the gift

---

17. §VI, also cited in objection 5, below.

of God, and thus not the giver of all things. I respond, Someone can give himself
to another, as God gives himself to his own through the covenant of grace when
he wills to be their God (Heb. 8:10; 1 Tim. 2:6; Titus 2:14). And (8) that he
changes location (Luke 3:21–22). I respond, It is denied that he changes, except
symbolically as God does (Gen. 18:19–21). (9) That he prays for Christ to come
in judgment (Rev. 22:17). I respond, He prays efficiently (as they say) in believers, not formally in himself—although it also can be said that "the spirit and
the bride" through hendiadys denotes a spiritual bride. (10) That the baptized
did not know that there was a Spirit (Acts 19:2). I respond: (a) Because they
did not know it, does he therefore not exist? (b) They did not know the Spirit's
extraordinary gifts, not his existence. (11) That he has an intellect distinct from
God's intellect, because he listens to him and is taught by him. I respond, This
is a stale repetition of arguments 3 and 4. Finally (12) that he has a will distinct
from the will of God, because he is said to intercede for the saints according to
the will of God (Rom. 8:26–27). I respond, Besides those things which we said
against objection 9, we say also that κατὰ θεὸν does not here mean according to
a will of God different from his own, but from verse 26, it means the same thing
as καθὸ δεῖ, namely, that the Holy Spirit causes believers to pray "as is fitting,"
and if you also prefer, "according to the will of God," but the same will with his
own. The celebrated Cloppenburg has expressly and accurately dealt with this
argument in his *Vindication of the Deity of the Holy Spirit against Biddle*.

3. Does the worship of the Holy Spirit have any basis in Scripture?
XIX. It is asked, third, whether the worship of the Holy Spirit has any basis in
Scripture. The Socinians, because they deny the eternal deity of the Holy Spirit,
also are compelled to deny that his worship has any basis in Scripture, that is,
lest from his worship we infer his deity. The Remonstrant Apologists, out of love
for the Socinians, although they otherwise wish to appear to acknowledge the
eternal deity of the Holy Spirit, nevertheless deny that his worship has any basis
in Scripture. The Reformed, although they acknowledge that the Scriptures
speak more sparingly about the worship of the Holy Spirit because by office
he is rather the cause of worship in us than its terminus (Rom. 8:15, 26; Gal.
4:6), nevertheless affirm that his worship does have a basis in Scripture, because:
(1) through the Scriptures, the Holy Spirit is God consubstantial with the
Father and the Son, just as we have demonstrated in the dogmatic part, and
even our opponents confess this is so; and also through the Scriptures it is commanded that God be worshiped (Deut. 6:13; Matt. 4:10), whereas it would be
quite absurd for the worship of him who is true God to have no commandment or example in the Scriptures. (2) Also there are clear examples of this

worship in our baptism (Matt. 28:19), in Paul's prayer (2 Cor. 13:14; cf. Rev. 1:4). (3) It breathes of atheism not to worship him who is truly God. Nor is it valid to argue on the contrary: (1) that in 1 John 1:3 we are said to have communion with the Father and the Son, but not with the Holy Spirit. I respond, This occurs in this way because the Holy Spirit is rather the bond and the deepest cause of this communion than its terminus. Nor also does this derogate from his worship whatsoever. (2) That believers are said to be and to abide in the Father and the Son (1 John 4:13; cf. 2:6; etc.), but not in the Holy Spirit. I respond: (a) This makes no difference for worship. (b) This occurs because he and his anointing is and abides in us rather than we in him (1 John 2:20, 27). (c) That Scripture speaks less frequently about the Holy Spirit than about the others. I respond, This occurs first because he continually speaks in Scripture, and next because he makes himself known in the minds of believers by internal operations. See Hoornbeeck, *Socinianism Confounded* (vol. 1, p. 447) and Alting, *New Elenctic Theology.*[18]

4. Does the Holy Spirit proceed from the Father and the Son?
Differences of opinion
XX. It is asked, fourth, whether the Holy Spirit proceeds from the Father alone or in fact from the Father and the Son. Weigel and his fanatics stated that the Holy Spirit under the Old Testament proceeded from the Father alone, whereas under the New Testament he proceeded from the Father and the Son, perhaps because he did not frankly enough acknowledge the existence of the Son under the Old Testament. Long ago in AD 381, the Greeks, since in the recitation of the Constantinopolitan Creed they observed only these words, τὸ ἐκ τοῦ πατρὸς ἐκπορευόμενον, "who proceeds from the Father," and that by the Latins there had been added "ex Patre *Filioque*," "from the Father *and the Son*," and thus not only that the public canons of the church were being changed by the private authority of the Latins, but also that in the judgment of the faith they were raising themselves above the rest, indeed that they wanted to correct Scripture itself, from which the words of the Creed had been taken (namely from John 15:26), thus took occasion to deny altogether that the Holy Spirit proceeds from the Son as from the origin of his hypostasis. Nor was the schism taken away by the decree of the Council of Florence (AD 1438) that the Holy Spirit proceeded from the Father and the Son eternally, as from one principle and by a single spiration, but rather it was augmented by the fact that though up to the

---

18. See bk. 2, ch. 5, sec. 2, §VI, Hoornbeeck, *Socianismus confutatus*, 1:447–51; cited as *loc. 3, contr. 2*: Alting, *Theologia elenctica nova*, 187–91.

time of the council the dogma was not yet necessary, now the Latins were urging it as a necessary article of faith. There was sin here on both sides: by the Latins because they added something to the Constantinopolitan Creed, and in so doing intended obliquely to extend the authority of the pope to the Greeks; but by the Greeks because they rashly rejected a dogma consistent with the Scriptures and acknowledged by the more ancient Fathers of the church, out of mere ill-will toward the name of the Latins. Nevertheless, there are many who think that both the ancient and especially the more recent Greeks intend nothing other than that the Holy Spirit proceeds from the Father alone, *through* the Son. Thus their opinion would be more tolerable, since the Father works all things through the Son, and in this way the controversy would almost fade into a mere contest over words.

The opinion of the Reformed with their reasons
Meanwhile, the Reformed think with the Latins that the Holy Spirit proceeds from the Father and the Son, generally for these reasons: (1) because he is called not only the Spirit of Elohim, that is, of the divine persons, but also particularly the Spirit of the Father (Matt. 10:20) and the Spirit of the Son (Gal. 4:6; Rom. 8:9; Phil. 1:19). Accordingly, just as he is the Spirit of the Father by procession (1 Cor. 2:11), so he is the Spirit of the Son by the same procession. (2) He is called the Spirit of the mouth of the Lord Jesus (2 Thess. 2:8), in the same way as in Psalm 33:6 he is called the Spirit of the mouth of the Father. (3) The river of the water of life, bright as crystal (by which nothing more fitting is understood than the Holy Spirit; cf. Isa. 44:3; John 7:38; Ezek. 36:25–26) is said to proceed from the throne of God and of the Lamb (Rev. 22:1). (4) He is said to be sent by the Son as well as by the Father (Luke 24:49; John 15:26; 16:17), and moreover in the name of the Son (John 14:26), just as in turn the Son sends the Holy Spirit from the Father (John 15:26), and thus he is understood to proceed from both in a similar way. (5) Christ in John 16:14–15 says of the Holy Spirit, "He will receive of what is mine," just as he says of himself, "All things that the Father has are mine." But he did not receive in time what he would declare, so then he received it from eternity—and how from eternity unless by procession? (6) If his procession from the Son is denied, then the order of subsisting and of operating in the Trinity will be disturbed in no small measure: if the Holy Spirit immediately proceeds from the Father just like the Son does, there will hardly be anything, besides generation and spiration, by which the procession of the Son and the Holy Spirit might be sufficiently distinguished from each other.

Objections

The chief arguments by which the Greeks strive to support their own opinion are: (1) the passage in John 15:26, "When the Paraclete has come, whom I will send to you from the Father, the Spirit of truth, who proceeds from the Father...." I respond: (a) That passage, because of the lack of an exclusive, does not extend in meaning further than to say that the Holy Spirit proceeds from Father, which is not disputed. (b) If they do not intend anything other than that the Holy Spirit proceeds from the Father alone, but through the Son, then it does not supply me much that I would oppose. Meanwhile, (c) the passage seems to speak not so much about his hypostatic procession as about his economic procession, which occurs in time. (2) That Scripture has nothing about the procession of the Holy Spirit from the Son. But we oppose to this all those arguments which we have already brought forth in favor of the opinion of the Latins. If they should allege (3) that as a result of the opinion of the Latins the order of the persons in the Trinity is disturbed in no small measure, and that perhaps it is more cor- rectly said that the Holy Spirit proceeds from the Father through the Son, the same way the particles ἐκ, διά, and εἰς seem to be employed in Romans 11:36, just as Basil, Theophylact, John of Damascus, and others have said, as witnessed by Cardinal Basilios Bessarion in the Council of Florence,[19] I respond: (a) I do not object greatly, although (b) the passage in Romans 11:36 does not seem to be occupied with the procession of the Holy Spirit, and much less to speak about his hypostatic procession, but only about the production of creatures by God, and the conservation of them through providence, and the direction of the same to his glorification. But (c) notwithstanding, the order of subsisting will obtain accurately enough if it is stated that the Holy Spirit proceeds from the Father and from the Son, when the Father is said simply not to proceed from any, the Son to proceed from the Father by eternal generation, and the Holy Spirit to proceed from both by one procession or active spiration.

5. *Now after the canon of Scripture has been closed, does the Holy Spirit teach in the same way and degree as he once taught the patriarchs, prophets, and apostles?*
XXI. It is asked, fifth, whether now after the canon of Scripture has been closed the Holy Spirit teaches and leads believers in the same way and degree as he taught and led the patriarchs, prophets, apostles, and others inspired by God.

---

19. This is the argument, for example, of Marcus Ephesius at the Council of Florence, as refuted by Cardinal Basilios Bessarion (1403–1472). See Bessarion, Δογματικός Λόγος ἢ περὶ ἑνώσεως (*Oratio dogmatica sive de unione*) in PG 161:558–614; cf. idem, Ἀπόκρισις πρὸς τὰ τοῦ Ἐφέσου κεφαλαία (*Responsio ad Ephesii capita*) in PG 161:137–244; esp. 166, 168.

The pseudo-Enthusiasts, Weigel, Franck, Schwenckfeld, David Joris, and other fanatics of this sort, want, even after the closing of the canon, the Holy Spirit (if only they genuinely acknowledge his personality and teaching office, and do not rather understand by "their Spirit" their own reason and its dictates) to teach and lead people, as once he did the patriarchs, prophets, and the apostles, by enthusiasms and divine inspirations,[20] by inspiring them with new axioms different from the Scriptures. But since we have already aired this controversy in both its parts in book 1, chapter 2, §XXXIII, it will suffice at present for the completion of this elenctic part to have pointed our finger there and left the reader to it.

The Practical Part

Practice urges that we strive: 1. To obtain the Holy Spirit

XXII.[21] Therefore as respects practice, here there is reason, first, that we should with every effort strive toward the communication of the Holy Spirit (2 Cor. 13:14), that by it we may be made partakers of the Holy Spirit, that we may receive him (Acts 19:2). For this, there is required on God's part: (1) that the Holy Spirit be freely given to us, for which reason he is called the gift of God (Neh. 9:20; John 14:16; 20:22; Acts 2:38; Rom. 5:5); (2) that he be sent to us from the Father, in the name of the Son, that is, that he come to us as if by the authority, indeed in the name of the whole Trinity (John 15:26); (3) that he be poured out upon us (Joel 2:28) like a cleansing stream (Isa. 44:3; Titus 3:6). In order that we may receive the Spirit, there is required on our part: (1) faith (Gal. 3:2, 14; John 7:39), that is, the faith by which we take hold of him as the Spirit of promise (Eph. 1:13), for such things as are promised we obtain by faith (Gal. 3:14); (2) prayers (Luke 11:13), from which also he is called the Spirit of prayers (Zech. 12:10); (3) expectation (Acts 1:4); (4) hearing of the word (Acts 10:44; 2 Cor. 3:8), and other means of this kind (Acts 2:1); (5) repentance from sins (Acts 2:38); (6) religious worship, by which we offer ourselves as temples of the Holy Spirit in which he would desire to dwell (1 Cor. 6:19); (7) obedience, by which we carefully compose ourselves to his movements (Rom. 8:14). The following things will stimulate this effort to obtain the Holy Spirit: (1) the excellence of his person, by which he is God consubstantial with the Father and the Son, equal in power, wisdom, and goodness, through which we can promise ourselves all those things from him that we promise ourselves from the Father and the Son. (2) The goal of his economic office, namely to consummate the work

---

20. θεοπνευγίας
21. The Latin repeats the paragraph number XXI; as in the Dutch translation, it is corrected here through the end of the chapter, §§XXII–XXVII.

of human salvation, that is, to communicate to us the grace of our Lord Jesus Christ, the love of the Father, and whatever those persons can communicate to us (2 Cor. 13:14). (3) The abundance and preciousness of his economic operations and benefits, of regeneration, direction, establishment, and consolation. (4) His absolute necessity, inasmuch as without him we cannot even hail Christ as Lord (1 Cor. 12:3), nor can we have any communion with Christ (Rom. 8:9).

2. To preserve the Holy Spirit

XXIII. Second, there is reason that we should zealously preserve and cherish the Holy Spirit once acquired, so that he may not so much lodge in us as a guest only for a time, but rather dwell in us (Rom. 8:11) as in his own temple (1 Cor. 6:19), indeed, that he may abide with us forever (John 14:16).

To what extent he can be lost

For the Holy Spirit can be lost, and indeed lost totally and finally with respect to common gifts, as is evident in the case of Saul (1 Sam. 16:14; Heb. 6:4–6): he can to that extent be quenched (1 Thess. 5:19). With respect to saving gifts, the sense of the presence of the Holy Spirit can be lost (Ps. 119:8), which occurs in spiritual desertions (Ps. 13:1). He can be lost with respect to pleasant gifts, as regards full assurance, joy, peace, and consolation (Ps. 51:11–12; 30:7; 77:7–9; 88:14). He can be so diminished, with respect to saving fruits, to faith, hope, and love, that you ask, "Where is your faith?" (Luke 8:25; Rev. 2:4–5; Isa. 6:13). Therefore because the Holy Spirit can be lost in so many and such great ways (although he cannot be lost absolutely and finally), surely there is reason that we should zealously labor to preserve the Holy Spirit and all his fruits, following the example of David (Ps. 51:11). For it is well worth our labor to preserve and cherish not only the Holy Spirit himself, but also his gifts; not only his saving gifts, but also his common gifts; not only his honorable fruits but also his pleasant fruits; not only the presence of all these, but also the sense and evidence of them.

The means of preserving the Spirit

Moreover, the means of preserving the Holy Spirit are: (1) concern for the movements of the Holy Spirit in our hearts, so that we not only diligently observe them, as the bride (Song 2:8) and John (Rev. 1:10), who observe a voice speaking to them and turn themselves toward it, but that we also immediately yield to him, that we may hear the Spirit disputing with us (Gen. 6:3), and admit him when he knocks (Rev. 3:20; Song 5:2, 5–6). (2) The use of the gifts of the Holy Spirit, by which the Spirit as it were lives in us (Gal. 5:25), and we fan into flame the gifts of the Spirit (2 Tim. 1:6), for little by little, what is unused vanishes.

(3) The use of the means by which the Spirit can be acquired, roused, and augmented, such as: (a) the hearing of the Word (Acts 10:44; 1 Peter 1:12; Gal. 3:2); (b) meditation on the same (Rom. 8:6); (c) prayers (Luke 11:13); (d) conversation with the godly (Eph. 4:29–30). (4) Taking heed to ourselves regarding all things by which the Holy Spirit can be extinguished or driven away, such as: (a) any sins committed against knowledge and conscience, more shameful and serious sins especially, for example, the adultery and murder of David (Ps. 51:1, 11–12), drunkenness (Eph. 5:18), immoderate love of the world (1 John 2:15), sluggishness in spiritual things (Rom. 12:11), lukewarmness and satisfaction, in which we rest in what we have already attained and do not attempt to make progress (Rev. 3:15–17). (b) Those sins specifically in which we particularly and as it were expressly struggle against the Holy Spirit, such as quenching the Spirit (1 Thess. 5:19), grieving him (Eph. 4:30), resisting him (Acts 7:51), provoking him (Isa. 63:10), blaspheming him (Heb. 10:29), all concerning which we will deal with expressly below.

3. To follow the leading of the Holy Spirit

XXIV. Third, there is reason that we should turn ourselves toward and follow the movements and leadings of the Holy Spirit (Rom. 8:14), that we should live according to the Spirit (Rom. 8:1), and that we should walk in the Spirit (Gal. 5:25). Moreover, we understand by the leading of the Holy Spirit all those operations by which that Spirit is occupied with our soul, which we have already divided into three kinds:[22] (1) teaching and establishment: "He will teach you all things." And we obey him by religiously hearing him as he teaches inwardly and outwardly, by not suppressing the truth in unrighteousness (Rom. 1:18); (2) sanctification, by which he labors: (a) to regenerate, renew, and vivify, as the Spirit of life (Rom. 8:2), with whom, inasmuch as we are dead in sins, we cannot cooperate (Eph. 2:1); (b) to convert, or to lead us once vivified to faith in Christ, by convicting us concerning our sin, our misery, the guilt of our eternal condemnation, and our natural powerlessness in good (John 16:8–10), from which things he is called the Spirit of bondage to fear (Rom. 8:15; 2 Tim. 1:7); (c) to effectively draw us once converted back from vices and to incite us to virtue, from which he is called preeminently the Holy Spirit and the Spirit of sanctification (Rom. 1:4); (d) to strengthen us once sanctified in zeal for good (2 Cor. 1:21); (e) to seal and confirm us for the day of redemption (Eph. 4:30); and (f) to comfort us in whatever hostile adversities, from which he is particularly named

---

22.Teaching, sanctifying, and comforting, §§XII–XIV, above. Here the third is included in the second.

the Paraclete (John 14:26). Now in all these things, it is our duty: (1) to zeal-ously observe these movements, and if at any time good thoughts of any sort arise in our hearts, immediately to hear, to recognize them to be the voice, to be the impulse of the Holy Spirit, to be the Holy Spirit, in the same way as Samuel says, "Speak Lord, your servant hears" (1 Sam. 3:10), and the bride, "It is the voice of my beloved! Behold him, he comes" (Song 2:8). (2) To carefully search out the goal of these movements, what is the mind of the Spirit (Rom. 8:27), namely, toward what end those movements tend: for example, do they tend toward a knowledge, sense, and detestation of sin? Toward pious desperation concerning ourselves and toward conversion? Toward faith? Toward sanctification? Toward consolation? As with Saul, we should ask, "What do you desire, Lord?" (Acts 9:6). (3) When the movements of the Holy Spirit have been recognized, to promptly obey them, to turn ourselves toward them, as it were, just like John (Rev. 1:12), to cooperate with them, to run as ones who have been drawn to them (Song 1:4), to open to him as he knocks (Rev. 3:20), as the bride: "I will rise, I will open: she rose, she opened" (Song 5:3, 5–6), to follow him readily as he leads, as Peter did (Acts 12:8–9). (4) At the least, especially to take heed that we never neglect the acknowledged movements of the Holy Spirit, that we never hold them in indifference, which is to quench the Spirit (1 Thess. 5:19), much less to strive against them with carnal reasonings (Gal. 1:16; 2 Cor. 10:5) or the enticements of the world, just like Saul strove against the movements of the evil spirit with the psalmody of David (1 Sam. 16:14–16).

4. To test the Spirit. The signs of the Holy Spirit
XXV. There is, fourth, that we should test the Spirit, whether it is from God (1 John 4:1; 1 Thess. 5:21). We should test: (1) whether we have obtained the Holy Spirit: "Have you received the Holy Spirit?" (Acts 19:2), that is, do we sense some good movements in our hearts? And if we sense them, are they movements of the Holy Spirit, or movements of the natural conscience (Rom. 2:14–15), movements of a more honorable nature? (2) If they are movements of the Holy Spirit, then of what sort are they? Are they common (Heb. 6:4) or saving movements, ones that accompany salvation (Heb. 6:9)? We will pursue this inquiry fruitfully if we should studiously consider the nature of the Holy Spirit, which produces homogeneous movements, and compare them with our hearts. He is (1) the Spirit of life (Rom. 8:2), who vivifies (John 6:63), just as the spirit, or the presence of the soul, vivifies the body (Acts 20:10). Accordingly, the Holy Spirit is called life (Rom. 8:10), the one who raised us, for, "If the Spirit of him who raised Jesus from the dead dwells in you, he who raised Christ from the dead will also give life to your mortal bodies through his Spirit who dwells

in you" (Rom. 8:11). Therefore if we sense in ourselves spiritual life, by which we in turn live for the Spirit (Rom. 8:12) and put to death the actions of our body (Rom. 8:13), then certainly we are led by the Spirit of God, and thus we are sons of God (Rom. 8:14). The Holy Spirit is (2) the Spirit of holiness (Rom. 1:4). If therefore we should observe in ourselves a serious zeal for holiness and a detesting of all impurity, we will be able for that reason safely to confess that we have obtained the Holy Spirit. He is (3) the Spirit of light, from whom all spiritual light arises (Eph. 1:17–18), for the natural man does not perceive those things which are of the Spirit of God (1 Cor. 2:14). Therefore if we perceive that there is present to our mind a new light by which we spiritually judge spiritual things (1 Cor. 2:14–15), then the conclusion follows. He is (4) the fiery and burning Spirit (Matt. 3:11; Mark 9:49), and thus he is communicated under the appearance of flaming tongues (Acts 2:3–4). And also, those whom he indwells he makes fervent in spirit (Rom. 12:11), and wherever he is present he does not lazily snore, but urges on to action (Rom. 8:14). Therefore if we are not cold, lukewarm, or lazy in any good thing, but rather fervent, we obtain an evidence of the Holy Spirit. He is (5) the Spirit of Christ (Rom. 8:9), through whom Christ lives in us (Gal. 2:20), who glorifies Christ (John 16:14), through whom his holiness, love, obedience, humility, longsuffering, contempt of the world, and heavenly conversation live and thrive in us. Therefore if we have discovered that these things belong to us, we may be persuaded more certainly than certain that we have infallibly gained the Spirit of Christ. Finally, (6) it will be made known to us from the fruits of the Holy Spirit which the apostle mentions in Galatians 5:22–25.

5. *To take heed to ourselves of sins against the Holy Spirit.* What those sins are
XXVI. There is, fifth, that we should most studiously take heed to ourselves of all those sins which particularly resist the Holy Spirit, such as: (1) extinguishing the Spirit, neglecting and holding in indifference (like Felix in Acts 24:25) the movements and leadings of the Holy Spirit, concerning which we already spoke in the preceding sections. (2) Resisting the Holy Spirit (Acts 7:51; Ps. 81:8, 12, 13) by suppressing the truth in unrighteousness (Rom. 1:18); stopping up the mouth of the Holy Spirit, as it were, by opposing his leadings with the reasonings of the flesh, by living according to the flesh, not according to the Spirit (Rom. 8:1, 13). (3) Grieving the Spirit, by whom we were sealed for the day of redemption (Eph. 4:30), by doing that by which, if possible, the Holy Spirit might be grieved, whether in ourselves or others, which occurs in the more shameful sins—in impurity, lasciviousness, drunkenness, and others—and likewise by indulging in those things by which joy, peace, comfort, and readiness

of spirit can be obscured, and grieved as it were. (4) Provoking the Holy Spirit (Isa. 63:10), by frequently resisting his leadings, by murmuring against them (Ps. 95:8–11). (5) Lying to the Holy Spirit, just as Ananias and Sapphira did (Acts 5:3), which occurs especially in hypocrisy and sacrilege. Finally, (6) by blaspheming the Spirit of holiness (Heb. 10:29), which is that great sin against the Holy Spirit, the unforgivable sin (Matt. 12:32), in which the whole Trinity, the Father and the Son, from whom and in whose name the Holy Spirit is sent and comes, are insulted. Toward this sin the other preceding sins lay steps. Therefore, we should take heed of all these sins against the Holy Spirit, more than we would a dog or snake.

For what reasons we should take heed of them
Otherwise: (1) the Holy Spirit will in turn neglect us and hold us in indifference, he will resist us, he will grieve us, he will provoke us, that is, by the right of retribution[23] (Prov. 1:24ff.). (2) He will swear an oath against us, and so forth (Ps. 95:11), he will desert us like Saul, and indeed like David (Ps. 51:11–12), whether for a time as in the latter case, or for eternity as in the former. In addition, (3) after the Holy Spirit has been quenched, the spirit of the devil will be kindled, or the flaming arrows of the devil (Eph. 6:16), after the example of Saul (1 Sam. 16:14). A wicked spirit will follow, taking with him seven spirits who are more wicked than himself, and thus the latter state will be worse than the former (Matt. 12:44–45). Also, (4) by quenching the fire of the Holy Spirit we will kindle against ourselves the fire of divine fury (2 Kings 22:17), by calling down upon ourselves all the judgments of God, as much spiritual (Rev. 2:4–5) as eternal, the unquenchable fire (Isa. 66:24; Mark 9:43, 46, 48). I need not add that (5) by the previous sins against the Holy Spirit, little by little the steps are laid to that last great and fearful sin, blasphemy against the Holy Spirit, the thought of which should deservedly strike fear into anyone. For when: (1) you have allowed the neglect of the Spirit, and thus have quenched him, as it were, what will be easier than (2) also to resist him with raked-up little reasons, and in addition, (3) with more serious and shameful sins, and by these as it were to grieve the Holy Spirit; and moreover, (4) by doing this frequently and by murmuring against his movements and leadings, also to exasperate him; and indeed such that also (5) in covering up these sins, you employ hypocrisy as a remedy, and thus lie to the Holy Spirit with Ananias and Sapphira; finally, (6) what will draw you back, once prepared by all these things and carried to the closest step, from finally ascending to this step and taking in blasphemy the Spirit of holiness,

---

23. *jure talionis*

who comes in the name of the entire holy Trinity, and thus bringing down upon yourself inescapable destruction? Therefore so that you may be far from this, take heed to yourself of the first step toward this sin.

6. *To flee whatever spirit is adverse to the Holy Spirit.*
What spirits are adverse to him?
XXVII. Finally, there is reason, sixth, that we should carefully flee whatever spirit is adverse to the Holy Spirit, namely: (1) the spirit of error, and the seducing spirit (1 Tim. 4:1), the spirit of a lie, which was in the mouth of the false prophets (1 Kings 22:22), the spirit of antichrist (1 John 4:3), by which name is indicated everyone who teaches perverse things in the business of religion, namely the pseudo-Enthusiasts, who believe in the Spirit without and contrary to the Word. Thus we are commanded to test the spirits (1 John 4:1). (2) A perverse spirit, or a spirit of perversity (Isa. 19:14), which blinds a person so that he takes up and manages all his business in a perverse order. (3) The spirit of this world (1 Cor. 2:12), which allures toward worldly wisdom and all other worldly things (1 John 2:15–16). (4) The spirit of impurity (Mark 1:23), which is opposed to a pure and right spirit (Psalm 51:10), and casts men headlong into all lusts. Finally, (5) the wicked spirit, Satan (Matt. 12:43), to whom belongs the authority of the air, "the one at work in the sons of disobedience" (Eph. 2:2).

For what reason these spirits should be fled
We should therefore flee with such earnestness every one of these spirits which are adversaries of the Holy Spirit, because otherwise there can be no communion for us with the Holy Spirit (2 Cor. 13:14). For what communion does righteousness have with unrighteousness? Light with darkness? Christ with Belial? (2 Cor. 6:14–15; 1 Cor. 10:21).

Scripture Index

Subject Index